BOTTOM LINE'S

BIG BOOK OF
SERIOUS
SYMPTOMS AND
SIMPLE
SOLUTIONS

**Bottom Line
Books**

www.BottomLinePublications.com

Bottom Line's Big Book of Serious Symptoms and Simple Solutions

Copyright © 2012 by Boardroom® Inc.

First printing

ISBN 0-88723-675-8

Bottom Line Books® publishes the advice of expert authorities in many fields. The use of this material is no substitute for health, legal, accounting or other professional services. Consult competent professionals for answers to your specific questions.

Telephone numbers, addresses, prices, offers and Web sites listed in this book are accurate at the time of publication, but they are subject to frequent change.

Bottom Line Books® is a registered trademark of Boardroom® Inc.
281 Tresser Boulevard, Stamford, CT 06901

www.bottomlinepublications.com

Bottom Line Books® is an imprint of Boardroom® Inc., publisher of print periodicals, e-letters and books. We are dedicated to bringing you the best information from the most knowledgeable sources in the world. Our goal is to help you gain greater wealth, better health, more wisdom, extra time and increased happiness.

Printed in the United States of America

Bottom Line's Big Book of SERIOUS Symptoms and SIMPLE Solutions

Contents

Contents

6. Brain-Boosting Foods and Supplements

7. Brain-Boosting Tricks and Techniques

PART 3: Diabetes Prevention & Management

8. Preventing Diabetes

Contents

9. Managing Diabetes

Contents

Preface

We are proud to bring you *Bottom Line's Big Book of Serious Symptoms and Simple Solutions*. We trust that you'll find the latest discoveries, best treatments and money-saving solutions to your health concerns.

Whether it's quality medical care, new heart therapies, breakthrough cancer treatments or cutting-edge nutritional advice, our editors talk to the people—from top research scientists to consumer health advocates—who are creating the true innovations in health care.

How do we find all these top-notch medical professionals? Over the past two decades, we have built a network of literally thousands of leading physicians in both alternative and conventional medicine. They are affiliated with the premier medical institutions and the best universities throughout the world. We read the important medical journals and follow the latest research that is reported at medical conferences. And we regularly talk to our advisers in major teaching hospitals, private practices and government health agencies.

Bottom Line's Big Book of Serious Symptoms and Simple Solutions is a result of our ongoing research and contact with these experts, and is a distillation of their latest findings and advice. We trust that you will enjoy the presentation and glean new, helpful and affordable information about the health topics that concern you and your family.

As a reader of a *Bottom Line* book, please be assured that you are receiving reliable and well-researched information from a trusted source.

But, please use prudence in health matters. Always speak to your physician before taking vitamins, supplements or over-the-counter medication...changing your diet... or beginning an exercise program. If you experience side effects from any regimen, contact your doctor immediately.

The Editors, Bottom Line Books, Stamford, Connecticut.

PART 1

High Blood Pressure &
Heart Health Essentials

Delicious Fixes for High Blood Pressure

Eat Your Way to Health: DASH Diet

Marla Heller, MS, RD, author of *The DASH Diet Action Plan* (Amidon), based in Chicago. Her Web site is *http://dash diet.org/marla.asp.*

Maintaining normal blood pressure is vital to staying healthy, but perhaps we've been trained by the mainstream medical community to rely too much on drugs to do it. For many people, there can be a better—and safer—way that requires nothing more than your spoon and fork.

During a five-center study in the 1990s sponsored by the National Institutes of Health, researchers found that participants with high blood pressure (hypertension) who followed a specific dietary plan called DASH (Dietary Approaches to Stop Hypertension) lowered systolic pressure (the higher number in a blood pressure reading) by 11.4 millimeters of mercury (mmHg) and diastolic pressure by 6 mmHg. More recent studies gave the DASH diet added value—at Brigham and Women's Hospital in Boston, an analysis of data from the long-term Nurses' Health Study and Health Professionals Follow-Up Study found that following the DASH diet was associated with lower risk for kidney stones. Other studies find that a DASH diet lowers risk for cardiac disease and stroke...and most recently, at Utah State University in Logan, an 11-year study has demonstrated that elderly adults who followed DASH stayed mentally sharp longer.

How to Do DASH

The diet basically consists of eating healthy foods with some specific tweaking, plus a salt limitation. Given that the typical diet of Americans today is filled with processed foods high in sugar, salt and fat, DASH is often described as "difficult to follow." But it isn't! Marla Heller, MS, RD, author of *The DASH Diet Action Plan,* explains that it usually takes time to overcome a lifetime of bad habits such as living on french fries and soft drinks...but the DASH plan includes a wide variety of delicious, satisfying foods. It is important to follow this dietary plan closely, she says, because in addition to restricting sodium, eating the recommended amounts of foods on DASH provides high amounts of magnesium, potassium and calcium. A diet that is rich in foods with this combination of nutrients is what helps to control blood pressure.

In a nutshell, here's the DASH diet...

• **Whole grains**—six to eight servings a day of products made from 100% whole grains...a serving is one slice of bread, one ounce of dry cereal, or one-half cup of cooked cereal, whole-grain pasta or brown rice.

• **Fruits and vegetables**—eight to 10 servings a day...a serving is defined as one cup of raw, leafy vegetables or one-half cup of cooked veggies, one medium fruit, one-half cup low-sodium vegetable juice, one cup of fresh fruit, or one-half cup of frozen or canned fruit. To reduce calories, Heller suggests limiting starchy vegetables, such as potatoes, corn and the like, but the good news is that you can eat as much as you like of the nonstarchy ones, for example, to-matoes, green beans, leafy greens, peppers and others.

• **Low-fat or nonfat dairy**—two to three servings a day. A serving is one cup of milk or yogurt or one and one-half ounces of cheese.

• **Lean meat, fish and poultry**—six or fewer ounces a day. A three-ounce serving is the size of a pack of cards, which is sufficient with a meal.

• **Nuts, seeds and beans**—four to five servings per week...servings include one-half cup of cooked dried beans or peas, one-quarter cup of nuts or two tablespoons of peanut butter. Heller says it is okay to have more beans than this each week, but if you do, you should eat less meat, fish and poultry.

• **Fats and oils**—two to three servings a day...with a serving being one teaspoon of margarine or vegetable oil, one tablespoon of mayonnaise or two tablespoons of salad dressing.

• **Sweets**—up to five servings a week ...such as one-half cup sorbet, one tablespoon of sugar, jelly or jam, or one cup of lemonade.

• **Sodium**—The National Academy of Science's Institute of Medicine recommends not exceeding 1,500 milligrams (mg) to 2,400 mg of salt per day (1,500 mg is about two-thirds teaspoon of table salt).

Note: Factors such as medications you are on, exercise and diet history should be considered in determining your optimal sodium intake.

Make DASH Delicious...

Here's another reason the DASH diet is tastier and easier to follow than you might think: It follows many of the same principles as the Mediterranean diet that is so popular today, in particular its focus on a daily

Enjoy a Bit of Chocolate Every Day

Antioxidants known as polyphenols in dark chocolate may lower blood pressure by improving blood vessel functioning. In a recent German trial, adults with prehypertension or stage 1 hypertension who consumed 6.3 grams (g) of dark chocolate (less than two chocolate kisses) daily for 18 weeks lowered systolic pressure by an average of 2.9 mmHg and diastolic pressure by 1.9 mmHg, without increasing weight, cholesterol or insulin levels. For a modest blood pressure–lowering effect, enjoy a bite or two of dark chocolate daily. Skip milk chocolate, which contains too few polyphenols to curb blood pressure.

Mark Houston, MD, associate clinical professor of medicine, Vanderbilt University School of Medicine, and director, Hypertension Institute, both in Nashville.

Blueberries to the Rescue

In one of the first population-based studies to look at the effect of flavonoids on high blood pressure, researchers from the University of East Anglia in England found that blueberries' powerful antioxidant flavonoid *anthocyanin* can help keep pressure down. Eat one-half cup of blueberries (fresh or frozen) five times weekly.

A. Cassidy, et al., "Habitual Intake of Flavonoid Subclasses and Incident Hypertension in Adults," *American Journal of Clinical Nutrition* (2011).

bounty of fresh vegetables. It's easy to find restaurants serving these foods.

While many new DASH followers complain about a lack of flavor, what they really are reacting to is the lack of salt. Heller offers cooking tips for flavorful food—and she notes that reducing salt intake is easier if you make the change gradually. She often uses a base of onions, garlic and red wine, which she says makes just about everything tasty. "For sautéing foods, I start with onions and garlic together and at the very end of the dish I add a little bit of red wine and cook it down to evaporate the alcohol," she explains. Herbs add flavor, too—for instance, try a bit of oregano or thyme on vegetables. A sprinkle of reduced-sodium cheese can also be delicious, as is, surprisingly, cinnamon. Another trick of Heller's is to drizzle a bit of olive oil (a tablespoon, she suggests) over foods, which enhances their flavor and adds fat, making them more satisfying and also helping with absorption of nutrients.

To get started on DASH, Heller says, it is vital to clear your kitchen and pantry of all foods that are not on the diet. Then stock up with a wide variety of fresh, tasty and healthy DASH foods. That way, when your stomach rumbles, you will have plenty of satisfying no-cheat choices. For more

information on DASH, suggested menus and recipes, go to *www.dashdiet.org*.

Can Beets Beat High Blood Pressure?

Amrita Ahluwalia, PhD, professor of vascular pharmacology, Centre for Clinical Pharmacology, William Harvey Research Institute, Barts and The London School of Medicine and Dentistry, Queen Mary, University of London, London, UK.

Beyond being a treat for the eyes, with its gorgeous deep red color, beet juice serves up some pretty attractive health benefits—especially for people who need to bring down their blood pressure. Drinking beet juice appears to have a protective effect on blood vessels, which helps keep blood pressure under control, according to researcher Amrita Ahluwalia, PhD, a professor of vascular pharmacology at Barts and The London School of Medicine and Dentistry.

Nitrates in Beets Protect Blood Vessels

In the study, 14 people with normal blood pressure drank two cups of either pure beet juice (with no additives) or water. Dr. Ahluwalia and her colleagues checked the participants' blood pressure at regular intervals both before and after ingestion. *They found that…*

● **Blood pressure began to drop in the beet group about 60 minutes after drinking the juice.**

● **Blood pressure reached its lowest level in the beet group two to three hours after drinking the juice** (a reduction of approximately 10 mmHg systolic at two and a half hours and 8 mmHg diastolic at three hours).

● **No similar impact was observed in the control group, who drank water.**

Dr. Ahluwalia believes the nitrates in beets are what help control blood pressure by protecting blood vessels. She explains that colonies of bacteria on the back of our tongues chemically change nitrate to nitrite. When we swallow saliva, this nitrite enters the stomach and then crosses into circulation, where it is changed into a very important molecule called nitric oxide (NO). This is a "vasodilator," which means that it opens up blood vessels so blood flows more easily. With less resistance to blood flow, blood pressure comes down.

Results of the study were published in *Hypertension*.

HBP RX: Beets

"Our hope is that simple dietary interventions—such as including more beets and other fresh produce in the diet—may one day replace some blood pressure medicines," says Dr. Ahluwalia. We're not there yet, however. She advises people with high blood pressure to carefully discuss all treatment options with their doctors before stopping any medication. In the meantime, you can buy fresh beet juice at most health–food stores or make it yourself by steaming and juicing several whole beets. If you find beet juice too heavy, lighten it with apple juice. Other excellent sources of nitrates are spinach, lettuce and root vegetables. Two cups of beet juice is a lot, Dr. Ahluwalia notes, so she's currently testing the effect of lesser amounts on people who have high blood pressure.

Melon Lowers Blood Pressure

Lona Sandon, MEd, RD, LD, assistant professor, department of clinical nutrition, University of Texas Southwestern Medical Center, Dallas. Sandon is a national spokesperson for the American Dietetic Association. *www.eatright.org*

As though anyone needs an excuse to indulge in a cool, juicy slice of melon on a hot summer day, these popular fruits—including watermelon, cantaloupe, honeydew and casaba melons—are a rich source of potassium and a host of other nutrients as well. Refreshing and delicious, they also are a healthy, natural way to help lower your blood pressure, notes Lona Sandon, MEd, RD, LD, an assistant professor at University of Texas Southwestern Medical Center in Dallas, and a national spokesperson for the American Dietetic Association (*www.eatright.org*).

The "Whey" to Better Blood Pressure Readings

Recent study: Seventy-one adults with hypertension who drank a beverage containing 28 grams of powdered whey (a by-product of cow's milk) daily for six weeks had an average six-point drop in blood pressure.

Theory: Whey protein increases production of nitric oxide, a compound that expands blood vessels.

If you have high blood pressure: Ask your doctor about whey protein powder (available at health-food stores). Try adding it to smoothies or sprinkling it on cereal or yogurt.

Susan Fluegel, PhD, nutritional biochemist, department of food science and human nutrition, Washington State University, Pullman.

Shake Off Blood Pressure Worries

If you have salt-sensitive high blood pressure, you probably know already that you should watch your sodium intake. Too much salt—both from the salt shaker and from processed foods—causes fluid retention and blood vessel contraction that contribute to hypertension. What you may not know is that potassium also plays an important role in this equation. A study published last year in the *Archives of Internal Medicine* noted that people with a low sodium-to-potassium ratio—that is, those who made a point of both consuming less salt and eating more potassium-rich fresh produce than is typical for the American diet—were less likely to experience high blood pressure. Because it is a vasodilator and helps get rid of sodium and water, potassium helps curb fluid retention and blood vessel contraction.

According to the American Heart Association, the recommended daily intake of potassium for adults is 4,700 milligrams (mg). Many people don't normally consume this much potassium, but melons provide a tasty solution. Two cups of cubed melon contain more than 1,000 mg of potassium, or nearly one-fourth of your daily requirement.

Other rich dietary sources of this mineral include apricots, artichokes, avocados, bananas, beans, kiwis, oranges, peas, potatoes, prunes, raisins, tomatoes, spinach, Swiss chard and other green leafy vegetables.

Melon at Every Meal?

Melons are much more versatile than most people realize, and you can easily incorporate them into a wide variety of dishes. Instead of reserving them for breakfast or a snack, take advantage of the season's bounty and put melons on your family's summer menu of soups, salads and salsas...

Walnuts Curb Stress Response

After eating 18 walnut halves and taking one tablespoon of walnut oil daily for six weeks, study participants had lower blood pressure when exposed to stressors than participants who did not consume walnuts and walnut oil. Healthful omega-3 fatty acids in walnuts are likely responsible for lowering the body's stress response.

Sheila G. West, PhD, associate professor of biobehavioral health and nutritional sciences, Pennsylvania State University, University Park, and leader of a study published in *Journal of the American College of Nutrition.*

- **Melon soup.** Puree chunks of ripe honeydew and cantaloupe with orange juice and chill.
- **Luscious melon salad.** Combine small chunks of your favorite melon with raspberries, strawberries or orange sections and drizzle with honey and lime or lemon juice.
- **Fish or chicken with melon.** Serve the grilled or broiled meats on a bed of diced ripe melon. Or make a melon salsa to accompany the main dish—combine finely diced honeydew and cantaloupe, diced tomatoes, minced red onion, orange juice, lime juice, cilantro and salt.
- **Grilled melon.** Cube honeydew, and toss in lemon juice, brown sugar and ginger. Thread onto skewers and grill for three to four minutes or until slightly soft and beginning to brown.

Note: Potassium affects the balance of fluids in the body, so too much can be a problem for older people and those with heart or kidney disease. If you take a diuretic drug or have issues with fluid retention, talk to your doctor before adding significant amounts of melon to your diet.

Peas Help Reduce Blood Pressure

Rotimi Aluko, PhD, professor, department of human nutritional sciences, University of Manitoba, Winnipeg, Canada.

Peas, once viewed as a starchy vegetable, are now being recognized as nutritional blockbusters, packed with protein, assorted nutrients and fiber, and free of fat and cholesterol. Even better, Canadian food chemists have discovered a protein in yellow garden peas that shows promise in treating high blood pressure and chronic kidney disease (CKD).

While researching treatment options for patients with kidney disease, Rotimi Aluko, PhD, a professor in the department of human nutritional sciences at the University of Manitoba in Winnipeg, Canada, and colleagues purified a mixture of proteins—pea protein hydrolysate—from yellow peas. They fed this to rats with severe kidney disease every day for eight weeks. *At the end of this period, Dr. Aluko and his team found that...*

• **Blood pressure decreased by 20% in rats who consumed the pea mixture,** compared with a control group of rats who did not.

• **Urine production,** which typically decreases with kidney disease, improved by 30% in treated rats, bringing it to a normal level.

What's next: Pea pills for the heart and kidneys.

Given these promising results, trials are now under way in humans with mild hypertension, and—subject to regulatory approval—Dr. Aluko estimates that an edible product derived from peas could be available in a few years. In the not-too-distant future, you may be able to stroll into your local pharmacy or health-food store and purchase pea extract in pill form or as a powder to add to food or beverages. As for eating peas themselves, Dr. Aluko explains that for this purpose pea proteins must be treated with special enzymes in order to become active. But he believes that they're healthy anyway—so tell the kids and adults at the table to eat their peas, please.

Salt-Free Seasoning Made Easy

Judith Wylie-Rosett, EdD, RD, professor of epidemiology and population division head for health behavior and nutrition research at Albert Einstein College of Medicine in New York City. She is the author of *The Complete Weight Loss Workbook: Proven Techniques for Controlling Weight-Related Health Problems* (American Diabetes Association) and has published more than 130 journal articles on nutrition and health.

Have you had much luck in getting your loved ones (not to mention yourself) to put down the salt shaker? Most people are more bothered by the taste of bland, boring food than by the increased threat of a heart attack or stroke.

More than half of Americans age 60 and older have hypertension. If you or someone you cook for is among them, you may have

Mineral Water May Help Lower Blood Pressure

After drinking one liter of mineral water per day for one month, people between the ages of 45 and 64 with borderline hypertension (high blood pressure) experienced a significant decrease in blood pressure.

Theory: Most mineral waters contain significant amounts of magnesium and calcium, both of which help to reduce blood pressure.

Study of 70 people by researchers at Gothenburg University, Gothenburg, Sweden, published in *BMC Public Health.*

Hibiscus Tea Curbs Blood Pressure

Recent research: In a study of 65 adults with prehypertension or mild hypertension, those who drank hibiscus tea had a 7.2-point drop, on average, in systolic (top number) blood pressure, compared with a one-point drop, on average, in the placebo group.

Theory: Antioxidant flavonoids in hibiscus help lower blood pressure.

If you have been diagnosed with prehypertension or hypertension: Three cups daily of hibiscus tea may benefit you.

Diane L. McKay, PhD, assistant professor of nutrition, science and policy, Tufts University, Boston.

tried to fool the taste buds with a commercial salt substitute but found the flavor too bitter.

Well, take heart. Nutrition researcher Judith Wylie-Rosett, EdD, RD, whose book *The Complete Weight Loss Workbook* includes many health-promoting recipes, suggests some much better ways to put zing into low-salt foods. *To get started…*

- **It can take a lot of seasoning to make up for the missing salt**—so when you drop salt from a recipe, try doubling one or more of the other seasonings the recipe calls for.

- **For maximum flavor from herbs and spices, opt for fresh rather than dried.**

- **Choose herb-infused oils and vinegars instead of unflavored ones.**

Tasty, salt-free ways to spice up…

- **Beef.** For seasoning that stands up to red meat's strong flavor, marinate beef for two to three hours in pineapple juice or orange juice mixed with balsamic vinegar, red wine, diced onions and/or chopped garlic.

- **Chicken.** For delicate-flavored lemon chicken, add chopped tarragon, which is subtly bittersweet and minty. Robust chicken Parmesan needs more aggressive seasonings, such as fennel, basil, rosemary, garlic and/or oregano. For stews, add a bay leaf (remove before eating) plus mustard, marjoram and freshly ground black pepper…or use strong spices, such as cumin, turmeric and/or ginger.

- **Fish.** Complement a mild-flavored white fish with the tangy taste of yogurt. Mix plain low-fat or nonfat yogurt with dill, ginger, mustard and garlic, then add one tablespoon of mayonnaise per cup of yogurt to keep the yogurt from separating. Use this as a marinade…or serve with the fish as a sauce. Fatty fish (mackerel, bluefish) have a strong flavor that blends well with the hearty taste of curry, lemon pepper and garlic.

- **Pasta.** Instead of salting the cooking water, use a splash of flavored olive oil (this also keeps your pasta from sticking). Drain pasta one minute earlier than you normally would, return it to the pot, stir in whatever sauce you're going to use and cook them together for that final minute—so the pasta absorbs more flavor from the sauce.

- **Soups.** For delicate-flavored soups, such as chicken soup, use chopped sage, parsley and thyme to enhance but not overwhelm the flavor. To give zest to hearty-tasting soups, add a splash of balsamic vinegar and/or wine when the soup is almost done.

- **Vegetables.** Stir together two or more types of cooked veggies before serving—they taste more interesting that way than alone—and boost flavor with a generous amount of fresh-squeezed lemon juice. Simmer root vegetables in reduced-fat coconut milk mixed with curry. Dress salads with herb-infused olive or sunflower oil…champagne vinegar or vinegar made from sweeter fruits (pears, figs, raspberries)…and some flat-leaf parsley, chervil or tarragon.

Salt? Who needs it?

Tomato Extract Lowers Blood Pressure

New finding: In a study of 54 adults with moderately high blood pressure (above 135 mmHg/80 mmHg), a dietary supplement derived from tomatoes reduced average systolic (top number) readings by 12 mmHg and diastolic (bottom number) readings by 6 mmHg after two to four weeks. The 250-mg capsule given daily was equivalent to eating four medium tomatoes.

Theory: High levels of lycopene and vitamins C and E improve function of the arterial wall, which can lower blood pressure.

Esther Paran, MD, hypertension unit, Soroka University Hospital, Ben-Gurion University of the Negev, Israel.

■ ■ ■ ■

Try "Celery Therapy" To Reduce Blood Pressure Meds

Mao Shing Ni, PhD, DOM, LAc, chancellor and cofounder of Yo San University in Los Angeles and cofounder of Tao of Wellness, an acupuncture and Chinese medicine clinic in Santa Monica and Newport Beach, California. He is the author of 12 books, including *Secrets of Longevity: Dr. Mao's 8-Week Program* (Chronicle). *www.taoofwellness.com*

If you have hypertension (high blood pressure), you know it can be tricky to find the right drug or combination of drugs to bring blood pressure back under control. Often the meds do not reduce blood pressure enough…or they become less effective over time, so you have to keep increasing the dose.

Mao Shing Ni, PhD, DOM, LAc, author of *Secrets of Longevity: Dr. Mao's 8-Week Program—Simple Steps that Add Years to Your Life,* says a simple way to help solve such problems is by drinking celery juice. Used as a complement to hypertension medication, "celery juice therapy" can aid in normalizing blood pressure and even can allow some patients to eventually reduce or discontinue their medication. (Of course, it is important not to alter dosages or discontinue medication without a doctor's approval.) Celery juice also can be a useful preventive measure for people at risk for hypertension.

Dr. Mao explains that celery contains compounds that relax the smooth muscles lining the arteries and also reduce the stress hormones that constrict the arteries. Both these mechanisms cause the blood vessels to dilate, thus improving blood flow and reducing blood pressure.

Who can be helped: Talk to your doctor about trying celery juice if you have hypertension (blood pressure of 140/90 mmHg or higher)…have prehypertension (blood pressure between 120/80 mmHg and 139/89 mmHg)…take medication that may elevate blood pressure (for instance, certain decongestants or antidepressants)…or have a family history of hypertension. If you decide to go ahead, have your doctor take a baseline reading of your blood pressure for later comparison. Celery juice generally is safe for everyone except people with a celery allergy.

Eggs May Help with Hypertension

Egg proteins have effects similar to those of ACE inhibitors—prescription medicines used to treat hypertension. Despite concerns about cholesterol in eggs, healthy people can eat them without raising heart disease risk.

Jianping Wu, PhD, researcher, department of agricultural, food and nutritional science, University of Alberta, Edmonton, Canada, and coauthor of a study published in *Journal of Agricultural and Food Chemistry.*

What to do: The first goal is to consume the equivalent of 12 to 16 celery stalks per day for one month. You could just chomp on the stalks, but that's a lot of celery to eat—so it's more efficient to make juice. Dr. Mao recommends using a juicer because you won't have to dilute the juice or strain out any fibrous strands. Three to four times per day, drink the juice of four stalks—each serving is about eight ounces.

If you don't have a juicer, you can use a blender instead. Cut four celery stalks into chunks and place in the blender…add enough water to cover the chunks (about four ounces)…blend well. Strain out the fibers before drinking, because otherwise the fibers would be "too much to bear," Dr. Mao says. For this diluted juice, the dose is three to four 12-ounce servings daily.

After one month: Visit your doctor and discuss how your original baseline blood pressure reading compares with your current blood pressure as indicated on a home blood pressure monitor or a new reading taken at your doctor's office. If your blood pressure has dropped, the celery therapy is working!

Continue drinking the juice daily until your blood pressure is under control. At that point, Dr. Mao advises, ask your doctor whether you can try lowering your hypertension medication dosage—do not reduce or discontinue medication on your own. When your blood pressure is completely stable, try gradually reducing your celery juice dosage to one glass daily as a maintenance dose. You may even be able to halt celery juice therapy if your blood pressure completely returns to normal and you are able to go off your blood pressure medication, Dr. Mao says.

Live Like a Caveman and Live Much Longer

Philip J. Goscienski, MD, retired clinical professor of pediatrics, department of community and family medicine at University of California, San Diego, School of Medicine. He is author of *Health Secrets of the Stone Age* (Better Life). *www.stoneagedoc.com*

Our bodies reached their current stage of development—in terms of genetics, chemistry and metabolism—during the Stone Age, tens of thousands of years ago. But our lifestyles, in particular our diets and exercise habits, have undergone changes that our bodies aren't equipped to handle.

In particular, the development of agriculture and domesticated livestock has led to a plentiful food supply. Humans don't have to work as hard to find a good meal, and those meals are served more frequently. Obesity, once rare, is now a leading health threat.

Yet in modern hunter-gatherer societies, people live much as they did in the Stone Age—that's how we can make con-

Whole Grains Linked to Lower Blood Pressure

New study: Researchers who reviewed health and nutrition data for 31,684 men found that those who consumed the most whole grains (about 52 grams [g] daily) were 19% less likely to develop high blood pressure than those who consumed the least whole grains (about 3 g daily).

Best sources: Oatmeal (instant or cooked)—one cup, 30 g to 35 g…popcorn —one cup, 10 g to 12 g…whole-wheat bread—one slice, about 15 g…and bran cereal—one cup, 5 g to 10 g.

Alan Flint, MD, DrPH, research scientist, department of nutrition, Harvard School of Public Health, Boston.

clusions about the health of our Stone Age ancestors. Obesity is virtually unheard of in these groups. Members rarely get diabetes, hypertension or heart disease. Cancer is rare. Even in the absence of medical care, they often are healthier than the rest of us.

Here's what worked for our Stone Age ancestors…

Stone Age Fruit

Our Stone Age ancestors gathered wild fruits, which were much smaller and less attractive than we are used to today. The fruits that we buy in supermarkets are bred for appearance, sweetness and size. They have less fiber and antioxidants and more sugars than fruits that grow in the wild without human intervention.

A USDA study published in *Journal of the American College of Nutrition* found that nutrient levels in produce have declined significantly in just the last 60 years. There have been drops in protein, calcium, vitamin A, riboflavin and thiamine.

Self-defense: Opt for smaller fruits (such as apricots, cherries and berries), which have a greater ratio of skin to flesh, relative to their size, than larger ones, such as peaches. This is important because the largest concentration of fiber and antioxidants is found in the skin and the layers just beneath.

Also, if possible, switch from standard supermarket produce (which tends to be larger) to organic, wild-grown or heirloom varieties. The produce that is available at farmers' markets usually hasn't been bred solely for appearance (or ease of shipping). It naturally will have a higher concentration of nutrients and fiber, thus making it a superior option.

Game Meats

Our ancestors ate plenty of meat, but they ate game meats (antelope, venison, bison), which have very little saturated fat. High intake of saturated fat leads to obesity, which is a leading cause of heart disease and cancer.

Most of the saturated fat in the American diet (apart from that found in processed and restaurant foods) comes from domestic animal meats. These animals are fed grains, which are not part of their natural diet. The meat of grain-fed animals is marbled with saturated fat, making it sweeter and more tender.

What we can learn: Avoid grain-fed beef and pork. Many specialty markets feature meats from grass-fed animals, which are superior to grain-fed.

Even better: Look for game meats, which are high in healthful mono-unsaturated fat and low in saturated fat. For example, a four-ounce serving of venison has 1.4 grams (g) of saturated fat, about one-third as much as the same amount of rib eye steak.

Water, Not Soda

During the Stone Age, people had only water to drink. Recent studies, including one that looked at the average diet of preschoolers in England, found that many children now drink no water. They get virtually all of their fluids from high-calorie, high-sugar soft drinks and juices.

The average American consumes about two-and-a-half sugary soft drinks daily. Many soft drinks contain about 150 calories per serving. Someone who drinks two nondiet soft drinks a day for a year is consuming the caloric equivalent of about 30 extra pounds.

Even diet soda has been linked to health problems. A recent study found that diet soda drinkers have a higher risk for stroke and heart attack.

What we can learn: Water is the healthiest liquid you can drink. Most adults need about 60 ounces a day—enough to make the urine clear or lightly colored, instead of dark. Opt for filtered water whenever possible. Stone Agers didn't have to worry about industrial chemicals.

Far Less Salt

Our ancient ancestors probably consumed about 700 milligrams (mg) of sodium daily, about the same amount as those who live in hunter-gatherer societies today. People in these societies have virtually no high blood pressure. The average American now consumes about four times this much salt, and high blood pressure raises the risk for heart disease and stroke, leading causes of death in the US.

What we can learn: No one needs extra sodium. Every natural food, including fruits and vegetables, contains enough sodium to keep us healthy. Anything "extra" is unnecessary—and often unhealthy.

Recommended: No more than 1,500 mg of sodium daily. Less is better. Relatively little of the sodium in the American diet comes from the salt shaker—most comes from processed foods. Read labels carefully, even when you think a food is "healthy." A glass of tomato juice, for example, has more than 800 mg of sodium. One tablespoon of soy sauce has 1,200 mg.

Minirobics

During the Stone Age, the average adult most likely expended between 3,500 and 5,000 calories a day. Back then, people didn't "do exercise," because their lives were exercise. They walked miles to gather food, chased down game and used only hand tools.

In modern hunter-gatherer societies, dieting is unheard of—and unnecessary. People are naturally lean. They stay strong even into old age, unlike the 25% of Americans over the age of 65 who need assistance getting out of bed or bathing. They have healthier hearts because they are always moving.

Today only about 10% of Americans regularly get intense physical exercise. On average, our level of daily activity is about 75% less than it was at the beginning of the 20th century.

What we can learn: Current guidelines call for about 30 minutes of moderately intense exercise daily. That's not enough. Our "caveman bodies" seem to function best when we get at least 60 minutes of moderately intense exercise daily. This means exercise that is intense enough to get you breathing hard. It could be working in the yard, doing housework, bicycling or lifting weights.

My advice: If you don't care for formal exercise, you still can get benefits from what I call "minirobics"—daily habits that keep you moving. These include things such as taking stairs instead of elevators…and using a push-type mower rather than one powered with gasoline.

The average person can burn an extra few hundred calories daily (and lose a pound or two a month) simply by moving more throughout the day. And you're never too old to start using your body more. Researchers in Boston conducted a study in which residents of a convalescent home were put on a strength-training program. Their average age was 90. In eight weeks, they had tripled their strength and increased their muscle mass by 10%.

Add Flavor Without Adding Salt

Limiting sodium often lowers high blood pressure and cardiovascular disease risk—but many Americans consume double the recommended limit.

Problem: Reducing salt can reduce a food's flavor, too.

Participants in a recent study reported that low-sodium foods prepared with a broth flavored with karebushi (dried bonito, a fish in the mackerel family) tasted better than other low-sodium foods.

Try it: Karebushi is sold as thin shaven flakes in Asian food stores and online. Add it to low-salt soups, sauces, rice and vegetables.

M. Manabe, PhD, associate professor, laboratory of cookery science, Doshisha Women's College of Liberal Arts, Kyoto, Japan, and leader of a study of 61 people.

Less Salt Solution

Eva Obarzanek, PhD, RD, research nutritionist, division of prevention and population sciences, National Heart, Lung and Blood Institute, Bethesda, Maryland.

Eat more fruits and vegetables for an easy cutback on salt. In a three-month study of 354 adults (median age 48) with prehypertension or high blood pressure (120/80 millimeters of mercury [mmHg] to 159/95 mmHg), participants ate diets with three different daily sodium levels, for 30 days at each level.

Result: Participants rated a diet with 1,200 milligrams (mg) of sodium and a diet with 2,300 mg of sodium (about one teaspoon of salt) equally acceptable to 3,500 mg daily.

Theory: A lower-salt diet—especially if it is rich in fruits and vegetables—can be satisfying. Also, limit your consumption of processed foods and restaurant meals, which tend to contain high amounts of sodium.

The New Blood Pressure Control Diet for Women

C. Tissa Kappagoda, MD, PhD, professor of medicine, director, cardiac rehabilitation program, University of California, Davis.

For the first time, high blood pressure that is uncontrolled is more common in women than in men—yet women are less likely to be prescribed treatment, such as blood pressure–lowering medication. High blood pressure, or hypertension, doesn't hurt or cause other obvious warning signs, but it damages arteries in ways that can lead to stroke, heart attack, kidney problems and cognitive impairment. *More concerns for women…*

• **Hypertension now affects nearly one in four American women.** Rates in women are rising even as rates in men are falling.

• **About 35% of women with hypertension go untreated.**

Blood pressure is the force that blood exerts against the arterial walls. It is reported as two numbers. The top number, or systolic pressure, is the pressure as the heart pumps. The bottom number, or diastolic pressure, is the pressure as the heart rests between beats. Normal, healthy blood pressure is below 120/80 millimeters of mercury (mmHg)…hypertension is diagnosed at 140/90 mmHg or higher.

Problem: Up to 70% of people who are told that they are fine because their blood pressure is in the "high normal" range actually are at serious risk. Systolic pressure of 120 to 139 and/or diastolic pressure of 80 to 89 indicates prehypertension—which often progresses to hypertension.

Good news: You can significantly reduce blood pressure by changing what you eat. You must do more than just cut back on salt—although following this common advice helps—but the simple strategies below are worth the effort.

If you already have hypertension or have "high normal" blood pressure...are at risk due to being overweight or having a family history of blood pressure problems...or simply want to be as healthy as possible, this diet is for you.

Bonus: These habits often lead to weight loss—which also lowers blood pressure.

Have more...

• **Berries.** Berries are high in polyphenols, micronutrients that relax blood vessels.

Study: Hypertension patients who ate berries daily for two months lowered their systolic blood pressure by up to seven points—which could reduce risk for heart-related death by up to 15%.

Action: Eat one cup of fresh or frozen berries daily.

• **Fat-free milk.** A study found that people who ingested the greatest amounts of low-fat dairy were 56% less likely to develop hypertension than those who ate the least.

Theory: The active components may be the milk proteins whey and/or casein, which help blood vessels dilate.

Action: Have eight to 16 ounces of fat-free milk per day. Evidence suggests that fat-free milk is best—higher fat milk and other dairy products may not work as well.

• **Potassium-rich produce.** Potassium counteracts the blood pressure–raising effects of sodium.

New study: Prehypertension patients with the highest sodium-to-potassium intake were up to 50% more likely to develop cardiovascular disease within 10 to 15 years, compared with those who had the lowest ratio.

Action: Among the generally recommended five or so daily servings of fruits and vegetables, include some potassium-rich choices, such as bananas, citrus fruits, lima beans, potatoes and sweet potatoes (with skin), tomatoes and yams. Talk to your doctor before increasing potassium if you take blood pressure or heart medication (diuretic, ACE inhibitor or ARB blocker) or if you have kidney problems.

• **Fiber.** Studies suggest that fiber lowers blood pressure, though the mechanism is unknown. The fiber must come from food—fiber supplements do not offer the same benefit.

Action: Check food labels, and aim for at least 25 grams of fiber daily.

Good sources: Whole fruits (juice has less fiber)...raw or lightly cooked vegetables (overcooking reduces fiber)...beans and lentils...high-fiber breakfast cereals...and whole grains, such as barley, brown rice, oats, quinoa and whole wheat.

Eat less...

• **Meat.** Often high in cholesterol and saturated fat, meat contributes to the build-up of plaque inside arteries—a condition called atherosclerosis. Hypertension significantly increases the risk that atherosclerosis will lead to a heart attack or stroke.

Action: If you have been diagnosed with both atherosclerosis and hypertension, a good way to reduce your cardiovascular risk is to adopt a vegetarian or near-vegetarian diet.

Also: Avoid other sources of saturated fats, such as high-fat dairy, and palm oil.

If you are concerned about getting enough protein, increase your intake of plant proteins.

Good sources: Soy foods (edamame, soy milk, tofu)...beans, lentils, peas...nuts and seeds.

If you have hypertension or prehypertension but no atherosclerosis, limit yourself to no more than three weekly four-ounce servings of animal protein, and stick with low-fat meat, fish or poultry.

• **Salt.** Sodium raises blood pressure by increasing blood volume and constricting blood vessels. Some people are more sensitive to salt than others—but limiting dietary salt is a good idea for everyone.

Recommended: Healthy people up to age 50 should limit sodium to 2,300 milligrams (mg) per day (about one teaspoon of salt)…older people and anyone with pre-hypertension or hypertension should stay under 1,500 mg daily (about two-thirds of a teaspoon of salt).

Action: Instead of salt, add flavor with pepper, garlic and other seasonings. Do not use seasoning blends that contain salt. Avoid processed and canned foods unless labeled "low sodium."

Pros and cons of…

• **Red wine.** Like berries, red wine contains heart-healthy polyphenols.

But: Polyphenols relax blood vessels only when exposure time is short, as with light-to-moderate alcohol consumption. Heavy drinking actually reduces the blood vessels' ability to relax, negating polyphenols' benefits.

Advised: If you choose to drink alcohol, opt for red wine and have no more than one glass per day.

Alcohol-free option: Polyphenol-rich unsweetened dark grape juice.

• **Coffee, tea and soda.** Some evidence links caffeine to increased blood pressure.

Advised: Opt for caffeine-free beverages.

Good choice: Herbal tea. A recent study suggests that drinking three cups daily of a blend that includes hibiscus can lower systolic blood pressure by about seven mmHg.

• **Chocolate.** Small studies suggest that dark chocolate helps lower blood pressure.

Theory: Cocoa contains antioxidant procyanidins, which boost the body's pro-duction of nitric oxide, a chemical that relaxes blood vessels.

But: Chocolate is high in sugar and fat, both of which contribute to weight gain.

Advised: If you want an occasional dessert, one-half ounce of dark chocolate is a good choice.

"Berry Good News" For the Heart

Bethany Thayer, RD, spokesperson for the American Dietetic Association.

Daily servings of berries are heart-protective. Berries are a treat with a cherry on top—delicious and very healthful in that they actually provide protection for your heart. Among other things, these luscious fruits are packed with a form of antioxidant called *polyphenols.* Previous studies have found that consumption of other polyphenol-rich foods, such as red wine, tea and cocoa, increase cardiovascular health…and now a new study from Europe has investigated whether berries have a similar effect.

Researcher Iris Erlund and her colleagues at the National Public Health Institute in Helsinki, Finland, studied 72 middle-aged subjects with cardiovascular risk factors, such as mild hypertension, elevated total cholesterol, or low HDL cholesterol. Half the subjects were instructed to eat two portions of berries daily. The other half did not have any berries. Every other day, the berry group consumed 100 grams (3½ ounces) of whole bilberries and a nectar containing 50 grams (1¾ ounces) of lingonberries. On alternate days, they ate 100 grams of black currant-strawberry puree and raspberry-chokeberry juice (2.5 ounces

Food Companies Are Using Less Salt

Good news for individuals with high blood pressure—more manufacturers are using less salt.

Examples: Campbell Soup Co. has reduced the sodium in more than 100 products, including Prego sauces and Pepperidge Farm breads, by 25% to 50%. ConAgra, maker of Chef Boyardee and Hebrew National, plans to cut salt by 20% in the next five years. Kraft will cut salt by an average of 10% in more than 1,000 of its products, including Oscar Mayer bologna and Velveeta, over the next two years.

USA Today

undiluted). The point of using a combination of different berries was to ensure a high intake of various polyphenols, such as flavonols, phenolic acids, anthocyanins and procyanidins.

After eight weeks, the berry eaters had consumed about three times the amount of polyphenols as the non-berry eaters. They experienced a "significant" increase in HDL cholesterol of 5.2%. Their systolic blood pressure decreased by 1.5 points on average, with a more notable decrease of seven points for those with the highest blood pressure. Berry consumption also inhibited platelet function by 11%, lowering the risk of clot formation, which can lead to cardiovascular problems.

The findings show that eating even moderate portions of berries, as the study subjects did, can result in significant changes that may mean a reduced risk of cardiovascular disease and even death. "Berries are a great source of polyphenols, and polyphenols are an important antioxidant," says Bethany Thayer, RD, a spokesperson for the American Dietetic Association. "There are a wide variety of berries available—find ways to include the ones you like in your diet." The berries used in the Finnish study are not widely available here…but, blueberries, raspberries, blackberries and strawberries are all good choices. You can toss berries into a salad or stir them into oatmeal or low-fat yogurt. Combine them with other fruit, blend them in a smoothie with milk or yogurt, or bake them in muffins. As with most fruit, the riper the berries the richer the nutrient content. And in the winter (or any time of year), frozen berries are an excellent option as they are picked and frozen at the peak of ripeness. "These are all great ways to boost the odds that you're getting the polyphenols you need," says Thayer.

■ ■ ■ ■

2

Blood Pressure Dangers Your Doctor May Miss

What Your Doctor May Not Tell You About High Blood Pressure

Mark C. Houston, MD, associate clinical professor of medicine at Vanderbilt University School of Medicine and director of the Hypertension Institute at Saint Thomas Medical Group, both in Nashville. He is the author of *What Your Doctor May Not Tell You About Hypertension* (Grand Central). *www.hypertensioninstitute.com*

A woman—let's call her Naomi—was diagnosed with high blood pressure and went on medication prescribed by her doctor. Within a few months, she was back at the doctor's office, her blood pressure heading up instead of down. It turned out that she was not taking her medication properly—and that the drug she had been given was not the most appropriate one for her.

Naomi is hardly alone. Nearly one-third of US adults have hypertension (blood pressure higher than 140/90), a symptomless disease that, if not appropriately managed, can result in a heart attack or stroke.

Mark C. Houston, MD, is director of the Hypertension Institute at Saint Thomas Medical Group in Nashville and author of

What Your Doctor May Not Tell You About Hypertension. He explains that failure to take medication properly is one primary reason why high blood pressure is often so hard to get under control.

Another problem is that finding the right medication or combination of medications can be tricky, and often doctors have resorted to a "try this, try that" approach.

Good news: Recent research has helped clarify which types of drugs are likely to work best for certain patients. *So if you have recently been diagnosed with hypertension or if your medication is not working, it's time to talk to your doctor about...*

• **Your levels of the blood pressure–modulating enzyme** *renin.* A recent study showed that people with different blood levels of renin responded differently to various hypertension drugs—and that taking the wrong kind of medication actually made blood pressure go up.

Patients with **high-renin hypertension** responded best to...

• Angiotensin-converting enzyme (ACE) inhibitors, which reduce blood pressure by blocking an enzyme that produces angiotensin II (a hormone that causes blood vessels to narrow)…dilating arteries…and reducing inflammation and oxidative stress. They also decrease clotting, further protecting against heart attack and stroke.

• Angiotensin receptor blockers (ARBs), which work by blocking receptors for angiotensin I (the precursor to angiotensin II). They also dilate blood vessels and ease inflammation and oxidative stress.

• Direct renin inhibitors, which reduce angiotensin I and relax blood vessels.

• Beta-blockers, which reduce blood pressure by reducing nerve signals to the heart and blood vessels and slowing the heart rate.

People with **low-renin hypertension** responded best to…

• Calcium channel blockers, which combat high blood pressure by preventing calcium from moving into arteries and heart muscle cells and allowing arteries to dilate.

• Diuretics, which cause kidneys to remove excess sodium and water from the body and dilate blood vessel walls.

• **How your blood pressure is being measured.** The blood pressure cuff in your doctor's office may not be reliable if you are prone to "white-coat hypertension" (blood pressure that rises from the anxiety of being in the doctor's office) or "masked hypertension" (lower blood pressure numbers in the doctor's office but consistently higher numbers at other times).

Ask your doctor if you might benefit from using a high-quality home blood pressure monitor (sold over the counter in pharmacies and online for $50 to $150) to keep track of your readings every day. Also discuss the option of using a 24-hour ambulatory blood pressure monitor. A cuff worn on your arm and a small device clipped to your belt record your pressure every 15 to 30 minutes for 24 hours…then your doctor analyzes that data.

• **How consistently you take your medicine.** The different types of hypertension drugs can cause a variety of side effects, such as fatigue, memory problems and sexual dysfunction. If you experience these or other problems, do not suffer in silence—and certainly do not keep silent if you sometimes skip doses to avoid side effects. Tell your doctor and discuss alternative drugs.

But if you are conscientious about taking your meds, be sure your doctor knows that, too. Otherwise he or she may wrongly assume that any lack of effectiveness is due to your noncompliance rather than to a need for a different medication.

• **When to take your medication.** Since blood pressure medications are effective for only 24 hours, it is important to take them at the same time every day. Don't drive yourself crazy if you are an hour early or an hour late, but do not be off by several hours.

Very important: Most heart attacks and strokes happen between 3 am and 10 am, which is when blood pressure typically is highest. That's why the new recommendation generally is to take your medicine at night, Dr. Houston says—to block that early morning blood pressure spike.

■ ■ ■ ■

Is Your Blood Pressure Really Under Control?

Stevo Julius, MD, ScD, professor emeritus of medicine and physiology in the division of cardiovascular medicine at the University of Michigan in Ann Arbor. Dr. Julius is a recipient of the American Heart Association's Irvine Page-Alva Bradley Lifetime Achievement Award, presented annually to an individual with at least 25 years of outstanding service, research and teaching in the field of hypertension.

It's been widely reported that an estimated 72 million Americans have high blood pressure (hypertension)—but the fact that only 35% of the people who are being treated for the condition actually have it under control comes as a surprise to most people.

There are a variety of effective treatments, ranging from diet, exercise and supplements to dozens of medications. So why don't more people keep their hypertension in check?

250,000 American Lives Are at Stake

Even though one in three adults has hypertension, about one-third of them don't know it. That's largely because hypertension—defined as a systolic (top) number of 140 millimeters of mercury (mmHg) or higher and/or a diastolic (bottom) number of 90 mmHg or higher—usually produces no outward symptoms until organ damage has occurred. (For example, blood vessels in the kidneys can be harmed by untreated hypertension, leading to kidney failure.) That's why it's important to have your blood pressure checked at least once a year.

Danger: If you have hypertension that is not being adequately treated, your risk for stroke, heart attack, heart failure and kidney failure is greatly increased. This year alone, uncontrolled hypertension will cause or contribute to the deaths of more than a quarter-million Americans, according to the American Heart Association (AHA). *How to protect yourself…*

Treat It Early

Many doctors still "start low and go slow" when prescribing antihypertensive medications—a holdover from the days when blood pressure drugs invariably produced unwanted side effects, such as cough, dizziness and headache. But many of today's antihypertensives, particularly the angiotensin II receptor blockers (ARBs)—a class

of hypertension drugs including *valsartan* (Diovan) and *losartan* (Cozaar)—are generally well-tolerated.*

Latest scientific evidence: At the University of Michigan, we recently completed a large-scale international clinical trial comparing the effectiveness of an ARB with that of a calcium channel blocker (CCB)—a class of hypertension medication including *amlodipine* (Norvasc) and *felodipine* (Plendil)—for reducing cardiac deaths in people with hypertension and at least one additional cardiovascular risk factor (such as diabetes, high cholesterol, previous heart attack or stroke). Over an average of four years, we didn't see a significant difference between the two drugs' abilities to control blood pressure and reduce related deaths. By the end of the study, patients in both treatment groups had achieved good blood pressure control.

What did appear to make a crucial difference was the speed with which blood pressure was lowered. Those patients who responded quickly to treatment—that is, their systolic blood pressure dropped by 10 mmHg or more within the first month—were significantly less likely to suffer sudden cardiac death (an abrupt cessation of the heartbeat), heart failure or stroke.

Self-defense: If you have hypertension and at least one other cardiovascular risk factor, work with your doctor to quickly bring your blood pressure under control. If you have hypertension but no other risk factors, aim to lower your blood pressure within six months.

Be aware that a diuretic (a water-excreting drug often prescribed for high blood pressure), such as *furosemide* (Lasix) or *chlorothiazide* (Diuril), when used alone probably won't bring your blood pressure

---

*Recent research shows that aggressive early treatment of hypertension can be lifesaving for patients who are at high risk for cardiovascular disease.

under control. Most people require two or more medications to achieve a normal blood pressure of less than 120/80 mmHg. Two or more low-dose drugs can achieve significantly greater reductions in blood pressure, with fewer side effects, than a single high-dose drug, according to research.

If you find it difficult to take more than one pill a day, ask your doctor about combination blood pressure medication (two anti-hypertensive drugs in a single pill), such as *enalapril* and *hydrochlorothiazide* (Vaseretic). In an analysis of studies, Columbia University researchers recently concluded that such medication reduces the risk for noncompliance (not taking medication as prescribed) by 24%.

Never Too Old for Treatment

Two-thirds of Americans age 75 and older have high blood pressure—and 90% of people in that age group will develop it by the end of their lives. As a result, many doctors accept high blood pressure as a "normal" part of aging and do not aggressively treat it in their oldest hypertensive patients.

Latest scientific evidence: A recent British trial comparing active treatment (with an ACE inhibitor plus a diuretic) with a placebo unequivocally showed that lowering blood pressure reduces both stroke and death in adults in their 80s. The advantages of treatment were so striking that the researchers prematurely halted the study to allow all patients to receive the drugs.

Self-defense: If you're over age 80 and have hypertension, lowering systolic blood pressure by 12 mmHg to 15 mmHg can reduce your stroke and heart failure risk by as much as 35%, and your heart attack risk by as much as 20%.

Warning: A normal or low diastolic pressure does not offset an elevated systolic pressure. In fact, isolated systolic

hypertension (high systolic pressure of 140 mmHg or higher accompanied by normal diastolic pressure of less than 90 mmHg) is the most common—and most dangerous—type of hypertension in older adults. This condition indicates that the arteries are stiff, which makes the heart work harder. If you have isolated systolic hypertension and your doctor is not treating it aggressively, find one who will.

Too Soon to Treat?

In May 2003, the AHA created a designation for "prehypertension"—systolic pressure of 120 mmHg to 139 mmHg and/or diastolic pressure of 80 mmHg to 89 mmHg.

Latest scientific evidence: In the recent Trial of Preventing Hypertension (TROPHY) study, researchers found that people with a systolic pressure of 130 mmHg to 139 mmHg have a 63% chance of developing full-blown

Blood Pressure Medication Warning

Women on certain blood pressure medications are at increased risk of dying from heart disease. When used together with diuretics in women with hypertension but no history of heart disease, calcium channel blockers—a class of drugs that includes *diltiazem* (Cardizem) and *amlodipine* (Norvasc)—increased risk more than a beta-blocker or ACE inhibitor taken with a diuretic. Calcium channel blockers used alone also increased risk, compared with diuretics used alone.

Self-defense: Consult your physician. Don't stop taking any blood pressure medication on your own.

Sylvia Wassertheil-Smoller, PhD, professor and head of epidemiology, Albert Einstein College of Medicine, Bronx, New York, and leader of a study of 30,219 women, published in *Journal of the American Medical Association.*

hypertension within four years. By giving prehypertensive patients an ARB drug for two years, and then stopping it, our study found that the progression to hypertension can be effectively postponed for up to two years, without side effects.

Self-defense: The TROPHY study results hold promise for the estimated 37% of American adults on the verge of high blood pressure, but more research is needed before we can recommend antihypertensive medication for people with prehypertension. If you are prehypertensive, speak to your doctor about blood pressure monitoring (it should be checked every six months) and preventive steps you can take, such as improving your diet and getting more exercise. Aim to exercise for 30 minutes every other day, with an activity, such as brisk walking, that raises your heart rate to 110 beats per minute.

I also recommend following the *Dietary Approaches to Stop Hypertension* (DASH) eating plan, which calls for eight to 10 servings of fruits and vegetables and two to three servings of low-fat dairy foods daily…sodium intake of no more than 2,400 mg daily… and moderate alcohol consumption (up to two drinks daily for men and up to one drink daily for women). (See page 3 for more information on the DASH diet.)

■ ■ ■ ■

When Your Blood Pressure Just Won't Go Down

David A. Calhoun, MD, professor of medicine in the Vascular Biology and Hypertension Program at the University of Alabama in Birmingham.

High blood pressure (hypertension) is widely known as a "silent" disease because it increases the risk for health problems ranging from stroke and heart at-

---

Blood Pressure Drugs Can Raise Blood Pressure

Researchers recently analyzed 945 adults with elevated systolic (top number) blood pressure.

Results: Among those who had low levels of the blood pressure–controlling enzyme renin and were treated with a beta-blocker or an angiotensin-converting enzyme (ACE) inhibitor, 16% had a significant increase in systolic pressure.

When prescribed a blood pressure drug: Ask your doctor to check your renin levels—a diuretic or calcium channel blocker may be a better medication option.

Michael Alderman, MD, professor of medicine, Albert Einstein College of Medicine, Bronx, New York.

---

tack to erectile dysfunction—often without causing symptoms. For this reason, half of people with hypertension don't even seek treatment.*

A more challenging health threat: There are many people who are trying to lower their blood pressure—but they are not successful. In fact, an estimated 20% to 30% of people being treated for high blood pressure are said to have *resistant hypertension* because their blood pressure remains high even though they are taking three or more medications simultaneously.

How to avoid—or overcome—this problem…

Why Treatment May Not Work

Resistant hypertension is on the rise in the US, in part due to the dramatic increase in overweight individuals and those with diabetes and chronic kidney disease—all of which make high blood pressure harder to

*For most people, hypertension is defined as blood pressure of 140/90 millimeters of mercury (mmHg) or higher. Optimal blood pressure is lower than 120/80 mmHg. More than one reading is needed to make a determination.

treat. When other health problems are diagnosed and effectively treated, blood pressure usually drops.

Other conditions that can play a role in resistant hypertension...

• **Obstructive sleep apnea.** In one study, 83% of people with resistant hypertension suffered from sleep apnea (the airway relaxes and shuts during sleep, causing a temporary drop in oxygen).

Symptoms to watch for: Snoring, gasping for air during sleep and daytime drowsiness.

• **Aldosteronism.** This condition occurs when the adrenal glands secrete too much of the hormone *aldosterone*, leading to fluid retention, which raises blood pressure. Aldosteronism is much more common than previously thought—it affects about 20% of people with resistant hypertension. Potassium levels often drop as a result of aldosteronism.

Symptoms to watch for: Weakness, muscle spasms and temporary paralysis—all of which can occur with low potassium.

Drugs That May Interfere

Drugs taken for other health problems can interfere with blood pressure treatment. *For example...*

• **Nonsteroidal anti-inflammatory drugs (NSAIDs)**—over-the-counter (OTC) painkillers such as *ibuprofen* (Motrin, Advil) and *naproxen* (Aleve)—often are overlooked as a factor in resistant hypertension. NSAIDs promote fluid retention. If you have trouble controlling your blood pressure, *acetaminophen* (Tylenol) often is a better choice for pain relief.

• **Decongestants and diet pills,** including OTC versions, can raise blood pressure by causing *vasoconstriction* (narrowing of blood vessels).

• **Stimulants and amphetamines may elevate blood pressure,** also through vaso-constriction. Such drugs—*methylphenidate* (Ritalin) and dextroamphetamine and *amphetamine* (Adderall), for example—are taken for attention deficit disorder.

• **Oral contraceptives may keep blood pressure high,** likely by promoting fluid retention.

Lifestyle Changes That Help

Factors that often contribute to resistant hypertension...

• **Salt is a double threat.** A high-sodium diet not only increases blood pressure in many people but also blunts the effectiveness of many antihypertensive drugs.

Not everyone with high blood pressure is sensitive to sodium, but nearly all people with resistant hypertension would benefit from cutting back to less than 2,300 milligrams (mg) daily.

• **Potassium in your bloodstream can become depleted if you take a diuretic (water pill).** If you develop symptoms of low potassium (described earlier), ask your doctor to check your potassium level with a blood test—and then take a potassium supplement if needed.

Otherwise, include potassium-rich foods (such as citrus fruits, bananas, dried apricots and avocados) in your diet.

Caution: Chronic kidney disease patients, who are at higher risk for *hyperkalemia* (abnormally high blood levels of potassium), should ask their nephrologist (kidney disease specialist) about an appropriate diet.

• **Physical activity has been shown to produce a small but significant drop in blood pressure**—4 mmHg in systolic (top number) pressure and 3 mmHg in diastolic (bottom number) pressure, on average. Exercise at least 30 minutes, most days of the week.

Which Drugs Are Best?

Drugs work in different ways to lower blood pressure and may be tried in different combinations. For example, if an *angiotensin converting enzyme* (ACE) inhibitor doesn't do the job, a calcium channel blocker or diuretic, rather than another ACE inhibitor, might be added to the regimen. *Two kinds of medications that are particularly important for resistant hypertension…*

• **Thiazide diuretics lower blood pressure by ridding the body of excess water and salt** and also appear to increase the effectiveness of other types of blood pressure medications. If you take two or three blood pressure drugs, one should be a thiazide diuretic, such as *hydrochlorothiazide* or *chlorthalidone*.

• **Mineralocorticoid receptor antagonists,** such as *spironolactone* (Aldactone) and *eplerenone* (Inspra), have been shown to reduce blood pressure substantially when added to combinations of other drugs that haven't done the job.

Important: Even the most effective medications won't work if they stay in the bottle. If your blood pressure remains high despite treatment, make sure you take all the pills, all the time.

Smart idea: A pill-organizer box may help you stick to your medication schedule.

Do You Need a Specialist?

If your blood pressure is still high after six months of treatment by your regular doctor, it may be time to see a hypertension expert. The American Society of Hypertension (ASH) maintains a directory of clinical hypertension specialists at *www.ash-us.org.* Or call the ASH at 212-696-9099. Your doctor also may know of a cardiologist or nephrologist with expertise in treating resistant hypertension.

Keep trying until you've found a treatment that works. All too often, resistant hypertension goes untreated, causing steady, silent damage for years.

Not Just a Warning: Prehypertension Can Be Life-Threatening

Adnan I. Qureshi, MD, executive director, Minnesota Stroke Institute and Zeenat Qureshi Stroke Research Center at the University of Minnesota, Minneapolis.

Prehypertension—it sounds like a warning, but in fact this condition, defined as blood pressure higher than 120/80 millimeters of mercury (mmHg) but not quite at the "high" level, identified as 140/90—is officially a diagnosis and one to take seriously. A recent study found that people with prehypertension are at higher risk for heart disease and heart attack. In fact, lead author Adnan I. Qureshi, MD, executive director of the Minnesota Stroke Institute and Zeenat Qureshi Stroke Research Center at the University of Minnesota, says this might well be the culprit in many so-called "inexplicable" heart attacks suffered by seemingly healthy people.

Serious Risks

The Joint National Committee on Prevention, Detection, Evaluation, and Treatment of High Blood Pressure issued guidelines in 2003 that blood pressure previously considered "high normal"—falling between normal (120/80) to just under the start of high (140/90)—was an official medical condition named *prehypertension.* Though studies had shown for years that high blood pressure (hypertension) is an important cardiovascular risk, no one was sure how much of a risk prehypertension might be—if any.

Dr. Qureshi's research reveals there is indeed a dramatic increase in risk. An analysis of data taken over 50 years from the long-term ongoing Framingham Heart Study showed that participants with the condition were three times more likely to have a heart attack and 1.7 times more likely to have heart disease than people with normal blood pressure.

Interestingly, the early data from the Framingham Heart Study didn't take into account metabolic syndrome since it was only identified in 1988. It is quite possible that the factors associated with this condition, including central obesity, insulin resistance and others, are part of the increased risk and that a number of prehypertensive participants also had these factors early on. Nonetheless, this study makes clear that if you have prehypertension, you need to discuss it with your doctor and get an overall evaluation to determine how serious your risk might be.

Take Action

The first step in treating prehypertension is recognizing there is a problem, not just a potential one. A healthy lifestyle is key to reducing risk. Quit smoking, exercise 30 minutes a day most days of the week, manage stress, reduce sodium, maintain a normal weight and limit alcohol to two drinks a day for men and one for women. The next line of defense against hypertension is diuretics, although they have potential side effects, including potassium loss from some and increased blood sugar levels and diabetes from thiazide diuretics, in particular. Even so, Dr. Qureshi notes that lifestyle and dietary changes alone may not be sufficient for all prehypertensive people. If you have diabetes or established cardiovascular disease, the benefits of diuretics or other blood-pressure medications may outweigh the risks and be worth considering.

OTC Drugs Can Raise Blood Pressure

Prevention, 33 E. Minor St., Emmaus, Pennsylvania 18098. *www.prevention.com*

If you have high blood pressure, consult your doctor before using over-the-counter (OTC) cold products. These also can be dangerous for people with diabetes, glaucoma or enlarged prostate. The products generally contain decongestants, such as *pseudoephedrine* and *phenylephrine*, that help clear a stuffy nose by narrowing blood vessels. That also can raise blood pressure and heart rate and alter blood sugar levels. Ask your doctor or pharmacist for details. To safely relieve cold symptoms if you have high blood pressure, consider zinc lozenges, which may help shorten the duration of a cold, and a saline nasal spray to reduce congestion.

Blood Pressure Danger

Blood pressure that varies widely increases stroke risk. When blood pressure varies significantly within a 24-hour period, arteries are subject to increased stress. High pressure can stretch or weaken a blood vessel's walls...then if pressure drops significantly, not enough blood moves through the vessel, increasing stroke risk.

Self-defense: If your blood pressure varies significantly between readings, talk to your doctor about having your pressure monitored over a 24-hour period.

Mark Houston, MD, associate clinical professor of medicine at Vanderbilt University School of Medicine, and director of The Hypertension Institute, both in Nashville.

Will Your Blood Pressure Pills Give You Cancer?

Ilke Sipahi, MD, assistant professor of medicine, Case Western Reserve University, and associate director, heart failure and transplantation, University Hospitals Case Medical Center, Cleveland.

T alk about trading one problem for another...new research has unearthed a link between the most commonly prescribed type of blood pressure medication and a higher risk for cancer. We're talking about the possibility of one additional cancer for every 105 people who take one of the angiotensin-receptor blocker (ARB) blood pressure medications...and if you're among the 10 million Americans in that category, this presents a bit of a dilemma. What to do?

According to the lead author of the study, Ilke Sipahi, MD, assistant professor of medicine at Case Western Reserve University, ARBs work by blocking the action of angiotensin II, a chemical that causes blood vessels to contract, creating pressure that can lead to high blood pressure. Since these medications may also support the growth of new blood vessels, the concern is that they might help tumors grow.

The research team analyzed five studies involving a total of more than 60,000 people over a four-year period—85% were on the ARB drug *telmisartan* (Micardis), while the remaining patients were on *losartan* (Cozaar) or *candesartan* (Atacand). Researchers found that patients taking ARBs had a higher (11%) risk for all cancers—and for lung cancer, in particular, the risk was 25% higher. Dr. Sipahi notes that questions remain—for instance, it's not yet clear whether this association holds for all ARBs or just the ones studied, nor is it known whether the people with lung cancer were smokers or not.

Stop the Drug or Not?

The implications are enormous. In 2010, 83 million prescriptions were written for ARBs in the US alone.

If you take an ARB, do call your doctor but do not stop the drug on your own, says Dr. Sipahi. "Discuss the benefits and the risks—after weighing both, you and your doctor can decide whether you should continue taking the drug," he advises.

For some folks, there is another option to consider, too—step up your efforts to make lifestyle changes that would eliminate your need for blood pressure medication. Exercising regularly, losing excess weight and restricting your sodium intake all are beneficial to your health—and safe.

■ ■ ■ ■

Are You Taking Blood Pressure Medications That You Don't Need?

Steven Burgess, MD, chief resident in family medicine at Texas Tech University Health Sciences Center, School of Medicine, Amarillo.

H ere's a disturbing bit of news: A recent study reports that 81% of blood pressure measurements taken by doctors and nurses are done improperly, resulting in numerous misdiagnoses. This means that many people are taking medications that they really don't need!

The American Heart Association has published guidelines recommending a particular methodology to follow when taking blood pressure measurements in a clinical setting, such as a doctor's office. In an earlier study, researchers evaluated pressure-taking techniques of 172 doctors and nurses and reported that none were following guidelines set by the American Heart Association—this inspired Steven Burgess,

Hot Weather Can Raise Blood Pressure

When researchers reviewed the records of 6,400 people, in those age 66 or older who were being treated for high blood pressure, nighttime systolic blood pressure (top number) averaged five points higher when the temperature ranged from 77.9° F to 90.5° F than when it was 30.7° F to 43.2° F.

If you have hypertension and are 66 or older: Ask your doctor to review your blood pressure treatment during the summer.

Pietro Amedeo Modesti, MD, PhD, associate professor of internal medicine, University of Florence, Italy.

MD, chief resident in family medicine at Texas Tech University Health Sciences Center School of Medicine in Amarillo, to undertake a new study to evaluate how these potentially erroneous measurements impact patient care.

What he learned is disconcerting. Mistakes made when taking blood pressure readings were significant enough to change treatment recommendations for more than half the patients in the study! "My study showed that if someone initially has elevated blood pressure and we redo the reading in accordance with the guidelines, over 50% of the time the new 'correct' pressure puts the patient into a different category, which would cause treatment to be different," he says, noting that the pressure is virtually always lower when taken "correctly."

Mistakes Are Made

The most common blood pressure measurement mistake being made by health-care practitioners is to take a blood pressure reading immediately after a patient sits down. The guidelines say that patients should rest quietly for five minutes first. Why? Because physical activity raises blood pressure, often by 10 millimeters of mercury (mmHg) or more.

In his 18-month study of 56 patients, Dr. Burgess found that when blood pressure is measured properly, the average patient's systolic (top number) reading is 15.7 mm Hg lower than when the guidelines aren't being followed. For more than half (56.4%) of the patients, using the correct technique—compared with doing it the wrong way—meant that patients were fine without medication or changes to their current therapy.

Measure by Measure

Here are the American Heart Association's guidelines regarding the proper technique for measuring blood pressure…

• Patients should not exercise, drink caffeine or smoke for 30 minutes prior to measurement and should sit quietly for five minutes immediately before.

• While the measurement is being taken, the patient should be comfortably seated with his/her back supported (not perched

High Blood Pressure Linked to Added Sugars

People who consumed more than 74 grams of fructose a day from sweeteners, such as table sugar, high fructose corn syrup and honey—about the amount in two-and-a-half sugary soft drinks—had an 87% higher risk for a blood pressure reading of 160/100 or higher. Normal blood pressure is 120/80.

Bottom line: Limit intake of sweetened foods, including bakery products, dairy desserts, candy, jams, jellies, syrups and sugar-sweetened soft drinks.

Diana Jalal, MD, assistant professor of renal medicine, University of Colorado at Denver School of Medicine, Aurora, and leader of a study of 4,528 adults, presented at a recent meeting of the American Society of Nephrology.

on a stool or a table) and with feet flat on the floor. The patient's bare arm (the sleeve can be rolled up or, if it is too constricting, the shirt can be removed) should be supported at the level of his heart. In other words, the patient should lean his arm on an armrest or table or the doctor or nurse taking the reading should hold the patient's arm, not let it hang at the patient's side.

• The cuff must fit properly according to specific guidelines. For most people, a standard cuff will satisfy these guidelines, but large or obese patients or those who are unusually small require special-sized equipment.

• For professional equipment (what's used by a health-care professional), the cuff should be placed one inch above the elbow. For digital monitors designed to be used at home, the cuff should be centered over the inside of the elbow.

• No talking—by either the patient or the practitioner. Speaking not only raises blood pressure but also interferes with the practitioner's ability to focus on your pulse while taking a reading.

• At an initial visit, two readings should be taken and the results should be averaged. If the readings differ by more than 5 mm Hg, a third reading should be taken and averaged with the other two. (Note: At subsequent visits, a single reading may be sufficient.)

Homework

Lots of people now monitor their blood pressure at home—so it's important that everyone recognizes that these readings must be done in the proper way. Be sure you are using the right type of equipment and following instructions. Also check to see whether your equipment gives you readings that match those taken in your doctor's office.

Salt by the Numbers: Startling Findings to Help You Live Longer

JoAnn E. Manson, MD, DrPH, professor of medicine and women's health at Harvard Medical School and chief of the division of preventive medicine at Brigham and Women's Hospital, both in Boston. She is author, with Shari Bassuk, ScD, of *Hot Flashes, Hormones & Your Health* (McGraw-Hill).

When patients ask me what they can do to live longer, one of the most important and simplest suggestions I give is to eat less salt. You probably know that the higher a person's intake of salt (which is 40% sodium), the higher his or her blood pressure is likely to be—which in turn increases the risk for stroke, heart attack, heart failure, chronic kidney disease and dementia.

What many people have not heard: Numerous studies are very specific about the health impact of excess salt. *The results are startling...*

• If US residents cut their daily sodium intake by 1,200 milligrams (mg) on average—that's only about half a teaspoon of salt per day—each year, there would be 32,000 to 66,000 fewer strokes...54,000 to 99,000 fewer heart attacks...and 44,000 to 92,000 fewer deaths from any cause.

Also: National health-care costs would decrease by $10 billion to $24 billion.

• An analysis of 13 studies involved 177,025 participants from around the world who were followed for 3.5 to 19 years.

Conclusion: Compared with people with an average daily salt intake of about two teaspoons, those who consumed only about half that much salt had a 23% lower risk for stroke and a 17% lower risk for cardiovascular disease.

• A multicenter clinical trial involved more than 3,000 participants who followed a fairly typical American diet or a reduced-sodium diet for 18 to 48 months. Those in the reduced-sodium group made only modest changes—decreasing their intake on average by less than half a teaspoon of salt per day. Yet this was enough to lower their risk for stroke, heart attack or other major cardiovascular event by 30% over the next 10 to 15 years.

How Salt Wreaks Havoc

To function properly, the body does need some sodium—but only about 500 mg per day. When sodium consumption is excessive, the kidneys cannot eliminate all of it. Fluid is retained in the blood vessels, which increases blood pressure. This damages blood vessel walls, accelerating the progression of atherosclerosis (thickening and hardening of the arteries). Salt also appears to thicken the muscle in the heart's left ventricle, the chamber that pumps blood throughout the body. In addition, a high-salt diet may contribute to a decline in kidney function and an increased risk for kidney stones.

The right number for you: Some people are more sensitive to salt than others. *As a general guideline, the American Heart Association recommends…*

• **If you are age 40 or older,** are African-American or have high blood pressure, limit yourself to 1,500 mg of sodium (about two-thirds of a teaspoon of salt) per day.

Note: About 70% of the US population falls into this group.

• **If you do not meet any of the conditions in the preceding paragraph,** limit yourself to 2,300 mg of sodium (just under one teaspoon of salt) per day.

Troubling comparison: Among US women, the average daily intake of sodium jumped nearly 70% from 1971 to 2000. The typical American woman now consumes about 3,000 mg per day—twice the amount that's recommended for most people.

What's a Woman to Do?

About 80% of the sodium in the average American's diet comes from canned and processed foods and restaurant meals. Vigilance is required to avoid sodium overload. (See "The New Blood Pressure Control Diet for Women" on page 14.)

When You Shop

• **Buy whole foods whenever possible,** rather than processed foods.

• **If you must buy frozen entrées,** choose ones with no more than 600 mg to 800 mg of sodium per serving.

• **Select snack foods with no more than 200 mg of sodium per serving** (and limit your portion to a single serving).

• **Avoid notoriously salty processed foods**—including canned goods (soups, vegetables, beans)…deli meats and sausage…condiments (ketchup, pickle relish, soy sauce)…bottled salad dressings…and snack foods (popcorn, chips). Look for low-sodium or unsalted versions.

When You Dine Out, Remember…

• **Some fast-food meals contain nearly triple the salt limit recommended for an entire day!** If you visit a fast-food restaurant, forgo the fries in favor of a salad (going light on the dressing)…choose a hamburger instead of a cheeseburger (one slice of American cheese adds almost 400 mg of sodium)… skip the pickles and mayonnaise.

• **Check to see if the menu includes a section of low-sodium dishes.** If not, request that your meal be prepared with little or no added salt.

At Home

• **Put away the salt shaker.** When cooking or at the table, use other seasonings—spices, herbs, vinegar, lemon juice—to bring out food's flavor.

The Blood Pressure Problem Too Many Doctors Don't Detect

Zeenat Safdar, MD, associate director of the Pulmonary Hypertension Service and assistant professor of medicine at Baylor College of Medicine in Houston.

High blood pressure, or hypertension, is easy to detect. A cuff around your upper arm measures the pressure of the blood against the walls of the main arteries...high numbers signal a need for treatment to prevent heart and blood vessel damage.

But it is much more difficult to spot *pulmonary hypertension*, a disorder in which high blood pressure develops in the pulmonary arteries that carry blood from the heart to the lungs. It is a progressive and potentially deadly disease that can appear at any age and often goes undiagnosed for months or years.

For unknown reasons, pulmonary hypertension affects women two to four times more often than men. Sometimes the initial symptoms—shortness of breath, dizziness, fatigue—appear during pregnancy when the fetus puts stress on the woman's heart and lungs.

Recognizing the Problem

Pulmonary hypertension develops when tiny arteries in the lungs become narrowed, stiffened or blocked due to cellular changes or scarring in the arteries' lining. As blood flow is constricted, pressure in the pulmonary arteries rises and blood backs up, forcing the heart to pump harder. *Symptoms include...*

• **Shortness of breath.**
• **Palpitations or racing heartbeat.**
• **Dizziness or light-headedness.**
• **Fatigue upon exertion.**
• **Swollen ankles, legs or belly.**
• **Bluish lips and skin.**

At first, symptoms occur only during exertion and often are misdiagnosed as asthma, anxiety or signs that a person is out of shape. As the disease progresses, symptoms become constant. The longer pulmonary hypertension goes untreated, the more damage is done. *Possible consequences...*

• **The heart's right ventricle (lower right chamber) becomes enlarged and thickened as it attempts to increase its capacity to hold and pump blood.** Eventually, heart failure develops when the heart can no longer pump

Loneliness and High Blood Pressure

A study of 229 men and women found that those who rated themselves as feeling the loneliest had an average blood pressure increase, over four years, of 14 millimeters more than those who reported feeling the most socially content.

Theory: Loneliness alters physiological functioning, including blood pressure.

Self-defense: Expand the number of friends and relatives with whom you connect...and have contact at least twice a month.

Louise Hawkley, PhD, senior research scientist, Center for Cognitive and Social Neuroscience, University of Chicago.

blood efficiently enough to meet the body's needs.

● **An irregular heartbeat may develop,** increasing the risk for stroke or sudden cardiac death.

● **Blood clots may form in the lungs' arteries...**and/or there may be bleeding into the lungs. These conditions can be deadly.

Self-defense: If you experience any possible symptoms of pulmonary hypertension, inform your doctor immediately. With a stethoscope, an experienced physician can detect a telltale heart murmur, a consequence of the backflow of blood from the lungs. An echocardiogram (ultrasound of the heart) and/or right heart catheterization (in which a catheter is inserted into a pulmonary artery to measure pressure) confirms the diagnosis.

Recommended: Have a pulmonologist or cardiologist oversee your treatment.

Referrals: Pulmonary Hypertension Association, 800-748-7274, *www.phassociation.org.*

Life After Diagnosis

Often the cause of pulmonary hypertension is unknown (though in some cases, there is a genetic link). It also can occur as a result of another medical problem, such as a congenital heart defect, chronic obstructive pulmonary disease, sleep apnea, a blood disorder, an autoimmune disorder or disease of the liver, kidney or thyroid.

For most patients, pulmonary hypertension can be controlled but not cured. *Keys to treatment...*

Lifestyle

To ease symptoms and slow the disease's progress...

● **Reduce sodium intake to no more than 1,500 mg** (or about two-thirds of a teaspoon of salt) per day. Salt increases blood volume, straining the heart.

● **Do not use a hot tub,** sauna or steam bath or take long, hot showers or baths. Doing so could lower blood pressure excessively, leading to fainting or even death.

● **With your doctor's okay, do moderate exercise (walking, yoga, low-impact aerobics).** To avoid serious increases in pulmonary artery pressure, refrain from strenuous aerobic activity and heavy lifting.

● **Stay away from secondhand smoke**—it can exacerbate your disease. If you smoke, quit now.

For help: Visit *www.smokefree.gov.*

● **Avoid high altitudes.** Thin air is harder to breathe.

● **No dietary supplements treat pulmonary hypertension**—but for overall immune support, consider asking your doctor about taking the amino acid L-arginine.

● **Avoid decongestants that have pseudoephedrine or phenylephrine,** which can narrow blood vessels.

● **Get a flu shot every year.** Also, get vaccinated against pneumonia (typically only one or two injections are needed) to minimize risk for respiratory infections that could worsen your condition.

● **Do not use oral contraceptives or estrogen therapy** because they may increase blood clot risk.

● **Maintain a normal weight.** If you notice a rapid weight gain (two pounds in a day or five pounds in a week), call your doctor—this could indicate a buildup of fluid caused by heart failure.

● **It is strongly advised that you not become pregnant** because there is a risk for death for both mother and baby. If you want a child or are already pregnant, it is vital to work closely with a pulmonary hypertension specialist.

Medication

You may need to take one or more of the following…

• **Vasodilators open blood vessels.** These are inhaled every few hours…or are continuously injected through a catheter attached to a small wearable pump.

• **Endothelin receptor antagonists help reverse the effects of a substance that narrows blood vessels.**

• **Calcium channel blockers relax blood vessel walls.**

• **Diuretics help rid the body of heart-straining excess fluid.**

• **Anticoagulants improve blood flow and reduce clotting risk.**

• **Supplemental oxygen may be needed occasionally or constantly.**

Pulmonary hypertension medications can minimize the disease's consequences and ease symptoms—allowing you to live more actively and comfortably.

■ ■ ■ ■

Hidden Cause of Stroke, High Blood Pressure And Aneurysm

Jeffrey W. Olin, DO, professor of cardiology at the Mount Sinai School of Medicine and director of vascular medicine at the Zena and Michael A. Wiener Cardiovascular Institute and the Marie-Josée and Henry R. Kravis Center for Cardiovascular Health at Mount Sinai, all in New York City.

Most people have never heard of the blood vessel disorder known as *fibromuscular dysplasia* (FMD), but doctors now recognize that it can be a hidden cause of high blood pressure (hypertension), strokes and brain aneurysms (due to bulging in the wall of an artery in the brain).

Recent development: Once considered a rare condition, FMD now appears to be more common than previously thought, possibly affecting up to 5 million adults in the US.

What you need to know…

What Is FMD?

In people with FMD, abnormal cell growth occurs on the walls of one or more arteries (blood vessels), typically in the carotid (neck) arteries (leading to the brain) and renal arteries (leading to the kidneys). The normally smooth artery wall develops bumps, often resulting in a "string of beads" that can be seen on imaging tests used to examine blood vessels, such as ultrasound, a computed tomography angiogram (CTA) or magnetic resonance angiogram (MRA).

When cell growth becomes extensive, the artery narrows, disrupting blood flow and possibly resulting in hypertension, a stroke or an aneurysm. While atherosclerosis—fatty buildup in the arteries—occurs at the opening of a blood vessel, FMD occurs at the middle and end of a blood vessel.

Are You at Risk?

Though FMD typically strikes adults under age 50, doctors now are finding more and more previously undiagnosed cases in people age 60 and older—perhaps due to the increasing use of imaging tests. FMD often is diagnosed as a result of an incidental finding on an unrelated radiological test. In many of these cases, the patient has no symptoms of the disorder.

No one knows what causes FMD. Genetics may play a role, but not everyone with FMD has a relative with the disease. FMD occurs more often in women (about 85% of cases) than in men. Researchers suspect that a gene predisposes an individual to the condition and that the gene is expressed due to outside influences, such as hormones.

Getting a Proper Diagnosis

FMD often goes undiagnosed because many doctors mistakenly believe that it is very rare. In fact, many medical schools don't even teach their students about FMD.

To complicate matters further, many people with FMD have no symptoms. When symptoms do occur, they are related to the arteries that are affected and the degree of narrowing that has developed.

Example: Since the majority of FMD cases occur in the arteries leading to the kidneys, high blood pressure may develop (due to narrowing of the renal arteries, which triggers a series of adverse effects). Abnormal kidney function and flank pain (occurring on one side of the body between the upper abdomen and the back) also can occur.

In about 25% to 30% of FMD patients, the disease affects the carotid arteries. In these people, symptoms may include severe and unrelenting headaches…dizziness…ringing in the ears (tinnitus)…and neck pain.

FMD in the carotid artery also may lead to a swishing sound in the ears…temporary or permanent loss of vision in one or both eyes…brain aneurysms…and transient ischemic attacks (TIAs)—or "ministrokes"…as well as full-blown strokes.

Though less likely, FMD can affect the arteries supplying the liver, spleen and intestines, which may cause abdominal pain after eating, unexplained weight loss or gangrene of the bowel. If the arteries to the legs or arms are affected, pain or fatigue when using the affected limb can occur. In very rare cases, FMD may affect the coronary arteries in the heart, leading to angina (chest pain) or a heart attack.

Helpful: Regardless of your age, ask your doctor during all routine physicals to place a stethoscope on your neck and abdomen and listen for a *bruit*, a noise that indicates a narrowing of a blood vessel. If a bruit is heard, your doctor can follow up with the appropriate test, such as an ultrasound or CTA.

Important: Not all FMD patients have an audible bruit.

Best Treatment Options

FMD has no cure. The goal is to improve blood flow in the affected artery. Treatment depends on which artery is narrowed and the severity of the symptoms. Medication that alleviates high blood pressure, such as an angiotensin-converting enzyme (ACE) inhibitor, may be prescribed. Many patients take daily aspirin to help prevent clots from forming, thus reducing stroke risk.

FMD patients who have "new-onset" hypertension may require *percutaneous transluminal renal angioplasty* (PTRA). This procedure (usually outpatient) involves inserting a catheter into the affected artery

Cutting-Edge Research On FMD

Several medical centers in the US, including the Mount Sinai Medical Center in New York City and the Cleveland Clinic, participate in an international registry of FMD patients to help scientists conduct cutting-edge research to unravel some of the mysteries of the disease.

If you or a family member has been diagnosed with FMD, contact the Fibromuscular Dysplasia Society of America (FMDSA), 888-709-7089, *www.fmdsa.org*, which can provide information about the registry closest to you.

Lowering Blood Pressure Early May Limit Bleeding Stroke Severity

Hemorrhagic strokes affect about 60,000 people in the US every year—and up to 50% of these strokes are fatal. In a recent study of 404 stroke patients, half the stroke victims had systolic pressure (the top number) lowered to 180 by intravenous drugs—and half had it reduced to 140. Patients whose blood pressure was treated more aggressively had about one-third less bleeding, and the treatment caused no major side effects. Further research is needed.

Philip Gorelick, MD, neurology chief at University of Illinois Medical Center at Chicago and chairman of the International Stroke Conference 2008.

and inflating a small balloon to open the narrowed area.

Important finding: A study published in the *Journal of Vascular Surgery* showed that renal artery angioplasty reduced high blood pressure in 72% of the 29 FMD patients studied—and the reduction was still evident five years after the procedure.

Finding the Right Doctor

If you have FMD—or suspect that you may—see a vascular specialist or a physician who is experienced in treating the organ affected by the disease.

For example: A nephrologist (kidney doctor) if FMD affects your renal arteries (or you are having kidney problems such as those described above)…or a neurologist if the carotid arteries are affected.

What a Fainting Spell Could Really Mean…and Why You Should Never Ignore One

Lewis A. Lipsitz, MD, professor of medicine at Harvard Medical School, vice president for academic medicine and codirector of the Institute for Aging Research at Hebrew SeniorLife in Boston. He is the chief of the gerontology division at Beth Israel Deaconess Medical Center, also in Boston.

Even though some people faint for seemingly harmless reasons, such as the sight of blood, there are several potential causes. This temporary loss of consciousness that lasts no more than a few minutes can occur any time the brain isn't getting enough oxygen-rich blood.

What you need to know about the most common causes of *syncope* (pronounced "SIN ko-pe"), the medical term for fainting…

• **Heart conditions.** Arrhythmias, in which the heart beats too fast (*tachycardia*), too slow (*bradycardia*) or in an irregular pattern, cause fainting in up to 12% of older adults who suffer from syncope. With an arrhythmia, ineffective pumping of blood can result in an insufficient amount of blood going to the brain.

Typical treatment: Medication to help control the underlying heart condition.

• **Medications.** Certain drugs, such as medications for high blood pressure, heart failure, depression and Parkinson's disease, can cause fainting, especially when you first start taking them and/or if the dosage is too high. Men who take excessive doses of medication for an enlarged prostate, such as *tamsulosin* (Flomax), also may faint.

Typical treatment: Your doctor may lower the dosage or prescribe a different medication. Never stop taking a prescription drug without speaking to your physician.

• *Orthostatic* (postural) *hypotension* (low blood pressure). Standing up after sitting or lying down shifts your center of gravity and causes blood to pool in the legs—often reducing blood flow to the brain. Normally, blood vessels constrict in response to this postural change, ensuring that your brain continues to get enough blood. But in people with orthostatic hypotension, this mechanism is defective.

Typical treatment: Drinking enough water (which increases blood volume and prevents dehydration)…avoiding alcohol (which is dehydrating)…and wearing support hose (to prevent blood from pooling in the legs). Some people may be prescribed *fludrocortisone* (Florinef) to increase blood volume (including that to the brain) and *midodrine* (ProAmitine) to constrict blood vessels.

• **Postprandial hypotension.** After a meal (postprandial), blood pools in the intestines, thus reducing blood flow to the brain. In healthy people, the body responds by increasing heart rate and constricting blood vessels to maintain normal blood pressure. This mechanism fails in people with postprandial hypotension.

If You or Someone Else Faints

If you're feeling faint: Lie or sit down immediately. If you're sitting, put your head between your knees to help restore blood flow to your brain. *If someone else faints…*

• **Get the person into a supine position (lying down with the face up).** Raise the legs so they're higher than the head to bring blood back to the heart and head.

• **Check breathing.** If breathing has stopped, call 911 and perform cardiopulmonary resuscitation (CPR)—about 100 uninterrupted chest compressions per minute.

Typical treatment: Eat smaller, more frequent meals with fewer carbohydrates.

• **Vasovagal syncope.** This type of fainting, which can be triggered by emotional distress, exertion (such as straining on the toilet), heat or the sight of blood, leads to an exaggerated bodily process. The heart rate slows and blood vessels in the legs widen, allowing blood to pool in the legs. This lowers blood pressure, reduces blood flow to the brain and can result in fainting.

In some people, vasovagal syncope results from overly sensitive reflexes involved in swallowing, urinating or defecating. Vasovagal syncope also can occur in people who have a condition known as carotid sinus hypersensitivity, which causes fainting when excess pressure is placed on the carotid (neck) artery—for example, when a shirt collar is too tight.

Typical treatment: Avoiding situations that trigger vasovagal syncope. In people with swallowing syncope, eating smaller, more frequent meals can help. Men should sit on the toilet while urinating if they have this form of syncope. Adding more fiber to your diet helps prevent constipation.

• **Illnesses.** In people with anemia (deficiency of red blood cells), fainting may occur if they bleed excessively (due to an injury, for example), because blood loss can trigger a sharp drop in blood pressure. Hypoglycemia (low blood sugar), which can occur in people with or without diabetes, also can lead to fainting.

Typical treatment: People who have anemia should see their doctors regularly for treatment and monitoring of the condition. People with diabetes should control their blood sugar levels.

Identifying the Cause

Syncope is sometimes misdiagnosed as a stroke, brain tumor or seizure—all of

Dangerous High-Salt Diets

High-salt diets cause more than just heart attacks and strokes. High-salt intake is linked to an increased risk for stomach cancer because salty foods irritate the stomach lining, which can allow *H. pylori* infection that can lead to cancer. Too much salt raises risk for osteoporosis by increasing calcium loss and weakening bones. Diabetes risk also increases from too much salt because salt promotes insulin resistance.

Prevention, 33 E. Minor St., Emmaus, Pennsylvania 18098. *www.prevention.com*

which can cause loss of consciousness. But strokes, tumors and seizures are more apt to also cause slurred speech and/or vision loss. According to a recent study, doctors often rush to perform costly heart tests, such as cardiac enzyme tests, which measure possible heart damage, while overlooking much less expensive postural blood pressure testing.

Simple test: When assuming a standing position after lying down, you may have orthostatic hypotension if systolic (top number) blood pressure drops by more than 20 millimeters of mercury (mmHg) or if systolic pressure drops below 100 mmHg.

Another important tool: **The tilt table test.** For this test, you lie down and are strapped to a table, which is then tilted to raise the upper body to simulate what happens when you go from a lying to a standing position. Your body's response to the change in position may indicate whether you have orthostatic hypotension.

The tilt table test may be used in addition to postural blood pressure testing (mentioned above).

If your doctor suspects that your fainting is due to a heart problem, you may receive an electrocardiogram (which measures electrical activity of the heart) and an echocardiogram (a type of ultrasound test that helps detect abnormalities in heart rate or rhythm).

Salt May Weaken Bones

Caryl Nowson, PhD, chair, Nutrition and Aging, Deakin University, Victoria, Australia.

When 92 women with pre- or mild hypertension ate a low-sodium diet or a high-carbohydrate/low-fat diet for 14 weeks, those on the low-sodium diet excreted significantly less bone-building calcium through their urine than did the other dieters.

Theory: Calcium binds with sodium and is excreted via urine.

To maintain healthy bones: Men and women should limit sodium to the daily recommended intake of 2,300 milligrams (mg). People with hypertension should consume no more than 1,500 mg daily.

What Not to Drink

Did you know cola, not coffee, raises blood pressure in women? The association between hypertension and caffeine had been attributed to coffee, but a new study shows that caffeinated colas increase women's risk of hypertension. Researchers speculate that some other compound in soda is responsible for increased risk.

Wolfgang Winkelmayer, MD, department of pharmacoepidemiology and pharmacoeconomics, Brigham and Women's Hospital, Boston, and leader of an analysis of 12 years of data from 155,594 women, published in *The Journal of the American Medical Association.*

Blood Pressure Medication Breakthrough

Michael H. Alderman, MD, former president of the American Society of Hypertension and professor of medicine at Albert Einstein College of Medicine of Yeshiva University, Bronx, New York.

People who take blood pressure medications may not realize how unscientific doctors have been in their approach to finding the right drug or drugs for their condition—in fact, the expression, "Throw enough mud at the wall and some is bound to stick," seems an apt description. Commonly, drugs for hypertension are prescribed on top of others in the hope that the growing pile will keep blood pressure under control. As a result, many patients end up taking three or even more different drugs daily to manage their blood pressure.

Drugs aren't the only tool that people can use to get blood pressure under control, of course. Many patients find that losing weight, exercising and making other lifestyle changes can do the trick. But for those who do require blood pressure medication, scientists have now developed a more precise method of predicting which drug will control hypertension in a particular individual—and this could be very good news for drug-saturated blood pressure patients!

ABCs of HBP

Let me start by introducing you to renin, an enzyme produced by the kidneys that plays a critical role in modulating blood pressure. Renin regulates blood volume and vascular resistance as the body's needs change—but having too much renin is one cause of hypertension. Until recently, doctors have had no way to identify the patients in whom this is the root cause of the problem.

Of the two types of drugs that treat hypertension, there is one category called "R"

Another Hypertension Cause

High blood pressure, memory problems and fatigue can be linked to insulin resistance, reports Allan Magaziner, DO. People who are insulin resistant have an impaired ability to control their bodies' blood glucose levels. In addition to diabetes, the condition can lead to cardiovascular disease, decreased immunity, depression, increased inflammation, weight gain and breast and colon cancers.

Self-defense: Ask your doctor about getting tested for insulin resistance.

Allan Magaziner, DO, founder and director of Magaziner Center for Wellness, Cherry Hill, New Jersey, and author of *The All-Natural Cardio Cure* (Avery). *www. drmagaziner.com*

drugs (beta-blockers and ACE inhibitors) that works to control pressure by blocking the effect of blood renin levels. The other type, called "V" drugs (diuretics and calcium channel blockers), controls pressure by reducing blood volume. Since doctors have not had any easy techniques to help them determine whether a patient would benefit more from one or the other, some people with hypertension end up taking both types. For instance, they may take a pill that combines an R and a V drug along with another that is either an R or a V on its own. This new research may dramatically reduce the need for such guesswork.

Better Than a Crystal Ball

Done at the Albert Einstein College of Medicine of Yeshiva University, New York City, this recent research was published in the *American Journal of Hypertension.* Researchers measured renin levels in 945 previously untreated participants diagnosed with hypertension (a systolic, or top blood pressure, reading of at least 140 mmHg) before assigning them to either a V or R drug. A follow-up blood pressure reading was done one to three months later, and researchers found that the patients who had had high renin levels (more than 2.5 ng/mg/h) at the start of the study achieved better blood pressure control with an R drug, while those who had had low renin levels (below about 0.74 ng/mg/h) did better on a V drug. The conclusion—renin levels can indeed be useful as a predictor of how a particular patient will respond to a particular type of blood pressure drug.

A very important finding: For some patients, being on the wrong drug actually elevated their blood pressure, making the situation especially dangerous. The researchers found that 16% of patients with the lowest levels of renin who took an R drug experienced an increase of 10 or more points in their blood pressure. This rise, called a "pressor response," is not at all uncommon—doctors have tended to assume it was caused by "noncompliance," blaming the patients for failing to take their medications. The study shows, though, that the pressor response often is caused by giving patients the wrong drug.

Talk to Your Doctor

Study author Michael Alderman, MD, former president of the American Society of Hypertension, recommends that doctors measure renin levels in newly diagnosed hypertension patients as well as in those now taking multiple antihypertensive medications—most particularly when the drugs don't seem to be helping. Dr. Alderman says that it will likely be a few years before testing renin levels in advance of prescribing blood pressure medications becomes a standard practice, but he expects that it eventually will. If you need blood pressure medications, ask to have your renin level tested before you get a prescription—trial and error is not the way you want to find out what works!

Fascinating Blood Pressure Percentages

19%…Young adults (ages 24 to 32) in the US who have high blood pressure. Many of those affected are unaware that they have this potentially life-threatening condition.
Epidemiology

40%…Increased risk for heart disease among female workers who experienced "high job strain," as compared with female workers who reported low job strain.
Women's Health Study

42%…Increased risk of death among Americans ages 25 to 74 who have high blood pressure, as compared with those who do not have high blood pressure.

Circulation: Journal of the American Heart Association

3

Natural Remedies for Hypertension

Natural Ways to Lower High Blood Pressure

Elson M. Haas, MD, founder and director of the Preventive Medical Center of Marin in San Rafael, California, an integrated health-care facility. *www.elsonhaas.com.* He is coauthor, with Buck Levin, PhD, RD, of *Staying Healthy with Nutrition* (Celestial Arts).

Nearly everyone eventually suffers from high blood pressure. According to the National Heart, Lung and Blood Institute, adults age 55 and older who don't already have hypertension face about a 90% chance of developing it at some time in their lives.

Untreated hypertension greatly increases the risk of atherosclerosis (hardening and thickening of the arteries), kidney disease, heart failure and even dementia. People with severe hypertension—a reading of 160/100 or higher—almost always require treatment with medications. Your blood pressure is normal if it's below 120/80.

Good news: People with borderline or moderate hypertension can lower their numbers by 10 to 20 points with dietary changes and/or the use of supplements. That's often enough to make medications unnecessary. Even patients who are already taking blood pressure drugs may be able to reduce the doses or get off the drugs entirely.

Caution: Always talk to your doctor before taking any supplement or reducing or eliminating any medications.

To keep blood pressure at healthful levels, limit (or eliminate) red meat and processed foods…increase consumption of fruits, vegetables and whole grains…stop smoking…and exercise for at least 30 minutes most days. *Also important…*

Water

About 20% of Americans drink no water, and 42% drink only two glasses or less daily. Inadequate water intake causes a decrease in total blood volume, constriction of blood vessels and an increase in blood pressure.

The average adult needs almost 100 ounces of water daily. About one-third of this comes from the water contained within food. This means that most people need at least eight eight-ounce glasses of water daily.

My recommendation: Spring water that is naturally rich in minerals or that has minerals added, particularly magnesium. Magnesium is an alkaline mineral that relaxes blood vessels and helps lower blood pressure (see magnesium, next column). If you don't like water, try juices or herbal teas.

Sodium-to-Potassium Ratio

Most people know that a high-salt (high-sodium) diet can increase blood pressure, but the ratio of sodium to potassium in the diet may be more important. Only about 15% to 25% of Americans are salt-sensitive—a condition in which salt intake is directly correlated to sharp rises in blood pressure. Lowering salt intake can help, but increasing potassium helps more.

Potassium enters cells more readily than sodium and helps balance the sodium in your cells. If you don't consume or retain enough potassium, you may accumulate too much sodium in your blood, which can lead to high blood pressure. Increasing potassium intake also relaxes blood vessels and causes a drop in blood pressure.

People who eat a plant-based diet (and relatively few processed foods) rarely get hypertension, probably because these foods tend to be both low in sodium and high in potassium.

My recommendation: No more than 2,000 milligrams (mg) of sodium daily—many Americans consume more than 12,000 mg—and about 3,500 mg of potassium. A potassium-to-sodium ratio of 2:1 is optimal.

Good potassium sources: Virtually all fruits and vegetables are high in potassium and low in sodium. Particularly good sources include bananas, dried fruit and squash.

Other good sources: Lentils, nuts and seeds.

Helpful: Replace processed snacks with hulled unsalted sunflower seeds. One cup has 1,300 mg of potassium and only 4 mg of sodium.

If your diet is low in potassium, you may need a potassium supplement. I recommend to my patients two 99-mg tablets, three times a day.

Magnesium

Millions of Americans don't get enough magnesium, a mineral that's involved in literally hundreds of enzymatic reactions in the body, many of which are related to the heart and blood vessels. Low levels of magnesium have been linked to hypertension, heart disease and heart attacks.

Magnesium has been called an "anti-stress" mineral because it relaxes muscles in blood vessels, as well as skeletal muscles. People who increase their intake of magnesium can experience significant drops in blood pressure.

Important: The diuretic drugs commonly used to treat high blood pressure can cause a decrease of magnesium. Soft water (treated tap water that contains few minerals), common in the US, contributes to low magnesium intake.

My recommendation: At least 320 mg a day of magnesium for women and 420 mg a day for men. Many researchers now believe that higher amounts—up to 700 mg daily for men and women—may be optimal. Legumes, whole grains and dark green vegetables are all high in magnesium. People who don't eat a lot of vegetables or other plant foods should take daily supplements (150 mg, three times a day).

Fish Oil

I advise all patients with hypertension and/or heart disease to consume adequate fish oil, either by eating fish or taking fish oil supplements.

Two of the fats in fish—*eicosapentaenoic acid* (EPA) and *docosahexaenoic acid* (DHA)—reduce risk of atherosclerosis. Fish

Vinegar Fix for Hypertension?

There have been no human studies to determine whether daily vinegar consumption lowers blood pressure, but research on laboratory rats with high blood pressure (hypertension) shows promising results. After scientists fed laboratory rats either rice vinegar or water with their food for eight weeks, the rats that ingested vinegar had a 20-point drop, on average, in systolic (top number) blood pressure. Vinegar also has been shown to modestly inhibit the angiotensin converting enzyme (ACE) in rats. This enzyme forms a substance that narrows blood vessels. Since ACE inhibitor drugs, such as *benazepril* (Lotensin) or *enalapril* (Vasotec), commonly are prescribed to treat hypertension in adults, human trials may be performed to see if regular intake of vinegar inhibits ACE concentrations in humans and improves blood pressure.

Carol Johnston, PhD, RD, department of nutrition, Arizona State University, Mesa, Arizona.

oil makes platelets less sticky, increasing blood flow.

My recommendation: Two to three servings of fish a week.

Best choices: Mackerel, trout and salmon.

Large fish, such as tuna, often have higher levels of mercury than smaller species. To reduce mercury exposure, eat a variety of fish, not a single type.

Or take supplements. Most manufacturers screen out mercury and other heavy metals. The dose I recommend to patients is three grams of fish oil daily. Strict vegetarians may want to use flaxseed oil or hemp oil (one tablespoon or usually three capsules, twice a day).

Limit Caffeine

Caffeine is a central nervous system stimulant that causes the adrenal glands to produce more cortisol—a "stress" hormone that constricts blood vessels and raises blood pressure.

My recommendation: Limit coffee to a cup or two a day (or one or two soft drinks with caffeine daily). However, many people find it difficult to cut back. It may be easier in the long run just to give up caffeine altogether.

■ ■ ■ ■

Lower Blood Pressure With Melatonin

Mark Houston, MD, associate clinical professor of medicine at Vanderbilt University School of Medicine and director of the Hypertension Institute at Saint Thomas Hospital, both in Nashville.

The supplemental form of this "sleep" hormone may alleviate nocturnal hypertension (a form of high blood pressure that occurs during sleep). In most people, blood pressure drops by 10% to 20% during sleep. But about one-quarter of people with prehypertension or hypertension are "non-dippers"—their sleeping pressure is about as high as or higher than their waking pressure.

High blood pressure during sleep (which is diagnosed by a 24-hour blood pressure monitor) is particularly common among blacks and people with chronic kidney disease, and it worsens their risk for heart attack, stroke and kidney failure. Researchers at Boston's Brigham and Women's Hospital have found that 2.5 milligrams (mg) of melatonin, taken one hour before bedtime, may lower systolic (top number) pressure by an average of 6 millimeters of mercury (mmHg) and diastolic (bottom number) pressure by 4 mmHg during sleep.

My advice: If you know that you have nocturnal hypertension, or if you have hypertension plus insomnia or chronic kidney disease, ask your doctor about taking melatonin. At the very least, it may help you sleep better.

■ ■ ■ ■

Stress Busters for Women That Help Beat High Blood Pressure

C. Tissa Kappagoda, MBBS, PhD, professor of medicine in the Preventive Cardiology Program at the University of California, Davis. Dr. Kappagoda has published more than 200 medical journal articles on matters relating to cardiology and cardiovascular health.

A recent study in the journal *Circulation* found an alarming trend—that rates of uncontrolled hypertension are increasing among women even as rates among men are decreasing.

The Centers for Disease Control and Prevention reports that more than one-third of women age 45 to 54 now have high blood pressure…while among women age 75 and older, 80% do!

A report from the National Center for Health Statistics states that, in the past decade, there has been a 62% increase in the number of visits to the doctor due to high blood pressure.

These days, chronic stress—due to lack of job stability or other factors at home—is a significant contributor to hypertension. As C. Tissa Kappagoda, MBBS, PhD, a professor in the preventive cardiology program at the University of California, Davis, explains, "Chronic stress raises blood pressure by increasing levels of adrenaline and cortisol, hormones that promote artery spasm and salt retention. It also increases vascular resistance, the resistance to flow that must be overcome to move blood through the blood vessels, which is a primary cause of hypertension." (For a contrary finding on chronic stress and blood pressure, see page 64.) Stress also can impede basic self-care, such as eating healthfully and exercising—which probably explains why stress is such a "massive multiplier of the effects of conventional risk factors," Dr. Kappagoda adds.

Though high blood pressure doesn't cause pain or other obvious symptoms, it does damage arteries—increasing the risk for heart attack, diabetes, stroke and kidney problems. How high is too high? Hypertension is diagnosed when blood pressure hits 140/90 millimeters of mercury (mmHg) or higher…but doctors now realize that prehypertension (blood pressure between 120/80 and 139/89) also is risky.

Of course, it's important to follow your doctor's advice regarding blood pressure lowering lifestyle changes, such as limiting salt and alcohol and losing excess weight. But stress reduction should be a priority, too, Dr. Kappagoda says—and may reduce the need for hypertension medication. That's good, because these drugs can have side effects, such as dizziness, chronic cough and muscle cramps, and often are taken for the rest of a person's life.

Research shows that the following stress-lowering techniques help reduce blood pressure. *If you have hypertension or prehypertension, consider…*

● **Breathing control.** When you're relaxed, your breathing naturally slows…and if you slow down your breathing, your body naturally relaxes. This encourages constricted blood vessels to dilate, improving blood flow.

Target: Practice slow breathing for 15 minutes twice daily, aiming to take six breaths per minute.

If you find it difficult (or even stressful!) to count and time your breaths, consider using a biofeedback device instead. One example designed for home use is Resperate (877-988-9388, *www.resperate.com*, from $299.95), which looks like a portable CD player with headphones and uses musical tones to guide you to an optimal breathing pattern. Typically, it's used for 15 minutes three or four times per week, and results are seen within several weeks. In studies, users experienced significant reductions in systolic pressure (the top number of a blood pressure reading) and diastolic pressure (bottom number) (For more information on Resperate, see pages 52–53.) There are many similar and effective devices, says Dr. Kappagoda, so ask your doctor about the options. Biofeedback devices are safe and have no side effects.

● **Meditation.** A recent analysis of nine clinical trials, published in *American Journal of Hypertension*, found that regular practice of transcendental meditation reduced blood pressure, on average, by 4.7 mmHg systolic and 3.2 mmHg diastolic. Though these results are for transcendental meditation specifically, many experts believe that any type of meditation works.

Goal: Meditate for 20 minutes daily.

● **Exercise.** Regular physical activity reduces blood pressure not only by alleviating stress, but also by promoting weight loss and improving heart and blood vessel health. Research shows that becoming more active can reduce systolic pressure by 5 mmHg to 10 mmHg, on average. An excellent all-around exercise is walking, Dr. Kappagoda says—so with your doctor's OK, take a 30-minute walk at least three times weekly.

Caution: Weight training can trigger a temporary increase in blood pressure during the exercise, especially when heavy weights are used. To minimize this blood pressure spike, use lighter weights to do more repetitions...and don't hold your breath during the exertion.

What's Causing Your High Blood Pressure?

Jamison Starbuck, ND, naturopathic physician in family practice in Missoula, Montana. She is past president of the American Association of Naturopathic Physicians and a contributing editor to *The Alternative Advisor: The Complete Guide to Natural Therapies and Alternative Treatments* (Time Life).

You probably know that about one of every three American adults has high blood pressure (hypertension). But you may not realize that there are two types of hypertension—primary and secondary. The distinction is crucial since primary and secondary hypertension require different treatment. With the wrong treatment, hypertension can go uncontrolled, which can lead to kidney failure, stroke or even death.

The cause of primary hypertension is unknown, but genetics is among the most likely culprits. Primary hypertension often starts in a person's mid-20s, with readings creeping upward as the years go by. It's treated with diet and exercise and/or anti-hypertensive drugs.

Secondary hypertension, which usually comes on quickly and can occur in people with no family history of high blood pressure, is actually a symptom of a preexisting problem. Underlying health problems can be the trigger for secondary hypertension. The most common include congenital heart defects, kidney disorders (including a tumor on the adrenal gland at the top of the kidney) or hormonal disorders (including overactive thyroid or overproduction of the steroid hormone aldosterone). Secondary hypertension also can result from medications, including steroids, migraine drugs, the antidepressant *bupropion* (Wellbutrin) and nonsteroidal anti-inflammatory medicines, such as *ibuprofen* (Motrin). Or the underlying cause may be lifestyle issues, such as sleep deprivation, obesity, chronic stress, pregnancy or excessive alcohol consumption.

When I see a patient with high blood pressure, I look for an underlying cause. I do a physical exam and order a variety of blood and urine tests. I also inquire about personal habits, including sleep, exercise and diet, and review the patient's prescription and over-the-counter (OTC) medications and supplements (ones with licorice, ephedra or an ingredient to which a person is allergic can raise blood pressure). I also ask about major life shifts, such as a move, divorce or job change—all can affect blood pressure.

When the underlying cause is treated, secondary hypertension usually goes away. A change in prescription or OTC medication may be needed. Hormonal problems often are resolved with hormone therapy. Kidney disorders may require the care of a specialist. With some patients, I treat the underlying problem and prescribe antihypertensive medicines.

A healthful diet is essential for anyone with high blood pressure. My favorite is the so-called DASH diet, Dietary Approaches to Stop Hypertension. To learn more about this diet, which is high in fruits, vegetables, dietary fiber, magnesium and potassium, check *www.dashdiet.org.* Daily yoga and breathing exercises also help both primary and secondary hypertension.

Try this: Hold one finger over your right nostril and breathe in and out through the left nostril for 15 breaths, then repeat with the other nostril. Usually, this immediately lowers the blood pressure and can be done as often as you wish. Results may last for an hour or all day, depending on the person.

Home Blood Pressure Monitoring May Save Your Life

Mark C. Houston, MD, associate clinical professor of medicine at Vanderbilt University School of Medicine and director of the Hypertension Institute at Saint Thomas Medical Group, both in Nashville. He is the author of *What Your Doctor May Not Tell You About Hypertension* (Grand Central). *www.hypertensioninstitute.com*

The twenty-first-century version of the standard doctor's advice may be "take your blood pressure twice a day and call or e-mail me in the morning."

As our collective blood pressure keeps rising and more and more research affirms the benefit of at-home monitoring to better manage hypertension, patients are being instructed to keep close track of their own highs and lows. According to new guidelines from the American Heart Association, the American Society of Hypertension and the Preventive Cardiovascular Nurses' Association, most Americans with known or suspected hypertension (74 million adults, at least) should take regular blood pressure readings at home—especially those with high blood pressure of 140/90 millimeters of mercury (mmHg) or higher.

Not only will this help keep hypertension in check, but it also may be the only accurate way to get measurements for people who suffer from what's come to be known as "white coat hypertension," where the mere fact that a health care professional is checking makes blood pressure soar.

Why the big push for home blood pressure monitoring? Hypertension and vascular specialist Mark C. Houston, MD, author of *What Your Doctor May Not Tell You About Hypertension: The Revolutionary Nutrition and Lifestyle Program to Help Fight High Blood Pressure* (Grand Central) explains the benefits.

By providing a more accurate representation of day-to-day rises and falls, home monitoring can confirm suspected or newly diagnosed hypertension or it can be used to evaluate and fine-tune your response to antihypertensive treatment, says Dr. Houston. Continuous monitoring may also be valuable for people with borderline or pre-hypertension (between 120/80 and 139/89), as it can help determine whether to initiate treatment and at what level.

Best Buy: Digital Monitors

The two most common types of home monitors are aneroid and digital. Aneroid monitors are the old-fashioned ones that have a stethoscope, a bulb you pump to inflate, a cuff and a gauge. Digital monitors are more convenient and easier to use on yourself, with built-in sensors and easy-to-read number displays, plus most automatically inflate and deflate. According to Dr. Houston, the arm monitors are the most accurate. Although wrist and finger versions are also available, Dr. Houston does not recommend using them.

Those who are instructed to begin home monitoring should do it twice daily, as close to the same time as you can—once in the morning, before you take medication, and again in the evening. If you plan to exercise or drink anything with caffeine—or have a cigarette, which you shouldn't be doing anyway—take your blood pressure first. Also, make sure to sit quietly for five minutes before taking a reading.

Monitors are widely available at pharmacies, medical supply stores and online. Prices vary from about $30 to over $100, depending on options (e.g., memory recall that allows you to view blood pressure history, built-in printers and a USB cable or AC adapter to hook up to a computer to transmit data directly to your doctor's office). Dr.

Houston likes those by Omron (*www.omronhealthcare.com*).

Whatever monitor you choose, make sure your doctor sees and approves it and also tests it against what's used in the office. Ask for some training in proper use as well. Establish in advance what type of reading merits a phone call or visit.

It may require a little extra work, but home blood pressure monitoring can pay off with a lower risk of serious complications and greater peace of mind.

■ ■ ■ ■

Heart Supplements That Can Save Your Life

Dennis Goodman, MD, clinical associate professor of medicine at New York University School of Medicine in New York City and at the University of California in San Diego. *www.dennisgoodmanmd.com*

One of the most common reasons that people take nutritional supplements is to improve their heart health.

Nighttime Aspirin Lowers Blood Pressure

Previous studies have linked nighttime aspirin use with lower blood pressure, but there has been no explanation for the drug's effect.

New research: Bedtime aspirin use was found to lower blood and urine levels of naturally occurring chemicals associated with high blood pressure in a study of 16 adults with untreated, mildly elevated blood pressure.

If your doctor has prescribed daily aspirin: Ask about taking the pill at night.

Jaapjan Snoep, MSc, researcher, department of clinical epidemiology, Leiden University Medical Center, the Netherlands.

Problem: Very few cardiologists are aware of the ways in which heart supplements work synergistically—that is, by taking carefully selected supplements in combinations, you will heighten the effectiveness of each one. Over the past 22 years, I have treated thousands of heart patients with this approach.

What you need to know to make the most of your nondrug regimen for better heart health…*

The Essential Three

There are three daily supplements that I recommend to anyone who is concerned about heart health…

● **Fish oil** capsules primarily lower harmful blood fats known as triglycerides but also have a mild blood pressure–lowering effect.

Typical dose: 1 gram (g) total of the omega-3 fatty acids *eicosapentaenoic acid* (EPA) and *docosahexaenoic acid* (DHA) for blood pressure benefits. To reduce triglyceride levels, the typical daily dose is 2 g to 4 g total of EPA and DHA.

Caution: Fish oil can increase bleeding risk, so talk to your doctor if you take a blood thinner, such as *warfarin* (Coumadin).

● **CoQ10** helps enhance energy production in cells and inhibits blood clot formation.

Typical dose: 50 milligrams (mg) to 100 mg per day. CoQ10, which is commonly taken with the classic HDL-boosting treatment niacin (vitamin B-3), also helps minimize side effects, such as muscle weakness, in people taking cholesterol-lowering statin drugs.

● **Red yeast rice** is an extract of red yeast that is fermented on rice and is available in tablet, capsule, powder and liquid form. Long used by the Chinese, it mimics the action of cholesterol-lowering statin drugs.

Typical dose: 600 mg twice daily.

Red yeast rice is often used in combination with plant sterols, naturally occurring chemical compounds found in small amounts in fruits, vegetables and nuts… and added to food products, including butter substitutes, such as Promise activ and Benecol spreads.

Typical dose: About 400 mg daily of plant sterols.

Also important: Low levels of vitamin D (below 15 nanograms per deciliter [ng/dL]) have been linked to a 62% increase, on average, in heart attack risk.

Typical dose: 5,000 international units (IU) of vitamin D-3 per day for those who are deficient in the vitamin…at least 1,000 IU daily for all other adults.

Better Blood Pressure Control

The heart-friendly properties of fish oil are so well documented that the American Heart Association endorses its use (by

---

*To find a doctor to oversee your heart-health supplement regimen, consult the American Board of Integrative Holistic Medicine, *www.holisticboard.org.*

eating fatty fish at least twice weekly and/or taking fish oil capsules).

To enhance fish oil's blood pressure–lowering effect, ask your doctor about adding...

• **L-arginine.** This amino acid boosts the body's production of the chemical compound nitric oxide, which causes the blood vessels to dilate, thereby lowering blood pressure.

Typical dose: 150 mg daily.

L-arginine is also used to treat erectile dysfunction and claudication (impeded blood flow in the extremities) and has a mild and beneficial HDL-boosting effect.

Caution: L-arginine should not be taken by children or pregnant or nursing women, or by anyone with genital herpes—it can stimulate activity of the herpes virus. Possible side effects include indigestion, nausea and headache.

• **Lycopene.** This phytochemical is found in tomatoes—especially processed tomato sauce—watermelon, pink grapefruit, red bell peppers and papaya. I usually recommend that patients try L-arginine first, then add lycopene, if necessary, for blood pressure reduction.

Research conducted at Ben-Gurion University in Israel has shown that lycopene lowers systolic (top number) blood pressure by up to 10 points and diastolic (bottom number) by up to four points.

A potent antioxidant, lycopene is also thought to have potential cancer-preventive effects, but this has not been proven.

Typical dose: 10 mg daily.

In rare cases, lycopene supplements can cause diarrhea and/or nausea. Because tomatoes and other acidic foods can aggravate ulcer pain, people with stomach ulcers should consult their doctors before consuming tomatoes and tomato-based products regularly.

Better Blood Pressure Treatment

A thiazide diuretic, such as *chlorthalidone* (Combipres), typically is prescribed as the initial therapy for high blood pressure (hypertension), but these drugs can deplete potassium. Potassium loss has been linked to sudden cardiac death (an abrupt loss of heart function).

New finding: Hypertension patients treated with both a thiazide diuretic and a "potassium-sparing" drug, such as *amiloride* (Midamor), had a 40% lower risk for sudden cardiac death than those who took a placebo.

If you take a thiazide diuretic: Ask your doctor about adding a potassium-sparing drug to your regimen.

John Oates, MD, Thomas F. Frist senior professor of medicine, Vanderbilt University Medical Center, Nashville.

Boost HDL Cholesterol

In addition to taking CoQ10 and niacin, ask your doctor about trying...

• **Policosanol.** This plant-wax derivative has been found to boost HDL levels by more than 7%. The research on policosanol is considered controversial by some, but I have found it to be an effective HDL booster in my practice.

Typical dose: 10 mg daily.

There is also some evidence that policosanol may have LDL- and triglyceride-lowering benefits. There are no known side effects associated with policosanol.

Bonus: Used together, CoQ10, niacin and policosanol will allow you to raise your HDL levels while taking much lower doses of niacin (about 20 mg daily). A lower niacin dose reduces the risk for facial flushing, a common side effect in people who take the vitamin.

Lower Blood Pressure With Even a Small Reduction in Salt

Lower blood pressure with even a small reduction in salt. University of London researchers have determined that even a slight reduction—from two teaspoons to about one-and-a-half teaspoons of salt daily—can help lower blood pressure. For those who have moderate-to-high blood pressure, aim to reduce the table salt you add to food to less than one teaspoon—and ideally one-half teaspoon—daily.

Mark A. Stengler, NMD, naturopathic medical doctor and leading authority on the practice of alternative and integrated medicine. Dr. Stengler is author of the *Health Revelations* newsletter, author of *The Natural Physician's Healing Therapies* (Bottom Line Books), founder and medical director of the Stengler Center for Integrative Medicine, Encinitas, California, and adjunct associate clinical professor at the National College of Natural Medicine in Portland, Oregon. *http://markstengler.com*

Reduce LDL Cholesterol

Red yeast rice extract and plant sterols (both described earlier) are well-known natural methods of lowering LDL cholesterol levels.

To lower your LDL cholesterol further, ask your doctor about adding policosanol (described earlier), along with…

• **Pantethine.** This is a more biologically active form of pantothenic acid (vitamin B-5).

Typical dose: 600 mg daily.

Numerous small studies have found that pantethine significantly lowers LDL cholesterol and triglycerides.

• **Grape seed extract.** This antioxidant-rich substance reduces the blood's tendency to clot and helps lower blood pressure by boosting levels of the chemical compound nitric oxide found in the body. Some research shows that grape seed extract also reduces LDL cholesterol.

Typical dose: 200 mg daily.

In addition, studies suggest that grape seed extract helps protect against Alzheimer's disease.

Caution: Because grape seed extract has a blood-thinning effect, it should not be taken by anyone who uses warfarin or other blood-thinning medications or supplements.

Easy Walking Is an Easy Way to Control Blood Pressure

Kate Woolf-May, PhD, senior research fellow, department of sport science, tourism and leisure, Canterbury Christ Church University, Canterbury, UK.

If controlling your blood pressure is a goal of your exercise program, it may be as easy as a stroll in the park. It turns out that regular 30-minute walks at a comfortable pace are quite effective, say British researchers. While it sounds almost too good to be true, scientists at Canterbury Christ Church University in the UK recently found that a half-hour stroll at a moderate pace was just as beneficial to systolic blood pressure as walking faster or longer. With such significant benefits to be reaped from such relatively little effort, this news should get even the most reluctant among us up and moving.

Small Workouts Lead to Big Results

The British scientists examined a small group of 13 nonsmoking middle-aged men with normal blood pressure or prehypertension (blood pressure readings higher than the normal 120 over 80 millimeters of mercury mmHg, but below 140 over 80). Studies have shown that pre-hypertension may

Crack Down on Blood Pressure

Chiropractors have long claimed that neck manipulations can lower blood pressure.

Now: Scientists have recently learned that neck muscles do help control heart rate and breathing as well as blood pressure.

University of Leeds

be associated with an increased risk of atherosclerosis (formation of plaques in arteries) and heart attacks.

A baseline blood pressure reading was taken for all participants. Then, to determine what rate of walking produced the greatest reduction in blood pressure, the men walked for 30 minutes at 45% max effort, 60 minutes at 45% max effort and 30 minutes at 65% max effort (the study used as a measure VO2 max, which is maximum oxygen consumption). Systolic blood pressure was measured before and immediately after the walk and at one hour, four hours and 24 hours afterward. Researchers found that systolic blood pressure significantly decreased for at least four hours on all three occasions, but not for the control group. Systolic blood pressure returned to baseline values at 24 hours for all three groups.

This is good news for all those people who say they don't have time or energy to exercise, notes study coauthor Kate Woolf-May, PhD, a senior research fellow in the department of sport science, tourism and leisure. There's no need to feel pressure to squeeze in long exercise sessions every weekend or train to run a marathon—just put on your sneakers and take a walk. The American College of Sports Medicine recommends that healthy adults get 30 minutes of moderate exercise five days a week.

Prehypertension Alert

Shawna D. Nesbitt, MD, associate professor of internal medicine, University of Texas Southwestern Medical Center, Dallas.

Prehypertension—blood pressure of 120 to 139 millimeters of mercury (mmHg)/80 to 89 mmHg—usually is treated with lifestyle measures, such as weight loss, salt restriction and exercise.

New finding: In a study of 800 prehypertension patients, those who took the blood pressure medication *candesartan* (Atacand) for two years while making lifestyle changes had a 15.6% lower risk of developing hypertension than those who didn't take medication.

If your blood pressure is in the upper range of prehypertension: Ask your doctor about medication in addition to lifestyle changes.

A Quick Check-In With Your Doc Can Fix High BP

Try this simple strategy to lower blood pressure.

Recent study: Researchers tracked 5,042 adults with diabetes and high blood pressure for four years. Those who saw their doctors at least once a month reduced their blood pressure to healthy levels in 1.8 months, on average, compared with 29.4 months, on average, for those with doctor visits twice a year.

If you have high blood pressure: Discuss with your doctor the optimal frequency of doctor visits. Seeing a physician's assistant or e-mailing your doctor with the results of at-home blood pressure monitoring also may be options.

Alexander Turchin, MD, assistant professor of medicine, division of endocrinology, diabetes and hypertension, Brigham and Women's Hospital, Boston.

Pycnogenol: Good for What Ails You?

Mark A. Stengler, NMD, naturopathic medical doctor and leading authority on the practice of alternative and integrated medicine. Dr. Stengler is author of the *Health Revelations* newsletter, author of *The Natural Physician's Healing Therapies* (Bottom Line Books), founder and medical director of the Stengler Center for Integrative Medicine, Encinitas, California, and adjunct associate clinical professor at the National College of Natural Medicine in Portland, Oregon. *http://markstengler.com*

When a nutritional supplement is said to provide a multitude of health benefits, it is reasonable to ask if the claims are too good to be true. That is why I have taken a close look at Pycnogenol (pronounced pik-NOJ-en-all), the brand name of an extract from the bark of the maritime pine tree that grows in France. Numerous manufacturers use Pycnogenol in various supplement formulations.

The flavonoids (plant pigments) in Pycnogenol are potent anti-inflammatories and antioxidants (chemicals that protect cells from harmful molecules called free radicals). *Studies show the extract to be effective in treating…*

• **Hypertension (high blood pressure).** In a study published in the peer-reviewed international journal *Life Sciences*, 58 participants who were on prescription hypertension medication took either a placebo or 100 milligrams (mg) per day of Pycnogenol. After 12 weeks, 57% of the Pycnogenol users were able to halve their drug dosage while continuing to take the extract.

• **Diabetes.** A study published in *Life Sciences* involved 77 people with type 2 diabetes. Participants who took 100 mg of Pycnogenol daily for 12 weeks showed significantly lower blood-sugar levels than those who took a placebo.

• **Perimenopausal symptoms.** In a Taiwanese study, 155 women in perimenopause (the years of transition to menopause) took either a placebo or 200 mg of Pycnogenol daily…and assigned scores for the severity of their symptoms, such as hot flashes, sleep problems, poor memory and anxiety. After six months, symptom scores improved for everyone in the Pycnogenol group, while the placebo users' scores did not change significantly.

Bonus: Among Pycnogenol users, blood tests showed that LDL "bad" cholesterol dropped by 10% and antioxidant levels increased.

Studies suggest that Pycnogenol also may alleviate…

• **Circulatory problems,** including varicose veins, coronary artery disease, congestive heart failure, erectile dysfunction and retinopathy (a disorder of the retina).

Best Nutrients for Heart Health

Food is our best source of nutrients. That's because food sources offer a variety of minerals, vitamins and antioxidants that work synergistically to boost the nutritional value of each. *I urge all of my patients to get ample amounts of the following heart-healthy nutrients from food…*

• **Antioxidants, which help prevent plaque formation on the walls of your arteries.**

Good sources: Pomegranate, blueberries, and fruits and vegetables in general.

• **Magnesium, which helps regulate blood pressure and stabilize heart rhythm.**

Good sources: Dark green, leafy vegetables…soybeans…almonds…cashews…black-eyed peas…and peanut butter.

• **Potassium, which helps regulate blood pressure and heart function.**

Good sources: Apricots, cantaloupe, melons, kiwi, oranges (and orange juice), bananas, lima beans, tomatoes, prunes, avocados…as well as meat, fish and poultry.

Caution: If you have kidney disease, consult your doctor before consuming potassium-rich foods. —*Dr. Mark Stengler*

Keep Still

For an accurate blood pressure reading: Empty your bladder because a full bladder can affect the reading. Avoid smoking, drinking anything caffeinated and exercising 30 minutes before the test. Keep your feet flat on the floor for five minutes prior to checking your blood pressure. During the reading, keep still and rest your arm on a table so that it is at heart level.

Consumer Reports on Health, 101 Truman Ave., Yonkers, New York 10703. *www.consumerreports.org/health*

• **Respiratory disorders,** such as allergies and asthma.

• **Pain in muscles and joints,** such as postexercise soreness and osteoarthritis.

• **Lymphedema** (abnormal swelling due to accumulation of lymph fluid), common among postsurgical breast cancer patients.

Bottom line: I recommend Pycnogenol for adults and children age five and up with any of the conditions above. Dosage varies depending on your overall health, so talk to a holisitic physician.

Important: Check with your doctor before using Pycnogenol if you take blood-thinning drugs, such as aspirin or *warfarin* (Coumadin), because it also thins blood…if you take drugs for diabetes, because Pycnogenol can lower blood sugar…or if you are pregnant or nursing, as a general precaution. Otherwise, Pycnogenol generally is safe to take indefinitely. Side effects may include hives and tightness in the chest or throat.

Pycnogenol products are sold in health-food stores. Prices start at around $30 for 60 capsules of 50 mg to 100 mg. High-quality brands include Source Naturals (800-815-2333, *www.sourcenaturals.com*) and Country Life (800-645-5768, *www.country-life.com*).

■ ■ ■ ■

Simple At-Home Device Eases Hypertension Naturally

Mark A. Stengler, NMD, naturopathic medical doctor and leading authority on the practice of alternative and integrated medicine. Dr. Stengler is author of the *Health Revelations* newsletter, author of *The Natural Physician's Healing Therapies* (Bottom Line Books), founder and medical director of the Stengler Center for Integrative Medicine, Encinitas, California, and adjunct associate clinical professor at the National College of Natural Medicine in Portland, Oregon. *http://markstengler.com*

Blood pressure regulation is a complex process, which is one reason why blood pressure problems are so common. Half of people over age 60 have high blood pressure, or hypertension—pressure of 140/90 or greater, measured in millimeters of mercury (mmHg)—and some develop it as early as their mid-30s.

Blood pressure is determined by the amount of blood your heart pumps and by the arteries' resistance to blood flow. Excess weight, a high-salt diet, stress and high cholesterol can contribute to hypertension. In such instances, dietary changes, exercise, relaxation techniques and/or cholesterol-lowering therapies can help.

In 95% of hypertension cases, however, the cause is unknown—and often the therapies above are not enough to keep blood pressure in check. Uncontrolled hypertension raises the risk for heart failure, heart attack, stroke, kidney damage and diabetes.

Reason: When blood pressure rises, arteries take a beating as blood pounds through them. The body responds by patching damaged arterial walls with plaque (a mix of fat and cholesterol)…but this makes arteries narrower, increasing blood pressure even more.

Often medication can lower blood pressure—but it may take considerable experimentation to find the most effective drug or drugs for an individual. Also,

Lowering Blood Pressure When Your Mobility Is Limited

If your mobility is limited because you are in a wheelchair or some other injury, and you would like to lower your blood pressure, start by eating plenty of whole grains, vegetables and fruits. Several natural supplements also can help, such as hawthorn berry extract (which comes from the berry of this thorny shrub)...the enzyme coenzyme Q10...and calcium and magnesium. Hand-gripping exercises (in which you squeeze a handheld device, hold and release) can help as well. The Zona Plus (866-669-9662, *www.zona.com*), which has been shown in studies to improve blood pressure, uses hand-gripping exercises to improve blood flow and make blood vessels more flexible. The device is expensive ($399). Researchers believe that the same benefit can be had with a hand-gripping device from a sporting goods store, but studies have not confirmed this.

Mark A. Stengler, NMD, naturopathic medical doctor and leading authority on the practice of alternative and integrated medicine. Dr. Stengler is author of the *Health Revelations* newsletter, author of *The Natural Physician's Healing Therapies* (Bottom Line Books), founder and medical director of the Stengler Center for Integrative Medicine, Encinitas, California, and adjunct associate clinical professor at the National College of Natural Medicine in Portland, Oregon. *http://markstengler.com*

these drugs can have side effects, such as dizziness, chronic cough, muscle cramps, fatigue and erectile dysfunction.

That's why I am always exploring natural ways to reduce blood pressure—and why I am so enthusiastic about a device with the brand name Resperate, designed for use at home.

Encouraging Evidence

So far, nine clinical trials published in medical journals confirm that Resperate successfully lowers blood pressure. The first, from the *Journal of Human Hypertension*, involved 61 men and women with blood pressure averaging 155/95. For 10 minutes daily, one group of participants used the Resperate device and the other listened to quiet music on a portable CD player. After eight weeks, Resperate users' average reduction was 15.2 points for systolic pressure (top number) and 10 points for diastolic pressure (bottom number)...compared with the CD player group's reduction of 11.3 points (systolic) and 5.6 points (diastolic). Six months after treatment stopped, the Resperate group's diastolic pressure remained lower than the CD player group's.

The principle behind Resperate—sustained deep breathing—is not new. Yet the way the device accomplishes this goal is quite innovative. Before I describe this, let me explain some important facts about breathing. Most people breathe shallowly, taking air only into the tops of the lungs... unconsciously hold their breath whenever they feel anxious or are concentrating on a task...and hold in their stomachs, a practice that slims the silhouette but prevents the long, deep "belly breaths" that carry oxygen all the way down into the lungs.

Breathing slowly and fully from the abdomen helps to reduce blood pressure, because it balances the messages from the nervous system that constrict or relax the arteries and helps control the "fight or flight" stress response. As the body relaxes and anxiety eases, constricted blood vessels dilate and blood flows more easily.

How Resperate Works

Resperate has three components—a small computer unit, a headphone set and a sensor belt. The first time you use the device, it detects your baseline (normal) breathing pattern. Using this information, the computer develops a personalized melody—with high tones indicating inhalation and low tones indicating exhalation—that gradually guides you into a slower breathing pattern. You can follow this tailor-made breathing pattern effortlessly and almost unconsciously, the same way your toes automatically tap out the rhythm as you listen to music.

Resperate is designed to slow your respiration rate from the average of 12 to 19 breaths per minute to the hypertension-lowering rate of 10 or fewer breaths per minute. You use it for at least 40 minutes per week, typically in three or four 15-minute sessions. After you complete a session, your breathing returns to its normal rate—but the decreased blood pressure achieved during your session usually remains throughout the day. The more you use Resperate, the greater its effects are likely to be.

A blood pressure reduction of 10 points systolic and five points diastolic yields measurable health benefits. After three to four weeks of use, Resperate reduces blood pressure, on average, by 14 points systolic and eight points diastolic. Some users have experienced decreases of as much as 36 points systolic and 20 points diastolic. Among my own patients, 15 have used Resperate in the last six months—and 13 have successfully lowered their blood pressure by 10 to 14 points systolic and five to 10 points diastolic.

This device is safe for everyone and has no side effects. It can be used in conjunction with blood pressure drugs. After 10 weeks of regular use of Resperate, many patients can reduce their hypertension drug dosage, under a doctor's supervision.

Note: For sustained health benefits, you must use Resperate for the rest of your life—just as it is necessary to exercise regularly and eat healthfully for life.

To order: Resperate is available without a prescription from the manufacturer, InterCure (877-988-9388, *www.resperate. com*) and at some pharmacies. The cost is $299.95, plus tax and shipping. It is not covered by insurance, though it may be tax-deductible (ask your accountant) or reimbursible through a flexible spending account. I consider it money well spent.

Nondrug Approaches To Help Control Blood Pressure

Mark C. Houston, MD, associate clinical professor of medicine at Vanderbilt University School of Medicine and director of the Hypertension Institute at Saint Thomas Medical Group, both in Nashville. He is the author of *What Your Doctor May Not Tell You About Hypertension* (Grand Central). *www. hypertensioninstitute.com*

High blood pressure (hypertension) is so common in the US that many people don't take it as seriously as they should.

One out of every three American adults has hypertension, but only about half of them are being treated—and a far smaller percentage is being treated successfully.

Frightening statistic: About 58 million Americans are living with uncontrolled hypertension—a condition that dramatically increases their risk for heart attack, stroke, dementia, heart failure and kidney failure.

So why aren't we doing a better job of keeping our blood pressure under control?

Even though regular exercise and a low-fat and low-sodium diet can help reduce blood pressure in many people, the overwhelming majority of doctors end up treating hypertension with medication. In some cases, medication is required to control blood pressure, but its use can have drawbacks.

Blood pressure drugs are notorious for causing side effects, including headache and dizziness…and many hypertension medications (especially the newer ones) can be costly. Not surprisingly, studies show that only about 20% of patients over age 65 take their hypertension medication as prescribed.

Caution: Do not stop taking any blood pressure medication—or reduce your dosage—without first consulting your doctor.

Solutions that get overlooked: There are a number of natural approaches that can reduce your blood pressure or even eliminate your need for blood pressure medication. Unfortunately, most doctors have not been trained in these therapies, and there is rarely enough time during rushed office visits to discuss them.

My favorite nondrug approaches to help control blood pressure…

1. Get more potassium. Muscles in the heart and blood vessels require this mineral to contract normally and maintain a healthy blood pressure. We should consume five times more potassium than sodium, yet most of us get eight to 10 times more sodium than potassium.

If we increased our potassium intakes to the recommended amount of 4,700 milligrams (mg) daily and restricted our sodium intakes to the recommended levels of 2,300 mg or less daily, studies show that we could see a 10% drop in hypertension rates.

My advice: Avoid processed foods (typically salt-saturated) and eat eight to 10 daily servings of vegetables and fruits, which are naturally high in potassium and low in sodium.

Good potassium sources: Sweet potatoes, bananas, green beans, cantaloupe, orange juice, tomatoes (fresh or cooked) and prunes.

Caution: Never use potassium supplements unless prescribed by your doctor—they can be dangerous if you take certain medications or have kidney disease.

2. Add nuts to your diet. In a Pennsylvania State University study, men who consumed 1.5 ounces of pistachios (about 60 nuts) daily for four weeks averaged a 4.8 millimeters of mercury (mmHg) drop in systolic (top number) blood pressure.

The benefits likely stem from pistachios' healthful fats—one ounce has fewer than 2 grams (g) of potentially harmful saturated fat and nearly 11 g of healthful mono- and polyunsaturated fats, which help lower blood pressure by reducing arterial inflammation and improving blood vessel dilation. Reductions in blood pressure also have been found with a similar daily intake of almonds and walnuts.

My advice: Get 30% of your calories from mono- and polyunsaturated fats (unsalted nuts are a good source)…restrict saturated fat to no more than 10% of total daily fat intake. Eliminate all trans fats from your diet.

Good sources of mono- and polyunsaturated fats: In addition to nuts—salmon, ground flaxseed, olive oil and canola oil.

3. Get enough protein. Hypertension rates are lower in populations that consume high amounts of protein—possibly due to natural compounds in protein that inhibit the production of a chemical that constricts blood vessels.

The milk proteins casein and whey are especially abundant sources of amino acids that may also lower blood pressure. In a recent six-week trial, people with prehypertension or mild-to-moderate hypertension who consumed 20 g daily of whey protein saw their systolic pressure drop by an average of 8 mmHg and their diastolic (bottom number) pressure fall by an average of 5.5 mmHg.

My advice: Consume approximately 1.5 g of protein daily for every 2.2 pounds of body weight. (For example, if you weigh 160 pounds, aim for 109 g of protein daily.) Include 30 g of whey protein (available at health-food stores in drink powders and shake mixes), with the balance coming from high-protein foods such as fish, poultry, grass-fed beef (grass contains healthful omega-3 fatty acids), low-fat dairy products and beans.

4. Boost your vitamin D levels. The lower your vitamin D levels, the higher your risk for hypertension, diabetes and certain cancers, according to recent studies. Our bodies produce vitamin D when sunlight hits our skin, but few Americans get enough sun to manufacture sufficient levels of the vitamin. Even in Nashville, where I practice, 90% of my patients are vitamin D deficient.

My advice: Because sun exposure increases skin cancer risk (and sunscreen blocks the production of vitamin D), take daily supplements totaling 2,000 international units (IU) to 4,000 IU of vitamin D3 (the most active form). That's higher than the federally recommended 400 IU to 600 IU daily, but most researchers now agree that more is needed to safeguard health. Do not exceed 10,000 IU daily—high doses can cause adverse effects, such as nausea and headache.

5. Consult a chiropractor. For a recent study at the University of Chicago Medical Center, 25 patients with stage 1 hypertension underwent a treatment known as the National Upper Cervical Chiropractic Association (NUCCA) technique, which involves realignment of the topmost vertebra. Another 25 patients received a placebo treatment. Eight weeks later, doctors found that those who had had the real chiropractic adjustment averaged a 14-mmHg greater drop in systolic pressure and an 8-mmHg greater drop in diastolic pressure than those in the other group. Researchers theorize that misaligned vertebra may pinch arteries and nerves, affecting blood flow.

My advice: While more studies are needed, it may be worth consulting a chiropractor, particularly if you suffer from both neck pain and hypertension.

Important: Only licensed chiropractors certified in NUCCA techniques are qualified to perform this procedure. To find a qualified chiropractor, consult the National Upper Cervical Chiropractic Association (800-541-5799, *www.nucca.org*).

6. Try audio relaxation programs. Researchers at Seattle University College of Nursing found that when older adults listened for 12 minutes three times weekly to an audio relaxation program, their systolic blood pressure dropped by an average of 9 mmHg.

The audio program consisted of a soothing voice guiding the listener through a progressive muscle relaxation sequence with the sound of ocean waves in the background. Progressive relaxation calms the parasympathetic nervous system, which controls blood vessel function.

My advice: Buy audio relaxation CDs online or look for such programs at your local library.

7. Consider taking certain supplements. Several nutritional supplements are advertised as having blood pressure–lowering effects. But the strongest evidence supports the use of...*

• **Coenzyme Q10.** Studies indicate 39% of patients with hypertension also have a coenzyme Q10 (CoQ10) deficiency, compared with only about 6% of people without hypertension. Meanwhile, a dozen clinical

*All of these supplements can be used in combination—with or without blood pressure medication. Consult your doctor.

trials have found CoQ10 to lower systolic blood pressure by up to 17 mmHg and diastolic pressure by up to 10 mmHg, without adverse side effects.

My advice: Ask your doctor about trying 200 mg of CoQ10 daily.

● **Alpha-lipoic acid and acetyl L-carnitine.** In a recent Boston University School of Medicine study, researchers found that systolic pressure dropped by nine points in patients with coronary artery disease who combined these supplements for eight weeks—largely due to a relaxation of the arteries.

My advice: Try 100 mg of R-lipoic acid (the natural form of alpha-lipoic acid) twice daily…and 500 mg twice daily of acetyl L-carnitine.

More Natural Ways to Lower Blood Pressure

To lower your blood pressure, take all of the following natural substances for eight weeks. Then, if blood pressure readings show that you've improved, continue indefinitely. Supplements are sold in health-food stores and, unless noted, generally are safe.

Best: Use these natural therapies in conjunction with Resperate (see pages 52–53).

Important: Do not stop taking your blood-pressure medication without your doctor's approval.

● **Calcium—500 milligrams (mg) twice daily.** This mineral aids normal transmission of nerve impulses as well as muscle relaxation andcontraction.

● **Coenzyme Q10 (CoQ10)—300 mg daily.** For unknown reasons, many people with hypertension have low levels of this vitamin-like substance. It is especially beneficial if you have type 2 diabetes.

● **Hawthorne extract—250 mg three times daily.** This herb has a mild blood-thinning

effect, which improves blood flow. Ask your doctor before using if you take a blood thinner, such as aspirin or *warfarin* (Coumadin).

● **Magnesium—250 mg twice daily.** This mineral is involved in nerve and muscle function. Reduce dosage if stools become loose.

● **Vegetable juice high in potassium and low in salt (such as Low Sodium V8)—**four ounces twice daily. Potassium helps to normalize blood volume. If you have a history of kidney disease, ask your doctor before drinking high-potassium juice.

Fun fact: In a recent German study of 44 adults with hypertension, participants who ate about one-quarter of an ounce (30 calories) of dark chocolate daily for 18 weeks reduced their blood pressure by about three points systolic and two points diastolic.

Mark A. Stengler, NMD, naturopathic medical doctor and leading authority on the practice of alternative and integrated medicine. Dr. Stengler is author of the *Health Revelations* newsletter, author of *The Natural Physician's Healing Therapies* (Bottom Line Books), founder and medical director of the Stengler Center for Integrative Medicine, Encinitas, California, and adjunct associate clinical professor at the National College of Natural Medicine in Portland, Oregon. *http://markstengler.com*

Easy 20-Minute Way to Prevent Heart Disease— Anyone Can Do It!

Norman E. Rosenthal, MD, clinical professor of psychiatry at Georgetown University School of Medicine, who maintains a private practice in the Washington, DC, area. He is author of *Transcendence: Healing and Transformation Through Transcendental Meditation* (Tarcher). *www.normanrosenthal.com*

Wouldn't it be great if there were a simple way to lower blood pressure, reverse heart disease and sharpen your brain? There is! It's called transcendental meditation, or TM for short.

Many people think of TM as a vestige of the 1960s, a vaguely religious practice that was popularized when the Beatles went to India to study with Maharishi Mahesh Yogi.

TM is not a religious practice. It does not involve immersing yourself in a particular belief system. It's a mental technique that changes brain wave patterns and alters, in beneficial ways, physiological processes, such as blood pressure, heart rate and hormone levels.

Bonus: TM is easier to do than many other forms of meditation and relaxation therapy. And beginners exhibit the same brain wave changes as longtime practitioners, sometimes within just a few weeks after starting TM.

What It Involves

Various relaxation techniques require you to sit with your eyes closed, focus on your breathing and/or visualize a particular scene. TM requires the repetition of a mantra, a meaningless word that you mentally focus on.

There's nothing mystical about the mantra. It's simply a tool for quieting the mind and "transcending" stressful thoughts, worries and concerns.

Most people who practice TM do so twice a day for 20 minutes each time. During a session, the breathing slows and the brain (as measured on an EEG) produces a preponderance of alpha waves, slow frequency signals (eight to 12 cycles per second) that indicate deep relaxation. There's also an increase in brain wave coherence, in which activity in different parts of the brain is roughly synchronized.

TM has been studied more than most other forms of meditation and relaxation—and, in some cases, appears to have more pronounced health effects. Researchers have published approximately 340 peer-reviewed articles on TM, many of which appeared in respected medical journals. *Important benefits*…

Lowers Blood Pressure

A University of Kentucky meta-analysis that looked at data from 711 participants found that those who practiced TM averaged a five-point reduction in systolic pressure (top number) and three points in diastolic (bottom number). This might sound like a modest benefit, but it's enough to potentially reduce the incidence of cardiovascular disease by 15% to 20%.

Scientists speculate that TM lowers blood pressure by reducing the body's output of hormones, such as *epinephrine*, that accompany and stimulate the natural stress response. People with hypertension who meditate twice a day for more than three months require, on average, 23% less blood pressure medication.

Other nondrug treatments for hypertension, including biofeedback, progressive relaxation and stress-management training, don't have these same effects.

Reverses Heart Disease

Researchers divided participants with hypertension into two groups. Those in one group were given health education (the control group), while those in the second group practiced TM for six to nine months. The thickness of the *intima* (inner lining) of the carotid artery was measured at the beginning and end of the study.

Result: The intima thickened slightly in the control group, indicating that cardiovascular disease had progressed. In the TM group, the thickness of the intima decreased. This study, published in *Stroke*, indicates that TM actually can reverse cardiovascular disease.

It's not known why TM has this effect. We suspect that it's more effective in patients with early-stage disease. In those with advanced atherosclerosis, which is accompanied by calcification of plaques (fatty deposits) in the coronary arteries, TM might slow disease progression but is unlikely to remove plaque that has already accumulated.

Sharpens Your Brain

When people meditate, the coherence of alpha brain waves throughout the brain is accompanied by slightly faster beta waves in the prefrontal region of the brain, behind the forehead. The alpha waves produce relaxation, while the beta waves increase focus and decision-making.

Brain studies of top-level managers show that they have higher levels of both alpha and beta coherence than lower-level workers. A similar thing occurs in elite athletes.

Practice helps: Some of the physiological changes produced by TM occur immediately, but people who keep doing it for several months tend to have better results, probably because of increased synaptic connections (connections between brain cells). The brain may literally rewire itself, with practice.

How to Start

During a TM session, you'll achieve a state of restful alertness, during which your thoughts are clear but without the distractions of the internal noise that we live with. How people achieve this is highly individual. I like to relax in a comfortable chair in a quiet room. I dim the lights, turn off the telephones and start repeating my mantra. A friend of mine who has practiced TM for 40 years can enjoy a brief session in the back of a taxi.

You might find it tricky to keep mentally repeating the mantra. You might be distracted by physical sensations, outside sounds, etc. All of this is natural and expected. At some point during the session, you'll

feel mentally silent. You will be present in the moment but removed from it.

Important: TM is easy to practice but difficult to learn on your own. People start with one-on-one sessions with an instructor. In general, each teaching session lasts about 90 minutes. Your instructor will assign a mantra and give instructions for using it. Sometimes people wonder why they can't pick their own mantras. One reason is that it is a tradition not to. Another is that someone who chooses his/her own mantra might do so because of underlying meanings or associations. A mantra from a teacher won't have this baggage.

You will work with the instructor once a day for four consecutive days. After that, you might return once every month to make sure that your technique is working. The Web site *www.tm.org* can provide referrals to instructors in your area.

Use Yoga to Treat High Blood Pressure

Beryl Bender Birch, founder of The Hard & The Soft Yoga Institute and the nonprofit Give Back Yoga Foundation, *www.givebackyoga.org*, both based in East Hampton, New York. She is the author of *Power Yoga* (Simon & Schuster), *Beyond Power Yoga* (Fireside) and *Boomer Yoga* (Sellers).

Yoga has long been known to reduce stress while also boosting strength, flexibility and overall well-being.

Now: More and more scientific studies are showing that yoga helps treat specific medical conditions such as high blood pressure. Unfortunately, many people never even try yoga because they assume that it's too difficult or unconventional.

What you should know…

Yoga for Everyone

Yoga is easy to do at home and requires a minimal investment in special equipment. It is best performed in your bare feet (so your feet won't slide) while wearing comfortable clothing. Many people perform yoga on a bare floor or clean carpeting, but a yoga mat keeps your feet even more secure (available in some sports-equipment stores and from online retailers such as *www.yogadirect.com*, 800-331-8233…and *www.jadeyoga.com*, 888-784-7237).

For postures below: Hold for at least five "slow breaths" (close your mouth and breathe in through your nose for a few seconds as your lower belly rises…exhale slowly for about six seconds). Poses can be repeated two to three times at each session (one to three per week).

For High Blood Pressure

A single 10-minute session of "slow breathing" can result in a temporary lowering of both systolic (top number) and diastolic (bottom number) blood pressure. How much depends on such factors as diet, stress level and genetics.

My recommendation: Do Face Up Dog Posture and Face Down Dog Posture followed by Child's Pose.

What to do: For Face Up Dog, start by lying facedown on the floor with your feet (tops flat on floor) in line with your hips. Place your arms at the sides of your chest and hands directly under your shoulders. While keeping your knees on the floor, push into your arms straightening them, roll your shoulders back, arch your back slightly and keep your neck aligned with your spine. Hold for five breaths. Then exhale into Face Down Dog (by turning your feet so that your heels are flat on the ground, and pushing up and back into an upside-down V). For Child's Pose, kneel with your feet folded under flat and extend your arms straight in front of your head, palms flat on your mat. Touch your forehead to the ground if possible.

■ ■ ■ ■

Lower Blood Pressure 15 Points While Watching TV

Maureen MacDonald, PhD, associate professor, department of kinesiology, McMaster University, Hamilton, Ontario.

Isometrics may be making a comeback… as an effective way to control blood pressure. Recent studies show that isometric hand exercises can help you to quite literally get a grip on blood pressure problems. In the 1960s a researcher made the serendipitous discovery of a link between the

---

Yoga Safety 101

If you have a chronic medical condition, check with your doctor before beginning a yoga program, and consider consulting a qualified yoga teacher for a customized "prescription" of yoga poses.*

Caution: While doing yoga, don't hold your breath! That may raise your blood pressure. If you have high blood pressure, any eye condition where increased pressure should be avoided or neck injuries, forgo postures in which your head is inverted, such as headstands—these poses can significantly increase blood flow to the brain, increasing your risk for a stroke or other cardiac event.

*To find a qualified yoga therapist, consult the International Association of Yoga Therapists, 928-541-0004, *www.iayt.org*.

hand grips used by fighter pilots to help them tolerate gravitational forces while flying and their subsequently lower blood pressure. The aim of the gripping during flight is to increase blood pressure to maintain the flow to the brain and prevent blackout. The beneficial side effect was that when pilots were not flying, they experienced training-induced reductions in their resting blood pressure.

Easy and Very Effective

A research team at McMaster University in Hamilton, Ontario, gathered people taking medication for high blood pressure for a study on the effects of isometric hand-grip training using a device called Zona Plus. One of the two groups exercised with both arms while the other group used just one arm. All were taking antihypertensive medications (a wide variety) before and throughout the study. After eight weeks of thrice-weekly isometric hand exercises (four sets of two-minute isometric contractions), the group exercising with both arms decreased their systolic (the upper number) blood pressure by an average of 15 millimeters of mercury (mmHg). The diastolic pressure dropped about 3 mmHg—a lesser amount, but this figure is also less relevant. In a more recent study, researchers from the same university found that patients in their 60s, all with normal blood pressure, had significantly reduced resting blood pressure after completing eight weeks of isometric hand-grip training, using inexpensive spring hand-grip devices.

Maureen MacDonald, PhD, one of the lead investigators, explains that isometric hand exercises seem to somehow reprogram the way the nervous system sets its control level of blood pressure, sending a message that a high resting blood pressure isn't necessary. More research has to be done on the whys and wherefores, but

Sleep More to Lower Blood Pressure

People who get five hours or less of sleep a night were more than twice as likely to develop high blood pressure as people who slept seven to eight hours, according to a study.

Theory: Blood pressure drops by 10% to 20% during sleep, so a sleep deficit raises average 24-hour blood pressure and increases the workload on the cardiovascular system. Lack of sleep also boosts stress, which increases appetite for salt and decreases salt excretion—further raising hypertension risk in some people.

James E. Gangwisch, PhD, assistant professor, department of psychiatry, Columbia University, New York City, and leader of a study of 4,810 people, published in *Hypertension.*

evidence is building for the benefits of using this as a lifestyle modification for hypertension.

Get a Grip

Hand-gripping devices are inexpensive and easy to find in sporting goods stores. Grips come in a variety of resistances that feel different, so check around until you find one that is comfortable for you. To determine whether the grip is sufficiently intense, hold the device steady, keeping your body relaxed and your breath normal. If your hand tires after two minutes of squeezing the grip and holding the contraction (like when you reach your limit when lifting weights), you have found the correct grip—Dr. MacDonald says you need to grip at least 30% of your maximum strength; less than that does not have any impact.

Here is an exercise sequence that Dr. MacDonald advises should be performed three to five times each week. Remember to breathe normally throughout.

• **Squeeze the grip and hold the contraction with your left hand for two minutes.**

• **Remove it and rest for two minutes.**

• **Squeeze the grip and hold the contraction with your right hand for two minutes.**

• **Remove it and rest for two minutes.**

• **Now repeat this process until you have done four complete sets.**

The Deluxe Solution: Zona Plus

Another option is to buy an electronic hand grip called the Zona Plus that measures the grip to the correct level and also guides the user through the series of exercises. The price is $399. (The research team used the Zona Plus in some of their experiments.) Dr. MacDonald says that the Zona Plus is ergonomically designed so it is more comfortable to grip. Go to *www. zona.com* or call 866-669-9662 for more information.

According to Dr. MacDonald, so long as you continue to do these exercises regularly, your blood pressure will remain at a lower level—but, you should know that when research subjects did not exercise for eight weeks, their blood pressure returned to its elevated state.

Note: There are concerns that this form of exercise can be dangerous for individuals who have an aneurysm or a mitral valve problem, so if you fall into that category, check with your doctor before trying it.

Heart Health Essentials

The Verdict Is In—Fish Oil Can Save Your Life

Carl Lavie, MD, medical director of Cardiac Rehabilitation and Prevention at the Ochsner Heart and Vascular Institute in New Orleans.

What if there were just one food or one pill that could dramatically reduce your risk of the heart problems that bedevil and kill more Americans than any other disease...

• **Coronary artery disease,** the slow, toxic accumulation of arterial plaque, choking off the flow of blood and oxygen to the heart.

• **Heart attack,** the disastrous and sometimes deadly blockage of blood flow to the heart.

• **Sudden cardiac death,** electrical mayhem in the rhythms of the heart (arrhythmia), causing cardiac arrest.

• **Atrial fibrillation,** a quiver rather than a beat in the upper chambers of the heart, increasing the risk of blood clots and strokes.

• **Heart failure,** a weakened heart (perhaps damaged by one or more heart attacks) that can't pump blood normally, choking the body of oxygen.

Fortunately, there is one food and one pill that can help prevent or treat all these conditions.

The food is oily fish. The pill is a fish oil supplement.

Three Decades of Evidence

A recent "state-of-the-art" paper in the *Journal of the American College Cardiology*—by cardiologist and fish oil expert Carl Lavie, MD, medical director of Cardiac Rehabilitation and Prevention at the Ochsner Heart and Vascular Institute in New Orleans, Louisiana, and his colleagues—details three decades of studies on fish oil and heart health, involving more than 40,000 people.

And the scientific evidence that fish oil—specifically, the omega-3 fatty acids EPA (eicosapentaenoic acid) and DHA (docosahexaenoic acid)—is good for your heart isn't just "suggestive," as cautious scientists like to say. It's incontrovertible.

"We now have tremendous and compelling evidence from very large studies, some dating back 20 and 30 years, that demonstrate the protective benefits of omega-3 fish oil in multiple aspects of preventive cardiology," says Dr. Lavie.

Why it works: The body incorporates fish oil into the membranes (outer envelopes) of red blood cells and the cells of your blood vessels. *From there, it works to…*

• **Reduce triglycerides,** blood fats that can damage the heart;

• **Stabilize plaque**—crucial, because a chunk of plaque can break off an artery wall and become an artery-closing blood clot;

• **Stop the deposition of collagen,** a protein fiber that stiffens flexible arteries;

• **Boost the functioning of the endothelium,** the lining of the artery, which generates artery-relaxing, clot-dissolving nitric oxide;

• **Reduce inflammation**—and chronic, low-grade inflammation fuels heart disease;

• **Lower blood pressure,** a major risk factor for heart attacks and strokes;

• **Thin the blood by decreasing platelet aggregation,** the clumping of tiny structures in the blood that form blood clots;

• **Prevent arrhythmias,** the chaotic electrical episodes that can cause sudden cardiac death;

• **Tone the autonomic nervous system,** which controls the heartbeat—another way to decrease the risk of arrhythmia.

Two Fish Meals a Week

"You can get fish oil into your diet by eating oily fish, such as herring, mackerel, salmon, albacore tuna, sardines and oysters, or by taking fish oil supplements or cod liver oil," says Dr. Lavie.

Recommended intake: If you have heart disease, the American Heart Association recommends a daily dose of 1,000 milligrams (mg) (1 gram) of EPA and DHA.

If you don't have heart disease, the AHA recommends you eat two oily fish meals a week, which is the equivalent of about 500 mg a day of EPA and DHA—the amount linked to the lowest risk of developing heart disease.

As a cardiologist, Dr. Lavie adds these recommendations…

• **To prevent heart failure,** a supplement containing 800 to 1,000 mg a day of combined EPA and DHA.

• **To lower triglycerides,** supplements supplying 4 grams a day of EPA and DHA (a therapeutic dose taken with the approval and supervision of a doctor).

Dr. Lavie notes that your doctor can safely combine a high-dose fish oil supplement with statins, fibrates, niacin and other "lipid therapies."

Bottom line: "It's really good to get your fish oil through diet—because you replace bad food with good food, and you don't have to take a supplement," says Dr. Lavie.

However: "Very few people probably have two fish meals per week—the amount you need to get 500 mg a day," he says. And the dosage that showed benefits in heart disease would require five fish meals a week. So it may be far more practical to take a fish oil supplement.

"If you have heart disease, you should talk to your doctor about whether a fish oil supplement is needed, and what the right amount is for maximum heart protection in your case."

Smart idea: "I eat a lot of fish, including sushi," he says.

"And I take a supplement on the days I don't eat fish. If I ate sushi the evening before, I skip the supplement the next day."

Product: Dr. Lavie recommends Lovaza, a prescription omega-3 supplement, which is guaranteed to deliver the specified amount of DHA and EPA.

For over-the-counter brands, he prefers Nordic Naturals and GNC.

• **Don't worry about mercury.** You may be scared of eating a lot of fish—particularly if you're pregnant or nursing—because you've heard it's contaminated with mercury or other pollutants.

Not to worry, says Dr. Lavie.

"A study of nearly 12,000 British women during their pregnancy and beyond found that women who exceeded the US FDA recommendation for fish intake actually had offspring with better cognitive and behavioral development than the offspring of women who consumed less fish," he says. (DHA nourishes the brain and nervous system.)

Dr. Lavie also points to a risk-benefit analysis from researchers at Harvard Medical School that looked at hundreds of studies on fish and fish oil. It showed that oily fish and/or supplements reduced deaths from heart disease by 36% and premature deaths from any cause by 17%—and did not increase the risk of "subclinical neuro-developmental deficits" in children caused by mercury, or the risk of cancer in adults caused by the fish-borne pollutants PCBs and dioxin.

"The most commonly consumed dietary sources of omega-3—salmon, sardines, trout, oysters and herring—are quite low in mercury," says Dr. Lavie. "And because mercury is water soluble and protein bound, it's present in the muscle of the fish but not in the oil, so fish oil supplements should contain negligible amounts of mercury."

Red flag: The Harvard researchers warn consumers away from three mercury-laden species—swordfish, shark and golden bass (tilefish) from the Gulf of Mexico.

Did You Have a Heart Attack—and Not Know It?

Wilbert Aronow, MD, professor of medicine in the divisions of cardiology, geriatrics and pulmonary/critical medicine, and chief of the cardiology clinic at Westchester Medical Center/New York Medical College in Valhalla, New York. Dr. Aronow has edited eight books and is author or coauthor of more than 2,250 scientific papers, abstracts and commentaries that have appeared in *The Lancet*, *The New England Journal of Medicine*, *Circulation* and other medical journals.

Up to 60% of all heart attacks in people over age 45 are "silent." Detection and treatment are a must.

When you have a heart attack, you know it because the main symptom—crushing chest pain—is overwhelmingly obvious. That's what most of us believe about heart attacks. But it's not always true.

What few people realize: Studies show that 20% to 60% of all heart attacks in people over age 45 are unrecognized or "silent." And the older you are, the more likely it is that you've already had a silent heart attack. In a study of 110 people with a mean age of 82, an astounding 68% had suffered a silent heart attack.

What happens during a silent heart attack? You may have no symptoms at all. Or you may have symptoms that are so mild—for example, a bout of breathlessness, digestive upset or neurological symptoms such as fainting—that neither you nor your doctor connects them with a heart attack.

Scientists don't know why some people have unrecognized heart attacks. But they do know that a silent heart attack is a real heart attack and can cause as much damage to heart muscle as a nonsilent heart attack. And just like a person with a known heart attack, anyone who has had a silent heart attack is at higher risk for another heart attack, heart failure, stroke…or sudden death from an irregular heartbeat.

Recent scientific evidence: In a six-year study by cardiologists from the University of California in San Diego and San Francisco —published in *Clinical Research in Cardiology*—people who were diagnosed with a silent heart attack at the beginning of the study were 80% more likely to have another "cardiovascular event," such as a heart attack or stroke, by the end of the study period.

In a five-year study by cardiologists at the Mayo Clinic, people with an unrecognized heart attack were seven times more likely to die of heart disease than people who didn't have an unrecognized heart attack.

If you have risk factors for heart disease, it is vitally important to your health that you find out if you have had a silent heart attack. *Here's how…*

The Key to Detection

If you're at high risk for heart disease, your primary care physician should perform an electrocardiogram (EKG)—a test that checks for problems with the electrical activity of your heart—every year during your regular checkup. If the EKG reveals significant "Q-waves"—markers of damaged heart tissue—you have had a silent heart attack.

"High risk" means that you have two or more risk factors for heart disease. These risk factors include a family history of heart disease (in a first-degree relative such as a sibling or parent)…high blood pressure…smoking…inactivity…obesity…high LDL "bad" cholesterol…low HDL "good" cholesterol…high triglycerides… and type 2 diabetes.

The groups at highest risk for having an unrecognized heart attack are adults over age 65…women…and people of any age with type 2 diabetes.

The Treatment You Need

If your EKG reveals a previously unrecognized heart attack, it's wise to see a cardiologist and receive the exact same treatment that you would get if you had a recognized heart attack. *Elements of that treatment should include…*

● **Treadmill stress test.** The cardiologist will check for and interpret many variables, such as your symptoms (if any), the electrical patterns of your heart rhythms and your blood pressure while you are on a treadmill.

Important: Be sure to get your cardiologist's advice on special steps to take to ensure accurate results. For example, you should have no caffeine within 24 hours of the test.

If the results of the stress test indicate "severe myocardial ischemia"—poor blood flow to the heart muscle—it may be necessary to have a coronary angiogram (X-rays of the heart's arteries) to accurately diagnose the degree of blockage and decide whether you should pursue such options as angioplasty (in which a balloon is inserted into the coronary artery and inflated to restore normal blood flow) or coronary bypass surgery (in which a blood vessel is grafted from another part of the body to give blood a new pathway to the heart).

However, in most cases, heart disease that is associated with a silent heart attack can be managed with lifestyle changes, such as not smoking…losing weight if you're overweight…and getting regular exercise. *In addition, medications may include…*

● **Aspirin.** A daily dose of 81 milligrams (mg) of aspirin is the best choice for an antiplatelet drug to reduce the risk for blood clots.

Very important: A higher dose does not increase the cardiovascular benefit—but does increase the risk for gastrointestinal bleeding.

• **Beta-blocker.** This class of drugs slows the heart rate, relaxing the heart and helping to manage high blood pressure.

• **Angiotensin-converting enzyme (ACE) inhibitor.** These drugs expand blood vessels, improving blood flow and lowering blood pressure—thus allowing the heart to work less.

• **Statin.** If you have heart disease, this cholesterol-lowering medication reduces your risk for another heart attack or dying from heart disease—regardless of whether your levels of LDL "bad" cholesterol are high or low.

In addition, statin use should be accompanied by a diet that is low in cholesterol (less than 200 mg per day) and low in saturated fat (less than 7% of total calories).

Also important: It's crucial that people with diabetes maintain tight control of their HbA1C levels. This measure of long-term blood sugar control should be less than 7%.

However, HbA1C levels should not be aggressively lowered below 6.5% in diabetes patients with cardiovascular disease, according to the *Action to Control Cardiovascular Risk in Diabetes* study—that increases the risk for death because it would indicate that blood glucose is at times too low.

In general, the best way for people with diabetes to protect against heart attacks and strokes is to give up cigarettes if they smoke...lose weight if necessary...reduce blood pressure to 130–139/80–89 millimeters of mercury (mmHg)...and reduce LDL cholesterol to less than 70 milligrams per deciliter (mg/dL).

If these lifestyle measures do not also sufficiently lower the person's HbA1C level, standard antidiabetes medication can be used.

■ ■ ■ ■

Can You Have Sex After Heart Disease?

Patients recovering from stroke or heart disease can safely enjoy sex as long as their cardiovascular disease is stable and they experience minimal or no symptoms, such as chest pains or shortness of breath, during routine activities. Sex with a familiar partner in a familiar setting is generally no more strenuous than an activity that requires moderate exertion, such as golf—and resuming sexual activity can be an important part of healing.

John Moran, MD, professor of medicine, Loyola University Chicago Stritch School of Medicine.

Six Ways to Liven Up Your Heart-Healthy Diet

Janet Bond Brill, PhD, RD, an expert in nutrition and cardiovascular disease prevention based in Valley Forge, Pennsylvania. She is director of nutrition for Fitness Together, a franchise company of almost 500 personal fitness-training studios, has served as a nutrition consultant for several corporations and is author of *Prevent a Second Heart Attack* (Three Rivers). *www.drjanet.com*

Just about everyone knows that a Mediterranean-style diet can help prevent heart disease. Even if you've already had a heart attack, this style of eating—emphasizing such foods as fish and vegetables—can reduce the risk for a second heart attack by up to 70%.

Problem: About 80% of patients with heart disease quit following dietary advice within one year after their initial diagnosis. That's often because they want more choices but aren't sure which foods have been proven to work.

Solution: Whether you already have heart disease or want to prevent it, you can liven up your diet by trying foods that usually don't get much attention for their heart-protective benefits...

Secret 1. Popcorn. It's more than just a snack. It's a whole grain that's high in cholesterol-lowering fiber. Surprisingly, popcorn contains more fiber, per ounce, than whole-wheat bread or brown rice.

Scientific evidence: Data from the 1999–2002 National Health and Nutrition Examination Survey found that people who eat popcorn daily get 22% more fiber than those who don't eat it.

Important: Eat "natural" popcorn, preferably air-popped or microwaved in a brown paper bag, without added oil. The commercially prepared popcorn packets generally contain too much salt, butter and other additives. Three cups of popped popcorn, which contains almost 6 grams (g) of fiber and 90 calories, is considered a serving of whole grains. Studies have shown that at least three servings of whole grains a day (other choices include oatmeal and brown rice) may help reduce the risk for heart disease, high cholesterol and obesity.

Secret 2. Chia seeds. You're probably familiar with Chia pets—those terra-cotta figures that sprout thick layers of grassy "fur." The same seeds, native to Mexico and Guatemala, are increasingly available in health-food stores. I consider them a superfood because they have a nutrient profile that rivals heart-healthy flaxseed.

In fact, chia seeds contain more omega-3 fatty acids than flaxseed. Omega-3s increase the body's production of anti-inflammatory eicosanoids, hormonelike substances that help prevent "adhesion molecules" from causing plaque buildup and increasing atherosclerosis.

Scientific evidence: A study published in the *Journal of the American College of Cardiology*, which looked at nearly 40,000 participants, found that an omega-3–rich diet can prevent and even reverse existing cardiovascular disease.

Other benefits: One ounce of chia seeds has 10 g of fiber, 5 g of alpha-linolenic acid and 18% of the Recommended Dietary Allowance for calcium for adults ages 19 to 50.

Chia seeds look and taste something like poppy seeds. You can add them to baked goods, such as muffins, or sprinkle them on salads and oatmeal or other cereals.

Secret 3. Figs. They're extraordinarily rich in antioxidants with an oxygen radical absorbance capacity (ORAC) score of 3,383. Scientists use this ORAC scale to determine the antioxidant capacity of various foods. An orange, by comparison, scores only about 1,819. Fresh figs are among the best sources of beta-carotene and other heart-healthy carotenoids.

Scientific evidence: In a study published in the *Journal of the American College of Nutrition*, two groups of participants were "challenged" with sugary soft drinks, which are known to increase arterial oxidation. Oxidation in the arteries triggers atherosclerosis, a main risk factor for heart disease. Those who were given only soda had a drop in healthful antioxidant activity in the blood...those who were given figs as well as soda had an increase in blood antioxidant levels.

Bonus: Ten dried figs contain 140 milligrams (mg) of calcium. Other compounds in figs, such as quercetin, reduce inflammation and dilate the arteries. Perhaps for these reasons, people who eat figs regularly have much less heart disease than those who don't eat them, according to studies. Most dried figs contain added sulfites, so it's best to buy organic, sulfite-free dried figs.

Secret 4. Soy protein. Tofu, soy milk and other soy foods are "complete proteins"—

that is, they supply all of the essential amino acids that your body needs but without the cholesterol and large amount of saturated fat found in meat.

Scientific evidence: People who replace dairy or meat protein with soy will have an average drop in LDL "bad" cholesterol of 2% to 7%, according to research from the American Heart Association. Every 1% drop in LDL lowers heart disease risk about 2%.

A one-half cup serving of tofu provides 10 g of protein. An eight-ounce glass of soy milk gives about 7 g. Edamame (steamed or boiled green soybeans) has about 9 g per half cup. Avoid processed soy products, such as hydrogenated soybean oil (a trans fat), soy isoflavone powders and soy products with excess added sodium.

Secret 5. Lentils. I call these "longevity legumes" because studies have shown that they can literally extend your life.

Best choices: Brown or black lentils.

Scientific evidence: In one study, published in the *Asia Pacific Journal of Clinical Nutrition*, the eating habits of five groups of older adults were compared. For every 20 g (a little less than three-fourths of an ounce) increase in the daily intake of lentils and/or other legumes, there was an 8% reduction in the risk of dying within seven years.

Lentils contain large amounts of fiber, plant protein and antioxidants along with folate, iron and magnesium—all of which are important for cardiovascular health.

Similarly, a Harvard study found that people who ate one serving of cooked beans (one-third cup) a day were 38% less likely to have a heart attack than those who ate beans less than once a month.

Caution: Beans have been shown to cause gout flare-ups in some people.

Important: Lentils cook much faster than other beans. They don't need presoaking. When simmered in water, they're ready in 20 to 30 minutes. You need about one-half cup of cooked lentils, beans or peas each day for heart health.

Secret 6. Pinot Noir and Cabernet Sauvignon. All types of alcohol seem to have some heart-protective properties, but red wine offers the most.

Scientific evidence: People who drink alcohol regularly in moderation (one five-ounce glass of wine daily for women, and no more than two for men) have a 30% to 50% lower risk of dying from a heart attack than those who don't drink, according to research published in *Archives of Internal Medicine.*

Best choices: Pinot Noir, Cabernet Sauvignon and Tannat wines (made from Tannat red grapes). These wines have the highest concentrations of flavonoids, antioxidants that reduce arterial inflammation and inhibit the oxidation of LDL cholesterol. Oxidation is the process that makes cholesterol more likely to accumulate within artery walls.

Bonus: Red wines also contain resveratrol, a type of polyphenol that is thought to increase the synthesis of proteins that slow aging. Red wine has 10 times more polyphenols than white varieties.

In a four-year study of nearly 7,700 men and women nondrinkers, those who began to drink a moderate amount of red wine cut their risk for heart attack by 38% compared with nondrinkers.

If you are a nondrinker or currently drink less than the amounts described above, talk to your doctor before changing your alcohol intake. If you cannot drink alcohol, pomegranate or purple grape juice is a good alternative.

Foods That Help Your Heart

James A. Duke, PhD, former chief of the US Department of Agriculture's medicinal plant laboratory. He is author of more than 25 books, including *The Green Pharmacy* (St. Martin's) and editor of *CRC Handbook of Medicinal Spices* (CRC). He teaches at Tai Sophia Institute's Botanical Healing Program in Laurel, Maryland, conducts ecotours of the Amazon and cultivates his own Green Farmacy Garden, which has more than 300 medicinal plants.

These days, fish and garlic get so much attention for promoting heart health that many people are unaware of foods that confer similar health benefits.

Numerous scientific studies have shown that many foods besides fish and garlic have some of the same healing properties as prescription heart medications. *Best heart-healthy foods…*

Greens

• **Chicory, dandelion, endive, kale and spinach** are rich sources of heart-friendly antioxidant and anti-inflammatory polyphenols (plant chemicals, known as phytochemicals, that help prevent cardiovascular disease), vitamins and minerals. When eaten on a regular basis, they help reduce triglyceride (a type of blood fat) and LDL "bad" cholesterol levels. I enjoy greens as a raw snack or added to salads.

My recommendation: Cook greens with heart-friendly garlic and onion and top with an olive oil and vinegar dressing. Aim to eat a half cup to one cup of greens daily.

Herbs

• **Onions and leeks** share most of the important phytochemicals that are in garlic, and some people find them easier to digest. Leeks are available at many grocery and health-food stores. I add several diced leaves of leeks, a few garlic cloves and an onion to my soups.

My recommendation: Add onions and leeks to bean dishes.

Legumes

• **Beans, peas and lentils** are all pulses (a subcategory of the legume family). Power-packed with protein, B vitamins, minerals and antioxidant phytonutrients, pulses are also low in fat and high in fiber. I use pulses in soups.

My recommendation: Boil or stir-fry pulses with garlic and olive oil or use in a cold mixed-bean salad with a garlic, olive oil and vinegar dressing. Aim for a half cup of pulses daily.

Caution: People with estrogen-sensitive malignancies, including some breast and uterine cancers, should avoid phytoestrogenic beans, such as soybeans.

Fruit

• **Berries and cherries.** Blackberries, blueberries, cherries and cranberries are excellent sources of antioxidant and anti-inflammatory phytochemicals, including polyphenols and anthocyanins. Berries and cherries help lower blood pressure as well as cholesterol and blood sugar (glucose) levels, all of which tend to rise as we age. I squeeze four black cherries or blueberries into my lemonade.

My recommendation: Add berries or cherries to your daily cereal, or eat as a fresh fruit dish for a total of one cup daily.

• **Grapes.** The phytochemical resveratrol, which acts as a blood thinner and relaxes blood vessels, makes grapes a potent food for heart health. Red wine—and to a lesser extent white wine—is a rich source of resveratrol. Believe it or not, grape leaves—especially tart and wild ones—have more resveratrol than the fruit or wine. I regularly eat grape leaves and grapes from my organic farm.

My recommendation: Eat one cup of grapes or a handful of raisins each day. Consider drinking one small glass of wine or grape juice daily.

Nuts and Seeds

• **Walnuts and flaxseeds** are excellent plant sources of omega-3 fatty acids, which reduce the risk for blood clots and lower blood triglyceride levels as well as blood pressure. Most walnuts sold in the US are English walnuts, which have about twice as many omega-3s as black walnuts. I have a handful of mixed nuts before dinner.

My recommendation: Aim for a handful of walnuts daily or add flaxseed or walnut oil to a homemade salad dressing.

Vegetables

• **Celery** contains numerous anti-inflammatory, blood-thinning and blood pressure- and cholesterol-lowering compounds. I often munch on up to four stalks of celery a day.

My recommendation: Try a celery soup by simmering four stalks, diced, with one teaspoon of mustard, a dash of curry powder and hot sauce, and black pepper. Munch on raw celery sticks or top them with heart-healthy peanut butter.

Caution: Celery is relatively high in sodium—about 50 milligrams (mg) of sodium per stalk.

■ ■ ■ ■

Think You Know Your True Risk for Heart Attack and Stroke?

James Ehrlich, MD, clinical associate professor of endocrinology at the University of Colorado, Denver. The chief medical officer of United Cardio Systems, based in Castle Rock, Colorado, Dr. Ehrlich advises physicians on best practices involving biomarkers, imaging technologies and radiation protection. He is a founding member of the Society of Atherosclerosis Imaging and Prevention and coauthor of *The Physician's Guide to Coronary Imaging,* a multimedia CD (available to physicians only).

You may think that you are at low risk for a heart attack because the heart tests that your doctor has ordered had "negative" results. The standard blood test that you received may show that your cholesterol and triglyceride levels are fine. And you may have even received a clean bill of health after taking a cardiac stress test (exercising on a treadmill while heart rhythms are electronically monitored).

Surprising fact: Those two standard heart tests miss many high-risk individuals with early heart disease. For example, a study published in the *Journal of the American College of Cardiology* found that 95% of women who had heart attacks at age 65 or younger were considered low risk.

For the greatest protection: In addition to the standard heart tests, all adults should consider receiving the highly accurate heart tests described in this article, which are not regularly ordered by most physicians but serve as stronger predictors of cardiovascular disease.

Why don't more doctors have conversations with their patients about these important tests? Many physicians closely adhere to the guidelines of the government's Preventive Services Task Force, whose evidence-based recommendations tend to include tests that are less sophisticated and less expensive.

But if your primary care physician or cardiologist does not mention these tests, ask him/her which ones might be right for you. The results will provide the best possible information for your doctor to create a customized medical and lifestyle regimen that can help prevent heart attacks and strokes.

Coronary Calcium CT Scan

This radiological imaging test—also called a CT heart scan—detects and quantifies calcified plaque, a marker for atherosclerosis (fatty buildup in the arteries). This test is up to 10 times more predictive of future heart problems than a cholesterol test and can detect early heart disease that often goes undetected by a stress test.

My advice: Men over age 35 and women over age 40 with one to two risk factors for cardiovascular disease are good candidates for screening with a heart scan. Risk factors include being overweight…having hypertension, diabetes (or prediabetes), high LDL "bad" cholesterol, low HDL "good" cholesterol, elevated triglycerides, a family history of heart disease…and/or smoking.

Risks: Cardiac CT tests expose patients to ionizing radiation (the same type used in X-rays), which has been linked to an increased risk for cancer. Heart scans, such as electron-beam CT scans and late-generation spiral CT scans, now are performed at lower radiation doses—the equivalent of 10 to 25 chest X-rays is typical. These CT scans use faster speeds than standard CT scans to produce the image, are accurate and expose you to less radiation.

Cost and coverage: $150 to $500 and may be covered by insurance.

Carotid Test

An ultrasound test of the carotid (neck) arteries leading to the brain does not involve radiation and measures two important conditions that help predict cardiovascular disease—the dangerous presence of plaque and the thickness of the two inner layers of each artery (the intima and media).

The carotid test is a stronger predictor of a future stroke than coronary calcium and a moderate predictor of heart attack risk.

My advice: I recommend this test for men over age 35 and women over age 40 with one to two risk factors such as hypertension and/or a family history of heart disease or stroke. People with such risk factors as high cholesterol and type 2 diabetes also may benefit from the test.

Results: If there is any noticeable plaque or the thickness of the intima/media is in the top 25% for people of your age, sex and ethnicity, you are at a higher than desirable cardiovascular risk and should pay close attention to all risk factors—especially hypertension.

Cost and coverage: $100 to $500 and often is covered by insurance.

Advanced Lipoprotein Analysis

Advanced lipoprotein analysis includes blood tests that measure hidden risk factors such as…

• **Lp(a),** a dangerous particle that often is elevated in families with a history of premature heart attacks.

• **ApoB/ApoAI,** a ratio of dangerous particles to protective particles.

My advice: This analysis is especially useful for people with heart disease that occurs in the absence of risk factors or who have a family history of premature heart disease (heart attack before age 55 in a father or brother and before age 65 in a mother or sister, for example). Those with type 2 diabetes (or prediabetes) or "metabolic syndrome"—often with a bulging waistline, hypertension, low HDL, elevated triglycerides and/or elevated blood sugar—also are good candidates.

Cost and coverage: Varies widely from as little as $40 to as much as $400—often covered by insurance.

However, not all labs perform these tests.

Labs that perform advanced lipoprotein analysis: Atherotech (*www.atherotech.com*)...Berkeley Heart Lab (*www.bhlinc.com*)...Boston Heart Diagnostics (*www.bostonheart diagnostics.com*)...Health Diagnostic Laboratory (*www.hdlabinc.com*)...LipoScience (*www.liposcience.com*)...and SpectraCell (*www.spectracell.com*).

Other Biomarkers

• **Lp-PLA2 (PLAC test).** This blood test, which measures inflammation in blood vessels themselves, is a powerful predictor of the most common type of stroke (ischemic stroke). The test is more specific for vascular disease than the commonly ordered test for C-reactive protein (which is elevated with any type of inflammation in the body).

Cost and coverage: About $50 to $200 and may be covered by insurance.

• **BNP or NT-proBNP (B-type natriuretic peptide).** This is an early indicator of a weakening heart muscle (even before overt heart failure) and an excellent test for managing patients with heart failure. The test can also be used to help predict risk for heart attack.

Cost and coverage: About $50 to $250 and may be covered by insurance.

Aspirin Resistance Testing

Aspirin helps stop blood components called platelets from sticking together, which reduces the risk for an artery-plugging blood clot. A daily "baby" aspirin (81 milligrams [mg]) or higher doses usually are prescribed for anyone who has had a heart attack or stroke...or for someone who is at risk for either condition.

However, 25% of people are aspirin resistant—the drug doesn't effectively prevent platelet "stickiness."

Aspirin resistance testing measures a urinary metabolite (11-dehydrothromboxane B2), which is high if you are aspirin resistant.

Who should be tested: Anyone taking aspirin to treat or prevent cardiovascular disease.

Cost and coverage: $30 to $150 and often covered by insurance.

Good news: Recent research published in the *Journal of the American College of Cardiology* shows that supplementing the diet with omega-3 fatty acids can overcome aspirin resistance.

Sobering Statistics

About 81 million American adults have cardiovascular disease. This may include

---

Exercise Cuts Your Risk of Dying from Heart Disease

Recent finding: Men at high risk for heart disease (due to hypertension, high cholesterol and/or other risk factors) who exercised for 30 minutes four to five days per week reduced their risk of dying from a heart attack or stroke by 50%.

Self-defense: Everyone—especially those who are at risk for heart disease—should perform aerobic exercise, such as walking or swimming, for at least 30 minutes four to five days a week.

Peter T. Katzmarzyk, PhD, professor and associate executive director for population science, Pennington Biomedical Research Center, Baton Rouge, Louisiana.

narrowed, blocked arteries (coronary artery disease)…irregular heartbeats (arrhythmia)…and/or a weakened heart muscle (heart failure).

Every year, 1.5 million of those Americans have heart attacks and 500,000 of them die. Another 800,000 have strokes, 140,000 of whom die.

■ ■ ■ ■

Heart Disease: What Women—and Their Doctors—Often Overlook

Nieca Goldberg, MD, a cardiologist and nationally recognized pioneer in women's heart health. Her New York City practice, Total Heart Care, focuses primarily on caring for women. Dr. Goldberg is clinical associate professor of medicine and medical director of the New York University Women's Heart Program. She is author of *The Women's Healthy Heart Program* (Ballantine).

Most women now know that heart disease is their single greatest health risk—greater than stroke and all cancers, including breast malignancies, combined.

However, many doctors still associate heart disease with men—and overlook it in women. That's partially because a woman's symptoms of heart disease or a heart attack are different from symptoms in men—but no less dangerous.

Consider these facts…

• **A woman has a one in two lifetime risk of dying from heart disease.** (Her lifetime risk of dying from breast cancer is one in 25.)

• **Women are twice as likely as men to die in the first few weeks following a heart attack.**

Fortunately, recent research has revealed ways to help protect women.

Delayed Onset

Heart disease in women tends to become apparent about 10 years later than it does for men. The same risk factors that cause men to have heart attacks in middle age are initially masked in women by the protective effects of estrogen, which is associated with healthy cholesterol levels. After menopause, sharp declines in estrogen dramatically increase a woman's risk for heart attack.

Different Symptoms

The "classic" heart attack symptoms, such as crushing chest pain or pain that radiates down an arm, can affect women, but is more common in men. Women have their own classic symptoms, which doctors often fail to recognize.

They include…

• **Unusual fatigue.**

• **Heart palpitations.**

• **Pressure or pain in the upper abdomen.**

• **Back pain or symptoms resembling indigestion.**

• **Angina,** mild to severe chest pain caused by insufficient blood to the heart and often the initial symptom of a heart attack, occurs less often in women than in men. Women are more likely than men to suffer angina-equivalent symptoms—shortness of breath, tightness or tingling in the arm and/or lower chest.

Doctors who don't recognize heart attack symptoms in women may delay lifesaving treatments—and women may not go to a hospital because they don't understand the significance of the symptoms.

Missed Risk Factors

About 80% of women who die suddenly of a heart attack have modifiable risk factors, such as obesity or a history of smoking, but women are less likely to receive adequate counseling regarding preventive strategies.

Important: Because heart disease is strongly associated with lifestyle issues, women must begin addressing key risk factors, such as weight, exercise levels, diabetes and smoking, years before menopause.

Different Lipid Profiles

Elevated cholesterol levels can be associated with heart disease in men as well as in women—but elevated levels of blood fats known as triglycerides present a greater risk for women, even when their cholesterol levels are low. Women with high triglycerides also tend to have high total and LDL cholesterol, and low levels of HDL cholesterol.

Recommendation 1: A woman's triglycerides should be less than 150 milligrams per deciliter (mg/dL). Her HDL should be 50 mg/dL or higher, and her LDL should be less than 100 mg/dL. In men, triglycerides and LDL levels should be the same, and HDL should be 40 mg/dL or higher.

A recent study published in the journal *Circulation* found that nearly two-thirds of women at very high risk for heart disease had unacceptably high levels of cholesterol, but only about one-third were receiving statins or other appropriate medication, as recommended by the American Heart Association.

Recommendation 2: Every woman age 20 or older should ask her doctor for a fasting lipoprotein profile, which measures total, LDL and HDL cholesterol, along with triglycerides (a 12-hour fast ensures that triglycerides are not falsely elevated). If the first test is normal, repeat it in five years. Abnormal tests are usually repeated in six months to a year, following medical or lifestyle interventions to control cholesterol and triglyceride levels.

Insufficient Testing

When women undergo angiography, an imaging test that examines the blood vessels of the heart, doctors usually find that they have fewer diseased arteries than the typical male patient—yet women have a higher death rate from heart disease. This is primarily because women often have other conditions, such as hypertension, diabetes or even heart failure, that increase risk for heart attack and stroke but aren't treated as aggressively as they are in men.

Important: Every woman should know her blood pressure…her cholesterol levels…and other heart disease risk factors. If her doctor doesn't routinely order these tests—and recommend treatment when required—she should insist on it.

A standard test for heart disease is the exercise stress test, in which a person walks on a treadmill while being monitored by an electrocardiogram (ECG), a test that measures the electrical activity of the heartbeat.

The stress test increases the work of the heart and reveals angina or other symptoms that are present only during exertion. The test can help detect coronary artery disease in men about 90% of the time—but for reasons that are not yet known, it is not as accurate in women.

In about half of cases, women with coronary artery disease who receive an ECG during a stress test will appear to have normal coronary arteries. This false-negative reading may occur if a woman doesn't achieve a high enough heart rate during the test, or if beta blocker or other medications she's taking keep her heart rate artificially low.

Important: Women with heart disease symptoms should get a stress test that includes imaging studies, such as a nuclear exercise stress test (which involves the injection of a radioactive substance to produce images of the heart muscle) or an exercise echocardiogram (which uses ultrasound waves to view the heart). These tests provide more accurate results and are typically covered by insurance.

Ask About Aspirin

Doctors routinely recommend aspirin therapy for patients with an elevated risk for heart disease.

Recent finding: Aspirin does not reduce the risk for heart attack in healthy women under age 65…and is more likely to cause gastrointestinal upset or bleeding problems in women than in men. In women over age 65, the heart benefits of aspirin may outweigh the risks for stomach problems.

In my opinion, women with heart disease or risk factors benefit from taking aspirin. Get your doctor's advice before starting aspirin therapy.

Overlooked Stress

Women often must balance more life roles and responsibilities than men but may feel that they have less control at home or in the workplace. This situation can foster anxiety, anger or depression, all of which are major risk factors for heart disease, according to reliable scientific studies.

Elevated stress hormones, particularly cortisol and adrenaline, raise blood pressure and/or heart rate. Elevated cortisol levels also increase the coronary arteries' susceptibility to plaque buildup. Central adiposity, a condition associated with elevated cortisol and characterized by accumulations of abdominal fat, greatly increases heart disease risk.

Women with untreated depression and/or high levels of anxiety or stress should talk to a counselor or therapist. Social support also helps.

In a recent pilot study, women with heart disease participated in either coed exercise sessions using weight machines…or joined a women-only aerobics class. Levels of depression and anxiety were significantly decreased in the aerobics group, probably because of the social support the women got from working out with each other.

When Cholesterol Just Won't Go Down

Anne Carol Goldberg, MD, associate professor of medicine in the division of endocrinology, metabolism and lipid research at Washington University School of Medicine in St. Louis. A former president of the National Lipid Association, she has participated in numerous clinical trials involving the use of lipid-modifying agents, including the Lipid Research Clinic Coronary Primary Prevention Trial, which was one of the first to show that lowering blood cholesterol levels decreases risk for coronary artery disease.

Most of the estimated 42 million Americans with high cholesterol can successfully lower it with diet and exercise—or, when necessary, with statins or other cholesterol-lowering drugs.

But what if your cholesterol levels do not improve substantially with these standard therapies?

About one in every 500 Americans has an inherited (genetic) predisposition to high cholesterol—a condition known as familial hypercholesterolemia (FH), which is marked by LDL "bad" cholesterol levels ranging from 150 milligrams per deciliter (mg/dL) to 1,000 mg/dL.

Dietary changes may have some positive effect on people with FH but typically do not lower LDL levels to a normal range. Cholesterol-lowering medication is sometimes sufficient for people with FH—but not always.

What most people don't know: A high-tech treatment that filters LDL from the blood (described at right) can reduce LDL levels by as much as 75% in people with FH whose cholesterol is not controlled with standard therapies. The procedure also can be used by others, including people who cannot tolerate statin drugs due to side effects.

Skyrocketing LDL

On the surfaces of a healthy person's cells, there are LDL receptors that remove LDL from the blood. Lower levels of LDL cholesterol reduce the risk for atherosclerosis (the accumulation of cholesterol and other fatty substances on artery walls). A genetic mutation in people with FH results in a greatly reduced number of LDL receptors—or none at all.

People who inherit a defective gene from one parent (the heterozygous form of FH) typically have cholesterol levels of 250 mg/dL to 500 mg/dL, while those with two defective copies of the gene (the homozygous form) can have cholesterol readings as high as 1,000 mg/dL. Genetic tests are available to detect the defective genes, but most doctors diagnose FH based on such factors as very high LDL levels and the presence of fatty deposits on certain parts of the body.

Important red flag: Cholesterol levels in people with FH may be so high that they develop xanthomas (deposits of cholesterol that accumulate). These occur most often in the Achilles tendons (backs of the ankles) but also over the knuckles, elbows, knees and bottom of the feet. They're most commonly seen in people with FH who have LDL levels above 200 mg/dL. If you have any such deposits, see a doctor for an evaluation.

Medication to Try

Most people with FH can achieve normal—or nearly normal—cholesterol levels with the use of medication. Typically, more potent statins are prescribed at the upper end of the daily dose range—for example, *simvastatin* (Zocor)—40 mg to 80 mg…*atorvastatin* (Lipitor)—80 mg…or *rosuvastatin* (Crestor)—40 mg.

Good news about side effects: Even though statin-related side effects, such as muscle pain, are more likely to occur when high doses are used, people with FH who take such doses of these drugs don't appear to have more side effects than individuals without FH who take lower doses.

Most patients with FH require combination therapy—treatment with a statin plus one or more additional cholesterol-lowering drugs, such as *ezetimibe* (Zetia)… bile-acid resins, such as *cholestyramine*…or high-dose niacin.

"Dialysis" for LDL

A relatively new procedure, known as LDL apheresis, filters LDL from the blood—similar to the way dialysis filters toxins from the blood when the kidneys are unable to do so. LDL apheresis can reduce LDL levels by at least 50% and sometimes by as much as 75%.

How it works: At an outpatient clinic, a needle attached to a catheter is inserted into a vein in the arm. Over a period of about 90 minutes, up to three quarts of blood are withdrawn from the body and passed through a series of filters that remove the LDL. The "cleansed" blood is then returned to the body through another vein.

Who can benefit: LDL apheresis is recommended for people who don't have atherosclerotic cardiovascular disease and whose LDL levels are 300 mg/dL or above and who can't significantly lower their LDL after maximum therapy, including medication. Additionally, if you have been diagnosed with atherosclerotic cardiovascular disease and your LDL level is 200 mg/dL or above after maximum treatment, you may benefit from LDL apheresis. Patients with cardiovascular disease whose LDL levels are above 200 mg/dL and who cannot tolerate the side effects of statins also are eligible.

The results of apheresis are immediate. Cholesterol levels are tested before and after the procedure. It's not uncommon for LDL to drop from levels greater than 300 mg/dL to as low as 35 mg/dL. The procedure also causes a reduction in C-reactive protein and fibrinogen, substances that increase the risk for blood clots.

Not a cure: Because apheresis does not eliminate the underlying genetic defect in people with FH, LDL levels start to rise immediately after the procedure is completed. Patients who opt for LDL apheresis must repeat the treatment every two weeks, possibly for the rest of their lives.

LDL apheresis is very safe. There is a potential risk for unwanted bleeding (both internally or from the needle site) because the blood thinner heparin is used to keep blood flowing during the procedure. However, this type of bleeding rarely occurs because the patient's "bleeding times" (how fast small blood vessels close to stop bleeding) are frequently tested and the dose of heparin is adjusted as needed.

Doctors don't yet know how effective LDL apheresis is at reducing cardiovascular disease, but patients who receive the therapy often report a rapid reduction in cardiovascular symptoms, such as leg discomfort (caused by insufficient blood flow) and chest pain from angina.

People who are eligible for LDL apheresis should ask their doctors where they need to go for the procedure. It is currently offered at more than 40 medical centers across the US. Each treatment costs, on average, $2,500 to $3,000 and is covered by Medicare and most insurance plans.

Heart Attack Prevention Update

Stephen R. Devries, MD, a preventive cardiologist and associate professor of medicine in the division of cardiology at the Center for Integrative Medicine at the Feinberg School of Medicine at Northwestern University in Chicago. He is author of *What Your Doctor May Not Tell You About Cholesterol* (Warner Wellness).

Conventional medicine is very effective for treating existing and/or severe heart disease, but most doctors don't give nearly enough attention to prevention.

What you may not know: An estimated eight out of 10 heart attack deaths can be prevented—but not by focusing mainly on high cholesterol and prescribing powerful drugs, as most doctors do. With integrative heart care—which combines conventional medicine and alternative therapies—patients get much better results than either type of treatment can offer when used alone.

Problem: Too many doctors have not stayed up to date on a number of important heart disease risk factors that have been discovered only in recent years. To protect yourself—or a loved one…

• **Don't be fooled by a "normal" cholesterol reading.** A "normal" total cholesterol level is typically defined as less than 200 milligrams per deciliter (mg/dL). But one-third of patients with heart disease have cholesterol levels that are less than 200 mg/dL.

How does this happen? Total cholesterol is the combined total of LDL "bad" cholesterol…VLDL (very-low-density lipoprotein, also a "bad" cholesterol because high levels are linked to heart disease)…and HDL "good" cholesterol levels. Many people who have "normal" total cholesterol levels have dangerously low levels of the beneficial HDL cholesterol. HDL is responsible for removing LDL "bad" cholesterol from the arteries and carrying it to the liver for disposal. HDL also has antioxidant properties that can reduce arterial blockages (atherosclerosis).

Conversely, a total cholesterol reading that is 200 mg/dL or higher might be due to elevated HDL. These patients are less likely to get heart disease than those with the same total cholesterol level and a lower HDL level—but the standard cholesterol test would indicate that they are at increased risk.

Example: A 39-year-old woman I know had a total cholesterol reading of 125 mg/dL. Her doctor thought she was in great health—but her HDL was only 15 mg/dL, and she went on to develop coronary artery disease. (HDL should be at least 50 mg/dL in women…and at least 40 mg/dL in men.)

To raise "good" HDL: Ask your doctor about niacin. At doses of 1,000 mg to 2,000 mg daily, this form of vitamin B can increase HDL by 29%—that's more effective than the prescription drug *gemfibrozil* (Lopid), which is used to raise HDL.

Caution: Niacin at these doses can worsen gastroesophageal reflux disease and ulcers, elevate blood sugar, trigger gout (a type of arthritis) and cause liver irritation. Therefore, it should be taken only under a physician's supervision.

Helpful: To reduce flushing, a common side effect of high-dose niacin, take it with food. Do not take popular "flush-free" niacin—anecdotal evidence shows that it isn't as effective as standard types.

• **Don't settle for a traditional cholesterol test.** These tests measure levels of total, HDL and LDL cholesterol, along with blood fats known as triglycerides. Newer tests—which still aren't used by most doctors—look at cholesterol subfractions, blood fat measurements that may be more predictive of heart disease than total cholesterol, HDL and LDL alone. *Ask for a cholesterol test that looks at…*

• **Lp(a).** This is a particle that includes both LDL and a potentially dangerous blood-clotting chemical. People with an elevated Lp(a) are one-and-a-half times more likely to get heart disease than those whose level is normal.

Optimal Lp(a) level: Below 30 mg/dL.

Treatment: Niacin—500 mg to 2,000 mg daily—can lower Lp(a) by up to one-third.

Also helpful: Eating 10 walnuts daily will lower Lp(a) by up to 6%.

• **LDL size.** LDL particles are either small and dense or large and fluffy. Patients with a relatively high percentage of large particles are said to have Pattern A distribution. They're three times less likely to have heart disease than those with a higher percentage of small particles (Pattern B)—even when LDL readings are the same in both groups.

Treatment: If you have Pattern B distribution, fish oil may be beneficial because it can convert small particles into large ones.

Typical dosage: 1,000 mg to 4,000 mg of fish oil daily, from supplements containing at least 1,000 mg of combined eicosapentaenoic acid (EPA) and docosahexaenoic acid (DHA).

Caution: Fish oil can cause gastrointestinal upset and has a mild blood-thinning effect. It should not be used by patients who take the blood thinner *warfarin* (Coumadin) and should not be taken two weeks before and after any surgical procedure.

Exercise also decreases the concentration of small LDL particles. Aim for 30 to 60 minutes of aerobic exercise five to seven days a week.

Peanuts for Your Heart

Heart disease is the leading cause of death for American men and women.

Simple home remedy: Eat peanuts. They're the richest source of L-arginine, an amino acid that increases the blood's level of nitric oxide.

This molecule, naturally produced by the body, dilates arteries and can lower blood pressure 10 to 60 points. Nitric oxide also reduces cholesterol levels and interferes with clot formation, the cause of most heart attacks.

You need about 5 grams (5,000 milligrams [mg]) of dietary L-arginine daily to significantly elevate nitric oxide. You get that much in one cup of peanuts. However, even raw, unsalted peanuts have about 800 calories per cup, so alternate sources of L-arginine also are required. Not surprisingly, peanut butter contains L-arginine, and salmon, shrimp, eggs, kidney beans and chicken giblets are also good sources.

To ensure adequate intake: Consider taking 2,000 mg to 3,000 mg daily of supplemental L-arginine—for a total of 4,000 mg to 6,000 mg daily. Studies show that patients who take it have better blood flow than those taking placebos. (L-arginine may raise blood sugar in some people, so check with your doctor.)

Supplemental L-arginine doesn't enter cells as readily as the L-arginine in foods unless it's combined with L-citrulline, an amino acid that is found in watermelon and cucumbers. Because it is difficult to get enough L-citrulline in foods, take 400 mg to 600 mg daily in supplement form.

Louis J. Ignarro, PhD, was awarded the 1998 Nobel Prize in Physiology or Medicine for his research on nitric oxide and named Distinguished Scientist by the American Heart Association in 2008. He is distinguished professor of pharmacology at the University of California, Los Angeles, School of Medicine, and author of *No More Heart Disease* (St. Martin's).

● **Find out your high-sensitivity C-reactive protein (hs-CRP) level.** Hs-CRP is linked to higher rates of heart disease, yet few doctors test for it routinely. Insist on it. Elevated hs-CRP greatly increases heart attack risk, even in patients with normal cholesterol.

Optimal hs-CRP level: Below 1 mg/L.

Treatment: Cholesterol-lowering statin drugs, such as *atorvastatin* (Lipitor) or *simvastatin* (Zocor), can lower hs-CRP by up to 40%.

Also helpful: Weight loss (excess fat tissue, especially in the abdominal area, produces inflammatory chemicals that promote hardening of the arteries)…daily brushing and flossing (lowers risk for gum inflammation and dental infections, which are linked to heart disease)…exercise…and combining a statin drug with 1,000 mg to 4,000 mg of fish oil daily.

● **Take stress seriously.** Mainstream medicine greatly underestimates the effects of chronic stress on heart health. Patients with frequent stress maintain high levels of adrenaline and other potentially harmful chemicals and hormones that increase blood pressure and hs-CRP.

Treatment: Add stress reducers, such as exercise, yoga and/or meditation, to your daily schedule.

● **Consider supplements.** People without heart disease who have high blood pressure and mildly elevated cholesterol (requiring an LDL decrease of less than 25%) as well as those who can't tolerate prescription drugs may be good candidates for treatment with over-the-counter (OTC) supplements. *Use of the following supplements should be supervised by a physician—they have potential side effects and may interact with medications or other supplements…*

● Red yeast rice is an OTC product that can lower LDL by nearly 25%. Red yeast rice is helpful for patients with mildly elevated cholesterol (described above)…those who have experienced side effects from prescription statin drugs...or those who simply do not want to take a prescription statin.

Typical dosage: 600 mg twice daily. If stronger effects are needed, a maximum dosage of 1,200 mg twice daily.

Caution: Red yeast rice has the potential to cause liver and/or muscle irritation. Use it only under the supervision of a doctor, who can monitor its effectiveness and any side effects. Stop taking red yeast rice if you develop unexplained muscle aches or pain.

• **Coenzyme Q10** (CoQ10) is a vitamin-like substance that's naturally present in cells. In supplement form, it lowers blood pressure and improves symptoms of heart failure.

Important: Statins lower CoQ10 levels.

Typical dosage: 100 mg daily when taking statins...or 200 mg to 300 mg daily when taken for hypertension and/or congestive heart failure.

Caution: CoQ10 is a mild blood thinner, so it should not be taken by people on warfarin.

Heart Attack Myths

Ronald M. Krauss, MD, senior scientist and director of atherosclerosis research at Children's Hospital Oakland Research Institute. He is an adjunct professor in the department of medicine at the University of California, San Francisco, and in the department of nutritional sciences at the University of California, Berkeley. He is a member of one of the US National Cholesterol Education Program's expert panels, and founder and past chair of the American Heart Association's Council on Nutrition, Physical Activity and Metabolism.

For years, we have been told that high cholesterol causes heart attacks. But that is a dangerous oversimplification.

What most people don't know: Nearly 50% of heart attack patients who are tested for cholesterol turn out to have normal levels, according to data from the large Framingham Heart study.

What's true—and what's not—about cholesterol and heart attack risk...

Myth 1. LDL cholesterol is always bad. This type of cholesterol is often referred to simply as "bad" cholesterol. But we now know that LDL cholesterol isn't a single entity. Scientists have identified seven different subtypes, and there are probably more. Some forms of LDL do contribute much more to atherosclerosis and heart attacks—others are not as harmful.

Yet the standard cholesterol tests don't make this distinction. A patient with high LDL is assumed to have an elevated risk for heart disease and probably will be treated with a cholesterol-lowering statin drug, even though his/her LDL might consist primarily of one of the less harmful forms.

Fact: Some LDL subtypes are large and buoyant—and less likely to cause heart disease than others that are small and dense. Small forms are most likely to settle into artery walls and cause inflammation and atherosclerosis, increasing risk for a heart attack.

Example: A person with high levels of Lp(a), an extremely dense form of LDL, is up to three times more likely to develop heart disease or have a heart attack than someone with lower levels, even when the total LDL is the same in both people.

Implication: Newer, expanded cholesterol tests that measure individual types of LDL particles may prove to be more useful than standard cholesterol tests. Lp(a) screening is not yet widely used—ask your doctor whether you should have it. Some insurers cover the cost of this test.

Myth 2. High cholesterol numbers mean high risk. Depending on an individual's risks and other factors, optimal cholesterol is roughly defined as having a total number below

200 milligrams per deciliter (mg/dL)…LDL below 100 mg/dL…and HDL, the so-called "good" cholesterol, greater than 40 mg/dL for men and 50 mg/dL for women.

Fact: The standard test numbers may matter less than experts once thought.

More important: The ratio of small-to-large LDL particles, known as the size pattern.

Patients with Pattern A have a higher concentration of large, buoyant particles. Those with Pattern B have a higher concentration of small, dense particles. A patient with Pattern A is at least three times less likely to develop heart disease than someone with Pattern B.

Implication: Don't assume that you need a statin drug just because your LDL is high.

Example: Suppose that your LDL is 160. If you happen to have Pattern A, taking a statin may provide only a modest benefit. If you happen to have the more dangerous Pattern B, taking a statin may not provide maximal benefit either, so other treatment may be necessary to reduce heart disease risk. Taking high doses of a statin may result in side effects such as muscle pain or weakness. Advanced lipid testing determines one's LDL size pattern.

Myth 3. Saturated fat is the enemy. We've all been told that reducing dietary fat, particularly saturated fat, is among the most important ways to lower cholesterol and protect the heart.

Fact: A diet high in saturated fat clearly increases LDL. However, much of this increase is due to a corresponding increase in large, buoyant particles. In other words, saturated fat seems to trigger the less harmful Pattern A composition. Also, saturated fat increases the beneficial HDL cholesterol.

Implication: For years, Americans have been advised to keep their intake of dietary fat under 30% of total calories, with less than 7% of the fat calories coming from saturated fat. This now seems overly cautious. Americans who slightly exceed 10% saturated fat in their diets probably experience no increase in cardiovascular risks. However, people should avoid harmful trans fats in partially hydrogenated vegetable oils, found in packaged baked goods and fast foods.

Myth 4. It's OK to replace fat with carbohydrates. Doctors have routinely advised patients to eat more carbs and less fat to help manage their cholesterol levels.

Fact: A high-carbohydrate diet may be more likely than a diet high in fat to increase cardiovascular risks.

Reason: Replacing fat with carbohydrates seems to shift LDL to the more dangerous Pattern B.

Important: Researchers suspect that it's mainly refined carbohydrates, such as soft drinks, white rice, white pasta, sugary desserts, etc., that cause this shift. Unprocessed carbohydrates that are high in fiber, such as whole grains, legumes, fruits and vegetables, are less likely to increase risk.

Implication: It's more important to cut back on refined carbohydrates than to cut back on fat. Danish researchers who followed 53,644 adults for an average of 12 years found that those who replaced saturated fat with refined carbohydrates were 33% more likely to have a heart attack. Those who ate healthier carbohydrates, on the other hand, had a slightly lower risk.

Myth 5. Statins are the best way to prevent a heart attack. Estimates show that 20 million Americans take statin drugs, such as *atorvastatin* (Lipitor), *pravastatin* (Pravachol) and *simvastatin* (Zocor).

Fact: Even though statins do lower LDL, these drugs appear to have a limited ability to change LDL size pattern.

Implications: If you have high LDL, first control your diet and get more exercise. If your LDL level is still high, ask your doctor about advanced lipid testing to determine your LDL size pattern. Especially if you have Pattern B, discuss taking a statin with your doctor.

If necessary, also talk to your doctor about adding niacin. In high doses, niacin lowers Lp(a) by about 30% in some patients.

If you use niacin, you should be supervised by a physician and receive periodic blood tests to ensure that your liver is functioning properly. If too much niacin is taken, it can damage the liver.

The Great American Heart Hoax: Needless Cardiac Surgery

Michael D. Ozner, MD, cardiologist and medical director of Cardiovascular Prevention Institute of South Florida in Miami. He is the symposium director for "Cardiovascular Disease Prevention," an annual international meeting highlighting advances in cardiology. He is author of *The Great American Heart Hoax: Lifesaving Advice Your Doctor Should Tell You About Heart Disease Prevention (But Probably Never Will)* (BenBella). His Web site is *www.drozner.com.*

Americans get more than 1.5 million cardiac bypass surgeries and angioplasty procedures a year, which makes heart surgery among the most commonly performed surgical procedures in the US.

Fact: These procedures have not been proved to extend lives or to prevent future heart attacks except in a minority of patients. More than one million people get needless cardiac surgery every year. Between 70% and 90% of angioplasties and bypass surgeries are unnecessary in stable patients with coronary artery disease.

Macadamia Nuts May Lower Cholesterol

New finding: In a study of 25 adults with slightly elevated cholesterol levels, participants ate a diet that included 1.5 ounces (a small handful) of macadamia nuts daily or a standard American diet for five weeks, then switched diets for another five weeks. Both diets contained 33% of daily calories from fat.

Result: After eating the macadamia nut diet, participants' total cholesterol was 9.4% lower, on average, than when they ate a standard diet. In previous research, almonds, walnuts and pistachios have been shown to reduce cholesterol.

Penny Kris-Etherton, PhD, RD, distinguished professor of nutrition, Pennsylvania State University, University Park.

While American patients are seven times more likely to undergo coronary angioplasty procedures and bypass surgery than patients in Canada and Sweden, the number of Canadians and Swedes who die from cardiovascular disease is nearly identical (per capita) to the number of people who die from heart disease in this country.

These are not harmless procedures. About 30% of angioplasties fail, requiring patients to repeat the procedure—and eventually, many of these angioplasty patients will undergo bypass surgery. People who have bypass surgery are nearly four times more likely to suffer a stroke at the time of surgery and are vulnerable to postsurgical infections. Between 3% and 5% of patients die from bypass surgery—that's 15,000 to 25,000 lives lost a year.

So why do we keep doing these procedures?

A Flawed Model

Cardiologists used to compare the coronary arteries to simple pipes under a sink. The thinking went that these arteries sometimes accumulated sludge, called plaque (cholesterol deposits within an artery wall), that impeded the flow of blood to the heart. Treating this sludge with angioplasty or shunting blood around it with bypass surgery seemed obvious.

That approach, however, is flawed. We now know that the arteries are highly dynamic structures. What happens within the artery wall is more significant than blockages that obstruct the lumen (arterial openings).

The majority of heart attacks can be linked to small, yet highly inflamed, plaques. These small plaques have no effect on circulation, because they take up little space within the lumen. Yet they may rupture and cause a sudden heart attack due to a clot that forms at the site of the rupture.

What happens: Cholesterol-carrying particles that enter an artery wall undergo oxidation and modification that trigger an immune response. White blood cells flood the area and engulf the oxidized cholesterol particles and cause plaque to form. Then the white blood cells secrete substances, such as proteinases, that break down the fibrous cap that covers the plaque. When the fibrous cap ruptures, blood enters the plaque and a blood clot forms that can block the artery.

Sudden clots that form following plaque rupture are the cause of most heart attacks. Angioplasties and bypass surgery do nothing to prevent plaque rupture or clot formation.

Heart-Saving Steps

The following steps may save lives. *Of course, always ask your doctor about the best heart-health strategies for you...*

● **Test for high sensitivity (hs)-C-reactive protein (CRP).** It's a "marker" that indicates simmering inflammation in blood vessel walls and can be measured with a simple blood test. Inflammation within arterial plaques contributes to plaque rupture and clot formation and subsequent heart attacks.

The landmark JUPITER study looked at more than 17,000 participants with elevated hs-CRP (above 2 milligrams per deciliter [mg/dL]) and normal cholesterol. Those who were treated with medication to lower hs-CRP were significantly less likely to have a heart attack or stroke or to die than those in the control group. CRP can be lowered with lifestyle changes (diet, exercise, weight loss, smoking cessation) and medical therapy (including statin drugs).

● **Test for apolipoprotein B (apoB).** This is a better indicator of heart disease than standard cholesterol levels (including HDL, LDL and triglycerides). Even if your LDL "bad" cholesterol level is normal, you still could have elevated particle numbers, which means that your LDL cholesterol is distributed across a lot of very small, dense particles. These small, dense particles are the most dangerous kind—they are more likely to squeeze through the lining of the artery and more likely to become oxidized once they're there, leading to atherosclerosis (hardening of the arteries). You can check your "bad" particle number by testing for apoB. Blood tests for apoB are performed routinely in Europe and Canada but not in the US. Ask for this test when you have your usual cholesterol screening.

The optimal level of apoB is less than 90 mg/dL (or even lower for high-risk patients). To lower apoB, follow the recommendations for lowering CRP.

● **Choose an anti-inflammatory diet.** People who follow a Mediterranean-style diet—

high in plant foods and cold-water fish (such as salmon) and low in red meat and processed foods—can reduce inflammation.

The Lyon Diet Heart Study compared a Mediterranean diet to a diet resembling the American Heart Association's cholesterol-lowering Step 1 Diet. Participants on the Mediterranean plan were 70% less likely to die from all causes and 73% less likely to have a recurrent cardiac event than those on the standard "healthy" diet.

The Mediterranean diet is effective partly because it limits saturated fat and does not contain trans fat. The fat present in the Mediterranean diet, mainly from olive oil and fish, has anti-inflammatory effects. Also, the antioxidants in fruits and vegetables reduce the oxidation of cholesterol-containing particles within artery walls.

Avoid high-fructose corn syrup, which goes straight to the liver, where it causes an increase in triglycerides, a major risk factor for heart disease.

• **Laugh, pray, get a pet.** Anything that reduces stress can significantly reduce your risk for heart disease. Research at the University of Maryland Medical Center, for example, found that laughing is almost as effective as exercise at improving arterial health.

Laughter relaxes blood vessels and improves circulation to the heart. And like other stress-control strategies, including prayer, loving relationships (with pets as well as people) and yoga, it lowers cortisol, a stress-related hormone.

• **Get moving.** There is a dose-response relationship between exercise and the heart—more exercise gives a greater benefit. Aim for 30 to 45 minutes of exercise most days of the week.

Good news: Walking for as little as 30 minutes five to seven days a week can significantly decrease the risk of dying from heart disease.

■ ■ ■ ■

More from Michael Ozner...

Who Needs Surgery?

Americans often undergo needless heart surgery, but stents or bypass surgery can be lifesavers for a select group of patients, including those with…

• **Unstable angina with increasing frequency and intensity of chest pain,** often occurring at rest.

• **Disabling chest pain that does not respond to lifestyle intervention** or optimal medical therapy.

• **Significant obstructions** in the left, right or other coronary arteries and a weak heart muscle.

• **Significant blockage in the main trunk of the left coronary artery.**

■ ■ ■ ■

The 15-Minute Test That Could Save Your Life

Rebecca Shannonhouse, editor of *Bottom Line/Health,* Boardroom Inc., 281 Tresser Blvd., Stamford, Connecticut 06901.

The standard risk factors used to predict cardiovascular disease, such as age, sex, low HDL ("good") cholesterol, smoking and high blood pressure, don't tell the whole story.

You can appear to be relatively healthy and at low risk for coronary artery disease but actually have a higher risk than you realize—and an increased risk for such conditions as heart attack and stroke.

Underrecognized marker for coronary artery disease: The thickness of the carotid (neck) arteries, which carry blood from the heart to the brain.

Important new finding: When ultrasound was used to measure the thickness of the carotid artery wall and to detect the presence of plaque in 13,145 patients, about 12% who would have been classified as having a low or intermediate risk of developing heart disease were found to actually belong in a higher-risk group—and may require treatment, such as medication.

There should be no plaque in the carotid artery, says cardiologist Vijay Nambi, MD, lead author of the study, which recently appeared in the *Journal of the American College of Cardiology*. Patients with plaque have a significantly higher risk of developing cardiovascular disease, regardless of their other risk factors.

Used in combination with other tests (such as those for blood pressure and cholesterol), carotid imaging with ultrasound allows doctors to more accurately determine who is at higher risk for heart disease. This 15-minute test is noninvasive, painless and usually costs $150 to $200. Patients should ask if the test is covered by their insurance.

After Heart Surgery, Have a Drink

Umberto Benedetto, MD, PhD, the University of Rome La Sapienza, Italy.

Simona Costanzo, MD, Catholic University of Campobasso, Italy.

Eric Rimm, ScD, associate professor at the Harvard School of Public Health and the Channing Laboratory at the Harvard Medical School.

Licia Iacoviello, MD, PhD, research associate professor in the Department of Social and Preventive Medicine at the School of Public Health and Health Professions at the University of Buffalo.

More than 80 scientific studies link moderate alcohol intake—an average of one to two drinks a day for men, and one drink a day for women—to a healthier cardiovascular system. *The benefits of imbibing may include…*

● **Lower risk of heart disease and heart attack**

● **Lower risk of stroke**

● **Lower risk of congestive heart failure**

● **Lower risk of death in people with atrial fibrillation (irregular heartbeat)**

● **Lower risk of heart disease with diabetes.**

Latest findings: Several recent studies show that moderate drinking may also help after you've had coronary bypass surgery …after you've had a heart attack…or after you've had a stroke.

More Drinks, Fewer Deaths

Italian researchers studied more than 1,000 men who had bypass surgery, following their habits and health for 3½ years after the operation.

Those who drank moderately had 25% fewer heart attacks, strokes, additional bypass surgeries and deaths compared with nondrinkers, reported the researchers at a meeting of the American Heart Association.

However: Bypass patients with heart failure who drank four or more drinks a day were twice as likely to die of heart disease, compared with nondrinkers.

"The benefits of moderate amounts of alcohol have been documented in healthy individuals, but our analysis showed a benefit from moderate alcohol intake in post-coronary bypass patients," says Umberto Benedetto, MD, PhD, a study researcher from the University of Rome La Sapienza in Italy.

In another study of more than 16,000 people who had a heart attack or stroke, those who drank moderately after the event had a 20% lower risk of dying from any cause, reported Italian researchers in the *Journal of the American College of Cardiology.*

"We observed that regular and moderate consumption of alcohol has beneficial effects even for people already affected by a heart attack or stroke," says Simona Costanzo, MD, the study leader.

And in a study of 325 people who had a heart attack, those who drank moderately before the attack and continued to drink afterward were 35% less likely to have angina, 21% less likely to be hospitalized again for heart disease, and 25% less likely to die within three years of the heart attack compared with moderate drinkers who quit drinking after the heart attack.

"There are no adverse effects for moderate drinkers to continue consuming alcohol after an acute myocardial infarction [heart attack], and they may have better physical functioning compared to those who quit," concluded the researchers in the *American Journal of Cardiology*.

Gin Is Tonic

How does alcohol help the heart?

To answer that question, Harvard scientists examined 13 well-known biomarkers for heart disease in more than 50,000 men and women, says Eric Rimm, ScD, an associate professor at the Harvard School of Public Health. *Among moderate drinkers, three biomarkers were common in 100% of the men and 80% of the women…*

• **High HDL, the "good" cholesterol that carries fat away from arteries.**

• **Low fibrinogen, a protein that increases the risk of artery-clogging clots.**

• **Low hemoglobin A1c, a biomarker for long-term control of blood sugar.** (Diabetes doubles the risk of heart disease.)

Important: Many studies show that these three biomarkers are improved not by any particular element in wine, beer or spirits, says Dr. Rimm, but by ethanol—the alcohol in alcoholic drinks.

In other words, one or two drinks a day of any alcoholic drink—not just red wine or imported beer or double-malt Scotch—protects the heart.

Example: A drink is 5 ounces of wine, 12 ounces of beer, or 1½ ounces of 80% distilled spirits or liquor, such as whiskey or vodka.

And the study found the greatest degree of protection among those who drank regularly. One or two drinks a day, three to seven days a week, was the healthiest pattern, says Dr. Rimm.

But one or two drinks a day does not mean seven to 14 drinks on Saturday night, he adds. "Immoderate drinking—binge-drinking, or consistently drinking three or more drinks a day—puts you at higher risk for heart disease and many other chronic health problems."

"When we talk about moderate alcohol consumption, we mean drinking regularly, at low doses, within a healthy lifestyle, such as the Mediterranean diet," agrees Licia Iacoviello, MD, PhD, a research associate professor at the University of Buffalo who has studied alcohol and health. "A glass of wine or beer during meals has always been an integral part of the Mediterranean way of eating.

"And the heart-healthy research shows drinking has to be not only moderate, but also regular. A moderate consumption throughout the week is positive. The same amount of weekly alcohol, concentrated in a couple of days, is definitely harmful."

Who Shouldn't Drink

Immoderate or unsafe alcohol intake is a serious public health problem, says Dr. Rimm, with 16,000 people dying every year in alcohol-related car accidents. Needless to say, there are many people who shouldn't drink. *Don't drink if…*

• **You're pregnant**

- **Your father or mother suffered from alcoholism**

- **You're on a blood-thinning medication like warfarin**

- **You have breast cancer,** or a family history of the disease

- **You're about to drive,** operate heavy machinery or do anything that requires normal reaction time.

"Those are only a few examples of the many scenarios where drinking is inappropriate, moderate or otherwise," says Dr. Rimm. "Discuss your alcohol intake with your doctor."

■ ■ ■ ■

Protect Yourself from Heart-Hurting Pollution

Robert D. Brook, MD, associate professor of medicine, Division of Cardiovascular Medicine, University of Michigan, Ann Arbor.

Ryan W. Allen, PhD, assistant professor, faculty of health sciences, Simon Fraser University, Burnaby, British Columbia, Canada.

Here's the dirty little truth about tiny particles of air pollution—they can and do cause deadly cardiovascular disease (CVD), such as heart attack and stroke.

And it's not a whistle blower at a power plant making that claim.

It's a new scientific statement from the American Heart Association, which reviewed the last six years of research on the link between air pollution and CVD—and found a very strong link.

The Polluted Heart

"It looks like the cardiovascular system is uniquely sensitive to air pollution levels," says Robert D. Brook, MD, associate pro-

fessor of internal medicine in the Division of Cardiovascular Medicine at the University of Michigan, and an author of the statement.

The type of pollution that does the dirtiest work is fine particulate matter—the congealed specks of floating carbon, metals and other compounds that spew from exhaust pipes, industrial smokestacks and coal-fired power plants.

The risk from fine particulate matter is both short term and long term, says Dr. Brook.

In "susceptible individuals," just a few hours or days of exposure to air pollution can increase the risk of irregular heartbeats (arrhythmias), heart attack, stroke, heart failure and death, he says.

And susceptible doesn't mean you're on your last legs. *You're susceptible if…*

- **You're 60 or over** (aging is a risk factor for heart disease).

- **You have diabetes,** which can damage arteries.

- **You're overweight or obese,** which studies link to susceptibility.

- **You're at high risk for CVD,** which means you have two or more risk factors, such as high blood pressure and high LDL cholesterol.

- **You have CVD, which means you have angina…**or you've already had a heart attack or stroke…or you've had a cardiovascular procedure such as angioplasty or bypass surgery…or you have heart failure (a weak heart muscle).

Several years or more of exposure to air pollution may increase anyone's risk for CVD, says Dr. Brook.

Air pollution can also increase the risk for premature death from any cause, shortening life from a few months to several years.

And there's no "safe" level of exposure to fine particulate matter, just as there's no "safe" level of exposure to secondary smoke—even a little air pollution can do a lot of damage, he says.

What happens: There are "multiple pathways" by which fine particulate matter affects the cardiovascular system, says Dr. Brook.

• **It can spark artery-damaging inflammation**—just as smoking and excess saturated fat (to cite two examples) can inflame and damage your arteries.

• **It can weaken the cells of the endothelium,** which line the artery and generate artery-relaxing nitric oxide.

• **It irritates the sympathetic nervous system,** which regulates heart rate.

And any one, or several, or all of these pathways can lead to high blood pressure, blood clots, clogged and weakened arteries and irregular heartbeats, which in turn can lead to heart attack, stroke and death, says Dr. Brook.

Bottom line: The fine particulate matter of air pollution should be recognized as a "modifiable risk factor" for CVD and for premature death, concluded the American Heart Association in its scientific statement.

Protecting Yourself

Fortunately, there are several ways you can modify this risk factor.

• **Modify your other CVD risk factors.** "The main message for susceptible people is to use medical care and lifestyle changes to control their other modifiable risk factors, such as high blood pressure, high cholesterol, diabetes and smoking," says Dr. Brook.

• **Know when the air is unhealthy—and stay indoors.** You can find a map that displays daily air-quality levels across America at the Web site *www.airnow.gov.* It shows where air quality is good…moderate…unhealthy for sensitive groups…very unhealthy…and hazardous.

"Limit your exposure as much as possible by decreasing time outside when particle levels are high and the air is unhealthy," says Dr. Brook.

That's particularly important if you're susceptible (or "sensitive," as the Web site calls it)—one of the many people with an older or weaker cardiovascular system that is more vulnerable to air pollution.

• **Reduce your time in traffic.** "In today's world, traffic is a common source of exposure to particulate matter," says Dr. Brook.

Healthful strategy: Don't exercise next to highly trafficked roads or outside during rush hour.

• **Use a HEPA filter.** Researchers studied 45 healthy people in a small town in Canada where wood-burning stoves—which generate fine particulate matter—were the main source of air pollution. For one week, the participants used high-efficiency particle air (HEPA) filters in their homes. For another week, they used the same filters—but with the filters removed.

Results: The HEPA filters reduced the amount of indoor fine particulate matter by 60%.

When people used the working HEPA filters, they had 9% better endothelial function (as indicated by a test for blood flow) and 33% lower levels of C-reactive protein (a biomarker of inflammation).

"This simple intervention can improve air quality indoors—where the majority of time is spent—and reduce cardiovascular-related health risks," concluded Ryan Allen, PhD, assistant professor at Simon Fraser University in Burnaby, British Columbia, and the study leader, in the

American Journal of Respiratory and Critical Care Medicine.

"We were surprised to see the magnitude of effects from air pollution in the people we studied—people who didn't have many of the underlying problems that make you more susceptible to air pollution, such as aging and diabetes," says Dr. Allen. "You wouldn't expect those young and relatively healthy people to be susceptible to the cardiovascular effects of air pollution—but they were."

For the greatest benefit: "There's enough evidence to recommend HEPA filters—which are relatively inexpensive to purchase and operate—as a possible intervention against air pollution, particularly for susceptible groups, such as those with cardiovascular disease," says Dr. Allen.

He points out that a previous study showed the ability of HEPA filters to reduce fine particulate matter in homes in a heavily trafficked area of a big city—and also to reduce endothelial damage in those who used them.

The researchers used two HEPA filters in the study: the Honeywell model 50300 in the main activity room, and the quieter Honeywell 18150 in the bedroom.

■ ■ ■ ■

The Fat That Guarantees Longevity

Andrew Shao, PhD, senior vice president of scientific and regulatory affairs, Council for Responsible Nutrition, Washington, DC.

Floyd H. Chilton, PhD, professor in the Department of Physiology and Pharmacology at Wake Forest University in North Carolina and author of *The Gene Smart Diet* (Rodale).

The government's Centers for Disease Control and Prevention (CDC) recently funded an analysis by researchers at the Harvard School of Public Health that ranked from number 1 to number 12 the health activities that could have done the most good in preventing the early deaths of Americans—the 12 most effective actions Americans could have taken to save their lives. But didn't.

Top Eight Ways to Stay Alive

The seven biggest lifesaving actions weren't a big surprise.

The analysis—"The Preventable Causes of Death in the United States: Comparative Risk Assessment of Dietary, Lifestyle and Metabolic Risk Factors," published in *PLoS Medicine*—outlined the top ways to prevent death. *They were...*

1. Stop smoking. Yearly preventable deaths 467,000.

2. Control high blood pressure. 395,000.

3. Maintain healthy weight. 216,000.

4. Exercise regularly. 191,000.

5. Control high blood sugar levels. 190,000.

6. Lower LDL "bad" cholesterol. 113,000.

7. Reduce salt intake. 102,000.

But number 8 on the list was a big surprise.

The researchers determined that diets deficient in omega-3 fatty acids cause 84,000 preventable deaths every year in the US.

In fact, a low intake of omega-3s—the EPA (eicosapentaenoic acid) and DHA (docosahexaenoic acid) found mainly in oily fish such as sardines, anchovies, salmon and mackerel, and in fish oil supplements—may cause more preventable deaths than a high intake of the artery-clogging trans fats found in many baked goods, snacks and crackers. Low omega-3 intake also appears to cause more preventable deaths than a low intake of fruits and vegetables.

"This analysis reinforces the idea that diet has a tremendously powerful impact on health and longevity—and that the consumption of omega-3s by Americans is far from adequate," says Andrew Shao, PhD, senior vice president of scientific and regulatory affairs at the Council for Responsible Nutrition, an industry trade group for supplement manufacturers.

More Omega-3

"Chronic inflammation causes or complicates many diseases, and omega-3 fatty acids have an important effect on reducing chronic inflammation," says Floyd H. Chilton, PhD, a professor in the Department of Physiology and Pharmacology at Wake Forest University in North Carolina, and author of *The Gene Smart Diet* (Rodale). "Omega-3s have been found to prevent and reverse heart disease and stroke, and also produce positive effects in diabetes, arthritis, cancer, age-related cognitive decline, depression, chronic obstructive pulmonary disease, asthma, psoriasis, and inflammatory bowel disease."

● **Take a fish oil supplement daily.** "Unless you eat fish at every meal, it's difficult to get enough omega-3 fatty acids from your diet," says Dr. Chilton. He suggests taking a fish oil supplement.

Red flag: According to Dr. Chilton, many fish oil supplements don't contain as much EPA and DHA as advertised. For example, a study that analyzed 20 fish oil supplements found that EPA concentration was typically 50% to 75% lower than stated on the label.

Recommended: "Buy fish oil supplements that contain at least 500 milligrams (mg) each of EPA and DHA per capsule—typically in a 1,000- to 1,200-mg capsule of total oil, which allows you to achieve your

targeted omega-3 intake with just one or two capsules a day," says Dr. Chilton.

If you'd rather get your omega-3 fatty acids through the food you eat, your best source is fish. *To get to the recommended daily level of 1,000 mg, Dr. Chilton suggests…*

● **As often as possible, eat fish high in omega-3.**

Analyses in his laboratory show the following fish contain more than 500 mg of omega-3s per 3.5-ounce serving—mackerel, coho salmon, sockeye salmon, Copper River salmon, canned wild Alaskan salmon, canned gourmet salmon (prime fillet), canned skinless pink salmon, trout and canned albacore tuna.

● **Occasionally, eat fish with moderate levels of omega-3.**

These fish contain between 150 and 500 mg of omega-3 per 3.5-ounce serving—haddock, cod, hake, halibut, shrimp, sole, flounder, perch, black bass, swordfish, oysters, Alaska king crab and farmed Atlantic salmon.

Resource: Dr. Chilton has studied omega-3 fatty acids for 30 years and has formulated a supplement—Gene Smart Omega-3—that he says is ideal for delivering an adequate daily level of EPA and DHA. You can order the supplement at *www.genesmart.com*, or by calling 888-571-0112.

The Web site also offers a blood test—the Gene Smart Omega 3 Index Home Blood Test Kit—that allows you to find out if you have adequate blood levels of omega-3s to promote optimal health and protect against heart disease and other chronic inflammatory conditions.

The Ultimate Cholesterol Profile

Michael D. Ozner, MD, cardiologist and medical director of Cardiovascular Prevention Institute of South Florida in Miami. He is the symposium director for "Cardiovascular Disease Prevention," an annual international meeting highlighting advances in cardiology. He is author of *The Great American Heart Hoax: Lifesaving Advice Your Doctor Should Tell You About Heart Disease Prevention (But Probably Never Will)* (BenBella). His Web site is *www.drozner.com.*

For years, doctors have performed routine cholesterol tests to help identify people who are at risk for a heart attack or stroke.

Problem: Traditional cholesterol tests that provide basic readings—such as total cholesterol…HDL "good" cholesterol…and LDL "bad" cholesterol levels—identify only 40% of people at risk for cardiovascular disease.

Each year, about 830,000 Americans die of heart attack or sudden cardiac death (abrupt loss of heart function). Unfortunately, for the majority of people, heart attack or sudden cardiac death is the initial symptom of heart disease. A test that more accurately predicts heart disease risks could prevent many of these deaths.

New approach: Expanded lipid testing identifies up to 90% of patients at risk for heart disease, according to researchers at Duke University.

LDL Alone Is Not Enough

LDL is the form of cholesterol most closely linked to cardiovascular disease. Yet the long-running Framingham Heart Study has reported that 80% of patients who suffered a heart attack had the same LDL levels as those who did not have a heart attack.

Reason: Risk is determined not only by the level of LDL cholesterol measured in a blood test, but also by the size of the LDL particles.

Example: Two patients could both have normal LDL readings of 98 milligrams per deciliter (mg/dL). The patient with a higher percentage of small LDL particles is more likely to have a heart attack or stroke than the patient with more of the large LDL particles.

LDL Subclasses

Expanded lipid testing includes a variety of LDL subclasses.

Most important…

• **Lp(a) is a very small, dense form of LDL.** Lp(a) particles readily penetrate the endothelium (the artery lining) and enter the artery wall itself, causing deadly inflammation and atherosclerosis (fatty buildup in the arteries). In fact, patients with elevated Lp(a) are up to 10 times more likely to have a heart attack than those with lower levels.

Treatment: Initial treatment for patients with elevated Lp(a) focuses on lowering their LDL levels, then addressing Lp(a) levels. Niacin (vitamin B-3) can lower LDL and Lp(a) levels and increase HDL. Patients with high Lp(a) also may need to take the triglyceride-lowering drug *fenofibrate* (Tricor), which can help reduce Lp(a) levels.

• **IDL stands for intermediate-density lipoprotein** (a type of protein combined with lipids). It's a mid-sized particle that's more likely to cause atherosclerosis than an equal amount of LDL.

Treatment: A cholesterol-lowering statin drug, such as *atorvastatin* (Lipitor) or *simvastatin* (Zocor), used in combination with niacin.

• **Size pattern.** Pattern A means that a patient has a high percentage of large particles, which are desirable. Pattern B indicates a higher percentage of dangerous small particles. A patient with Pattern B is up to six times more likely to suffer a heart attack than a patient with Pattern A.

Treatment: Usually a statin drug, combined with niacin and/or fenofibrate.

• **Total number of particles.** The higher the number of LDL particles, the higher the risk for cardiovascular disease. That's because a greater amount increases the likelihood that particles will penetrate the endothelium and travel to the artery wall.

Treatment: Typically, a statin drug.

HDL Subclasses

The HDL form of cholesterol is protective because it helps to remove LDL from arterial walls. Like LDL, it can be subdivided into different particle sizes. *Most important…*

• **HDL-2.** These are the larger HDL particles. They transport LDL out of the arterial wall and into the liver for disposal. They also have antioxidant/anti-inflammatory effects.

Treatment: Niacin increases total HDL as well as HDL-2.

• **HDL-3.** Like HDL-2, these particles lower LDL and can help prevent the dangerous oxidation of cholesterol that's already present in artery walls. However, HDL-3 is smaller than HDL-2 and may not be quite as protective.

Treatment: Niacin helps to increase the size of HDL particles, changing them from HDL-3 to HDL-2 particles.

Are These Tests for You?

All patients with cardiovascular risk factors such as hypertension…diabetes… family history of heart attack or stroke… or smoking should ask their doctors about getting expanded lipid testing. This testing is not necessary for people with no known risk factors for cardiovascular disease, but it could help uncover hidden risks in such individuals.

Expanded lipid testing costs about the same as the older cholesterol tests and may be covered by insurance, depending on the patient's medical history. Even if it's not covered, this type of testing, which costs about $100, on average, is far less expensive than the cost of being treated for a heart attack or stroke.

The Whole Truth About Heart Tests

Michael D. Ozner, MD, cardiologist and medical director of Cardiovascular Prevention Institute of South Florida in Miami. He is the symposium director for "Cardiovascular Disease Prevention," an annual international meeting highlighting advances in cardiology. He is author of *The Great American Heart Hoax: Lifesaving Advice Your Doctor Should Tell You About Heart Disease Prevention (But Probably Never Will)* (BenBella). His Web site is *www.drozner.com.*

We've all heard of someone who dies of a heart problem soon after receiving a clean bill of health from a doctor. When this kind of tragedy occurs, people often wonder why the deadly condition was not detected by one of the sophisticated medical tests now available.

What most people don't realize: Even among some doctors, including cardiologists, there's a great deal of confusion about the use of heart tests and how to interpret the results. *Common misconceptions…*

Stress Testing

Stress testing, which measures a person's capacity for exercise while walking on a treadmill or riding a stationary bicycle, is used to detect coronary artery disease and to help determine overall fitness. But a person who "passes" a stress test can still be at increased risk for a heart attack. *Here's why...*

There are three varieties—a standard stress test (which uses an electrocardiogram, or ECG, a noninvasive test that involves attaching electrodes to the patient's chest to record the heart's electrical activity during exercise)...a nuclear stress test (which uses a radioactive contrast agent that can be viewed with a special scanner to measure blood flow to the heart)... and a stress echocardiogram (which uses ultrasound, a noninvasive procedure that produces images of the heart with high-frequency sound waves).

A nuclear stress test or stress echocardiogram gives the doctor more detailed information about the health of the heart than the standard ECG stress test, but none of the tests spots decreased blood flow to the heart unless at least 70% of a coronary artery is blocked by plaque (fatty buildup).

A shortcoming of stress testing: Plaque buildup that is not severe enough to be detected by a stress test still can rupture. This rupture can, in turn, trigger the formation of a blood clot that completely blocks the artery, leading to a heart attack or sudden death.

Self-defense: If your doctor recommends any type of stress test, remember that you can be at increased risk for a heart attack even if the test result is normal. People with normal stress test results still should follow lifestyle recommendations for heart-disease prevention, including eating a healthful diet, exercising regularly and giving up cigarettes if they smoke.

CT Heart Scan

Many people think that a computed tomography (CT) scan of the arteries is the new gold standard for assessing heart health. That is not true.

CT heart scans provide detailed images of plaque buildup in the coronary arteries via a series of X-rays that produces a single image of the beating heart. The technology has become more popular since 2004, when a new generation of the CT heart scan was introduced. The new test, known as a 64-slice CT scan, creates an extremely detailed, three-dimensional image of the heart by combining thousands of X-ray images taken during rotations around the torso over a period of about 15 seconds.

Many cardiologists are concerned that multislice CT scans, which are heavily advertised to consumers, are overused, thus subjecting patients to unnecessary risks. For example, a single 64-slice CT scan exposes the patient to radiation levels that are roughly the equivalent of more than 100 chest X-rays, resulting in a small but significant increase in cancer risk. In addition, there is little evidence supporting the common use of the CT heart scan—as a screening test for coronary artery disease in people without heart disease symptoms.

A shortcoming of the CT heart scan: If a CT heart scan identifies arterial blockages, doctors still don't know which plaques are likely to rupture.

Even so, doctors may recommend the placement of a stent (tiny mesh tube) to prop open the blocked artery or coronary bypass surgery (an invasive procedure that involves grafting veins or arteries from another part of the body, such as the leg, to reroute—or bypass—the blocked artery). The data show that in most cases, neither procedure prolongs life or prevents future heart attacks in people who have no heart disease symptoms.

Self-defense: A multislice CT scan should be used only in certain situations. For example, if you go to an emergency room because of severe chest pain, your doctor may order a CT heart scan. The test can quickly determine whether a heart problem is causing the chest pain—and, in this case, the benefits of the test outweigh the risks previously described.

Coronary Angiogram

Some people who are worried about the radiation risks associated with a CT heart scan assume that a coronary angiogram is a good, lower-risk alternative. But other risks that are associated with the coronary angiogram make it inappropriate for many people.

During a coronary angiogram, dye that can be seen on X-rays is injected into the arteries. When combined with cardiac catheterization (which involves the insertion of a catheter that is threaded through an artery in the groin and into the heart chambers), a coronary angiogram is the most accurate way to diagnose coronary artery disease.

A shortcoming of coronary angiogram: During cardiac catheterization with coronary angiogram, one of every 1,000 patients has a serious complication, such as a heart attack or stroke, or dies. As with CT scans, these tests help identify the location of large plaque deposits but do not pinpoint which plaques are at risk of rupturing and causing a heart attack.

Self-defense: A cardiac catheterization with coronary angiogram should not be used simply as a screening tool. However, these tests are appropriate if your doctor believes that you are already in the throes of a heart attack or are about to suffer one.

Should You Take "Mega-Doses" of Omega-3?

Doug Hansen, MD, assistant professor of medicine at the University of Colorado and medical director of Altitude Family Medicine in Denver, Colorado. *www.altitudemedicine.com*

Dave Woynarowski, MD, a physician in private practice in Lancaster, Pennsylvania, and coauthor of *The Immortality Edge: Realize the Secrets of Your Telomeres for a Longer, Healthier Life* (Wiley). *www.drdavesbest.com*

Hardly anybody seriously questions whether or not the omega-3 fatty acids found in fish oil—EPA (eicosapentaenoic acid) and DHA (docosahexaenoic acid)—can help the heart. *Decades of studies link a higher intake of omega-3s to…*

● **Less chronic inflammation,** which fuels heart disease

● **Lower triglycerides,** a heart-hurting blood fat

● **Lower levels of the small,** dense LDL particles that experts say are the true bad guys in "bad" LDL cholesterol

● **Higher levels of good HDL cholesterol**

● **Less platelet aggregation,** which helps stop blood from clumping into artery-clogging clots

● **Lower blood pressure**

● **A steadier heartbeat.**

But what's still very much debated is how much omega-3 you need to protect your heart.

The American Heart Association recommends people without heart disease eat two servings of fish a week, emphasizing fatty fish such as salmon. (Two servings of salmon supply 2 to 4 grams [g] omega-3s, or about 400 milligrams [mg] daily.) They also recommend that people with heart disease take 1 gram a day of EPA/DHA. But is that really enough?

Now: A recent study points to the amount that might be optimal. And it's a lot more than you're probably getting.

20 Times Higher, A Whole Lot Healthier

Pointing out that most studies on omega-3 and health have looked at people with low intakes of the nutrient, a team of researchers from the Fred Hutchinson Cancer Research Center in Seattle studied 330 people (average age 45) among Yup'ik Eskimos in Alaska—many of whom consume 20 times more omega-3s than the average American.

Yup'ik men get an average of 3.7 g EPA/DHA daily; the average American male gets 140 mg. Yup'ik women get an average of 2.4 g; the average American woman gets 90 mg.

But one thing that wasn't different about the Yup'iks and the average American was weight—70% of the Yup'iks were overweight or obese, the same percentage as the rest of the US population.

But perhaps because of all that "extra" omega-3 in their diet, the overweight Yup'iks had uniquely healthy levels of several risk factors for heart disease—levels you wouldn't typically find in an overweight person. *Their high blood levels of EPA and/ or DHA were linked to…*

- **Lower triglycerides**
- **Higher HDL cholesterol**
- **Lower LDL cholesterol**
- **Lower total cholesterol**
- **Lower C-reactive protein,** a biomarker of inflammation.

"Increasing EPA and DHA intakes to amounts well above those consumed by the general US population may have strong beneficial effects on chronic disease risk," concluded the researchers in the *American Journal of Clinical Nutrition.*

More Research

Other recent research links omega-3s to a healthier heart…

- **Sturdier telomeres.** Telomeres are a fibrous type of DNA that form a protective cap on the end of chromosomes; the faster the fibers shorten, the faster you age, say some experts. In a five-year study of 608 people with coronary heart disease, researchers in the Division of Cardiology at University of California, San Francisco, found that those with the highest blood levels of omega-3s also had the slowest rate of telomere shortening. "Omega-3 fatty acids may protect against cellular aging in patients with coronary heart disease," concluded the researchers in the *Journal of the American Medical Association.*

- **More stable plaque.** Many heart attacks and strokes happen when a chunk of plaque breaks off and plugs an artery. Plaques with higher levels of EPA are more stable, reported UK researchers in the journal *Atherosclerosis.*

- **Less metabolic syndrome.** In a study of 3,500 people aged 40 to 69, those eating a serving of fish a day were 57% less likely to develop metabolic syndrome—a constellation of risk factors for heart disease that includes high blood pressure, low HDL and high triglycerides.

- **Omega-3 and statins better than statins alone.** Adding omega-3 supplements to statin therapy tripled the reduction of triglycerides compared with taking just statins, reported Korean researchers in the *European Journal of Clinical Nutrition.*

- **More flexible arteries.** People who ate a meal supplemented with 4.7 g of omega-3s had more flexible arteries after the meal than people who ate a meal without the supplement, reported UK researchers in the journal *Clinical Nutrition.*

Optimal Levels of Omega-3

Omega-3 is good for your heart. But should you try to get the 3 to 4 g daily consumed by the Yup'iks? Maybe, says one doctor. Definitely, says another.

"Even though the American Heart Association recommends 1 g of fish oil daily as a heart-protecting dose, going over that level doesn't seem to have any downside—and there doesn't seem to be a level of intake over which omega-3s stops having benefits," says Doug Hansen, MD, an assistant professor of medicine at the University of Colorado and medical director of Altitude Family Medicine in Denver, Colorado.

Dr. Hansen points to a recent study showing that a dosage from 3 to 6 g daily was the level that reduced the risk of sudden cardiac death—a type of lethal heart stoppage that strikes more than 250,000 Americans yearly. "Clearly, there is a risk that the 1 g daily recommendation is underestimating," he says.

Recommended intake: For patients without heart disease, he recommends 1 to 1.5 g a day and eating two to three servings of fatty fish a week.

For people with high triglycerides or heart failure, he often increases the dose to 3 to 4 g.

Dr. Hansen favors several over-the-counter brands for a safe, pure fish oil, including fish oils from Carlson, Nordic Naturals and NOW Foods. For the "least expensive omega-3 on the market" that is also of high quality, he recommends Kirkland Omega 3 One Per Day Fish Oil, the Costco house brand.

Trap: Many people who think they're getting 1 g a day of omega-3s from a supplement probably aren't, he says. "Three out of four of my patients who take fish oil are misreading the label. They look at the total grams of fish oil, which is larger than the total dosage of EPA and DHA—and they end up not taking 1 g a day of the omega-3s."

● **The 6-gram solution.** A dose of 6 grams daily is recommended by Dave Woynarowski, MD, a physician in private practice in Lancaster, Pennsylvania, and coauthor of *The Immortality Edge: Realize the Secrets of Your Telomeres for a Longer, Healthier Life* (Wiley).

"I think fish oil is the missing link to human health," he says. "I conducted a meta-analysis of more than 500 studies on fish oil for heart disease, rheumatoid arthritis and many other conditions—and found that 5.8 grams daily was the level that was most protective and curative. An intake of about 6 g daily is also the level that creates a ratio of 4-to-1 omega-3s to omega-6 fatty acids in the bloodstream—and that's the ratio shown to be most effective in preventing heart disease.

"People might say this is an inordinately high level of omega-3 to be recommending. In response, I say that the conventional recommendations are inordinately low."

And like Dr. Hansen, he says safety is not an issue. "Unless a patient is in the midst of a stroke, there is no risk of increased bleeding with omega-3s, even when taking a blood-thinning medication. The idea that usage of high doses of fish oil would create spontaneous bleeding is nonsense."

What Most People Don't Know About Heart Disease

Mimi Guarneri, MD, founder and medical director of Scripps Center for Integrative Medicine and attending physician in cardiovascular disease at Scripps Clinic, both in La Jolla, California. She is author of *The Heart Speaks: A Cardiologist Reveals the Secret Language of Healing* (Touchstone).

The physical risk factors for heart disease—smoking, elevated cholesterol, high blood pressure, diabetes, etc.—are well known. What very few people realize is that these factors contribute to only about half of the cases of coronary artery disease.

Surprising: Emotional factors, such as stress, anger and depression, may be even more predictive of heart disease than traditional risk factors, according to research. For example, a study reported in *The New England Journal of Medicine* found that heart attack survivors who were socially isolated and had a high degree of stress had more than four times the risk for death from heart attack and other causes over a three-year period than those with low levels of isolation and stress.

Each day, 2,600 Americans die of cardiovascular disease—one every 33 seconds. Many of these deaths are preventable through risk factor modification and lifestyle changes.

At Healing Hearts, a lifestyle change program at Scripps Center for Integrative Medicine in La Jolla, California, heart patients' physical and emotional risk factors are treated with a variety of personalized approaches, including medication, exercise and nutrition programs, group therapy, yoga and meditation. Research shows that patients who undergo these major lifestyle changes have half the number of hospital admissions for recurring cardiac events as those who receive only traditional cardiac care.*

Stress

The chronic release of stress hormones is one of the most potent risk factors for the heart. Research has shown that chronic stress—from job pressures, financial worries, etc.—is comparable to hypertension as a risk factor for cardiovascular disease. Highly stressed individuals have elevated

*To find a medical center near you that offers integrative heart care, go to the Consortium of Academic Health Centers for Integrative Medicine, 612-624-9166, *www.imconsortium.org* or the Bravewell Collaborative, 612-377-8400, *www.bravewell.org*.

levels of cortisol and epinephrine, hormones that can raise cholesterol and/or blood pressure by 20% to 50%.

Helpful: Suppose you're late to work and have to stop at a railroad crossing to let a train pass. A "stress response" might be to get angry at the delay.

Better: Count yourself lucky to have a short break in the day. Take the time to relax and listen to the radio or talk to a companion…and remind yourself that the brief delay isn't likely to make much of a difference.

Also helpful: Take a few deep breaths whenever you feel yourself getting stressed. Breathe in deeply for about five seconds, then take another five seconds to exhale. Within a few seconds, your nervous system will begin to shift from an excited state to a relaxed state. Deep breathing helps lower stress hormones along with blood pressure and heart rate.

Anger

Anger and hostility are the most toxic emotions for the heart. Studies have shown that men who are rated as "hostile" on personality tests are much more likely to experience angina (chest pain) and episodes of high blood pressure.

Feelings of hostility sharply increase blood pressure and heart rate and cause elevations in blood sugar, cholesterol and interleukin-6 (IL-6), a blood protein that acts as a marker for arterial inflammation. An outburst of anger more than doubles the risk for a heart attack in the next two hours.

Helpful: Biofeedback, in which a monitoring device and sensors record heartbeat, muscle tension and other bodily processes, is very effective. It helps you recognize and manage your anger triggers. To find a licensed biofeedback practitioner, consult the Biofeedback Certification Institute of America, 866-908-8713, *www.bcia.org*.

Also helpful: Anger management support groups, where people are encouraged to let down their emotional barriers, express feelings and listen compassionately to others. If you'd like to find a local group, ask your doctor for a referral to a psychologist, who can refer you to an anger management group.

Depression

Nearly one in 10 Americans suffers from a depressive disorder in a given year, and the incidence of depression is 10 times higher now than it was 50 years ago. Depression, which may be caused by social isolation as well as a chemical imbalance in the brain, is at least as serious as high cholesterol and hypertension as a risk factor for heart disease.

Patients with heart disease who also suffer from depression are up to four times more likely to die during the six months after a heart attack than those who aren't depressed. Studies have shown that depression, along with other emotional factors, such as anxiety, may be a better predictor of illness and death than the severity of coronary artery disease—even when arteries are blocked by as much as 70%.

Important: Antidepressant medications alone do not appear to reduce the risk for coronary artery disease, even when they significantly improve depressive symptoms. However, antidepressants help people change destructive behavior, such as not exercising or eating a poor diet, and allow them to make lifestyle choices that affect risk for heart disease.

Helpful: For some people, forming social connections is among the most effective ways to reduce depression as well as the risk for heart disease—and may explain why integrative approaches to heart disease are so effective. People who participate in such programs exercise together, join support groups and sometimes eat together.

Also helpful: Volunteer work. People who serve others have a stronger sense of purpose and self-worth. People often say that they'd like to volunteer, but aren't sure what to do.

Try this: What is your passion? It may be playing the piano, working with animals or taking care of children. Look around and find a volunteer program that includes the activities that you like best. To find volunteer activities in your area, go to Volunteer-Match, 415-241-6868, *www.volunteermatch. org*.

Isolation

Research shows that people who are socially isolated are two to three times more likely to die from heart disease and other causes over a nine-year period than those with strong social connections.

A long-running study that looked at residents of Roseto, Pennsylvania, found that over a 10-year period, people died of heart attack at a rate only half that of the surrounding communities—despite their high rates of smoking, a fatty diet and hazardous work in local slate quarries. Researchers concluded that their robust cardiac health was due, in part, to a tight civic community—extended families, frequent religious festivals, social clubs, etc.

Important: Stay socially engaged—attend church or synagogue services or engage in other community activities...do volunteer work...and encourage friends to visit.

■ ■ ■ ■

You Don't Need Drugs to Control Your Cholesterol

Allan Magaziner, DO, a clinical instructor in the department of family practice at the Robert Wood Johnson University of Medicine and Dentistry in New Brunswick, New Jersey, and founder and medical director of the Magaziner Center for Wellness in Cherry Hill, New Jersey (*www.drma gaziner.com*). A past president of the American College for Advancement in Medicine, he is author of *The All-Natural Cardio Cure* (Avery).

It's widely known that low cholesterol levels help prevent heart attack and stroke. But that's only part of the story. Levels of HDL "good" cholesterol must be high enough to carry harmful forms of cholesterol to the liver to be excreted.

Recent finding: Research has shown that decreasing LDL "bad" cholesterol by 40% and increasing HDL by 30% lowers the risk for heart attack or stroke by 70%—a much greater reduction of risk than occurs from lowering either total cholesterol or LDL levels.

The pharmaceutical industry has worked feverishly to develop a prescription medication that significantly increases HDL levels, to be used as a complement to cholesterol-lowering statins that focus primarily on lowering LDL levels.

Examples: The new drug *torcetrapib* was pegged as a blockbuster that increases HDL levels by 60%—that is, until late-stage clinical trials showed that torcetrapib actually increased heart problems and death rates.

What you may not know: Therapeutic doses of niacin (vitamin B-3) effectively boost HDL levels—and lower LDL and total cholesterol.

The "Cholesterol Vitamin"

Over fifty years ago, Canadian scientists discovered that high doses of nicotinic acid—a form of niacin—could lower total cholesterol. In a 1975 study of men with heart disease, niacin was shown to reduce the rate of second heart attacks. Later, niacin was found to boost heart-protective HDL levels.

Although niacin alone cannot help everyone with abnormal cholesterol levels—often it is best used in combination with a statin—the vitamin is one of the most effective nondrug therapies available.

Ask your doctor about taking niacin if after trying cholesterol-lowering medication you have suffered side effects or your cholesterol levels have not improved within three months of getting a cholesterol test. Or consider trying niacin with the nondrug therapies described on the next page.

How to use: Start with 100 milligrams (mg) of niacin daily and build up over one week to 500 mg a day. Every week, increase the dose by 500 mg until you reach 2,000 mg a day, taken in three divided doses, with meals. Be certain to use nicotinic acid, not niacinamide, a form of B vitamin that does not improve cholesterol levels. Consult your doctor before taking niacin.

The most common side effect of niacin is flushing—a warm, itchy, rashlike reddening of the face, neck and chest, which lasts about 10 minutes. Flushing is caused by niacin's ability to trigger vasodilation (widening of blood vessels).

To lessen this side effect, choose a form of niacin known as inositol hexanicotinate. It helps prevent the flush without reducing niacin's effectiveness.

Caution: Niacin should be avoided by people with a history of liver disease or stomach ulcers and used with caution by patients with diabetes and/or gallbladder disease. In addition, high-dose niacin (2,000 mg or more) may interact with certain medications, including alpha-blockers, such as *doxazosin* (Cardura), and the diabetes drug *metformin* (Glucophage).

Other Nondrug Therapies

A diet that keeps sugar and processed food to an absolute minimum and emphasizes fruits and vegetables…whole grains…beans…fish…lean meats…and nuts and seeds can help lower LDL cholesterol and raise HDL levels. So can regular exercise, such as brisk walking, and losing excess weight.

Other nondrug approaches can lower total and LDL cholesterol and boost HDL. *Combine the following nondrug therapies with niacin for maximum effectiveness…*

• **Red yeast rice.** This Chinese medicine—a yeast that is grown on white rice, then fermented—contains monacolins, substances that act as naturally occurring statins. Research in China shows that red yeast rice can lower total cholesterol by 11% to 30%.

Typical use: Take 1,200 to 2,400 mg a day of red yeast rice, in two to four doses, with meals.

Not recommended: Policosanol—a supplement derived from cane sugar that also contains natural statins—has been widely promoted as effective for lowering cholesterol. However, several recent studies show that policosanol has no significant effect on cholesterol.

• **Fish oil and flaxseed.** Fish oil and flaxseed supply omega-3 fatty acids, which lower total cholesterol and LDL levels and raise HDL levels.

Typical dose: For fish oil, take supplements containing a total of 3 grams (g) daily of eicosapentaenoic acid (EPA) and docosahexaenoic acid (DHA). If you take a blood-thinning drug, such as aspirin or *warfarin* (Coumadin), check with your doctor before taking this dose of fish oil. Or use one to three teaspoons of ground flaxseed a day, sprinkled on food or mixed with water or juice. Flaxseed also can help relieve constipation and ease arthritis pain.

• **Soy.** Many studies show that soy can help lower total and LDL cholesterol.

Typical use: Try to get 20 g of soy protein a day—the equivalent of eight ounces of tofu…or one cup of edamame (soy) beans.

Important: Soy ice cream and other processed soy foods don't deliver enough soy to help reduce cholesterol.

Caution: If you have been diagnosed with a hormone-dependent cancer, such as some breast malignancies, or are at risk for such a condition, check with your doctor before adding soy to your diet.

• **Plant sterols.** These natural substances, which block the absorption of cholesterol in the intestines, are found in fruits, vegetables, beans, grains and other plants. Regular intake can reduce total cholesterol by 10% and LDL by 14%. Products with plant sterols (or a similar form, plant stanols) include spreads, salad dressings, snack bars and dietary supplements.

Typical use: Aim for 1 g to 2 g daily of plant sterols.

• **Walnuts.** A recent study published in the medical journal *Angiology* showed that people who ate a handful of walnuts daily for eight weeks had a 9% increase in HDL. Walnuts contain polyphenol antioxidants, which also inhibit oxidation of LDL cholesterol.

Recommended intake: One ounce of raw walnuts three times daily.

A Twice-a-Day Heart-Healthy Practice

Peter Jones, PhD, professor of nutrition and food science at the University of Manitoba in Canada.

Some plants have very high cholesterol. Or rather, they have very high sterols, a chemical cousin to cholesterol that does the same thing for a plant that cholesterol does for you—maintains and strengthens cellular membranes, the envelope around every cell.

When you eat plant sterols (or stanols, their twin), they act in your body as if they were dietary cholesterol, blocking the real thing at every turn—beating it to the punch before it's absorbed through the intestines…and shoving it aside before it's packaged into the lipoproteins that carry it through the bloodstream (LDL stands for low-density lipoprotein).

Dozens of studies show that a daily intake of 2.5 grams (g; 2,500 milligrams [mg]) of plant sterols can help lower LDL cholesterol levels up to 15%—dramatically lowering your risk of heart disease. In fact, if you're taking a cholesterol-lowering statin, adding a goodly amount of plant sterols to your diet is more effective than doubling the dose of the drug.

To get more plant sterols, you just eat more plants, right?

Well, our hunter-and-gatherer ancestors managed to consume only about 1.2 g (1,200 mg) of plant sterols a day, as they spent endless hours munching and crunching their way through a diet of seeds, berries, leaves and the like. Today even the most determined vegetarians consume no more than 500 mg a day. The average American eats about 250 mg.

To make up for the shortfall, food scientists began enriching everyday foods with plant sterols—starting with heart-healthy margarines such as Benecol and Take Control, and expanding to sterol-enriched salad dressings, yogurts, chocolate bars, juices and a supermarket aisle's worth of other sterol-filled products.

But are each of those foods equally effective at lowering LDL cholesterol?

Latest development: Recent research shows that some sterol-enriched foods do a much better job than others at lowering LDL—and that when you eat sterols can make all the difference in whether or not sterols work to protect your heart.

Newest Research

A team of researchers at McGill University in Canada analyzed 59 studies on the cholesterol-lowering ability of sterol-enriched foods.

They found the highest reduction in LDL when plant sterols were combined with fat—in margarine, mayonnaise, salad dressing, milk or yogurt.

They found the lowest reduction from other sterol-enriched foods, such as croissants, muffins, orange juice, nonfat beverages, cereal bars, chocolate and meat.

They also found that eating all your sterols at one meal—such as spreading sterol-enriched margarine on your toast at breakfast and then calling it a day—failed to lower LDL.

Best: Eating sterol-enriched foods two or three times a day.

A confirming study conducted a few months later showed that eating sterol-enriched margarine three times a day lowered cholesterol 6% more than eating the same amount of margarine once a day.

What to Do

● **Eat in divided dosages.** "If you want the biggest cholesterol-lowering bang for your buck, eat sterols in smaller doses, two or three times a day, rather than in one large dose," says Peter Jones, PhD, the lead researcher on those studies and professor of nutrition and food science at the University of Manitoba in Canada.

● **Focus on fat.** "Our research shows that the most effective way to ingest plant sterols is in the company of fat," says Dr. Jones. "That might seem odd because fat is supposedly bad for your heart. But we have to eat some fat to live, and research shows the right kinds of fats, eaten in moderation, are actually good for your heart.

Recommended: A sterol-rich margarine that also includes heart-protecting mono-unsaturated and omega-3 fatty acids, such as Smart Balance.

"Smear the margarine liberally on a piece of toast at breakfast and on your sandwich bread at lunch," says Dr. Jones. "You get the sterols, you get the benefits of the good fats in the margarine and your timing maximizes the cholesterol-lowering power of the sterols."

The greatest reduction in LDL cholesterol is from 2.5 g of sterols a day.

Trap: Eating more than 2.5 g a day doesn't cut cholesterol any further.

● **Or take a sterol supplement.** If you don't like margarine, Dr. Jones recommends a sterol supplement, taking 2.5 g a day, in two doses.

Best: For maximum cholesterol-lowering power, look for a supplement in a soft gel (rather than a pill), with the sterols suspended in a healthy oil (such as omega-3 or monounsaturated fat).

Can't Tolerate Statins? Try Red Yeast Rice

Joshua Levitt, ND, naturopathic physician in private practice in Hamden, Connecticut. *www.wholehealthct.com.*

Statins work—really well. By reducing high blood levels of artery-clogging "bad" LDL cholesterol, they can reduce the risk of a heart attack by up to 40%, compared with people not taking statins.

That's why more than 15 million Americans take the drug. Or at least start taking it. Two out of five people who start a statin—a drug intended to be a lifelong therapy—stop it within a year.

The likely reason—a side effect.

The most common statin side effect (bothering three out of five people who reported a side effect to the Statin Effects Study at the University of California–San Diego) is muscle pain and weakness, or myalgia. In fact, some people who take a statin find their muscles become so achy and fatigued they can no longer exercise!

Other side effects commonly reported in the Statin Effects Study include digestive upset…cloudy memory and thinking…neuropathy (burning, tingling and numbness in the hands and feet)…irritability…insomnia…and sexual problems such as erectile dysfunction or low libido.

And switching from one statin to another isn't necessarily a solution—nearly 60% of people who develop myalgia from their first statin still have it after switching to a second or third.

Are there any LDL-lowering alternatives for people who can't handle statins? Yes, says a team of physicians from the University of Pennsylvania School of Medicine.

The ancient Chinese heart remedy, red yeast rice.

Red yeast rice is the granddaddy of all statins. When the yeast monascus purpureus grows on rice, it produces compounds called monacolins that block the action of HMG-CoA reductase, an enzyme with a key role in manufacturing cholesterol.

A few decades ago, Western scientists took a closer look at this intriguing Chinese heart medicine, identified its active ingredients, synthesized one (monacolin K), and produced *lovastatin* (Mevacor)…which was followed by *simvastatin* (Zocor), *atorvastatin* (Lipitor), *rosuvastatin* (Crestor) and all the other statins…now the most-prescribed medicines in the US.

Same Effect but No Side Effects

The researchers tested the effectiveness of red yeast rice in 62 people (average age 61) who had stopped taking a statin because of myalgia, and whose muscle pain cleared up after they discontinued the drug.

They divided them into two groups, giving one red yeast rice and the other a placebo. (Those taking red yeast rice also attended classes in "therapeutic lifestyle changes," learning about a low-fat Mediterranean diet, regular exercise and relaxation techniques.)

Results: After six months, LDL cholesterol in the red yeast rice group fell from 163 mg/dL (milligrams per deciliter) to 128, a 21% drop. In the placebo group, LDL fell from 165 to 150, a 9% decline.

Total cholesterol fell in the red yeast rice group from 245 to 208, or 15%. In the placebo group, it dropped from 246 to 230, or 5%.

And What About Myalgia?

Red yeast rice is a statinlike supplement—it caused myalgia in 2 people, who stopped taking it. But the other 27 people taking red yeast rice were myalgia-free!

"Red yeast rice significantly decreased LDL and total cholesterol levels compared with the placebo, and did not increase the incidence of myalgias," summed up the researchers in the *Annals of Internal Medicine*. "The regimen of red yeast rice," they continued, "may offer a lipid-lowering option for patients with a history of intolerance to statin therapy."

In an earlier study, the researchers conducted a head-to-head test of Zocor and red yeast rice (along with the therapeutic lifestyle changes and fish oil supplements) in 74 people with high LDL.

After three months, those taking the red yeast rice had a 42% drop in LDL; those taking the Zocor, 40%.

But can red yeast rice prevent heart attacks like statins?

Latest development: Researchers at the Peking Union Medical College in Beijing treated more than 1,500 older individuals who had suffered a heart attack with either red yeast rice or a placebo. *After four years, red yeast rice had…*

- **Reduced the risk of heart attack by 38%**

- **Reduced the risk of death from heart disease by 29%.**

The findings were published in the *Journal of Clinical Pharmacology*.

Supplement with Supervision

The University of Pennsylvania researchers note that the amount of lovastatin delivered by red yeast rice is equivalent to 6 milligrams (mg) of Zocor, which is usually given in 20- to 40-mg doses. So why does red yeast rice work as well as Zocor? And why is it less likely to cause myalgia? Nobody knows for sure, but there are theories.

"Red yeast rice has several monacolins in small amounts," says Joshua Levitt, ND, a naturopathic physician in private practice in Hamden, Connecticut. "They might work additively or synergistically, accomplishing the same effect as a pharmaceutical product with only one agent. Also, red yeast rice has compounds other than monacolins, which might enhance their effectiveness."

Suggested dosage: 1,800 mg, twice a day.

Products: The study doctors used a red yeast rice manufactured by Sylvan Bio-products, which is available at GNC stores (*www.gnc.com*) as Red Yeast Rice, from Traditional Supplements. The Sylvan formulation is also used in Naturals Organic Red Yeast Rice, at *www.naturals-supplements.com*, or call 866-352-7520.

In his practice, Dr. Levitt uses the product Choleast, from Thorne Research, which includes both red yeast rice and the antioxidant CoQ10 (a nutrient often recommended to counter statin side effects). It is available at many Web sites, including *www.thorne.com* (or call 800-228-1966), *www.amazon.com* and *www.pureprescriptions.com* (or call 800-860-9583).

Red flags: "Just because red yeast rice is a natural, over-the-counter product doesn't mean it's safe," says Dr. Levitt. "It has statinlike activity, and carries the risk of all the same side effects, including rare but serious conditions that can cause extensive muscle damage.

"I feel very strongly that this supplement should be taken only under the supervision of a licensed health professional, who can monitor your health, which includes periodic laboratory tests to ensure that there is no liver damage—a possible risk of statins—and that the therapy is effectively lowering LDL."

There have also been questions about the purity and potency of over-the-counter red yeast rice supplements, says Dr. Levitt—some have been contaminated with toxins, and some contained only minuscule amounts of monacolins.

The Sylvan Bioproducts formulation used in the study and the product recommended by Dr. Levitt both have strict quality controls.

■ ■ ■ ■

Juice Up Your Heart

Gale Maleskey, RD, clinical dietitian and author of Nature's Medicines (Rodale). *www.galemaleskey.com.*

Tinna Traustadóttir, PhD, associate director of exercise sciences, Kronos Longevity Research Institute (KLRI), Phoenix, Arizona.

Michael Davidson, MD, director of preventive cardiology, University of Chicago Medical Center.

Christine Morand, PhD, senior research scientist, biochemist and nutritionist, Centre Hospitalier Universitaire, Clermont-Ferrand, France.

"Juice has gotten a bad rap," says Gale Maleskey, RD, a clinical dietitian and author of *Nature's Medicines* (Rodale). "That's because when people heard soda was bad for you, many stopped drinking 32 ounces or more of soda a day and started drinking the same amount of juice. But drinking large quantities of any sugar-rich beverage is not a healthy choice, because of the extra calories and the risk of diabetes."

However: Several recent studies show that drinking a glass or two a day of a juice packed with cell-nourishing, cell-protecting plant antioxidants called polyphenols can be a healthy choice—particularly for your heart.

Striking Research Findings

• **Tart cherry juice, a powerful antioxidant.** Researchers at the Kronos Longevity Institute in Phoenix, Arizona, asked 12 people, average age 69, to drink either 8 ounces of tart cherry juice twice a day, or a look-alike juice.

Two weeks later, those drinking the true cherry juice had triple the ability to resist oxidative damage, the injury to cells and genes from molecules called free radicals that is a main cause of heart disease.

"Tart cherries are very rich in protective antioxidants, such as flavonols and anthocyanins," says Tinna Traustadóttir, PhD, the study leader.

"It's often hard to eat four to five servings of antioxidant-rich fruit every day," Dr. Traustadóttir says. "This is a very convenient way of maximizing antioxidant intake."

Product: The product used in the study was Cheribundi, a 100% juice with 50 tart cherries per bottle. You can order the juice online at *www.cheribundi.com* or use the Web site to find a retailer near you.

● **Pomegranate juice, for cleaner arteries.** Researchers at the University of Chicago studied 289 people, aged 45 to 74, all of whom had one or more risk factors for heart disease, such as high cholesterol. They divided them into two groups—one drank 8 ounces a day of pomegranate juice, and one didn't.

After one year, the pomegranate drinkers with the most risk factors for heart disease had a much slower accumulation of artery-clogging plaque, compared with the high-risk folks not drinking the juice.

The findings were in *American Journal of Cardiology*.

"I was surprised by the results," says Michael Davidson, MD, the study leader and director of preventive cardiology at the University of Chicago Medical Center. "Pomegranate juice slowed the progression of atherosclerosis in the group most at risk for heart disease and stroke."

Theory: The powerful antioxidants in pomegranate juice slow or stop the oxidation of LDL cholesterol, the process that creates arterial plaque.

Dr. Davidson says that larger studies are needed to prove that pomegranate juice is truly protective against cardiovascular disease. But he calls the results "encouraging"—and recommends talking to your doctor about whether pomegranate juice is right for you.

Product: POM Wonderful was the juice used in the study.

Smart idea: If you're overweight or have diabetes, drinking 8 ounces of juice a day may not be advisable because of the amount of calories and sugar. If that's the case, says Dr. Davidson, you can get the same amount of pomegranate antioxidants found in an 8-ounce glass of juice by taking a one teaspoon liquid extract of the juice or a pomegranate extract pill, both called POM-X.

● **Orange juice, for lower blood pressure.** Research links a diet rich in flavonols, a class of polyphenols, to less risk for heart disease. French researchers decided to see if the most abundant flavonol in orange juice—hesperidin—might help control high blood pressure, a risk factor for heart disease and stroke.

To find out, they studied 24 men, aged 50 to 64, dividing them into three groups. One group drank 16 ounces of orange juice a day. One group drank a placebo beverage and also took a pill containing 292 milligrams (mg) of hesperidin, the amount in 16 ounces of orange juice. And one group drank the placebo beverage and took a placebo pill.

After one month, those drinking the orange juice and taking the hesperidin had a significant drop in blood pressure. There was no change in the placebo group.

The researchers also noted that orange juice quickly increased levels of nitric oxide, a biochemical that relaxes and strengthens arteries.

And the men drinking OJ or taking hesperidin had more activity in hundreds of genes linked to control of CVD.

Important: "Whole fruit contains up to two times as much hesperidin as the equivalent amount of juice," says Christine Morand, PhD, the study leader. "Eating 1 to 1¼ oranges provides as much hesperidin as drinking 16 ounces of juice."

Juicing Judiciously

"These and other studies make clear that some juices have very unique polyphenols and drinking more of them is worthwhile," says Maleskey. *Her suggestions for drinking juice healthfully…*

● **Don't overdo it.** "Pure fruit juice can have more calories per ounce than soda— for example, 20 calories for grape juice, compared with 12 calories for cola," she says. "That's 160 calories for an 8-ounce glass of juice—a lot of calories, if you're trying to control or lose weight. Plus, it's easy to overconsume juice, because your body doesn't register 'fullness' the way it does with solid food."

What to do: Stick to 4 to 6 ounces a day, or ½ to ¾ of a cup.

Red flag: If you have diabetes, avoid juices. "They can upset your blood sugar levels," says Maleskey.

● **Drink unfiltered juice.** "It has a lot more heart-healthy polyphenols in it than filtered juice," says Maleskey. Unfiltered juice is usually cloudy in the bottle.

● **Drink juice with a high-fiber, high-protein snack.** A handful of nuts are a good choice, says Maleskey. Or drink juice with a meal. "With this strategy, the sugar from the juice enters the bloodstream more slowly, preventing an unhealthy spike of blood sugar."

● **Mix juice with a soluble fiber supplement.** "It helps slow the absorption of sugars—and reduces cholesterol, too. And a soluble fiber supplement made from methylcellulose doesn't thicken the juice, so you won't even know it's there."

Product: Benefiber, from Novartis.

■ ■ ■ ■

Why Your Heart Adores Chocolate

Yerem Yeghiazarians, MD, associate professor of medicine and researcher in the Eli and Edythe Broad Center of Regeneration at the University of California-San Francisco.

Carl Keen, PhD, professor of nutrition and internal medicine at the University of California-Davis.

Janet Bond Brill, PhD, RD, an expert in nutrition and cardiovascular disease prevention based in Valley Forge, Pennsylvania. She is director of nutrition for Fitness Together, a franchise company of almost 500 personal fitness-training studios, has served as a nutrition consultant for several corporations and is author of *Prevent a Second Heart Attack* (Three Rivers). *www.drjanet.com*

Deborah Klein, RD, registered dietitian in California (*www.livitician.com*) and author of *The 200 SuperFoods That Will Save Your Life* (McGraw-Hill).

Now there's a reason other than romance for putting chocolates in heart-shaped boxes—recent studies confirm that eating a little bit of the confection every day is one of the best gifts you can give your heart, your arteries and your entire cardiovascular system.

Here's a sampler of recent research…

High Blood Pressure

High blood pressure—a reading of 140/90 to 159/99—damages arteries and is a major risk factor for heart attack and stroke. Chocolate can help keep high blood pressure under control.

● **Safer exercise for people with high blood pressure.** If you're overweight, your blood pressure can shoot up during exercise because your arteries don't widen as well as they should.

Cocoa flavanols—potent plant compounds found mainly in dark chocolate—improve the health of the endothelium, the arterial lining that generates the chemical nitric oxide, which signals arteries to expand.

Researchers from the University of South Australia studied 24 overweight people, with an average age of 55 and an average blood pressure of 134/87 (an unhealthy level just below high blood pressure, called prehypertension). They divided them into two groups. One group drank a daily high-flavanol cocoa beverage and the other drank a low-flavanol beverage. A week later the groups switched, with the group drinking the high-flavanol cocoa now drinking the low, and vice versa.

Two hours after downing the beverage, the participants exercised at moderate intensity for 10 minutes on a stationary bike, while their blood pressure was continuously monitored.

The researchers also measured flow-mediated dilation (FMD)—the amount of blood flowing in an artery, an indicator of endothelial health. (The more flow, the better.)

Results: The people who drank the high-flavanol cocoa had a 14% lower increase in blood pressure during exercise, and a 68% lower increase in the diastolic (lower) reading. (Higher diastolic pressure is, by itself, a risk factor for heart attack and stroke.)

The high-flavanol group also had a 44% greater FMD.

"The consumption of cocoa flavanols could allow for safer and more efficient exercise performance in a population" at risk for heart attack and stroke, "thus placing less stress on the cardiovascular system," wrote the researchers in the *British Journal of Nutrition*. The study, they continued, "adds to the growing evidence that high flavanol cocoa consumption may benefit individuals with cardiovascular risk factors."

● **Lowering high blood pressure.** Researchers at the University of Adelaide in Australia analyzed 15 studies on dark chocolate and high blood pressure—and found an average drop of 5 points systolic and 3 points diastolic in people with hypertension and prehypertension.

Benefit: That's the same drop in blood pressure you're likely to achieve with 30 minutes a day of physical activity, say the researchers—and it can reduce the risk of a heart attack or stroke by 20%.

Reversing Heart Disease

Chocolate may help strengthen the weakened arteries of people with heart disease.

● **Repairing damaged arteries.** Researchers from the University of California-San Francisco studied 16 people (average age 64) under medical treatment for coronary artery disease. The study participants drank a high-flavanol cocoa beverage twice a day for 30 days, and then switched to a low-flavanol cocoa beverage for 30 days.

Their FMD was 47% better when they were drinking the high-flavanol cocoa.

They also had twice as many endothelial progenitor cells, a type of cell that helps repair and maintain the endothelium.

"This benefit is similar to that achieved by statins and with lifestyle changes such as exercise and smoking cessation," says Yerem Yeghiazarians, MD, the leader of the study, which appeared in the *Journal of the American College of Cardiology*.

The participants also had a drop in high blood pressure.

"It's not often that we're able to identify a natural food compound that can demonstrate a benefit on top of traditional medical treatment," says Carl Keen, PhD, professor of nutrition and internal medicine at the University of California-Davis, and a study author. "And perhaps most importantly, for the first time, we found that cocoa flavanols might even directly mobilize important cells that could repair damaged blood vessels."

Product: The study participants drank cocoa made from CocoaVia from Mars, a high-flavanol cocoa powder that delivers 350 milligrams (mg) of cocoa flavanols and 50 calories per serving.

• **Lowering LDL cholesterol.** Chinese scientists analyzed eight studies on dark chocolate and cholesterol, involving 215 people. They found that "cocoa consumption significantly lowered" bad LDL cholesterol by 6 milligrams per deciliter (mg/dL) in people with risk factors for heart disease, such as diabetes.

How it works: Flavanols inhibit the production and absorption of cholesterol… help cells process LDL so it doesn't stick to arteries…and cocoa butter contains a type of monounsaturated fatty acid that studies link to an "ideal profile" of cholesterol levels, explained the researchers in the *American Journal of Clinical Nutrition.*

Preventing Heart Attack and Stroke

But chocolate does more than help people who already have risk factors for cardiovascular disease or the disease itself. It can also help prevent the problem.

• **Less than an ounce does it.** In an eight-year study by German researchers involving nearly 20,000 people, those who ate the most chocolate (an average 7.5 grams [g] daily, about ¼ ounce, or one square of a 100-g chocolate bar) had a 39% lower risk of a heart attack or stroke than those who ate the least (1.7 g daily, about ⅟₁₆ of an ounce).

"Chocolate consumption appears to lower cardiovascular disease risk," concluded the researchers in the *European Heart Journal.*

• **Five times a week for protection.** Researchers from Harvard Medical School analyzed health data from nearly 5,000 people with an average age of 52. Those who ate chocolate at least five times a week were 57% less likely to develop heart disease than those who didn't eat chocolate. The results were in the journal *Clinical Nutrition.*

• **Staying out of the hospital**—and the cemetery. In a 10-year study of more than 1,200 women aged 70 and older, German researchers found that those who ate chocolate at least once a week were 35% less likely to be hospitalized or die from heart disease compared with those who rarely ate chocolate. The findings were in the *Archives of Internal Medicine.*

• **Less heart failure.** In a study of more than 31,000 women aged 48 to 83, those who ate one to two servings of dark chocolate a week had a 32% lower risk of developing heart failure compared with women who ate less chocolate, reported researchers from Harvard Medical School in the journal *Circulation: Heart Failure.*

• **Fewer strokes**—and fewer deaths from stroke. Researchers from the University of Toronto in Canada investigated the link between chocolate consumption and the risk of stroke—and found one serving of chocolate a week was linked to a 22% lower risk of stroke, and eating 50 g of chocolate a week (just under 2 ounces) was linked to a 46% lower risk of dying after a stroke.

The Chocolate Cure

"Dark chocolate is now the new, guilt-free superfood—isn't this the best nutrition news to come along in decades!" says Janet Brill, PhD, RD, a diet and nutrition expert, and author of *Prevent a Second Heart Attack* (Three Rivers). *Her recommendations for healthfully increasing your intake of dark chocolate…*

- **"It's the cocoa component of chocolate that contains the flavanols,** and dark chocolate has the higher percentage of cocoa," she says. "Sample several dark chocolate products until you find one that appeals to you."

Trap: "Watch out for impostors such as white chocolate, hot chocolate mixes, chocolate syrups and milk chocolate bars—all of which are low in flavanols."

Suggested intake: "I recommend you eat no more than an ounce [28 g] of dark chocolate a day, choosing a product with 70% cocoa," says Dr. Brill. "Keep in mind that chocolate is a treat and certainly not a low-calorie food. Most of the mammoth premium chocolate bars sold in the supermarket are 100 g, with a serving described as three or four squares. That's about 40 g—and that's much more than you should eat."

- **Cocoa powder: low calorie, low sugar, high flavanol.** Perhaps the healthiest way to increase cocoa flavanols in your diet is cocoa powder, says Dr. Brill. "Natural cocoa powders have the highest level of flavanols, followed by unsweetened baking chocolates, dark chocolates, and semisweet baking chips." *When choosing a cocoa powder, look for...*

- The words natural cocoa powder unsweetened on the label. (*Example:* Scharffen Berger unsweetened natural cocoa powder.)

- Cocoa powder produced using the Broma process—not using Dutch processing with alkali, which strips cocoa of flavanols. (Check for the word alkali on the label.)

Try this: "The best way to get your chocolate is with unsweetened cocoa powder," agrees Deborah Klein, RD, a registered dietitian in California and author of *The 200 Superfoods That Will Save Your Life* (McGraw-Hill). *Her suggestion...*

"For a delicious daily drink, mix one tablespoon of unsweetened cocoa powder with a teaspoon of agave nectar, in a mug of hot water, with a dash of cinnamon."

PART 2

Memory Problems &
Brain-Boosting Techniques

5

Prevent and Treat Alzheimer's/Dementia

The Real Truth About Alzheimer's Prevention

Marwan Sabbagh, MD, a geriatric neurologist and founding director of the Cleo Roberts Center for Clinical Research under the umbrella of the Sun Health Research Institute in Sun City, Arizona, one of 29 NIH-sponsored Alzheimer's Disease Centers in the US. He is author of *The Alzheimer's Answer* (Wiley).

We all want to do everything possible to avoid developing Alzheimer's disease and dementia.

The problem: Experts don't agree on whether anything we do to change our lifestyles will actually help.

The news media has recently reported a statement made by a panel of 15 scientists in the *Annals of Internal Medicine* that there's not enough evidence to recommend any particular lifestyle strategies to prevent Alzheimer's.

How could the panel make such a bold statement?

What the headlines missed: There is, in reality, a large body of scientific evidence suggesting that certain strategies do help protect against Alzheimer's disease—it is just that these interventions have yet to be definitively proven in clinical settings. Instead, the evidence we have at this time is basic scientific research, such as cellular and animal studies, as well as epidemiological research that analyzes large groups of people to discover factors that could be linked to either increased or decreased risk for Alzheimer's.

Clinical research, which tests a specific agent such as medication along with a placebo, always lags behind basic and epidemiological research because it is costly and difficult to conduct.

My advice: Follow well-known Alzheimer's prevention strategies. For starters, eat healthfully—ideally the Mediterranean diet, which features brain-healthy omega-3–rich fish and antioxidant-rich fruits, vegetables and nuts. And get regular aerobic exercise to stimulate blood flow to the brain. The most recent research links 45 to 60 minutes four days per week to reduced Alzheimer's risk. Pace yourself, and consult your doctor before starting any exercise program. *In addition, keep up with the latest research, and consult your doctor about incorporating simple, underrecognized strategies such as those described here…*

Avoid Copper

Current evidence: In basic research on animals and on the brain cells of people who have died of Alzheimer's, scientists at the University of Rochester Medical Center in New York recently found that copper damages the molecule that shuttles *beta-amyloid* out of the brain. Beta-amyloid is a protein that forms toxic chunks (plaque) in the brains of people with Alzheimer's, and it may play a key role in the development of the disease. This research builds on a decade of research linking excessive levels of copper in the body to Alzheimer's.

What to do: According to research published in *Chemical Research in Toxicology*, people over age 50 should avoid nutritional supplements that contain copper…take a 15-milligram (mg) zinc supplement daily, as zinc helps the body remove excess copper …limit intake of red meat, which contains a lot of copper…and use an effective filtering system to remove copper from drinking water.

My personal approach: Depending on the water source, tap water may contain significant amounts of copper even if the water isn't flowing through copper pipes. For this reason, I have stopped drinking unfiltered tap water. To remove copper from my drinking water, I use a reverse osmosis water filter to separate the water from potentially harmful substances.

Reverse osmosis filtration systems are found at home-improvement stores and online in tap or under-the-sink models (about $150) or whole-house models (up to $3,000).

Get Enough Vitamin E

Vitamin E has been studied for Alzheimer's for more than a decade, with a landmark study in *The New England Journal of Medicine* in 1997 showing that high doses of vitamin E were more effective than a placebo at delaying specific outcomes of Alzheimer's disease, such as nursing home placement. Now, a recent study connects high dietary intake of vitamin E to a reduced risk for the disease.

Current evidence: In a 10-year study involving more than 5,000 individuals, those with the highest dietary intake of vitamin E were 25% less likely to develop Alzheimer's than those with the lowest intake, reported Dutch researchers in *Archives of Neurology*.

What to do: Eat vitamin E–rich foods, which provide the full range of vitamin E nutrients. Most vitamin E supplements do not contain the entire class of these nutrients. The data now clearly support dietary sources of vitamin E over supplements. Aim to get 15 mg of vitamin E daily.

Top sources: Wheat germ oil (20 mg per tablespoon)…almonds (7 mg per ounce)… sunflower seeds (6 mg per ounce)…spinach (4 mg per cup, boiled).

Beware of Hospitalization And Anesthesia

Doctors have long known that some older adults develop Alzheimer's symptoms soon after being hospitalized.

Current evidence: Researchers conducted a six-year study involving almost 3,000 people age 65 and older who did not have dementia (cognitive decline most commonly caused by Alzheimer's). As reported in the *Journal of the American Medical Association*, those who were hospitalized for a noncritical illness, such as broken bones, experienced a 40% higher risk of developing dementia.

The researchers speculated that several factors might play a role in increasing dementia after the hospitalization, such as hospital-acquired infections…general anesthesia, tranquilizers and painkillers taken in the hospital…and the blood pressure and blood sugar problems that frequently arise during hospitalization. Research has linked each of these factors, in varying degrees, to the development of Alzheimer's.

What to do: If you are hospitalized, try to stay in the hospital for as short a period as possible. If you need anesthesia and have a choice between general anesthesia or local or spinal anesthesia, opt for the local or spinal. As much as possible, minimize the use of optional *psychoactive medications*, such as tranquilizers and sleeping pills.

Have a Purpose in Life

No one knows why people who feel that they have a purpose in life tend to be less likely to develop Alzheimer's, but it does seem to help.

Current evidence: In a study published in *Archives of General Psychiatry*, researchers at the Rush University Medical Center in Chicago found that older adults with a high score on a questionnaire evaluating one's sense of purpose in life (feeling that life has meaning and having goals that guide behavior) were 2.4 times more likely to remain free of Alzheimer's than adults with a low score.

Living Alone Raises Dementia Risk

In a study of 1,449 men and women, researchers found that those who were single or divorced during middle age had twice the risk for dementia later in life as those who were married or living with partners. The risk was seven times higher for those who were widowed during middle age and still lived without a partner 21 years later.

Theory: Social engagement promotes healthy brain function.

If you live alone: Aim to stay engaged by participating in social, cultural and recreational activities.

Krister Hakansson, research fellow, Aging Research Center, Karolinska Institute, Stockholm, Sweden.

What to do: Look for ways to add meaning to your life—for example, volunteer for your neighborhood association or for local organizations that strive to improve your community. The social involvement associated with volunteering also may help guard against Alzheimer's. Research has linked social connectedness to a decreased risk for the disease.

Alzheimer's Disease: Myths and Truths

Alzheimer's Association, 225 N. Michigan Ave., Chicago 60601, *www.alz.org.*

Alzheimer's disease is a frightening diagnosis—one that we all hope never to face. Unfortunately, there are many myths about what can cause Alzheimer's or increase your risk for the disease.

Here, we set the record straight…

Myth: Use of aluminum is linked to the disease.

Truth: No study has confirmed any link between Alzheimer's and aluminum.

Myth: The low-calorie sweetener *aspartame* causes memory loss.

Truth: There is no scientific evidence of this.

Myth: Flu vaccinations raise Alzheimer's risk.

Truth: Several studies show the opposite—that flu shots reduce risk for Alzheimer's. Previous exposure to specific types of vaccines may be related to a lower risk for Alzheimer's because aging and Alzheimer's may involve changes in immune responses.

Myth: Amalgam tooth fillings raise Alzheimer's risk.

Truth: There is no evidence that these fillings—which contain 50% mercury—are linked to Alzheimer's disease.

Reduce Alzheimer's Risk by 60%: Latest Breakthroughs in Prevention and Treatment

Marwan Sabbagh, MD, a geriatric neurologist and founding director of the Cleo Roberts Center for Clinical Research under the umbrella of the Sun Health Research Institute in Sun City, Arizona, one of 29 NIH-sponsored Alzheimer's Disease Centers in the US. He is author of *The Alzheimer's Answer* (Wiley).

The Alzheimer's Association has reported that one in eight Americans age 65 and over suffer from Alzheimer's disease. Two-thirds of those with the disease are women. (More women get Alzheimer's, in part, because they tend to live longer.) Many people think that not getting Alzheimer's is more about good genes than good health, but new research suggests that lifestyle factors, such as diet and exercise, play key roles.

Here's what you need to know about the latest scientific advances in the battle against Alzheimer's disease...

Prevention

The research shows that the primary feature of Alzheimer's disease—the accumulation of *beta-amyloid*, a protein by-product that wrecks brain cells—starts decades before the symptoms begin, perhaps even in a person's 30s.

How to help prevent or forestall that process...

● **Statins.** Researchers from the Netherlands studied nearly 7,000 people age 55 and older. They found that those who regularly took a cholesterol-lowering statin drug had a 43% lower risk for developing Alzheimer's than those who didn't take the drug.

Theory: Cholesterol may be a "cofactor" in beta-amyloid production.

Bottom line: More studies are needed to show that taking a statin can prevent Alzheimer's, so it's premature for your doctor to prescribe the drug for that purpose. But if you take a statin to control cholesterol, you may experience this very positive "side effect."

● **Weight control.** Researchers at the National Institutes of Health analyzed 23 years of data from more than 2,300 people. Women who were obese at ages 30, 35 or 50, with excess belly fat, had a nearly seven times higher risk for developing Alzheimer's. Men who gained a lot of weight between ages 30 and 50 had a nearly four times higher risk.

Theory: Excess pounds increase chronic low-grade inflammation...increase insulin resistance (prediabetes)...and may increase production of amyloid precursor protein—all factors that may increase the likelihood of Alzheimer's.

Bottom line: Keep your body weight within a healthy range by controlling calories and exercising regularly.

● **Fruits and vegetables.** Oxidative stress—a kind of "internal rust" caused by factors such as a diet loaded up with fat and refined carbohydrates...air pollution...and hormones triggered from stress—is believed to play a role in the development of Alzheimer's. In the laboratory, researchers at Cornell University exposed brain cells to oxidative stress and added extracts of apples, bananas and oranges to the mix. The extracts reduced *neurotoxicity*—damage to brain cells.

Theory: Fruits and vegetables are filled with cell-protecting and strengthening antioxidants that fight the oxidative stress that contributes to Alzheimer's.

Bottom line: Fruits that deliver the most antioxidants include blueberries, blackberries, cherries, red grapes, oranges, plums, raspberries and strawberries. Best vegetables include arugula, bell peppers, broccoli, bok choy, cabbage, collard greens, kale and spinach.

● **Alcohol.** Researchers at Stritch School of Medicine at Loyola University in Chicago reviewed data on alcohol intake and health and found that more than half the studies showed that a moderate intake of alcohol (one drink a day for women, one to two drinks a day for men) was associated with a lower risk for cognitive decline and dementia, including Alzheimer's.

Theory: Alcohol delivers potent antioxidants, and moderate intake helps reduce inflammation.

Bottom line: One to two drinks a day may slightly decrease Alzheimer's risk. One drink is five ounces of wine, 12 ounces of beer or 1.5 ounces of 80-proof liquor, such as vodka or gin.

● **Exercise.** Research shows that regular exercise can reduce Alzheimer's risk by up to 60%. A new study shows that it also may help slow the progression of the disease. Scientists at University of Kansas School of Medicine studied 57 people with early-stage Alzheimer's disease and found that those who were sedentary had four times more brain shrinkage (a sign of Alzheimer's) than those who were physically fit.

Bottom line: Aim for 30 minutes a day of exercise, such as brisk walking outdoors or on a treadmill.

Combination Treatment

Medicines can slow the development of Alzheimer's symptoms. Research now shows that combining particular drugs maximizes their effectiveness. The FDA has approved two types of drugs to treat Alzheimer's—*cholinesterase inhibitors*, such as *donepezil* (Aricept), which work by slowing the breakdown of *acetylcholine*, a neurotransmitter that helps brain cells communicate…and *memantine* (Namenda), which calms *excitotoxicity*, a type of cellular hyperactivity that harms neurons.

In a 30-month study of nearly 400 people with Alzheimer's, researchers at Harvard Medical School found that taking both drugs together is more effective in reducing Alzheimer's symptoms than taking either a cholinesterase inhibitor alone or a placebo.

Bottom line: Patients who begin both drugs at the time of diagnosis may significantly slow the progress of Alzheimer's disease.

What Doesn't Work

The following do not seem to be effective against Alzheimer's…

● **NSAIDs.** Various studies have linked regular intake of a nonsteroidal anti-inflammatory drug (or NSAID)—such as aspirin, *ibuprofen* (Advil), *naproxen* (Aleve) and *celecoxib* (Celebrex)—with a lower incidence of Alzheimer's. However in the Alzheimer's Disease Anti-Inflammatory Prevention Trial (ADAPT)—a study conducted by more than 125 researchers, involving more than 2,000 people age 70 and older—celecoxib didn't reduce the risk for developing Alzheimer's. Naproxen offered a minor effect that was

---

Veggie Juice Can Delay Alzheimer's

Delay the onset of Alzheimer's by drinking fresh vegetable juice. It has a concentrated array of anti-inflammatory vitamins, minerals and trace elements that promote cognitive health. Try juicing broccoli, celery, carrots and peeled cucumber with apples for sweetness to enhance day-to-day brain performance.

Best: Drink eight to 12 ounces per day, preferably using organic produce to avoid harmful chemicals.

Dharma Singh Khalsa, MD, president and medical director, Alzheimer's Prevention Foundation International, Tucson, Arizona, *www.drdharma.com*

outweighed by the fact that it increased the rate of heart attacks and strokes.

● **Ginkgo biloba.** A team of dozens of researchers led by scientists at University of Pittsburgh studied more than 3,000 people age 75 and older, dividing them into two groups. One group took a daily dose of 240 milligrams (mg) of ginkgo biloba extract, which is widely touted for invigorating the brain and improving memory. The second group took a placebo. Those taking ginkgo did not have a lower rate of developing Alzheimer's disease. See a doctor before using.

● **B vitamins.** Elevated blood levels of the amino acid *homocysteine* have been linked to Alzheimer's. Because B vitamins can lower homocysteine, scientists wondered if B vitamins could slow the development of Alzheimer's.

Researchers in the department of neurosciences at University of California, San Diego, studied 340 people with mild-to-moderate Alzheimer's disease for about four years and found that B vitamins reduced homocysteine levels but did not slow the progression of Alzheimer's disease.

● **Antipsychotics.** Alzheimer's patients often develop behavioral disturbances, such as wandering, agitation, aggression, paranoia, delusions, anxiety and hallucinations. A standard treatment is an antipsychotic drug, such as *risperidone* (Risperdal), *ziprasidone* (Geodon), *olanzapine* (Zyprexa), *quetiapine* (Seroquel) or *aripiprazole* (Abilify).

New danger: For three years, researchers in England monitored 165 Alzheimer's patients who had taken antipsychotics—continuing the drug in half the patients and switching the other half to placebos. After three years, 59% of those on the placebo were alive, compared with 30% on the medication. In other words, those who continued the drug had twice the risk of dying.

New approach: Researchers at Indiana University Center for Aging Research reviewed nine studies on the use of a cholinesterase inhibitor to manage behavioral symptoms and found it to be a "safe and effective alternative" to antipsychotics.

Alzheimer's Symptoms

● **Severe memory loss.**
● **Language problems, including difficulty finding the right word.**
● **Difficulty performing familiar tasks.**
● **Disorientation in regard to time and place.**
● **Changes in personality, such as increased irritability and hostility.**

■ ■ ■ ■

How to Cut Your Risk for Alzheimer's by HALF... With Simple Strategies

Majid Fotuhi, MD, PhD, assistant professor of neurology at Johns Hopkins University and director of the Center for Memory and Brain Health at Sinai Hospital, both in Baltimore. He is the author of *The Memory Cure* (McGraw-Hill) and co-author of *The New York Times Crosswords to Keep Your Brain Young* (St. Martin's Griffin).

Recent research shows that the prevalence of memory and thinking problems—including Alzheimer's disease and other forms of dementia—declined in the US by nearly 30% during a recent nine-year period.

Why did this happen? Partly because many adults are doing a better job at controlling significant dementia risk factors, including blood pressure (below 120/80 millimeters of mercury [mmHg] is optimal) and cholesterol (below 200 milligrams per deciliter [mg/dL] is the target for most people's total cholesterol).

But there are other strategies to reduce dementia risk even further. Although some vulnerability to Alzheimer's and other forms

118

of dementia can be genetic, an ever-increasing body of evidence shows that adopting a healthful lifestyle often can cut a person's risk by half. *What you need to know…*

Overlooked Risk Factors

Dementia will occur when cells in the brain are progressively damaged from excessive accumulation of proteins, such as *amyloid*. These proteins trigger inflammation, causing more damage to nearby brain cells. But that's not the only trigger. The brain needs a constant supply of oxygen, hormones and nutrients such as blood sugar (glucose). Interruptions in the supply—due to narrowed and blocked blood vessels, multiple small strokes that may pass unnoticed and even heart failure, kidney disease and chronic lung disease—can kill brain cells.

Other dementia risk factors that are sometimes overlooked…

• **Belly fat.** Abdominal fat is strongly linked to an increased risk for heart disease, and two recent studies have shown an association between belly fat and dementia.

Recent evidence: A study of more than 6,500 men and women, published in *Neurology*, found that those with the most belly fat during their 40s were nearly three times as likely to develop dementia over the next 30 to 40 years, compared with those who had the least belly fat.

Alzheimer's prevention step: Regardless of your age, strive for a fit body. Your waist measurement in inches should be no more than half your height, in inches.

• **Diabetes.** Recent findings support a link between diabetes and dementia. One Swedish study of 2,269 men found that those whose secretion of the hormone insulin was low in response to glucose at age 50 (a sign of impaired glucose metabolism that is likely to progress to diabetes) were significantly more likely to develop dementia over the next 32 years.

Excess Weight Linked to Dementia

Compared with people of normal weight, obese people were 42% more likely to develop some type of dementia…and 73% to 80% more likely to develop one of the most common types, *vascular dementia* (from reduced blood flow) or Alzheimer's disease (caused by waxy plaques in the brain). Underweight people had a 36% increased risk for dementia.

Best: Maintain an optimal weight.

Youfa Wang, MD, PhD, associate professor of international health and epidemiology, Johns Hopkins Bloomberg School of Public Health, Baltimore, and leader of an analysis of 10 studies on dementia, published in *Obesity Review.*

Alzheimer's prevention step: Your blood glucose level after fasting overnight should be less than 100 mg/dL. People with levels of 100 mg/dL to 125 mg/dL may be at risk for diabetes and should be closely monitored by their physicians. Readings of 126 mg/dL and higher indicate diabetes. Follow your doctor's advice on the frequency of fasting blood-glucose testing.

• **Smoking and heavy drinking.** People with a history of smoking or heavy drinking appear to develop Alzheimer's sooner than others.

Recent evidence: In a Florida study of approximately 1,000 people diagnosed with Alzheimer's, those who smoked more than a pack per day developed Alzheimer's 2.3 years before people who were not heavy smokers. Those who drank more than two drinks per day developed it 4.8 years earlier than those who drank less.

Alzheimer's prevention step: If you're a smoker, quit now. If you drink, ask your doctor whether moderate drinking is beneficial for you. Moderate alcohol consumption has been shown in some studies to

Memory Self-Test

Questions to ask yourself…

1. Have you ever gotten lost when you drive home?
2. Have you forgotten being at major appointments or events? Forgetting names of people you met at a recent party is not cause for concern, but forgetting that you attended the party could signal a possible memory problem.
3. Has anyone around you complained that you tend to repeat the same questions four or five times?
4. Have you stopped any of your hobbies or routines because of memory problems?
5. Have you reduced your work responsibilities or hours mainly due to poor memory? For example, did you take early retirement because you can't keep up with the same work you've done for years?

If you answered "yes" to any of these questions, speak to your doctor about getting a neurological evaluation.

help circumvent cognitive decline. Women should not exceed one drink (wine, beer or hard liquor) daily…men, no more than two drinks daily.

Exercise Really Does Help

Even if you are aware that exercise helps protect against dementia, few people realize just how important it is. Besides maintaining good circulation to ensure a steady supply of nutrients and oxygen to the brain, physical activity increases production of brain-derived *neurotrophic factor*—a protein that triggers brain cell growth.

Recent evidence: Sedentary retirees began walking three times a week. Just six months later, their brains—as measured by *magnetic resonance imaging* (MRI) *scans*—

had grown by 3%, on average, roughly the equivalent of taking three years off the age of their brains.

Alzheimer's prevention strategy: Get at least 30 minutes of moderate exercise (such as brisk walking) most days of the week. If you don't like walking, try dancing, cycling or golf. Any physical activity is better than nothing—and the more, the better.

Get the Right Brain Foods

Foods that help protect your brain…

- **The omega-3 fatty acids** are the most abundant of the *polyunsaturated fatty acids* that comprise up to 20% of the brain's volume. Some people get their omega-3s from fish-oil capsules—which contain both *eicosapentaenoic acid* (EPA) and *docosahexaenoic acid* (DHA). DHA is the most important for brain health and is recommended (along with EPA) for heart health by the American Heart Association.

Alzheimer's prevention step: Ask your physician about taking an omega-3 supplement that contains at least 400 mg of DHA per daily dose. Or eat two to three servings of cold-water fish (wild salmon, mackerel or sardines) weekly.

- **Antioxidants** protect the brain against cumulative damage caused by highly reactive chemicals known as "free radicals." A new eight-year study of 5,000 people identified vitamins E and C as particularly important for brain health.

Alzheimer's prevention step: Whenever possible, try to get your vitamins E and C from fruits and vegetables—this also will increase your intake of other powerful antioxidants. Kiwifruit, papaya and pomegranates are particularly good sources. Aim for four to five servings daily of fruits and vegetables. If you prefer a supplement, take 300 international units (IU) of vitamin E and 500 mg of vitamin C daily.

● **Curcumin** is the yellow pigment of turmeric, the primary ingredient in curry powder. Laboratory tests have shown that curcumin helps dissolve the abnormal amyloid formations of Alzheimer's disease.

Alzheimer's prevention step: Cook with curcumin (try it in curried chicken, soups and vegetables) or take a supplement.

Also helpful: A consistent regimen of "brain fitness" activities.

■ ■ ■ ■

The Power of Curry

Curcumin may *prevent* and *treat* Alzheimer's. This antioxidant and anti-inflammatory herb, used in curry powder, improves cognitive functions in Alzheimer's patients and decreases the inflammatory response that may lead to the disease's onset. Add curry to meals, or take a 95% curcumin supplement (daily dosage 250 mg to 500 mg).

Shrikant Mishra, MD, professor of neurology, University of Southern California, Los Angeles.

How to Cut Your Risk For Alzheimer's by 50%: "Brain Fitness" Activities Help Ward Off Cognitive Decline

Pierce J. Howard, PhD, a leading cognitive researcher and cofounder and director of research at the Center for Applied Cognitive Studies in Charlotte, North Carolina. He is the author of *The Owner's Manual for the Brain: Everyday Applications from Mind-Brain Research* (Bard).

It's so easy to blame fading memory and waning cognitive skills on advancing age. But in reality, age doesn't hurt the brain as much as unhealthful habits, such as a sedentary lifestyle…poor choices of food… excessive alcohol use…and chronic health problems, such as heart disease, high blood pressure, diabetes, obesity and depression.

Latest development: Although the evidence is not yet definitive, a growing body of scientific research suggests that people who incorporate a steady dose of mental challenges into their daily activities are less likely to suffer cognitive decline—including that associated with Alzheimer's disease.

For example, a landmark study of 678 nuns reported that although autopsies revealed some of them had late-stage Alzheimer's disease upon death, those who were mentally active did not develop behavioral symptoms of the disease while they were alive—perhaps because they had reserves of brain cells.

While some neurologists recommend crossword puzzles and the widely popular number-placement activity Sudoku to help promote brain fitness, there is a variety of other activities that are less well-known but perhaps just as effective—if not more so. By varying your brain-fitness workout, you will maximize the benefits.

My five favorites…

1. Adopt a "back-to-school" attitude. Until recently, scientists believed that we had a finite number of brain cells. Now, research has indicated that we are able to generate new brain cells (*neurons*) and connections (*synapses*) between them. Acquiring new knowledge and skills—no matter what your age—is one of the best ways to stimulate brain activity.

Even if you do develop all the classic brain changes associated with Alzheimer's disease, having a ready supply of additional brain cells may help protect you from the signs and symptoms of dementia. The key is to learn something brand new and mentally challenging.

What to try: If you enjoy books, read about an unfamiliar topic and grapple with it until you understand it. If you play music, learn a new piece—or better yet, a new instrument—and practice until you master it. Learning a foreign language (CDs are available at most public libraries) also promotes brain health.

Helpful: Devote the first part of the day to learning. At that time of day, you are less likely to be fatigued, and your attention will be better. During the day, review the material and other information you learned on previous days.

Smart idea: You can study a wide variety of subjects, ranging from pure science and the humanities to architecture and engineering, by enrolling in one of the 1,800 free college-level online classes offered by the Massachusetts Institute of Technology. To learn more, go to MIT OpenCourseWare at *http://ocw.mit.edu.* To learn a new vocabulary word each day, sign up for A.Word.A.Day at *www.wordsmith.org.*

2. Involve others in your brain workouts. Research shows that people who interact socially on a regular basis are less likely to suffer from cognitive decline—perhaps due to the soothing effects of the brain chemicals *serotonin* and *endorphins*, which are secreted during positive interactions with others. This, in turn, reduces levels of the hormone *cortisol*, which contributes to deterioration of the *hippocampus*, the brain's memory storage center. By involving other people in your brain activities, you not only challenge your cognitive abilities but also increase your social connections, thus further protecting your brain.

What to try: Chess, bridge, backgammon or board games, such as Stratego or Risk, that test your ability to strategize.

Also helpful: Increase your social interactions by joining a book club, a civic organization or a religious group. Or get involved in volunteer work.

3. Do brain-sharpening exercises online. For times when you are alone, online brain-training games are a good option. Researchers at the University of Michigan in Ann Arbor recently found that people who performed computer-based brain-training exercises for about 30 minutes daily boosted their ability to reason and solve new problems.

What to try: Play different games on different days. This helps to thicken the *myelin sheath* (fatty tissue surrounding nerve fibers) on existing neural pathways and fosters the emergence of new synapses. For a wide variety of free online games and brain teasers, go to *www.gamesforthebrain.com* or *www.sharpbrains.com.*

4. Surprise your brain with new habits. Experts call these exercises "neurobics," activities that jar the brain into forming new synapses by creating new associations. The idea is to do something familiar—but in an unfamiliar way. A good plan for doing this is to tweak one old habit every week. Find a pattern that works for you. Later, disrupt the pattern—to keep yourself on your toes!

What to try: Drive a different route to work…eat a type of ethnic food you've never experienced…if you wear your watch on your left wrist, try putting it on your right… switch the part in your hair to the other side…and brush your teeth or hold eating utensils with your nondominant hand.

5. Preserve your brain's equilibrium. As we age, changes occur in our sense of balance, which is controlled by signals that the brain receives from certain sensory systems. To adapt gradually to this change, we need to force ourselves to experiment with unaccustomed postures, which helps us become familiar with our new "internal gyroscope."

What to try: Whenever you're waiting in line, lift one foot off the ground and balance your weight on the other foot for as long as possible. Then, switch feet and rest your weight on the other foot. A good sense of balance helps prevent falls and preserves the brain's equilibrium.

Caution: If you feel unsteady on your feet, do not attempt this activity unless you can support yourself by holding on to a counter or railing.

■ ■ ■ ■

Alzheimer's Disease and Low-Calorie Diets: Small Dietary Changes May Protect the Brain

Giulio Maria Pasinetti, MD, PhD, director of Neuroinflammation Research Laboratories and professor of psychiatry and neuroscience and geriatrics, Mount Sinai School of Medicine, New York City.

Much of the newest research on Alzheimer's disease (or AD) has shown that lifestyle choices—exercise, eating a nutritious diet, not smoking and the like—may directly impact our risk for developing the disease, just as they do with cardiovascular disease. Some researchers at Mount Sinai School of Medicine in New York City have shifted their focus slightly, and are investigating if how much people eat might impact AD risk.

Previously the Mount Sinai researchers put mice that had been specially bred to develop Alzheimer's on a diet that was 30% lower in calories than normal. Surprisingly, the mice following this dietary regimen revealed at death a significant reduction of AD brain plaques.

In a follow-up study, the research team used squirrel monkeys—whose responses are that much closer to those of humans—and again put one group on a similar calorie-restricted diet. This time, monkeys were restricted not only to one macronutrient, but to an overall reduced access to food. When the monkeys died, the researchers discovered that the ones in the low-calorie groups were much less likely to have developed AD-type brain changes than those in the group eating a normal diet. Most interestingly, the researchers found that the calorie-restricted monkeys also had higher levels of *SIRT1*, one protein that has been linked to longer life spans and better health in old age and is receiving major attention because of being a target molecule involved in the treatment of AD plaques.

One of the lead researchers of the later study is Giulio Maria Pasinetti, MD, PhD, director of Neuroinflammation Research Laboratories at Mount Sinai School of Medicine. He says he is surprised by how even a minor change in what we eat seems to result in major changes in metabolic pathways and cognitive deterioration. He adds that there is now evidence that restriction of calories influences the way the brain utilizes glucose and consumes energy, and this might have a fundamental role in helping prevent Alzheimer's.

But most people would find a 30% reduction in calories from their normal diet draconian and impossible to maintain. Fortunately, it appears we won't have to—Dr. Pasinetti says that another mouse study is showing that even a 15% reduction would be sufficient to lower AD risk. And in yet another mouse study, the researchers found that a modest amount of red wine daily also produces a positive effect (making for some happy mice, one assumes), probably from the grape seeds used in making red wine and the fermentation process itself, says Dr. Pasinetti.

While his dietary studies continue, Dr. Pasinetti says they have enough findings now to advise healthy people to cut down calories by 15% each day (after consulting with your physician, of course—especially if you are on a low-calorie diet). For example, on a 2,000-calorie-a-day diet that would equal 300 calories. That's equal to just one serving of ice cream. Dr. Pasinetti points out that might be a small sacrifice for keeping your brain healthy as well as your body.

A Tasty Juice for The Brain

Journal of Alzheimer's Disease, www.j-alz.com.

Mice given the human equivalent of two glasses of apple juice per day produce less *beta-amyloid*, the harmful protein that's commonly found in the brains of Alzheimer's patients. The finding suggests that apple juice may be recommended in the future to help delay onset of the disease.

An Apple a Day Keeps Alzheimer's Away

Chang Y. Lee, PhD, professor and department chairman, department of food science and technology, Cornell University, Geneva, New York.

Apple skins fight Alzheimer's disease and cancer. They contain high levels of *quercetin*, an antioxidant that may fight cell damage linked with these diseases.

Best: Eat at least one red apple a day.

Quercetin also can be found in onions, raspberries, cherries, red wine, red grapes, citrus fruits, broccoli, leafy greens and green and black tea.

A Good Reason to Drink Fruit Juice!

Qi Dai, MD, PhD, assistant professor of medicine, division of general internal medicine and public health, Vanderbilt School of Medicine, Nashville, and leader of a study of 1,836 people of Japanese descent, published in *The American Journal of Medicine.*

Fruit juice may lower the risk for Alzheimer's disease.

Recent finding: Individuals who report drinking at least three servings of juice a week are 76% less likely to develop Alzheimer's than those who drink juice less than once a week. The research is preliminary and not conclusive—drinkers of juice may lead a more healthful life in general.

Popular Drink May Reduce Alzheimer's Risk an Impressive 65%

Study of 1,409 people over a 21-year period by researchers at University of Kuopio, Finland, in collaboration with Karolinska Institutet, Stockholm, Sweden, and the National Public Health Institute, Helsinki, Finland, published in *Journal of Alzheimer's Disease.*

Coffee may lower dementia risk. People who drink three to five cups of coffee daily in midlife are up to 65% less likely to develop Alzheimer's disease or other forms of dementia as they age, according to a European study. Further research is needed.

Can Olive Oil Fight Alzheimer's?

William L. Klein, PhD, professor of neurobiology and physiology at Northwestern University, Evanston, Illinois, and coauthor of a lab study.

A recent lab study looked at *oleocanthal,* a compound in extra-virgin olive oil.

An intriguing finding: Oleocanthal may protect brain cells from toxic proteins called *ADDLs* that are thought to contribute to Alzheimer's disease.

Theory: Oleocanthal alters the structure of ADDLs, inhibiting the toxins' ability to bind to and damage the synapses that allow nerve cells to communicate with each other. More research is underway—in the meantime, include extra-virgin olive oil in your diet.

■ ■ ■ ■

Can French Fries Cause Alzheimer's?

Richard M. LoPachin, PhD, neurochemist and director of research, department of anesthesiology, Montefiore Medical Center, Albert Einstein College of Medicine, Bronx, New York.

Researchers now have an abundance of theories on what causes Alzheimer's disease, but it's been challenging to nail down the scientific proof. Though the central cause has been elusive, one thing that all these researchers agree on is that early in the disease process, nerve endings in the brain get demolished. Now we have revealing research reported in the *Journal of Neurochemistry* that has unearthed one potential agent of destruction—a group of toxic chemicals called *type-2 alkenes* that damage nerve endings when they accumulate in the brain. The brain itself produces some of these *neurotoxicants* naturally, but others come from our environment.

A Dangerous Path

Richard M. LoPachin, PhD, a neurochemist and director of research in the department of anesthesiology at Montefiore Medical Center, Bronx, New York, and a researcher in Alzheimer's disease, says that years ago, he did animal research demonstrating that type-2 alkenes destroy nerve endings in the brain. Other studies have found an excess of these neurotoxicants in the brains of Alzheimer's patients. The recent research suggests that the damage originates when some of the brain's *mitochondria* (the power producers that exist in all cells) become dysfunctional, creating free radicals that ultimately generate the type-2 alkenes. Some individuals may be genetically predisposed to this type of mitochondria failure, and in these folks, the destruction is "a low-grade event that accumulates damage over many years," Dr. LoPachin says. It seems that such damage can be sped up with exposure to type-2 alkenes that we eat or breathe.

For instance, we do know that people who smoke are at higher risk for Alzheimer's—Dr. LoPachin says that he believes it is the type-2 alkenes in tobacco that cause this higher risk and notes that these neurotoxicants exist in other places, too, including in vehicle exhaust, industrial pollution and smoke from burning organic material, including fireplaces and coal stoves. As to those french fries, Dr. LoPachin explains that potatoes have a certain amino acid (*asparagine*) that reacts with potatoes' natural sugar at high temperatures to produce dangerous type-2 alkenes.

No More Fries?

Does this mean that you have to forever avoid fireplaces and french fries? Well, it's not a bad idea (especially the fries)—but fortunately research has identified natural compounds that are quite helpful in partially protecting the brain from the type-2 alkenes.

In particular, Dr. LoPachin says that *curcumin* (found in the spice turmeric and in curries that use it)...*resveratrol* (in red wine and grape skins)...and *phloretin* (apple skins) are strong *neuroprotectors*, but he adds that they are only a few among thousands of other protective *phytopolyphenols* in various fruits and vegetables. Researchers are attempting to isolate some of these compounds for potential use as therapeutic mediums, but Dr. LoPachin advises getting phytopolyphenols in their natural state by eating them in foods, where they are accompanied by other helpful cofactors and offer greater bioavailability.

Once again it seems that the real secret to minimizing the risk for dire health problems is quite simple—eat lots and lots of fruits and vegetables!

Another Reason to Lower Your BP

Cyrus Raji, MD, PhD, University of Pittsburgh School of Medicine and coauthor of a study of blood flow in the brains of older adults, presented at a recent meeting of the Radiological Society of North America.

High blood pressure may raise Alzheimer's risk. High blood pressure reduces blood flow to the part of the brain that controls memory and learning.

Self-defense: Exercise and proper diet are very effective at keeping blood pressure down. Ask your doctor what is best for you.

Dementia Danger

T. Jared Bunch, MD, assistant professor, department of cardiology, Intermountain Medical Center, Murray, Utah.

In a new study of 37,025 men and women, researchers found that patients with *atrial fibrillation* (AF)—irregular heartbeat—were 44% more likely to develop dementia than those without the condition.

Theory: AF increases risk for stroke, and multiple small strokes over time can lead to dementia.

If you have AF: Ask your doctor about treatment options to lower high blood pressure, reduce stroke risk and restore your heart to a normal rhythm.

Can Alzheimer's Be Prevented with BP Meds?

Benjamin Wolozin, MD, PhD, professor of pharmacology and neurology, Boston University School of Medicine, Boston.

A recent study finds that a type of blood pressure medication—*angiotensin receptor blocker* (ARB)—was associated with a decreased risk for dementia in seniors and slows its progress in cases where it is already diagnosed.

A study of the medical records of five million people found that patients taking ARBs had a 35% to 40% lower chance of getting Alzheimer's disease or other forms of dementia, while patients taking ARBs who were already suffering from Alzheimer's or other forms of dementia had up to a 45% lower chance of developing delirium, being admitted to nursing homes or dying. How ARBs might produce this benefit is not certain. Consult your doctor.

Hypertension Drugs May Fight Alzheimer's One Day

Giulio Maria Pasinetti, MD, PhD, Mount Sinai School of Medicine, New York City, and leader of the mouse study, published in *The Journal of Clinical Investigation.*

In experiments on mice genetically at risk for Alzheimer's, seven of 55 hypertension drugs tested slowed the buildup of *beta-amyloid proteins*, which form plaque in the brains of people with Alzheimer's.

Hormone That Increases Alzheimer's Risk

Mirjam I. Geerlings, PhD, associate professor, University Medical Center Utrecht, the Netherlands.

Estrogen has been linked to Alzheimer's disease in older men.

Background: Men typically have lower levels of the hormone estrogen than women. However, beyond menopause women have lower estrogen levels than men of the same age.

Recent study: Over an average of six years, researchers evaluated hormone levels and cognitive function in 2,974 men ages 71 to 93.

Result: The risk for Alzheimer's rose with increasing levels of estrogen.

Theory: The production of estrogen involves *aromatase*, an enzyme that, in some cases, may serve as a marker for Alzheimer's. Previous research found a similar link in women. More studies are needed.

Alzheimer's May Be Associated with Lead Poisoning

Nasser Zawia, PhD, associate professor of pharmacology and toxicology, University of Rhode Island, Kingston, and lead author of a study published in *The Journal of Neuroscience.*

Alzheimer's may be linked to lead poisoning during infancy, according to an animal study.

Recent finding: After 23 years, monkeys that had been given a lead-laced baby formula had higher levels of Alzheimer's-related proteins and damage to DNA than monkeys given ordinary formula.

Dementia/Infection Connection

Theodore J. Iwashyna, MD, PhD, assistant professor of internal medicine, University of Michigan Medical School, Ann Arbor, and lead author of a study of 5,093 patients, published in *The Journal of the American Medical Association,* online at *http:jama.ama-assn.org.*

Dementia may be linked to *sepsis.* Sepsis, a life-threatening blood infection, kills about one-third of those affected.

Recent finding: Elderly patients who survive severe sepsis are more than three times as likely as other elderly patients to experience long-term impairment of cognitive function.

Talk to your doctor about steps to prevent and treat sepsis.

Cold Sore/Alzheimer's Link?

University of Rochester Medical Center, www.urmc. rochester.edu.

In animal studies, a gene that increases risk for Alzheimer's was associated with a hospitable environment for the *herpes simplex 1 virus* that causes cold sores. Researchers will continue to investigate how herpes might affect the development of Alzheimer's disease.

Maternal Genes Raise Alzheimer's Risk

Lisa Mosconi, PhD, research assistant professor of psychiatry, New York University School of Medicine, New York City, and leader of a study of 49 people, published online in *Proceedings of the National Academy of Sciences.*

People whose mothers had Alzheimer's might be at higher risk for the disease than people whose fathers had it.

Recent finding: Adult children of women who had Alzheimer's showed reductions in utilization of sugar in the brain—glucose (sugar) was available, but the brain wasn't using it properly. Decreased sugar utilization is common in Alzheimer's patients.

Theory: Maternally inherited genes may alter brain metabolism. Identifying individuals at risk may enable earlier intervention.

Also, for people with a maternal link it may help to keep weight and blood pressure down and to stay mentally active.

A Little-Known Finding

Nikolaos Scarmeas, MD, assistant professor of neurology, Taub Institute, Columbia University, New York City, and leader of a study of 312 Alzheimer's patients, published in *Journal of Neurology, Neurosurgery and Psychiatry.*

Alzheimer's often develops more quickly in people with higher educations than in less-educated people.

Study: Although highly educated people typically are diagnosed with Alzheimer's disease later in life than less-educated people—probably because they can compensate for the memory loss for a longer time—once the disease becomes apparent, they lose their memory at a faster rate.

A Dementia-Safe Personality?

Rush University Medical Center, www.rush.edu.

In one recent finding, people with organized and purposeful personalities were less likely to get Alzheimer's disease. It is possible that these people develop more *neural connections*, which can protect against mental decline.

Calm Disposition = Reduced Dementia Risk

Hui-Xin Wang, PhD, research scientist at Aging Research Center, Karolinska Institute, Stockholm, Sweden.

Calm people are less likely to develop dementia.

Recent finding: In a study of 506 older adults (median age 82), researchers found that those with calm, laid-back personalities were 50% less likely to develop dementia than those who were prone to distress.

Theory: Chronic stress can affect the *hippocampus*—the portion of the brain that helps regulate memory and emotion—possibly leading to dementia.

To guard against this ill effect of stress: Participate in physical, social and mentally challenging activities.

Alzheimer's Indicator

Stephen McConnell, PhD, vice president for advocacy and public policy, Alzheimer's Association, Chicago.

One of the first signs of early-stage Alzheimer's disease is difficulty handling financial affairs. So for that reason, people who have even mild symptoms should immediately get help managing their affairs before the disease progresses. They also should speak to their doctors about treatment options.

Symptoms to watch for: Forgetting to pay bills or paying them more than once… difficulty balancing the checkbook or doing simple calculations…increased susceptibility to scam artists.

If you or a loved one is showing any of these signs: A relative or close friend can be given "financial power of attorney" to handle financial duties if it becomes necessary.

Early Alzheimer's Harms Driving Skills

Jeffrey Dawson, ScD, departments of biostatistics and neurology, University of Iowa, Iowa City, and leader of a study of 155 older people, including 40 with early-stage Alzheimer's, funded by the National Institute on Aging and published in *Neurology.*

Warning signs of Alzheimer's include loss of memory and cognitive abilities, such as needing more help than before with directions or a new route…getting lost on once-familiar roads…having trouble with turns, especially left turns…becoming very confused when exiting the highway…being honked at frequently by other drivers…and drifting in and out of the proper lane.

What to do: If you notice these signs in yourself or a family member, talk to a doctor.

An idea: Consider consulting a driver-rehabilitation specialist who can provide a comprehensive evaluation to determine one's ability to drive a car and/or provide rehabilitation to strengthen driving skills—find one from the American Occupational Therapy Association, 301-652-2682, *www.aota.org/olderdriver.*

Eye Test for Alzheimer's

Cell Death & Disease, www.nature.com/cddis/index.html.

A simple, noninvasive test that measures damage to cells in the retina of the eye can reveal stages of cell death in the brain. The technique is being tested and could allow doctors to diagnose and treat Alzheimer's at an earlier stage.

Test Detects Alzheimer's *Early*

Leslie Shaw, PhD, professor, department of pathology and lab medicine at University of Pennsylvania Medical School, Philadelphia.

A spinal test can detect Alzheimer's early. The test measures proteins in the spinal fluid and is *87% accurate* in predicting Alzheimer's in patients who have early cognitive impairment but before full dementia symptoms appear. Early diagnosis allows doctors to provide medication to slow the progression of the disease.

Note: The test was also 95% accurate in ruling out Alzheimer's in those tested in a clinical study.

A Computer Diagnosis That's 96% Accurate!

Wellcome Trust, www.wellcome.ac.uk.

Computers diagnose Alzheimer's disease with up to 96% accuracy, compared with the 86% accuracy rate for diagnoses by physicians. Computers can analyze a *magnetic resonance imaging* (MRI) *scan* and pick up characteristic Alzheimer's brain changes.

Alzheimer's Symptoms Reversed?

Edward Tobinick, MD, director, Institute of Neurological Research, University of California, Los Angeles, and leader of several studies involving a total of 18 Alzheimer's patients.

The immune disorder drug *etanercept* (Enbrel) deactivates *tumor necrosis factor-alpha* (TNF), part of the immune system. Excess TNF is present in the *cerebrospinal fluid* of Alzheimer's patients.

In preliminary studies: Alzheimer's patients receiving weekly etanercept spinal injections showed improved attention, memory and language—in one case, within minutes of the first injection. More research is needed.

Drugs for Alzheimer's Need to Be Started *Early*

Richard Powers, MD, chair of the medical advisory board, Alzheimer's Foundation of America (*alzfdn.org*), and senior scientist/associate director, Alzheimer's Disease Research Center, University of Alabama, Birmingham.

Drugs that slow Alzheimer's disease work best when taken early on.

Problem: Many Alzheimer's patients exhibit symptoms years prior to being diagnosed. Warning signals include short-term loss of memory, confusion about time and place, and changes in mood or personality. If you detect symptoms, consult a geriatrician who can do an evaluation.

Treatments for Behavioral Problems in Alzheimer's

Noll L. Campbell, PharmD, clinical pharmacy specialist in geriatrics, Wishard Health Services, Indianapolis.

Cholinesterase inhibitor medicines, such as *donepezil* (Aricept) and *rivastigmine* (Exelon), which are prescribed to help slow progression of cognitive impairment in Alzheimer's disease patients, also decrease such symptoms as aggression, paranoia and wandering, with no significant side effects, according to a recent review of nine studies.

Important: The cholinesterase inhibitors typically are advised for less than 10% of Alzheimer's patients seen in primary care practice—and for fewer than three months, on average—even though 90% of patients have some type of behavioral and psychological symptoms.

Possible reasons: Dementia often goes unrecognized by primary care physicians… and because of the stigma attached to a dementia diagnosis, many patients and doctors may not pursue treatment options. If a family member has Alzheimer's disease, ask his/her doctor whether a cholinesterase inhibitor might be helpful. A growing body of evidence shows that atypical antipsychotics, such as *risperidone* (Risperdal) and *quetiapine* (Seroquel), which have been used for behavioral problems in elderly dementia patients, may hasten their death (due to cardiovascular events or pneumonia).

Skin Patch for Alzheimer's

William Thies, PhD, vice president, medical and scientific relations, Alzheimer's Association, Chicago.

A skin patch treats dementia in people with a mild-to-moderate case of Alzheimer's. The patch contains *rivastigmine* (Exelon), a drug previously available only in capsule form and as an oral solution. The patch delivers the drug continuously throughout the day and causes fewer gastrointestinal side effects, such as nausea and vomiting, than the oral forms.

When Less Is More...

Jacqueline Birks, senior medical statistician, Centre for Statistics in Medicine, University of Oxford, UK, and lead author of a review of studies involving 4,775 people.

The *rivastigmine* (Exelon) skin patch improves symptoms of Alzheimer's disease, but very often causes side effects (diarrhea, vomiting, poor appetite, dizziness).

Finding: Two-thirds of patients using a 17.4-milligram (mg) patch daily had one or more side effects...versus only half of patients using a 9.6-mg skin patch. Both groups scored similarly on cognitive tests.

Help for Severe Alzheimer's

Sandra E. Black, MD, professor of neurology, Sunnybrook Health Sciences Centre, University of Toronto, Canada, and leader of a study of 343 people, published in *Neurology*.

The drug *donepezil*—already prescribed for mild-to-moderate-stage Alzheimer's symptoms—preserves cognitive function in late-stage Alzheimer's patients as well.

A recent finding: 63% of patients who took donepezil exhibited stable or improved memory, speech, attention and recognition of their own names. The donepezil patients also showed slower declines in overall social functioning than the placebo users.

Alzheimer's Antidote?

The Lancet, www.thelancet.com.

The drug Dimebon, originally approved as an antihistamine in Russia, may improve cognitive and functional abilities in Alzheimer's patients—it is the first drug to promote continued improvement over a 12-month period. More research is needed.

Bacteria for Alzheimer's?

American Friends of Tel Aviv University, www.aftau.org.

In a novel approach to Alzheimer's, a bacterial virus (*phage*) is introduced through the nose, goes to the brain and dissolves disease-causing plaques. Mice given phage for one year had 80% fewer plaques than untreated mice.

Better Therapy for Alzheimer's/Sleep Apnea Sufferers

Sonia Ancoli-Israel, PhD, professor of psychiatry at University of California, San Diego School of Medicine.

Fifty-two Alzheimer's patients who also had obstructive sleep apnea (repeated breathing interruptions throughout sleep) received *continuous positive airway pressure* (CPAP) *treatment* (a special device is worn over the nose to assist breathing during sleep).

Result: After three weeks, the patients' neurological scores significantly improved.

Theory: Decreased oxygen levels and interrupted sleep could worsen cognitive function.

■ ■ ■ ■

Combined Dementia Therapy

Sandy Burgener, PhD, associate professor, University of Illinois, Urbana, and leader of a study of 46 people published in *American Journal of Alzheimer's Disease and Other Dementias.*

Early-stage dementia patients participated in sessions of *tai chi* (gentle martial arts movements with meditation) three times every week...plus biweekly support groups, mental exercise sessions and cognitive behavioral therapy (which bolsters positive thoughts and behaviors). After 20 weeks, patients showed improved self-esteem and cognitive function. A control group that did not attend showed no improvement.

Referrals: American Tai Chi Association (*www.americantaichi.net*)...Association for Behavioral and Cognitive Therapies (212-647-1890, *www.abct.org*).

■ ■ ■ ■

For the Alzheimer's Caregiver: How to Cope With Behavior Problems

Victor A. Molinari, PhD, a psychologist and professor in the department of aging and mental health disparities at Florida Mental Health Institute of the University of South Florida in Tampa. He is coeditor with Sheila LoboPrabhu, MD, and James Lomax, MD, of *Supporting the Caregiver in Dementia* (Johns Hopkins University Press).

Alzheimer's disease robs its victims not only of memories and mental abilities, but also of the ability to control their behavior. This leaves the family caregivers struggling to cope with their loved ones' behavioral problems—and even can provoke regrettable behavior from frustrated caregivers themselves. *Why this happens...*

• **Nine out of 10 Alzheimer's disease patients display some behavioral and psychological symptoms,** such as yelling, restlessness and/or delusions, at some point. Often family members are on the receiving end of verbal or physical aggression. For caregivers who are constantly giving of themselves, this can be very upsetting.

• **Spending an average of 100 hours a week taking care of a loved one leaves caregivers with no time to exercise or see friends.** Isolation is one reason why depression is more common among caregivers than non-caregivers.

• **Family caregivers often deplete their own finances to deal with their loved ones' needs.** Caregivers with full-time jobs miss more than three weeks of work per year, on average...20% quit their jobs. The financial burden is extremely stressful.

As the strain mounts, many caregivers cannot help lashing out.

Recent study: 52% of people caring for a relative with dementia admit to screaming at, swearing at or threatening their loved ones. Caregivers then feel guilty, which can add to their stress. *What helps…*

Working with the Doctor

The more effectively you can communicate with your loved one's doctor, the more likely the patient is to receive treatment that minimizes behavioral difficulties. *Ask the doctor about…*

● **Cholinesterase inhibitors.** These prescription drugs, such as *donepezil* (Aricept) and *rivastigmine* (Exelon), generally are used to treat cognitive symptoms of Alzheimer's.

New finding: These drugs also reduce behavioral/psychological symptoms, such as aggression, wandering and paranoia.

How: Alzheimer's patients have depleted levels of *acetylcholine*, the brain chemical that helps with cognition, memory and judgment. By raising acetylcholine, cholinesterase inhibitors promote communication between the nerve cells, stabilizing or even improving symptoms. If your loved one experiences digestive problems with one drug, consider trying a different one.

● **Sleep disorders.** Up to 80% of Alzheimer's patients exhibit sleep apnea (frequent breaks in breathing when sleeping). Apnea reduces oxygen in the brain, impairs cognition and triggers sleep deprivation—all of which can negatively impact behavior.

New hope: Patients showed cognitive improvement after three weeks of *continuous positive airway pressure* (CPAP) *treatment.* The CPAP machine provides pressurized air via a face mask worn during sleep.

Handling Problem Behaviors

Practical strategies help reduce negative behaviors. *Here's how to deal with your loved one's…*

● **Agitation.** Alzheimer's patients often get upset, act restless or pace around. Keep a log to help you identify circumstances that provoke these reactions, then develop a plan to work around such triggers.

Example: If your loved one gets upset when you try to bathe him in the morning, try it in the afternoon instead. Once you find a routine that is comfortable for your loved one, stick with it. Isolation and understimulation also can provoke agitation, so strive to keep your loved one active and engaged during the day—for instance, by listening to music or going for a walk together.

● **Aggression.** Shouting, shoving and hitting can be signs of frustration or pain.

To avoid triggers: Protect your loved one from overstimulation (from extra clutter or noise)…confusion (from being given too many instructions)…and physical discomfort (from medication side effects or an unnoticed injury).

Soothing: Try to maintain a calm and reassuring demeanor, refrain from arguing or lecturing—and do not take your loved one's behavior personally.

● **Wandering.** Place a substantial, solid-colored, dark, rubber-backed mat in front of each door to the outside. Your loved one probably won't remember if you say not to go past that point—but mats act as visual deterrents, discouraging an Alzheimer's patient from leaving home unattended.

Also: Install sliding bolts high enough on each door that a person must reach up to unlock them (but not so high as to impede the family's departure in an emergency, such as a fire). Chances are that a person with advanced Alzheimer's will not figure out how to open them.

New technology: The Alzheimer's Association Comfort Zone program includes a GPS-like service that alerts you (via telephone or the Internet) to your loved one's location.

Information: 877-259-4850, *www.alz.org/ comfortzone.*

● **Restlessness at nightime.** Many Alzheimer's patients suffer disturbances in *circadian rhythms* that affect sleep cycles and alertness. Keep the house brightly lit between 7 pm and 9 pm each evening…then help your loved one get ready for bed, following a consistent routine. This helps normalize his/her body clock, improving sleep and decreasing nocturnal disturbances.

Finding Support

Compared with caregivers who have little support from others, those who obtain the most support keep their loved ones at home longer…feel healthier…and find caregiving more rewarding. *Best…*

● **Ask family and friends for help.** Be specific. Instead of saying, "Can you help me out sometime?" say, "Can you watch Mom for three hours on Monday?" Having even a few hours off a week helps significantly.

● **Reach out to support organizations.** The Alzheimer's Association (800-272-3900, *www.alz.org*) offers a toll-free helpline, guidance on financial and legal matters, online message boards, information on local support groups and more.

Also helpful: Alzheimer's Disease Education and Referral Center (800-438-4380, *www.nia.nih.gov/alzheimers*).

● **Consider professional aid.** Your local Alzheimer's Association office can connect you with geriatric health-care professionals, meal-delivery programs, adult day-care centers and respite-care providers (who come to your home so you can have time off).

● **Recognize the rewards.** Many family caregivers report that they receive significant emotional benefits from taking care of their loved ones. You can, too, if you allow yourself to take pride in your ability to help and to find joy in your deepened sense of devotion.

Caregiver Relationship May Slow Disease

In a recent finding, patients who had close relationships with their caregivers retained more mind and brain function over time than patients who were not close to their caregivers. It is not very clear why—further research is planned—but closer caregivers may provide better supportive and overall health care. Also, Alzheimer's patients whose caregivers feel closer to them may be less prone to depression and have a better quality of life.

Constantine Lyketsos, MD, MHS, Elizabeth Plank Althouse Professor in Alzheimer's Disease Research and director, Johns Hopkins Memory and Alzheimer's Treatment Center, Baltimore, and leader of a multistate study of 167 pairs of caregivers and patients, published in *The Journals of Gerontology Series B: Psychological Sciences and Social Sciences.*

How to Talk to Those With Dementia So They Can Hear You

Kristine N. Williams, RN, PhD, associate professor, University of Kansas School of Nursing, Kansas City, Kansas.

Have you noticed how loudly some people talk when attempting to communicate with a person who doesn't speak English? They seem to think turning up the volume will bridge the language gap. Similarly it is common for many, including some trained professional caregivers, to use "elderspeak" with people who are old and infirm. It sounds a lot like baby talk, with very simple grammar and vocabulary and liberal use of terms of endearment, such as honey, sweetie and dearie. Though it may be done with the best intentions, a new study finds that when elderly patients are spoken to in this way, they often become angry, less responsive and harder to care for.

The study, led by researcher Kristine N. Williams, RN, PhD, an associate professor at the University of Kansas School of Nursing, videotaped interactions between caregivers (nursing assistants, nurses, therapists and social workers) and 20 nursing home residents with moderate dementia.

Using a measure called the "Resistiveness to Care Scale" to quantify the intensity of various care-disrupting behaviors (acts of withdrawal or aggression, such as grabbing onto a person or pulling one's own limbs tightly into the body, hitting, sobbing and kicking), researchers reviewed the tapes. When they witnessed such episodes, they rewound the tapes to see what kind of communications occurred in the preceding seven seconds.

Often (about 55% of the time), it turned out that the caregivers had been using "elderspeak," compared with the 26% of the time these behaviors arose when caregivers utilized normal adult communication. It seemed that the elders objected to being talked to in this childlike way. The researchers hypothesized that this form of communication often imparts a negative message of incompetence, which ends up irritating rather than soothing listeners.

Respect Your Elders

The National Institute on Aging and Dr. Williams offer these tips for communicating with those who have Alzheimer's disease or dementia...

- **Before speaking,** attract the person's full attention. Use his/her name.
- **While interacting,** turn off distractions such as the TV or radio.

Don't Talk Down

Don't talk down to Alzheimer's patients.

Recent finding: Individuals with Alzheimer's disease living in nursing homes who are spoken to as if they are children are more likely to resist care designed to improve their quality of life. There is not a need to use overly simplified grammar and vocabulary or intimate childlike expressions of endearment with individuals who have Alzheimer's. See more details at left and below.

Sam Fazio, PhD, director, medical and scientific relations, Alzheimer's Association, Chicago.

- **Speak in a tone that is calm and gentle,** without infantilizing. Dr. Williams also points out that nonverbal cues such as establishing eye contact convey your focus and willingness to communicate.
- **Use simple words and short, clear sentences**—but not baby talk.
- **If someone is having trouble finding the right words,** it's fine to help him/her out by gently making suggestions.
- **Be patient,** providing ample time to think and respond. It is important to give people with dementia time to compose and communicate their thoughts, says Dr. Williams. When you are patient, it shows you believe that what they have to say is important and that you are paying attention to them.
- **Do not talk about a person with AD or dementia** in front of him/her as if he/she was not present.

It is not so hard, actually—doesn't it really come down to using the same good manners we should be using anyway?

Cancer and Alzheimer's

Catherine M. Roe, PhD, research assistant professor, neurology, Washington University School of Medicine, St. Louis, and author of a study based on data from the Cardiovascular Health Study, published online in *Neurology*.

According to a recent study, Alzheimer's patients are less likely to develop cancer…and cancer patients are less likely to develop Alzheimer's. Patients who had Alzheimer's at the start were 69% less likely to be hospitalized for cancer after eight years than those who did not have Alzheimer's. People who had cancer were 43% less likely to develop Alzheimer's after five years than those who didn't have cancer. The links between the conditions may help researchers discover new treatments.

When It's NOT Alzheimer's: Little-Known Brain Disorders Can Cause Memory Loss and Unusual Behaviors

Muriel R. Gillick, MD, associate professor in the department of ambulatory care and prevention at Harvard Medical School/Harvard Pilgrim Health Care, and staff geriatrician at Harvard Vanguard Medical Associates, all in Boston. She is the author of *Tangled Minds: Understanding Alzheimer's Disease and Other Dementias* (Plume).

Memory-robbing Alzheimer's disease is the most common form of dementia, affecting more than five million Americans.

What you may not know: One-third to one-half of patients with dementia suffer from a non-Alzheimer's neurological disease that typically starts with symptoms other than memory loss.

In advanced stages, the symptoms of these other dementias resemble those of Alzheimer's disease. Besides suffering from memory loss, patients eventually have minimal ability to speak and/or limited ability to move.

Anyone who has problems with walking, planning activities or mood (such as apathy or depression) should be evaluated by a neurologist or geriatrician, who may suggest treatments that can help improve symptoms.

Non-Alzheimer's dementias…

Vascular Dementia

It's the second most common form of dementia in older adults, and the one that's potentially the most preventable.

Key symptoms: Difficulty performing mental tasks, such as balancing a checkbook or planning an activity, and problems with walking, bladder control and/or vision. Although memory loss is one of the first symptoms experienced by people with Alzheimer's disease, it typically occurs later in most patients with *vascular dementia*.

Vascular dementia can be caused by a single large stroke, multiple small strokes or narrowing of small blood vessels to the brain due to plaque formation (*atherosclerosis*).

Some patients experience symptoms of vascular dementia abruptly—for example, immediately after a stroke. More often, damage to the brain occurs over a period of years. A *magnetic resonance imaging* (MRI) *scan* of the brain often shows abnormalities in people with vascular dementia.

The same conditions that increase the risk for stroke—elevated blood pressure, diabetes and high cholesterol—also increase the risk for vascular dementia. Treatment of these conditions will not reverse cognitive changes but can play a significant role in prevention.

Recent finding: European researchers followed a number of patients age 60 and older for four years. All had hypertension, but none had signs of dementia. Those who were given the drug *nitrendipine*—a calcium channel blocker similar to the US drug *nifedipine* (Procardia)—to control hypertension were half as likely to develop vascular dementia over a four-year period as those who weren't given the drug.

Treatment: Alzheimer's drugs known as *cholinesterase inhibitors*, such as *donepezil* (Aricept) and *rivastigmine* (Exelon), may reduce symptoms of vascular dementia in some patients.

Lewy Body Dementia

Lewy body dementia, which typically occurs in adults age 65 and older, is named for Dr. Friederich H. Lewy, the scientist who discovered the disease's characteristic abnormal protein deposits that form inside nerve cells in the brain.

Key symptoms: Some are typical of Alzheimer's disease, such as memory loss and confusion, but others resemble those caused by Parkinson's disease, such as muscle rigidity. Lewy body dementia also causes visual hallucinations (seeing objects or people that are not really there)…delusions (a false belief that cannot be altered by a rational argument)…and fluctuations in alertness.

No one knows exactly what brings on Lewy body dementia. The protein deposits are often present in patients with Alzheimer's and Parkinson's diseases, suggesting that the conditions may be linked in some way.

To diagnose Lewy body dementia, physicians look for any progressive decline in cognitive abilities, along with intermittent episodes of hallucinations, a lack of alertness and Parkinson's-like symptoms.

Treatment: Parkinson's disease drugs, such as *carbidopa* and *levadopa* (Sinemet), to improve motor symptoms.

Warning: In some Lewy body patients, Sinemet may worsen hallucinations.

For hallucinations and delusions, low doses of antipsychotics, such as *quetiapine* (Seroquel) or *olanzapine* (Zyprexa), if necessary.

Warning: The antipsychotic medicines *haloperidol* (Haldol) and *risperidone* (Risperdal) worsen Parkinson's-like symptoms in patients who have Lewy body dementia. And some antipsychotics can cause dangerous side effects.

Frontotemporal Dementia

This is a rare form of dementia in which portions of the brain shrink, causing extreme changes in personality. Unlike other forms of dementia, which are most common in older adults, *frontotemporal dementia* typically appears between ages 40 and 60.

Key symptoms: Inappropriate public behavior, such as getting undressed in public…rude comments…a lack of inhibition…apathy and a loss of interest in day-to-day life…short-term memory loss…and compulsive behavior, such as constantly shutting doors.

No one test is able to diagnose frontotemporal dementia. Imaging studies of the brain, such as MRI, will sometimes show shrinkage of the frontal or temporal lobes. There are no treatments that can stop frontotemporal dementia or temper its progression. Most patients die within two to 10 years after the initial diagnosis.

Treatment for symptoms: Antipsychotic drugs (preferably low-dose) may be used to decrease agitation or compulsive behavior. However, research shows that these drugs are not very effective for this purpose and may even hasten death in older dementia patients.

Memory Robbers That Are Often Overlooked

Cynthia R. Green, PhD, assistant clinical professor of psychiatry at Mount Sinai School of Medicine in New York City and president of Memory Arts, LLC, *http://totalbrainhealth.com.* She is the author of *Total Memory Workout* (Bantam).

Alzheimer's disease is such a dreaded diagnosis that you may be filled with panic if you experience an occasional memory loss. But these worries may be unnecessary.

As people age, the brain undergoes changes that may lead to some decline in short-term memory. This is normal.

Of course memory loss that truly concerns you is another matter. *Ask your primary care physician to refer you to a neurologist or geriatrician for an evaluation if…*

• **You have noticed a significant change** in your everyday memory over the past six months.

• **Friends or family members have expressed concern** about your memory.

• **You have begun forgetting** even recent conversations.

In the meantime, think about whether your occasional forgetfulness may be due to one of the following causes, all of which can be easily corrected…

Not Enough Sleep

Poor sleep is probably the most common cause of occasional lapses in memory. The ability to concentrate suffers with insufficient rest. Sleep also appears to be essential for consolidating memory—whatever information you learn during the day, whether it's the name of a colleague or the street where a new restaurant opened, you need sleep to make it stick in your mind.

Self-defense: If you're not sleeping seven to eight hours nightly, make it a priority to get more sleep. If you are unable to improve your sleep on your own, talk to your doctor.

Widely Used Drugs

Impaired memory is a potential side effect of many medications. The obvious suspects include prescription sleeping pills…opiate painkillers, such as *meperidine* (Demerol)… and antianxiety drugs, such as *diazepam* (Valium) and *alprazolam* (Xanax).

Certain blood pressure–lowering medications, such as beta-blockers, and antidepressants also cause memory problems in some people. Even the over-the-counter antihistamines, including *diphenhydramine* (Benadryl), can have this effect.

If you're taking multiple medications, more than one may cause impaired memory, making it even more difficult to identify the culprit.

Timing is often a tip-off: When impaired memory is an adverse drug effect, it's most likely to appear when you start taking a new medication or increase the dosage. But not always.

As we grow older, our bodies become less efficient at clearing medications from the body, so the same dose you've been taking safely for years may cause problems you never had before.

Self-defense: If you think medication might be affecting your memory, do not stop taking the drug or reduce the dosage on your own. Talk to your doctor or pharmacist for advice.

Emotional Upset

Whenever you're anxious, stressed or depressed, your ability to concentrate suffers. Whatever it is that worries or preoccupies you keeps your mind from focusing on facts, names, faces and places, so they aren't absorbed into memory.

Self-defense: To help keep everyday tensions from undercutting your memory, practice some form of relaxation or stress reduction. Yoga, meditation, deep breathing—or something as simple as allowing yourself a soothing time-out to walk or chat with a friend—can all relieve accumulated stress and bolster your recall.

True depression is something else: Even mild-to-moderate depression can sap your energy, take pleasure out of life and affect your memory. If you suspect that you may be depressed, be alert for other symptoms—such as difficulty sleeping, sadness, apathy and a negative outlook—and see your doctor or a mental-health professional.

Too Much Alcohol

Moderate red wine consumption has been shown to promote the health of your heart and arteries. Because of this cardiovascular health benefit, red wine also may reduce risk for dementia.

Excessive drinking, on the other hand, is harmful to the brain. Among its devastating toxic effects is a severe and often irreversible form of memory loss called *Korsakoff's syndrome*, a condition that occurs in alcoholics.

Alcohol's effect on memory could be subtle. Some people find that even a glass or two of wine daily is enough to interfere with learning facts and recalling information. Pay attention to how mentally sharp you feel after having a drink. If you think your alcohol intake may be causing forgetfulness, cut back. Remember, tolerance for alcohol generally declines with age, giving the same drink more impact.

Self-defense: There is more scientific evidence supporting red wine's brain-protective effect than for any other form of alcohol. If you are a man, do not exceed two glasses of red wine daily, and if you are a woman, limit yourself to one glass daily.

Illness

A simple cold or headache is enough to interfere with your concentration and recall.

Illnesses that commonly go undiagnosed also may play a role. For example, when the thyroid gland (which regulates metabolism) is underactive, the mind slows down along with the body. (Other signs of an underactive thyroid include weight gain, constipation, thin or brittle hair and depression.) An overactive thyroid can affect your memory by making you anxious, "wired" and easily distracted.

Memory impairment also may be a symptom of other disorders, such as Parkinson's disease, multiple sclerosis or Lyme disease.

Nutritional Deficiency

An easily overlooked memory robber is a vitamin B-12 deficiency, often marked by general fatigue and slowed thinking. Older people are especially at risk—as we age, our ability to absorb vitamin B-12 from foods diminishes.

Self-defense: If you have occasional memory lapses, ask your doctor for a blood test to check your vitamin B-12 level.

Safeguarding Your Memory

Even if you've identified a relatively harmless cause for occasional forgetfulness, it's still wise to take steps to guard against cognitive decline in the future. *My advice…*

• **Get enough exercise.** Exercise helps prevent a wide range of serious health problems, including heart disease, diabetes and some types of cancer. The evidence also is strong that exercise protects against dementia—and enhances everyday memory performance by improving overall circulation and lowering risk for disorders that can affect memory, such as high blood pressure and obesity.

Self-defense: A leisurely stroll around the block may be relaxing, but you must get 30 minutes of moderate exertion (such as brisk walking or swimming), three to four days a week, to keep your memory intact.

● **Stay on top of chronic health problems.** Studies have shown repeatedly that people with high blood pressure, *atherosclerosis* (fatty buildup in the arteries), obesity and/ or diabetes are at dramatically increased risk of getting dementia in their later years.

But the effect of these chronic medical conditions on day-to-day memory is not so clear. Research indicates that memory declines when blood sugar rises in people with diabetes and improves when they take dietary steps to stabilize it.

Self-defense: If you have any chronic health problem, work with your doctor to keep your symptoms under control.

● **Give your brain a timed workout.** A growing body of research shows that mental exercise can help to fend off occasional forgetfulness.

Self-defense: Crossword puzzles and the number game Sudoku have gotten a lot of attention as "brain" workouts, but I prefer timed games, such as the word game Boggle or the card game Set (both available online or at discount stores). Racing against the clock gives your mental muscles a real workout.

■ ■ ■ ■

¿Hablas Español?

When researchers examined clinical records of 211 adults diagnosed with probable Alzheimer's disease, those who spoke multiple languages over their lifetimes showed initial symptoms of Alzheimer's an average of five years later than individuals who spoke one language.

Fergus Craik, PhD, senior scientist, The Rotman Research Institute, Toronto, Canada.

"Dementia" May Be a Drug Side Effect

Samuel Gandy, MD, PhD, professor, Alzheimer's disease research, Mount Sinai School of Medicine, New York City, *www.mountsinai.org.*

Don't assume that a diagnosis of dementia is accurate. Up to 10% of seniors diagnosed with Alzheimer's or other forms of dementia may really be suffering from drug side effects.

Most likely culprits: Sleeping pills, tranquilizers and beta-blockers used to treat high blood pressure, among other ailments. When you take several drugs of any kind (including over-the-counter drugs), unexpected interactions can bring on dementia-like symptoms.

Safety: Call your doctor at the first sign of memory problems arising after taking a new drug.

■ ■ ■ ■

Memory Loss Can Be Prevented!

Majid Fotuhi, MD, PhD, assistant professor of neurology at Johns Hopkins University and director of the Center for Memory and Brain Health at Sinai Hospital, both in Baltimore. He is the author of *The Memory Cure* (McGraw-Hill) and co-author of *The New York Times Crosswords to Keep Your Brain Young* (St. Martin's Griffin).

Alzheimer's disease is the most widely recognized variety of dementia. But there's another cause of memory loss that people should know about—but usually don't.

Vascular cognitive impairment (or VCI), which is typically caused by multiple small strokes, has been estimated to affect 1% to 4% of adults over age 65. However, because there is no agreement on the exact definition of this condition, the actual number of affected individuals is not known. Most older adults with vascular risk factors—such as high blood pressure (hypertension) and diabetes—may have varying levels of VCI.

Blood Vessels and Your Brain

The brain needs a substantial amount of blood—about 20% of the heart's output—to function normally. Even a slight reduction in circulation—such as that caused by small strokes—can result in symptoms, including slowed thinking, that can mimic Alzheimer's disease.

While genetics can play a role in Alzheimer's disease, VCI is widely recognized as the most preventable form of dementia. Even if you've begun to suffer early signs of this form of cognitive impairment (see symptoms at right), you may be able to avoid the devastating effects of full-blown dementia.

Hidden Blockages

Most people imagine stroke as a life-threatening event that brings on dramatic symptoms. This is true of major strokes. It is not the case with ministrokes, also known as *transient ischemic attacks* (TIAs).

When researchers at Johns Hopkins searched for the evidence of microscopic strokes—areas of brain damage that are too small to be visible on a *magnetic resonance imaging* (MRI) *scan*—they found that such strokes are extremely common. Millions of Americans with normal cognition, including healthy adults, have probably experienced one or more of these minor ministrokes.

What happens: Small, transitory blood clots can momentarily prevent circulation to small portions of the brain. Or *vascular hypertrophy*, an abnormal growth of cells inside blood vessels, may impede normal circulation. In either case, certain portions of the brain receive insufficient blood and oxygen. The damaged areas can be much smaller than a grain of rice.

Symptoms—assuming that there are noticeable symptoms—tend to be minor. People who have experienced multiple ministrokes that affect larger or more diverse areas of the brain are those most likely to develop dementia, but it might take years or even decades before the problem is severe enough to be diagnosed.

Symptoms to Watch For

Specific symptoms of VCI depend on the part of the brain affected. Patients who have suffered multiple ministrokes may walk or think more slowly than they did previously. Some will have trouble following directions. Others may feel apathetic or confused.

Some ministrokes, however, affect only the part of the brain involved in decision-making and judgment. The changes might be so subtle that a patient isn't aware of them—at least, until subsequent ministrokes affect larger or different areas of the brain.

Getting the Right Diagnosis

People who exhibit marked cognitive changes usually will be given an MRI or *computed tomography* (CT) *scan*. These tests sometimes reveal white, cloudy areas in the brain (*infarcts*) that have suffered damage from impaired circulation due to ministrokes.

Often, however, the ministrokes are too small to be detected. In these cases, patients may be incorrectly diagnosed with Alzheimer's disease. (The abnormal proteins that are characteristic of Alzheimer's cannot be detected by standard imaging tests.)

The distinction is important. There is no cure for Alzheimer's disease. In patients with VCI, there are a number of ways to stop the disease's progression and maintain long-term cognitive health.

Better Vascular Health

Brain damage that's caused by ministrokes cannot be reversed. Medication—including *cholinesterase inhibitors*, such as *donepezil* (Aricept)—may modestly decrease some symptoms in patients with dementia but cannot cure it.

Preventive strategies, however, can be very effective in people with VCI alone. *Most important…*

• **Don't let high blood pressure shrink your brain.** Chronic hypertension is one of the main causes of dementia because the vascular trauma is constant. People with uncontrolled high blood pressure actually have smaller brains because of impaired circulation. Their risk for developing dementia is two to three times higher than that of people with normal blood pressure.

My advice: Blood pressure should be no higher than 120/80 millimeters of mercury (mmHg)—and 115/75 mmHg is better. Most people can achieve good blood pressure control with regular exercise and weight loss, and by limiting sodium and, when necessary, taking one or more blood pressure–lowering drugs, such as diuretics, beta-blockers or ACE inhibitors.

• **Avoid the other "D" word.** By itself, diabetes can double the risk for dementia. The actual risk tends to be higher because many people with diabetes are obese, which is also a dementia risk factor.

Important research: One study found that patients with multiple risk factors, including diabetes and obesity, were up to 16 times more likely to develop dementia than those without these risk factors.

My advice: By adopting strategies that prevent hypertension, including weight loss and regular exercise, you will also help to stabilize your blood sugar—important for preventing or controlling the health complications associated with diabetes.

• **Keep an eye on your waist.** Obesity increases the risk for hypertension and diabetes and has been associated with damage to the *hippocampus* (the brain's main memory center). Obese patients also have a much higher risk for *obstructive sleep apnea*, interruptions in breathing during sleep that can increase brain shrinkage (*atrophy*) by up to 18%.

My advice: Measure your waist. For optimal health, the size of your waist should be no more than half of your height. Someone who's 68 inches tall, for example, should have a waist measurement of 34 inches or less.

• **If you drink, keep it light.** People who drink in moderation (no more than two drinks daily for men and one for women) tend to have higher HDL, so-called "good," cholesterol…less risk for blood clots…and a lower risk for stroke and dementia.

My advice: If you already drink alcohol, be sure that you don't exceed the amounts described above. Drinking too much alcohol increases brain atrophy.

• **Get the right cholesterol-lowering drug.** People with high cholesterol are more likely to develop *atherosclerosis* (fatty buildup in the arteries) and suffer a ministroke or stroke than those with normal cholesterol levels.

My advice: Talk to your doctor about statins, such as *atorvastatin* (Lipitor) and *simvastatin* (Zocor). These drugs not only reduce cholesterol but also may fight blood-vessel inflammation. Other cholesterol-lowering drugs—such as *resins*, which bind in the intestines with bile acids that contain cholesterol and are then eliminated in the stool—don't provide this dual benefit.

• **Ask your doctor for a vitamin B-12 test.** If your blood level is low, you may benefit from B-12 supplements or injections.

How's Your Memory?

Rebecca Shannonhouse, editor of *Bottom Line/Health*, Boardroom Inc., 281 Tresser Blvd., Stamford, Connecticut 06901, *www.bottomlinepublications.com.*

D octors have long believed that it is normal for the brain to shrink with age.

Now: Recent research suggests that loss of brain cells—especially in the *hippocampus* (a brain structure associated with memory)—mainly happens in people with neurological disorders that can lead to cognitive declines.

Even if you have a healthy brain, virtually everyone experiences some degree of memory loss. The challenge is to distinguish normal memory loss from that due to a disorder such as dementia.

Primary care physicians, neurologists and psychologists can evaluate a person's memory using a wide variety of tests. These may include tests that assess your ability to recall lists of words and visual information such as shapes and faces.

If you're unsure whether your memory should be tested by a doctor, says Paul R. Solomon, PhD, clinical director of the Memory Clinic in Bennington, Vermont, ask yourself...

• **Is it getting worse?** It's normal to occasionally forget a name or an appointment. Memory lapses that occur with increasing frequency could be a sign of dementia.

• **Is it causing any problems?** Abnormal memory loss often interferes with daily life—for example, you may chronically forget appointments or neglect to take medication.

Since half of people with Alzheimer's disease have not been diagnosed, you may want to also ask a loved one about your memory. If either of the questions above applies to you, see your doctor.

6

Brain-Boosting Foods And Supplements

The Ultimate Brain Foods: What to Eat and Drink to Keep Your Mind Sharp

Alan C. Logan, ND, a naturopathic physician and an invited faculty member in Harvard's School of Continuing Medical Education, Boston. Dr. Logan is author of *The Brain Diet* (Cumberland House). His Web site is *www.drlogan.com.*

If you are trying to do everything possible to keep your brain in good health, chances are your diet incorporates well-known brain-boosting foods, such as salmon (with its beneficial fatty acids) and blueberries (with their high antioxidant and anti-inflammatory content).

Exciting development: While scientists have long relied on animal studies to support blueberries' positive effect on memory, a recent study confirms a similar effect in humans. A recent study published in the *Journal of Agricultural and Food Chemistry* reported that when nine adults in their 70s who were experiencing early memory decline drank 2 to 2½ cups of juice made from frozen wild blueberries each day for three months, they significantly improved their performance on memory and learning tests

compared with seven adults who consumed a placebo drink.

Below are some less well-known options that can also confer significant brain-protecting effects (because the foods here contain a wide variety of important nutrients, it's wise to consume them even if you take brain-boosting supplements, such as fish oil or vitamin B-12)…

• **Purple sweet potatoes.** Like yellow or orange sweet potatoes, the purple variety is loaded with antioxidants. But purple sweet potatoes also have special antioxidants—purple pigments called *anthocyanins*. These pigments help to preserve the integrity of blood vessels that transport oxygen to the brain and improve signaling between nerve cells in the brain (*neurons*).

As we age, the integrity of small blood vessels delivering nutrients and energy—in the form of blood sugar (*glucose*)—to the brain diminishes. But our mental sharpness is dependent on a healthy blood supply.

For the greatest benefits: Aim to eat one medium purple sweet potato (available in gourmet supermarkets and Asian grocery stores) or one yellow or orange sweet potato twice a week. Instead of topping them with

Green Tea Boosts Brainpower

In a recent Japanese study of cognitive function in people age 70 or older, participants who drank two or more cups of green tea daily had a 54% lower prevalence of cognitive decline—measured via memory, attention and language-use tests—than people who drank three cups or less weekly.

Theory: Antioxidants in green tea may reduce the buildup of a type of plaque in the brain that is responsible for memory loss in Alzheimer's disease.

Self-defense: Drink two or more cups of green tea daily to help promote brain health.

Shinichi Kuriyama, MD, PhD, associate professor of epidemiology, Tohoku University Graduate School of Medicine, Sendai, Japan.

butter and/or salt, try eating oven-roasted sweet potatoes with the nutrient-rich skins.

- **Sardines.** When it comes to fish that provide the most brain-boosting omega-3 fatty acids, most people think of salmon, mackerel and herring.

Even better: Sardines (along with salmon, mackerel and herring) are less likely than larger fish, such as swordfish, shark and tilefish, to have high amounts of mercury and *polychlorinated biphenyls* (PCBs). Plus, sardines are budget-friendly and convenient because they are typically canned and require no cooking.

For the greatest benefits: Eat three to four servings of omega-3–rich fish, including sardines—about 3.5 ounces per serving (the size of a deck of cards) weekly. When cooking fish, trim the skin—this practice significantly reduces PCB content.

- **Omega-3–enriched eggs.** As a leading source of a valuable nutrient known as *choline*, eggs help protect against cognitive decline by facilitating efficient communication between neurons.

For the greatest benefits: Try omega-3–enriched eggs, which have an anti-inflammatory effect that also promotes brain health. Eat four to five omega-3 eggs per week.

Also important: The omega-3 content of eggs remains generally stable during scrambling and poaching, according to research. Hard-boiling may be somewhat less beneficial due to the breakdown of brain-boosting fats within eggs during boiling.

- **Ginger.** As an anti-inflammatory, ginger can preempt the manufacture of inflammatory brain chemicals and potentially can delay or slow down the progression of inflammation-related brain conditions, such as Alzheimer's disease.

For the greatest benefits: Add just one teaspoon of freshly grated ginger to your meals two or three times a week…or about one-half teaspoon of powdered ginger. If you prefer pill form, take one 500-milligram (mg) ginger capsule daily.

- **Green tea.** Green tea contains *epigallocatechin-3-gallate* (EGCG), an antioxidant that curbs brain-damaging inflammation.

Promising research: One recent study found that mice that drank water with EGCG for six months showed a 50% decrease, on average, in the *amyloid plaques* characteristic of Alzheimer's disease.

For the greatest benefits: Drink three to four (eight-ounce) cups daily. Decaffeinated green tea also promotes brain health but is less potent than caffeinated.

- **Coffee.** Regular consumption of caffeinated coffee can reduce risk for cognitive decline as well as *neurodegenerative diseases*, such as Alzheimer's and Parkinson's.

This brain-protective effect may be due to coffee's ability to protect the fat component of cells against oxidative stress. Since the brain is 60% fat, this could account for the positive link between coffee consumption and lower risk for neurodegenerative diseases.

For the greatest benefits: Consider consuming two to four (eight-ounce) cups per day of home-brewed coffee, which tends to have less caffeine than coffee bought at a coffee shop.

Helpful: If you are especially sensitive to the effects of caffeine or you suffer from insomnia, anxiety, high blood pressure or irregular heartbeat, moderate your intake of caffeine and/or try decaffeinated coffee, which still is a good, though somewhat less potent, source of antioxidants.

■ ■ ■ ■

The Most Powerful Brain-Building Nutrients And Herbs

Mao Shing Ni ("Dr. Mao"), PhD, DOM (doctor of oriental medicine), LAc (licensed acupuncturist), chancellor and cofounder of Yo San University in Los Angeles, and codirector of Tao of Wellness, a clinic in Santa Monica, California. He is author of numerous books, including *Second Spring: Dr. Mao's Hundreds of Natural Secrets for Women to Revitalize and Regenerate at Any Age* (Free Press). Go to *www.taoofwellness.com* for more information.

You open your cupboard but then can't recall what you wanted…you're introducing two friends and suddenly draw a blank on one's name.

Such instances of "brain fog" are common, but they are not an inevitable part of aging. Many people remain remarkably sharp all their lives—and the right nutritional strategies can help you be one of them.

Cognitive declines can be caused by hormonal changes and reductions in *neurotransmitters*, chemicals that help brain cells to communicate with each other. Increasing your intake of certain nutrients

helps balance hormones and protect neurotransmitters. *You can obtain these nutrients from…*

● **Foods.** Eating brain-boosting foods is an ideal way to get needed nutrients.

Reasons: The body is designed to absorb nutrients from foods rather than from isolated or manufactured chemicals (such as in supplements)…and foods contain complementary components that enhance nutrient absorption.

● **Herbs.** The healthful aromatic oils are most active when herbs are fresh, but dried herbs also will do.

● **Supplements.** These are an option if you cannot find the foods that provide certain nutrients, or if you need specific nutrients in quantities beyond what you typically get from food. Unless otherwise noted, the following supplements generally are safe, have few side effects and may be used indefinitely. All are sold at health-food stores.

Important: Ask your doctor before supplementing, especially if you have a health condition…take a medication…or are pregnant or breast-feeding. To reduce the risk for interactions, do not take supplements within 30 minutes of medication…and limit your use of these supplements to any four of the following.

Nutrients Your Mind Needs

For the following recommended foods, one serving equals four ounces of meat, poultry, fish or soy products…eight ounces of milk…two ounces of nuts…two eggs (with yolks)…one-half cup of vegetables or fruit… and one cup of leafy greens.

● **Choline.** The neurotransmitter *acetylcholine* plays a crucial role in learning and memory. Choline is a precursor to acetylcholine that is produced in the liver. Production of choline declines with age, as does the body's ability to efficiently use the choline that remains.

Brain boost: Eat one or more servings daily of choline-rich broccoli, cauliflower, eggs, kidney beans, navy beans, liver, milk or peanuts.

Supplement option: 1,200 milligrams (mg) daily.

• **DMAE (2-dimethylaminoethanol).** The body uses fatty acids to create brain cells and neurotransmitters. DMAE, a chemical in fatty acids, helps produce acetylcholine.

Brain boost: Have two servings weekly of DMAE-rich anchovies or sardines. If fresh fish is not available, consume canned water-packed sardines or anchovies and rinse before eating to reduce salt.

Supplement option: 500 mg twice daily after meals.

• **L-carnitine.** *Mitochondria* are the engines of cells. The amino acid L-carnitine transports fatty acids to mitochondria for use as fuel and provides nutrients to brain cells.

Brain boost: Have two weekly servings of lamb or poultry, which are both rich in L-carnitine.

Supplement option: 500 mg to 1,000 mg before breakfast and again in the afternoon.

Supplement option: 500 mg to 1,000 mg before breakfast and again in the afternoon.

• **Vitamin B-12.** This is key to red blood cell formation and nerve cell health. The body's ability to absorb vitamin B-12 diminishes with age—about 10% to 15% of people over age 60 are deficient in it.

Brain boost: Have two servings weekly of beef or lamb…halibut, salmon, sardines or sea bass…eggs…or vitamin B-12–enriched soybean products (miso, tempeh).

Supplement option: 500 micrograms (mcg) to 1,000 mcg daily.

The Most Helpful Herbs

An easy way to get the benefits of mind-sharpening herbs is to brew them into a tisane, or herbal infusion—more commonly called herbal tea.

To brew: Pour eight ounces of very hot water over one heaping tablespoon of fresh herbs or one teaspoon of dried herbs. Steep for five minutes, strain and drink.

Convenient: To reduce the number of cups needed to meet the daily recommendations below, brew two or more herbs together.

• **Chinese club moss.** This herb contains the chemical *huperzine A*, which helps conserve acetylcholine.

Brain boost: Drink one to two cups of Chinese club moss tea each day.

Supplement option: 50 mcg of huperzine A twice daily (discontinue if supplements cause gastric upset or hyperactivity).

• **Ginkgo biloba.** An herb, it increases blood flow to the brain's small capillaries and combats DNA damage caused by free radicals.

Caution: Do not use ginkgo if you take blood-thinning medication, such as *warfarin* (Coumadin).

Brain boost: Drink three cups of ginkgo tea daily.

Supplement option: 120 mg daily.

• **Kitchen herbs.** Oregano, peppermint, rosemary and sage have oils that may increase blood flow in the brain and/or support neurotransmitters, promoting alertness.

Brain boost: Use any or all of these herbs to brew a cup of tea for a pick-me-up in the morning and again in the afternoon.

Also: Use herbs liberally when cooking.

Supplement option: About 150 mg each of any or all of these herbs daily, alone or in combination.

● **Mugwort (wormwood).** This herb improves circulation, aiding delivery of nutrients to brain cells.

Brain boost: Twice a week, drink one cup of mugwort tea…or add a half-dozen leaves of fresh mugwort to salad…or sauté leaves with garlic or onions.

Supplement option: 300 mg daily.

Caution: Be sure to avoid mugwort during pregnancy, as it can stimulate uterine contractions.

Don't Forget Green Tea

Strictly speaking, an herb is a flowering plant whose stem above ground does not become woody. In that sense, the leaf of the *Camellia sinensis shrub*—otherwise known as tea—is not an herb. Yet green tea (which is less oxidized than black) is so helpful that it must be listed among the top brain boosters.

Along with antioxidant *polyphenols,* green tea provides the amino acid *theanine,* which can stimulate soothing alpha brain waves and strengthen concentration. Green tea also has been linked to a reduced risk for Alzheimer's disease.

To brew: Pour about eight ounces of very hot water over one teaspoon of loose, fresh green tea leaves (or a tea bag if fresh is not available) and steep for three to five minutes. You needn't strain the tea. As you empty your cup, you can add more warm water to the remaining leaves—as long as the water turns green, the tea still contains polyphenols.

Brain boost: Drink three cups of green tea (caffeinated or decaffeinated) daily.

Supplement option: 350 mg of green tea extract daily.

■ ■ ■ ■

Brain-Boosting Nutrients Women (and Men) Need

JoAnn E. Manson, MD, DrPH, professor of medicine and women's health at Harvard Medical School and chair of the division of preventive medicine at Brigham and Women's Hospital, both in Boston. She is one of the lead investigators for two highly influential studies on women's health—the Harvard Nurses' Health Study and the Women's Health Initiative. Dr. Manson is also author, with Shari Bassuk, ScD, of *Hot Flashes, Hormones & Your Health* (McGraw-Hill).

Certain foods may help ward off subtle age-related cognitive decline or even full-blown dementia, recent research suggests. *Nutrients linked with a clear mind and sharp memory…*

● **Folate.** In studies of people 70 years and older, those with low blood levels of folate had about twice the risk for Alzheimer's disease as those with normal levels. Folate reduces *homocysteine,* a dietary by-product linked to inflammation, blood clots and small blood vessel damage.

Best: Each day, eat two or more servings of folate-rich dark green leafy or cruciferous vegetables, such as spinach, romaine lettuce, broccoli and brussels sprouts. As insurance, consider using a daily multivitamin that provides 400 micrograms (mcg) of folic acid (synthetic folate). Many doctors recommend up to 1,000 mcg.

● **Marine omega-3 fatty acids.** Fish provide the *eicosapentaenoic acid* (EPA) and *docosahexaenoic acid* (DHA) in the omega-3s. Studies show that people who eat fish five or more times weekly are 30% less likely to have a stroke than those who rarely eat fish. Habitual fish consumption also is associated with fewer "silent" (symptomless) brain lesions, as seen on imaging tests…and may reduce Alzheimer's risk. Fish oil also improves function of nerve cell membranes and boosts production of brain chemicals that allow nerve cells to communicate.

Eating Fish Daily Improves Memory

According to a recent study, men as well as women between the ages of 70 and 74 who ate an average of more than 10 grams (0.35 ounces) of fish daily scored higher on memory, visual conception, attention, verbal fluency and orientation tests. The effect was even stronger as fish consumption increased to as high as 80 grams (2.8 ounces) per day.

A. David Smith, PhD, professor emeritus, pharmacology, University of Oxford, England.

Wise: Eat salmon, tuna, herring, sardines or mackerel at least twice weekly…or take daily fish oil supplements with 400 milligrams (mg) to 1,000 mg of combined EPA and DHA.

Important: Watch consumption of large fish such as tuna and salmon. These may have higher levels of mercury and PCBs.

• **Flavonoids.** Oxidation, a chemical reaction that can damage blood vessels, may be a key contributor to brain aging. Antioxidant plant pigments called *flavonoids* may counteract this—particularly the *anthocyanins* in deep-colored fruits such as berries, cherries and Concord grapes. In animal research, berry extracts reversed age-related declines in spatial learning and memory as measured by how quickly the animals figured out how to navigate a maze.

Goal: Eat berries or deep-colored fruit at least two to three times per week.

• **Coffee.** In a study of 7,017 people age 65 and older, women who drank at least three cups of caffeinated coffee or six cups of caffeinated tea per day experienced less decline in memory over four years than those who drank one cup or less. However, caffeine can trigger digestive upset, insomnia and migraine.

Advised: Have no more than four eight-ounce cups of coffee daily.

The alcohol question: Moderate alcohol intake is linked with less cognitive decline—though this may simply reflect that people who already have cognitive problems are less likely to imbibe.

Recommended: Do not begin drinking alcohol specifically to stave off cognitive decline. If you already drink, limit consumption to no more than one alcoholic beverage daily.

■ ■ ■ ■

Superfoods, Superbrain

Mark Hyman, MD, founder of The UltraWellness Center (*www.ultrawellness.com*) in Lenox, Massachusetts, and author of *The UltraMind Solution* (Scribner).

The aging American population is facing a sharp increase in diagnosed cases of dementia. Alzheimer's disease and other forms of dementia affect about 10% of people 65 and older. Among those in their mid-80s and older, up to half have a significant degree of cognitive impairment.

Millions of younger Americans suffer from less obvious mental impairments, including mild memory loss and diminished alertness, as well as brain-related disorders, such as depression and chronic anxiety.

The research clearly shows that some foods can strengthen mental performance and help prevent long-term damage. *Best choices…*

• **Sardines.** They provide two to three times more omega-3 fatty acids than most other fatty fish. Our bodies use omega-3s for the efficient transmission of brain signals. People who don't get enough omega-3s in their diets are more likely to experience learning disabilities, dementia and depression.

Bonus: Omega-3s decrease inflammation and inhibit blood clots, the underlying cause of most strokes.

Fatty fish also are high in *choline*, a substance used to manufacture one of the main neurotransmitters (*acetylcholine*) involved in memory.

Recommended: Three cans of sardines a week. Sardines are less likely to accumulate mercury and other toxins than larger fish.

A caution: Many people believe that flaxseed is an adequate substitute for fish. Although it does contain *alpha-linolenic acid* (ALA), a type of omega-3, only about 10% of ALA is converted to *docosahexaenoic acid* (DHA) or *eicosapentaenoic acid* (EPA), the most beneficial forms of omega-3s and the ones that are plentiful in fish oil.

If you don't like sardines, you can take fish oil supplements (1,000 milligrams twice a day).

- **Omega-3 eggs.** They are among the best foods for the brain because they contain folate along with omega-3s and choline. Folate is a B vitamin that's strongly linked to mood and mental performance. A Finnish study of 2,682 men found that those with the smallest dietary intakes of folate were 67% more likely to experience depression than those with adequate amounts.

Recommended: Up to eight eggs each week. Only buy eggs that say "Omega-3" on the label. It means that the chickens were given a fish meal diet. Eggs without this label contain little or no omega-3s.

- **Low-glycemic carbohydrates.** The glycemic index ranks foods according to how quickly they elevate glucose in the blood. Foods with low glycemic ratings include legumes (beans and lentils) and whole-grain breads. They slow the release of sugars into the bloodstream and prevent sharp rises in insulin.

Why it matters: Elevated insulin is associated with dementia. For example, diabetics with elevated insulin in the blood have four times the rate of dementia as people without diabetes. Elevated insulin damages blood vessels as well as neurons. The damage is so pronounced that some researchers call Alzheimer's disease "type 3 diabetes."

Recommended: Always eat all-natural, minimally processed foods. They're almost always low on the glycemic index. For example, eat apples instead of applesauce… whole-grain bread instead of white bread… or any of the legumes, such as chickpeas, lentils or soybeans.

- **Nuts.** They're among the few plant foods that contain appreciable amounts of the omega-3 fatty acids. They also contain antioxidants, which reduce brain and arterial inflammation that can lead to cognitive decline.

Most of the fat in nuts is monounsaturated—it lowers harmful LDL cholesterol without depressing beneficial HDL cholesterol—important for preventing stroke.

Recommended: One to two handfuls per day. Walnuts and macadamia nuts are among the highest in omega-3s, but all nuts are beneficial. Avoid highly salted and roasted nuts (the roasting changes the composition of the oils). Lightly toasted is okay.

- **Cruciferous vegetables, such as broccoli, brussels sprouts, cauliflower and kale.** They contain detoxifying compounds that help the liver eliminate toxins that can damage the *hippocampus* and other areas of the brain involved in cognition.

Recommended: One cup daily is optimal, but at least four cups a week. Cooked usually is easier to digest than raw.

- **B-12 foods.** Meat, dairy products and seafood are our only sources (apart from supplements) of vitamin B-12 in the diet. This nutrient is critical for brain health. A study published in *American Journal of*

Leafy Greens Help Your Mind Stay Sharp

People who eat lots of green vegetables, such as spinach, kale and collard greens, have a 40% slower rate of mental decline than people who eat less than one serving per day.

Best: Aim for at least three one-cup servings of leafy green vegetables every day to protect memory and thinking speed.

Martha Clare Morris, PhD, associate professor, department of internal medicine, Rush University Medical Center, Chicago, and leader of a study of 3,718 people ages 65 and older, published in *Neurology*.

Clinical Nutrition found that older adults with low levels of vitamin B-12 were more likely to experience rapid declines in cognition. Older adults have the highest risk for B-12 deficiency because the age-related decline in stomach acid impairs its absorption.

Recommended: Get two to three daily servings of organic lean meat, low-fat dairy (including yogurt) or seafood.

Also important: I advise everyone to take a multinutrient supplement that provides all of the B vitamins.

• **Green tea.** It's a powerful antioxidant and anti-inflammatory that also stimulates the liver's ability to break down toxins. New research indicates that green tea improves insulin sensitivity—important for preventing diabetes and neuro-damaging increases in insulin.

Recommended: One to two cups daily.

• **Berries, including blueberries, raspberries and strawberries.** The darker the berry, the higher the concentration of antioxidant compounds. In studies at Tufts University, animals given blueberries exhibited virtually no oxidative brain damage. They also performed better on cognitive tests than animals given a standard diet.

Recommended: One-half cup daily. Frozen berries contain roughly the same level of protective compounds as fresh berries.

Delicious Memory Boosters

Fred Gage, PhD, professor, laboratory of genetics, Salk Institute for Biological Studies, La Jolla, California, and leader of a study of the effects of *epicatechin* on mice, published in *The Journal of Neuroscience*.

Consuming foods with *epicatechin*, such as black or green tea, cocoa, blueberries and grapes, may improve memory. Epicatechin is an antioxidant, which reduces damage triggered by harmful molecules called free radicals.

Recent finding: Epicatechin helps increase the size of blood vessels in an area of the brain that is important for memory.

For a bigger boost: Exercise increases epicatechin's effect on memory.

Memory Loss Linked to Low Levels of "Good" Cholesterol

Archana Singh-Manoux, PhD, senior research fellow, French National Institute for Health and Medical Research, Saint-Maurice, France.

When 3,673 men and women were followed over seven years, researchers found that those who had low levels of *high-density lipoprotein* (HDL) "good" cholesterol (less than 40 milligrams per deciliter [mg/dL]) at age 60 were 53% more likely to experience memory loss than those with high HDL levels (60 mg/dL or higher).

To increase HDL levels: Exercise regularly…do not consume trans fats…and replace saturated fat with monounsaturated fat, such as olive oil, whenever possible.

■ ■ ■ ■

Seeds for Brain Health

Larry McCleary, MD, a retired pediatric neurosurgeon in Incline Village, Nevada, and author of *The Brain Trust Program* (Perigee).

Flaxseeds, sunflower seeds, sesame seeds and pumpkin seeds all contain high levels of *polyunsaturated oils*, as well as protein, vitamins and minerals, including magnesium, which is especially crucial for brain health.

Best: Nibble on seeds instead of other snacks, or add them to salads. There is no need to measure precisely—about three to four tablespoons a day is ideal.

■ ■ ■ ■

A Mineral for a Better Memory

Robert Krikorian, PhD, associate professor of clinical psychiatry, University of Cincinnati, Ohio.

When 26 adults with mild memory loss took a 1,000-microgram (mcg) *chromium picolinate* supplement or a placebo daily for 12 weeks, the supplement group performed better on memory tests while the placebo group showed no change.

Theory: This trace mineral reduces insulin resistance, a condition in which the body's cells don't use insulin properly. Too little insulin in the brain may contribute to poor memory.

If you're concerned about your memory: Ask your doctor about taking 400 mcg of chromium picolinate daily.

Caution: This supplement may affect dosage requirements for various diabetes medications.

■ ■ ■ ■

Study Shows Iron Improves Memory in Women

Laura E. Murray-Kolb, PhD, assistant professor, department of international health, Center for Human Nutrition, The Johns Hopkins University, Baltimore, and leader of a study of 113 women, published in *American Journal of Clinical Nutrition.*

In a recent study, young women who had sufficient levels of iron performed better on cognitive tasks than women who were deficient in iron. Iron supplementation for women with iron deficiencies for 16 weeks led to noticeably better learning, memory and attention. Further research is needed to find out if iron also can benefit older women and men.

Caution: Do not start iron supplementation on your own—be sure to see your doctor first.

A Brain-Boosting Diet That Helped a Doctor Conquer a Dreaded Neurological Disease: How It Can Help You, Too!

Terry L. Wahls, MD, an internist and clinical professor of medicine at the University of Iowa Carver College of Medicine in Iowa City and president of the Wahls Foundation, *www.thewahlsfoundation.com*, which supports research and provides education to the public about managing multiple sclerosis and other chronic diseases. She is the author of *Minding My Mitochondria: How I Overcame Secondary Progressive Multiple Sclerosis and Got Out of My Wheelchair* (TZ).

At age 44, I was diagnosed with multiple sclerosis (MS). Three years later, when I became dependent on a wheelchair, my MS got classified as "secondary progressive," meaning that the disease was steadily progressing with no stints of improvement. I kept getting weaker, even though I was receiving broadly used treatments for MS including chemotherapy and immune-suppressing medications.

Now: Thanks to the regimen I designed, I have not required a wheelchair or even a cane for more than three years. I ride to work on my bicycle, my energy is good and I've stopped taking medication to treat my MS. What happened?

Here is what I credit for my dramatic turnaround—with a description of how it might help you, as well. Because MS is a neurological disease, this diet plan is designed to also help those people who are concerned about dementia or Parkinson's disease, have depression or have suffered a traumatic brain injury or stroke.

Finding a Solution

With the help of my medical training, I began poring over the medical literature and designed my own treatment protocol in 2007 based on my theories of what allowed MS to develop and progress.

In people with MS, immune cells damage the *myelin sheath*, protein and fatty substances that surround nerve cells in the brain and spinal cord. This results in slower nerve signals, which lead to muscle weakness, a lack of balance and muscle coordination, bladder or bowel spasms, blurred vision and other symptoms.

Medications can decrease symptoms, but they do not accelerate nerve signals. As a result, MS patients battle with physical and neurological disability—experienced either episodically or in a continual, unrelenting course. The disease often continues to worsen despite therapy. Within 10 years of initial diagnosis, half of MS patients are unable to work because of disabling levels of fatigue, and one-third need a cane, scooter or wheelchair.

After thoroughly reviewing all the research, I decided to put myself on a diet that helps boost the efficiency of *mitochondria*, units within cells that supply the energy that's needed for nerve activity. Although the effect of diet on MS was not proven, I firmly believed that this was my best hope for fighting MS.

My eating plan was designed to improve the balance of neurotransmitters and supply the mitochondria with the building blocks needed for healthy nerve activity.

My Brain-Health Diet

People who follow this diet typically notice improvements in neurological symptoms in just weeks.*

Because natural foods contain a variety of nutrients that can work synergistically, I recommend taking supplements only when you are unable to get the following

*Consult your doctor before trying the diet and/or supplements described here—especially if you take any medication or have kidney or liver disease.

nutrients in your diet. Be sure to discuss the supplements (and dosages) with your physician if you take blood-thinning medication—some supplements may produce a blood-thinning effect.

In addition to taking such general steps as avoiding sugary and/or processed foods that are low in key nutrients, make sure you get enough…

• **Sulfur vegetables.** Cabbage, kale, collard greens and asparagus are all excellent sources of sulfur, which is utilized by the body to produce *gamma-aminobutyric acid* (GABA). This "inhibitory" neurotransmitter counteracts the early brain-cell death that can occur if the neurotransmitter *glutamate* reaches excessive levels.

My advice: Consume about three cups of greens every day, including one to three cups of sulfur-rich vegetables daily.

Also: To get other important nutrients, consume one to three cups of brightly colored vegetables or berries each day.

• **Coenzyme Q10.** Exposure to environmental toxins, such as detergents, pesticide residues and mercury, has been linked to MS and other neurological conditions, such as dementia and Parkinson's disease. Coenzyme Q10 is a fat-soluble compound that helps minimize the effects of these toxins while increasing the amount of energy produced by mitochondria.

Organ meats, such as calf liver and chicken liver, are among the best sources for coenzyme Q10. In particular, I recommend organ meats for older adults because coenzyme Q10 production declines with age. It's also suppressed by cholesterol-lowering statin drugs.

My advice: Eat organ meats at least once a week. If you don't like organ meats, sardines, herring and rainbow trout are also high in coenzyme Q10. Coenzyme Q10 is available in supplement form, too.

• **Omega-3 fatty acids.** Omega-3 fatty acids coming from cold-water fish, such as salmon and sardines, are used by the body to produce the *myelin* that insulates brain and spinal cord cells. Myelin is also used to repair damage caused by MS. Omega-3s are concentrated in the brain and are necessary to help prevent depression and cognitive disorders.

My advice: To avoid any worry about mercury and other toxins in cold-water fish, such as salmon, get your omega-3s from fish oil supplements that are purified.

Recommended dose: 1 gram (g) to 3 g daily.

• **Kelp and algae.** These detoxify the body by binding to heavy metals in the intestine and removing them in the stool.

My advice: Take supplements—one to two 500-milligram (mg) to 600-mg capsules of kelp and one to four 500-mg capsules of algae daily. Or, as an alternative, add about one tablespoon of powdered algae—different types include *Klamath blue green algae*, *spirulina* and *chlorella*—to morning smoothies.

• **Green tea.** It's very high in *quercetin*, an antioxidant that reduces inflammation. Green tea also changes the molecular structure of fat-soluble toxins and allows them to dissolve in water. This accelerates their excretion from the body.

My advice: Drink several cups of green tea daily.

The best choice: Finely milled Matcha green tea. It has more antioxidants than the typical tea brewed with dried leaves.

Note: Most types of green tea contain caffeine—on average, approximately 25 mg per cup.

■ ■ ■ ■

Foods That Trigger Inflammation

Leo Galland, MD, an internationally known expert in nutritional medicine. He is director of the Foundation for Integrated Medicine in New York City and author of several books, including *The Fat Resistance Diet* (Three Rivers).

Most of us tend to associate inflammation with the redness, pain, heat and swelling that accompany an injury or infection. This is part of the normal healing process. However, when the inflammatory process neglects to turn itself off when it should, inflammation becomes chronic—and potentially quite damaging.

Chronic inflammation (CI) works slowly and silently at the cellular level. One cause is poor diet. This may trigger inflammation, which can impair immunity and contribute to artery damage and *insulin resistance* (the inability of the body's cells to effectively use the hormone insulin to regulate blood sugar levels). These factors may increase the risk for heart disease, stroke, diabetes, osteoporosis, cancer and arthritis.

Despite all these dangers, many people with CI go undiagnosed, in part because the symptoms are so vague. Many doctors, not yet fully aware of CI, might not suspect inflammation. Only a blood test can confirm its presence. The best is the *high-sensitivity C-reactive protein* (or hs-CRP) *screening test*, which detects levels of CRP, a marker for inflammation in the bloodstream. Health insurance often covers the cost.

What Not to Eat...

Avoid these common inflammation-producing foods...

• **Trans fats.** They are created by adding hydrogen to vegetable oil (a process called *hydrogenation*). Consuming trans fats may damage cells that line blood vessels, causing inflammation.

To do: Check labels and avoid foods with hydrogenated or partially hydrogenated vegetable oil (or aliases, such as shortening or margarine). Most commercial baked goods, such as cookies and crackers, and many fried foods have trans fats.

• **Omega-6 fatty acids.** Needed for good health, omega-6s can be found naturally in meats, poultry, shellfish, milk, eggs, vegetable oils and some seeds. They are harmful only when eaten out of proportion to omega-3s, another essential fatty acid. A good ratio of omega-6s to omega-3s is about three to one. A typical American diet has a ratio of up to 20 to one—which allows omega-6s to crowd out omega-3s, changing the body's metabolic processes and creating inflammatory chemicals.

To do: Boost your intake of foods rich in omega-3s.

• **Processed sugar.** Table sugar, candy, soft drinks and other sweets contribute to insulin resistance and extra pounds, both of which increase inflammation.

To do: Satisfy your sweet tooth with a wide variety of fruits.

Note: If you have diabetes, talk to your doctor before increasing fruit intake.

■ ■ ■ ■

7

Brain-Boosting Tricks and Techniques

Your Memory Problems Solved!

Scott Hagwood, founder and president of The Center for Creative Memory Leadership, a corporate training center in Fayetteville, North Carolina. He is author of *Memory Power: You Can Develop a Great Memory—America's Grand Master Shows You How* (Free Press).

Scott Hagwood had an average memory growing up. Then, in 1999, at age 36, the chemical engineer learned that he had cancer and that the radiation treatments he needed often cause forgetfulness. Determined to ward off memory loss, Hagwood performed mental exercises for several hours a day. He would do such things as remember the exact order of cards in a shuffled deck and all the names of the doctors and nurses on his hospital floor.

He became so proficient that he entered the US National Memory Championships in 2001 and won. He is now one of 50 Grand Masters of Memory in the world. *Here, his easy solutions to common memory problems...*

Problem: You call directory assistance for a phone number, but you don't have a pen to write it down.

Solution: After you hang up, repeat the number out loud. There's something about hearing yourself say what you want to remember that resonates in the brain and enhances recall. Speak slowly. The faster you go, the less you remember. It's much more effective to say the phone number once or twice in a deliberate rhythm than to repeat it over and over in a hurried manner.

Problem: You can't remember the name of a coworker's spouse even though it is on the tip of your tongue.

Solution: Your forgetfulness is caused by stress. The more you try to recall something, the more frustrated and agitated you will get. First, take a few deep breaths. Then jog your memory by sorting through related information in your head. Visualize the coworker's name, the last time you saw him with his wife, their car, their home, etc.

If after a minute this doesn't work, distract and calm yourself by thinking about another topic. For instance, I enjoy golf, so I'll focus on my favorite course—the sand traps, the greens. While I'm doing this, the information I need often bubbles up in my mind.

Problem: You spend hours memorizing a presentation or studying for a test, then you cannot remember key information the next day.

Solution: Last-minute memorizing isn't effective. You need to give your brain time to digest information. Do not spend more than 50 minutes at a time trying to learn anything. Take a 10-minute break and then review your notes.

I practice the "Rule of 1s"—I review material after one hour, one day, one week, one month, etc., to log it into my long-term memory.

Problem: You need to remember a specific errand to do later in the day.

Solution: Scientists often refer to this as "prospective memory" because you are trying to recall a specific time in the future, not in the past. Even people with excellent memories find this difficult without a small, external reminder.

Examples: If I need to remember that I have clothes in the dryer, I'll leave the light on in the laundry room. If I have to return books to the library, I'll leave my library card sticking out of my wallet or my books on the front seat of the car.

Problem: You misplaced your keys or the TV remote.

Solution: You sometimes can jog your memory by recalling where you last saw the missing object and retracing your steps—but an object usually is misplaced because you were not paying attention, so you are unlikely to recall where you left it. Create a forget-me-not spot—for example, a hook for your keys or on top of the TV for the remote—and get in the habit of using that spot.

Problem: You forget a set of numbers, such as your bank ATM code.

Solution: Your brain is not built to remember abstract information such as numbers or names. What it remembers best are vivid images. The more you can associate information with pictures in your mind that are meaningful to you, the more powerful your memory.

Example: If you're trying to remember your bank code, 6052, associate each two digits with either a person, place or action. I might connect "60" with Babe Ruth hitting 60 home runs in a single season...and "52" with the pop group, the B-52s, singing their hit song "Love Shack." So my ATM code is an unforgettable visual image—Babe Ruth trotting around the bases as the B-52s sing.

Problem: You're at a business convention and want to remember the names of a dozen people you have met.

Solution: I use the powerful technique called the *Roman Room Method*. You associate bits of information with images in your house. So if I am trying to remember the names of one dozen acquaintances, I might visualize my office, going around the room, assigning each name to an easily retrievable mental hook.

Example: Let's say I want to remember a woman whose last name is Penny. My hook for her might be the closet door in my office and her emerging from the closet. This often is enough to trigger the name. If I find that association is not strong enough, I add one element to the mental picture. It may be one particular characteristic—her color of hair, her nose, how she gestures. In this case, I see her coming out of the closet with her pockets overflowing with pennies. I might "hook" another person to my computer, another to the bookcase, a third to a painting.

You can link different rooms with different categories of information. For instance, I might use triggers in my office to remember business contacts and triggers in the kids' playroom to remember people with whom I discuss parenting.

Helpful: Once you've used a particular room, don't use it again for a few days or weeks. Otherwise, previous associations can interfere with new ones.

■ ■ ■ ■

A Doctor's Secrets for Getting Your Memory Back in Gear

Gary Small, MD, professor of psychiatry and biobehavioral sciences, and director, University of California, Los Angeles, Center on Aging. Dr. Small is one of the world's leading physician/scientists in the fields of memory and longevity. He's author of *The Memory Bible* and *The Longevity Bible* (both from Hyperion). His Web site is *www.drgarysmall.com.*

Age is the biggest factor for memory loss. We all have memory problems of some sort by age 60, such as momentarily forgetting someone's name, or briefly wondering why we just walked into a room. We can't stop the effects of aging, but we can slow them down.

At the University of California, Los Angeles, Center on Aging, where I am director, we find that using very simple techniques and lifestyle changes—such as reading regularly and playing board games—can have a positive impact on memory retention. Scientific research shows that whenever we push ourselves to solve problems in a new way, we may be strengthening the connections between our brain cells.

Memory Techniques

Some people are so good at memorizing things that they test their talent in competitive matches involving knowledge of trivia or the recall of remarkably large numbers. Scientists have found that those people are no different from the rest of us. There is nothing out of the ordinary in their brain structure nor are there any indications of unusual intelligence. They simply often tap into a memory technique used since antiquity called the *Roman Room Method.*

This method is simple. Visualize yourself walking a familiar route, such as the rooms of your home. Mentally place images of the items to be remembered on specific points on the route. It might be helpful to place items where they may logically be—if you want to remember to buy coffee beans, perhaps they're best mentally placed on the kitchen counter. When you want to recall them, mentally retrace your steps.

Over time, you can add more objects to the rooms. If one day you want to remember to pick up the newspaper, add it next to the coffee beans on the counter. If it is airline tickets, visualize them taped to the fridge door. You can also extend your route or even add other familiar locations for certain kinds of memory tasks.

The Roman Room Method is a very useful technique. Orators back in Ancient Rome would remember lengthy speeches this way, imagining each progression of a speech by mentally walking through rooms where they had placed objects to remind themselves of lines. Yet since today we all have much more clutter coming at us, I also

Speak Out for a Better Memory

Speak out loud to improve memory when studying. Reading words aloud makes them easier to remember. Identify which information is most important for you to remember, and read only that material out loud.

Colin MacLeod, PhD, professor, department of psychology, University of Waterloo in Waterloo, Ontario, Canada, and leader of a study of more than 200 people, published in *Journal of Experimental Psychology: Learning, Memory, and Cognition.*

teach my patients an additional memory technique that I call *Look, Snap, Connect...*

• **Look** reminds us to focus our attention. The most common explanation for memory loss is that the information never gets into our minds in the first place. Because we are distracted, we don't take in the information or don't allow ourselves to absorb it. Simply reminding ourselves to focus our attention will dramatically boost memory power.

• **Snap** stands for creating a mental snapshot or visual image in your mind's eye of the information to be remembered. For most people, visual images are much easier to remember than other forms of information.

• **Connect** means we need to link up the visual images from Snap in meaningful ways. These associations are key to recalling memories when we want them later. When linking your mental images, create a story that has action and detail.

Example: Say that you want to remember five words on your "to do" list: Mail, gasoline, grandson, sweater, airline. Come up with a story linking them. For instance, I imagine a grandson knitting a sweater on a plane, then mailing it at the airport, when the plane lands to refuel.

Whatever your story winds up being, having detail, action and, for me, humor, all help to imprint the information.

This linking technique works very well with everyday memory tasks, such as grocery lists or errands to run.

When trying to remember faces and names, create an image either linked to the person whose name you need to remember or a distinguishing feature of his/her face. A redhead named Lucy could be remembered by noting that the red hair reminds you of Lucille Ball. You could remember the last name of a woman named Potvin by imagining that she landscaped her yard with pots full of vines.

Mental Aerobics

It's never too late to improve your memory. Recent studies show that even people in the early stages of Alzheimer's can be taught significant face and name retention under the guidance of a professional. For those of us looking to overcome the common forgetfulness in daily life, we can tackle much of that ourselves by doing activities that involve lateral thinking.

Lateral thinking means that we are trying to solve a problem from many angles instead of tackling it head on. *Here are some mental aerobic exercises to get you started and, hopefully, suggest further how to invoke lateral thinking in your life...*

Quiz Time

A lot of memory loss is simply being too hectic to take in what people are saying. These exercises are meant to remind you to slow down, pay attention and consider what is at hand. *In doing so, your memory will improve...*

1. Brush your hair using your nondominant hand. You may find it awkward at first, but over a few days notice how much easier it gets. This and other exercises don't directly help your memory (after all, how often will any of us need to remember to brush with the opposite hand?). What these mental exercises do is challenge your mind to think differently and examine tasks we often do without thinking, and which lead to our minds getting "flabby."

2. Fill in a grid so that every row, column and two-by-two box contains the numbers 1, 2, 3 and 4.

3. Say "silk" six times. Then answer the following question: What do cows drink?

This exercise will help you be more thoughtful about things, which in turn is conducive to better memory.

A Simple Trick to Help You Remember

In a study of 57 adults (average age 72), participants were told to push a computer's "F1" key once while performing a series of cognitive and perceptual tasks. One group also was asked to touch the top of their heads when they pressed the key.

Result: Those who had touched their heads were much more likely to remember having hit the F1 key.

Theory: It's easier to recall having completed a habitual task if it is accompanied by some kind of motor task, such as touching your head or crossing your arms.

If you have trouble remembering whether you've completed a daily activity (such as taking pills): Try making a specific motion each time you perform the task.

Mark McDaniel, PhD, professor of psychology at Washington University, St. Louis.

4. See how many words you can spell from these letters: LIGOBATE

No letter may be used twice in any given word, and each word must contain the letter L.

5. How many months have 28 days?

6. All of the vowels have been removed from the following saying. The remaining consonants are in the correct sequence, broken into groups of two to five letters. What is the saying below?

STRK WHLTH RNS HT

How well did you do? Regardless, this is just a start to remembering more and living better.

Answers to Quiz

2. *Across row 1:* 1, 2, 3, 4 or 1, 2, 4, 3. *Row 2:* 4, 3, 1, 2. *Row 3:* 2, 1, 4, 3 or 2, 1, 3, 4. *Row 4:* 3, 4, 2, 1.

3. Cows drink water. If you said "milk," you need to focus your attention.

4. agile, ail, aale, bagel, bail, bale, blog, boil, el, Gail, gale, gel, glib, glob, globe, goal, goalie, lab, lag, lea, leg, lib, lie, lob, lobe, log, loge, oblige.

5. All of them. (If you say only one month has 28 days, it's an example of not paying attention to the matter at hand—all months have 28 days, after all.)

6. Strike while the iron is hot.

How to Remember People's Names and Faces

Tony Buzan, a renowned expert on thinking visually, a leading lecturer on the brain and learning and the inventor of Mind Mapping, ThinkBuzan.com.

Forgetting names as quickly as you hear them is one common problem. Yet, putting names and faces together correctly only takes a little practice…if you know the *Mnemonic Method of Memorization.*

The Mnemonic Method is simple. All you have to do is take the time to link a person's name to a mental picture you create in your own mind. *Here's how to do it…*

• **Listen very carefully to the name.** Does the name or part of the name conjure up an image?

Example: If you hear the name Gene Mapley, associate the name with blue jeans and a map. (Jeans for Gene and a map for Mapley.)

• **Coordinate.** Search Mr. Mapley's head and face for unique features that you can link up to the image of blue jeans and a map.

Example: If Gene Mapley has a deeply furrowed brow, you could pretend that the furrows are the roads found on a map.

• **Visualize.** See Gene Mapley's face as a caricaturist might, drawn in exaggerated and ludicrous form—with the blue jeans dancing frantically along the lines of the map on Mapley's face. The more absurd the link and the mental picture you associate with the person, the more impossible it is to forget his/her name.

If you push yourself to use this technique every time you meet a new person over the next few days, you'll be amazed at how quickly you get good at it. By the time you attend your net gathering, you'll be able to put on a dazzling display of memory—whether you're shaking hands with just one new person or 100.

Forget to Take Your Medication? A Memory Expert's Secrets for Remembering

Harry Lorayne, a renowned memory-training specialist known for the feats of recall he performed during frequent appearances on *The Tonight Show.* Based in New York City, he is author of several books about memory, including the best-selling *Ageless Memory: Keep Your Mind Young Forever* (Black Dog & Leventhal). His Web site is *www.harrylorayne.com.*

Taking medications on schedule is often a challenge. Here are memory tricks that help. They may seem complicated, but in reality, they take only minutes to learn.

Bonus: Research has shown that this type of mental "exercise" can help prevent age-related memory loss and keep your brain sharp.

Which Drugs to Take

Mentally link the names of your prescription drugs to memorable images, then link these visual images together. Absurd or jarring visual images are best because they stick in the mind.

Example: Say I take four prescription medications. The first is Altace, a blood pressure drug. The visual image that the word Altace brings to my mind is an Old Ace because the pronunciation is similar. I visualize the Ace of Spades with a long gray beard.

My second medication is special eyedrops prescribed after cataract surgery. I picture my Old Ace with bloodshot eyes, putting in eyedrops.

My third drug is Micardis, for hypertension. The words "my card" sound like the drug "Micardis." I imagine that the label on the Old Ace's eyedropper is my business card, and I visualize myself thinking, "That's my card," when I see it.

My final drug is Lipitor, for high cholesterol, so I picture my business card giving the Old Ace a very bad paper cut on his mouth, tearing his lip open. The words "lip tore" remind me of Lipitor.

In this way, the silly Old Ace image leads you to the other "reminder images." When my medications change, I simply create a new set of linked images. The old links disappear from my memory after a few days of disuse.

When to Take Them

To remember to take pills at different times, associate each hour of the day with a similar-sounding and easy-to-visualize word. *The words I use are…*

one (o'clock)–run	**seven**–heaven
two–shoe	**eight**–date
three–tree	**nine**–dine
four–door	**ten**–hen
five–dive	**eleven**–leaven
six–sticks	**twelve**–shelf

Most people can remember these associations with a few minutes of practice. Now create a mental image that links the hour with your medication.

Example: You need to take Lipitor every day at six. Picture a bunch of sticks hitting you in the face and tearing open your lip. Now when you glance at a clock and see that it is six, the time will remind you of sticks, which in turn reminds you of a torn lip, which means it is time for your Lipitor.

Mentally go over your "time words" a few times during the day. Each time you do, you'll be reminded of a medication and when to take it.

Did I Take My Pills Already?

You were supposed to take your pills at 4:00. Now it is 5:30, and you cannot remember whether you took your daily dose. A great way to remember is to pause and visualize a memorable image (different from the images above) just before you take the medicine.

Example: You want to remember that you took your daily dose of the allergy drug Benadryl. Just before you take it, you picture a friend named Ben using a drill on your throat ("Ben" and "drill" sound like "Benadryl"). You imagine the pain this drill would cause you. The powerful image greatly increases the chances that you will later remember that you took the medication.

■ ■ ■ ■

Aerobic Exercise Slows Mental Decline

The brain starts to shrink during middle age, so it processes information more slowly.

Recent finding: As little as three hours per week of walking triggers biochemical changes that increase the volume of brain regions responsible for memory and cognitive function.

Arthur Kramer, PhD, department of neuroscience and psychology, University of Illinois, Urbana, and leader of a study published in *Journal of Gerontology.*

Memory Boosters for Busy People

Cynthia R. Green, PhD, founder of the Memory Enhancement Program and assistant clinical professor of psychiatry, both at Mount Sinai School of Medicine, New York City, and president of Memory Arts, LLC, which provides memory fitness training, Upper Montclair, New Jersey. She is author of *Total Memory Workout: 8 Easy Steps to Maximum Memory Fitness* (Bantam). For more, go to *http://totalbrainhealth.com.*

Have you misplaced your keys…again? Or forgotten your best friend's phone number? You may blame age for these memory lapses, but for most people, the real culprit is a hyperactive life. Having too much competing for your attention is challenging no matter what your age—and attention is a key component in memory.

To improve your focus, organize your life in memory-boosting ways…

• **Build new brain cells by squeezing exercise into your schedule**—walk while you talk on the phone, do leg lifts while stirring a pot on the stove. Exercise increases blood flow to the brain, including the hippocampus, which processes memories. Exercise also appears to promote *neurogenesis*—the creation of new brain cells—and to combat the normal age-related memory decline that typically begins around age 30. This may explain why people who work out regularly do better on memory tests.

• **Don't stay up late or wake up too early to get more done.** This is necessary sometimes, but as a regular coping strategy, it is counterproductive. One function of sleeping is to consolidate memory—to convert new memories into long-term ones. Lack of sleep also dulls concentration, which is critical to memory.

• **Use mindfulness meditation,** in which you focus on the here and now. Just remind yourself while walking, dining or at the supermarket to pay close attention to what is around you. Focus on the beauty of the trees or the cool breeze on your skin. Revel in awareness of what is happening at this moment. This lowers stress and helps you to feel less overwhelmed. Prolonged stress may alter brain cells and structure, contributing to memory problems.

• **Teach yourself to pay attention.** Often the problem is not that we've forgotten something, but that we didn't focus on acquiring the information in the first place. Did you "forget" where you put your glasses, or did your mind wander as you were setting them down?

• **Devise a system to make remembering automatic.** Learn to routinely put your car keys in one place—on a hook in the garage, for instance. Make sure the system fits your habits. You may think it is wise to hang a cute key holder in your kitchen, but if you always enter the house through the garage, take off your coat in the mudroom and enjoy an enthusiastic reunion with your dog, the keys will get dropped elsewhere long before you reach the kitchen.

• **Free your mind of clutter by using memory tools.** Ask yourself, "Do I need to memorize this information or merely record it so I know where to find it?" Most of life's details (grocery lists, dinner dates) can be jotted down for reference when you need the information. Calendars, personal digital assistants and "to do" lists are excellent memory devices. Choose a memory aid that is compatible with your lifestyle. A wall calendar won't work if you're always on the go.

• **Make getting yourself organized a habit.** On Sundays, list and prioritize tasks for the coming week on your calendar. Every morning, review what is coming up. Each evening, reevaluate tasks that did not get done. Reschedule the important ones—and give yourself permission to forget about the rest.

A Noted Psychiatrist Tells How to Keep Your Brain Sharp

Gene D. Cohen, MD, PhD, professor of health-care sciences and psychiatry, and director of The Center on Aging, Health & Humanities at The George Washington University in Washington, DC. He is founding chief of the Center on Aging at the National Institute of Mental Health, past president of the Gerontological Society of America and author of *The Mature Mind* (Basic).

Scientists used to assume that elderly adults don't learn as well as younger people and children…that creativity is strongest in youth…and that mental abilities in general go south after age 50. These long-standing myths prevailed even though there was virtually no science to back them up.

New findings: The brain has enormous plasticity—the ability to form new *neurons* (brain cells) and new connections between neurons. Brain plasticity does not decline with age. It can actually increase as people get older.

Example: The *hippocampus* is the part of the brain that processes information and integrates all thinking and emotions. Nerve endings (*dendrites*) and the connections between dendrites (*synapses*) increase in this area between the ages of 50 and 80.

The brain is not immune to age-related changes. Brain cells "wear out" and die with age. Older adults can't process math problems as quickly as younger people, and they experience declines in short-term memory storage.

However, other kinds of brain changes aren't caused by aging, but by underlying conditions, such as Alzheimer's, stroke and depression. *Assuming that you take care of yourself and stay healthy, you can improve mental function by doing the following…*

Stimulate Your Brain

People who push themselves mentally can increase synaptic connections by at least 20%. They also experience increased *neurogenesis*, the formation of new neurons. The result is quicker thinking, better memory, etc. Mental challenges even can delay the onset of Alzheimer's disease. A study in *The New England Journal of Medicine* reported that patients at high risk for Alzheimer's who engaged in difficult mental activities, such as playing a musical instrument or word games, significantly delayed disease onset. Apparently, they built up a brain "reserve," which kept their minds robust longer.

Choose mental activities that really expand your capacities.

Examples: Learning a language or instrument…doing challenging crossword puzzles…playing Scrabble or chess.

Exercise

People who exercise do better mentally and diminish the risk of Alzheimer's disease and other forms of dementia than those who are sedentary. Aerobic exercise in particular improves brain circulation and oxygenation. It appears to stimulate the release of chemicals in the body that increase synaptic connections as well as the formation of new neurons.

Example: One study of older women indicated that those who increased their physical activity by walking had less cognitive decline and dementia over a period of six to eight years.

More is better. Just as vigorous exercise of the brain is good for cognition, vigorous physical activity is necessary for brain health.

Exercise for 30 to 45 minutes at least four days a week. Aerobic activities, such as brisk walking and swimming, are better for the brain than weight training. Aerobic workouts improve cardiovascular fitness, which is thought to increase networks of blood vessels in the frontal part of the brain and stimulate the release of chemicals that improve brain cell survival and plasticity.

Achieve Mastery

Older adults who work hard to get good at something experience feelings of empowerment and control. These feelings produce higher levels of T cells and natural killer cells—immune cells that battle disease and help keep brain tissue and blood vessels robust.

One study compared 150 older adults, average age of 80, who were all involved in rigorous arts programs with a comparable group not enrolled in the programs. People in the arts group met weekly for a period of about nine months a year for two years and completed between-session assignments.

Many of the adults in the arts group showed no physical or mental health declines during the study—and some showed significant improvement. Those who didn't participate in the arts programs tended to have a reduction in overall mental health.

It is less important what you do—it could be embroidery, learning how to paint or understanding your computer better—than learning to do it well.

Strengthen Both Sides of the Brain

It is not true that some people are "right-brained" and others are "left-brained." We use both sides of our brain throughout life, but younger adults are more likely to use only one side at a time—for things such as reading, recognizing patterns, etc. After middle age, however, people are more likely to use both sides simultaneously. This is probably a protective mechanism that allows the brain to overcome some degenerative changes associated with aging.

Phone a Friend, Boost Brainpower

Chatting for 10 minutes a day benefits your brain as much as doing the daily crossword puzzle.

A recent finding: Social interaction—such as talking on the phone and getting together with friends—will boost memory and mental performance as effectively as more traditional kinds of mental exercise, such as word and number puzzles.

Oscar Ybarra, PhD, psychologist, University of Michigan Institute for Social Research, Ann Arbor, and lead author of a study of 3,610 people, published in *Personality and Social Psychology Bulletin.*

Older adults who cultivate this capacity have quicker reaction times and improved cognitive abilities.

Best: Creative activities draw on both the right and left sides of the brain and improve the ability of both sides to work together. Take drawing classes. Join a book club. Write your autobiography.

Strengthen Social Networks

Close relationships are important throughout life, particularly for older adults. People who maintain active social schedules—going to church, getting together with friends and spending time with family—have lower blood pressure and less risk of stroke. They have lower levels of stress hormones, the chemicals that damage brain tissue and increase the risk of anxiety and depression.

New finding: Older adults experience undesirable emotions less often—including fear and anger, which interfere with relationships—than younger individuals. Imaging studies show that the *amygdalae* (the parts of the brain that generate some of our most intense emotions) get less active

with age. We experience less intense negative emotions as we get older, but positive ones remain robust. We have an improved capacity to ride out emotional storms that often roil relationships.

Spend time with people you really do care about. Volunteer and get involved in your community. Even the people who described themselves as wallflowers during their younger years often find that social connections get easier—and more rewarding—later in life. And they help keep your brain healthy.

Common Myths About The Brain

Sandra Aamodt, PhD, and *Sam Wang, PhD,* coauthors of *Welcome to Your Brain: Why You Lose Your Car Keys but Never Forget How to Drive and Other Puzzles of Everyday Life* (Bloomsbury). Based in northern California, Dr. Aamodt is editor in chief of *Nature Neuroscience*, a scientific journal on brain research. Dr. Wang is associate professor of neuroscience at Princeton University, Princeton, New Jersey. He has published more than 40 articles on the brain.

We use our brains every moment of our lives, but a lot of what we accept as fact about our brains is really just folklore. Today, cutting-edge scientific techniques are helping us unravel the secrets responsible for everything from creating and storing memories to avoiding jet lag and senility. *The truth behind common myths...*

Myth: You can't reverse memory loss.

Some of the erosion of memory that comes with aging can be slowed or even reversed. For example, when aging cells in the front part of your brain, known as the prefrontal cortex, shrink, it causes a loss of "executive function," skills that let you multitask and focus intently on what you are doing. But you can improve executive function through physical exercise, which increases the blood flow and the availability of oxygen and glucose to your brain cells.

To do this, you will need at least 30 minutes of cardiovascular exercise, such as aerobics or fast walking, three times a week. Even if you have been sedentary for a while, your ability to focus can improve markedly within a few months of starting an exercise program.

Myth: We use just 10% of our brains.

This myth is based on the erroneous and simplistic view of the brain as a single unified structure, like a computer hard drive. The brain actually consists of various parts, and you use every part every day. There are no large, unused or unexplored reserves of gray matter waiting to be tapped.

Myth: Alcohol kills brain cells.

Chronic heavy drinking can cause your brain to shrink, and that is associated with many disorders, ranging from an inability to concentrate to a form of dementia in which you lose old memories and can't form new ones. But the brain shrinkage is not caused by brain cells dying. Heavy drinking shrinks *dendrites*, the microscopic, highly branched connections between brain cells. The distinction is important because, unlike brain cells, dendrites are capable of expansive regrowth. An alcoholic who gives up drinking can improve cognitive abilities.

The more relevant question for most people is whether moderate drinking damages the brain. The answer is no. In general, men can have up to three drinks a day and women up to two without adversely affecting brain function long-term. In fact, the widely held belief that red wine is beneficial for your brain's health as you age is true. For example, as little as one glass every three or four days decreases stroke risk.

Myth: Jet lag can be cured only with time.

When you travel across time zones, it often takes several days to feel normal again. Meanwhile, you're falling asleep at 7 pm or waking up at 4 am. This is because the internal clock in your brain, known as the *circadian rhythm*, requires some time to resynchronize.

There's a reliable way to speed up this process. Doses of bright sunlight can resynchronize your internal clock more quickly than time.

Rule of thumb: Plan ahead to determine the best arrival time for light exposure. On the first day at your destination, it is optimal to get as much bright sunshine as possible. This fools your body into speeding up its circadian rhythm. For example, if you fly east—say, an overnight trip from the US to Europe—get bright light for a few hours after you arrive. Exposure to sunlight around noon will help you get up more easily the next day without feeling so sluggish.

Myth: Listening to classical music can make babies and children smarter.

The origin of this popular misconception stems from one 1993 study of college students who improved their performance doing tasks that involved paper folding and cutting after listening to a Mozart sonata. Neuroscientists have not been able to replicate the results, but that hasn't stopped parents from trying to use the "Mozart Effect" to foster their children's intellectual development.

If you really want to improve a child's intelligence, have him/her learn to play a musical instrument. The children who take music lessons have better spatial reasoning skills than those who don't take music lessons, perhaps because music and spatial reasoning are processed by similar brain systems.

Learn a Word a Day and Other Fun Ways to Add Healthy Years to Your Life

The late Robert N. Butler, MD, former president and chief executive officer, International Longevity Center-USA. He also was professor of geriatrics at Brookdale Department of Geriatrics and Adult Development at Mount Sinai Medical Center in New York City. Dr. Butler was the author of *The Longevity Prescription: The 8 Proven Keys to a Long, Healthy Life* (Avery) and won the 1976 Pulitzer Prize for his book *Why Survive? Being Old in America* (The Johns Hopkins University Press).

We all know that eating right and exercising can boost our chances of a long, healthy life. But sometimes it seems as if the changes we have to make to live a healthier life are simply too overwhelming. The good news is that just a few little changes can have a significant impact on our health. *Here, the little changes that can make a big difference…*

• **Learn a word a day.** Pick a word out of the paper or dictionary every day. Or have a word e-mailed to you daily (*http://diction ary.reference.com/wordoftheday*). Put it on an index card, and drill yourself. This type of cognitive calisthenic keeps your brain sharp.

The brain will continue to regenerate nerve cells throughout life. This process, known as *neurogenesis*, helps older adults to improve memory and other cognitive functions as they age.

Example: A study published in *The Journal of the American Medical Association* compared two groups of older adults. Those in one group were given training in memory, reasoning and mental processing. After just 10 sessions of 60 to 75 minutes each, the participants had immediate and long-lasting improvements, compared with those who didn't get the training.

If learning a word a day doesn't appeal to you, pick an activity that you enjoy and find mentally challenging.

Examples: Reading books on history, learning chess or memorizing poems. When the activity starts getting easier, move on to harder challenges.

People who do this can regain as much as two decades of memory power. In other words, someone who starts at age 70 could achieve the memory of the average 50-year-old.

• **Take a trip.** Go on a cruise. Take a bus tour. Go to a reunion. All of these are great ways to connect with people. Why bother? Because emotional connections add years to your life.

Example: Studies published in the last 10 years show that people in happy marriages have less heart disease and live longer than those in unhappy relationships or who are divorced or widowed. Being happily married at age 50 is a better predictor of good health at age 80 than having low cholesterol.

The same benefits occur when people maintain any close relationship—with friends, children or even pets. People who are emotionally bonded with others suffer less depression. They also tend to have less stress and lower levels of disease-triggering stress hormones. And inviting new people into your life can help you cope with the dislocations—due to death, divorce, retirement, etc.—that occur over time.

Emotional connections don't just happen—people have to work at them. Think of the friendships that are important to you. If you are like most people, maybe a few of these relationships are active, but others have gone dormant for a variety of reasons. Ask yourself why some relationships have lapsed and what you can do to revive them. If you have lost touch with someone special, send an e-mail or pick up the phone.

We all have "relationship opportunities" that we can take advantage of. Talk to the stranger next to you at a concert or a sports event. If you volunteer, invite one of your coworkers for coffee.

● **Take a nap.** It is a myth that older people need less sleep than younger adults. They often do sleep less, but this is mainly because they're more likely to have physical issues, such as arthritis or the need to use the bathroom at night, that interfere with restful sleep.

People who don't get enough sleep often have declines in immune function, which can increase the risk for cancer as well as infections. They also have a higher risk for hypertension and possibly prediabetes.

A short nap—no more than 20 to 30 minutes—can make up for a bad night of sleep. But beware of excessive napping. A long nap or more than one short nap per day can ruin a good night's sleep. Napping late in the day, say, after 3:00, also can interfere with a night's sleep.

● **Climb the stairs.** It takes very little time but is a great way to get your heart and lungs working. Most guidelines for exercise recommend at least 20 to 30 minutes of exercise most days of the week. That much exercise, or more, is clearly beneficial, but short amounts of activity can have a significant impact.

In one study of 5,000 people over age 70, all the participants had some physical limitations, but those who got even minimal exercise (defined as the equivalent of walking a mile at least once a week) were 55% less likely to develop more serious physical limitations (defined as severe joint pain or muscle weakness) that could compromise independence.

● **Watch the birds.** For many people, contact with the natural world has a restorative effect. A few minutes observing birds at a feeder or watching a sunset can restore our equilibrium. The natural world has a pace that reminds us that life does not have to be lived in a rush.

Taking a few moments to destress is worth doing because an estimated 60% to 90% of doctor visits are for stress-related disorders.

Connecting with nature also can boost our performance. A study at Kansas State University had 90 women do a five-minute typing assignment. The researchers found that those who worked with a bouquet of flowers nearby outperformed those with no flowers.

● **See a funny movie.** A good guffaw is more complicated than most people imagine. Laughter uses 15 facial muscles, along with the lungs, larynx and epiglottis. It even seems to protect against heart disease.

One study at Loma Linda University School of Medicine found that volunteers who watched a humorous video had lower levels of the stress hormones *cortisol* and *epinephrine*. These and other stress-related chemicals have been linked with increased inflammation and an elevated risk for heart disease and many other conditions.

■ ■ ■ ■

Can Ping-Pong Be a Brain Exercise?

Pierce J. Howard, PhD, managing director, research and development, Center for Applied Cognitive Studies, Charlotte, North Carolina.

Two things could make Ping-Pong a "brain exercise"—if you're learning something new, and if it provides aerobic exercise. The initial condition involves developing fresh branches and connections between brain cells (*neurons*), as well as reinforcing established neural pathways. Aerobic exercise provides more oxygen to the brain, thereby increasing mental energy. If you are already an accomplished Ping-Pong player, then the first condition would not apply (unless you learn to play with your nondominant hand). If you play competitively and/or vigorously, you will reap the benefits of the second condition. Additionally, new research indicates that social interaction boosts brainpower. If owning a Ping-Pong table increases time spent with family and friends, it's a bonus for the brain.

■ ■ ■ ■

How to Get the Nap You Need

Sara Mednick, PhD, assistant professor of psychiatry at the University of California, San Diego. In addition to authoring numerous published studies on napping, she is coauthor of *Take a Nap! Change Your Life* (Workman) and the recipient of a National Institute of Mental Health Mentored Research Career Scientist Award. See *www.saramednick.com* for more.

What if there were a secure, nontoxic, simple, costless way to amplify your alertness…boost your creativity…improve your memory…decrease your stress …and even reduce your risk for heart disease, all in just 20 minutes a day? There is. It's called a nap.

Napping Without Guilt

In our work-driven, activity-driven society, the hardest part of taking a nap is getting past that little voice in your head telling you that napping is a sign of laziness.

Reality: People who nap tend to be more productive, not less.

When you allow yourself that brief period of rest and refreshment, you wake up alert and energized, ready to be active for the rest of the day. The time you spend sleeping is more than made up for by the improved work or activity time a nap can give you.

Instead of a nap, you could just have coffee or another form of caffeine to perk yourself up, but a nap is a better idea. Caffeine makes you more alert, but it doesn't give you any of the other benefits of napping.

Example: Napping will enhance performance on a wide range of memory tests. Studies show that a 90-minute nap is as good as a full night's sleep for improving memory.

The Sleep Cycle

To understand why napping can be so valuable, it helps to understand the basic concept of the sleep cycle and how it applies to both nighttime sleeping and daytime napping.

Through the night, your sleep moves through a consistent pattern of four distinct phases…

• **Stage 1.** This occurs when you're just falling asleep and generally lasts for only a few minutes. Your structured thinking gradually gives way to dreamlike imagery.

• **Stage 2.** After you have fallen asleep, stage 2 sleep takes over. During this time, many parts of your brain are less active, but stage 2 sleep is the sleep that restores alertness and consolidates all motor learning—anything that involves muscle movements such as dancing or driving.

• **Stage 3.** When you move into stage 3 sleep, your brain waves slow down, so much so that this stage is also called *slow-wave sleep* (SWS). In SWS, your body repairs itself because growth hormone is secreted during this phase, which helps with muscle fiber growth and repair as well as bone growth—basically, the antidote to *cortisol*, a stress hormone—and consolidates memory, such as new information you've just learned (a phone number, for example) so that you'll remember it.

• **Stage 4.** During stage 4, you move into *rapid eye movement* (REM) *sleep*, or dreaming. REM sleep is when you consolidate more complex information and learning, such as a vocabulary list in a foreign language.

In the course of the night, you generally go through stage 1 sleep only once, just as you fall asleep. After that, you cycle through stage 2, stage 3 (SWS) and stage 4 (REM) sleep several times through the night. Each cycle takes about 90 minutes. Of that, about 60% is spent in stage 2 sleep. The amount of time spent in SWS and REM sleep varies through the cycles.

Your Optimum Nap

Most people feel a natural lull in their energy levels sometime during the afternoon. That's the natural time for napping—and in many countries, the traditional siesta takes place then. Ideally, because one sleep cycle takes about 90 minutes, you would nap for that long and awaken feeling refreshed and alert.

Not too many of us can manage a full 90 minutes in the middle of the day, however, and not everyone feels the need to nap that long. *To choose the best nap length for you, decide what you want to get from your nap…*

• **Stage 2 nap.** It decreases sleepiness, heightens alertness, increases concentration, enhances motor performance and elevates mood.

Sleep for: 15 to 20 minutes.

• **Stage 3 (SWS) nap.** Clears away useless information, improves conscious memory recall and restores and repairs tissues.

Sleep for: 60 minutes.

• **Stage 4 (REM sleep) nap.** Increases creativity, improves perceptual and sensory processing, and improves memory for complex information.

Sleep for: 90 minutes.

The best time for your nap depends on several factors, including when you woke up and what type of sleep you want

to get from your nap. I've created a handy Nap Wheel to help you determine when the ideal time for your nap is. (See the box on the next page to learn more.)

Napping and Your Health

We know that lack of sleep is definitely bad for your health, but is napping good for it? That has actually been a hotly debated question. Over the years, some studies seemed to show that people who often napped had greater risk for death, especially from heart disease.

One recent Harvard University study, however, emphatically suggests the opposite. In the study, more than 23,000 people in Greece were followed for an average of 6.3 years. None of the individuals had a history of heart disease, stroke or cancer at the start of the study, and they ranged in age from 20 to 86. The results showed that the people who regularly napped for at least 30 minutes at least three times a week had a 37% lower risk for death from heart disease than the non-nappers.

Taking a nap in the afternoon doesn't typically affect a person's ability to get to sleep at his/her normal bedtime or to sleep for the normal number of hours at night. In fact, many people who start taking daytime naps report that they fall asleep more easily at bedtime and feel more refreshed in the morning.

Exception: Do not nap within two to three hours of your usual bedtime—it could keep you from getting to sleep on schedule.

Sleep and Age

Older adults often find themselves waking up earlier than they used to and having trouble getting back to sleep. Shifting to an earlier wake-up time—and feeling the need for an earlier bedtime—is a natural part of the changes in body rhythm that can come with aging. Rather than fighting your body's normal needs, accept them. A great way to make up for the lost sleep and help yourself stay up later? Take a nap!

Customize Your Nap

Use the *Nap Wheel* to design your own custom nap based on the time you wake up in the morning. To access the Nap Wheel, go to *www.saramednick.com* and click on "Nap Wheel" under "Take a Nap Book."

How: Drag the "wake-up time" dial to the hour that you got up. Then follow the hours clockwise until you reach the point when the rapid eye movement (REM) sleep and the slow-wave sleep (SWS) cross—the point of ultimate balance.

Example: If you woke up at 7 am, that balance point would be 2 pm. Naps taken before the crossing point will have more REM sleep…naps taken after it will have more SWS. All you have to do is decide what type of nap you want.

Six-Minute Memory Booster

Olaf Lahl, PhD, researcher, Institute of Experimental Psychology, University of Dusseldorf, Germany.

Boost your memory in a few minutes by simply taking a nap. Napping during the day—for as little as six minutes—produces better performance on memory exercises.

A possible reason: The act of falling asleep might trigger a neurological process that improves memory—even if actual sleep time is minimal.

Cut Your Risk for Alzheimer's…with These Simple Brain-Boosting Exercises

Majid Fotuhi, MD, PhD, assistant professor of neurology at Johns Hopkins University and director of the Center for Memory and Brain Health at Sinai Hospital, both in Baltimore. He is the author of *The Memory Cure* (McGraw-Hill) and co-author of *The New York Times Crosswords to Keep Your Brain Young* (St. Martin's Griffin).

Anyone who has ever done a sit-up or bicep curl knows that exercises are generally targeted to specific parts of the body.

But what about brain exercises?

What most people do not realize: Even though it's common to assume that a daily crossword puzzle or game of bridge or chess gives your brain a full workout, that's not true.

There are, in fact, particular activities that can be done on a regular basis to "exercise" all parts of your brain so that you have the best possible chance of retaining your mental capacities as you age.

Brain-boosting exercises are most effective when performed as part of an overall brain-health regimen that also includes regular aerobic exercise to increase blood flow to the brain.

Brain Exercise Really Does Help

The *hippocampus*, the part of the brain responsible for such functions as short-term memory and learning new facts, tends to gradually shrink as we get older. But studies have found that this shrinkage can not only be forestalled, but actually reversed, if you stimulate your brain with challenging new activities.

Improvements in brain functioning are possible for most people because the brain will remain very "plastic" throughout one's life—that is, capable of growing in size and developing significant new capacities at virtually any age.

Exciting scientific finding: A brain-imaging study of cab drivers in London, who typically require years to memorize the big sprawling maze of local streets, found that those who had been working the longest also possessed the largest-sized posterior hippocampus—perhaps because their work requires them to constantly enhance their spatial memory and navigation skills.

To achieve optimal brain health, it is also important to turn off the TV. A recent study that compared Alzheimer's patients to people of the same age without cognitive impairment found that the Alzheimer's group had been less active during middle age than the healthy group had in virtually every activity except for TV-watching. Conversely, various types of brain-stimulating activities have been found by researchers at the Rush Alzheimer's Disease Center to cut the risk for Alzheimer's disease nearly in half.

Top 10 Brain Boosters

The brain exercises described below are not only a lot of fun to do, but also challenge a person's reasoning, planning, memory and spatial skills.

All of these exercises have been found to engage most areas of the brain to some degree—but each is particularly effective at stimulating the specific brain regions noted. There is no evidence indicating the optimal frequency and duration of these exercises, but I suggest doing as many as possible as often as you can. *For a full-brain workout…*

1. Challenge your powers of navigation. If you have a GPS navigation device in your car, turn it off when driving to an unfamiliar destination and use a map to find your way. If you don't have a GPS and use maps

anyway, concentrate on remembering the route so that you can make most of the return trip by memory.

Also helpful: When you're walking inside a large building, keep track of where north and south are.

Good for: Right parietal lobe, the part of your brain that's responsible for judging your orientation in space.

2. Engage in math on the fly. While grocery shopping, tally the cost of your purchases in your head.

Also helpful: When driving a distance of any length, keep track of your elapsed time and miles covered, and use this information to periodically calculate your average speed.

Good for: Left parietal lobe, the part of your brain used to make mathematical calculations.

3. Play mind games. When you have some "downtime"—if you're stuck in traffic, for example, or waiting on line at the store—memorize your credit card numbers or the phone numbers of friends.

Also helpful: Spell the names of cities and states backward.

Good for: Frontal lobes, used in planning and in abstract thinking…left parietal lobe…and left temporal lobe, specialized for language functions, including speech, language comprehension and verbal memory.

4. Take a class in ballroom dancing. You need to pay attention to the sequence of steps, memorize them and then perform them while following the rhythm of the music and the movements of your partner.

Good for: Parietal lobes (spatial awareness)…frontal lobes (for planning of movement)…and the cerebellum (balance and physical movement). The right frontal lobe and cerebellum are activated with the music component of dancing.

5. Prepare new recipes. Preparing an unfamiliar dish forces you to carefully follow instructions and coordinate the order and timing of each step, thereby strengthening the parts of your frontal lobes used for following directions and planning. Get adventurous. The more unfamiliar the ingredients and cooking style, the more you will have to focus.

Good for: Both frontal lobes.

6. Do tai chi. In addition to giving a workout to the cerebellum and frontal lobes on both sides, remembering sequences of the slow-motion movements used in tai chi relaxes the brain.

Added bonus: Tai chi reduces levels of the stress hormone *cortisol.*

Good for: The cerebellum…and frontal lobes.

7. Purchase furniture you have to assemble yourself. Or fix things at home, such as malfunctioning remote controls and clogged sinks. Having to figure out the parts and steps required is certain to give your brain's frontal lobes a stimulating workout.

Good for: Both frontal lobes…and the cerebellum.

8. Learn to play a musical instrument. Mastering the technique of any new instrument exercises parts of your brain used for fine motor control, auditory processing and procedural thinking, among others. If you already play a musical instrument, challenge yourself by learning a new song.

Good for: Both parietal lobes and both frontal lobes…and the cerebellum.

9. Enroll in a drawing, painting or sculpture class. Learning a new art form exercises your "right brain," which is responsible for visual memory, as well as creative imagination. People who already practice an art form should push themselves with new works.

Good for: Right parietal lobe and right frontal lobe.

10. Read the news actively every day. Reading about political events—not just in the US but around the world—requires and activates "attention" centers of the brain, mostly the frontal lobes.

Remembering scores of sports events also helps heighten and sharpen the frontal lobes.

Good for: Both frontal lobes.

■ ■ ■ ■

What You Can Do *Today* to Protect Your Brainpower

Vincent M. Fortanasce, MD, assistant clinical professor, department of neurology and School of Biokinesiology, University of Southern California, Los Angeles. He is founder and medical director of Fortanasce Anti-Alzheimer's Clinic in Arcadia, California, and author of four books, including *The Anti-Alzheimer's Prescription* (Gotham).

In the past five decades, the incidence of Alzheimer's disease—which accounts for 60% to 80% of all cases of dementia (loss of mental functioning)—has increased dramatically among people under age 75. Overall, the rate of Alzheimer's is expected to increase by 70% by the year 2030.

Alzheimer's disease is characterized by increasingly severe problems with memory and speech and impairment of the ability to recognize familiar people and places. It is caused by a type of brain aging in which plaques of *amyloid*—a waxy protein—grow inside of the brain, destroying impulse-conducting *neurons* (nerve cells). Women are more likely than men to develop Alzheimer's disease.

Good news: New studies suggest that up to 70% of people can prevent Alzheimer's…and that even those with strong genetic risk factors, such as having a parent who has or had the disease, can delay its onset by up to 20 years. How? By controlling factors that cause brain aging. *What you need, starting today…*

Less Stress, More Sleep

Long-term sleep deprivation coupled with chronic stress lowers levels of the mood-regulating brain chemicals *dopamine* and *serotonin*. This in turn could drain you of the willpower required to maintain brain-protecting habits, such as exercising regularly and eating healthfully.

Crucial point: Preliminary studies suggest that chronic stress may quadruple a person's risk for Alzheimer's disease. *Self-defense…*

• **Cut down on responsibilities.** When asked to take on yet another task, consider whether it would contribute to your stress. If so, say no. Reevaluate all your commitments weekly, continuing only with those that are most important to you.

• **Meditate for 15 minutes per day—and any time that you feel stressed.**

Easy technique: Focus on the sensation of each breath as it moves in and out of your body…when your attention wanders, simply refocus on your breath.

Crucial point: A century ago, the average American slept nine hours per night. Now some research suggests that the average is less than 6.5 hours. *What you can do…*

• **Take a 10- to 30-minute nap daily—** during your lunch break or preferably in the midafternoon, when sleep-inducing hormones typically are elevated.

• **Clear your mind at bedtime.** As you're falling asleep (or if you wake up during the night), again focus on your breath. Let go of intrusive thoughts about the day that is ending and what's to come the next day.

• **Reduce bedroom light and noise.** A small night-light is fine—but bright or flickering lights disrupt sleep. Wear earplugs to bed if you often are awakened by noises.

The Brain Bank

The brain is like a bank account that pays interest—if you make regular deposits by doing brain-building mental exercises.

Crucial point: A key to building neuron-to-neuron connections that strengthen the brain is novelty—doing things that you're not used to doing. *Examples…*

• **Build up brainpower during dinner.** If you're right-handed, try eating with your left hand…or use chopsticks instead of silverware…or if you always eat in the kitchen, try dining in a different room.

• **Learn a new word daily**—in a new language. Pick an object that you see often… look up how to say it in a foreign language… then say the word aloud throughout the day whenever you see that object. For instance, "car" is *coche* in Spanish…*voiture* in French…*auto* in German.

Resource: Access the free translator at *www.freetranslation.com*.

• **Search your memory.** Several times a day, select an image from the scene around you, then think of a pleasant memory you can associate with it.

Example: Seeing a tractor might remind you of childhood summers at your uncle's farm.

• **Play games that challenge your brain—** such as Scrabble, Boggle, bridge or charades. When you don't have a partner, do a crossword or Sudoku puzzle (visit *www.bestcrosswords.com* and/or *www.websudoku.com*)…or play some chess online at *www.chessmaniac.com*.

Strong Body, Strong Mind

Hormones can be classified as either youthful or aging. The youthful hormones include *estrogen*, *thyroid hormone*, *growth hormone* and *testosterone*. From ages 20 to 70, levels of each of these hormones plummet by about 90%. Aging hormones are *cortisol* and *adrenaline*...and the detrimental effects of these increase as you get older.

Crucial point: Physical exercise helps reduce aging hormones and boost youthful ones...strengthens the connections between neurons...increases brain size...and improves blood flow to the brain. *Best*...

• **Take at least 8,000 steps each day.** A six-year study of nearly 2,000 people age 65 and older found that those who took a walk three times or more weekly—even for as little as 15 minutes each time—reduced their Alzheimer's risk by up to 38%, compared with nonwalkers.

Motivating tip: Wear a pedometer to count steps. To accrue extra steps, get up from your desk hourly and walk in place for several minutes...get off the bus one stop ahead of your destination...use stairs, not elevators.

• **Vary your workout**—to exercise body and brain simultaneously. Enroll in a dance class to learn new choreography...attempt squash instead of your usual tennis...bike around town instead of using a stationary cycle.

• **Do isometric strength-training exercises,** which may quickly strengthen muscles and neurons. With isometric exercises, your body remains in a static position throughout the exercise.

Example: Get into a push-up position and start lowering yourself as if doing a regular push-up, but stop halfway down...then remain there, without moving, for as long as possible.

Crucial point: Diet has an enormous effect on hormone balance. Certain foods trigger spikes and drops in blood sugar, leading to elevated levels of insulin. This makes the insulin-degrading enzyme in the brain work overtime to remove excess insulin rather than doing its other job of removing amyloid plaques. *To protect yourself*...

• **Stay away from simple carbohydrates.** Among the worst offenders in triggering blood sugar fluctuations are white sugar, white flour and white rice.

• **Follow the "one-thirds" diet.** Get one-third of your daily calories from complex carbohydrates (fruits, vegetables, high-fiber whole grains)...one-third from protein (fish, poultry, lean meats, soy, eggs, nuts, seeds, low-fat dairy)...and one-third from healthful fats (olive, grape seed and flaxseed oils, nuts, avocados). This keeps blood sugar and insulin levels stable, helping to minimize buildup of amyloid plaque and protect brainpower.

■ ■ ■ ■

A Brain Exercise for Every Day of the Week!

Pierce J. Howard, PhD, a leading cognitive researcher and cofounder and director of research at the Center for Applied Cognitive Studies in Charlotte, North Carolina. He is the author of *The Owner's Manual for the Brain: Everyday Applications from Mind-Brain Research* (Bard).

Try this regimen for brain fitness, which includes fun activities for every day of the week...

Sunday: Create something in an artistic medium that you've never tried (such as painting with watercolors or sculpting clay)...repair or clean something that you have neglected (such as reorganizing messy files).

Monday: Switch left-pocket contents to the right pocket...contact a high school or college friend with whom you haven't communicated since then (or for years).

Tuesday: Write a love poem or note to your partner, child or friend...plant something (such as orchids) that you've never tried to grow before.

Wednesday: Tackle a word or number game that you do not usually do...write a thank-you note to someone who has meant a great deal to you.

Thursday: Listen closely to music by a composer whose work you've never listened to and identify what you like and don't like about the piece...or begin learning a new language.

Friday: Write a letter to an editor or blogger about an issue that you feel strongly about...begin constructing a model of an airplane, a house or another object that you've never built.

Saturday: Learn the words to a poem or song and recite and/or perform the piece at least three times for yourself and/or others...learn to do something new in a computer software program you use regularly (such as organizing messages into folders in your e-mail program).

■ ■ ■ ■

Stress Kills Brain Cells— Protect Yourself

Richard O'Connor, PhD, a psychotherapist with offices in Canaan, Connecticut, and New York City. He is the author of *Undoing Perpetual Stress: The Missing Connection Between Depression, Anxiety, and 21st Century Illness* (Berkley), *Undoing Depression: What Therapy Doesn't Teach You and Medication Can't Give You* (Berkley) and *Active Treatment of Depression* (Norton).

Everyone knows that stress can contribute to weight gain, diabetes and many other ailments, but few people realize how harmful stress can be for your brain.

Latest development: Although chronic stress has long been known to trigger the release of excessive amounts of stress hormones, such as *cortisol* and *adrenaline*, new studies show that both hormones actually kill brain cells and interfere with the production of new ones.

But fortunately, new research on the brain suggests that there may be ways to minimize, slow down and perhaps even reverse this damage. For advice on the most effective brain-protection strategies, we spoke to Richard O'Connor, PhD, a renowned psychotherapist who has extensively studied the harmful effects of stress. Below he answers important questions...

Why has stress become such a serious health threat in recent years?

It is a long-term historical trend that involves culture and economics. Before the Industrial Revolution (in the late 18th century), people tended to awaken in the morning when it became light and to go to bed when it turned dark. They also had a great deal of leisure time. That's been changing— and just in the past 25 years, it has changed dramatically. We're working 25% longer and harder to attain the same standard of living we did a quarter of a century ago. In fact, Americans now work as many hours as anyone in the world, including the Japanese, who are known for working incredibly long hours.

Doesn't a certain amount of stress make people more productive?

Yes, people are more productive when their work provides enough of a challenge to help them grow. But when the work is too difficult or the hours are too long, or our home life provides no relief, then stress becomes chronic. Research has consistently shown that chronic stress disrupts the functions of the immune, endocrine and digestive systems. This can result in a variety of health problems, such as asthma, heart disease and immune system deficiencies.

During the last 15 years, advances in technology have given scientists an opportunity to examine the human brain in great detail. For example, imaging studies have allowed researchers to visualize the significant reduction of *gray matter* (the brain's information processing center) that can result from years of stress-related conditions, such as depression and anxiety. Unfortunately, no one knows for sure whether these effects are permanent.

Are most people aware of the degree to which they are suffering from stress?

By no means. We have an interest in denying all the effects of stress. Our society admires people who maintain grace under pressure, and we all want to believe we can handle whatever life dishes out.

Given the nature of our lives today, is it really possible to avoid stress? Yes, absolutely. The first step is to believe that you have some degree of control over your own life. Many people feel out of control—as if events are driving them rather than the other way around. Many people think that they must work 60 hours a week, but that's simply not so. If your job requires long, stressful hours, consider changing professions or finding a job in your profession that offers shorter hours.

The stakes are high. People who can't reduce chronic stress live shorter lives, suffer more illness and disability, have less satisfying relationships and often are plagued by anxiety and/or depression.

What if it's not practical to make such a drastic change?

Changing our thought patterns helps. This can allow us to prevent and even reverse some of the adverse changes, such as loss of gray matter, that occur in our brain's neural circuitry as a result of chronic stress. Meditation is an effective stress-decreasing strategy. Research has shown that people who spend just 20 minutes a day focusing on their breath or on calming thoughts achieve such benefits as lower blood pressure, less anxiety and reduced chronic pain.

What do you recommend in addition to meditation?

As we all know, exercise also is an excellent stress fighter. However, few people appreciate the importance of intimate communication. When we feel like we have a partner or are part of a group, we feel safer and more secure. As a result, the stress hormone cascade is reduced. Feeling that we have a purpose in life—having a child or pet to care for, a cause that's meaningful to us, people who need us—these are good stress fighters.

In one landmark study, residents of a nursing home were split into two groups. Half of these residents were told that they were responsible for taking care of a plant. The other half were told not to worry about the plant. After one year, the people who were caring for a plant were healthier and had fewer illnesses. They also lived longer.

How can we improve the way we communicate with others?

Communication always takes place on two levels. It is not only about the content of what's being said, but also the nature of the relationship between the people. Content communication is generally conveyed through words…but relationship communication comes through tone, face and body language. It's perfectly possible to say the words "I love you" but contradict the words through a dismissive tone or a frown. Content communication should be consistent with relationship communication.

What if these strategies aren't effective?

For some people, self-help practices are just not sufficient. Some of the newer antidepressants, such as *selective serotonin reuptake inhibitors* (or SSRIs), appear to reverse stress-related brain damage and help people regain the ability to grow new brain cells.

We have evidence that psychotherapy can do the same thing. Cognitive behavior therapy, which trains patients to see how their psychological problems are the result of faulty thought patterns, has been around for more than 40 years now, and it works to fight the effects of stress. To find a cognitive behavior therapist in your area, consult the Academy of Cognitive Therapy, *www.academyofct.org*, 267-350-7683.

Acupressure for Memory Problems and More

Michael Reed Gach, PhD, founder of the Acupressure Institute in Berkeley, California, and author of self-healing instructional DVDs and CDs and many books, including *Acupressure's Potent Points* (Bantam), *Acupressure for Lovers* (Bantam) and *Arthritis Relief at Your Fingertips* (Warner). For more, go to *www.acupressure.com.*

The *Mind Clearing* acupressure points can improve recall instantly—for example, when you've forgotten a name or gone to the supermarket without your shopping list.

Location: One finger width (about one-half inch) directly above the center of each eyebrow.

What to do: Gently place your right thumb above your right eyebrow and your middle fingertip above the eyebrow on the left side. Hold very gently. You should feel a slight dip or indentation in the bone structure—the acupoints on both sides are in the dip. Press the indentation very lightly, hold and breathe deeply. After a minute or two, you'll experience more mental clarity and sharper memory.

The *Inner Gate* acupoint can reduce emotional problems—such as anxiety, depression and irritability—in two to three minutes.

Location: On the inner side of the forearm, three finger widths up from the center of the wrist crease, in between two thick tendons.

What to do: Place your thumb on the point and your fingers directly behind the outside of the forearm between the two bones. Squeeze in slowly and firmly, hold for two to three minutes, breathing deeply. Repeat on the other arm for the same amount of time.

Also good for: Carpal tunnel syndrome, insomnia, indigestion and nausea.

The acupoints *Gates of Consciousness* relieve a tension headache or migraine.

Location: Underneath the base of your skull to either side of your spine, about three to four inches apart, depending on the size of your head.

What to do: Using your fingers, thumbs or knuckles, press on the points under the base of your skull. At the same time, slowly tilt your head back so that the angle of your head relaxes your neck muscles. Press forward (toward your throat), upward (underneath the base of your skull) and slightly inward, angling the pressure toward the center of your brain. Continue to apply pressure for two minutes, breathing.

Also good for: Neck pain, insomnia or high blood pressure.

Boost Memory, Ease Anxiety, Erase Pain...with Your Brain Waves

Paul G. Swingle, PhD, RPsych, registered psychologist board-certified in biofeedback and neurotherapy and the author of *Biofeedback for the Brain* (Rutgers University). Formerly a professor of psychology at the University of Ottawa in Canada, he currently is in private practice in Vancouver, British Columbia, *www.swingleandassociates.com.*

Imagine finding relief from medical or psychological problems by changing the way your brain works. You can—with *neurofeedback*, a type of biofeedback in which you learn to control brain wave activity. As

Which Brain Waves Do What...

Common brain wave frequencies (in hertz), the mental states they are normally associated with and the consequences of excess or deficiency...

Type of Wave	Normal State	Too Much Leads to...	Too Little Leads to...
Delta: 0-3 hz	Asleep	Mental fog, Pain	Poor sleep
Theta: 4-7 hz	Drowsy	Poor memory	Inability to relax
Alpha: 8-13 hz	Relaxed	Insomnia	Mental chatter
Beta: 14-30 hz	Alert	Anxiety	Distraction

brain function improves, symptoms associated with inefficient brain function also improve. Even physical pain is eased, because pain management has a psychological component—and there are no drug side effects to worry about.

How it works: The brain produces electrical signals in the form of waves that correspond to specific mental states (see the box above). Neurofeedback increases your ability to produce particular brain waves that have specific desired effects. The process is painless and noninvasive.

You don't even have to be ill or in pain to reap the advantages. Many healthy executives, musicians and athletes use neurofeedback to sharpen the mind, ease stage fright or just perform at their peak.

Useful to You?

To explore whether neurofeedback can help you, consult a *neurotherapist*—a specially trained psychologist, psychiatrist, naturopathic doctor, medical doctor, chiropractor or other health-care professional.

Recommended: Choose one who is certified in neurofeedback by the Biofeedback Certification Institute of America (866-908-8713, *www.bcia.org*).

At your initial diagnostic meeting, the neurotherapist will use an *electroencephalogram* (EEG) *machine* to map your brain wave activity. For relatively straightforward problems, such as depression or sleep disorders, or in cases where the goal is simply to maximize cognitive performance, several electrodes (sensors) are dabbed with conductive gel and attached to specific spots on your head. For complex problems, such as traumatic brain injury or epilepsy, you wear a close-fitting cap with 19 sensors.

These sensors, connected with wires to a computer, measure electrical impulses produced by your brain. The practitioner reads these impulses while your eyes are open, while your eyes are shut and while you are reading—because some brain abnormalities are apparent only under certain circumstances.

Example: With one form of attention deficit disorder, brain waves look normal when the mind is not challenged—but when given a task, such as reading, the brain produces a wave that is not conducive to concentrating.

Your brain map is compared with internationally recognized reference data showing which brain patterns are normal under which circumstances. This identifies areas of the brain that are functioning abnormally or suboptimally. These areas are then targeted for treatment.

During a Treatment Session

A typical treatment session lasts about 50 minutes. The practitioner places an electrode at the spot where your brain needs to become more or less active when producing a specific frequency. The electrode is connected to a computer that gives you feedback. When you succeed in changing your brain waves to the target frequency, the computer produces a special sound or visual cue.

Neurofeedback Helps...

- Age-related cognitive decline
- Alcohol and drug cravings
- Anxiety
- Attention disorders (such as ADD and ADHD)
- Brain damage from head injury
- Depression
- Epilepsy, seizures
- Fibromyalgia
- Migraine
- Post-traumatic stress
- Sleep problems
- Stroke effects

At first, achieving this is a matter of trial and error—more the result of passively observing the mental and physical states that seem to work rather than actively trying to think or do something specific. For instance, if you are trying to create alpha waves to ease anxiety, you may notice that the tone sounded when you closed your eyes and pictured a ship sailing into the horizon but not when you imagined yourself in a meadow. With practice, your brain learns to regulate these brain waves.

The severity of the problem determines the length of treatment. Some people have 10 to 30 weekly treatments...others come three times a week for up to 100 sessions. A follow-up session assures that the brain wave change is stable. Some patients get "tune-ups"—many older clients come four times a year to adjust the frequencies associated with mental focus. Cost varies but typically runs about $100 per session. Insurance sometimes covers treatment.

Recommendation: Neurofeedback is a complementary therapy, best used in conjunction with psychotherapy, physical therapy, nutritional counseling, medical care or other treatment.

For instance: Neurofeedback can ease cravings for alcohol or drugs—but a person with a substance use disorder also needs counseling to learn how to create a new social environment that does not include drinking or drugs.

Important: Inform your medical doctor and other health-care providers before beginning neurofeedback (as you should with any new treatment) to make sure that none of your therapies conflict.

Computers Make Life Easier for the Elderly— Better Memory, Sharper Focus and Expanded Social Network

Scott Rains, senior advisor to with-tv.com and former director of programs and services, SeniorNet.org.

"There are three signs of old age," the old joke goes. "First is loss of memory. And I forget the other two." That makes us smile—but what's underlying this common stereotype about seniors is really not very funny. We all know that age-related mental decline takes simple forgetfulness to much more painful levels.

Computers, of all things, can help you, and not just because they store so much information. It has been demonstrated that brain-teasers and games can help to keep mental faculties sharp, and in the past, studies have hinted that computer-based brain games can be especially helpful. (We say "hinted" since many were funded or conducted by software companies with a stake in the outcome.) One particularly interesting study was conducted at the Tel Aviv Sourasky Medical Center of Tel Aviv University in Israel, where a clinical trial compared the cognitive improvements of 121 participants age 50 and older. They were asked to use a sophisticated brain-training program called MindFit or classic computer games (such as Tetris or Labyrinth) 30 minutes a day, three times a week for three months.

Pick a Game...Any Game

Yes, this was one of those studies that received funding by a software company to test their products, so please take their conclusions on that front with a grain of salt. But what grabbed our attention was that in this case, regardless of which computer game or program they used, both the study groups experienced improvements in areas such as short-term memory, memory recall and focused attention. The very act of focusing—attentive participation involving higher order thinking, information integration and judgment—on mental computer tasks appears to be what helps keep the mind sharp...and that is consistent with past research.

Add to that some of the other ways computers can expand horizons—including building or maintaining social connections, providing access to information on virtually any topic, and even offering the potential to contribute a valued service to a business or nonprofit—and it seems an excellent idea to encourage computer use by seniors in your life who aren't already connected.

Providing Tech Support

A common problem is that computers can be frustratingly difficult for people who lack experience with them. Memory issues, lack of confidence and often sensory problems and decreasing motor skills present obstacles that could seem insurmountable—but they need not be.

Scott Rains is senior advisor to with-tv. com (a television station serving people

Cell Phone Games Are Great for Your Brain

Games on your cell phone are better for your brain than crossword or Sudoku puzzles.

Reason: Because they have a timing component.

As you age, your brain faces more challenges with short-term memory and the cognitive tasks of paying attention and juggling multiple abilities. It's important to challenge these skills, and playing games against the clock provides a better brain workout than puzzles and board games.

Cynthia R. Green, PhD, president, Memory Arts, LLC, Upper Montclair, New Jersey, *http://totalbrainhealth.com.*

with disabilities) and former director of programs and services at SeniorNet.org, a nonprofit organization that specializes in computer and Internet education for older adults and seniors. *He offers advice on how to help computer-cautious seniors get started and/or become more comfortable with the computer...*

● **Focus on their interests.** Rains suggests starting with a conversation to assess how a computer can (and actually will) be used, before buying any equipment and software. For instance, says Rains, grandparents may be interested in staying in touch with family through e-mail or receiving regular digital photo updates, while people who enjoy travel may like the convenience of the many travel resources on the Internet. A benefit for housebound seniors may be that they can let their "fingers do their shopping."

● **Get the right equipment.** Seniors who have physical disabilities, such as arthritis or poor eyesight, may believe these barriers stand in the way of using a computer. That's not usually the case, as specialized equipment is available to adapt computers for just about any disability or challenge. For example, arthritis sufferers can benefit from large-key keyboards, such as those made by BigKeys Keyboards (go to *www.bigkeys.com*) and also specialized "mice" like those from EnableMart (*www.enablemart.com*). People with vision problems do better with large-print keyboards, such as boards offered by ZoomText or screen magnification programs like BigShot (both available at *www. aisquared.com*).

• **Take a class.** For most inexperienced computer users, success depends on learning how to use the hardware and software. Fortunately there are many resources. "You can register for classes at continuing education centers, adult education centers, senior centers, community colleges, libraries and more," says Rains, noting that there are more than 200 SeniorNet Learning Centers across the country, as well. The very best senior-oriented computer classes are small, use lots of visual aids, provide a handbook for use at home, work at a pace that allows for plenty of questions and repetition, and are focused on personal enrichment—not speed, competition or job certification, he says. Ask questions about what classes emphasize before signing up.

• **Enlist a friendly tech expert.** There are plenty of resources for people who need in-home help setting up computers or solving problems—including the national franchises such as Best Buy, which has partnered with Geek Squad. There is also GeeksonTime.com. But, says Rains, for computer beginners it can be best to enlist the help of a tech-savvy friend or family member. "You're going to obtain the best results through an interaction between friends," Rains insists. "There's a level of comfort and trust, and a shared culture and language that helps them relate to one another."

Online Games That Improve Your Mind

Andrew Carle, an authority on technology for older adults. He is assistant professor at the College of Health and Human Services at George Mason University in Fairfax, Virginia. Carle's work has been featured on National Public Radio and *Fox Morning News* as well as in *The Washington Post, USA Today* and *The Chronicle of Higher Education.*

Electronic games have been around for many years, but they recently reached a new level with computer programs designed specifically to help older adults hone their mental abilities.

These games—including some that are better described as mental exercises—are aimed at improving several important abilities, including memory, eye-hand coordination, audio perception and visual acuity. And they're fun!

The best of these programs continually offer new challenges to customers via the Internet, so games you played last week won't necessarily be the same as those you play this week. That's a big advantage over bridge, chess and other classic games that are challenging but require the same skill regardless of how long you play them.

New Challenges

The new mental exercises generally fall into two categories. The "Brain Gyms" are designed to be personalized and comprehensive, which gives you an incentive to play—just as working out at the actual gym may be more enjoyable than, say, getting on a treadmill in your den. They're also likely to adjust more often according to your performance.

"Brain Trainers" usually have a smaller selection of games—though many can be very entertaining—and they're aimed at a broad range of users, not just older adults.

Most new training games are sold on a subscription basis, but some can also be purchased on a CD.

A potential drawback of the new games is that few of them can be played directly against an opponent, although two or more people can sometimes challenge each other by playing separately and then comparing scores.

Before making a purchase...

• **Try out the program,** which most companies let you do online for free.

• **Even if a trial game appears to work well,** check the "system requirements" page of the manufacturer's Internet site to make sure that your computer can play the game you're interested in. The new games typically require a computer with at least 256 megabytes (and preferably 512 megabytes) of random access memory (RAM) and 500 megabytes (and preferably 1 gigabyte) of free disk space on your hard drive. You may also need headphones for some of the games that involve auditory skills.

Working Out in the "Gym"

Popular brain gyms include...

• **CogniFit.** Dozens of entertaining exercises are aimed at improving reaction time, short-term memory, eye-hand coordination and the ability to recognize signs and symbols.

In one game, a room with different-colored walls is displayed on the screen. A colored ball bounces off one wall and then another. The objective is to make sure that the ball bounces off only the wall that's the same color as the ball. The game is more difficult than it first appears.

Price: Contact CogniFit.

Information: *www.cognifit.com.*

• **Posit Science.** One exercise program sharpens your eyesight while another is aimed at improving your hearing.

Exercises for eyesight are designed to widen your field of view and improve your ability to locate certain colors and shapes.

Auditory games give you practice in telling sounds apart, responding to different sounds and remembering what you hear. Exercises of this kind are helpful in many ways, from improving driving skills to enjoying a Broadway show.

Price: $345.

Information: 866-599-6463, *www.posit science.com.*

• **Vigorous Mind.** I am on the advisory board of this company, which provides a variety of entertaining games designed to improve memory as well as skills in language, perception, mathematics, eye-hand coordination and reasoning.

In the "Take 2" exercise, for example, the challenge is to memorize pairs of identical pictures on the computer screen. The pictures are then "turned over," and you're asked to remember the location of every pair. In more advanced levels, when the pictures are turned over, their reverse side may show another picture—a maneuver designed to challenge the player.

Price: Contact Vigorous Mind.

Information: 888-769-6463, *www.vigor ousmind.com.*

"Trainers" on the Web

Some of the most popular brain trainers...

• **Lumosity.** By accessing a Web site, you can play games designed to improve attention span, speed at performing tasks and other cognitive abilities, such as concentration and memory for both names and numbers.

Games are colorful and entertaining. A game created around bird-watching, for instance, aims at improving the ability to process visual information, an important skill in such activities as driving and playing sports. In another game, you're given three letters and challenged to think of as many words as you can that start with them. In each game, as your skill improves, tasks become progressively difficult.

Price: Contact Lumosity.

Information: *www.lumosity.com.*

• **MyBrainTrainer.** This company's 21-day online training program aims to help you process more information, perform simultaneous tasks, retrieve information from memory and improve concentration. The program records daily and monthly scores so that you can keep track of improvements and know where you still need practice.

Exercises include dozens of games that require you to respond to visual and/or audio signals. In one game, for example, one playing card appears in a box on the screen for half a second, followed by a display of three cards in the middle of the screen for a much shorter period of time (0.016 second). The object is to determine which of the three cards matches the first one. To complete the exercise, players must respond correctly 20 times in a row.

Price: $9.95 for three months or $29.95 for one year.

Information: *www.mybraintrainer.com.*

No Computer Needed

If you don't want to rely on a computer for playing mind-expanding games, consider…

• **Big Brain Academy.** Each of their 15 games is played on a Nintendo DS handheld device. You can play alone to improve your score or with as many as seven other competitors. These games are designed to test your ability to think logically, analyze, compute, visually identify and memorize. At the end of a game, you receive a label that describes your brain—from "caveman" to "Isaac Newton."

Typical price: $19.99 plus about $100 for a Nintendo DS, on which you can play dozens of other games suitable for adults, including Crosswords DS and Scrabble.

Information: 800-895-1672, *www.ninten do.com.* Games and the DS device are also available from such retailers as Amazon. com and Office Depot.

• **Platinum Solitaire 3.** A dozen variations of the game can be played on many mobile-phone models, including BlackBerry, Nokia, Samsung and Sony Ericsson. In the "casino mode," Platinum Solitaire 3 lets you place simulated bets on your talent.

Note: The higher the bet, the more difficult the game becomes.

Typical price: $3 and over. The game is also available free with some cell-phone subscriptions that include a Nokia phone.

Information: 212-993-3000, *www.game loft.com.*

Web Surfing Builds Brain Function

Gary Small, MD, director, Center on Aging, University of California, Los Angeles.

Surfing the Web can be beneficial for the brain.

Recent study: Researchers measured brain activity in 24 healthy adults (ages 55 to 76) while they performed either Internet searches or read books.

The result: Internet searching triggered more extensive brain activity than did reading. Experienced Web surfers showed nearly twice the level of brain function as those unfamiliar with the Internet.

Theory: Searching the Internet requires the ability to quickly evaluate significant amounts of information.

Meditation for People Who Don't Like to Meditate

Roger Walsh, MD, PhD, professor of psychiatry and human behavior in the School of Medicine, and of anthropology and philosophy in the School of Humanities, both at the University of California, Irvine. He has done extensive research on Asian philosophies, religion and the effects of meditation and has received more than 20 national/international awards. He is author of *Essential Spirituality: The 7 Central Practices to Awaken Heart and Mind* (Wiley), which contains a foreword by the Dalai Lama.

We have heard all about the benefits of meditating. For decades, studies have shown that meditation helps with depression, anxiety, stress, insomnia, pain, high blood pressure, self-esteem, self-control, concentration and creativity. Yet for many people, meditation seems daunting. Maybe you find it hard to sit still…to clear your mind…to make the time…or to stick with it long enough to experience the effects.

Secret to success: Choose a technique that suits your personality, schedule and level of experience, then do it consistently. Twenty minutes or more per day is a good goal, but even five minutes is helpful if you do it every day—and some techniques take almost no time at all.

If You Are a Beginner…

The methods below are effective yet simple enough for a novice. Start with just a few minutes, and work your way up.

● **Single-tasking.** A time-crunched society encourages multitasking—so you sort mail while on the phone and listen to audiobooks while driving.

What you may not know: The simple act of focusing fully on a single task is a meditative exercise. It improves your powers of concentration, alleviates stress and boosts mood by enhancing your appreciation of the here-and-now.

Try: Once or twice each day, give your complete attention to just one activity.

Example: When you fold the laundry, don't turn on the TV—just enjoy the softness of the fabrics and the soothing rhythm of your hand motions.

● **Focused breathing.** Sit in a quiet place, on the floor or in a chair, keeping your back straight so your lungs can expand. Pay attention to your breathing. Feel the air moving through your nostrils when you slowly inhale and exhale…feel your abdomen rise and fall. Then choose either of these sites (nostrils or abdomen) and focus fully on all the sensations there. Soon you may notice that your mind has wandered. Don't berate yourself—this happens even to experienced meditators. Simply return your attention to the breath.

● **Centering prayer.** Choose a phrase or a word that is spiritually meaningful for you, such as *God is love* or *shalom*. With each breath, repeat it silently to yourself. Again, if your thoughts start to stray, just calmly return to your prayer.

If You Hate to Sit Still…

Some people cannot stop squirming when they try to meditate.

Solution: Moving meditation.

● **Qigong, tai chi or yoga.** These practices combine specific movements with a contemplative focus on the body, so you exercise while you meditate. Many health clubs, adult-education centers and hospitals offer classes in these techniques.

Referrals: National Qigong Association (888-815-1893, *www.nqa.org*)…American Tai Chi Association (703-477-8878, *www.americantaichi.net*)…Yoga Alliance (888-921-9642, *www.yogaalliance.org*).

● **Mindful eating.** Eat a meal alone, in silence, savoring the experience. When you first sit down, spend a moment enjoying the colors and aromas of the food. Take a bite and chew slowly. How do the taste and texture change as you chew? What sensations do you perceive as you swallow?

Surprise: You are meditating. Continue to eat each bite as consciously as you can, never rushing.

If You Can't Find the Time...

Some days you may not have even five minutes to meditate—but you can take just a moment.

• **Three long breaths.** Whenever you get tense, take three long, deep breaths. Even a few conscious inhalations and exhalations will calm you. Also use cues in your environment as regular reminders to focus and breathe deeply.

Example: Take three slow breaths every time you hang up the phone...walk through a doorway...or get into your car.

• **Beauty in the moment.** Three times a day, look around you and notice something lovely—the scent of someone's perfume, the happy sound of children playing. Explore the experience with your full attention.

Example: A mellow breeze is blowing. Watch the graceful way it makes the grass sway...listen to it whispering as it moves through the trees...feel its gentle touch on your cheeks. Notice your emotions of pleasure and appreciation—and carry them with you as you continue through your day.

If You Already Love to Meditate...

If you are an accomplished meditator and want to enrich your experience, try these more advanced techniques...

• **Contemplative reading.** Select a brief passage (just two or three sentences) from a philosophy book, religious text or other writing that is meaningful to you. Read it slowly and reflectively, over and over. If your reading brings up insights, ponder them. If your mind drifts to unrelated thoughts, return to reading.

• **Inquiry.** Sit and focus on your breathing. When a thought, feeling, sound or other sensation enters your awareness, instead of turning your attention back to the breath, simply explore the experience. Does it seem to have a shape/image associated with it? Does it change or fade away as you examine it?

Some examples...

• You notice a tickle in your shoulder. As you study it, you note that it feels diffuse... then localizes in one spot...then moves to a different area and prickles...then disappears completely.

• You are feeling anxious. Rather than trying to figure out what is causing this, note where the anxiety manifests in your body (a fluttery stomach, a tight muscle)...any images and thoughts associated with it...and how all those images and thoughts change as you observe them.

When a particular sensation passes, return your full attention to your breath until the next sensation enters your awareness... then explore this new one. Over time, this enhances awareness and acceptance.

PART 3

Diabetes Prevention
& Management

8

Preventing Diabetes

Surprising Symptoms of Prediabetes

Frederic J. Vagnini, MD, a cardiovascular surgeon and medical director of the Heart, Diabetes & Weight Loss Centers of New York in Lake Success, *www.vagnini.com.* He is coauthor of *The Weight Loss Plan for Beating Diabetes* (Fair Winds).

One of the best ways to prevent diabetes is to spot blood sugar (glucose) problems before the full-blown disease develops. But most people don't realize that diabetes—and its precursor, prediabetes—can cause no symptoms at all or a wide range of symptoms that often are misinterpreted.

Common mistake: Because type 2 diabetes is strongly linked to excess body weight, many people who are a normal weight assume that they won't develop the disease. But that's not always true. About 15% of people who are diagnosed with diabetes are not overweight. And paradoxically, even weight loss can be a symptom of this complex disorder in people (normal weight or overweight) who have uncontrolled high glucose levels.

Shocking recent finding: The Centers for Disease Control and Prevention now estimates that 40% of Americans ages 40 to 74 have prediabetes, and nearly two out of three Americans over age 65 have prediabetes or diabetes—most likely due to the increasing numbers of people who are overweight and inactive, both of which boost diabetes risk.

However, most primary care doctors aren't diagnosing and treating prediabetes early enough in their patients—often because they fail to order the necessary screening tests (see page 191). And because the symptoms of prediabetes can be subtle, especially in its early stages, most people are not reporting potential red flags to their doctors.

Fortunately, prediabetes can virtually always be prevented from progressing to diabetes if the condition is identified and treated in its early stages (by following a healthful diet, exercising regularly and taking nutritional supplements and medications, if necessary).

What Is Prediabetes?

Prediabetes occurs when the body's cells no longer respond correctly to *insulin*, a hormone that regulates blood sugar. With prediabetes, blood sugar levels are higher than normal but not high enough to warrant a diagnosis of diabetes.

Prediabetes affects about 57 million Americans—most of whom are unaware that they have the condition.

Red Flags for Diabetes

Being overweight (defined as having a body mass index, or BMI, of 25 or higher) is perhaps the best-known risk factor for type 2 diabetes.* The more excess body weight you have, the more resistant your cells become to the blood sugar–regulating effects of the hormone insulin, ultimately causing blood glucose levels to rise.

Greatest danger: Abdominal fat, in particular, further boosts diabetes risk. That's because belly (visceral) fat hinders the processing of insulin. The single biggest risk factor for prediabetes is having a waistline of 40 inches or more if you're a man...or 35 inches or more if you're a woman. *Lesser-known red flags for prediabetes (and diabetes)—if you have one of these symptoms, see your doctor...*

• **Increased thirst and need to urinate.** Because excess blood glucose draws water from the body's tissues, people with elevated blood glucose levels feel thirsty much of the time. Even when they drink fluids, their thirst is rarely quenched. Therefore, they drink even more, causing them to urinate more often than is normal for them.

• **Unexplained weight loss.** While being overweight is a significant risk factor for prediabetes, the condition also can paradoxically lead to unexplained weight loss. This weight loss results from a lack of energy supply to the body's cells and a loss of glucose-related calories due to excessive urination.

*For a BMI calculator, go to the Web site of the National Heart, Lung and Blood Institute, *www.nhlbi support.com/bmi.*

• **Dry, itchy skin.** Excess blood glucose also draws moisture from the skin, leaving it dry and prone to itching and cracking—especially on the legs, feet and elbows.

• **Blurred vision.** Glucose can change the shape of the eye lens, making it difficult to focus properly.

• **Slow-healing cuts, sores or bruises and frequent infections.** For unknown reasons, excess blood glucose appears to interfere with the body's healing processes and its ability to fight off infection. In particular, women with prediabetes and diabetes are prone to urinary tract and vaginal infections.

• **Red, swollen and tender gums.** Because the body's ability to heal can be compromised by prediabetes, gum inflammation, involving red, swollen, tender and/or bleeding gums, may develop.

• **Persistent feelings of hunger.** When the body's cells do not get enough glucose due to prediabetes, the cells send signals to the brain that are interpreted as hunger, typically about one hour after consuming a meal.

• **Lack of energy.** Because their cells are starved of energy-boosting glucose, people with prediabetes tend to tire quickly after even mild physical effort. Dehydration due to excess blood glucose also can contribute to fatigue.

• **Falling asleep after eating.** An hour or so after eating, our digestive systems convert the food we've eaten into glucose. In people with prediabetes, the process is exaggerated—blood glucose levels spike, triggering a surge of insulin as the body attempts to stabilize high glucose levels. This insulin surge is ineffective in lowering blood glucose, causing the person to become drowsy. If you feel sleepy after meals, it can be a sign that your blood glucose levels are riding this prediabetic roller coaster.

• **Moodiness and irritability.** Lack of energy production in your cells, together with sharp rises and dips in blood glucose levels, can trigger feelings of restlessness, irritability and exaggerated emotional responses to stress.

• **Tingling or numbness in the hands and feet.** Excess blood glucose can damage small blood vessels feeding the body's peripheral nerves, often causing tingling, loss of sensation or burning pain in the hands, arms, legs or feet.

• **Loss of sex drive and erectile dysfunction in men.** Prediabetes is associated with low testosterone in men, which often reduces libido. In addition, glucose-related damage to the body's small blood vessels often impairs the ability of prediabetic men to have an erection.

■ ■ ■ ■

More from Dr. Frederic Vagnini...

Three Key Diabetes Tests

If you suspect that you may have prediabetes, ask your doctor to order the following tests...

• **Fasting blood glucose.** This traditional blood test for diabetes is usually part of a standard physical. Until recently, a result over 125 milligrams per deciliter (mg/dL) was considered a sign of diabetes, while 100 mg/dL to 125 mg/dL indicated prediabetes.

New finding: Standard guidelines established by the American Diabetes Association have not changed, but recent data suggest that a person who has a fasting blood glucose reading over 90 mg/dL should be evaluated by a physician.

• **Hemoglobin A1C.** This blood test, also included in many annual checkups, measures the average blood glucose level over a two- to three-month period. An A1C result of 4.5% to 5.9% is considered normal...6% to 6.5% indicates prediabetes...and two separate readings of 6.5% or above indicate diabetes.

New danger level: Standard guidelines still use 6% as the lower end of the prediabetes range, but recent data suggest that results as low as 5.6% or 5.7% may signal prediabetes.

• **Oral glucose tolerance test.** Administered over two hours in your doctor's office, this test can spot problems with blood-sugar regulation that may not show up in the other tests. For the oral glucose tolerance test, blood levels of glucose are checked immediately before drinking a premixed glucose formula and two hours afterward.

A result of 140 mg/dL to 159 mg/dL is a sign of increased risk for diabetes...160 mg/dL to 200 mg/dL indicates high risk for diabetes...and over 200 mg/dL signals full-blown diabetes. Also ask your doctor to measure your insulin levels—insulin fluctuations can be an even earlier predictor of prediabetes than the tests described above.

■ ■ ■ ■

Lifestyle vs. Drugs for Preventing Diabetes— Lifestyle Wins!

Jill Crandall, MD, director, Diabetes Clinical Trials Unit at the Albert Einstein College of Medicine in New York City.

Neil H. White, MD, professor of pediatrics, division of endocrinology and metabolism, Washington University School of Medicine, St. Louis.

More than a decade ago, researchers launched the Diabetes Prevention Program study (DPP) to discover the best way to prevent or delay type 2 diabetes. The study involved more than 3,200 individuals with prediabetes—people who were overweight and had higher-than-normal blood sugar (glucose), and were therefore at high risk for developing type 2 diabetes.

The researchers divided them into three groups. One group took the glucose-lowering drug *metformin* (Glucophage, Glucophage XR, Fortamet, Riomet). One group took a placebo. And one group went through a "Lifestyle Balance Program," learning new and healthy habits, such as exercising regularly and eating a low-fat diet.

After three years, the researchers tallied the new cases of diabetes to see which approach had worked best—and lifestyle was the winner. It reduced the rate of diabetes by 58%, compared with the placebo group. Metformin also worked, but not as well, reducing the rate by 31%.

After the DPP study was over, researchers offered the participants the opportunity to keep going with the lifestyle program or the drug—a continuation of the study, called the Diabetes Prevention Program Outcome Study (DPPOS). About nine out of 10 of the study participants opted to continue.

And now more than 10 years after the start of DPP, and more than seven years after the start of DPPOS, the latest results are in, published in the prestigious medical journal *The Lancet*…And the winner is—lifestyle!

Reducing Risk by Nearly 50%

Compared with the placebo group, those in the lifestyle group had a 34% lower rate of developing diabetes.

And among those in the study who were aged 60 or older, lifestyle reduced the rate of developing diabetes by nearly 50%.

Those in the metformin group had an 18% lower rate.

Important: On average, the people in the lifestyle group regained 10 of the 15 pounds they lost during the three years of the DPP study. But 10 years of regular exercise and a healthier eating regimen was still protective against the development of diabetes. In other words, you don't have to lose a whole lot of weight to get a whole lot of benefit!

"Moderate weight loss through a lower-calorie, low-fat lifestyle, and regular exercise—usually walking—seems to be effective in lowering the risk for diabetes in people at very high risk for developing the disease, and that's certainly a positive finding," says Jill Crandall, MD, a study author, and director of the Diabetes Clinical Trials Unit at the Albert Einstein College of Medicine in New York City.

The Diabetes Prevention Program

"Changing your lifestyle to better health habits—including those aimed at reducing weight, improving diet and increasing exercise—can have long-term, sustained impact on preventing diabetes," agrees Neil H. White, MD, a study author at the Washington University School of Medicine in St. Louis.

Here are some recommendations for lifestyle changes from the Diabetes Prevention Program…

• **Do 2½ hours of physical activity a week.** This will burn about 700 calories a week. Pick an easy activity you like, such as brisk walking. Spread the 2½ hours a week over 3 to 4 days (or more)—for example, ½ hour a day, on five days.

• **Eat less fat—three smart ways.** Incorporate the following straightforward lifestyle practices to reduce fat in your diet.

• Eat high-fat foods less often. *Example:* Don't eat french fries every day—have them only once a week.

• Eat smaller amounts of high-fat foods. *Example:* At the salad bar, don't use the ladle to pour on salad dressing—use a regular spoon from your place setting.

• Eat lower-fat foods instead of high-fat foods. *Examples:* choose pretzels instead of potato chips...use low-fat margarine instead of regular margarine...use salsa instead of sour cream on a baked potato.

• **Watch out for hidden fat.** Nearly 70% of the fat you eat isn't obvious, like a pat of butter—it's hidden in foods.

Example: The hidden fat in a typical fast-food meal—a fried fish sandwich (5 teaspoons of fat), large french fries (6 teaspoons), apple pie (4 teaspoons) and a milkshake (5 teaspoons)—equals 20 teaspoons of fat. That's close to eating a whole stick of butter!

• **Lower the fats in the meat you eat.** Meats are a major source of dietary fat. Buy lean cuts (round loin, sirloin, leg). Trim all the fat you see. Instead of frying—bake, roast, broil, barbecue or grill. Remove the skin from chicken and turkey. Drain off fat after cooking. Flavor meats with low-fat flavorings, such as Tabasco, ketchup, lemon juice or Worcestershire sauce.

• **Healthy eating out.** Restaurant meals are often a major source of fat. If you are planning to eat dinner out, eat less fat and fewer calories at other meals during the day. Eat a little something before you go out, or drink a large, low-calorie beverage. Split a dessert.

Look for these low-fat choices on the menu...

• Pizza. Plain cheese pizza—and ask for half the cheese.

• Mexican. The grilled chicken or beef fajitas.

• Chinese. Stir-fried chicken or stir-fried vegetables.

• Italian. Spaghetti with meatless tomato sauce.

• Seafood. Broiled, baked or boiled—not fried.

• Steakhouses. Broiled chicken or fish, with a plain baked potato.

One in Three US Adults Could Have Diabetes By 2050?

Currently one in nine people has the disease. The predicted increase in cases is attributable to aging of the population, obesity, sedentary lifestyle, people with diabetes living longer and an increase in the population of minority groups that are at higher risk for type 2 diabetes.

Ann Albright, PhD, RD, director, Division of Diabetes Translation, Centers for Disease Control and Prevention, Atlanta. *www.cdc.gov*

Resource: You can find guidelines for the entire Lifestyle Balance Program on the Web site of the Diabetes Prevention Program, *www.bsc.gwu.edu/dpp/index.htmlvdoc.* Click on "Manuals."

How to Beat "Diabesity"— Fight Fat with Fat

Neal Barnard, MD, author of *Dr. Neal Barnard's Program for Reversing Diabetes* (Rodale).

Martha Belury, PhD, RD, professor, department of human nutrition at Ohio State University, Columbus.

Almost 90% of people with type 2 diabetes are overweight. In fact, these two problems are so closely related that one expert combined the words diabetes and obesity, calling the problem diabesity.

What happens: Insulin is the hormone that helps blood sugar (glucose) leave the bloodstream and enter cells. Now, imagine your cells are locks and insulin is the key, says Neal Barnard, MD, author of *Dr. Neal Barnard's Program for Reversing Diabetes*

(Rodale). Extra fat clogs the locks, so insulin can't do its job.

Which is why losing even a little body fat can help prevent or delay diabetes, or help normalize glucose levels if you've already developed the disease.

And shedding extra body fat may be as easy as slightly increasing the fat in your diet, according to a surprising new study from researchers at Ohio State University.

Study Details

Researchers studied 35 overweight, postmenopausal women (average age 60) with diabetes, dividing them into two groups.

One group took a daily supplement of *conjugated linoleic acid*, a saturated fat found in beef, lamb and dairy products. Studies have shown CLA can help burn body fat. (In one such study, people taking 3.4 grams a day of CLA lost an average of 4.5 pounds of fat and gained an average of 1.5 pounds of fat-burning muscle in three months—without cutting calories or increasing exercise.)

The other group took a supplement containing about two teaspoons of *safflower oil,* a vegetable oil rich in *omega-6 polyunsaturated fats*. (Omega-6 is a scientific term describing the specific chemical composition of a fat.)

After four months, the women taking CLA had lost a few pounds and an average of 3.2% of their body fat—without losing any muscle. (Losing muscle rather than fat is an unfortunate result of many diets.)

The women taking safflower oil didn't lose any weight. But they shed an average 6.3% of their belly fat and had a 1.6% increase in muscle.

Important: Excess belly fat is a risk factor for diabetes, possibly because it leads to a fattier pancreas and liver, two organs that play key roles in regulating glucose levels.

The women taking safflower oil also had an improvement in glucose control.

And they had a 20% increase in *adiponectin*, a hormone produced by fat cells that helps control glucose.

What to Do

"The big surprise of this study was the effect of safflower oil on body fat and blood sugar—a result never seen before in scientific research," says Martha Belury, PhD, RD, professor of human nutrition and the study leader.

Why safflower oil had that effect, she doesn't know. But that doesn't mean you can't benefit from it.

• **Safflower oil.** "If you're overweight and trying to improve blood sugar control, you should definitely begin to get two teaspoons a day of safflower oil in your diet," says Dr. Belury. "It's easy to do and it's inexpensive." You can also use another type of vegetable oil rich in omega-6 polyunsaturated fats, such as sunflower or corn.

• **Use the oil as a salad dressing, along with vinegar.** "I try to have a salad with oil and vinegar almost every day, because I know it's good for me," says Dr. Belury. Or cook with vegetable oil instead of butter.

• **CLA supplements.** Taking a CLA supplement is a personal decision, based on the cost of the supplement and the possible benefit, says Dr. Belury. "If I had 50 pounds to lose, and I could afford to take CLA, I would—because the supplement might help me lose that weight," she says.

Caution: Take the dosage recommended on the label—a larger dose won't speed or increase weight loss, says Dr. Belury. And take the supplement for at least three to six months, the time it takes for CLA to produce results.

■ ■ ■ ■

Let the Sun Shine— For Your Health

Frederic J. Vagnini, MD, a cardiovascular surgeon and medical director of the Heart, Diabetes & Weight Loss Centers of New York in Lake Success, *www.vagnini.com.* He is coauthor of *The Weight Loss Plan for Beating Diabetes* (Fair Winds).

Everyone knows that diet and exercise can help prevent type 2 diabetes. *Here's a simple preventative remedy that you might enjoy…*

To prevent diabetes, also be sure to get plenty of sunshine, which can provide most of the vitamin D that you need. The National Public Health Institute in Helsinki, Finland, recently reported that people with the highest vitamin D levels were 40% less likely to develop type 2 diabetes than those with lower levels. Studies indicate that adequate vitamin D also reduces insulin resistance, a hallmark of diabetes.

For a healthy vitamin D level, spend about 15 minutes in the sun a few times a week with your arms, hands and, if possible, legs exposed. Do this during the brightest part of the day (10 am to 3 pm). Wear sunscreen only on your face during timed sun exposure to prevent sun damage. If you have a history of skin cancer or you are at high risk for it, check with your doctor before practicing timed sun exposure.

If you live above 33° latitude—roughly north of Atlanta—you will not be able to produce significant amounts of vitamin D from sun exposure during the winter. Dark-skinned individuals are at increased risk for vitamin D deficiency.

To ensure adequate levels: Ask your doctor to test your vitamin D level. If you're deficient, you will be prescribed a therapeutic dose that is taken for about 12 weeks, followed by a regular daily dose to be determined by your physician.

How Full Fat Helps Diabetes

Dariush Mozaffarian, MD, DrPH, associate professor, department of epidemiology, Harvard School of Public Health, Boston.

After all these years of reading and writing about health, we can't help but notice that certain basic nutritional truths keep reasserting themselves. For instance, it seems blatantly obvious that we could save lots of money researching the root causes of chronic illness by saying simply this—always eat in moderation, and choose foods that are as close to their natural states as possible.

As the latest example, here's some research that says people who consume whole-fat dairy products—as opposed to their processed, lower-fat versions—have a 60% lower incidence of diabetes! This flies in the face of what experts have been advising for decades—that everyone but babies and toddlers should choose milk, cheese, yogurt and other dairy products with the lowest possible fat content, because the saturated fat that's prominent in dairy products is bad for your health.

Fat Is Beautiful?

Now, in a study from Harvard published in *Annals of Internal Medicine,* a team of researchers has found that people with the highest circulating levels of a type of fatty acid that is found only in whole-fat dairy are one-third as likely to get diabetes as those with the lowest circulating levels. Higher levels of the fatty acid—called *transpalmitoleic acid*—were also associated with lower body mass index (BMI)…smaller waist circumference…lower triglycerides (potentially harmful blood fats)…higher levels of HDL "good" cholesterol…less insulin resistance…and lower levels of *C-reactive protein,* a marker for general inflammation.

How the study was done: At the study's start, researchers began with baseline measurements of glucose, insulin, inflammatory markers, circulating fatty acids and blood lipids (such as triglycerides and cholesterol) from stored 1992 blood samples of 3,736 participants in the National Heart, Lung, and Blood Institute–funded Cardiovascular Health Study. Those data were compared with the same participants' dietary records and recorded health outcomes (including the incidence of diabetes) over the following 10 years. During this period, 304 new cases of diabetes were recorded. When the participants were grouped according to their circulating levels of trans-palmitoleic acid, the researchers discovered that those with higher levels had the lowest rates of diabetes.

How Much Dairy?

The study's lead researcher, Dariush Mozaffarian, MD, DrPH, associate professor of epidemiology at Harvard School of Public Health, says that other studies have suggested a similar phenomenon with dairy consumption, but that his is the first to have used objective chemical markers in the blood to determine the relationship between this specific fatty acid and the onset of diabetes. The participants with the highest levels averaged about two servings of whole-fat dairy foods a day.

This is not a license to indulge yourself in a daily serving of strawberry shortcake with extra whipped cream or a giant ice cream from Cold Stone Creamery...but you might want to consider switching from skim milk to whole milk with your morning cereal and selecting full-fat yogurt over low-fat or nonfat. The difference in calories isn't great—and you may be getting some real metabolic and cardiovascular benefits.

■ ■ ■ ■

Try a Blue Treat!

Researchers from Louisiana State University have found that drinking two blueberry smoothies daily helped obese, prediabetic adults improve their blood sugar control. The blueberry smoothie contained 22.5 grams of freeze-dried blueberry powder. Everyone can benefit from eating blueberries year-round. You can buy them frozen in the off-season...and freeze-dried blueberry powder is available online and at health-food stores. Sprinkle a teaspoon of the powder on toast (instead of jam), or stir a half cup of fresh blueberries into yogurt.

Mark A. Stengler, NMD, naturopathic medical doctor and leading authority on the practice of alternative and integrated medicine. Dr. Stengler is author of the *Health Revelations* newsletter, author of *The Natural Physician's Healing Therapies* (Bottom Line Books), founder and medical director of the Stengler Center for Integrative Medicine, Encinitas, California, and adjunct associate clinical professor at the National College of Natural Medicine in Portland, Oregon. *http://markstengler.com*

Do Sweets Give You Diabetes?

Steven Edelman, MD, clinical professor of medicine at the University of California, San Diego, and founder and director of *Taking Control of Your Diabetes,* a not-for-profit diabetes education organization based in Del Mar, California.

Many people believe this myth, but in fact there is no direct link between eating excessive amounts of sugar and developing diabetes. However, if you are already at risk for type 2 diabetes and you become overweight or obese from eating too much sugar—or too much of anything, for that matter—you can bring on diabetes.

The factors that put you at increased risk for diabetes include high cholesterol… high blood pressure…a history of gestational diabetes or giving birth to a baby who weighed more than nine pounds…a family history of type 2 diabetes…or being of African-American, Hispanic, Native American, Pacific Islander or Asian-Indian descent. If you have none of these risk factors, gaining weight from overindulging in sugar is not likely to lead to diabetes. But it certainly can contribute to many other health problems, such as heart disease and cancer—so it's still best to eat sweets only in moderation.

■ ■ ■ ■

"Healthy" Whole Wheat Linked to Diabetes and Other Diseases

William Davis, MD, a preventive cardiologist and medical director of Track Your Plaque, an international heart disease prevention program. Based in Milwaukee, Wisconsin, he is author of *Wheat Belly: Lose the Wheat, Lose the Weight, and Find Your Path Back to Health* (Rodale). *www.wheatbelly blog.com*

What could be more wholesome than whole-wheat bread? For decades, nutritionists and public health experts have almost begged Americans to eat more whole wheat and other grains.

It's Bad Advice

Most of us know that white bread is bad for us, but even whole-wheat bread is bad, too. In fact, on the Glycemic Index (GI), which compares the blood sugar effects of carbohydrates, both white bread and whole-wheat bread increase blood glucose more than pure sugar. Aside from some extra fiber, eating two slices of whole-wheat bread is little different from eating a sugary candy bar.

What's particularly troubling is that a high-wheat diet has been linked to obesity, digestive diseases, arthritis, diabetes, dementia and heart disease.

Example: When researchers from the Mayo Clinic and University of Iowa put 215 patients on a wheat-free diet, the obese patients lost an average of nearly 30 pounds in just six months. The patients in the study had *celiac disease* (a form of wheat sensitivity), but I have seen similar results in nearly everyone who is obese and gives up wheat.

New Dangers from a New Grain

How can a supposedly healthy grain be so bad for you? Because the whole wheat that we eat today has little in common with the truly natural grain. Decades of selective breeding and hybridization by the food industry to increase yield and confer certain baking and aesthetic characteristics in flour have created new proteins in wheat that the human body isn't designed to handle.

The gluten protein in modern wheat is different in structure from the gluten in older forms of wheat. In fact, the structure of modern gluten is something that humans have never before experienced in their 10,000 years of consuming wheat.

Modern wheat also is high in *amylopectin A*, a carbohydrate that is converted to glucose faster than just about any other carbohydrate. I have found it to be a potent appetite stimulant because the rapid rise and fall in blood sugar causes nearly constant feelings of hunger. The *gliadin* in wheat, another protein, also stimulates the appetite. When people quit eating wheat and are no longer exposed to gliadin and amylopectin A, they typically consume about 400 fewer calories a day.

Not Just Celiac Disease

Celiac disease, also known as celiac sprue, is an intense form of wheat sensitivity that damages the small intestine and can lead to chronic diarrhea and cramping, along with impaired absorption of nutrients. But wheat has been linked to dozens of other chronic diseases, including lupus and rheumatoid arthritis. *It also has been linked to…*

• **Insulin resistance and diabetes.** It's not a coincidence that the diabetes epidemic (nearly 26 million Americans have it) parallels the increasing consumption of modern wheat (an average of 134 pounds per person per year) in the US. The surge in blood sugar and insulin that occurs when you eat any kind of wheat eventually causes an increase in *visceral* (internal) *fat*. This fat makes the body more resistant to insulin and increases the risk for diabetes.

• **Weaker bones.** A wheat-rich diet shifts the body's chemistry to an acidic (low-pH) state. This condition, known as *acidosis*, leaches calcium from the bones. Grains—and particularly wheat—account for 38% of the average American's "acid load." This probably is the reason that osteoporosis is virtually universal in older adults.

• **More heart disease.** A diet high in carbohydrates causes an increase in small LDL particles, the type of cholesterol that is most likely to lead to atherosclerosis and cardiovascular diseases. Studies at University of California, Berkeley, found that the concentration of these particles increases dramatically with a high-wheat diet. The increase in small-particle LDL, combined with diabetes and visceral fat, increases the risk for heart disease.

A Wheat-Free Life

People who crave wheat actually are experiencing an addiction. When the gluten in wheat is digested, it releases molecules known as *exorphins*, morphine-like compounds that produce mild euphoria. About one-third of people who give up wheat will experience some withdrawal symptoms, including anxiety, moodiness and insomnia. *My advice…*

• **Go cold turkey.** It's the most effective way to break the addiction to wheat. The withdrawal symptoms rarely last more than one week. If you're really suffering, you might want to taper off. Give up wheat at breakfast for a week, and then at breakfast and lunch for another week. Then give it up altogether.

• **Beware of gluten-free products.** People who give up wheat often are tempted to satisfy their craving by buying gluten-free bread or pasta. Don't do it. The manufacturers use substitutes such as brown rice, rice bran, rice starch, corn starch and tapioca starch, which also increase blood glucose and cause insulin surges. Even oatmeal can cause blood sugar to skyrocket.

• **Switch grains.** Small supermarkets now stock quite a few nonwheat grains, such as millet, quinoa, buckwheat and amaranth. They're easy to cook, and they taste good—and they don't have the gluten and other wheat proteins that trigger weight gain, inflammation and insulin resistance.

Helpful: If you aren't willing to give up wheat altogether, you can substitute an older form of wheat, such as spelt or kamut. These grains haven't undergone all of the genetic modifications, so they're somewhat better for you than modern wheat. Any form of wheat can be a problem, however. You'll want to limit yourself to small servings—say, a few ounces once or twice a week.

• **Get plenty of protein.** Protein satisfies the appetite more effectively than carbohydrates. Eat eggs for breakfast and chicken salad for lunch. For dinner, you can have fish or even steak.

Recent finding: Research has shown that people who eat a reasonable amount of saturated fat in, say, red meat (about 10% or a little more of total fat calories) have a reduction in small LDL particles, as well as an increase in protective HDL cholesterol.

■ ■ ■ ■

More Diabetes with Your Steak?

Lawrence de Koning, PhD, research fellow, department of nutrition, Harvard School of Public Health, Boston.

Many health-conscious consumers adopt low-carb eating habits to lose weight and ward off heart disease and diabetes. But be careful—it can backfire. A recent study warns that a low-carbohydrate, Atkins-style diet with lots of animal protein actually may increase your risk for type 2 diabetes.

At the Harvard School of Public Health in Boston, postdoctoral research fellow Lawrence de Koning, PhD, and his colleagues analyzed the medical records of 41,140 men (all free of heart disease, cancer and diabetes at the start) in the Health Professionals Follow-Up study. The participants completed questionnaires about their eating habits once every four years for more than 20 years, during which time 2,761 of the men developed type 2 diabetes.

After taking into account risk factors such as body mass index, physical activity, family history of diabetes, smoking, coffee and alcohol consumption and total caloric intake, Dr. de Koning and his team found that the men whose diets were lowest in carbohydrates (averaging 37% of calories) but high in animal protein (18% of calories) and animal fat (26% of calories) had a 41% higher risk for type 2 diabetes than men

consuming a higher carbohydrate (57% of calories) diet where animal protein (10% of calories) and animal fat (12% of calories) were lower.

The findings are preliminary, based on an observational study, and further research is necessary.

What to Eat?

Dr. de Koning says it isn't that low-carbohydrate, high-protein and high-fat diets are inherently harmful, but it's the type of protein and fat you consume. The problem with animal sources of protein, especially red and processed meat, relates to their fat and iron content. Taking in lots of saturated fats (as found in these meats) can reduce insulin sensitivity. Additionally, iron can accumulate in body tissue, generating oxidative stress, insulin resistance and (if the iron accumulates in the pancreas) problems in secreting insulin.

Note: Iron is an important nutrient, and deficiency brings its own set of problems so people who are anemic may be advised to eat meat. Red meat (beef, of course, but also lamb, pork and veal) is rich in *heme iron*, which is the most effective at reversing iron deficiency, since it is absorbed better than nonheme. Moderation and balance are key.

A better way: The Nurses' Health Study (also from Harvard) found that eating greater quantities of vegetable proteins and vegetable fats as part of a low-carbohydrate diet was inversely associated with diabetes risk, says Dr. de Koning.

For most folks, the best high-protein, low-carb diet includes very little red or processed meat, a smattering of chicken and fish, and lots of vegetable proteins (including legumes and nuts) and vegetable fats. Good protein sources include tofu (10.3 grams of protein per one-half cup)...black beans (15.2 grams of protein per cup)...

roasted beets (3.9 grams of protein per one-half cup)…and almonds (6 grams of protein per quarter cup).

Eating a low-carb diet can be all-around healthy. It helps control your weight and, says Dr. de Koning, "may actually reduce your risk for chronic diseases if your sources of fat and protein (what you replace the carbs with) are chosen carefully." That means that red meat should be ordered rarely…rather than rare, medium or well done.

■ ■ ■ ■

A Diabetes-Fighting Diet That Helps You Look and Feel 20 Years Younger

David A. Colbert, MD, founder and head physician of New York Dermatology Group in New York City. He is coauthor, with Terry Reed, of *The High School Reunion Diet: Younger, Thinner and Smarter in 30 Days* (Simon & Schuster, *www.highschoolreuniondiet.com*).

Patients who first try Botox often say that they want to look good for an upcoming wedding, high school reunion or other important event. Botox is very effective at treating some wrinkles, but it doesn't improve the aged look of skin. Nor can it reverse the aging effects of obesity, including lack of vitality.

The right diet can not only help you lose weight but also can make you feel and look 10 to 20 years younger…

• **Eat low-glycemic carbohydrates.** The Glycemic Index (GI) is a measure of how quickly the carbohydrates in foods turn into glucose (sugar) in the blood. A food on the GI is ranked relative to pure glucose, which is given the ranking 100.

High-GI foods cause a spike in blood sugar and a consequent dip, which causes cravings for more sugar. A consistently high-GI diet not only causes weight gain and risk for insulin resistance and diabetes, it compromises the radiance and suppleness of skin.

A food with a low GI causes a more even rise and fall in blood sugar than a food with a high GI. I advise patients to eat lots of fresh whole foods. Many green vegetables, such as spinach, broccoli and asparagus, have GI rankings under 20 and are full of the antioxidants that promote beautiful skin (see the next page). Slightly higher on the GI but still wholesome are whole-grain products.

Example: Oat bran bread has a 68 GI versus a French baguette with a 136 GI.

To find the GI ratings of foods, go to *www.glycemicindex.com.*

• **Limit refined sugar.** The trick to looking years younger just by changing your daily diet is sugar control—know how sugars work in your system and where they lurk in processed foods and avoid them.

Beans Lower Blood Sugar as Well as Meds

In a recent study, diabetics who ate one-half cup of beans a day—garbanzo, black, white, pinto or kidney beans—had significantly lower fasting glucose, insulin and *hemoglobin A1C,* a marker of long-term glucose control. When eaten as a regular part of a high-fiber, low-glycemic-index diet, beans lower hemoglobin A1C by an average of 0.48%, which is at the lower level of effectiveness for medications such as *metformin* (Glucophage).

Cyril Kendall, PhD, leader of research analyzing 41 trials regarding the effects of beans on blood sugar levels, published in *Diabetologia.*

The sugars added to many packaged foods trigger a process known as *glycosylation,* which causes the skin to become stiff and discolored.

Don't buy any product that lists sugar in the top three ingredients. Be aware that sugar goes by different names including *dextrose, galactose, high-fructose corn syrup* and *caramel.*

Fruits have a lot of fructose (sugar), but if eaten whole, they are full of fiber that slows down the sugar. I tell patients to avoid drinking fruit juices, though, and to go for the whole fruit.

• **Eat antioxidant-rich foods.** Much of the skin damage that accompanies aging is caused by free radicals, oxygen-based molecules that are produced in higher-than-normal amounts when we're exposed to sun or environmental toxins (such as cigarette smoke). Free radicals damage cells and alter genetic material, leading to skin aging, including wrinkling, and skin cancer.

Antioxidants can fight free radicals. *Here are a few of the powerful antioxidants that can help repair skin…*

• **Allium**—found in garlic, onions and scallions.

• **Anthocyanin**—in berries, pomegranates, cherries, blood oranges, black beans and soybeans.

Helpful: Blueberries are particularly good for skin. I recommend one-half cup to one cup a day. If you get tired of blueberries, switch to blackberries.

• **Beta-carotene**—in carrots, sweet potatoes, pumpkins and squash.

• **Lutein**—in spinach, kale, broccoli and brussels sprouts.

• **Lycopene**—in tomatoes, watermelon and pink grapefruit.

• **Quercetin**—in broccoli, cranberries, onions and apples.

• **Eat fish three to four times weekly.** The omega-3 fatty acids in cold-water fish, such as salmon and sardines, can help reduce acne, rosacea and other forms of skin infection and inflammation. The omega-3s also help reduce joint inflammation—important for maintaining youthful flexibility.

If you don't like fish, take a supplement of 1,000 milligrams of omega-3s daily.

• **Eat plain unsweetened yogurt.** It's high in protein as well as calcium—important for skin collagen as well as healthy muscles and joints. Yogurt also aids weight loss. One study found that people who ate one serving of yogurt with blueberries daily lost an average of 12 pounds in a year without doing anything else.

Look for Greek yogurt, which is strained longer and therefore is thicker—it delivers the highest amount of protein. You can add berries, nuts or a touch of honey.

• **Drink water**—at least eight (and preferably more) tall glasses a day.

Water literally plumps the skin and makes wrinkles less apparent.

■ ■ ■ ■

You Can Extend Your Life Span by 50%

Paul McGlothin and *Meredith Averill,* who have practiced calorie restriction for about 20 years. They are the directors of the CR Way Longevity Center in Ossining, New York, and leaders of the CR Society International. They are the authors of *The CR Way* (Harper). Their Web site is *www.livingthecrway.com.*

Seventy years of scientific research shows that restricting calories to 30% below normal intake can extend life span by up to 50% in laboratory animals. Recent research shows that calorie restriction may extend the life span of human beings as well.

Paul McGlothin and Meredith Averill, internationally recognized experts on calorie restriction and authors of *The CR Way: Using the Secrets of Calorie Restriction for a Longer, Healthier Life*, discuss some of their important findings below…

Less Diabetes and Other Deadly Conditions

Reporting in *Science*, researchers from the University of Wisconsin revealed the results of a study on calorie restriction in rhesus monkeys, our closest "relatives." The researchers studied 76 adult rhesus monkeys (which live an average of 27 years and a maximum of 40), dividing them into two groups. One group ate a calorie-restricted diet, and one didn't. After 20 years, 37% of the monkeys in the nonrestricted group had died, compared with only 13% in the calorie-restricted group. The calorie-restricted monkeys also had fewer incidences of heart disease, diabetes, cancer and brain disease.

Scientists at Washington University School of Medicine in St. Louis studied the biomarkers of aging of 33 people, average age 51, who ate a calorie-restricted diet for an average of six years. Compared with another group of people who ate a typical American diet, the calorie-restricted practitioners had lab results that are typical of people much younger than themselves. They had lower cholesterol, lower blood pressure, less body fat and lower glucose (blood sugar) levels.

The study participants also had lower levels of *insulin* (the hormone that regulates blood sugar)…*C-reactive protein* (a biomarker for disease-causing inflammation)… *tumor necrosis factor* (a biomarker for an overactive immune system)…and *thyroid hormone T3* (lower levels indicate a slower, cell-preserving metabolic rate).

Why It Works

There are several theories as to why calorie restriction improves health and may increase life span. *It may…*

- **Reduce DNA damage.**
- **Reduce daily energy expenditure,** the most basic of metabolic processes, thereby reducing *oxidative stress*, the internal "rust" that damages cells.
- **Decrease core body temperature.** The higher your normal body temperature, the faster you age.
- **Improve how cells handle insulin,** which controls glucose. Poor glucose regulation damages cells.
- **Improve the neuroendocrine system,** the crucial link between the brain and the hormones that regulate many of the body's functions.
- **Activate a type of gene called sirtuins,** which protect *mitochondria*, tiny energy factories in the cells. Mitochondrial failure speeds aging.

Easy Way to Cut Back

The level of calorie restriction probably required to extend life in humans—about 20% to 30% of typical intake—is more than most people are willing to do on a regular basis, but reducing calories by even 5% can produce significant health benefits.

Estimated calorie requirements for a moderately active person age 51 or older are 2,200 to 2,400 calories a day for a man and 1,800 for a woman. Reducing calories by 5% would mean cutting between 110 and 120 daily calories for a man and 90 for a woman.

With just a few changes in your dietary routine, you easily can reduce calories by 5% or more and improve your health…

- **Favor nutrient-dense foods.** A nutrient-dense food has a high amount of nutrients per calorie. They're the healthiest foods to eat. *They include…*

•Animal protein. Salmon (Alaskan wild, canned, fresh or frozen), sardines, tuna.

•Good fats. Nuts…avocados…grape-seed oil, extra-virgin olive oil.

•Beans. Adzuki, limas, black-eyed peas, black turtle beans, garbanzos (chickpeas), lentils (red or green), mung, pinto, soy.

•Veggies. Arugula, beets, bok choy, broccoli, cabbage, carrots, chard, collard greens, garlic, kale, kohlrabi, leeks, mushrooms (maitake, portobello, shiitake), mustard greens, onions, romaine lettuce, spinach, squash (butternut, summer), sweet potatoes, tomatoes.

•Grains. Barley, quinoa, wild rice, sprouted-grain breads.

•Fruit. Apricots, blackberries, blueberries, cantaloupe, cranberries, kiwi, lemons, limes, oranges, peaches, raspberries, strawberries, tangerines.

•Spices and herbs. Season foods with herbs and spices rather than salt, butter or sugar. Examples include basil, chives, ginger, parsley and turmeric.

• Focus on foods with low-to-moderate Glycemic Index (GI) rankings. High levels of glucose and insulin are linked to faster aging and disease. It's just as important to limit glucose as it is to limit calories.

The best way to regulate glucose and insulin is to choose carbohydrates with a low-to-moderate score on the GI—carbohydrates that digest slowly so that glucose and insulin levels don't suddenly skyrocket.

The beans, veggies, grains and fruits that are nutrient-dense (listed above) have low-to-moderate GIs.

Other ways to keep glucose low…

• Start your meal with one cup of water with one tablespoon of lemon juice, which lowers glucose.

• Finish your last meal of the day as early as possible, eating complex carbohydrates and a fat source.

• After your evening meal, take a 45-minute or longer walk.

• Keep protein intake moderate. Excess protein can increase blood levels of the hormone *Insulin-Like Growth Factor-I* (IGF-I), which deactivates a sirtuin gene and accelerates aging.

Each day, eat 0.36 grams of protein per pound of body weight—at your healthiest, ideal body weight. That's 43 grams of protein a day for a woman whose ideal weight is 120 pounds and 55 grams of protein a day for a man whose ideal weight is 154 pounds. For comparison, typical intake for US adults is 65 grams to 90 grams. One ounce of meat or fish contains about seven grams of protein.

• Stop eating before you're full. Always leave the table slightly hungry. This helps you cut calories and prompts the *hypothalamus*—the emotion-generating part of the brain—to produce the hormone *orexin*, which boosts feelings of happiness. The Japanese have a concept for this healthful practice—*Hara hachi bu*—which means eat until you're 80% full.

Balance Hormones for Weight Loss, Great Health

Michael Aziz, MD, internist, Lenox Hill Hospital, and founder and director, Midtown Integrative Medicine, both in New York City. He is author of *The Perfect 10 Diet* (Cumberland House).

Diets come and go, many of the most popular weight-loss plans these days being a variation on the popular low-fat or low-carb approaches. However, few people succeed long term on any of these eating plans. Here is a science-based diet approach that has been particularly effective for many people.

It's called *The Perfect 10 Diet Plan*, named for the way it helps the body balance 10 hormones that are important to weight loss. Internist Michael Aziz, MD, founder and director of Midtown Integrative Medicine and attending physician at Lenox Hill Hospital, both in New York City, developed the program, which guides people in losing weight rapidly and comfortably while also optimizing long-term health. A year after its introduction, thousands of people have successfully lost weight and noticed an improvement in their health.

How the Diets Stack Up

According to Dr. Aziz, we are a nation in "hormonal chaos" and that flawed research was behind the initial popularity of low-fat diets. Few doctors understood the difference between good fats and bad, Dr. Aziz says, so dieters were urged to shun all fats and eat lots of carbohydrates instead. However, eating like this triggers excessive *insulin*, a hormone that stores fat…makes people hungry…and can start people down a path toward diabetes.

Other disadvantages: Dr. Aziz says that eating so many carbs also negatively impacts other hormones, including *human growth hormone* (HGH), which helps people stay youthful…*leptin* (an appetite-regulating hormone)…and the *sex hormones* (testosterone, estrogen and progesterone). All this leads to a sluggish metabolism that makes weight loss harder.

On the other hand, low-carb diets (including the popular Atkins diet) urge people to minimize carbohydrates and load up on fats in order to keep insulin in check. This helps you shed pounds but doesn't address the problems related to other hormones. Plus, it also overloads people with

unhealthy amounts of protein—reducing thyroid function, which is crucial for weight control. Furthermore, Atkins and the other low-carb eating plans allow lots of nitrite-rich processed meats, including bacon and cold cuts, which are linked to several types of cancer.

In contrast, The Perfect 10 Diet Plan considers all 10 hormones that are key to weight loss and control, which are…

- **Insulin**
- **Leptin**
- **Human growth hormone** (HGH)
- **Thyroid hormones**
- **Cortisol** (the "stress hormone")
- **Glucagon** (which controls blood sugar)
- **Dehydroepiandrosterone** (DHEA, which combats depression and fatigue)
- **Testosterone**
- **Estrogen**
- **Progesterone**

Perfect 10 Foods

In his book, *The Perfect 10 Diet,* Dr. Aziz explains that calorie restriction is not the key to successful and lasting weight loss —rather the point is to avoid "diet" foods (he calls them "fake foods") that have chemical ingredients added. Instead choose whole foods that contribute to a healthy metabolism, helping with weight loss while also satisfying your hunger.

To follow the Perfect 10 Diet, you should base your daily caloric intake on a 40/40/20 formula—get 40% of your calories from carbohydrates, 40% from fats and 20% from protein. *You can select from the following foods…*

- **Vegetables**—you may have unlimited amounts of greens (including peas and beans) and other nonstarchy veggies, while starchy ones (such as potatoes and corn) are allowed only occasionally, in very small amounts.

- **Fruits**—especially berries and citrus fruits packed with vitamin C. Limit yourself to two servings a day since fruit is high in fructose, which is used only by the liver, leaving the excess stored as fat.

- **Proteins**—mostly seafood, poultry (including zinc-rich dark meat, important for the production of sex hormones)… whole eggs…and if you like it, a serving of red meat once in a while.

- **Saturated fats**—you may have one serving per day of butter (one pat) and use coconut oil (one serving is one tablespoon) as needed both for cooking or to spread on vegetables. Dr. Aziz explains that many studies over the years have confirmed that saturated fats can be helpful because they boost production of sex hormones, thus contributing to more rapid weight loss.

Other allowable fats: Olives and olive oil…avocados and avocado oil…and nuts, all of which are rich in nutrients.

Forbidden Foods

The Perfect 10 Diet strictly forbids foods that act against good hormone balance. *In addition to those fake fats, you should avoid…*

- **Artificially "fat-free" and "low-fat foods"** (including dairy). Foods in this group are manipulated to have less fat than their unprocessed forms, and as a result, they usually have higher amounts of sugar that spike insulin release.

- **Soy protein isolates.** This food ingredient may sound healthful, but it is in fact highly processed and may disrupt hormonal balance due to increased concentrations and potential imbalances in *isoflavones* (antioxidants found in plants). Be on the alert for this ingredient in weight-loss shakes, protein bars, low-carb products and many other processed foods that are labeled "healthy."

Off to a Quick Start

To help you take off and then keep off excess pounds, the Perfect 10 Diet includes three stages…

- **Stage One gets you off to a rapid start.** Each day, you may have three meals plus one or two snacks from the accepted food list, but no grains of any sort or alcohol. Follow this for about three weeks.

- **Stage Two supports continuous weight loss but provides additional choices** (whole grains and a bit of alcohol). Once weight loss has begun in earnest and you have grown accustomed to following the diet regimen and exercising regularly, you may add one to three servings of whole grains per day, including whole-grain pasta, and an occasional glass of organic wine.

- **Stage Three is a weight-maintenance plan** that also is an excellent choice for general good health, says Dr. Aziz. Now you may add yet another whole-grain serving each day and even have an occasional sweet treat such as a piece of dark chocolate.

In summary, eating whole foods that nourish rather than challenge your body will result in naturally balanced hormones, which will help you lose weight and feel great. Since it is smart to continue to keep a close eye on your hormone balance, in his book Dr. Aziz also provides advice on what lab tests you should ask your doctor to perform at the start of your diet and periodically thereafter. He also includes recipes and other suggestions for making this way of eating satisfying and one that can be healthfully maintained as time goes on…the true measure of a successful diet for health!

Eat Leafy Greens

Recent study: People who ate the most greens, such as Chinese cabbage, kale and spinach, had a 14% lower risk for type 2 diabetes than those who ate the least.

Possible reason: Leafy greens have magnesium, an antioxidant involved with glucose metabolism. And the *alpha-linoleic acid* in leafy greens helps increase insulin sensitivity.

Patrice Carter, PhD, research nutritionist, University of Leicester, England, and leader of an analysis of six studies, published online in *British Medical Journal*.

Another Healthy Approach To Your Diet

Dawn Jackson Blatner, RD, Chicago-based nutritionist in private practice and author of *The Flexitarian Diet* (McGraw-Hill). *www.dawnjacksonblatner.com*

Are you wondering what the buzzword *flexitarian* means? It's a simple plan that helps keep down the risk of diabetes and other diseases.

The word flexitarian combines the words flexible and vegetarian. It's a way of eating that is less restrictive than a completely plant-based diet yet still provides many of its health benefits, such as weight loss and reduced risk for heart attack, diabetes and cancer. A flexitarian eats a diet rich in whole grains, fruits, vegetables, beans, nuts and healthy fats while limiting meat intake—but not excluding it entirely. Add fish based on personal preference. You probably already have a few vegetarian meals each week—from peanut butter sandwiches to vegetable burritos. For flexitarians, vegetarian meals outnumber meaty meals.

To adopt a flexitarian diet: Adjust the foods on your plate at mealtime so that 25% is lean meat or beans, 25% is whole grains and 50% is fruits and veggies. You can also swap beans for meat in recipes (use one-quarter cup of beans per ounce of meat).

The Best and Worst Foods

Philip P. Cavicchia, PhD, environmental preparedness epidemiologist, Florida Department of Health, Tallahasee, Florida.

Andrew L. Rubman, ND, medical director, Southbury Clinic for Traditional Medicines, Southbury, Connecticut. *www.southburyclinic.com*

Recently, scientists proudly announced their creation of an index to rank how particular foods encourage or discourage inflammation—a well-known contributor to chronic health conditions such as heart disease, diabetes, cancer and dementia. This is great in theory, but scientists being scientists, it's all obscure algorithms and formulas—hardly a useful list to take to the grocery store. We consulted contributing medical editor and nutrition expert Andrew L. Rubman, ND, to give us his easy-to-follow list of foods that reduce inflammation—making us healthier—along with the most inflammatory foods that should be avoided. *But first, the latest findings by researchers...*

How Do Foods Spark Inflammation?

While a PhD student in the department of epidemiology at the Norman J. Arnold School of Public Health at the University of South Carolina, Philip Cavicchia helped design this new inflammatory index. He and his colleagues scored 41 foods and food components thought to positively or negatively affect levels of inflammation, based on a review of all the English language, peer-reviewed studies relating to diet and inflammation that were published between 1950 and 2007.

Carbohydrates, fat and cholesterol were among the food components most likely to encourage inflammation, while magnesium, beta-carotene, vitamins A, B-6, C, D and E, fiber, omega-3 fatty acids, flavonoids, turmeric and tea were the strongest anti-inflammatories.

Next, using data from the Seasonal Variation of Cholesterol Levels Study (SEASONS), they examined the records of 494 men and women (average age 48), looking specifically at the relationship between the inflammatory index (what they ate) and their blood levels of *C-reactive protein* (typically called CRP). Manufactured by the liver, CRP predicts vulnerability to inflammation and is also elevated in people with obesity, allergies and immune disorders—a lower CRP is thought to translate to reduced risk for heart disease, cancer and other inflammation-related chronic health conditions.

After factoring in variables such as age, weight and smoking status, Cavicchia and his team found that there is indeed a relationship between an anti-inflammatory diet based on the inflammatory index and a reduced level of CRP. These findings appeared in *The Journal of Nutrition.*

Now, here are Dr. Rubman's picks of the best and worst foods if you want to reduce inflammation in your body…

10 Best Anti-Inflammatory Foods

- **Wild salmon,** mackerel and other fish rich in omega-3 fatty acids.
- **Berries.**
- **Green, leafy vegetables** (e.g., spinach and kale).
- **Cruciferous vegetables** (broccoli, brussels sprouts, cabbage, etc.).
- **Deeply pigmented produce,** such as sweet potatoes, eggplant and pomegranate …along with carrots, plums, oranges, peppers, peas and red grapes.
- **Nuts.**
- **Whole grains.**

- **Tea**—specifically black, green and white teas.
- **Cold-pressed fresh oils,** including avocado, flaxseed and olive oils in particular.
- **Spices** (specifically, garlic, ginger, turmeric, saffron).

10 Worst Inflammatory Foods

- **Desserts made with lots of sugar** (cookies, candy, ice cream and so on).
- **Sweetened cereals.**
- **"White" carbohydrates** (white bread, white rice, white potatoes, English muffins, etc.).
- **Non-diet soft drinks.**
- **Anything containing high-fructose corn syrup.**
- **Processed meats** (bologna, salami, hotdogs, sausage and others made with preservatives and additives).

Another "Worst" Habit

Dr. Rubman adds one more bit of information to this "highly inflammatory" list. "It should also include almost any food eaten quickly, especially if you drink a lot of liquid while eating," he says, noting that this is all the more true for people who then end up soothing their predictable digestive distress by taking anti-heartburn medication. His advice is to eat slowly…chew thoroughly…avoid liquids during a meal so that you don't dilute the stomach acid and reduce its ability to help digest food…and include items from the "best" list in every meal, every day, while eliminating those from the "worst" list or at least reserving them for an occasional treat. "Within weeks, you will decrease your risk for disease, improve your digestion, enjoy more energy and feel better overall," he promises.

Andrew L. Rubman, ND, medical director, Southbury Clinic for Traditional Medicines, Southbury, Connecticut. *www.southburyclinic.com*

- **French fries,** potato chips and other fried snack foods.

- **Fast foods,** most specifically the ones that are high-fat, high-calorie, high-simple carbohydrate—which describes most of the inexpensive offerings at quick-serve restaurants.

- **Margarine,** because it contains processed *sterols* called *stanols* that have been implicated in both *atherosclerosis* and various fatty-deposit diseases.

- **Organ meats such as liver,** because these often contain undesirable products including antibiotics, fertilizer and other unwanted residues.

■ ■ ■ ■

What Not to Drink to Prevent Diabetes

Frank B. Hu, MD, PhD, professor of nutrition and epidemiology at the Harvard School of Public Health, Boston.

Vasanti Malik, research fellow in the department of nutrition, Harvard School of Public Health, Boston.

Lora Krulak, healthy foods chef and "nutritional muse" in Miami, Florida. *www.lorakrulak.com*

Ann Lee, ND, LAc, naturopathic doctor and licensed acupuncturist, Health for Life Clinic, Lancaster, Pennsylvania. *www.doctornaturalmedicine.com*

To prevent diabetes, we're often told by health experts what not to eat, such as too many refined carbohydrates from breads, pasta and ice cream.

But, what not to drink may be just as important.

Latest finding: Researchers at the Harvard School of Public Health analyzed health data from 310,000 people who participated in 11 studies that explored the connection between *sugar-sweetened beverages* (SSBs) and diabetes.

Fact: SSBs include soda, fruit drinks (not 100% fruit juice), sweetened ice teas, energy drinks and vitamin water drinks. And in the last few decades, the average daily intake of calories from SSBs in the US has more than doubled, from 64 to 141. The beverages are now "the primary source of added sugars in the US diet," wrote the Harvard researchers in *Diabetes Care.*

The researchers found…

Drinking one to two 12-ounce servings of SSBs per day was linked to a 26% increased risk of type 2 diabetes, compared with people who drink one or less SSB per month.

The increased risk for diabetes among those drinking SSBs was true even for people who weren't overweight, a common risk factor for diabetes. The researchers concluded that while SSBs are a risk factor for overweight, they're also a risk factor for diabetes whether you gain weight or not.

"The association that we observed between sodas and risk of diabetes is likely a cause-and-effect relationship," says Frank B. Hu, PhD, professor of nutrition and epidemiology at the Harvard School of Public Health.

Theory: A typical 12-ounce serving of soda delivers 10 teaspoons of sugar. That big dose of quickly absorbed sugar drives up blood sugar (*glucose*) levels…in turn driving up blood levels of *insulin*, the hormone that moves glucose out of the bloodstream and into cells…leading to *insulin resistance*, with cells no longer responding to the hormone and blood sugar levels staying high…eventually leading to diabetes.

SSBs also increase *C-reactive protein*, a biomarker of chronic, low-grade inflammation, which is also linked to a higher risk for diabetes.

"Cola-type beverages" also contain high levels of *advanced glycation end products*, a type of compound linked to diabetes, say the researchers.

And many SSBs are loaded with *fructose*, a type of sugar that can cause extra abdominal fat, another risk factor for diabetes.

Bottom line: "People should limit how much sugar-sweetened beverages they drink and replace them with healthy alternatives, such as water, to reduce the risk of diabetes, as well as obesity, gout, tooth decay and cardiovascular disease," says Vasanti Malik, a study researcher at the Harvard School of Public Health.

Good-for-You Beverages

"I help many of my clients break the habit of regularly drinking soda, sweetened ice tea and other sugary beverages," says Lora Krulak, a healthy foods chef and "nutritional muse" in Miami, Florida. "I show them how to make other beverages that have natural sugar or are naturally sweetened, so they don't miss the sugary drinks."

One of her favorite thirst-quenching combinations...

2 to 3 liters of water (sparkling or regular)

Juice of 2 lemons

Juice of 2 limes

Small bunch of mint

Pinch of salt

1 tablespoon of maple syrup, honey or coconut sugar or stevia to taste (stevia is a natural, low-calorie sweetener)

Let the mixture steep for 30 minutes before drinking.

"It's good to make a lot of this drink, so it's in your refrigerator and you can grab it any time," says Krulak. When leaving home, put some in a water bottle and carry it with you.

Cut Sugar Cravings

"If one of my patients is craving sugary drinks, it means his or her blood sugar levels aren't under control," says Ann Lee, ND, LAc, a naturopathic doctor and licensed acupuncturist in Lancaster, Pennsylvania.

To balance blood sugar levels and control sugar cravings, she recommends eating every three to four hours, emphasizing high-protein foods (lean meats, chicken, fish, eggs, nuts and seeds), good fats (such as the monounsaturated fats found in avocados and olive oil) and high-fiber foods (such as beans, whole grains and vegetables).

She also advises her clients to take nutritional supplements that strengthen the adrenal glands, which play a key role in regulating blood sugar levels.

Recommended: Daily B-complex supplement (B-50 or B-100) and vitamin C (2,000 to 5,000 milligrams daily, in three divided doses, with meals).

For healthy drinks, she recommends green tea sweetened with honey or stevia, or a combination of three parts seltzer and one part fruit juice.

Mineral Supplements Can Be Toxic

Leo Galland, MD, internist, author and internationally recognized leader in integrated medicine. For more information about supplements and drugs and free access to Dr. Galland's Web application, visit *http://pilladvised.com.*

You take your vitamin and mineral supplements to improve your health, but are you sure they're not making you ill?

For a variety of reasons, including a few that are quite surprising, it turns out that the supplements you take to achieve optimal health may be harmful. This caution applies not only to individual supplements, but even to the ingredients in multivitamins.

Leo Galland, MD, is an internist and creator of Pill Advised, an online resource for information and interactions involving medications, supplements and food. Here, he explains the risks and benefits of the most commonly used vitamins and minerals so you can be confident that what you're taking will help you feel good, not bad.

What Are You Taking?

While most people believe that the only potential harm with vitamins and minerals is with megadoses, that's not true, Dr. Galland stresses, adding that "research has indicated that adhering to that belief may cost people their lives."

What people need to know about mineral supplements…

• **Calcium.** You've been hearing lots about this mineral in the news lately. While it may help prevent colon cancer and improve bone health, it may also increase the risk for heart attack or prostate cancer. This danger is due to the way calcium interacts with vitamin D. If your calcium consumption is high but your vitamin D level is low, calcium can render the vitamin D in your body less active. That, in turn, increases heart and cancer risk. Meanwhile, the lack of vitamin D also means that your bones, heart and other tissues absorb less calcium, which increases the risk for heart attack and kidney stones.

The research: An analysis of 11 studies published in *BMJ* found that women taking high doses of calcium (averaging 1,000 milligrams [mg] a day) without vitamin D, and also getting about 800 mg/day of dietary calcium in their diets, had an increased risk for heart attacks. Another study, the Harvard Health Professionals Follow-Up Study, involving 48,000 men with no history of cancer (other than nonmelanoma skin cancer), found that high calcium intake from supplements or food was associated with an increased risk for highly invasive prostate cancer.

Dr. Galland's advice: Most people should limit calcium supplementation to 500 mg a day, to be taken with 1,000 international units (IU) of vitamin D after dinner. He advises aiming to get another 500 mg daily from food (for instance, one ounce of cheddar cheese has 204 mg of calcium) but adds that if you have a history of kidney stones, speak first to your doctor about how much calcium in any form you should consume.

• **Selenium.** This powerful antioxidant may decrease the risk for heart attacks and cancers of the stomach, lung, colon and prostate…but don't take it if you've had skin cancer or are at especially high risk for it due to personal or family history.

The danger: Some studies have found that selenium supplements increase the risk for skin cancer, while others suggest an elevated risk for type 2 diabetes.

Dr. Galland's advice: If you are not at high risk for skin cancer but are at risk for prostate, colon or breast cancer, take 50 micrograms (mcg) to 200 mcg of selenium a day.

• **Magnesium.** Magnesium has a calming effect on the nervous system and helps with stress-related conditions. It also boosts absorption of calcium. Magnesium supplements have many benefits, with studies showing that they may prevent some of the complications of diabetes, improve breathing and airflow in adults with asthma and reduce blood pressure in people who have hypertension.

Potential problems: In some people, magnesium has a laxative effect and can cause diarrhea. This is a particular danger for people with digestive disorders such as IBS or Crohn's disease. What's more, if your kidneys aren't working well enough to excrete the magnesium your body doesn't need, high blood levels can develop, leading to slowed heart rate, reduced blood pressure, slowed breathing and even coma and death.

Dr. Galland's advice: Twenty-six million Americans have chronic kidney disease and millions more are at increased risk, so do not take magnesium supplements unless you have first had a serum creatinine blood test (typically done during a normal physical), which indicates how well your kidneys are functioning. If your blood tests show that you would benefit from magnesium supplementation or your doctor advises it to address particular symptoms such as muscle spasms or tension, palpitations, difficulty falling asleep or anxiety, Dr. Galland says to start slowly, with 100 mg a day, and then work up to 400 mg/day if needed—but stop if you find that the supplements cause diarrhea.

• **Zinc.** A zinc deficiency can affect immune function, tissue repair and brain function. According to Dr. Galland, people who have problems resisting infection or whose cuts and wounds heal too slowly could have a zinc deficiency. Zinc is also known to improve mood and helps antidepressant medications work better. Zinc can be particularly helpful for elderly people—or for anyone—who will be undergoing surgery.

Caution: Zinc in excess of 40 mg/day may cause a deficiency of copper, which can cause unusual anemia and neurological problems. Zinc can also cause nausea in some people.

Dr. Galland's advice: Take zinc (15 mg to 40 mg/day) only if your doctor prescribes it based on a blood test.

• **Copper.** This mineral is taken primarily in multimineral supplements but sometimes on its own by people who are taking zinc supplements (to help prevent a copper deficiency).

The dangers: Copper can be very toxic, especially to the nervous system. High levels can cause neurological effects such as insomnia, depression, anxiety or liver or kidney damage, and some experts believe high levels may increase the risk for Alzheimer's disease. Because copper spurs the growth of new blood vessels, it's not recommended for anyone with cancer.

Dr. Galland's advice: Sources for dietary copper include chocolate, nuts, seafood, mushrooms and legumes. The usual dose for those who need supplemental copper is 0.5 mg a day, but people with low blood levels of copper (unusual but sometimes the case in patients with chronic disease) may need much more, 2 mg to 4 mg/day. If you take a copper supplement, it is important to have your serum copper level checked annually, as copper is absorbed more rapidly from a supplement than from food.

• **Iron.** Iron deficiency can cause anemia, fatigue and impaired cognitive function, so iron supplements have been standard fare for those who need them for many years.

Problems: Iron supplements are potentially toxic. Since the body eliminates iron slowly (except in bleeding episodes), it can accumulate in the liver, where it can cause cirrhosis...in the heart, causing heart failure...or in the pancreas, causing diabetes. When iron levels are too high, the toxicity can also generate free radicals that can contribute to cancer risk.

Dr. Galland's advice: Most adult men and postmenopausal women do not need iron supplements—they should be taken only if the level of blood ferritin is found to be low, and then only long enough to bring it up to the desired level. Dr. Galland notes that this is true even among premenopausal women. The usual dose for those who need iron is 20 mg to 30 mg a day.

Read Labels and Get Rid of What You Don't Need

In summary, Dr. Galland says that mineral supplements aren't for everyone. In fact, he says, "a lot of people shouldn't be taking them individually," adding that for a few vulnerable individuals even the amounts found in typical multivitamins can prove dangerous. He stresses that mineral supplementation must be tailored to individual needs, emphasizing the importance of taking minerals only under the supervision of a doctor trained in their use.

And one final tip: Noting that many people take supplements that are in combination pills or capsules, Dr. Galland points out that it's possible you aren't even aware of what minerals you are taking. He urges readers to look closely at the label of any supplements they take to be sure they're getting only what they need and aren't ingesting anything that could prove harmful.

■ ■ ■ ■

Eat Like a Caveman and Live Much Longer

Philip J. Goscienski, MD, retired clinical professor of pediatrics, department of community and family medicine at University of California, San Diego, School of Medicine. He is author of *Health Secrets of the Stone Age* (Better Life). *www. stoneagedoc.com*

Our bodies reached their current stage of development—in terms of genetics, chemistry and metabolism—during the Stone Age, tens of thousands of years ago. But our lifestyles, in particular our diets and exercise habits, have undergone changes that our bodies aren't equipped to handle.

In particular, the development of agriculture and domesticated livestock has led to a plentiful supply of food. Humans don't have to work as hard to find a good meal, and those meals are served more frequently. Obesity, once rare, is now a leading health threat.

Yet in modern hunter-gatherer societies, people live much as they did in the Stone Age—that's how we can make conclusions about the health of our Stone Age ancestors. Obesity is virtually unheard of in these groups. Members rarely get diabetes, hypertension or heart disease. Cancer is rare. Even in the absence of medical care, they often are healthier than the rest of us.

Here's what worked for our Stone Age ancestors…

Stone Age Fruit

Our Stone Age ancestors gathered wild fruits, which were much smaller and less attractive than we are used to today. The fruits that we buy in supermarkets are bred for appearance, sweetness and size. They have less fiber and antioxidants and more sugars than fruits that grow in the wild without human intervention.

A USDA study published in *Journal of the American College of Nutrition* found that nutrient levels in produce have declined significantly in just the last 60 years. There have been drops in protein, calcium, vitamin A, *riboflavin* and *thiamine*.

Self-defense: Opt for smaller fruits (such as apricots, cherries and berries), which have a greater ratio of skin to flesh, relative to their size, than larger ones, such as peaches. This is important because the largest concentration of fiber and antioxidants is found in the skin and the layers just beneath.

Also, if possible, switch from standard supermarket produce (which tends to be larger) to organic, wild-grown or heirloom varieties. The produce that is available at farmers' markets usually hasn't been bred solely for appearance (or ease of shipping). It naturally will have a higher concentration of nutrients and fiber, thus making it a superior option.

Game Meats

Our ancestors ate plenty of meat, but they ate game meats (antelope, venison, bison), which have very little saturated fat. High intake of saturated fat leads to obesity, which is a leading cause of heart disease and cancer.

Most of the saturated fat in the American diet (apart from that found in processed and restaurant foods) comes from domestic animal meats. These animals are fed grains, which are not part of their natural diet. The meat of grain-fed animals is marbled with saturated fat, making it sweeter and more tender.

What we can learn: Avoid grain-fed beef and pork. Many specialty markets feature meats from grass-fed animals, which are superior to grain-fed.

Even better: Look for game meats, which are high in healthful monounsaturated fat and low in saturated fat. For example, a four-ounce serving of venison has 1.4 grams (g) of saturated fat, about one-third as much as the same amount of rib eye steak.

Water, Not Soda

During the Stone Age, people had only water to drink. Recent studies, including one that looked at the average diet of preschoolers in England, found that many children now drink no water. They get virtually all of their fluids from high-calorie, high-sugar soft drinks and juices.

The average American consumes about two-and-a-half sugary soft drinks daily. Many soft drinks contain about 150 calories per serving. Someone who drinks two nondiet soft drinks a day for a year is consuming the caloric equivalent of about 30 extra pounds.

Even diet soda has been linked with health problems. A recent study found that diet soda drinkers have a higher risk for stroke and heart attack.

What we can learn: Water is the healthiest liquid you can drink. Most adults need about 60 ounces a day—enough to make the urine clear or lightly colored, instead of dark. Opt for filtered water whenever possible. Stone Agers didn't have to worry about industrial chemicals.

Far Less Salt

Our ancient ancestors probably consumed about 700 milligrams (mg) of sodium daily, about the same amount as those who live in hunter-gatherer societies today. People in these societies have virtually no high blood pressure. The average American now consumes about four times this much salt, and high blood pressure raises the risk for heart disease and stroke, leading causes of death in the US.

What we can learn: No one needs extra sodium. Every natural food, including fruits and vegetables, contains enough sodium to keep us healthy. Anything "extra" is unnecessary—and often unhealthy.

Recommended: No more than 1,500 mg of sodium daily. Less is better. Relatively little of the sodium in the American diet comes from the salt shaker—most comes from processed foods. Read labels carefully, even when you think a food is "healthy." A glass of tomato juice, for example, has more than 800 mg of sodium. One tablespoon of soy sauce has 1,200 mg.

Minirobics

During the Stone Age, the average adult most likely expended between 3,500 and 5,000 calories a day. Back then, people didn't "do exercise," because their lives were exercise. They walked miles to gather food, chased down game and used only hand tools.

In modern hunter-gatherer societies, dieting is unheard of—and unnecessary. People are naturally lean. They stay strong even into old age, unlike the 25% of Americans over the age of 65 who need assistance getting out of bed or bathing. They have healthier hearts because they are always moving.

Today only about 10% of Americans regularly get intense physical exercise. On average, our level of daily activity is about 75% less than it was at the beginning of the 20th century.

What we can learn: Current guidelines call for about 30 minutes of moderately intense exercise daily. That's not enough. Our "caveman bodies" seem to function best when we get at least 60 minutes of moderately intense exercise daily. This means exercise that is intense enough to get you breathing hard. It could be working in the yard, doing housework, bicycling or lifting weights.

My advice: If you don't care for formal exercise, you still can get benefits from what I call "minirobics"—daily habits that keep you moving. These include things such as taking stairs instead of elevators…and using a push-type mower rather than one powered with gasoline.

The average person can burn an extra few hundred calories daily (and lose a pound or two a month) simply by moving more throughout the day. And you're never too old to start using your body more. Researchers in Boston conducted a study in which residents of a convalescent home were put on a strength-training program. Their average age was 90. In eight weeks, they had tripled their strength and increased their muscle mass by 10%.

Can Resveratrol Replace Exercise?

Heather Hausenblas, PhD, an exercise psychologist and resveratrol researcher at University of Florida, Gainesville.

It is beginning to seem as if some people believe that *resveratrol*, a plant *polyphenol* found in red wine (among other places), might be a real-life magic potion—given that research has shown it can slow tumor growth, improve heart health, heal inflammation-related damage and slow the ravages of aging. And now here comes another study suggesting that it may be able to hold back the damage that is done when people don't exercise!

Space-Age Findings

Let's start by saying this is sort of an "out there" study that was inspired by space travel and involved rats—weightless ones, yet. Even so, it's intriguing.

The study: In an effort to examine the damage that weightlessness causes for astronauts spending long periods in space, which includes loss of muscle and bone, researchers at the University of Strasbourg in France suspended rats to approximate weightlessness. These rats were unable to move about as they usually do (though they were able to eat and drink normally). Half of these rats were dosed daily with resveratrol. After 15 days, the rats that had not received resveratrol were experiencing all the predictable problems, including loss of strength, muscle mass and bone density. They also developed *insulin resistance*, a precursor to diabetes. The resveratrol-taking rats, however, did not show any of these effects.

What's in It for You?

So resveratrol is obviously tremendously good for rodents that don't exercise…but is it reasonable to believe this is relevant to human beings when we don't exercise?

To get expert insight, we consulted Heather Hausenblas, PhD, an exercise psychologist and resveratrol researcher at the University of Florida and scientific adviser for ResVitále, a company that makes resveratrol products. Dr. Hausenblas and her colleagues recently completed a review of the human clinical studies already done on resveratrol. She says that findings from the weightless-rats study are in line with earlier studies that show resveratrol is a powerful antioxidant that has antiaging, anticarcinogenic and anti-inflammatory properties with few, if any, negative side effects. But no one is sure how or why resveratrol is so powerful, so more research needs to be done.

In the meantime, though, it's not surprising that resveratrol is becoming such a popular supplement. It is not easy to get from food sources—though red wine, grape juice, grapes and berries and, surprisingly, peanuts contain resveratrol, the amounts are not even close to the quantity that studies indicate would have helpful properties.

How to Buy

There now are dozens of resveratrol supplement brands on the market, but Dr. Hausenblas cautions that consumers should beware. You need to check the label carefully to be sure that the brand you choose is a high-quality product. *The label should show the following…*

• **The product doesn't contain fillers or additives,** such as sugar, starch, gluten or artificial colors or flavors. These other ingredients make it easier and cheaper for the manufacturer to produce resveratrol supplements but do not add any health value.

Look for products that contain "trans" not "cis" resveratrol—trans resveratrol is the bioactive form of the resveratrol polyphenol that has been scientifically proven to enhance cellular productivity, Dr. Hausenblas says. She adds that it has also been shown to increase the number of mitochondria in cells, thus boosting energy capacity.

• **The product was produced under "good manufacturing practices" (or GMP),** which are standards established by the US Food and Drug Administration (FDA) to which manufacturers adhere on a voluntary basis. These standards are intended to ensure that products are consistently produced with high-quality ingredients.

• **Also, resveratrol is light-sensitive,** so it should be protected in opaque capsules and in a bottle that shields the capsules from light.

The Daily Dose

Dr. Hausenblas says that research hasn't yet pinned down what an optimal dose of resveratrol is nor who would benefit most from taking it, but she says there is enough research to indicate that a dosage of up to 500 mg a day is helpful for most people. Since the body absorbs resveratrol rapidly and its activity is fairly short-lived, she suggests splitting the daily dosage into two smaller ones that will keep some in the body most of the time. Resveratrol is safe, Dr. Hausenblas says, but she suggests starting with a low dosage so your body can adjust to it gradually—some people experience digestive upset at first. Also, pregnant women, nursing mothers and people with a medical condition should check with the doctor before taking resveratrol to be sure it is appropriate for them.

The One Vitamin That Can Save Your Life

Michael F. Holick, MD, PhD, professor of medicine, physiology and biophysics at Boston University Medical Center. He is the author of *The Vitamin D Solution* (Hudson Street). Dr. Holick has been an outspoken critic of dermatologists' standard advice to avoid all sun exposure. *www. drholick.com*

The health benefits of vitamin D have been making news for some time now, but roughly two-thirds of Americans still are not getting enough of this vital nutrient.

Even though vitamin D has long been known to promote bone strength—it enables bone-building calcium to pass through the small intestine and into the bloodstream and the bones—many other health benefits are being discovered. *Most recently, research findings have shown that low vitamin D also is linked to chronic diseases, such as…*

Magnesium Benefits

When researchers studied 4,497 healthy adults' diets for 20 years, those who consumed the most magnesium (about 200 milligrams [mg] per 1,000 calories) were 47% less likely to develop diabetes than those who consumed the least (about 100 mg per 1,000 calories).

Theory: Magnesium enhances the enzymes that help the body process blood sugar.

Self-defense: Eat magnesium-filled foods, such as almonds (one-quarter cup roasted, 97 mg) and spinach (one-half cup cooked, 77 mg).

Ka He, MD, associate professor, departments of nutrition and epidemiology, University of North Carolina, Chapel Hill.

- **Diabetes.** People who get more than 800 international units (IU) of vitamin D daily may be about one-third less likely to develop type 2 diabetes.

- **Cancer.** For example, about half of colorectal cancers in the US are believed to be preventable by raising vitamin D levels in people who are deficient.

- **Dementia.** Adults age 65 and older with the lowest levels of vitamin D were found to be more than twice as likely to suffer cognitive impairment (which often precedes dementia) than those with optimal levels of the vitamin.

- **Heart disease.** Risk for heart disease was reduced by 31% in women who took vitamin D supplements as part of a study on osteoporosis-related fractures.

How could one vitamin have such a profound effect on overall health? Research now shows that vitamin D helps facilitate cellular health in virtually every cell in the body including those in the brain. If this cellular health is interrupted due to a vitamin D deficiency, health problems, such as those described earlier, may occur.

Little-Known Facts

What you may not know about vitamin D…

- **Few doctors recommend a blood test to measure 25-hydroxyvitamin D,** a form of vitamin D that acts as a marker for vitamin D status.

- **Adults over age 60 should ask to be tested.*** They are at increased risk for vitamin D deficiency since the skin becomes less able to manufacture the vitamin from sunlight as the body ages.

Recommended blood level of vitamin D: Thirty to 100 nanograms of 25-hydroxyvitamin D per milliliter (ng/mL) of blood. I like

*Vitamin D testing is covered by most health insurers, including Medicare.

to keep patients between 40 ng/mL and 60 ng/mL, but up to 100 ng/mL is safe.

Helpful: It's best to get tested in the winter, when levels are likely to be lower than in the summer. If you are deficient, your doctor will prescribe therapeutic doses of vitamin D. Get retested eight to 12 weeks later, then follow up once a year.

Warning Signs

• **Low energy,** bone pain (especially in the arms and legs) and/or lack of muscle strength can indicate a vitamin D deficiency. A condition known as *osteomalacia*, which causes softening of the bones, can result from vitamin D deficiency. Unlike osteoporosis, which occurs when existing bone is weakened, osteomalacia is an abnormality in the bone-building process. People with osteomalacia complain of throbbing and aching bone pain.

Simple self-test: Press firmly with your thumb or forefinger on your breastbone or your shins. If you feel pain in either of those areas, you're probably low in vitamin D and may have osteomalacia. See a doctor to have your vitamin D status tested.

• **The US recommendations for vitamin D are too low.** The Office of Dietary Supplements, part of the National Institutes of Health, advises Americans to get 600 international units (IU) of vitamin D daily from food and/or supplements if you're age 50 to 70…and 800 IU daily for those over age 70.

My advice: If you don't think you can get enough timed sun exposure without sunscreen (see below), get 1,500 IU to 2,000 IU of vitamin D daily. Foods that contain vitamin D (such as wild-caught salmon, mushrooms and vitamin D–fortified milk and breakfast cereals) do not provide significant amounts of the vitamin. Many people will also need to take a vitamin D supplement.

Important: A supplement is especially critical if you don't get much sun due to your distance from the equator—for example, you live in Seattle rather than Miami.

Supplements also are required for people who have been tested and are low in vitamin D…and are more frequently necessary for dark-skinned people because dark skin pigmentation naturally filters vitamin D–producing sun rays.

• **The vitamin D produced from sunlight is superior to that provided by supplements.** Sun-produced vitamin D has been shown to last at least twice as long in the blood as vitamin D from supplements.

There are no simple formulas to determine the amount of sun exposure needed to produce adequate amounts of vitamin D.

My general guideline: Three times a week—during the period of 10 am to 3 pm (virtually no vitamin D is produced at other times)—spend one-quarter to one-half the amount of time in the sun that it takes you to get the beginning of a sunburn.* For someone with dark skin, this might be 30 minutes three times weekly. If you're fair-skinned, five to 10 minutes might be enough. Expose your arms and legs—and, if possible, your abdomen and back—to sun. During timed exposures, put sunscreen on your face to help prevent sun damage. When you're not doing a timed exposure, cover all exposed skin with sunscreen to prevent sunburn.

Note: If you live above 33° latitude (roughly any area north of Atlanta), you cannot produce any significant vitamin D from sun exposure during the winter.

• **Inadequate sun exposure may increase your risk for melanoma and other cancers.** Sunburn increases the risk for skin cancer, but there is no scientific evidence that

*If you take a prescription drug or are at high risk for skin cancer or have a history of the disease, consult your doctor.

moderate sun exposure has the same effect. In fact, most melanomas (the most lethal form of skin cancer) occur on parts of the body that receive little sun. Research published in the *Journal of Investigative Dermatology* shows that people who get regular, moderate sun exposure are less likely to develop melanoma than those who get little or no sun.

Melanoma kills about 8,600 Americans annually. Colon, prostate and breast cancers combined claim about 115,000 lives. Each of these cancers has been linked to insufficient vitamin D.

Important finding: A study in the journal *Cancer* reported that insufficient sun exposure in the US accounted for 85,000 more cancer cases than would have occurred had the same people gotten more sun.

● **Certain medications reduce vitamin D levels.** Antiseizure drugs, such as *phenytoin* (Dilantin), the steroid *prednisone*, AIDs medications and some other drugs destroy vitamin D and increase one's risk for osteomalacia and other conditions associated with vitamin D deficiency. People taking such drugs may need double or triple the usual amounts of vitamin D.

Other medications that reduce vitamin D include the cholesterol-lowering drug *cholestyramine* (Questran)...the weight-loss medication *orlistat* (Xenical)...and the herb *St. John's wort*.

If you take one of these products, you may need to take a vitamin D supplement to maintain adequate blood levels of the vitamin.

■ ■ ■ ■

Healthy Habits That Make You Sick

Kent Holtorf, MD, medical director, Holtorf Medical Group, with locations in California and Pennsylvania (*www.holtorfmed.com*). Dr. Holtorf is a leading physician in the fields of preventive medicine, endocrine dysfunction and immune disorders and the founder of the National Academy of Hypothyroidism, a nonprofit organization that gives patients the latest information and studies on hypothyroidism (*www.nahypothyroidism.org*).

American consumers receive a steady stream of advice to drink lots of water, stay out of the sun, wash hands religiously, exercise regularly and on and on. Might we actually do ourselves harm with some of these seemingly healthful habits? Yes indeed, according to Kent Holtorf, MD, a leading physician in the fields of preventive medicine, endocrine dysfunction and immune disorders and founder of the National Academy of Hypothyroidism. He says that well-meaning efforts to improve our health can and often do backfire, sometimes with dangerous results. *Dr. Holtorf offers advice on how to walk the line between taking steps to stay healthy and going overboard...*

Drink Plenty of Water?

Not so fast—our water is not as safe as you think. According to the Environmental Protection Agency, as many as 19 million Americans are sickened each year by drinking water from the public supply. Not only has bacterial (and, though rarely, even viral) contamination been a problem, but traces of toxins including arsenic, uranium, radium, *tetrachloroethylene* and lead, along with minute amounts of pharmaceuticals and personal-care products, have been found. Bottled water isn't the solution you might think, either. Most disposable plastic bottles contain *bisphenol-A* (BPA), a chemical that has been linked with an increased risk for hormonal disturbances (especially thyroid), reproductive and fetal abnormalities, breast and prostate cancer, brain development issues and diseases, weight gain, neurological changes, type 2 diabetes, heart disease and liver disorders.

Best solution: Invest in a water filter for your home. Prices range from $20 for a basic water pitcher to hundreds of dollars for a home-wide filtration system. Shop at Web sites such as *www.brita.com* and *www. purwater.com*. Dr. Holtorf notes that *reverse osmosis* home-filtration systems are most effective in eliminating contaminants. Buy reusable, BPA-free bottles (e.g., from retailers such as *www.nalgene.com*) to bring drinking water along when you're away from home.

Stay Out of the Sun?

Rising skin cancer rates motivate many to avoid the midday sun and/or slather on layers of sunscreen…yet Dr. Holtorf points out that most Americans are deficient in vitamin D, a key nutrient that our bodies most efficiently synthesize through sun exposure. Inadequate vitamin D levels raise the risk for heart disease and certain cancers. As for sunscreen, many formulas contain chemicals such as *para-aminobenzoic acid* (PABA), which can cause allergic reactions and, potentially, liver problems as well.

The smart way: Do spend 10 to 20 minutes each day outdoors in the sunshine without sunscreen. If you want to sunbathe for longer, liberally apply a broad-spectrum sunscreen that protects against both UVA and UVB rays and has an SPF of 15. Sunscreen with a higher SPF won't hurt you, Dr. Holtorf says, but he views the extra strength as a waste of money.

Wash Hands Frequently?

It's important to wash your hands frequently to avoid cold and flu germs and prevent food-borne disease…but using antibacterial

soap causes more problems than it solves. One antibacterial agent of particular concern is *triclosan*, a common ingredient in liquid hand soaps and dishwashing detergent. Triclosan may disrupt thyroid function and has been implicated in liver toxicity, Dr. Holtorf says. In addition, antibacterial soap is no better at getting your hands clean than regular soap—but its use contributes to the development of drug-resistant "supergerms."

What to do: Keep washing your hands frequently with regular soap and warm water, but do not use antibacterial soaps—especially those that contain triclosan. To view a list of triclosan-free personal products, visit *www.ewg.org/triclosanguide*.

Fortifying Yourself Sick?

More and more packaged foods are fortified with supposedly good-for-you vitamins and other supplements, but these aren't always the best choices for your health. For some nutrients, such as folic acid, intake may climb too high if you are also taking a multivitamin and, in fact, research now links excessive folic acid consumption with cancer.

Instead: Choose whole, unprocessed, fiber-rich foods, and aim for a balanced diet that naturally provides a multitude of nutrients. One very good way to boost your nutrient intake is to drink freshly made vegetable juices, which contain an ideal balance of trace minerals and antioxidants along with thousands of beneficial *phytonutrients* that are not available in pill form.

Fat-Phobic and Unhealthy?

Our fat-phobic society has thrown out the baby with the bathwater. Trans fats should absolutely be avoided, but other fats—even saturated ones—are vital to our health. The benefits of unsaturated fats in fish and flax oil are well known, as are the benefits of monounsaturated fats found in nuts, avocado and olive oil—which help balance cholesterol levels. Though saturated fats are generally considered to be unhealthy, they are an essential component of every single cell in our bodies, and there is some evidence that the kind of saturated fat in products such as coconut oil may aid in weight loss, digestion and cardiovascular health.

Try this: Rather than worrying too much about reducing fat intake, avoid simple and concentrated sugars, such as high fructose corn syrup, and avoid simple carbohydrates such as baked goods and white bread. Research shows that these are the worst culprits in weight gain, *insulin resistance*, *high triglycerides* and *cardiovascular disease*.

Fruits, Vegetables…and Food Poisoning?

In the past, food-borne illness was primarily associated with meat and seafood, but recent outbreaks have been traced to fresh produce. Many disease-causing bacteria—such as *E. coli, listeria* and *salmonella*—routinely reside on fruits and vegetables, and this is true whether the produce is grown conventionally or organically.

To stay safe: Wash your hands before handling produce. Avoid cross contamination (especially from uncooked meats) by storing produce and proteins in separate parts of the refrigerator—also, use separate cutting boards. Don't nibble on unwashed produce…and wait until just before preparation of fruits and vegetables to wash them, as washing removes their natural coating and makes them spoil faster. You do not need to use any special detergents, soap or bleach—simple running tap water is effective. Rinse all parts of the fruit or vegetable that may come into contact with a paring knife (even parts that you don't intend to eat), and remove and discard the outer leaves of lettuce, cabbage and other greens. Scrub firmer fruits and vegetables with a vegetable brush.

Getting Too Much Sleep?

It's true that most American adults aren't getting enough sleep—and the trend is growing worse. Yet getting too much sleep is a problem, too. Excessive sleeping is a common symptom of depression and can indicate that something else is amiss—research shows that getting too much sleep (more than eight hours a night) is associated with risk for premature death as much as getting too little sleep, and it also contributes to back pain and memory problems.

Dr. Holtorf suggests: An underactive thyroid is one common cause of daytime sleepiness or an excessive need for sleep. It's a problem that often goes undiagnosed because the standard blood test for it—*the TSH test*—is inadequate. Having even "low normal" thyroid levels significantly increases your risk for heart disease, diabetes, weight gain, depression and fatigue. Other causes of oversleeping include depression, chronic fatigue syndrome, *fibromyalgia*, *hypersomnia* (a medical condition that causes sufferers to oversleep), alcohol and some medications. If you are suffering from excessive fatigue, discuss with your doctor what might be the cause.

So, as with everything else, it turns out that moderation is key. Maintaining perspective is important when following health advice—or you will indeed end up taking "the bad with the good."

Reset Your "Body Clock"

Steve A. Kay, PhD, dean and Richard C. Atkinson Chair in the division of biological sciences at the University of California, San Diego, where he is also a Distinguished Professor of Cell and Developmental Biology. He directs the Kay Laboratory, also at the University of California, San Diego, which investigates the role of circadian disorders in regulating sleep-wake cycles, glucose stability and weight control.

Chronobiology is the study of *circadian rhythms* —the body's 24-hour cycles of physical, mental and behavioral changes. Light and darkness are the main factors that influence one's circadian rhythms, affecting the body's temperature, sleep-wake cycles, hormone release and other important bodily functions.

For most of us, our bodies need a day or two to adjust when we travel across time zones or change the clock.

But increasing evidence now shows that chronic (or even occasional) interruptions in our circadian rhythms—the 24-hour cycles that regulate sleep and wakefulness—may affect our health more than we thought was possible.

What's new: The brain used to be considered the body's only biological "clock." Now researchers are finding that many cells in the body have "clock genes" that regulate their activity—for example, organs such as the liver also have cycles.

When Body Clocks Falter

Exposure to light is one of the main factors for maintaining, or changing, our daily rhythms. And our modern society has essentially turned night into day with near-constant exposure to lights, TVs, computers and other electronic gadgets. In many cases, our bodies haven't adapted, and it's putting us at increased risk for health problems.

Age is also a factor. Older adults tend to have a weaker circadian orchestration of physiology, which means the body's clocks are less able to work together—a problem that has been linked to heart disease.

What you can do: Here's how to help manage your body's internal clocks so that you minimize your risk for health problems, such as…

Diabetes

Several studies have shown that people with poor sleep habits (especially those who sleep five or fewer hours per night) are more likely to be overweight—and have a higher risk for diabetes. Now researchers are speculating that disruptions in circadian rhythms may be to blame.

Recent research: In lab studies, mice with a genetic mutation in the part of the brain that synchronizes circadian rhythms ate all day instead of just in the evening, the time that they're normally active. They were more likely to be obese and also had high blood sugar.

Why does this occur? A protein called *cryptochrome* stimulates the production of *hepatic glucose*, a sugar used for energy. In humans, cryptochrome is normally suppressed throughout the day, when energy is supplied by eating, and increased at night to provide energy while we're sleeping. Research has shown that a disruption in sleep-wake cycles causes a prolonged elevation of cryptochrome and an increased risk for obesity and diabetes.

Simple self-defense: To help minimize your risk for weight gain and diabetes, be sure to keep a regular sleep schedule. Go to bed at the same time every night, and get up at the same time in the morning. Aim for seven to eight hours' sleep each night, and don't change your routine on weekends. If you work at night, use heavy curtains to block sunlight, and turn off telephones so that you can sleep during the day.

Depression

Seasonal affective disorder (SAD), in which episodes of depression increase in the fall and winter when there are fewer hours of daylight, is thought to be caused in part by changes in the circadian cycles.

Simple self-defense: Light therapy, which involves the use of indoor light that mimics sunlight.

Light boxes, available at many pharmacies and online retailers for about $100 to $400, are typically used for a half hour or longer each morning. Exposure to the light increases alertness, and repeated exposure can help fight SAD.

Caution: If you have cataracts, glaucoma or another eye condition…or take medications that increase your skin's sensitivity to light, be sure to consult a doctor before using a light box. In addition, light boxes may trigger mania in people with bipolar disorder.

Heart Attack

More than half of heart attacks occur in the six hours between about 6 am and noon. The greater frequency probably is due to several circadian factors, including body position—most people experience about a 10- to 25-point increase in *systolic* (top number) blood pressure when they rise from bed in the morning. What's more, people who have a heart attack in the morning are likely to suffer more damage to the heart than those who have heart attacks later in the day.

New finding: In a study published in *Heart*, researchers analyzed data from 811 patients who had suffered heart attacks. Those whose attacks occurred in the morning were found to have about a 20% larger *infarct*, an area of dead tissue, than those whose attacks happened later in the day.

It's not known why morning heart attacks are more severe.

Caution: In most people, blood pressure rises in the morning, then dips slightly in the afternoon and falls during sleep. However, some people don't have these periodic declines. Known as "non-dippers," they're more likely to have a heart attack than those who experience normal cycling.

Simple self-defense: Get out of bed slowly. In addition, because high blood pressure is a leading risk factor for heart attack, people who take blood pressure–lowering medication may benefit from timing it so that they get the greatest reduction in the morning.

Example: The blood pressure medication *verapamil* (such as Verelan PM) is meant to be taken at bedtime. The active ingredient isn't released during the first hours of sleep (when blood pressure is already low)—more gets released in the morning, the time when blood pressure rises. Other drugs that are designed to provide greater benefit when taken at night include timed-release versions of *diltiazem* (Cardizem LA) and *propranolol* (InnoPran XL). If you take blood pressure medication, ask your doctor about timed-release drugs—or if you could take your current medication at night.

Asthma

People with asthma are more likely to need emergency treatment between 10 am and 11 am than at other times of the day, research has shown. The use of rescue inhalers also increases during the morning.

Reason: Lung movements are reduced during sleep and soon after waking up. This impairs the elimination of mucus, which can lead to congestion and difficulty breathing several hours later.

Simple self-defense: If you have asthma and use a bronchodilator, such as one containing *theophylline* (Uniphyl), talk to your doctor about taking your last dose of the day a few hours before bedtime. This allows the active ingredients to increase through the night and reach peak levels in the morning.

Drowsiness

Feel drowsy after lunch? Blame your circadian rhythms. It's normal for body temperature, blood pressure, metabolism and cognitive abilities to decline in the afternoon hours.

The peak mental hours for most adults are from about 7 am or 8 am until early afternoon. This is followed by a brief (one-to two-hour) dip, after which energy rises again until later in the evening.

Simple self-defense: If your job and lifestyle allow it, take a brief (20- to 30-minute) nap in the afternoon. Or, if that's not possible, try to schedule less demanding tasks during the "dip" period.

Childhood Trauma Link To Adult Diseases

Janice Kiecolt-Glaser, PhD, professor of psychiatry and psychology, The Ohio State University Wexner Medical Center, Columbus, and coleader of a study presented at the American Psychological Association Annual Convention.

Childhood trauma can shorten life span by as much as 15 years, says Janice Kiecolt-Glaser, PhD.

Recent finding: Adults who experienced emotional trauma as children had elevated levels of inflammation, which is linked to cardiovascular disease, type 2 diabetes, osteoporosis and other disorders. Experiencing multiple traumas during childhood may shorten life span by as much as

15 years. Emotional traumas include abuse or neglect, loss of a parent, lack of a close relationship with an adult, witnessing severe marital problems or having a family member who abused alcohol or had a mental illness.

Self-defense: Psychotherapy, exercise, meditation and yoga can help—even in middle age or beyond.

Good and Easy...Eating The Mediterranean Way

Wendy Kohatsu, MD, assistant clinical professor of family medicine at the University of California, San Francisco, and director of the Integrative Medicine Fellowship at the Santa Rosa Family Medicine Residency Program in Santa Rosa, California. Dr. Kohatsu is also a graduate of the Oregon Culinary Institute.

There is abundant scientific evidence on the health benefits of the so-called Mediterranean diet, which promotes the traditional eating habits of long-lived people in such countries as Greece and Italy.

Landmark research: Among the most compelling evidence is one long-term European study of healthy men and women ages 70 to 90.

It found that following the Mediterranean diet as part of an overall healthful lifestyle, including regular exercise, was associated with a more than 50% lower rate of death from all causes over a decade. Numerous studies have associated this type of eating with reduced risk for heart disease, cancer, cognitive decline, diabetes and obesity.

But many Americans are reluctant to try the Mediterranean diet for fear that it will be difficult or costly to follow because it emphasizes such foods as omega-3–rich fish, vegetables and nuts.

Surprising findings: Mediterranean eating does not increase food costs, according to a recent study—and this style of eating need not be complicated.

Wendy Kohatsu, MD, an assistant clinical professor of family medicine at the University of California, San Francisco, and a chef who conducts cooking demonstrations for patients and doctors, explains the best ways to incorporate Mediterranean eating into your daily diet…

Easy Ways to Get Started

To effectively tap into the Mediterranean diet's powerful health benefits, it's important to know exactly which foods should be eaten—and in what quantities.

Start by getting four to five daily servings of whole grains (one serving equals one-half cup of cooked quinoa, brown rice or whole-wheat pasta, for example, or one slice of whole-wheat bread) and two to three daily servings of low- or nonfat dairy products (such as yogurt, cottage cheese or milk), which are an important source of bone-protecting calcium. *In addition, be sure to consume…*

• **Oily fish.** This high-quality protein contains abundant omega-3 fatty acids, which help fight the inflammation that plays a role in cardiovascular disease, Alzheimer's disease and asthma.

The best choices: Follow the acronym SMASH—salmon (wild)…mackerel (Spanish, not king, which tends to have higher levels of mercury)…anchovies…sardines… and herring.

How much: Three ounces (the size of a deck of cards), twice a week.

Chef's secret: Drain canned sardines (the large size), grill briefly, sprinkle with fresh lemon juice and chopped parsley.

Beware: Some fish—such as shark, swordfish, golden bass (tilefish), king mackerel and albacore tuna—can be high in mercury. Avoid these. If you eat tuna, choose the "light" version, which contains less mercury than albacore tuna does.

If you don't like fish: Take a fish oil supplement (1,000 milligrams [mg] daily). Choose a brand that guarantees that no lead or mercury is present.

My favorite brands: Carlson's and Nordic Naturals.

Vegetarians can get omega-3s from flaxseed, walnuts and other nonfish sources. However, nonfish food sources of omega-3s are largely in the form of *alpha-linolenic acid* (ALA), which is not as potent as the more biologically powerful fatty acids found in fish. Algae-derived *docosahexaenoic acid* (DHA) capsules contain the omega-3s found in fish. The recommended dose of DHA capsules is 1,000 mg daily.

What most people don't know: A small but important study shows that eating oily fish with beans, such as lentils and chickpeas (also known as garbanzo beans), improves absorption of the iron found in beans.

• **Olive oil.** Olive oil contains about 77% healthful monounsaturated fats. Olive oil is also high in *sterols*, plant extracts that help reduce LDL "bad" cholesterol and increase HDL "good" cholesterol.

Best choice: Look for extra-virgin (or "first-press") olive oil. ("Extra virgin" means that the oil is derived from the first pressing of the olives.)

How much: Use olive oil as your primary fat—in salad dressings, marinades and sautées. To minimize your total daily intake of fat, do not exceed 18 grams (g) to 20 g of saturated fat and 0 g of trans fat from all food sources.

Chef's secret: If you dislike the "grassy" taste of some extra-virgin olive oils, look for Spanish and Moroccan versions, which tend to be more mellow. One good choice is olive oil made from the *arbequina olive*, which has a buttery taste.

What most people don't know: Nutrients in extra-virgin olive oil may offer some pain-relieving qualities over the long term.

● **Nuts.** Like extra-virgin olive oil, nuts are high in healthful monounsaturated fats. In fact, a recent Spanish study found that a Mediterranean diet that included walnuts significantly lowered risk for heart disease.

What kinds: Besides walnuts, best choices include almonds and peanuts. Be sure to choose plain raw nuts—not salted or honey-roasted.

How much: One-quarter cup daily.

Beware: A quarter cup of nuts contains about 200 calories. Eat only a small handful daily—for example, about 23 almonds or 35 peanuts. If you're allergic to nuts, try pumpkin, sunflower or sesame seeds instead.

Chef's secret: Store nuts in your freezer to prevent them from going rancid.

● **Fruits and vegetables.** Many of the most healthful vegetables—including those of the *brassica family*, such as cabbage, kale, broccoli and cauliflower—originated in the Mediterranean area.

What kinds: Choose brightly colored fruit, such as citrus and berries, and vegetables, such as spinach, watercress, beets, carrots and broccoli.

How much: Five to nine servings daily. (A serving is one-half cup of cooked vegetables, one cup of leafy greens, one medium orange or one-half cup of berries.)

Contrary to popular belief, frozen vegetables, which are often far less costly than fresh produce, are just as nutritious—if not more so because they're frozen at their peak level of freshness and don't spoil in the freezer.

Chef's secret: Cooking tomatoes in olive oil concentrates the tomatoes' levels of *lycopene*, a powerful antioxidant that has been associated with a decreased risk for prostate, lung and stomach cancers.

■ ■ ■ ■

Yoga Fights Inflammation

The compound *interleukin-6* (IL-6), part of the body's inflammatory response, is linked to heart disease, diabetes and other age-related diseases. Researchers compared yoga novices (who had done yoga no more than 12 times) with yoga experts (who had practiced at least weekly for two years) as the women performed stressful tasks, such as putting feet in extremely cold water or solving math problems. IL-6 blood levels of the yoga experts were 41% lower than those of the novices—a possible indicator of yoga's effectiveness at combating stress-induced inflammation.

Janice Kiecolt-Glaser, PhD, professor of psychiatry and psychology at The Ohio State University Wexner Medical Center in Columbus.

Belly Fat: It's Even Bad for Skinny People!

Robert F. Kushner, MD, clinical director, Northwestern Comprehensive Center on Obesity (NCCO) at Northwestern University Feinberg School of Medicine, Chicago.

It's well known that for overweight people, being "apple-shaped"—with the extra fat mostly around their middle—is particularly dangerous for their health, especially heart health. But if your weight is in the normal range, you don't have to worry about that little muffin top or beer belly, right?

Wrong. An analysis from the Mayo Clinic published in *Journal of the American College of Cardiology* looked at how belly, or *visceral*, fat impacts cardiac disease patients. It gathered data from six studies totaling nearly 16,000 heart patients, 40% of whom were of normal weight. These patients (all of whom had either had a heart attack or a procedure to open blocked arteries) were followed for just over two years after their attacks or treatment.

The studies revealed that among the normal-weight folks, their belly fat was associated with an early and unexpected death—an astonishing one in five deaths. Remember, these people were not overweight—they just had a little extra around the middle! Matters were even worse for the obese group, where belly fat caused one in three deaths…but that's not very surprising given how dangerous we all know obesity to be.

A Different Kind of "Bad Fat"

We consulted Robert Kushner, MD, clinical director at the Northwestern Comprehensive Center on Obesity at Northwestern University Feinberg School of Medicine. Most of us don't think of fat around the middle as anything more than unsightly "spare tires," but Dr. Kushner describes it as "angry fat that is biologically active." What he means is that this fat, unlike the thinner layer of fat that lies just beneath the skin (*subcutaneous fat*), produces chemicals that lead to *insulin resistance*, a precursor of diabetes. Diabetes, as we know too well, is a disease that puts people at high risk for cardiac disease and inflammation—making it harder for blood vessels to dilate and easier for blood to clot, all of which increases the risk for heart attacks and strokes.

While the Mayo Clinic's meta-analysis involved only people who already had cardiac disease, Dr. Kushner stresses that belly fat is dangerous for people with good health histories as well. In fact, several years ago, data from the long-range Nurses' Health Study, which tracked 44,000 women for 16 years, showed that women with greater waist circumferences were more likely to die early of cancer or heart attack than women with smaller waists—and the Nurses' Health Study data baseline was healthy women.

Should You Whittle Your Waistline?

You may already know that your weight is in the officially healthy range if your body mass index (BMI) is under 25 (to calculate your BMI, go to *www.nhlbisupport.com/bmi*). But to have a more accurate picture of your health, you need to know just how big your belly is, so go ahead and get out that tape measure. Do not worry about gauging your hip-to-waist ratio, a measurement that was widely used in the past as a measure of abdominal fat, says Dr. Kushner. Research now shows that waist circumference alone is a good indicator of the presence of that deep "angry fat." However, it is crucial that both men and women take this measurement at a very specific part of the body. Place the tape measure just above the top of the hip bones.

Reason: Hip bone position never changes, and it is easy to find even for people who are overweight. For men, you are at risk if your waist circumference is 40 inches or more…for women, 35 inches or more puts you into the danger zone.

Use Your Head—for Your Heart

For your health, it is crucial to lose belly fat if your waist measurement exceeds the above guidelines. Despite the promises you see on many magazine covers for both women and men—you know, "Bust That Belly Fat with One Simple Move!"—there is no way to spot reduce, says Dr. Kushner. The only way to get that fat to budge is to reduce your calorie intake via a healthy weight-loss program, such as the Mediterranean diet. For more on this fruit, veggie and whole-grain-heavy diet that most people find both delicious and filling, see the Mediterranean diet article starting on page 223. Exercise is a must as well, with aerobic exercise particularly good for both shedding pounds and boosting cardiovascular health.

Once you have lost some weight and reduced your waistline to a healthy number of inches, you'll need to be vigilant to keep that belly fat from doing what it does best—creeping back onto your body.

■ ■ ■ ■

More Polish for The Apple

Chang Yong Lee, PhD, professor in the department of food science at Cornell University, Ithaca, New York.

David Joachim, chef, based in Center Valley, Pennsylvania, and coauthor of numerous cookbooks, including *Perfect Light Desserts* (William Morrow), *The Science of Good Food* (Robert Rose) and *Fire It Up: More Than 400 Recipes for Grilling Everything* (Chronicle).

We've all heard the family wisdom, especially, "an apple a day keeps the doctor away." Well, not only does it turn out that Grandma was right about that—new research shows that apples can actually keep the grim reaper away, too. That's according to a study conducted at The Chinese University of Hong Kong and published in the *Journal of Agriculture and Food Chemistry*. The study shows that fruit flies (*Drosophila melanogaster*) fed a diet high in apple *polyphenols* (antioxidant substances) lived 10% longer than fruit flies fed the same diet without the polyphenols. Plus, the polyphenol-fed group retained the ability to walk, climb and move about for longer than the nonpolyphenol group.

Fruit flies are commonly used as human stand-ins in research because their genes are remarkably similar to ours. And the positive result of this apple polyphenol research simply adds to the loads of evidence that apples do a body good. Previous studies have shown that the chemicals in apples can be beneficial in reducing the risk for cancer, cardiovascular disease and diabetes. Apples also promote weight loss and improve pulmonary function.

The trick, of course, is figuring out how many apples you'd need to eat each day to see a benefit.

"We do not know yet the optimum amounts of antioxidants required per person per day," says Chang Yong Lee, PhD, a professor in the department of food science at Cornell University who specializes in bioactive phytochemicals. "But since there is no known negative effect from consuming large portions of natural fruits and vegetables, I would say that at least one to two apples a day is very reasonable." And, Dr. Lee points out, a recent USDA report has shown that Americans typically eat only about one-quarter of a raw apple a day, on average, so there's plenty of room for improvement.

It's not that hard to eat a few apples a day—for example, you can include one in your breakfast and then eat another after dinner. But if that seems a little monotonous, it's easy—and fun—to incorporate apples into more of your meals.

The rule of thumb: According to Dr. Lee, a raw, unpeeled apple retains the most beneficial chemicals—you can add it to meat salads and garden salads. Cooked apples with the skin still intact are nearly as beneficial and can be added to many dishes, ranging from pork chops to roast chicken to desserts like apple tarts and apple up-side-down cake. Or you could make simple baked apples. And of course, there are processed apple products (applesauce, juice) that have lower amounts of beneficial phytochemicals.

With this information in mind, we asked David Joachim, chef and coauthor of numerous cookbooks, including *Perfect Light Desserts, The Science of Good Food* and *Fire It Up: More Than 400 Recipes for Grilling Everything,* to give his thoughts on an interesting apple recipe.

"I'd make an apple-jicama salad, with an orange-lime vinaigrette," Joachim says. "The salad and dressing are colorful and sweet enough that even kids will gobble it up, and the ingredients pack a load of health-boosting nutrients. Plus it's easy to make any night of the week." Here's how to put it together. Try it tonight—and enjoy those apples!

Apple-Jicama Salad

Core two apples (a firm red variety is best—these include honeycrisp, jazz, empire, jonathan and others—with the skin intact) and julienne into matchsticks. Place in a bowl.

Then julienne a peeled medium-sized (about one pound) jicama (a crisp, slightly sweet root vegetable) and add to bowl.

Add in a handful of orange segments (cut into smaller pieces if you prefer) and a handful of chopped mint.

Mix this together with an orange-lime vinaigrette—one to two tablespoons each of orange juice and lime juice with two to three tablespoons of olive oil, plus salt and pepper to taste.

Serve on a bed of watercress with some toasted pecans scattered on top.

Serves four.

The Eskimo Diet for Good Health

Zeina Makhoul, PhD, RD, nutrition assessment specialist, SPOON Foundation, Portland, Oregon, *http:spoon foundation.org.* She was formerly a researcher at the Fred Hutchinson Cancer Research Center, Seattle.

Not surprisingly, the best thing that an overweight or obese person can do to improve his/her health is to lose weight…but it appears that the next best thing might be to take fish oil!

A recent study conducted in the rugged Yukon-Kuskokwim Delta in southwestern Alaska examined the diet of Yup'ik Eskimos, a native American people, many of whom have maintained a traditional lifestyle, including eating a diet that's especially rich in fish. About 70% of the Yup'ik Eskimos in the study were overweight or obese—a percentage that is consistent with the rest of the US.

Compared with overweight or obese folks in other parts of our country, these Yup'ik Eskimos have a far lower risk for heart disease and a lower rate for adult-onset diabetes. And that's what interested the researchers.

Fishing for the Facts

The Yup'ik Eskimos consume about 30 times more omega-3 fats in their diet on average than do other American adults. This led researchers at the Fred Hutchinson Cancer Research Center in Seattle to design a study measuring the association between their fish-rich diet and their good health.

Omega-3 fats, found mainly in saltwater fish such as salmon, halibut and herring, include *docosahexaenoic acid* (DHA) and *eicosapentaenoic acid* (EPA), which are the components of most fish oil supplements on the market today. If omega-3s help prevent adult-onset diabetes, the researchers reasoned that they might also reduce the threat for other conditions associated with being overweight, including heart disease, so the study was designed to measure the association between omega-3 fats and blood markers of chronic disease risk, including *C-reactive protein* (CRP) and *triglycerides*.

While at the Hutchinson Center, Zeina Makhoul, PhD, was the lead author of the study that resulted from the Center's research in Alaska.

Results of the study were clear: In the 330 Yup'ik Eskimos studied, the more omega-3 fats they ate, the lower the levels of CRP and triglycerides. Importantly, this was the case even in participants who were overweight or obese.

Fish Oil for All?

According to Dr. Makhoul, "It's very possible that foods rich in omega-3 protect Yup'ik Eskimos from some of the harmful effects of obesity." But, she says, this particular study was designed to measure only the association and it does not establish a cause-and-effect link between omega-3 fats and the levels of CRP and triglycerides. That, she says, would require clinical trials—and, as a result of the study, clinical trials are a likely next step.

If trials confirm what she and other researchers suspect, Dr. Makhoul says, the outlook is good that higher intake of omega-3 fats will be recommended for virtually everyone and most especially for people who are overweight.

Resveratrol—Setting the Record Straight

Joseph C. Maroon, MD, clinical professor of neurological surgery and Heindl Scholar in Neuroscience, University of Pittsburgh Medical Center, Pittsburgh. Dr. Maroon is the team neurosurgeon for the Pittsburgh Steelers and author of *The Longevity Factor: How Resveratrol and Red Wine Activate Genes for a Longer and Healthier Life* (Atria).

The red-wine supplement resveratrol has been very much in the news in recent years, but reports vary—while some cast doubt, many are very promising about its numerous health benefits. With sales soaring and more than 100 resveratrol supplements available, it's clear that lots of people want to believe that these products work miracles. Do they? How? And which work best?

We turned to Joseph C. Maroon, MD, a professor of neurological surgery at the University of Pittsburgh Medical Center and author of *The Longevity Factor: How Resveratrol and Red Wine Activate Genes for a Longer and Healthier Life* for answers. We talked about what scientists are sure of and what has yet to be proven. Dr. Maroon also shared his insights on how to safely and effectively use this supplement today.

Multiple Health Benefits

Where earlier studies demonstrated that resveratrol brought health benefits to animals, now new ones are examining what resveratrol does for humans (or human cells). *The findings suggest that resveratrol can be beneficial in areas such as...*

● **Inflammation control.** A University of Buffalo study published in the *Journal of Clinical Endocrinology & Metabolism* verified for the first time that resveratrol controls oxidative stress and inflammation in people. Twenty healthy volunteers took a 40-milligram (mg) resveratrol extract or a placebo for six weeks, and subsequent blood tests revealed lower levels of inflammatory *cytokines* in the resveratrol group. Inflammation is at the root of devastating age-related illnesses such as cancer, diabetes, heart disease, arthritis and Alzheimer's, Dr. Maroon notes.

● **Cancer prevention and treatment.** In a laboratory trial at the University of Rochester Medical Center, investigators discovered that resveratrol may help combat pancreatic cancer. They added 50 mg of the supplement to one group of human pancreatic cancer cells and nothing to the other and found that the cancer cells treated with resveratrol responded more positively to chemotherapy. Other research suggests that resveratrol guards against cancers of the skin, breast, liver, lung and colon.

● **Protection against diabetes.** Scientists at Albert Einstein College of Medicine of Yeshiva University report that resveratrol improves glucose metabolism in adults with prediabetes.

● **Improved heart and brain health.** A review in *Genes & Nutrition* summarized existing reports on the cardioprotective and longevity aspects of resveratrol, which protects the linings of blood vessels in the heart to prevent blood clots and other damage. In a randomized, double-blind, placebo-controlled trial of 22 healthy adults reported in the *American Journal of Clinical Nutrition*, British investigators at Northumbria University found that resveratrol increases oxygen uptake and blood flow to the frontal lobes of the brain (the site of cognition and problem solving).

Want to Try It?

To supplement your diet with resveratrol, Dr. Maroon says to look for products made with *trans-resveratrol*—the active form of resveratrol polyphenols made from the skins of red grapes. An average dose consists of 250 mg to 500 mg a day, and scientists have detected no significant side effects at these doses. Expect to pay on average $40 for a 30-day supply. *Dr. Maroon recommends the following brands…*

● **Vindure 900.** A mixed polyphenol supplement based on Harvard University's resveratrol research. It can be purchased directly from Vinomis Laboratories (*www. vinomis.com*, 877-484-6664).

● **ResVitále Resveratrol.** A resveratrol supplement from French red wine vineyards. *www.resvitale.com*, 877-787-5454).

● **GNC Longevity Factors Cellular Antioxidant Defense.** A combination of resveratrol, vitamin D (*cholecalciferol D-3*), grape seed extract and quercetin. Note that this product was developed by Dr. Maroon together with GNC, and that he does have a financial interest in it. Available at GNC stores or on their Web site (*www.gnc.com*, 877-462-4700).

Whether you choose to take supplements or not, it certainly makes sense to eat plenty of resveratrol- and polyphenol-rich foods. Go for variety in your diet, because different plant compounds interact synergistically with one another to provide more powerful health advantages. Choose items such as red grapes…red wines including Cabernet Sauvignon, Merlot and Pinot Noir (in moderation, of course)…pure red grape juice (high-quality organic, not from concentrate)…unroasted peanuts…dark chocolate (at least 70% cocoa)…green tea…and blueberries, cranberries and pomegranates.

Why Go Nuts for Nuts?

Richard D. Mattes, PhD, MPH, RD, professor of foods and nutrition at Purdue University in West Lafayette, Indiana. He has published numerous studies on nuts and appetite.

If you've relegated nuts to the "occasional snack" category, it's time to get more creative. Substitute nuts for some or all of the meat in a stir-fry entrée...sprinkle sliced or chopped nuts over vegetables, rice, soup or cereal...add ground nuts to a smoothie or yogurt...dress salads with nut oils...spread nut butter on celery sticks or apple slices.

Why do we push nuts? Because from all corners of the nutrition world, we hear from wellness professionals who are amazed by nuts' health benefits. *Recent research shows that eating a moderate amount of nuts on a regular basis may help...*

● **Control weight.** According to Richard D. Mattes, PhD, MPH, RD, a professor of foods and nutrition at Purdue University who has done extensive research on the topic, nut consumption increases your resting energy expenditure, which means that you burn more calories just sitting still than you otherwise would. Also, about 5% to 15% of the calories in nuts are excreted without being absorbed. And nuts' unique combination of protein, fiber, fatty acids and other characteristics quell hunger quickly and for prolonged periods.

● **Prevent heart disease.** Most of the fats in nuts are heart-healthy monounsaturated fats and omega-3 fatty acids that help lower LDL (bad) cholesterol and triglycerides... increase HDL (good) cholesterol...and prevent abnormal heart rhythms. Nuts also contain vitamin E, which inhibits arterial plaque buildup...and *l-arginine*, an amino acid that makes arteries more flexible and less vulnerable to clots.

● **Fight inflammation.** The soluble fiber in nuts appears to increase production of the anti-inflammatory protein *interleukin-4*. In addition, antioxidant vitamin E reduces inflammation.

● **Reduce diabetes risk.** A Harvard study found that women who ate five or more ounces of nuts weekly were almost 30% less likely to get type 2 diabetes than women who rarely or never ate nuts.

Also: Spanish researchers found that nuts were even more effective than olive oil in combating *metabolic syndrome*, a condition that puts you at risk for diabetes and heart disease.

● **Combat cancer.** Some nuts (including dried Brazil nuts and walnuts) are high in selenium, a mineral associated with a decreased risk for colorectal, skin and lung cancers. In animal studies, walnuts appeared to inhibit breast tumors—perhaps due to their disease-fighting omega-3s and antioxidants.

● **Support brain function.** Evidence suggests that nuts' omega-3s may ease depression and boost thinking and memory by improving neurotransmitter function. Nuts also provide folate—and low levels of this B-vitamin are linked to depression and poor cognition.

Nut Types to Try

Per ounce, nuts typically have 160 to 200 calories and 13 grams (g) to 22 g of fat. Eating 1.5 ounces of nuts per day (a small handful) is enough to provide health-promoting benefits. Nuts naturally contain only a trace of sodium, so they won't wreak havoc with blood pressure, especially if you choose brands with no added salt.

"All types of nuts are good for you, so there's no such thing as a 'best' type of nut," Dr. Mattes emphasizes. Still, each type does contain a different mix of nutrients—so for the widest range of benefits, eat a variety. Here are some excellent options and the nutrients that each is especially rich in. *Consider having...*

- **Almonds** for bone-building calcium… and inflammation-fighting vitamin E.
- **Brazil nuts** for their cancer-fighting selenium.
- **Cashews** for magnesium, which is linked to prevention of heart attacks and hypertension.
- **Hazelnuts** for potassium, which helps normalize blood pressure.
- **Peanuts** for folate, which helps lower levels of the artery-damaging amino acid *homocysteine.*
- **Pecans** for *beta-sitosterol*, a plant compound that combats cholesterol.
- **Pistachios** for *gamma-tocopherol*, a form of vitamin E that may reduce lung cancer risk.
- **Walnuts** for the heart- and brain-enhancing *omega-3 alpha-linolenic acid.*

■ ■ ■ ■

Five Cups of Coffee a Day Can Be Good for You!

Frank B. Hu, MD, PhD, an epidemiologist, nutritional specialist and professor of medicine at Harvard Medical School and the Harvard School of Public Health, both in Boston. He is codirector of Harvard's Program in Obesity Epidemiology and Prevention.

Even coffee drinkers find it hard to believe that their favorite pick-me-up is healthful, but it seems to be true. People who drink coffee regularly are less likely to have a stroke or get diabetes or Parkinson's disease than those who don't drink it. There's even some evidence that coffee can help prevent cancer, although the link between coffee and various cancers is preliminary and still being investigated.

Polyphenols and More

Coffee contains hundreds of antioxidants and other *bioactive compounds*, including some of the same *polyphenols* that are found in fruits, vegetables, wine and green tea. Polyphenols are potent antioxidants that inhibit inflammation as well as cell damage.

Both caffeinated and decaffeinated coffees contain antioxidants. However, some of the health benefits occur only with regular coffee. This suggests that caffeine also plays a role.

More coffee might be better for disease prevention. For example, coffee has a dose-response relationship with diabetes. People who drink five cups a day seem to benefit more than those who drink three cups…and two or three cups a day might be better than just one cup. But not everyone is better off with more. Some people get jittery with too much coffee, and it can cause other problems, such as stomach upset and bladder irritation.

Lower Diabetes Risk

More than 20 studies have found that coffee drinkers are less likely to get diabetes than those who don't drink coffee. When we analyzed the data from nine previous studies, which included a total of more than 193,000 people, we found that those who drank more than six or seven cups of coffee daily were 35% less likely to have type 2 diabetes (the most common form) than those who drank two cups or less. Those who consumed four to six cups daily had a 28% lower risk for diabetes.

Some of the studies were conducted in Europe, where people who drink a lot of coffee—up to 10 cups daily—are the ones least likely to have diabetes.

Both decaf and regular coffee seem to be protective against diabetes. This suggests that the antioxidants in coffee—not the caffeine—are the active agents. It's possible that these compounds protect insulin-producing cells in the pancreas. The minerals in coffee, such as chromium and magnesium, have been shown to improve insulin sensitivity.

Healthier Brain

It's not a coincidence that coffee is the beverage of choice at the workplace. People who drink coffee have short-term improvements in memory and other cognitive functions. Coffee also seems to improve long-term brain health.

Example: Coffee drinkers are at least 30% less likely to get Parkinson's disease than people who don't drink coffee. Parkinson's disease is characterized by a lack of *dopamine* in the brain.

Some researchers believe that coffee also can help reduce the risk for Alzheimer's disease. One study, which followed 1,400 participants for about 20 years, found that regular coffee consumption (three to five cups daily) reduced the risk for Alzheimer's and other forms of dementia by 65%, compared with those who drank little or no coffee.

You will get the brain benefits only if you drink regular coffee—decaf does not have the same effects. It's possible that caffeine contributes to the benefits.

Better Blood Pressure

Caffeinated coffee raises blood pressure temporarily, but people who drink it regularly have no increased risk for high blood pressure.

There is emerging evidence that coffee drinkers have a lower risk for stroke and other cardiovascular diseases.

Example: Data from the long-running Nurses' Health Study found that women who drank four or more cups of coffee a day had about a 20% lower risk for stroke than those who drank little or no coffee.

Other studies indicate that coffee may reduce the risk for heart disease, possibly by reducing arterial inflammation that can lead to atherosclerosis and blood clots. However, the evidence is not conclusive.

Less Cancer

It's not a substitute for sunscreen, but drinking coffee could protect you from the most common type of skin cancer.

In a report presented at the American Association of Cancer Research meeting in Boston, researchers found that coffee drinkers were less likely to develop basal-cell carcinoma than people who did not drink coffee.

In the study, researchers followed more than 112,000 people for up to 24 years. During this time, they tracked the incidence of basal-cell carcinomas and other skin cancers. Men who drank the most coffee had a 13% lower risk for basal-cell carcinomas than those who drank the least…in women, the risk was 18% lower.

Decaffeinated coffee didn't provide the same protection, so it appears that caffeine is responsible—but the reason isn't known.

Coffee reduced the risk for only this one type of skin cancer. Other skin cancers, such as melanoma and squamous-cell carcinoma, weren't affected. Because this is the first large study to find this effect, it will have to be repeated—by different researchers and with different groups of people—to confirm that coffee does, in fact, protect the skin.

Caffeine may protect against other cancers as well.

New finding: Women who drink four or more cups a day of caffeinated coffee reduced their risk for endometrial cancer by 30%. And drinking two or more cups of decaffeinated coffee reduced risk by about 22%.

Promising but Not Proved

It's important to remember that the majority of research about coffee is observational. Researchers interview large numbers of people…ask them about their coffee consumption and other habits…look at their health status…and then make conclusions about what caused what.

Unlike double-blind, randomized clinical trials, which are considered the gold standard of scientific research, observational studies cannot prove cause and effect, but they do offer evidence.

Caution

Some caveats about coffee…

• **Moderation matters.** Some people get the jitters or have insomnia when they drink coffee. In rare cases, the caffeine causes a dramatic rise in blood pressure. It's fine for most people to have three, four or five cups of coffee a day—or even more. But pay attention to how you feel. If you get jittery or anxious when you drink a certain amount, cut back. Or drink decaf some of the time.

• **Hold the milk and sugar.** Some of the coffee "beverages" at Starbucks and other coffee shops have more calories than a sweet dessert. Coffee may be good for you, but limit the add-ons.

• **Use a paper filter.** Boiled coffee, coffee made with a French press or coffee that drips through a metal filter has high levels of oils that can significantly raise levels of LDL, the dangerous form of cholesterol.

Better: A drip machine that uses a paper filter. It traps the oils and eliminates this risk.

It's Processed Meat— Not Red Meat!—That Harms You

Renata Micha, RD, PhD, research associate in the department of epidemiology at Harvard School of Public Health in Boston and leader of a review of 1,598 studies.

A recent analysis of data from 20 studies involving a total of more than 1.2 million people from 10 different countries who were followed for up to 18 years suggests that this advice is too broad.

Surprisingly, researchers found that eating unprocessed beef, pork or lamb was not associated with increased risk for either heart disease or diabetes. However, eating even a moderate amount of processed meats (those preserved by smoking, curing, salting or adding chemical preservatives, such as nitrates and including bacon, salami, sausage, hot dogs, many deli meats and perhaps processed poultry) was another story. Average daily consumption of one 1.8-ounce (50-gram) serving of processed meat (about one to two slices of deli meat or one hot dog) was associated with a 42% increase in heart disease risk and a 19% increase in diabetes risk.

The saturated fat and cholesterol in meat typically are the main focus of recommendations to cut back on red meat…yet researchers found that unprocessed and processed meats actually contained similar amounts of saturated fat and cholesterol.

Where meat products differed: The processed meats contained about four times as much sodium and about 50% more nitrates (since nitrates also naturally occur in meat) than unprocessed red meat—which suggests that these ingredients may be the true culprits to avoid when it comes to guarding against heart disease and diabetes.

Managing Diabetes

Straight Talk from a Doctor with Diabetes

Julian Seifter, MD, associate professor of medicine at Harvard Medical School in Boston. A nephrologist at Brigham and Women's Hospital, also in Boston, he has practiced medicine for 30 years. He is the author of *After the Diagnosis: Transcending Chronic Illness* (Simon & Schuster).

If you're one of the more than 90 million Americans who suffer from a chronic illness, such as high blood pressure, diabetes, kidney disease or asthma, chances are your doctor has recommended that you take medication and/or change your lifestyle.

Following your doctors' orders isn't always easy, but a bit of judicious "cheating" is almost always OK.

Julian Seifter, MD, is a Harvard nephrologist (kidney specialist) who has diabetes himself. *He shares some advice based on his personal experiences…*

My Health Challenges

As a nephrologist, I'm an expert in the complications of diabetes, but I've sometimes been unable to change my own habits to keep my diabetes under control. At different times, I've been out of shape and overweight and allowed my blood pressure and blood sugar to get too high. *What I've learned…*

Why We Cheat

Being diagnosed with a chronic illness profoundly affects your sense of identity. You may need to give up things that are important to you…forever. And doing what you're told by your doctor means that you're losing some control over your life.

It's only human that we often respond to these losses with denial. That's especially true if you don't feel particularly sick, as with high blood pressure. You can ignore dietary guidelines your doctor has given you or not take your medication—and if you're lucky enough to not suffer ill effects, this cheating lets you tell the world, and yourself, there's nothing wrong with you.

Even if you accept your illness, giving up favorite foods or pleasurable habits can hurt your quality of life. And letting your illness define you—becoming afraid to do things you enjoy and worrying about everything you eat—isn't healthy either. Life has to be worth living, which requires some compromise.

Find the Right Doctor

Doctors shouldn't just be instruction givers…they should be problem solvers. They should meet their patients halfway and help them figure out how to do what's necessary for their health while maintaining their pleasure in life.

If your doctor is rigid and moralistic, this creates a communication barrier that makes matters worse. You will be tempted to lie or simply cancel your appointment if you haven't followed your diet or you stopped taking medication that was causing uncomfortable side effects.

To find out if you can work with your doctor, say something like, "I'm worried that I'll never be able to have corned beef (or a glass of wine…or a piece of pie) again. Is there any way we can compromise on my diet?" You also may want to ask about larger worries, such as how you can continue to travel or participate in your favorite sport.

Strike a Balance

It's almost always possible to build flexibility into a diet or medical regimen and still achieve a high level of care.

Example: A pastrami sandwich is not part of a low-fat or low-salt diet. But one every other week won't make much difference to most people's health, and if you love pastrami, it's likely to make you a lot happier with the whole eating plan.

If you're prescribed a low-salt diet for hypertension, can you name three salty foods that you wouldn't mind giving up? And are there three foods that you would truly miss? Talk to your doctor about the foods you will miss most to see whether a compromise can be made. The "special foods" may need to be rotated or scheduled with appropriate portion sizes.

If you feel that you must cheat, work with your doctor to find a creative solution.

Example: When I told one of my patients that alcohol contributed to his high blood pressure, he insisted that he had to have his two martinis nightly. To compromise, I said he could have one martini per night but without the high-sodium olive.

Forget You're Sick

With my diabetes, the turning point for me came after I collapsed, due to poorly controlled blood sugar that was compounded by anxiety, while visiting Paris with my wife.

What I realized: Ironically, cheating less could give me what I wanted most—to simply forget about my illness. Thereafter, I made it a habit to check my blood sugar before and after meals, as well as to exercise, take my blood pressure pills and eat the right foods.

I'm not perfect. But I make repeated efforts to get it right, and this has allowed me to live with greater confidence and freedom—and simply have more fun. I aim for the art of the possible and try to help my patients do the same.

■ ■ ■ ■

You May Be Able to Throw Away Your Meds!

Stefan Ripich, ND, a naturopathic physician based in Santa Fe, New Mexico. He practiced for 10 years at the Palo Alto Veterans Administration Medical Center and established the first holistic clinic in the VA system. He is coauthor, with Jim Healthy, of *The 30-Day Diabetes Cure* (Bottom Line Books, *www.bottomlinepublications.com/diabetes*).

In the US, a new case of diabetes is diagnosed every 30 seconds. And many of those people will be given drugs to treat the disease.

You can control high blood sugar with medications, but they aren't a cure and they can have side effects. They also are expensive, costing $400 or more a month for many patients.

Much better: Dietary remedies that have been proven to reduce blood sugar, improve the effects of *insulin* (a hormone produced by the pancreas that controls blood sugar), promote weight loss and, in many cases, eliminate the need for medications. A UCLA study found that 50% of patients with type 2 diabetes (the most common form) were able to reverse it in three weeks with dietary changes and exercise.

How you can do it, too…

• **Eliminate all HFCS.** A Princeton study found that rats given water sweetened with *high-fructose corn syrup* (HFCS) gained more weight than rats that drank water sweetened with plain sugar, even though their calorie intake was exactly the same.

Reasons: The calories from HFCS fail to trigger *leptin*, the hormone that tells your body when to quit eating. Also, HFCS is more likely than natural sugar to be converted to fat…and being overweight is the main risk factor for diabetes.

What to do: Read food labels carefully. HFCS is the main sweetener in soft drinks and many processed foods, including baked goods such as cookies and cakes.

• **Don't drink diet soda.** If you give up HFCS-laden soft drinks, don't switch to diet soda. Diet sodas actually cause weight gain by boosting insulin production, leading to excessively high insulin in your blood that triggers greater fat accumulation and even more cravings for sugar.

A study published in *Diabetes Care* found that drinking diet soda every day increased the risk for type 2 diabetes by as much as 67%.

If you crave sweet bubbly beverages, pour one inch of pure fruit juice into a glass and then top it off with carbonated water.

• **Eat barley.** I advise patients to eat foods that are as close to their natural state as possible—whole-grain cereals and breads, brown rice, etc. These "slow carbohydrates" contain fiber and other substances that prevent the spikes in glucose and insulin that lead to diabetes.

Best choice: Barley. Researchers at the Creighton Diabetes Center in Omaha compared the effects of two breakfasts—one consisting of oatmeal (one of the best slow carbohydrates) and the other consisting of an even slower breakfast cereal made from barley. Participants who ate barley had a postmeal rise in blood sugar that was significantly lower than participants who ate the oatmeal breakfast.

You can eat cooked barley as a side dish…sprinkle it on salads…or mix it into tuna, chicken, tofu or lentil salad.

• **Season with cinnamon.** About one-quarter teaspoon of cinnamon daily reduces blood sugar, improves insulin sensitivity and reduces inflammation in the arteries—important for reducing the risk for heart disease, the leading cause of death in people who have diabetes.

Research published in *Diabetes Care* found that people with type 2 diabetes who ate at least one-quarter teaspoon of cinnamon daily reduced fasting blood sugar levels by up to 29%. They also had up to a 30% reduction in *triglycerides* (a blood fat) and up to a 27% drop in LDL (bad) cholesterol.

• **Eat protein at breakfast.** Protein at breakfast stabilizes blood sugar and makes people feel satisfied, which means that you will consume fewer calories overall. Lean protein includes eggs, chicken and fish.

• **Eat more meat (the good kind).** We've all been told that a diet high in meat (and therefore saturated fat) is inherently unhealthy. Not true. Other things being equal, people who eat more saturated fat actually tend to weigh less and have smaller waist

Your Best Friend

Dogs can detect blood sugar drops in diabetics. Trained dogs can detect a faint odor emitted by humans as much as 20 minutes before blood sugar drops to a critical level. Such drops can cause diabetics to collapse or go into a coma if they do not receive medication immediately. A trained dog is valued at $20,000, but Dogs4Diabetics and other providers often require only $150 for people in need.

Dogs4Diabetics, Nylabone Training Center, Concord, California. *www.dogs4diabetics.com*

measurements than similar adults who eat less.

The real danger is from processed meats, such as bacon, hot dogs and many cold cuts. These foods have more calories per serving than natural meats. They're higher in sodium. They have a lower percentage of heart-healthy omega-3 fatty acids and other beneficial fats that lower inflammation.

A large study that looked at data from 70,000 women found that those who ate processed meats with every meal were 52% more likely to develop diabetes than those who ate healthier meats and other foods.

I advise people to look for grass-fed beef. It's lower in calories and fat than industrialized grain-fed factory feedlot beef and higher in omega-3s.

• **Snack on nuts.** Healthful snacking between meals keeps blood sugar stable throughout the day. Nuts are the perfect snack because they're high in fiber (which reduces abrupt increases in glucose and insulin) and protein (for appetite control). They also are good sources of important nutrients and antioxidants.

A Harvard study of 83,000 women found that those who frequently ate almonds, pecans or other nuts were 27% less likely to develop diabetes than those who rarely ate nuts. A small handful every day is enough.

Caution: "Roasted" nuts usually are a bad choice because they often are deep-fried in coconut oil. They also have added salt and/or sugar. "Dry-roasted nuts" have not been fried in fat but usually have salt and sugar.

If you like roasted nuts, it's best to buy organically grown raw nuts and lightly toast them in a dry fry pan over very low heat (or in your oven).

• **Supplement with vitamin D.** In theory, we can get all the vitamin D that we need from sunshine—our bodies make it after the sun hits our skin. But about 90% of Americans don't get adequate amounts—either because they deliberately avoid sun exposure or because they live in climates without much sun.

A Finnish study found that participants with high levels of vitamin D were 40% less likely to develop diabetes than those with lower amounts. Vitamin D appears to improve insulin sensitivity and reduce the risk for diabetes-related complications, including heart disease.

Recommended: Take 1,000 international units (IU) to 2,000 IU of vitamin D-3 daily.

• **Remember to exercise.** It's just as important as a healthy diet for preventing and reversing diabetes. The Diabetes Prevention Program (a major multicenter clinical research study) found that people who walked as little as 17 minutes a day, on average, were 58% less likely to develop diabetes.

Walking for 30 minutes most days of the week is optimal.

■ ■ ■ ■

Black Tea Helps Treat Diabetes

When researchers compared concentrations of *polysaccharides* (a type of carbohydrate) in black, green and oolong teas, the polysaccharides in black tea were the best blood sugar (glucose) inhibitors.

Theory: Polysaccharides in black tea block an enzyme that converts starch into glucose.

If you have diabetes or prediabetes: Consider drinking three cups of black tea daily to better control blood sugar.

Haixia Chen, PhD, associate professor, department of Traditional Chinese Medicine, School of Pharmaceutical Science and Technology, Tianjin University, Tianjin, China.

A Reader's Dilemma

Mark A. Stengler, NMD, naturopathic medical doctor and leading authority on the practice of alternative and integrated medicine. Dr. Stengler is author of the *Health Revelations* newsletter, author of *The Natural Physician's Healing Therapies* (Bottom Line Books), founder and medical director of the Stengler Center for Integrative Medicine, Encinitas, California, and adjunct associate clinical professor at the National College of Natural Medicine in Portland, Oregon. *http://markstengler.com*

My 86-year-old mother has diabetes and refuses to follow a low-sugar/low-carbohydrate style of eating. Is there a supplement she can take when she has an especially unhealthful meal/snack?

Of course, for people with diabetes there is no substitute for consuming foods with a low Glycemic Index (GI value), such as proteins, vegetables and whole grains. (GI refers to the effect that eating a specific food has on blood sugar.) For information about the GI value of specific foods, go to *www.glycemicindex.com*. But your mother can speak with her doctor about taking a *glucomannan* supplement, which can help after she has an unhealthy meal. This soluble fiber is derived from *konjac root*, a plant native to subtropical and tropical eastern Asia. It reduces the rapid absorption of sugar from the digestive tract into the bloodstream. I generally recommend that patients take 1,000 milligrams (mg) of glucomannan either in capsule or powder form per meal and drink eight ounces of water with it. Glucomannan can expand when it comes in contact with water—so don't use tablets. They can swell up and become a choking hazard. Taking a 15-minute walk after a meal also can help to reduce blood sugar levels.

Just a Spoonful of Vinegar Helps the Blood Sugar Go Down

Carol S. Johnston, PhD, RD, associate director, nutrition program, Arizona State University, Mesa, and coauthor of a study published in *Diabetes Care.*

Adding vinegar to a meal slows the *glycemic response*—the rate at which carbohydrates are absorbed into the bloodstream —by 20%.

Reason: The *acetic acid* in vinegar seems to slow the emptying of the stomach, which reduces risk for *hyperglycemia* (high blood sugar), a risk factor for heart disease, and helps people with type 2 diabetes manage their condition.

Ways to add vinegar to meals: Use malt vinegar on thick-cut oven fries...marinate sliced tomatoes and onions in red-wine vinegar before adding the vegetables to a sandwich...mix two parts red wine vinegar with one part olive oil, and use two tablespoons on a green salad.

If You Have Diabetes, Not Just Any Workout Regimen Will Do

Timothy S. Church, MD, PhD, MPH, exercise researcher at the Pennington Biomedical Research Center at Louisiana State University System in Baton Rouge, and leader of a study of the effects of various exercise regimens on diabetes patients.

Exercise is essential for everybody, of course. But people with diabetes stand to benefit particularly—provided that their workouts include the right variety of physical activity. This finding, from a recent study published in the *Journal of the American Medical Association*, addresses questions that had not previously been well studied.

The Study

Researchers recruited 262 sedentary patients with type 2 diabetes, 63% of whom were women, with an average age of 56. Participants had an average blood test score of 7.7% for *hemoglobin A1C*, an indicator of how well blood sugar concentration has been controlled in the previous eight to 12 weeks (for comparison, levels under 6% generally are considered normal in people without diabetes). One group of participants did aerobic exercise, walking at a moderate pace for two-and-a-half hours per week...a second group did resistance training, performing a full-body routine (primarily with weight-lifting machines) three times per week...a third group combined the aerobic workout and resistance training, doing a shortened version of both routines so that the total exercise time was the same for the three groups. A fourth group, which did not exercise, served as a control.

Supplement Speeds Weight Loss

In a recent study, obese women with diabetes supplemented with 6.4 grams (g) daily of the fatty acid *conjugated linoleic acid* (CLA). In 16 weeks, they lost three pounds of fat, on average...and their body mass index (a calculation based on height and weight) fell by about half a point.

Reassuring: Earlier animal studies produced concerns that CLA might reduce beneficial lean muscle mass—but patients participating in this study did not lose any lean muscle.

Martha Belury, PhD, RD, professor of nutrition, Ohio State University, Columbus, and leader of a study of 35 women.

The Results

After nine months: Participants in all three exercise groups showed improvement in several areas, including reduced waist size, as compared with the nonexercisers—but improvement was greatest in the combination aerobics/resistance training group. Combination exercisers were the only ones who lowered the amount of diabetes medication they needed, lost weight and showed significant improvement in hemoglobin A1C levels...they also lost the most fat mass—about four pounds' worth, on average.

Bottom line: If you have diabetes, work with your doctor to develop an appropriate exercise regimen that includes both aerobics and resistance training.

Better Choice for Diabetes Medication

New study: Researchers examined data from 166 published studies to compare the safety and efficacy of several diabetes drugs.

Result: The generic drug *metformin* is just as effective as newer drugs but has fewer side effects. Metformin, which was FDA-approved in 1995, is also much less expensive than the newer drugs. All of the drugs reduce blood sugar levels, but measurement of long-term outcomes is not yet possible with the newer medications.

Wendy L. Bennett, MD, assistant professor of medicine, Johns Hopkins University School of Medicine, Baltimore.

Does Agave Health Claim Match Its Hype?

Jonny Bowden, CNS, board-certified nutritionist, member of the American Society for Nutrition and American College of Nutrition, and author of *The 150 Healthiest Foods on Earth* (Fair Winds). www.jonnybowden.com

Jeannette Bessinger, board-certified holistic health counselor, chef and coauthor of *Simple Food for Busy Families* (Celestial Arts), based in Newport, Rhode Island. www.balanceforlifellc.com

From the same cactus that gives us tequila, we now have a sweetener that is making health-food fanciers kick up their heels in delight—it is a syrup made from *agave*, a succulent native to Mexico. Even local supermarkets are now selling a variety of products proudly proclaiming that they are "sweetened with agave nectar," the implication being that this is healthier than regular sugar or *high-fructose corn syrup* (HFCS).

It's easy to understand how agave syrup got its great reputation. The cactus has been cultivated for thousands of years. Even its name, "agave," has a fine pedigree, coming from the Greek word for noble. Fresh extracts from the agave plant have been shown to have anti-inflammatory and some antioxidant properties—but unfortunately, there's zero evidence that any of those compounds are present in the commercially made syrup.

Agave Claims

Agave nectar is an amber-colored liquid that pours more easily than honey and is sweeter than white table sugar, according to Jeannette Bessinger, author of *Simple Food for Busy Families*. Among the health claims are that it's gluten-free (but so are all other refined sugars) and suitable for vegan diets (again, just like the rest of the sweeteners)—and, most especially, that it has a relatively low Glycemic Index (GI).

A large body of research shows that foods with low GIs, such as vegetables, beans and high-fiber foods in general, tend to be healthier for us than foods that quickly raise our blood sugar. But in the case of agave nectar, you have to ask, why does this sugar have a low GI? And the answer is that agave nectar is made largely of fructose, which, even though it has a low GI, is implicated in many long-term health problems. With the exception of pure liquid fructose, agave nectar has the highest fructose content of any commercial sweetener.

High Fructose Content

It's worth knowing that all sugars, from white table sugar to high-fructose corn syrup and even honey, include some mixture of fructose and glucose. For example, table sugar is 50% fructose/50% glucose and HFCS is 55/45. Agave nectar is a whopping 70% to 90% fructose.

"Fructose, which is basically the sugar found in fruit, is perfectly fine when it is ingested in whole foods like apples," says nutritionist Jonny Bowden, CNS, author of *The 150 Healthiest Foods on Earth* and *150 Ways to Boost Energy*. "That's because it also comes with a host of vitamins, antioxidants and fiber, so you are getting good stuff along with it. But, when fructose is extracted from fruit, concentrated and made into a sweetener, it plays havoc with the metabolism."

Special Concern for People with Diabetes

Research shows that fructose, more than other kinds of sugars, contributes to *insulin resistance* and often significantly raises blood levels of *triglycerides* (a risk factor for heart disease) in both obese and healthy people. It also has a greater propensity than other sugars to increase fat around the middle, which elevates risk for diabetes, heart disease and *metabolic syndrome*. And it's the sweetener most often linked to nonalcoholic fatty liver disease.

Spun Sugar

So, in the end, it's all marketing spin. "Agave nectar syrup ends up being a triumph of marketing over science," says Bowden.

"Agave nectar is not poison—it's okay to enjoy it from time to time," says Bowden. But don't believe the hype that it's a health food—that's just food-industry sweet talk.

Are Your Medications Making You Sick?

Hyla Cass, MD, board-certified psychiatrist and nationally recognized expert in nutritional and integrative medicine. She is the author of several books, including *8 Weeks to Vibrant Health* (Take Charge) and *Supplement Your Prescription: What Your Doctor Doesn't Know About Nutrition* (Basic Health). *www.cassmd.com*

When we think of drug side effects, what usually comes to mind are headache, dizziness, dry mouth and other such complaints.

Commonly ignored side effect: Many popular medications can deplete your body of crucial nutrients—an unintended effect that can increase your risk for diseases ranging from cancer to heart disease. *What you need to know…*

Are You at Risk?

Nutrient depletion, which causes such symptoms as fatigue, muscle cramps and even a rapid heartbeat, can potentially occur within weeks after starting a medication.

More often, such symptoms occur gradually, over months or even years—and, as a result, often are dismissed by people taking the drugs as mere annoyances or mistaken for signs of aging.

In some cases, a hidden nutrient deficiency increases one's risk for other illnesses—for example, a deficiency of *folate* (a B vitamin) may raise your risk for cancer or cause physiological changes that can set the stage for heart attack or stroke.

Important: If you take one or more medications regularly, ask your physician about nutrient depletion—and whether you should be tested. Doctors can do a basic blood screening profile for low blood levels of vitamins and minerals, such as B-12, folate, calcium, magnesium and potassium.

However, to more accurately measure your levels of all the important nutrients, your doctor should consider more sophisticated testing.

For example, SpectraCell's micronutrient test measures more than 31 vitamins, minerals, amino acids and antioxidants. Not all doctors are familiar with the test, but you can go to *www.spectracell.com* and click on "Find a Clinician" to locate a physician in your area who is. Or try the Metametrix Nutrient and Toxic Elements Profile, *www.metametrix.com*). Insurance may pay for some of the cost.

Helpful: Be sure to eat foods that are rich in nutrients that may be depleted by your medications. To ensure adequate levels of these nutrients, ask your doctor about taking the supplements described below. *Drugs that can deplete nutrients…*

Aspirin and Other NSAIDs

The *nonsteroidal anti-inflammatory drugs* (NSAIDs), such as aspirin, are commonly used to reduce pain and inflammation. Millions of Americans also take aspirin to "thin" the blood, reducing the risk for a heart attack or stroke.

Nutrients depleted: Folate and vitamin C. Insufficient folate is thought to increase the risk for a variety of cancers, including malignancies of the breast and colon. Low folate also has been linked to elevated levels of *homocysteine*, an amino acid that can raise risk for heart attack and stroke.

People who are low in vitamin C get more colds, flu and other infections than those with normal levels. A deficiency of vitamin C also can impair the body's ability to produce and repair cartilage—which may explain why people with osteoarthritis who regularly take an NSAID often suffer more joint pain in the long run.

My recommendation: Take 1,000 milligrams (mg) of vitamin C daily if you take an NSAID regularly. A Boston University study found that people who got the most vitamin C were three times less likely to develop osteoarthritis, or have an increase in symptoms, than those who got lower amounts.

Caution: High-dose vitamin C can cause loose stools in some people—if this occurs, reduce your dose to 500 mg daily.

In addition, take a 400-microgram (mcg) to 800-mcg folic acid (the man-made form of folate) supplement daily. Take vitamin B-12 (1,000 mcg daily) with folic acid—taking folic acid alone can mask a B-12 deficiency.

Also helpful: 1,000 mg to 2,000 mg of fish oil daily. One study found that 60% of people with osteoarthritis who took fish oil improved their joint pain within 75 days. Half improved so much that they no longer needed to take an NSAID.

Calcium Channel Blockers

When it comes to blood pressure medication, most people know that *diuretics* (water-excreting drugs) can deplete important nutrients, including potassium. It's less well-known that blood pressure drugs known as *calcium channel blockers*, including *amlodipine* (Norvasc) and *nicardipine* (Cardene), can have the same effect.

Nutrient depleted: Potassium. People with low potassium may experience muscle weakness and fatigue. Their blood pressure also may increase, which offsets the drug's effectiveness.

My recommendation: Take a 100-mg potassium supplement daily. Because many foods contain significant amounts of this mineral, you can eat a single extra serving of a high-potassium food as an alternative. A medium baked potato with the skin, for example, provides 850 mg of potassium…and a large banana has 487 mg. Check with your physician if you have kidney disease—extra potassium can worsen the condition.

Gemfibrozil

People who can't control elevated cholesterol with a statin, or who suffer muscle pain or other side effects when taking a statin, may be given a prescription for *gemfibrozil* (Lopid). This and similar drugs, known as *fibrates*, raise levels of HDL (good) cholesterol and reduce harmful LDL cholesterol and triglycerides.

Nutrients depleted: Vitamin E and the naturally occurring nutrient *coenzyme Q10* (CoQ10). A deficiency of vitamin E, a potent antioxidant, can increase risk for cancer, heart disease and other conditions, such as nerve disorders. Inadequate CoQ10 often results in muscle pain and weakness…and can impair the ability of the heart to beat efficiently.

My recommendation: Take 200 mg of CoQ10 and 100 mg of natural vitamin E (*mixed tocopherols*) daily.

Metformin

Metformin (Glucophage), the most popular oral diabetes drug, reduces blood sugar by making cells more responsive to insulin. It also causes less weight gain and fewer episodes of *hypoglycemia* (excessively low blood sugar) than other diabetes drugs.

Nutrients depleted: Vitamin B-12. A study in *Archives of Internal Medicine* found that patients taking metformin had average vitamin B-12 levels that were less than half of those in people who weren't taking the medication. Metformin also reduces levels of folate. A deficiency of these nutrients can cause fatigue, forgetfulness and depression.

My recommendation: Take 1,000 mcg of vitamin B-12 every day. Many multivitamins have only 200 mcg (or less) of B-12, so you'll have to supplement to reach the 1,000-mcg daily dose. For folic acid, take 400 mcg to 800 mcg daily.

Important: When increasing levels of vitamin B-12, people with diabetes may be more likely to experience episodes of hypoglycemia. Ask your doctor about getting an *A1C blood test*, which provides an estimate of blood sugar levels over many weeks rather than at a single point in time.

Do You Need a Personal Pharmacist?

Marie Chisholm-Burns, PharmD, MPH, dean of the College of Pharmacy at the University of Tennessee Health Science Center, Memphis.

Do you need a personal pharmacist? Perhaps—and even if "need" is too strong a word, it is quite likely that you would benefit from having one. This is especially true if you have a chronic illness or condition or are the caregiver for such a person.

Pharmacists are a great resource for improving your health. Many people don't realize how helpful pharmacists can be, says Marie Chisholm-Burns, PharmD, MPH, dean of the College of Pharmacy at the University of Tennessee and the lead author of a recent study on this topic. I called her to learn more about this research.

Today's pharmacists are becoming more directly involved in patient care and this is a very good development, according to the meta-analysis published in a recent issue of *Medical Care*, a journal devoted to health-care administration issues. Benefits include improvements in diabetes control, cholesterol and hypertension and lower rates of adverse drug reactions and medical errors. When pharmacists were directly involved in care, patients spent fewer days in the hospital, took their medications more regularly, often had lower health-care costs and were healthier overall.

The research: This multidisciplinary study from the University of Arizona analyzed nearly 300 trials comparing patient results with a variety of chronic conditions such as diabetes, hypertension and high cholesterol—when pharmacists were and were not closely involved. The researchers found compelling evidence favoring pharmacists' involvement, including the above-mentioned benefits and also an increase in the quality of life, patient knowledge, better outcomes and greater safety and efficacy.

Can We Meet?

How do you go about finding a pharmacist who can be "directly involved" with your care? A good place to start is with the pharmacy where you fill all or most of your prescriptions—or, if you do mail-order, you might ask your doctor for a recommendation for a pharmacist with whom you can consult.

Introduce yourself and ask to make an appointment for a medication review. *Here's a checklist to make the most of this consultation…*

• **Before your meeting it's important to create a complete and detailed list,** not only of all prescription medications you take but also all herbal supplements, vitamins and minerals.

• **Tell your pharmacist about all your medical conditions.** For example, if you're taking medications for hypertension and you also suffer seasonal allergies, discuss both the prescriptions and what over-the-counter (OTC) treatments you typically take for the allergies—ask which are okay and whether any should be avoided. If you

---

Statin Warning

Statins may raise risk for diabetes.

Recent findings: People taking high doses of the cholesterol-lowering drugs had a 12% higher risk for diabetes than those taking moderate statin doses. And users of high doses had a 20% higher risk for diabetes than people who do not take statins at all. But doctors say these statistics may be misleading. Statins increase blood sugar only a little, which may push a few patients over the threshold for diagnosis of diabetes.

Most experts agree that the cardiovascular benefits of statin use far outweigh the increase in diabetes risk.

Steven E. Nissen, MD, chairman of cardiology, Cleveland Clinic.

---

have a chronic condition (such as arthritis) for which you take any OTC drugs, tell the pharmacist about this as well, since certain prescription medications may affect your condition or interact with the OTC medication.

• **Be sure to discuss any herbs or other natural treatments** you take or are interested in taking. For each, ask whether it is okay to take it, and how does it fit in with the drugs you take?

• **Ask about drug and food interactions—** for instance, grapefruit juice interferes with some drugs.

This is a terrific way to improve your health—it's easy, important and many pharmacists are eager to get more involved in patient care. Some even are willing to provide this service over the phone for patients who can't come in for an appointment.

Safer Diabetes Medication

Frederic Vagnini, MD, cardiovascular surgeon and medical director, Heart, Diabetes and Weight Loss Centers of New York, Lake Success, *www.vagnini.com.* He is coauthor of *The Weight Loss Plan for Beating Diabetes* (Fair Winds).

In a recent development, an FDA panel voted to keep the diabetes drug *rosiglitazone* (Avandia) on the market but suggested tougher warning labels to reflect research showing that the drug is linked to an increased risk for heart attack and stroke in some people.

If you take rosiglitazone: Ask your doctor about switching to *pioglitazone* (Actos), a similar but safer medication. Both drugs lower blood sugar levels, but pioglitazone also helps improve cholesterol/triglyceride profiles.

If you have heart failure: Don't take either of these drugs as they may worsen this condition.

■ ■ ■ ■

Are You Overdosing on Supplements?

Alan R. Gaby, MD, a specialist in nutritional medicine, past president of the American Holistic Medical Association and a former professor of nutrition at Bastyr University in Kenmore, Washington. He is the chief science editor for *Aisle7*, a Web-based health and wellness resource, and the author of *Nutritional Medicine*, available from his Web site, *www.doctorgaby.com.*

With so much scientific research pointing to the health benefits of getting enough vitamins and minerals, it's not surprising that more than half of all American adults now take dietary supplements to boost their intakes of these nutrients.

Diabetes Drugs That Increase Fracture Risk

The diabetes medications Actos and Avandia may increase fracture risk in women over age 50. Higher doses are associated with greater risk. Postmenopausal women should be careful to consume adequate amounts of calcium and vitamin D to protect bone health.

William H. Herman, MD, MPH, director of the Michigan Center for Diabetes Translational Research, University of Michigan, Ann Arbor, and leader of a study published in *The Journal of Clinical Endocrinology & Metabolism.*

What you may not realize: Even though certain supplements may help prevent serious conditions such as heart disease, vision problems, osteoporosis and even certain types of cancer—some people are unknowingly endangering their health by taking doses that are too high.

Important: Because many foods are now fortified with vitamins and minerals, you should include those nutrients, as well as those found in multivitamins, when determining your total daily intake for the following nutrients.

To determine the average amount of nutrients you need to maintain good health: Aim for the *recommended dietary allowance* (RDA) set by the Food and Nutrition Board of the National Academy of Sciences.

Do not exceed the *Tolerable Upper Intake Level,* also set by the Food and Nutrition Board, unless you are doing so for a therapeutic reason under a doctor's supervision. *The Tolerable Upper Intake Level* is the highest level of nutrient intake, from food and supplements, that is likely to pose no risk for adverse health effects for almost all individuals in the general population.

What you need to know to safely use the following supplements…*

Vitamin D

Adequate vitamin D levels promote bone health and muscle strength. Low levels of this vitamin have been linked to a variety of medical conditions, such as colorectal cancer, dementia, osteoporosis and multiple sclerosis.

However, it is estimated that at least one-third of Americans do not get enough sunshine for their bodies to synthesize adequate levels of vitamin D. Food sources, such as vitamin D–fortified foods, egg yolks and fatty fish, provide relatively low levels of the vitamin.

The RDA for vitamin D is 600 international units (IU) daily for adults age 19 to 70…800 IU for those age 71 and older. The Tolerable Upper Intake Level is 4,000 IU daily.

When you get too much: Excessive vitamin D can interfere with calcium metabolism. Lab animals that are given the human equivalent of 11,500 IU a day develop arterial calcification that is indistinguishable from the appearance of coronary artery disease in bypass patients. Because vitamin D changes the way calcium is absorbed, in rare cases, high doses of the vitamin can bring on *hypercalciuria*, excessive calcium that can lead to kidney stones.

To be safe: I advise most patients to take 800 IU daily, depending on sun exposure and other factors.

Adults over age 65…people who are obese…or patients with intestinal diseases (such as Crohn's disease) may need to take

*Always consult your doctor before starting a supplemental vitamin or mineral regimen. Certain vitamin and mineral supplements can interact with medication and/or have side effects.

up to 2,000 IU daily because they don't utilize and/or synthesize vitamin D efficiently.

Vitamin C

Vitamin C is a potent antioxidant that plays a vital role in the formation of collagen and the health of your immune system. This vitamin also helps prevent high blood pressure, and the National Cancer Institute recommends adequate levels to help guard against cancer.

The RDA for vitamin C is 75 milligrams (mg) daily for women…90 mg for men. Because smoking depletes vitamin C from the body, smokers should get an additional 35 mg of vitamin C daily. The Tolerable Upper Intake Level is 2,000 mg daily.

When you get too much: Excessive vitamin C can lead to gastrointestinal (GI) problems, mainly diarrhea and stomach cramps. Some individuals experience GI discomfort when they take as little as 500 mg of vitamin C. More often, this occurs at doses exceeding 2,000 mg. To help avoid side effects, spread out the dosage throughout the day.

Caution: Even low doses of vitamin C could damage soft tissue, including the heart, in people with late-stage kidney disease. Anyone with a kidney disorder, including a history of kidney stones, should consult a doctor before supplementing with vitamin C.

To be safe: Don't take more than 1,000 mg twice daily without consulting a doctor. Taking it with food or using a buffered form (such as *sodium ascorbate* or *calcium ascorbate*) will help prevent GI discomfort. Avoid chewable ascorbic acid—the acid content can damage tooth enamel.

Many studies show that taking 1,500 mg to 4,000 mg of vitamin C daily during a cold will help reduce the duration and severity of the illness.

Vitamin E

Doctors used to recommend vitamin E to prevent heart disease—until a 2004 study concluded that people who took 400 IU of vitamin E daily had a 4% higher risk of dying from any cause than those who didn't take the supplement. However, this research has since been called into question because of the type of vitamin E taken by the study subjects and the fact that they also took *beta-carotene*, which increases lung cancer risk in smokers.

The RDA for vitamin E is 33 IU daily. The Tolerable Upper Intake Level is 1,500 IU daily.

When you get too much: Excessive vitamin E can lead to bleeding—in part because the vitamin inhibits the activity of platelets, cell-like structures involved in clotting.

To be safe: Limit doses to 200 IU to 400 IU daily. In this range, vitamin E probably does reduce the risk for heart disease as well as cancer.

Also important: Your vitamin E should contain mixed *tocopherols*, the types of vitamin E that are present in foods.

Talk to your doctor about taking higher doses of vitamin E if you have *peripheral artery disease*, arthritis, diabetes or high cholesterol.

Vitamin A

It's commonly used to treat some vision and skin disorders (such as acne). Multivitamins may contain 5,000 IU of vitamin A. That's nearly double the RDA, but vitamin A isn't harmful at that dose.

The RDA for vitamin A is 2,310 IU daily for women…3,000 IU for men. The Tolerable Upper Intake Level is 10,000 IU daily.

When you get too much: Excessive doses of vitamin A could cause dizziness, blurred vision, fatigue or reduced bone mineral density.

To be safe: Adults who are otherwise healthy should not exceed the RDA. Higher doses should be taken only if you're under a doctor's care. Women of childbearing age should not take more than 5,000 IU of vitamin A daily because of increased risk for birth defects.

People with liver disease, such as *cirrhosis* or *hepatitis*, should not take more than 5,000 IU daily of a vitamin A supplement without consulting a physician—this nutrient can cause liver damage in some people.

Talk to your doctor about taking higher doses of vitamin A if you have night blindness, celiac disease, excessive menstrual bleeding, acne or a respiratory or diarrheal infection.

Zinc

It's commonly used to improve immunity and treat infections, including the common cold.

When you get too much: High doses of zinc can cause copper deficiency, which can lead to neurological disorders, including a loss of coordination, vision impairments or *peripheral neuropathy* (numbness and/or tingling in the hands or feet). In severe cases, the neurological damage can be permanent.

The RDA for zinc is 8 mg daily for adult women…11 mg for adult men. The Tolerable Upper Intake Level is 40 mg daily.

Warning: Some denture adhesives contain zinc and have been linked to copper deficiency. If you use one of these products, follow the package directions exactly. Problems tend to occur when people use too much adhesive or apply it too often.

To be safe: Stick to the RDA for your daily zinc intake. If, under a doctor's supervision, you exceed the RDA for zinc for reasons such as treating an infection, combine it with copper. For each 30 mg of zinc, add 1 mg to 2 mg copper daily (to a maximum of 4 mg of copper per day).

Talk to your doctor about taking the higher doses of zinc if you have age-related macular degeneration, night blindness or an enlarged prostate. *Zinc gluconate lozenges* can be taken for colds.

Calcium

Millions of postmenopausal women use supplemental calcium (with or without vitamin D) to preserve bone strength and reduce the risk for osteoporosis and fractures.

The RDA for calcium is 1,000 mg daily for women age 19 to 50 and men age 19 to 70...1,200 mg for women age 51 and older and men age 71 and older. The Tolerable Upper Intake Level is 2,500 mg daily for adults age 19 to 50...2,000 mg for adults age 51 and older.

When you get too much: Excessive calcium can cause constipation. Recent preliminary research also links the use of calcium supplements (even at low doses such as 500 mg daily) to a 30% increase in heart attack risk.

Some researchers speculate that calcium supplements may increase heart disease risk by interfering with the absorption or utilization of magnesium, a mineral that is known to prevent heart disease. If that is the case, then taking magnesium along with calcium (usually in a ratio of two parts calcium to one part magnesium) would be expected to prevent any possible adverse effect of calcium on the heart.

Bottom line: If you're currently taking calcium, keep taking it until you can talk to your doctor.

To be safe: Strive to get as much calcium as possible from food sources, which have the added benefit of containing other nutrients.

Diabetes "App"

The *Point-of-Care Information Technology Center Diabetes Guide,* from Johns Hopkins physicians, provides up-to-date diabetes news. Find it at *www.hopkinsguides. com/hopkins/ub.*

The Johns Hopkins University School of Medicine, Baltimore, Maryland.

Good calcium sources: Dairy foods—such as plain, low-fat yogurt (eight ounces provide 415 mg of calcium)...soy milk (one cup, 340 mg)...and collard greens (one-half cup, 178 mg).

A Little Bit of Exercise Helps a Lot

Genevieve Healy, PhD, School of Population Health, The University of Queensland, Herston, Queensland, Australia, and leader of a study of 169 adults, published in *Diabetes Care.*

As little as one minute of standing and walking around can make a difference in waist circumference over time.

Example: People who get up regularly and switch TV channels by hand, instead of using the remote, have, on average, a waist circumference of six centimeters less than those who stay seated. People who do these small amounts of activity also have lower body mass indexes and lower glucose and triglyceride levels. Stand up to answer the phone...take a long route back to your desk...do some stretches before reading a new e-mail.

Say Good-Bye to Your Diabetes Medication

Mark A. Stengler, NMD, naturopathic medical doctor and leading authority on the practice of alternative and integrated medicine. Dr. Stengler is author of the *Health Revelations* newsletter, author of *The Natural Physician's Healing Therapies* (Bottom Line Books), founder and medical director of the Stengler Center for Integrative Medicine, Encinitas, California, and adjunct associate clinical professor at the National College of Natural Medicine in Portland, Oregon. *http://markstengler.com*

Some of my patients who have type 2 diabetes are able to keep the disease under control with diet, exercise and supplements. Lucky them! But for other diabetes patients, that's not enough and they must take pharmaceutical medications.

I'm happy to report that there is another natural treatment option for diabetes patients who currently take pharmaceutical medications. Research has found that a plant extract called *berberine* can control diabetes as well as, or better than, common medications such as *metformin* (Glucophage) and *rosiglitazone* (Avandia). And it does this with no side effects—and without damaging the liver, as some medications do. *Here's how berberine can help people with diabetes*…

A naturally occurring chemical compound, berberine is found in the roots and stems of several plants, including *Hydrastis canadensis* (goldenseal), *Coptis chinensis* (coptis or goldthread) and *Berberis aquifolium* (Oregon grape). Long used as a remedy in Chinese and Ayurvedic medicines, berberine is known for its antimicrobial properties and as a treatment for bacterial and fungal infections. Several decades ago, berberine was used to treat diarrhea in patients in China. That was when doctors noticed that the blood sugar levels of diabetes patients were lower after taking the herbal extract—and berberine began to be investigated for this purpose.

Over the past 20 years, there has been much research on berberine and its effectiveness in treating diabetes. Chinese researchers published a study in *Metabolism* in which adults with newly diagnosed type 2 diabetes were given 500 milligrams (mg) of either berberine or the drug metformin three times a day for three months. Researchers found that berberine did as good a job as metformin at regulating glucose metabolism, as indicated by *hemoglobin A1C* (a measure of blood glucose over several weeks)…fasting blood glucose…blood sugar after eating…and level of insulin after eating. Berberine even reduced the amount of insulin needed to turn glucose into energy by 45%! In addition, those taking berberine had noticeably lower trigylceride and total cholesterol levels than those taking metformin.

In another study published in *Journal of Clinical Endocrinology* and *Metabolism*, researchers found that type 2 diabetes patients who were given berberine had significant reductions in fasting and postmeal blood glucose, hemoglobin A1C, triglycerides, total cholesterol and LDL (bad) cholesterol—and also lost an average of five pounds, to boot, during the three-month study period.

In a study in *Metabolism*, Chinese researchers compared people with type 2 diabetes who took either 1,000 mg daily of berberine or daily doses of metformin or rosiglitazone. After two months, berberine had lowered subjects' fasting blood glucose levels by an average of about 30%, an improvement over the rosiglitazone group and almost as much as people in the metformin group. Berberine also reduced subjects' hemoglobin A1C by 18%—equal to rosiglitazone and, again, almost as good as metformin. In addition, berberine lowered serum insulin levels by 28.2% (indicating increased insulin sensitivity)…lowered triglycerides by 17.5%…and actually improved liver enzyme levels. Pharmaceutical medications, on the other hand, have the potential to harm the liver.

These were remarkable findings. Here was a botanical that was holding up to scientific scrutiny—and performing as well as, or better than, some drugs that patients had been taking for diabetes for years.

How Berberine Works in the Body

Berberine helps to lower blood glucose in several ways. One of its primary mechanisms involves stimulating the activity of the genes responsible for manufacturing and activating *insulin receptors*, which are critical for controlling blood glucose.

Berberine also has an effect on blood sugar regulation through activation of *incretins*, gastrointestinal hormones that affect the amount of insulin released by the body after eating.

How Berberine Can Help

I recommend berberine to my patients with newly diagnosed type 2 diabetes to reduce their blood sugar and prevent them from needing pharmaceutical drugs. When a diet, exercise and supplement program (including supplements such as chromium) is already helping a patient with diabetes, I don't recommend that he/she switch to berberine.

Some patients are able to take berberine—and make dietary changes—and stop taking diabetes drugs altogether. People with severe diabetes can use berberine in conjunction with medication—and this combination treatment allows for fewer side effects and better blood sugar control. I don't recommend berberine for prediabetes unless diet and exercise are not effective. Berberine is sold in health-food stores and online in tablet and capsule form. The

dosage I typically recommend for all diabetes patients is 500 mg twice daily.

For patients with diabetes who want to use berberine, I recommend talking to your doctor about taking this supplement. It's also important for every patient with diabetes to participate in a comprehensive diet and exercise program.

Note that berberine helps patients with type 2 diabetes, not type 1 diabetes (in which the body does not produce enough insulin).

■ ■ ■ ■

When to See a Physician Assistant or Nurse Practitioner

Robert L. Kane, MD, professor and Minnesota Chair in Long-Term Care and Aging in the division of health policy and management at the University of Minnesota School of Public Health and director of the university's Center on Aging, both in Minneapolis. He has published numerous articles on the care of older adults and was awarded the British Geriatric Society's Medal for the Relief of Suffering Amongst the Aged in 2008. Dr. Kane is coauthor of *Essentials of Clinical Geriatrics* (McGraw-Hill).

These days, when you visit your primary care doctor, a hospital emergency department or even some medical specialists, it's more likely than ever before that a physician assistant (PA) or nurse practitioner (NP) will be caring for you.

Who are these health-care providers—and when should they be relied upon?

Robert L. Kane, MD, a renowned expert on medical care in the US, answers these questions and more below...

A Growing Trend

There are currently more than 70,000 PAs and 140,000 NPs practicing in the US, and their numbers are expected to rise significantly over the next decade due, in part, to the increasing patient load from the aging baby-boomer population and soaring health-care costs.

Although these nonphysician providers are trained to diagnose and treat medical conditions on their own, all states require that PAs must be supervised by a physician either in person or by telephone or some other means of telecommunication. NPs are allowed to practice without direct physician supervision in 10 states, but most require collaboration with a physician as well.

In general, medical doctors have a more thorough and rigorous grounding in basic science and patient care than do the nonphysician providers. Medical doctors attend four years of medical school after college and complete three to seven years of residency training.

In addition to college, PAs and NPs are required to complete a two-year master's degree for their medical training. In the next few years, certification to become an NP will require a doctoral degree as well. While PAs often have previous health-care experience—as an emergency medical technician, for example—all NPs have previous nursing experience as registered nurses (RNs).

Because both PAs and NPs are state-licensed, their actual responsibilities vary somewhat from state to state, but in most states, they're allowed to record medical histories, conduct diagnostic exams and tests, prescribe drugs and treatment plans, and administer care with a growing range of medical devices such as electrocardiograms.

Important: If nonphysician providers play a role in your doctor's practice, you should be informed when you make your appointment whether you're going to see a physician or a nonphysician provider.

In your first meeting with the PA or NP, ask what the facility's policy is regarding when patients are seen by a physician versus a nonphysician provider. If you have a complex condition, such as unstable heart failure or difficult-to-manage blood pressure or diabetes, you should also double-check that the physician will be reviewing your chart or electronic medical record on a regular basis. It is reasonable to see your physician about every third visit to ensure that your treatment is on track.

When to Use a PA or NP

When it is—and isn't—appropriate to see a PA or NP in place of a physician…

• **Simple health problems.** It is OK to be treated by a PA or NP if you just need a checkup or treatment for a straightforward medical condition, such as a sore throat.

In the US, more than one-third of all PAs and two-thirds of NPs work in primary care. Studies have repeatedly found that their patient outcomes and patient satisfaction levels in this area are as good as—or better than—those of physicians.

Interesting research finding: In a trial that I helped conduct at New York-Presbyterian Hospital, more than 1,300 patients who had visited the emergency department or an urgent-care center were then randomly assigned for follow-up care to either a primary care physician or a primary care NP with full authority to treat and prescribe drugs. When tested six months later, patients who were treated by an NP were just as healthy, on average, as those treated by a physician. Patient satisfaction rates for the two groups were also equivalent after six months.

*Ask for a physician consult if…*your nonphysician provider appears uncertain regarding your condition's diagnosis…your condition poses a challenging diagnostic dilemma (such as pain that does not improve or fatigue for no clear reason)…the treatment regimen being prescribed is complex and involves multiple medications or other interventions…or you're not confident that the provider's diagnosis and/or treatment recommendations are appropriate.

● **Routine follow-up.** It's OK to be treated by a PA or NP if you're making a routine follow-up visit for a chronic condition. Following initial diagnosis and treatment, managing chronic diseases, such as diabetes or hypertension, largely involves ongoing monitoring and preventive care, including medical intervention such as adjusting the dosage of a medication if a condition begins to worsen. This is done through routine follow-up visits or, increasingly, by patients checking in via phone or e-mail.

Important benefit: PAs and NPs are able to spend more time with each patient, so nonphysician providers typically excel at encouraging patients to adhere to their prescribed medical regimens, ensuring that treatment plans are working effectively and identifying problems with diet, sleep, drug side effects, psychological stress, pain and other areas that may impact the condition being treated.

*Ask for a physician consult if…*your chronic condition changes significantly in some other way that your PA or NP can't account for.

● **Monitoring after seeing a specialist.** It's OK to be treated by a PA or NP if you need follow-up care after seeing a specialist. An increasing number of nonphysician providers now are working in specialty practices. For example, an NP might specialize in obstetrics/gynecology, while a PA might specialize in cardiology. If you are referred to a specialist who uses a PA or NP, the physician will typically evaluate you on your first visit.

But once a treatment plan has been established, it's appropriate for a PA or NP to conduct follow-up exams to monitor your treatment and overall health. Similarly, with a specialist that you see regularly for preventive care—a pulmonologist or urologist, for example—it's fine to see a PA or NP if you need to make an unscheduled visit for a straightforward complaint, such as a cough or urinary tract infection.

*Ask for a physician consult if…*you suspect that the PA or NP is not keeping your doctor sufficiently apprised of your ongoing treatment…you aren't happy with how your preventive care or treatment is progressing…or you think that your current complaint is too complex for the PA or NP to handle or you suspect that it hasn't been diagnosed properly by the nonphysician provider.

● **When you need a fast appointment.** It's OK to be treated by a PA or NP if you want to be seen quickly, but your doctor isn't immediately available. In certain cases, you may be given the option of seeing the doctor in, say, two weeks or seeing a PA or NP tomorrow.

If you have a routine condition, such as the flu, that requires immediate attention, seeing a nonphysician provider right away may be your best option. This also holds true for visits to the emergency department, where PAs and NPs are increasingly the frontline providers who diagnose medical conditions.

*Ask for a physician consult if…*you believe that your condition is extremely serious or life-threatening…your illness involves an ongoing medical condition, such as cancer or hepatitis, that the PA or NP is inexperienced at treating or that requires the skills of a physician specialist.

Breathe Like a Baby

Carol Krucoff, a registered yoga therapist at Duke Integrative Medicine and a yoga instructor at Duke University's Center for Living, both in Durham, North Carolina. She is also a certified personal trainer and the author of *Healing Yoga for Neck & Shoulder Pain* (New Harbinger). Ms. Krucoff's audiotaped lessons on breathing are available on her home-practice CD, *Healing Moves Yoga* (*www.healingmoves.com*).

As a yoga therapist, I see clients with different medical issues, from diabetes to chronic pain to cancer. No matter what they're dealing with, I always begin by teaching deep abdominal breathing—the way we all breathed when we were babies.

Deep abdominal breathing is one of the most effective ways to quickly reduce stress and unleash the body's natural vitality. By breathing this way, you calm down the *sympathetic nervous system* (involved in the body's "fight or flight" response)...reduce blood levels of stress hormones...increase the body's blood flow...reduce perception of pain...and induce the body's relaxation response, resulting in a slower heart rate, lower blood pressure, less muscle tension and a feeling of greater well-being.

These are powerful effects. If you're practicing breathing exercises but are not getting these benefits, or tried them before but gave up, you may simply be doing them improperly.

Soften Your Body

Abdominal breathing does not require a determined effort. You simply draw breath into the lower part of your lungs, the way babies do. I teach my clients to visualize their lungs as two big balloons that expand and contract in six directions when they inhale—front to back, top to bottom and side to side.

How to do it: Sit comfortably with one hand on your abdomen and the other on your chest. On an inhalation, breathe down to the deepest portion of your lungs, so that your belly rounds out into your hand as you fill with breath. On the exhalation, your belly gently contracts and your hand moves in. Continue for several slow, deep breaths, observing the out-and-in movement of your belly, while the hand at your chest stays relatively still. It may help to start by lying down and placing a book on your belly so that it rises and falls with each inhalation and exhalation.

Breathe Slowly

People often mistakenly think that abdominal breathing involves "gulping" air—taking big, swift inhalations. On the contrary, one of the most important aspects of abdominal breathing is that it slows and deepens the breath.

Why that's important: Slowing your breathing is the key to calming your nervous system and increasing oxygen flow throughout your body. One study of menopausal women, for example, found that lowering their breathing rates to seven to eight breath cycles (inhalations and exhalations) per minute, down from an average of 15 to 16, reduced hot flashes by about 50%.

To achieve this slow breathing rate, count slowly to five during each inhalation and again during each exhalation.

Make Exhalations Longer Than Inhalations

Once you're accustomed to the feeling of relaxed abdominal breathing, I recommend gradually extending your exhalation until it's twice as long as your inhalation. Start by exhaling to a count of five, then work up to seven and finally to 10. Doing this triggers another deep-seated response—when you take longer to breathe out than in, it signals your brain that all is well, amplifying the relaxation effect.

Breathe Through Your Nose

If you have chronic congestion or another nasal obstruction, this may not be possible. But if you're able to breathe comfortably through your nose, this will help you control your breathing rate better while also ensuring the air you breathe is optimally warmed, moistened and filtered—all functions the nose is designed to perform.

Practice in a Relaxing Environment

Pick a calm, relaxing setting when first learning this technique. Choose a time when you don't have pressing concerns or deadlines. Select a place that's quiet, comfortable and free of distractions. Then spend at least several minutes exploring the techniques outlined above.

As you become more experienced with abdominal breathing, you can begin practicing it throughout the day—including when you awaken or go to sleep or during stressful situations, such as sitting in a traffic jam.

Employ a Mantra

Once you've become comfortable with your practice of inhalation and exhalation, I recommend adding mantras that you can recite to yourself while breathing. This is often more interesting and can be even more effective—because you can choose a mantra with meaning to you or one that reinforces a desired emotional state.

Examples: The mantra offered by Zen master Thich Nhat Hanh, *Breathing in, I calm myself. Breathing out, I smile.* Or the Dorothy mantra, *There's no place like home.* You also can use a favorite phrase or make up a phrase to fit the situation, such as *In energy, out fatigue* or *In peace, out anger.*

Begin by repeating your mantra silently, once while inhaling and once while exhaling. Then play with extending your exhalation to cover two repetitions of the mantra. Feel free to change mantras whenever you want.

■ ■ ■ ■

Don't Let Stress Harm Your Health—It Can Raise Your Blood Sugar

Irene Louise Dejak, MD, an internal medicine specialist who focuses on preventive health, including counseling patients on the dangers of chronic stress. She is a clinical assistant professor at the Cleveland Clinic Lerner College of Medicine of Case Western Reserve University in Cleveland and an associate staff member at the Cleveland Clinic Family Health Center in Strongsville, Ohio.

It's widely known that acute stress can damage the heart. For example, the risk for sudden cardiac death is, on average, twice as high on Mondays as on other days of the week, presumably because of the stress many people feel about going back to work after the weekend. People also experience more heart attacks in the morning because of increased levels of *cortisol* and other stress hormones.

Important recent research: In a study of almost 1,000 adult men, those who had three or more major stressful life events in a single year, such as the death of a spouse, had a 50% higher risk of dying over a 30-year period.

But even low-level, ongoing stress, such as that from a demanding job, marriage or other family conflicts, financial worries or chronic health problems, can increase inflammation in the arteries. This damages the inner lining of the blood vessels, promotes the accumulation of cholesterol and increases risk for clots, the cause of most heart attacks.

Among the recently discovered physical effects of stress…

• **Increased blood sugar.** The body releases blood sugar (glucose) during physical and emotional stress. It is a survival mechanism that, in the past, gave people a jolt of energy when they faced a life-threatening emergency.

However, the same response is dangerous when stress occurs daily. It subjects the body to constantly elevated glucose, which damages blood vessels and increases the risk for *insulin resistance* (a condition that precedes diabetes) and heart disease.

What helps: Get regular exercise, which decreases levels of stress hormones.

• **More pain.** Studies have shown that people who are stressed tend to be more sensitive to pain, regardless of its cause. In fact, imaging studies show what's known as stress-induced *hyperalgesia*, an increase in activity in areas of the brain associated with pain. Similarly, patients with depression seem to experience more pain—and pain that's more intense—than those who are mentally healthy.

What helps: To help curb physical pain, find a distraction. One study found that postsurgical patients who had rooms with views of trees needed less pain medication than those who had no views. On a practical level, you can listen to music. Read a lighthearted book. Paint. Knit. These steps will also help relieve any stress that may be exacerbating your pain.

Also helpful: If you have a lot of pain that isn't well-controlled with medication, ask your doctor if you might be suffering from anxiety or depression. If so, you may benefit from taking an antidepressant, such as *duloxetine* (Cymbalta) or *venlafaxine* (Effexor), which can help reduce pain along with depression.

• **Impaired memory.** After just a few weeks of stress, nerves in the part of the brain associated with memory shrink and lose connections with other nerve cells, according to laboratory studies.

Result: You might find that you're forgetting names or where you put things. These lapses are often due to distraction—people who are stressed and always busy find it difficult to store new information in the brain. This type of memory loss is rarely a sign of dementia unless it's getting progressively worse.

What helps: Use memory tools to make your life easier. When you meet someone, say that person's name out loud to embed it in your memory. Put your keys in the same place every day.

Also: Make a conscious effort to pay attention. It's the only way to ensure that new information is stored. Sometimes the guidance of a counselor is necessary to help you learn how to manage stress. Self-help materials, such as tapes and books, may also be good tools.

• **Weight gain.** The fast-paced American lifestyle may be part of the reason why two-thirds of adults in this country are overweight or obese. People who are stressed tend to eat more—and the "comfort" foods they choose often promote weight gain. Some people eat less during stressful times, but they're in the minority.

What helps: If you tend to snack or eat larger servings when you are anxious, stressed or depressed, talk to a therapist. People who binge on "stress calories" usually have done so for decades—it's difficult to stop without professional help.

Also helpful: Pay attention when you catch yourself reaching for a high-calorie snack even though you're not really hungry at all.

Healthy zero-calorie snack: Ice chips.

Low-calorie options: Grapes, carrots and celery sticks.

Once you start noticing the pattern, you can make a conscious effort to replace eating with nonfood activities—working on a hobby, taking a quick walk, etc.

Stress-Fighting Plan

There are a number of ways to determine whether you are chronically stressed—you may feel short-tempered, anxious most of the time, have heart palpitations or suffer from insomnia.

However, I've found that many of my patients don't even realize how much stress they have in their lives until a friend, family member, coworker or doctor points it out to them. Once they understand the degree to which stress is affecting their health, they can explore ways to unwind and relax.

In general, it helps to…

• **Get organized.** So much of the stress that we experience comes from feeling overwhelmed. You can overcome this by organizing your life.

Examples: Use a day calendar to keep your activities and responsibilities on-track, and put reminder notes on the refrigerator.

• **Ask for help.** You don't have to become overwhelmed. If you're struggling at work, ask a mentor for advice. Tell your partner/spouse that you need help with the shopping or housework.

Taking charge of your life is among the best ways to reduce stress—and asking for help is one of the smartest ways to do this.

• **Write about your worries.** The anxieties and stresses floating around in our heads often dissipate, or at least seem more manageable, once we write them down.

• **Sleep for eight hours.** No one who is sleep-deprived can cope with stress very effectively.

What to Do If You Urinate Profusely

Stanley Mirsky, MD, associate clinical professor of medicine, endocrinology and diabetes, Mount Sinai School of Medicine, New York City.

Excessive urination is a well-known symptom of diabetes. Blood sugar over 156 milligrams per deciliter (mg/dL) (on average) will spill into the urine and increase urination. Consult your physician to confirm whether this is the cause. If so, you may need to modify your diet, exercise more and get a proper mix of medications to better control your blood sugar. If elevated blood sugar is not the issue, you may be drinking too many fluids. An enlarged prostate in men or a urinary tract infection in men or women also can cause excessive urination. Finally, aging could be the culprit—over time, the bladder wall and sphincter weaken. Speak to your doctor.

Consumer Alert

What does "net carbs" mean on food labels? This is a marketing term. It refers to the amount of fiber and sugar alcohols (both carbohydrates) subtracted from total carbohydrates in a product. Net carbs are of concern to people who follow the Atkins, Zone and South Beach diets.

Warning: Products with low net carbs often have more calories than you might expect—and can raise blood sugar levels in people with diabetes.

Suzanne Havala Hobbs, DrPH, RD, clinical associate professor, department of health policy and management, University of North Carolina, Chapel Hill.

Delicious Ways to Cut Back on Carbs—You Can Have Parfaits, Pizza—and Even Pumpkin Pie!

Sandra Woodruff, RD, LD/N, a registered dietitian and nutritionist based in Tallahassee, Florida, *www.eatsmart today.com.* She is a past president of the Florida Dietetic Association and the author of several books, including *Secrets of Good-Carb/Low-Carb Living* (Avery).

To lose weight and help control elevated blood sugar, many people resort to ultra–low-carb diets—only to find them boring and hard to sustain for the long term.

The good news: A reduced-carb diet—done right—can be satisfying and delicious while providing many of the benefits of low-carb plans.

Tasty Reduced-Carb Eating

If you're reducing carbs by simply avoiding refined and processed carbs, such as sugar and white flour, that's a huge accomplishment. But there may be more that you can do.

For example, many carb reducers still tend to overdo portions of starchy foods (such as bread, cereal and rice) and starchy vegetables (such as potatoes and corn).

Even though it's a good rule of thumb to limit starchy foods to no more than one-fourth of your plate, you do not have to feel deprived of all higher-carb foods. Just choose them carefully, and you'll be amazed at how tasty your meals can be.

What to do: When you do eat higher-carb foods, it's wise to opt for those with a *low glycemic index* (GI). Low-GI carbs are absorbed into the bloodstream slower than those with a high GI, which helps prevent spikes in blood glucose. Oatmeal, barley, bulgur wheat, dried beans, sweet potatoes,

berries, apples, milk and yogurt are examples of low-GI foods.

Good news: Within a week or two of reducing carb intake, many people find that their cravings subside—and that a big bagel or an ultra-sugary cookie becomes a lot less appetizing.

Best ways to eat a variety of delicious meals while also reducing your carbohydrate intake…

Breakfast

What to avoid: Cereal, toast and juice—a common but very high-carb breakfast.

Good choice: A yogurt parfait. Layer Greek-style yogurt (which is lower in carbs and higher in protein than regular yogurt) with fresh berries and a sprinkling of walnuts. Or try using cottage cheese instead of yogurt.

Tea or coffee without sugar is fine. If you like, add a bit of low-calorie sweetener such as stevia or sucralose.

Lunch

What to avoid: A sandwich on "big" bread (such as a large bagel or sub roll), chips and sweet tea.

Good choice: A sandwich made with bagel thins or a reduced-carb wrap (such as Flatout Flatbread or a Toufayan multigrain wrap) instead of regular bread.

Add a lean protein filling, such as tuna, turkey or chicken, and pile on vegetable toppings. Pair your sandwich with a cup of vegetable soup, a garden salad or fruit cup.

Best bets for beverages: Have some iced tea flavored with mint or lemon instead of sugar. Sparkling mineral water with lemon or lime is another good choice.

Milk is also relatively low-carb (12 grams [g] per glass), and it has a low GI—be sure to choose low-fat to save calories.

Nondairy options such as plain soy milk and almond milk are fine as well.

Dinner

What to avoid: Pasta and bread. Although pasta is low-GI, many people overdo portions and make matters worse with extra carbs in the bread.

Good choice: Try a reduced-carb personal pizza. Top a round of whole-grain pita bread with marinara sauce, part-skim mozzarella cheese and your favorite toppings (I enjoy turkey "pepperoni," olives, mushrooms, onions, roasted red bell peppers, cooked spinach and/or artichoke hearts). Bake at 400°F for eight to 10 minutes. Add a big side salad topped with lots of colorful vegetables.

Dessert

What to avoid: High-sugar, flour-based desserts, such as cake and cookies.

Good choices: Fruit pies with low-sugar fillings and whole-grain crust (see next column)...fruit crisps made with oatmeal and nut toppings. Try replacing half or more of the sugar in fruit pie and fruit crisp recipes with either stevia or sucralose. A reduced-carb pumpkin pie is also delicious (see below).

Pumpkin Pie

1 Flaky Oat Piecrust (see recipe at right)

1½ cups canned or cooked mashed pumpkin

¼ cup honey

Sugar substitute equal to ½ cup sugar (check the label)

2 to 2½ teaspoons pumpkin pie spice

⅛ teaspoon sea salt

1½ teaspoons vanilla extract

1¼ cups evaporated nonfat or low-fat milk

½ cup fat-free egg substitute or two large eggs, beaten

1. Preheat the oven to 400°F. Prick several holes in the crust with a fork, and bake for five minutes. Remove from the oven, and set aside.

2. Place the pumpkin, honey, sugar substitute, pumpkin pie spice, salt and vanilla in a large bowl, and stir with a wire whisk to mix well. Whisk in the evaporated milk and then the egg substitute or eggs.

3. Pour filling into the crust, and bake for 15 minutes. Reduce heat to 350°F, and bake for about 35 minutes more or until a sharp knife inserted near the center of the pie comes out clean. Cool to room temperature and refrigerate until ready to serve.

Flaky Oat Piecrust

¾ cup whole-wheat pastry flour

½ cup quick-cooking (one-minute) oats

⅛ teaspoon baking powder

⅛ teaspoon sea salt

¼ cup canola oil

2 tablespoons nonfat or low-fat milk

1. Place the flour, oats, baking powder and salt in a medium bowl, and stir to mix well. Add the oil and milk, and stir until the mixture is moist and crumbly and holds together when pinched. Add a little more milk, if needed. Set aside.

2. Place a 12-inch square of waxed paper on a flat surface. Shape the dough into a ball, and then pat into a seven-inch circle. Top with another 12-inch square of waxed paper, and use a rolling pin to roll the dough into a roughly 10-inch circle.

3. Coat a nine-inch pie pan with cooking spray. Carefully peel off the top sheet of waxed paper, and place the other sheet, crust side down, over the pie pan. Peel away the waxed paper, and press the crust into the pan.

Nutrition facts: 209 calories and 29 g of carbohydrates per serving. Yields eight servings.

Control Diabetes with Qigong

Guan-Cheng Sun, PhD, assistant research scientist at Bastyr University, Kenmore, Washington, qigong teacher and executive director and founder of the Institute of Qigong & Internal Alternative Medicine, Seattle.

Wouldn't it be great if you could just wave your arms to get better control over your blood sugar? A research scientist at Bastyr University in Washington has adapted the ancient Chinese practice of movement called *qigong* (pronounced chee-gong) to help people with type 2 diabetes achieve better blood sugar control...feel better...and even reduce their reliance on drugs.

Study author Guan-Cheng Sun, PhD, assistant research scientist at Bastyr University, qigong teacher and executive director and founder of the Institute of Qigong & Internal Alternative Medicine in Seattle, says there are many types of qigong. What makes his version unique is the way it explicitly incorporates an energy component.

Dr. Sun named his new system *Yi Ren Qigong* (Yi means "change" and Ren means "human") and says it works by teaching diabetic patients to calm the *chi*, or "life energy" of the liver (to slow production of glucose) and to enhance the *chi* of the pancreas (exhausted by overproducing insulin). The goal of this practice is to "improve the harmony between these organs and increase energy overall," he says, noting that his patients have achieved significant results—reduced blood glucose levels, lower stress and less insulin resistance. Some were even able to cut back the dosages of their medications.

How Do They Know It Worked?

Dr. Sun's research team studied 32 patients, all on medication for their diabetes.

They were divided into three groups: One group practiced qigong on their own at home twice a week for 30 minutes and also attended a one-hour weekly session led by an instructor. The second group engaged in a prescribed program of gentle exercise that included movements similar to the qigong practice but without the energy component for an equivalent period of time. And the third group continued their regular medication and medical care but did not engage in structured exercise.

The results: After 12 weeks, the qigong patients had lowered their fasting blood glucose and their levels of self-reported stress and improved their insulin resistance. The gentle exercise group also brought down blood glucose levels, though somewhat less...and lowered stress. It was worse yet for the third group—blood glucose levels climbed and so did insulin resistance, while there was no reported change in their stress levels. The study was published in *Diabetes Care.*

While Yi Ren Qigong is not available anywhere beyond Bastyr University, Dr. Sun is developing a training program for instructors who can then teach in their own communities.

Qigong for Beginners

Roger Jahnke, OMD, a board-certified doctor of oriental medicine and author of *The Healer Within* (HarperOne). He is director of the Institute of Integral Qigong and Tai Chi and CEO of Health Action Synergies, both in Santa Barbara, California. *www.instituteofintegralqigongandtaichi.org*

The Chinese wellness system qigong (chee-GONG) combines four ancient practices, all meant to harness the body's self-healing powers. The basics are easy to learn and easy on the body, and they can be done at home. Here are samples of qigong movements and methods. Practice each daily to generate vitality and promote healing.

Body Movement

Gentle bending of the spine

Slow, gentle exercises build awareness of posture...increase strength, endurance and flexibility...and unlike vigorous exercises, do not cause injury or consume internal resources (such as energy) to fuel muscles.

Stand with feet shoulder-width apart, knees slightly bent. Inhaling, raise arms above head, elbows slightly bent and palms facing skyward...tip head back and tilt the pelvis, arching back slightly. On the exhalation, bend elbows and bring arms down in front of you, hands fisted and pressed together...tuck chin to chest, tilt the pelvis under and round your back. Repeat five to 10 times.

Breath Practice

Gathering breath

Deep breathing sends more oxygen-rich blood toward tissues...and "pumps" lymph fluid through the lymphatic system, a major part of the immune system.

Sit with hands in your lap. Inhaling through the nose, move hands outward and upward, scooping up healing energy, until hands are just above face level, palms toward you and elbows slightly bent. Exhaling slowly, bring hands toward you, then downward past the chest and navel. Repeat five to 10 times.

Massage

Healing hand massage

Reflexes refer to areas of the body that are separated physically, yet linked via acupuncture and energy channels. Self-massage of points on the hands, ears and feet has a healing effect on the organs, joints or tissues to which these reflexes connect.

Grasp your left hand with your right hand, thumb against the palm and fingers on the back of the hand. Starting gently and gradually increasing the pressure, knead your left hand, including fingers and wrist. Spend extra time on any sore points—these areas are linked to body functions and organs that are not operating optimally. Continue for three to five minutes, then switch hands.

Meditation

Qigong meditation

Stress overstimulates the nervous system and exhausts the adrenal glands (which secrete stress hormones). Meditation counteracts stress, enhancing healing brain chemicals and hormones.

Stand, sit or lie comfortably. Inhale fully, imagining you are drawing in *qi* (vitality) from the universe through hundreds of energy gates (acupuncture points) all over your body's surface. Exhale slowly, visualizing healing resources circulating inside you. Continue for five to 15 minutes, mentally directing the healing flow to wherever your body needs it most.

Illustrations by Shawn Banner.

■ ■ ■ ■

Got Diabetes? The Extra Help You Need

Joel Zonszein, MD, CDE, FACE, FACP, professor of clinical medicine, Albert Einstein College of Medicine and director, Clinical Diabetes Center, Montefiore Medical Center, New York City.

If you've been diagnosed with type 2 diabetes, you may think that you have a good handle on keeping your blood sugar under control...and maybe you do. Research has shown that only 16% of individuals with type 2 diabetes properly carry out the recommended "self-care behaviors," such as eating healthy foods, staying active, taking medications and monitoring blood sugar. A new study has found that diabetics who get regular individual instruction from a nurse or dietitian do much better and feel much better.

Getting Face Time

To learn more about how much of an impact one-on-one instruction can have, we spoke to Joel Zonszein, MD, director of the clinical diabetes program at Montefiore Medical Center in New York City. He took a close look at the recent research, which was conducted in Minneapolis, Minnesota, and Albuquerque, New Mexico, and was published in *Archives of Internal Medicine.*

The participants included 623 patients (men and women, average age 62) who had had type 2 diabetes for 12 years, on average. Researchers considered only patients who had taken a type of blood test called the *A1C*, which measures the average blood sugar levels within the previous two to three months, and selected only those whose A1C scores were above 7%—that's higher than what is considered healthy, so it indicated that, like the vast majority of diabetics, these people were poorly managing their condition. These patients were then split into three groups—one group received individual education, another received group education and another received no education at all.

After seven months, the researchers asked participants to take the A1C test yet again. *And here's what they discovered...*

It was basically "no contest" when comparing the results from group to group. The no-education group lowered its A1C score by 24% (perhaps because they knew that they were being studied)...those who received group education reduced A1C by 27%...and individual-education participants lowered their A1C scores by a whopping 51%.

The proportion of participants who got their scores into a healthy range (under 7%) was highest among those who were individually educated—21% of those participants achieved this fantastic result. Meanwhile, only 13% of the no-education group and 14% of the group-education patients got into the healthy range.

What's even better is that the individual education didn't take up much time at all—it consisted of exactly three one-hour sessions with a certified diabetes educator (either a nurse or a dietitian) about one month apart. Three short visits! The educators focused on topics that included all the healthy behaviors mentioned above (eating right, staying active, taking medications and monitoring blood sugar) along with problem solving (for instance, if a patient doesn't take a pill, maybe it's because he doesn't understand why he needs it and what it does)…healthy coping (such as if a patient is frustrated, instead of grabbing a bag of chips, he's taught to go for a walk or listen to calming music)…and setting personalized, action-oriented goals (for example, scheduling an eye exam once per year to prevent diabetic complications such as retinal detachment or blindness).

Why It Works So Well

It is exciting research, but also a little curious, that such a little bit of one-on-one education can go such a long way. After all, these weren't newbies—these were people who had had diabetes and had been under doctors' care for it for many years.

We asked Dr. Zonszein to comment on this, and he stressed one word—accountability. Having to face someone regularly and acknowledge mistakes that you may be making is a powerful motivator—apparently more powerful than just the idea of being healthy, he says. "It is also about empowerment—teaching diabetics to be in charge of the disease rather than letting the disease control them," he adds. And there's another, slightly darker side to all of this—doctors aren't typically trained to give appropriate diabetes education, and they aren't reimbursed for the time they spend educating patients about it, as Dr. Zonszein notes. So in too many cases, after an initial diagnosis and a hastily written prescription, patients are essentially sent out into the cold to muddle through on their own—not a shining example of great health care.

So, what can you do for you? In Dr. Zonszein's opinion, the best diabetes education programs are hospital-based with certification from the American Diabetes Association (ADA), since these are regularly evaluated to ensure that they meet high standards. To find one in your area, check the ADA's site, *www.diabetes.org*. Call the programs in your area and ask them specifically if they offer one-on-one instruction, what it costs and whether it is covered by insurance. Dr. Zonszein suggests trying one-on-one counseling for at least three months.

At the very least, don't assume that you already know all that you need to know about managing your diabetes—ask your doctor for diabetes brochures and visit reputable Web sites such as *www.diabetes.org* for the latest information and advice. And then make a point to discuss the information with your doctor at your next appointment. (Don't expect him or her to bring it up.)

Though one-on-one counseling might make you feel embarrassed or might seem like a nuisance, it's clear that the more you know about your disease and the more accountable you are about taking care of yourself, the better you will manage it…it's just human nature…so get the help!

Indulgences with Proven Health Benefits

Michael Tompkins, RN, LMT, a registered nurse and a licensed massage therapist, who is president and general manager of Miraval Resort & Spa in Tucson, Arizona. *www.miravalresorts.com*

Luxuriating at a spa can make us feel pampered—but there is no reason to feel guilty about the pleasure. In fact, we're doing ourselves a world of good when we indulge in spa services that have been scientifically proven to promote health and well-being. The benefits include stress reduction, of course, but they go far beyond that.

Michael Tompkins, RN, LMT, a registered nurse, licensed massage therapist and president and general manager of Miraval Resort & Spa in Tucson, discusses the newest research behind health-boosting spa services—and the shift it is bringing in spa clients' expectations. He points out that clientele today are more selective, trending toward therapies with demonstrable results...and he cites as prime examples the following four spa services. Each generally is safe, Tompkins confirms, though it is important to check with your doctor first if you are pregnant or if you have a medical condition.

Prices vary greatly depending on location and the type of spa you choose, so inquire about prices directly at the facilities you are considering—and ask whether a particular service costs less when done as an add-on to another service. *Consider trying these services...*

• **Mud therapy.** Certain types of mud contain magnesium and other beneficial minerals that moisturize and nourish the skin and help draw toxins out of pores—which is why mud therapy may ease dermatologic conditions such as acne, eczema and psoriasis.

Therapeutic mud also may help relieve arthritis pain, as several recent studies show.

Evidence: An Israeli study showed that 20-minute mudpack treatments applied to the extremities, neck and back once daily for two weeks reduced stiffness and pain and improved grip strength in people with rheumatoid arthritis, with improvement lasting from one to three months. A Turkish study found that patients with knee osteoarthritis who were given 12 sessions of daily mud therapy experienced improvement in physical function that persisted for three months after treatment.

What to expect: At some spas, you can take an actual mud bath, immersed up to your neck in warm mud. More typically, warm mud is applied directly to body areas that are painful (such as joints) or to areas that you want to draw toxins from, such

as the face. The treated area is wrapped in gauze for 20 minutes or so...then the wrapping is removed and the mud rinsed away.

Note: Therapeutic mud usually has a strong sulfur smell, which some people may find unpleasant.

• **Mineral water bath.** The special water used for this treatment is rich in minerals such as magnesium, potassium, calcium, sodium and sulfur, which are thought to have anti-inflammatory, antibacterial and/or moisturizing properties. In addition to research demonstrating benefits for improving the skin condition psoriasis, several recent European studies showed encouraging results from treating osteoarthritis with mineral water baths. For instance, in a study of patients with arthritic knee pain, one group took 30-minute mineral water baths five days a week for four weeks...a second group bathed in tap water. Both groups reported significant improvement on measures of pain, stiffness and physical function—but only in the mineral water group did the benefits persist after three months.

How it is done: You soak some or all of your body (up to the neck) in a tub full of warm mineral water for 15 to 30 minutes.

• **Massage.** A massage not only feels fantastic and leaves you blissfully relaxed, it also loosens tight muscles and releases waste products (such as *lactic acid*) that can lead to muscle stiffness and soreness. Numerous studies show additional benefits—for instance, massage can help alleviate pain, including chronic low-back pain...reduce blood pressure...boost the immune response and promote healing in patients suffering from burns or cancer...reduce aggression...ease depression...and improve sleep.

There are many types of massage. While some people like intense hands-on pressure, massage does not have to be painful to be therapeutic. *Options*…

• Swedish massage, the most popular, combines kneading and long muscle strokes using light to medium pressure.

• Hot stone massage uses the warmth of basalt stones to penetrate muscles, loosening them prior to gentle, relaxing tissue manipulation.

• Shiatsu massage aims to restore the natural flow of energy to your meridian points through gentle finger and palm pressure.

• Thai massage combines rhythmic holds and stretches that promote energy flow while reducing tension.

• Deep tissue massage is intense, using maximum pressure to release chronic muscle tension.

• Athlete's massage involves intense, constant pressure with targeted stretching.

• **Reflexology.** This therapy is based on the concept that certain areas of the foot correspond to various parts of the body. For instance, the toes are associated with the head and neck…the arch of the foot corresponds to the internal organs…and the ball of the foot corresponds to the chest and lungs. By applying manual pressure to certain zones on the foot, reflexologists aim to remove energy blockages and bring the body into ideal balance. From a Western perspective, studies show that stimulating and massaging the foot can reduce fatigue and stress, promote circulation and strengthen immunity.

Evidence: In a Korean study, middle-aged women were trained to do reflexology on themselves daily for six weeks. By the end of the study, participants showed significant improvement in measures of stress, depression and immune system response, plus reduced systolic blood pressure.

Recommended: If you want a genuine reflexology experience (rather than a simple foot massage), confirm that the spa's reflexologist is certified by the American Reflexology Certification Board or a state certification program.

Poor Sleep Might Worsen Diabetes

Kristen L. Knutson, PhD, assistant professor, medicine, University of Chicago.

Joel Zonszein, MD, director, Clinical Diabetes Center, Montefiore Medical Center, New York City.

Diabetes Care.

People with diabetes who sleep poorly have higher blood glucose levels and a more difficult time controlling their disease, a study shows.

Researchers compared 40 people with type 2 diabetes to 531 people without the blood sugar disease. The investigators examined the potential links between sleep quality, blood glucose levels and other measures of diabetes control.

"We found that in those with diabetes, there was an association between poor sleep quality and worse glucose measures," says study leader Kristen Knutson, PhD, an assistant professor of medicine at the University of Chicago. "We did not see a relationship in people without diabetes," she adds. The study was published in the journal *Diabetes Care*.

Examining a Link

Previous research has found some linkage between diabetes and poor sleep. Dr. Knutson says it is just an association, not cause-and-effect. "It may be that people with diabetes are more vulnerable to the effects of impaired sleep," she says. "But it could go either way." Those who don't control their diabetes could have worse sleep than those who do, she went on to say. "We need to look more closely at the role of sleep in diabetes," she adds.

Study Details

For the study, Dr. Knutson monitored sleep by having people wear wrist activity monitors. "If you are moving your wrist a lot, you are probably awake," she says.

The participants also reported on their sleep quality. The researchers found that those with diabetes who had trouble sleeping had a 23% higher fasting blood glucose level, a 48% higher fasting insulin level and an 82% higher insulin resistance than the normal sleepers with diabetes.

Expert Reaction

The findings tend to reflect what is seen in clinical practice, says Joel Zonszein, MD, director of the Clinical Diabetes Center at Montefiore Medical Center in New York City.

He, too, points out that the results beg the "chicken-egg" question. "They cannot tell us if the higher sugars were caused by the poor sleep or if the patients who have higher sugars don't sleep well or there are other factors causing that," Dr. Zonszein says.

Often, he notes, those with type 2 diabetes are overweight and that excess weight may impair sleep quality. Obesity is linked with sleep apnea, in which the patient often stops breathing during the night and is then awakened, for instance.

Improving Sleep Is Key

The take-home message for those with diabetes is to pay attention to their sleep quality, agrees Drs. Zonszein and Knutson. "If no sleep studies have been done, they might want to ask their doctor [about doing some]," Dr. Zonszein says.

Reducing stress, which is easier said than done, should be another goal for those with diabetes and poor sleep, he adds. "A lot of people are stressed, and they don't sleep well," Dr. Zonszein says.

"Don't wait for your doctor to ask you about sleep," says Dr. Knutson. "People with diabetes need to take their sleep seriously and talk to their doctor about it."

To learn more about how improving sleep habits can help you manage diabetes, visit the Web site of the Mayo Clinic, *www.mayoclinic.com*.

■ ■ ■ ■

What Can an Antioxidant From the Ocean Do for You?

Mark A. Stengler, NMD, naturopathic medical doctor and leading authority on the practice of alternative and integrated medicine. Dr. Stengler is author of the *Health Revelations* newsletter, author of *The Natural Physician's Healing Therapies* (Bottom Line Books), founder and medical director of the Stengler Center for Integrative Medicine, Encinitas, California, and adjunct associate clinical professor at the National College of Natural Medicine in Portland, Oregon. *http://markstengler.com*

I am excited to tell you about a super antioxidant—*astaxanthin* (pronounced as-tuh-zan-thin)—that you might not have heard about. And if you have heard about it (there has been a lot of talk about it in the natural healing community), I'm going to set you straight on how it can best help you.

Astaxanthin is a type of red-orange-pink *carotenoid* that comes from the sea. Carotenoids are pigments that give food their color and have powerful antioxidant properties. Most of us are familiar with *beta-carotene*, the main carotenoid found in land plants. Well, astaxanthin is the main marine carotenoid. It is found in some types of algae as well as in some fungi and plants—and it gives salmon, shrimp, lobster and crawfish their bright color. You get some astaxanthin when you eat these foods, but most of us don't eat enough of them to benefit.

Astaxanthin is closely related to *lutein*, a carotenoid known to improve eye health, and it has long been used as a supplement to treat aging eyes. But new studies are finding that this carotenoid provides many other health benefits. In my own practice, I have found that astaxanthin can especially help patients with diabetes and heart disease. Laboratory studies also show that astaxanthin may fight cancer and enhance cognition, but these findings have not yet been tested in humans. *Here's how astaxanthin can help you…*

• **Diabetes.** High blood glucose levels, which can occur in people with uncontrolled diabetes, increase deposits of fatty materials on the insides of blood vessel walls. This affects blood flow and can result in clogged and rigid blood vessels, increasing the risk for heart attack and stroke. The antioxidant activity of astaxanthin helps keep blood vessels clog-free and flexible by minimizing oxidative damage to the cells that make up blood vessels.

• **LDL cholesterol.** A study published in *Atherosclerosis* found that astaxanthin significantly lowered triglyceride levels and increased HDL (good) cholesterol in adults who were not obese. Astaxanthin also prevents LDL (bad) cholesterol from oxidizing. Oxidized LDL contributes to inflammation and the formation of cholesterol deposits.

• **Blood flow.** Astaxanthin improves *blood rheology*—the velocity of blood moving through arteries and veins. In a small study of middle-aged men, Japanese researchers showed that taking 6 milligrams (mg) of astaxanthin daily for 10 days resulted in smoother, faster blood flow. Improved rheology eases the heart's workload.

An Immune Booster

In a Washington State University study, researchers gave college-age women 2 mg or 4 mg of astaxanthin or placebos daily for eight weeks. Astaxanthin increased the immune system's production of natural killer cells, which help us fight infections. The supplements also lowered the women's levels of *C-reactive protein*, a marker of inflammation.

My Recommendations

To boost immunity and for people with diabetes, I suggest taking 2 mg to 4 mg daily of astaxanthin. For people with coronary artery disease, I recommend taking 8 mg to 16 mg daily (the dose is determined by your weight) as part of a dietary and supplement regimen. You can speak to a holistic doctor about the amount that is right for you. There are no reported side effects. Astaxanthin is safe for everyone but should not be taken by pregnant and lactating women because it has not been studied in these populations. The supplements are derived from algae, so they are even safe for people who are allergic to shellfish (but read the label!).

One brand I like: Source Naturals (800-815-2333, *www.sourcenaturals.com*).

Using Viruses to Cure Diabetes

M. William Lensch, PhD, faculty director of education, Harvard Stem Cell Institute and instructor in pediatrics, Harvard Medical School, Boston.

We are accustomed to thinking of viruses as "bad guys" that the world would be better without—but now that scientists have used a virus to transform a non-insulin-producing pancreatic cell into one that produced insulin, we may need to reconsider that position. Adding to the achievement is that the "programming" of the cell was done without use of sometimes controversial stem cells. This is a major breakthrough in the field of regenerative medicine, which aims to regrow or repair missing or damaged tissue.

In the research, which was published in the journal *Nature*, Douglas A. Melton, PhD, codirector of the Harvard Stem Cell Institute, and his fellow researchers used a modified virus to activate three key genes in non-insulin-producing pancreatic cells in mice. Within three days, the "infected" cells started producing insulin—far faster than the several weeks it's known to take to transform stem cells into specific organ tissues.

The findings are incredibly exciting for other researchers in the field of regenerative medicine as well. "This paper really got a lot of people's attention," says M. William Lensch, PhD, faculty director of education at the Harvard Stem Cell Institute, who wasn't himself involved with Dr. Melton's research. "It expands the possible universe of where regenerated cells can come from and how to get there—that's exciting," Dr. Lensch adds.

Though remarkable, it's important to note that this type of cell reprogramming is still a long way from becoming a viable mainstream treatment—it has not yet been tried in humans, and long-term safety is still to be determined. Nonetheless it deserves attention because of the thinking behind it—the idea that you can quickly, relatively easily and with no political debate, change a cell that's close to what's needed into exactly what's needed, perhaps to treat cancer, liver disease, cardiovascular disease and more.

10

Diabetes Complications and Concerns

What Your Doctor May Not Tell You About Your Diabetes

Frederic J. Vagnini, MD, a cardiovascular surgeon and director of the Heart, Diabetes & Weight Loss Centers of New York in Lake Success, *www.vagnini.com.* His clinical interests include heart disease, diabetes, weight loss and nutrition. Dr. Vagnini hosts *The Heart Show* on WOR NewsTalk Radio 710, *www.wor710.com,* and is the author, with Lawrence D. Chilnick, of *The Weight Loss Plan for Beating Diabetes* (Fair Winds).

For most of the 19 million Americans diagnosed with type 2 diabetes, the main goal of treatment is simply to control their glucose (blood sugar) levels with diet, exercise and sometimes medication.

But there's much more that should be done to help prevent serious complications, which can shorten the life expectancy of a person with diabetes—by about 7.5 years in men and 8.2 years in women.

Sobering statistics: About 80% of people with diabetes die from cardiovascular complications, such as a heart attack. About half the patients with poor glucose control will eventually suffer from nerve damage (*neuropathy*). Another 20% to 30%

may experience *retinopathy* or other eye disorders.

Whether or not you're taking medication for diabetes, virtually all of these complications can be avoided—and, in some cases, reversed—with natural approaches.

Important: Be sure to speak to your doctor before following any of the steps in this article—some may affect diabetes drugs and other types of medication.

Best ways for people with diabetes to avoid complications...

Control Inflammation

People with diabetes typically have elevated levels of *C-reactive protein*, a blood protein that indicates chronic low-level inflammation, the underlying cause of most cardiovascular, eye and nerve disorders. Inflammation also exacerbates arthritis, which is more common in diabetics than in those without the disease. *Effective options...*

• **Stop eating wheat.** Many people with diabetes are allergic or sensitive to gluten, a protein found naturally in wheat, barley and rye—and sometimes in other grains, such as oats, because they become "cross-contaminated" during processing. Even trace amounts of gluten can stimulate the production of *cytokines*, substances that increase inflammation. (See self-test below to determine whether you are sensitive to gluten.)

In addition to increasing inflammation in these patients, exposure to gluten may lead to fatigue and joint problems. Gluten may also impair digestion in these people, making it harder to lose weight—a serious problem because excess body fat increases inflammation even more.

Important: Read food labels. Besides avoiding obvious sources of gluten such as wheat bread and wheat pasta, look for terms such as "amino peptide complex," "filler flour," "hydrolyzed protein" and "vegetable starch"—these indicate that gluten is or may be found in the product. Gluten is also present in unexpected sources, such as soy sauce, malt and graham flour, as well as thousands of nonfood products, including some medications. To determine if a medication contains gluten, call the drug manufacturer.

For helpful information, go to *www. mayoclinic.com/health/gluten-free-diet/ my01140.*

• **Give up dairy.** Oftentimes people who are sensitive to gluten also have problems digesting *casein*, a dairy protein.

To test for a gluten or dairy sensitivity: Eliminate each food type one at a time for several weeks. If you notice an improvement in energy, or a reduction in joint pain or digestion problems, you're probably sensitive to one or both. To make sure, reintroduce dairy and/or gluten foods one at a time to see if your symptoms return.

Important: Foods that are labeled "lactose-free" or "dairy-free" are not necessarily casein-free. Foods that are both gluten-free and casein-free can be found online at *www.*

traderjoes.com or *www.wholefoodsmarket. com.*

To keep it simple: Remember that all unprocessed meats, vegetables and fruits are gluten-free and dairy-free.

• **Supplement with omega-3 fatty acids.** The American Diabetes Association recommends a diet high in these fatty acids because of their ability to reduce inflammation and other diabetes complications. Unfortunately, many people find it difficult to eat enough omega-3–rich foods, such as salmon, mackerel and herring—two six-ounce servings a week are recommended—so supplements often are a good choice.

My advice: Take a daily supplement with at least 1,500 milligrams (mg) of *eicosapentaenoic acid* (EPA), the component in fish oil that helps reduce the inflammation that contributes to diabetes-related complications. If you are allergic to fish, you can use an omega-3 supplement derived from algae.

Omega-3 fatty acids, also found in flaxseed and walnuts, have the additional benefit of helping to lower *triglycerides*, blood fats that have been linked to atherosclerosis and cardiovascular disease.

Lower Your Risk for Heart Disease

The Rotterdam Heart Study, which looked at the dietary histories of more than 4,800 patients, found that those with low blood levels of vitamin K2 were 57% more likely to develop heart disease, due in part to an increase in calcium in the arteries. Paradoxically, these patients had lower bone levels of calcium, which increases the risk for fractures.

Because diabetic patients have an extremely high risk for heart disease, I routinely recommend a daily supplement (45 micrograms [mcg]) of vitamin K2. You can also get more of this nutrient by eating such foods as liver, eggs and certain cheeses.

Caution: Because there are different forms of vitamin K—some of which interfere with the effects of *warfarin* (Coumadin) and other blood thinners—always speak to your doctor before taking any vitamin K supplement.

Overcome Fatigue

Both inflammation and elevated blood sugar increase fatigue, making it one of the most common symptoms of diabetes. *Helpful…*

• **Coenzyme Q10 (CoQ10)** increases the body's production of *adenosine triphosphate* (ATP), a molecule that enhances the performance of *mitochondria*, the energy-producing components of cells. CoQ10 is also an antioxidant that helps to decrease inflammation.

Typical dose: 100 mg to 200 mg, twice daily.

• **Magnesium** is involved in glucose and insulin reactions and is typically lower than normal in people with diabetes who experience fatigue. Patients who eat a healthy diet, including magnesium-rich foods such as nuts and oatmeal, and supplement with magnesium often report an increase in energy. They also show improvements in blood pressure and cardiac performance. Talk to your doctor about the appropriate dosage of a magnesium supplement—especially if you have kidney disease or heart disease, both of which can be worsened by too much magnesium.

All forms of supplemental magnesium can be used, but *magnesium citrate* causes diarrhea in some people. If this happens to you, take a different form, such as *magnesium taurate* or *magnesium glycinate*.

Avoid Diabetic Neuropathy

Excess blood sugar can damage the tiny blood vessels that carry blood and nutrients to nerves in the fingers, legs and/or feet, causing *neuropathy*. Neuropathy can eventually lead to tissue damage that requires amputation. *What to try…*

• **Alpha-lipoic acid** makes the cells more sensitive to insulin and can relieve symptoms of diabetic neuropathy.

Typical dose: 600 mg to 1,200 mg daily for people with diabetes who have neuropathy. To help prevent neuropathy, 100 mg to 300 mg daily is the typical dose.

• **B-complex** supplement may help prevent neuropathy or reduce symptoms in patients who already have it.

Typical dose: Two B-100 complex supplements daily for people with diabetes who have neuropathy…one B-100 complex daily to help prevent neuropathy.

Prevent Eye Damage

High blood sugar can cause *diabetic retinopathy*, which can lead to blindness. It can also increase eye pressure and lead to glaucoma.

Self-defense: Eat more fresh fruits and vegetables. These foods contain antioxidants such as *lutein, zeaxanthin* and vitamin C, which strengthen eye capillaries, fight free radicals and reduce the risk for blindness. Frozen fruits and vegetables also can be used.

Best choice: Blueberries or bilberries—both contain *anthocyanins*, antioxidants that help prevent eye damage and appear to improve glucose levels.

Prevent Serious Complications of Diabetes

Neal D. Barnard, MD, adjunct associate professor of medicine at George Washington University School of Medicine and president of the nonprofit Physicians Committee for Responsible Medicine, a Washington, DC–based group that promotes preventive medicine and higher standards of effectiveness and ethics in research. He is author of *Dr. Neal Barnard's Program for Reversing Diabetes* (Rodale). *www.nealbarnard.org*

Diabetes is a slow and often "silent" disease. Most people who have it feel fine initially. By the time they develop symptoms, years of elevated blood sugar (glucose) have already caused widespread damage and complications, including cardiovascular disease, nerve damage and kidney disease.

Unfortunately, complications from diabetes can shorten life expectancy by about a decade.

Good news: Most people can reduce or eliminate these complications by maintaining optimal glucose control.

Here, the dangerous complications of diabetes and how to control them…

Peripheral Neuropathy

Excess blood sugar can damage capillaries—tiny blood vessels—in the fingers, legs and/or feet. A lack of circulation to nerves can cause *neuropathy*, which can be painful and produce sensations of numbness, tingling and burning.

An important finding: One of my colleagues had his patients with neuropathy eat a low-fat, vegan diet (no animal foods or dairy products) and take a daily 30-minute walk. In 17 out of 21 patients, leg pain stopped completely—the remaining four had partial relief.

Many patients with neuropathy eventually lose all sensation in the extremities.

This is dangerous because small injuries, such as cuts or an ingrown nail, for example, won't be noticed and can progress to serious infections and tissue damage—and, in some cases, require amputation. *What to do…*

• **Exercise daily.** It helps with weight loss and glucose control, which help reduce capillary damage and may reduce pain from neuropathy.

• **Check your feet every day.** Look for abrasions, cuts and blisters. See a doctor if an injury isn't healing.

Also, ask your doctor to examine your feet two to four times a year. Most doctors don't do this routinely.

Helpful: Take off your shoes and socks while you are waiting in the examination room. This makes it impossible for the doctor to ignore your feet.

Eye Damage

Diabetes is the leading cause of blindness in American adults. High blood sugar can lead to *glaucoma*, resulting in optic nerve damage, which causes loss of vision. It also can damage the retinas (*retinopathy*) or the lenses of the eyes (*cataracts*). *What to do…*

• **Avoid dairy.** Many people lack the enzyme needed to metabolize *galactose*, a sugar that is released when the lactose in dairy is digested. This can lead to lens damage and cataracts.

• **Eat more produce.** The antioxidants in fresh fruits and vegetables, such as vitamin C, *lutein* and *zeaxanthin*, appear to have a stabilizing effect on the retina and can reduce the risk for cataracts and other eye diseases.

I do not recommend supplements for eye health because natural foods provide large amounts of these nutrients. It's likely that the combination of nutrients in foods, rather than single-source nutrients, provide the most protection.

Periodontal Disease

Doctors have known for a long time that patients with diabetes have a high risk for *periodontal disease*, a chronic bacterial infection of the gums that can lead to tooth loss.

Recent finding: A review of research by the Cochrane Database of Systematic Reviews found that people with diabetes who were treated for periodontal disease achieved better blood sugar control, indicating that periodontal disease is both caused by and causes higher blood sugar. Periodontal treatment includes regular scaling, the removal of bacteria and inflammatory material from beneath the gums. *What to do…*

● **See your dentist four times a year.** The usual twice-a-year schedule might not be enough for people with diabetes.

● **Eat less sugar.** This is important for everyone, but more so for those with diabetes and periodontal disease. A high-sugar diet makes it easier for bacteria to proliferate.

● **Floss and brush your teeth after every meal**—not just once or twice a day.

Heart Disease

Most people in the US have some degree of *atherosclerosis*, plaque buildup in the arteries that increases the risk for heart attack. The risk for heart disease is much higher in people with diabetes, particularly when atherosclerosis is accompanied by hypertension and kidney disease.

Recent finding: People with diabetes who eat a typical American diet tend to accumulate *intramyocellular lipids*, tiny bits of fat inside muscle cells. This fat inhibits the ability of cells to respond to insulin, which leads to elevated blood sugar. *What to do…*

● **Avoid animal products and added fats.** Research by Dean Ornish, MD, showed that people who get no more than about 10% of total calories from fat (preferably unsaturated) can reverse blockages in the arteries. (Traditional diabetes diets allow up to 35% of calories from fat.)

● **Reduce cholesterol.** It's one of the best ways to reduce cardiovascular risks.

Helpful: Foods that are high in soluble fiber, such as oatmeal, fruits, whole grains and beans. People who eat beans regularly have average cholesterol readings that are about 7% lower than those who don't eat beans.

● **Reduce blood pressure.** The same strategies that reduce cholesterol and arterial blockages also reduce blood pressure.

Kidney Disease

The filtering units of the kidneys, or *nephrons*, consist of millions of small blood vessels that frequently are damaged by diabetes. Extensive damage can lead to kidney failure and the need for a transplant. *What to do…*

● **Give up animal protein.** The sulfur-containing amino acids in meats and eggs are harder for the nephrons to process than the proteins from plant foods. People with diabetes who switch to a vegetarian diet have a reduced risk of developing kidney disease.

● **Maintain healthy blood pressure.** Uncontrolled hypertension is a leading cause of kidney failure. The same low-fat, plant-based diet that reduces glucose and cholesterol also is effective for lowering blood pressure.

Alzheimer's Disease

A Japanese study reported in *Neurology* found that patients with type 2 diabetes or resistance to insulin were more likely to develop *brain plaques*, clusters of abnormal proteins that occur in those with Alzheimer's disease.

It's not yet clear whether diabetes increases the risk of getting Alzheimer's or there's an underlying process that causes both conditions. *What to do…*

• **Avoid meat.** Numerous studies have shown that people who eat diets that are high in meat, fat and cholesterol are more likely to develop Alzheimer's disease than those who eat a healthier diet. It's possible that the *heme iron* in meats is more likely than the non-heme iron in plant foods to be associated with brain plaques.

Supplement Helps Treat Diabetic Kidney Disease

Mahmood S. Mozaffari, PhD, DMD, teaching director for the pharmacology and therapeutics curriculum, Medical College of Georgia, Augusta.

Kidney disease is more common than you might guess—for instance, about 40% of people with diabetes will get kidney damage, or *nephropathy*, so news of a treatment that might ease the condition is certainly welcome. Here is that news—a study has found that the mineral supplement *chromium picolinate* may be helpful in staving off diabetic kidney disease, which is caused when high blood sugar destroys the small blood vessels of the kidneys. With 17.9 million Americans suffering from diabetes, this is welcome news.

First, a tiny bit of background on diabetic nephropathy. If it is left untreated, the kidneys won't filter waste from the blood efficiently, which will eventually lead to kidney failure and the need for dialysis. Conventional preventive advice for this condition focuses on regular exercise, known to improve insulin sensitivity… keeping blood glucose levels down…controlling blood pressure, since high blood pressure can also damage the kidney's blood vessels…keeping cholesterol down …eating a low-fat diet…limiting salt and protein…and not smoking. But diabetic kidney disease continues to cause morbidity and mortality, thus indicating the need for other measures.

Can Chromium Picolinate Help?

In research presented at a Conference of the American Physiological Society, Mahmood Mozaffari, PhD, DMD, teaching director at the Medical College of Georgia, and his colleague Babak Baban, PhD, tested the effectiveness and safety of the supplement chromium picolinate for people at risk for diabetic nephropathy. Chromium picolinate has been suggested to help enhance the action of insulin and control glucose levels in patients with diabetes, especially type 2.

The researchers compared three groups of mice—one healthy group and two groups that were genetically engineered for obesity and diabetes (two conditions that often coexist). For six months, the healthy mice and one group of diabetic mice were fed a regular rodent diet. The other group of diabetic mice was fed a diet enriched with chromium picolinate.

The researchers measured blood glucose levels and urinary *albumin*, a marker for kidney damage. As expected, they found that the untreated diabetic mice excreted nearly 10 times more *albumin* (an indication of kidney disease) than the healthy mice…but, the diabetic mice consuming the chromium picolinate–enriched diet excreted only about half as much albumin as the untreated diabetic mice. In addition, kidney tissue samples showed changes suggestive of less inflammation in the treated diabetic group than in the untreated group. However, chromium picolinate treatment resulted in only a mild improvement in glucose control. Thus the researchers believe that effects other than sugar control may underlie the impact of the chromium picolinate in reducing biomarkers of inflammation in the kidney.

Chromium picolinate supplements are sold at most pharmacies or online in doses from 200 micrograms (mcg) to 800 mcg.

Should You Try It?

While you can get some of the chromium you require from foods—such as broccoli, beef, chicken, turkey, red wine, wheat germ, eggs, black pepper and molasses or the probiotic brewer's yeast—dietary chromium is poorly absorbed from the gut.

Dr. Mozaffari cautions that this promising animal study must be substantiated in other studies including human clinical trials, so he is not yet advocating that people with diabetes should take chromium picolinate to help reduce the impact of diabetic nephropathy. And you definitely shouldn't be taking supplemental chromium if you are on medication for your diabetes, including if you are taking insulin, *metformin* (Glucophage) or *glyburide* (Diabeta), as it will affect the way your body reacts to the drugs…or if you take NSAIDs and antacids.

■ ■ ■ ■

Ineffective Heart Surgery Performed on Diabetics

William E. Boden, MD, FACC, clinical chief, division of cardiovascular medicine and professor of medicine and preventive medicine, University at Buffalo Schools of Medicine and Public Health, Buffalo, New York.

If you have diabetes and heart disease—and many Americans do, or will, since the two tend to go hand in hand—it is important to be aware of special considerations regarding your treatment, especially when it comes to invasive heart procedures.

A Landmark Study

Surprisingly, there is no clear consensus on how to treat diabetic patients with heart disease. That, coupled with concern about the exorbitant cost of treating diabetes (it now accounts for one out of every five federal health-care dollars spent), led researchers to undertake the Bypass Angioplasty Revascularization Investigation (BARI 2D) trial, which is a comparative effectiveness study of two different treatments for diabetic patients with heart disease.

In the five-year randomized, clinical trial of 2,368 diabetics with heart disease at 49 locations in six countries, researchers compared optimal medical therapy (medications and lifestyle counseling) with the same plus surgery to see which worked best in preventing a cardiovascular event and/or early death. These patients were generally considered to be at low risk for heart attack and stroke based on the extent of their coronary artery disease and symptoms, such as their degree of *angina* (chest pain), when the study began. The "optimal medical therapy" (e.g., medications such as beta-blockers and statins) was given to all participants to control blood pressure and cholesterol, and participants were also counseled, as appropriate, to quit smoking and/or lose weight, notes William E. Boden, MD, FACC, clinical chief of the division of cardiovascular medicine and professor of medicine, University at Buffalo Schools of Medicine and Public Health.

For the group that received medical therapy plus surgery, half the participants were randomly assigned to either undergo stent angioplasty or coronary-artery bypass grafting (CABG).

Over the five-year period following the intervention, Dr. Boden and his colleagues found that…

• **There was little or no difference in outcome between those who underwent angioplasty versus only optimal medical therapy**—angioplasty patients had a 10.8% death rate, compared with a 10.2% death rate for those on optimal medical therapy.

• **In the bypass group**—which included individuals with more severe heart disease—surgery was more effective than optimal medical therapy. Bypass recipients had a 22.4% chance of having a heart attack or stroke or dying in the next five years, compared with 30.5% of participants who only took medications.

These results were published in *The New England Journal of Medicine*.

High Tech Is Not Always the Answer

We are often inclined to believe that high-tech devices and interventions are superior, Dr. Boden observes. This is not always the case—sometimes conservative medical therapy is more effective, since it is less invasive and therefore less dangerous, and it costs less, too. The BARI 2D results confirm that intensive medical (nonsurgical) therapy can be an effective first line of treatment for diabetics with heart disease, particularly for those with less severe disease.

Eye Problems Can Signal Diabetes, Stroke and Other Serious Conditions

James Salz, MD, clinical professor of ophthalmology at the University of Southern California and attending ophthalmic surgeon at Cedars-Sinai Medical Center, both in Los Angeles, *www.drsalz.com.* He is a spokesman for the American Academy of Ophthalmology and founding editor of the *Journal of Refractive Surgery.*

We all know that regular eye exams are important to detect and correct vision changes and to diagnose eye problems that could lead to vision loss.

What few people realize: Looking in and at the eyes can also reveal diseases in other parts of the body. *Important warning signs…*

Blurred Vision Could Be Diabetes

It's not often talked about, but blurred vision is one of the most common symptoms in people with diabetes, particularly those who aren't controlling their blood glucose levels effectively.

What happens: High blood concentrations of glucose can cause the *macula* (central area of the retina) and/or the inner lens of the eye to retain fluids. This can lead to swelling and blurred vision.

Blurring caused by vision changes that can be corrected with glasses typically develops over a period of years. Blurring that occurs rapidly, within a few days, is characteristic of diabetes.

See your doctor immediately—even if you've already been diagnosed with diabetes. Blurred vision can be an early symptom of *diabetic retinopathy*, a leading cause of blindness.

Next step: You should receive blood tests that measure glucose levels and/or long-term glucose control. Depending on the test results, your doctor will recommend dietary changes, regular exercise, etc., and might prescribe or adjust medication to achieve better glucose control.

Sudden Vision Loss Could Be a Stroke

A sudden loss of vision could mean that you're about to have—or are at high risk of having—a stroke.

What happens: Prior to a stroke, patients may experience an almost total loss of vision in one eye caused by cholesterol plaque in the carotid artery in the neck. This loss of central vision is known as *amaurosis fugax*. Normal vision returns when the cholesterol deposit passes through, usually within a few minutes. Other patients may experience loss of peripheral vision, which is often permanent. Symptoms also may include temporary double vision or dim vision.

Next step: Using a stethoscope, the doctor will listen for an abnormal sound, called a *bruit*, in the carotid arteries. The sound is caused by blood turbulence around an obstruction or narrowed arteries.

If you have risk factors for stroke—such as high blood pressure, elevated cholesterol and smoking—you will probably be scheduled for additional tests even if the carotid sounds are normal.

Example: A carotid ultrasound will show whether arterial plaque has narrowed the arteries. Patients who are diagnosed with carotid artery disease may require surgery and/or medication to reduce the risk for stroke.

New Way to Prevent Diabetes-Related Blindness

Recent study: After a year of treatment, almost half of patients with *diabetic macular edema* (diabetes-related swelling of the central part of the retina) treated with lasers and the injectable drug *ranibizumab* (Lucentis) showed substantial visual improvement—versus 28% of patients treated with lasers alone.

Neil M. Bressler, MD, retina division chief and professor of ophthalmology, Wilmer Eye Institute, Johns Hopkins University School of Medicine, Baltimore, and coauthor of a study of 691 patients with diabetic macular edema, published in *Ophthalmology*.

Bulging Eyes Could Be Thyroid Disease

An overactive thyroid gland (*hyperthyroidism*) may lead to bulging eyes.

What happens: Most patients with hyperthyroidism have an autoimmune disorder known as Graves' disease. It causes the thyroid gland to overproduce the hormone *thyroxine*, which leads to tissue swelling that pushes the eyeballs forward. It can affect one or both eyes.

Other symptoms: An overly rapid metabolism that causes profuse sweating, weight loss and often insomnia and anxiety.

Next step: An eye doctor should measure the distance between the cornea and the surrounding bony structure (the orbit). In people with hyperthyroidism affecting the eyes, the distance is excessive.

If blood tests indicate Graves' disease, prescription medications, such as *methimazole* (Tapazole), will be prescribed to stop the overproduction of thyroid hormones.

Many patients will have a long-term remission—and a reversal of the eye bulge—after taking medication for about a year.

Because many patients will have a relapse within several years after stopping medication, they may eventually need surgery to remove the thyroid and/or treatment with radioactive iodine to permanently reduce hormone production.

Wavy Lines Could Be An Ocular Migraine

Migraine headaches are often preceded by a *visual aura*—flashes of light, wavy lines and other changes in vision. A related condition, known as an *ocular migraine*, can produce the same visual changes, but usually without the headache.

What happens: Ocular migraines occur when blood vessels in the part of the brain that controls vision constrict and reduce blood flow. Attacks usually last 15 to 20 minutes but can sometimes continue for up to an hour. Then vision returns to normal.

Next step: An ocular migraine can be diagnosed by a description of the symptoms. Imaging tests, such as an MRI, are rarely needed.

Triptan migraine medications, such as *sumatriptan* (Imitrex) and *naratriptan* (Amerge), will quickly decrease eye symptoms. Because the attacks are so brief, however, most people don't need medication.

Yellow Eyes Could Be Liver Disease

Jaundice, a yellowing of the whites (*sclera*) of the eyes, is due to high blood levels of *bilirubin*, a waste product that accumulates in patients with liver disease.

What happens: One of the liver's main functions is to remove toxins/wastes from the blood. Bilirubin, produced from the breakdown of red blood cells, is one such waste. It accumulates when the liver isn't working efficiently, often due to diseases such as hepatitis or cirrhosis.

Jaundice can also occur when the body produces too much bilirubin—for example, in individuals with *hemolytic anemia*, which breaks down red blood cells at an accelerated rate.

Next step: The primary challenge with jaundice is to correctly identify and treat the underlying disorder. In addition to a physical exam, most patients will be given a liver "panel," blood tests that detect liver abnormalities or blockages in the bile duct, and possibly imaging tests such as ultrasound or a CT scan. Treating the underlying condition generally eliminates jaundice.

More Eye Care— See Better at Night

Marc Grossman, OD, LAc, medical director of Natural Eye Care in New Paltz, New York. A holistic developmental/behavioral optometrist and licensed acupuncturist, he is the coauthor of *Greater Vision* and *Natural Eye Care* (both from McGraw-Hill). *www.naturaleyecare.com*

Marc Grossman, OD, LAc, a holistic developmental/behavioral optometrist and licensed acupuncturist in New Paltz, New York, and coauthor of *Greater Vision*, discussed night vision with us. He confirms that aging often brings a reduction in the ability to see well in low light.

Reasons: Night vision has two elements. First, the pupils must dilate to let in as much light as possible. Normally this happens within seconds of entering a darkened environment—but as we age, the muscles that control pupil dilation weaken, slowing down and/or limiting dilation. Second, chemical changes must occur in the light-sensitive *photoreceptors* (called rods and cones) of the retina at the back of the eyeball.

Some of these changes take several minutes and some take longer, so normally full night vision is not achieved for about 20 minutes. Even brief exposure to bright light (such as oncoming headlights) reverses these chemical changes, so the processes must start over. With age, these chemical changes occur more slowly...and some of our photoreceptors may be lost.

While we cannot restore the eyes' full youthful function, we can take steps to preserve and even improve our ability to see in low light, Dr. Grossman says. *Here's how...*

• **First, see your eye doctor to investigate possible underlying medical problems.** Various eye disorders can cause or contribute to reduced night vision, including *cataracts* (clouding of the eye's lens), *retinitis pigmentosa* (a disease that damages the retina's *rods and cones)* and *macular degeneration* (in which objects in the center of the field of vision cannot be seen). Night vision also can be compromised by *liver cirrhosis* or the digestive disorder *celiac disease*, which can lead to deficiencies of eye-protecting nutrients...or *diabetes*, which can damage eye nerves and blood vessels. Dr. Grossman says that diagnosing any underlying disorder is vital because the sooner it is treated, the better the outcome is likely to be.

• **Adopt an eye-healthy diet.** Eat foods rich in the vision-supporting nutrients below ...and ask your doctor whether supplementation is right for you. *Especially important nutrients...*

• *Lutein*, a yellow pigment and antioxidant found in corn, dark green leafy vegetables, egg yolks, kiwi fruit, oranges and yellow squash.

Typical supplement dosage: 6 milligrams (mg) daily.

• *Vitamin A*, found in carrots, Chinese cabbage, dark green leafy vegetables, pumpkin, sweet potatoes and winter squash.

Typical supplement dosage: 10,000 international units (IU) daily.

• *Zeaxanthin*, a yellow pigment and antioxidant found in corn, egg yolks, kiwi fruit, orange peppers and oranges.

Typical supplement dosage: 300 micrograms (mcg) daily.

• *Zinc*, found in beans, beef, crab, duck, lamb, oat bran, oysters, ricotta cheese, turkey and yogurt.

Typical supplement dosage: 20 mg per day.

• **Update prescription lenses.** Many people just keep wearing the same old glasses even though vision tends to change over time, Dr. Grossman says—so new glasses with the correct prescription often can improve night vision.

• **Keep eyeglasses and contacts clean.** Smudges bend rays of light and distort what you see.

Wear sunglasses outdoors on sunny days, especially between noon and 3 pm. This is particularly important for people with light-colored eyes, which are more vulnerable to the sun's damaging ultraviolet rays. Excessive sun exposure is a leading cause of eye disorders (such as cataracts) that can impair eyesight, including night vision. Amber or gray lenses are best for sunglasses, Dr. Grossman says, because they absorb light frequencies most evenly.

• **Do not use yellow-tinted lenses at night.** These often are marketed as "night driving" glasses, implying that they sharpen contrast and reduce glare in low light. However, Dr. Grossman cautions that any tint only further impairs night vision.

Safest: If you wear prescription glasses, stick to untinted, clear lenses—but do ask your optometrist about adding an anti-reflective or antiglare coating.

● **Exercise your night vision.** This won't speed up the eyes' process of adjusting to the dark, but may encourage a mental focus that helps the brain and eyes work better together—thus improving your ability to perceive objects in a darkened environment.

What to do: For 20 minutes four times per week, go into a familiar room at night and turn off the lights. As your eyes are adjusting, look directly at one specific object that you know is there...focus on it, trying to make out its shape and details and to distinguish it from surrounding shadows. With practice, your visual perception should improve. For an additional challenge, do the exercise outdoors at night...while looking at unfamiliar objects in a dark room...or while using peripheral vision rather than looking directly at an object.

● **When driving at night, avoid looking directly at oncoming headlights.** Shifting your gaze slightly to the right of center minimizes the eye changes that would temporarily impair your night vision, yet still allows you to see traffic.

Also: Use the night setting on rearview mirrors to reduce reflected glare.

● **Clean car windows and lights.** When was the last time you used glass cleaner on the inside of your windshield...or on rear and side windows...or on headlights and taillights? For the clearest possible view and minimal distortion from smudges, keep all windows and lights squeaky clean.

Natural Help for the Diabetic Heart

Seth Baum, MD, medical director of Integrative Heart Care in Boca Raton, Florida, and author of *The Total Guide to a Healthy Heart* (Kensington). *www.myvitalremedymd.com*

Kenneth Madden, MD, associate professor of geriatric medicine at the University of British Columbia.

Robb Wolf, owner of NorCal Strength Conditioning, Chico, California, and author of *The Paleo Solution: The Original Human Diet* (Victory Belt Publishing).

If you have type 2 diabetes, you've already had a heart attack—whether you've had one or not!

"The guidelines for physicians from the American Heart Association are to treat a person with diabetes as if that individual has already had a heart attack," says cardiologist Seth Baum, MD, medical director of Integrative Heart Care in Boca Raton, Florida, and author of *The Total Guide to a Healthy Heart.*

How Does Diabetes Hurt Your Heart?

As excess sugar careens through the bloodstream, it starts to rough up the linings of the arteries.

Insulin resistance (the subpar performance of the hormone that moves glucose out of the bloodstream and into muscle and fat cells) raises blood pressure, damaging arteries.

Diabetes also injures tiny blood vessels called capillaries, which hurts your kidneys and nerves—damage that in turn stresses the heart.

The end result—an up to seven-fold increase in the risk of heart disease and stroke, the *cardiovascular diseases* (CVD) that kill four out of five people with diabetes.

But recent studies show there are several natural ways for people with diabetes to reverse the risk factors that cause heart disease...

Recent Research

It's never too late to exercise—and a little goes a long way. Researchers at the University of British Columbia in Vancouver, Canada, studied 36 older people (average age 71) with type 2 diabetes, high blood pressure, and high cholesterol, dividing them into two groups.

One group walked on a treadmill or cycled on a stationary bicycle for 40 minutes, three days a week. The other group didn't.

To find out if the exercise was helping with CVD, the researchers measured the elasticity of the arteries—a fundamental indicator of arterial youth and health, with arterial stiffness increasing the risk of dying from CVD.

Results: After three months, the exercisers had a decrease in arterial stiffness of 15% to 20%.

"Aerobic exercise should be the first-line treatment to reduce arterial stiffness in older adults with type 2 diabetes, even if the patient has advanced cardiovascular risk factors" such as high blood pressure and high cholesterol, conclude the researchers, in *Diabetes Care*.

What to Do

Kenneth Madden, MD, the study leader, and associate professor of geriatric medicine at the University of British Columbia, says, "You can improve every risk factor for diabetes and heart disease—and you can do it in a very short period of time."

Dr. Madden recommends that older people with diabetes and cardiovascular disease see a doctor for a checkup before starting an exercise program.

Once you get the okay from your physician, he says to purchase and use a heart

Consider Surgery

For diabetes patients with severe heart disease, bypass surgery is more effective than medication.

Recent finding: Only 22.4% of diabetes patients with severe coronary disease who had immediate bypass surgery died or had a heart attack or stroke within the next five years, versus 30.5% who elected to take medication instead.

Study of 2,368 people by researchers at University of Pittsburgh Graduate School of Public Health, presented at a recent meeting of the American Diabetes Association.

monitor during exercise, so you are sure that you're exercising at the level used by the participants in his study—60% to 75% of maximum heart rate.

Example: An estimate of your maximum heart rate is 220, minus your age. If you're 60, that would be 220 – 60 = 160. Exercising at between 60% to 75% of your maximum heart rate means maintaining a heart rate of between 96 and 120 beats per minute.

Finally, Dr. Madden advises you exercise the amount proven to improve arterial elasticity—a minimum of three sessions of aerobic exercise a week, of 40 minutes each.

More Help for the Heart

● **Maximize magnesium.** Researchers in Mexico studied 79 people with diabetes and high blood pressure, dividing them into two groups. One group received a daily 450-milligram (mg) magnesium supplement; one didn't.

Results: After four months, those on magnesium had an average drop of 20 points *systolic* (the higher number in the blood pressure reading) and 9 points *diastolic* (the lower number). Those on the placebo had corresponding drops of 5 points and 1 point.

"Magnesium supplementation should be considered as an additional or alternative treatment for high blood pressure in people who have diabetes," says Fernando Guerrero-Romero, MD, research group on diabetes, University of San Luis Potosi, Mexico, and the study leader.

What to do: "Magnesium acts as a natural *vasodilator*, relaxing arteries and lowering blood pressure," says Dr. Baum. "People with diabetes should incorporate a magnesium supplement into their regimen."

He suggests a daily supplement of 400 mg, about the level used in the study.

"People with diabetes and high blood pressure should also be encouraged to increase their dietary intake of magnesium, through eating more whole grains, leafy green vegetables, legumes, nuts and fish," says Dr. Guerrero-Romero.

• **Eat like a Neanderthal.** Researchers in Sweden tested two diets in 13 people with type 2 diabetes—the diet recommended by the American Diabetes Association (ADA), a generally healthful diet limiting calories, fat and refined carbohydrates; and a "Paleolithic" diet, consisting of lean meat, fish, fruits, vegetables, root vegetables, eggs and nuts—and no dairy products, refined carbohydrates or highly processed foods, whatsoever.

In terms of lowering risk factors for heart disease, the Paleolithic diet clubbed the ADA diet.

Results: After three months, it had done a better job of decreasing…
• **High LDL "bad" cholesterol**
• **High blood pressure**
• **High triglycerides** (a blood fat linked to heart disease)
• **Large waist size** (excess stomach fat is linked to heart disease).

The diet was also more effective at increasing HDL "good" cholesterol. And it was superior in decreasing *glycated hemoglobin* (A1C), a measure of long-term blood sugar control.

"Foods that were regularly eaten during the Paleolithic, or 'Old Stone Age,' may be optimal for prevention and treatment of type 2 diabetes, cardiovascular disease and insulin resistance," concludes Tommy Jönsson, MD, department of clinical science, University of Lund, Sweden.

What to do: "Eating a Paleolithic diet is far easier than most people think," says Robb Wolf, owner of NorCal Strength & Conditioning in Chico, California, and author of *The Paleo Solution.*

The Basic Diet
Eat more—lean meat, fish, shellfish, fruits, vegetables, eggs and nuts. Eat less (or eliminate)—grains, dairy products, salt, refined fats and refined sugar.

Resource: You can order prepackaged Paleolithic snacks and meals at *www.paleo brands.com.*

• **Have a cup of hibiscus tea.** Researchers in Iran studied 53 people with type 2 diabetes, dividing them into two groups. One group drank a cup of hibiscus tea twice a day; the other drank two cups a day of black tea. (The hibiscus tea was made from *Hibiscus sabdariffa*, which is also known as red sorrel, Jamaican sorrel, Indian sorrel, roselle and Florida cranberry.)

Results: After one month, those drinking hibiscus had…
• **Higher HDL "good" cholesterol**
• **Lower LDL "bad" cholesterol**
• **Lower total cholesterol**
• **Lower blood pressure.**

The black tea group didn't have any significant changes in blood fats or blood pressure.

The findings were in *The Journal of Alternative and Complementary Medicine* and the *Journal of Human Hypertension.*

What to do: Consider drinking a cup or two of hibiscus tea a day, says Hassan Mozaffari-Khosravi, PhD, an assistant professor of nutrition, Shahid Sadoughi University of Medical Sciences and Health Services, Yazd, Iran, and the study leader.

■ ■ ■ ■

Kidney Disease: You Can Have It and Not Even Know It

Alexander Chang, MD, a nephrology fellow in the department of nephrology and hypertension at Loyola University Medical Center in Maywood, Illinois. He is a member of the American Society of Nephrology, the National Kidney Foundation and the American Society of Hypertension. Dr. Chang led the group of researchers who recently presented their findings on diet and kidney disease prevention at the National Kidney Foundation's Spring Clinical Meetings.

We hear a great deal about the best dietary strategies to help prevent heart disease and diabetes. But what about kidney disease?

Recent development: For the first time, researchers have identified some of the key eating habits that help prevent the onset of kidney disease.

Why this is important: Kidney disease, which affects all the body's main physiological functions, significantly increases one's risk for serious medical conditions such as cardiovascular disease, including heart attack and stroke...sexual dysfunction...and bone fractures. *What you need to know...*

Kidney Damage Occurs Slowly

Like hypertension and diabetes, kidney disease can progress over decades. Patients can

Key Facts About the Kidneys

The kidneys are fist-size organs that remove waste (about two quarts) from the approximately 200 quarts of blood that are processed daily. Each kidney contains about one million filtering units—tiny, delicate networks of blood vessels and tubes that are easily damaged by diabetes, high blood pressure and other chronic diseases.

lose up to 75% of their kidney function without experiencing kidney disease's eventual symptoms, which include fatigue and loss of appetite, difficulty concentrating, muscle cramps, swelling in the feet and/or ankles and/or low urine output. Increased risk for heart attack and stroke begins when kidney function has declined by about 50%—further declines usually require medication, dialysis or a kidney transplant.

Losing weight if you're overweight and following very specific dietary strategies are among the best ways to prevent kidney disease—and to minimize further damage if you are one of the 26 million Americans who already have it. Obesity increases the risk for hypertension and diabetes, which are the two most common causes of kidney disease.

Key dietary approaches recently identified by researchers...

• **Drink fewer sugar-sweetened drinks.** In a recent unpublished analysis of data from a 25-year study of young adults, Loyola researchers found that those who drank just 3.5 soft drinks or other sweetened beverages, such as energy drinks or fruit drinks, per week were 150% more likely to develop kidney disease than those who didn't drink them.

It's possible that the sweet beverages' high concentration of fructose (in refined sugar and high-fructose corn syrup), in particular is responsible for the increased risk.

My advice: In general, Americans consume too much sugar. Switch to diet soft drinks.

Even better: Choose unsweetened beverages, such as water with a lemon slice.

• **Get less animal protein.** In our analysis, people who ate an average of more than 1.5 servings a day of red meat or processed meat were 139% more likely to develop kidney disease than those who ate less than that. In patients with kidney disease, reducing overall protein intake lessens stress on the kidneys and can delay disease progression and the need for dialysis.

My advice: If you have kidney disease, consider working with a nutritionist to find healthful ways to limit daily protein to 40 grams (g) to 50 g. Fish (salmon, herring, mackerel and sardines) and lean meats provide high-quality protein with less saturated fat than you would get from typical red meat. Some research suggests vegetarian diets are especially beneficial for people with kidney disease.

For prevention: Include the most healthful protein sources. For example, beans and whole grains provide not only high-quality protein but also antioxidants, vitamins and minerals.

• **Consume much less salt.** For many people, a high-salt diet is a main cause of high blood pressure—a leading risk factor for kidney disease.

My advice: Even though some recent research raises questions about universal sodium restrictions, most health organizations recommend limiting daily sodium intake to 2,300 milligrams (mg).

For some people with hypertension, reducing salt to 1,500 mg daily can lower *systolic* (top number) and *diastolic* (bottom number) pressure by about 11 points. That is comparable to the reduction that typical-

ly occurs with the use of antihypertensive medications.

• **Drink low-fat milk.** A study published in the *American Journal of Clinical Nutrition* that looked at 2,245 participants found that those who consumed the most low-fat milk, along with other low-fat dairy products, reduced their risk of developing hypertension by about 7%. Keeping one's blood pressure under control also contributes to healthy kidneys.

It's possible that the proteins and minerals (such as calcium) in dairy foods are responsible. Even though full-fat dairy contains the same minerals and proteins, the higher level of saturated fat may offset the benefits.

My advice: Check the USDA's Web site, *www.choosemyplate.gov,* for general guidelines regarding daily intake of low-fat or nonfat dairy.

• **Limit phosphorus intake.** The RDA for phosphorus in adults is 700 mg daily. However, the average adult consumes about twice as much because phosphorus is found in nearly every food—and it's added to processed foods to preserve colors and improve taste and/or texture.

Healthy adults excrete excess phosphorus. But in those with impaired kidney function, phosphorus can accumulate and cause conditions such as *hyperphosphatemia*, a buildup of this naturally occurring element that can lead to accelerated bone loss.

My advice: If you have kidney disease, ask your doctor if you need to lower your phosphorus levels—and work with a nutritionist to find the best ways to stay within healthy limits. It's wise for everyone to stay away from processed foods. In general, foods that are high in protein, such as meats, are also high in phosphorus. So are cola soft drinks, starchy vegetables and hard cheeses.

Important: To avoid high-phosphorus processed foods, look for "phos" on food labels. High-phosphorus additives include *phosphoric acid*, *calcium phosphate* and *monopotassium phosphate*.

For more information on kidney disease, consult the National Kidney Foundation's Web site, *www.kidney.org*.

High-Fat Diet Helps Kidneys

Charles V. Mobbs, PhD, professor of neuroscience, geriatrics and palliative medicine, Mobbs's Aging and Metabolism Lab, Fishberg Department of Neuroscience, Mount Sinai School of Medicine, New York City.

Not only is diabetes a difficult disease in and of itself, but it also brings some terrible complications, some of which are life-threatening—including kidney damage, long thought to be irreversible. But maybe it's not...a fascinating recent study shows that there is a way to reverse kidney damage from diabetes (type 1 and type 2), and believe it or not, the key is eating a high-fat diet!

Is This for Real?

It's not quite as simple as dining regularly on marbled steaks and rich ice cream, however. This research focused on what's called a *ketogenic diet*, a type of diet that has been used for decades to control seizures in children with severe epilepsy. It's a rigid eating plan in which people typically eat about four times as much fat (described in detail later) as carbohydrates and protein, for a diet that is 75% to 80% fat.

Charles V. Mobbs, PhD, professor of neuroscience, geriatrics and palliative medicine at Mount Sinai School of Medicine in New York City, says that this study is the first one ever to suggest that dietary intervention can turn around kidney damage and possibly other diabetes-related complications as well.

At Mount Sinai, Dr. Mobbs and his team examined the effects of a ketogenic diet in mice bred to have diabetes. They allowed the diabetic mice to develop kidney failure and put half on the diet (in this case 87% fat, 8% protein, 5% carbohydrates) and half on a high-carbohydrate control diet of standard mouse chow (11% fat, 23% protein, 64% carbohydrates). After eight weeks, kidney failure was reversed—meaning that urine analysis showed normal, healthy levels of *albumin* and *creatinine*—in mice on the ketogenic diet. The mice on the control diet died.

Tricking the Body

Here's how the ketogenic diet works: Similar to the low-carb, high-fat Atkins diet, it essentially tricks the body into believing that it is in starvation mode, a condition that produces lowered blood glucose levels and higher blood fat levels. These cues trigger the body to manufacture molecules called *ketones*—an indication the body is using fat to provide fuel for energy to the cells. (Normally, the body uses glucose for fuel.)

People with diabetes have elevated blood sugar (as you know), causing excess glucose metabolism—this is what causes diabetes-related kidney failure, Dr. Mobbs explains. But once blood glucose is relatively low and ketones are high (providing an alternative source of energy), the kidneys can take a rest from glucose metabolism—and thereby regenerate themselves. These findings were published in *PLoS ONE*.

If this process is found to work in humans—and Dr. Mobbs says he believes it probably will—using a ketogenic diet would be a dramatic improvement over dialysis or a kidney transplant, which are at present, the only ways to treat kidney failure.

It Works Fast

The problem, however, is that the ketogenic diet is so strict and extreme in its requirements (for instance, even toothpaste is restricted in case it has sugar in it) that people find it hard to follow for any length of time.

To illustrate: Children put on this diet to control seizures are hospitalized and begin with a 24-hour water fast. Their diet is gradually modified, eventually comprising 75 to 100 calories per 2.2 pounds of body weight with a ratio of three or four times as much fat as carbohydrate and protein—emphasizing lots of butter, heavy whipping cream, mayonnaise and oils. The children are closely monitored for adverse reactions—since this is a high-calorie diet, their calorie intake is also watched to be sure that they don't gain weight—and if all goes well, they are sent home to continue the diet for several months.

So it's logical that the next question would be how long does a person have to follow this eating plan for it to work—forever? The answer is, probably not.

Dr. Mobbs says that he believes that following a ketogenic diet for a short period of time—perhaps only one month—may be enough to "reset" the kidneys to begin functioning normally. But this is only a guess, he says, noting that he and his team are conducting further mouse trials to determine exactly how many weeks or months are needed to reverse kidney damage.

The research team is also organizing trials in humans, and Dr. Mobbs sees great potential for additional future uses of the ketogenic diet. In years to come, we may see it prescribed to treat a variety of both diabetes-related and nondiabetes-related complications—for instance, age-related kidney failure not caused by diabetes.

No question, this is compelling stuff. Dr. Mobbs emphasizes that the ketogenic diet is a serious medical intervention that should be attempted only under a doctor's supervision. Do not try it on your own.

■ ■ ■ ■

When Hospitals Make Mistakes

E. Wesley Ely, MD, MPH, professor of medicine and critical care, Vanderbilt University Medical Center, Nashville. Dr. Ely is the founder of Vanderbilt's ICU Delirium and Cognitive Impairment Study Group and associate director of aging research for the VA Tennessee Valley Geriatric Research and Education Clinical Center (GRECC).

You explore the pros and cons and shop around before you buy a car—so why not compare all local hospitals in case you, or someone close to you, becomes ill or has an accident? Lack of accessible information may have discouraged you from taking a close look in the past, but the Centers for Medicare & Medicaid Services (CMS) now reports hospital error rates on its Web site. The information is right there at *www. hospitalcompare.hhs.gov,* making it easy to see how the various medical centers in your area stack up against each other. So what can you find out?

Adverse Events: More Common Than You Think

Hospital-acquired conditions (HACs) are also called "never events"—because they are serious problems that people develop in the hospital that should seldom, if ever, happen as long as proper procedures are followed. As an example, according to the Department of Health and Human Services' Office of the Inspector General, 13.5% of hospitalized patients on Medicare experience preventable adverse events such as falls and infections.

That's clearly way more than "never"…and way too many.

The CMS tracks hospitals' rates on these eight "never events"…

• **Foreign objects.** Yes, it really is true—sometimes surgeons accidentally leave a sponge or clamp in a patient's body.

• **Air embolism.** Without proper care and attention, a dangerous air bubble may develop in your bloodstream. This can happen with a central IV line and during vascular procedures.

• **Mismatched blood.** Hospitals occasionally administer the wrong type of blood in a transfusion.

• **Severe pressure sores.** If you cannot move around independently and caregivers don't help you shift position frequently, you could develop painful and potentially life-threatening pressure sores, what most people call bedsores.

• **Falls and injuries.** Without proper assistance, a simple trip to the bathroom may result in a fall and a debilitating injury.

• **Vascular catheter-associated infection.** This is a blood infection from *catheters*—small tubes that are used to treat heart disease or other disease and carry a risk for sepsis.

• **Catheter-associated urinary tract infections.** Catheters also are used to help patients urinate, and infections are a common complication.

• **Uncontrolled blood sugar.** Signs of poorly controlled blood sugar range from confusion, anxiety and sweating (low blood sugar or *hypoglycemia*) to headaches, blurred vision and fatigue (high blood sugar or *hyperglycemia*). This is a concern for hospital patients with diabetes and also for others—for instance, those for whom the stress of hospitalization is too much. Pregnancy can cause short-term hyperglycemia as well.

After reading through that list, are you ready to take yourself to just any old hospital? Think about it. It's clearly a good idea to track error rates, notes E. Wesley Ely, MD, MPH, a professor and specialist in pulmonary and critical care medicine at Vanderbilt University Medical Center—but, he adds, it's something that needs to be done very carefully for the benefit of both patients and the hospitals themselves. For example, it's reasonable and helpful to hold hospitals responsible for mistakes such as transfusing the wrong blood type or leaving a foreign object in a patient during a surgical procedure—but it's not helpful to automatically blame hospitals when patients develop delirium after surgery, as the CMS originally proposed, because delirium is not always preventable. Fortunately, the CMS reversed its position on this condition, says Dr. Ely.

What You Need to Know Before You Go

To increase your odds of a safe and successful hospital stay, become an educated consumer…

• **Check hospital ratings.** Visit CMS's Web site and read about hospital errors. You'll find the incidence rate for each of the eight HACs in the nation's 4,700 hospitals. That is how many times a HAC has occurred per 1,000 discharges. At *www.hospitalcompare.hhs.gov*, you also can learn how satisfied other people were with their hospital stays…how closely hospitals followed best practices of care…how many people died within 30 days of hospitalization for a heart attack, heart failure or pneumonia… and the 30-day readmission rates for these conditions.

• **Don't pay for their mistakes.** Medicare does not pay for treatment of conditions that result from hospitals' mistakes, and you don't have to either. If you develop any of the eight above conditions in the hospital, you can't be charged for the resulting necessary treatment, according to the *Deficit Reduction Act of 2005*.

• **Work with caregivers as a team.** For best results, Dr. Ely urges families to communicate closely with doctors, nurses and other health-care professionals.

Provide caregivers with a complete list of all prescription and over-the-counter medications and supplements that the patient takes so that nothing gets overlooked in an emergency. This is particularly important so that doctors can avoid drug interactions with new medications they might prescribe.

Ask questions about the risks and potential benefits of treatment options, and speak up about any other concerns, such as a patient being sedated too deeply or for too many days.

As well-meaning as most health-care professionals are, the demands of their jobs mean that a patient's quality of care isn't necessarily automatic.

• **Safer at home.** Dr. Ely also encourages you to keep talking to your hospitalized loved ones so they remain as oriented and aware as possible…so that they get out of bed sooner…recover and come back home where they belong. It's much safer there!

■ ■ ■ ■

Eat Your Way to a Healthy Mouth

Marvin A. Fier, DDS, executive vice president of the American Society for Dental Aesthetics and an adjunct professor of dentistry at Loma Linda University, California, and New York University College of Dentistry, New York City. *www.rocklandnydentist.com*

Within seconds after we eat, bacteria in the mouth convert sugars into acids that can damage tooth enamel, leading to decay and cavities. We all know that we need to brush and floss to keep our teeth and gums healthy, but certain foods also can dilute acids, cleanse the teeth and reduce inflammation—the underlying cause of *periodontal* (gum) *disease.*

Important: By reducing gum disease, you also reduce your risk for other diseases that are linked to inflammation. These include heart disease, diabetes and even cancer.

Here are the best foods and beverages to keep your teeth and gums healthy…

• **Crunchy clean.** Celery, apples and carrots are ideal for dental health. These and other crisp fruits and vegetables act like mini-toothbrushes. They scour off plaque, the bacteria-laden film that accumulates on teeth and beneath the gums. These foods also have a high water content, which dilutes oral acids.

• **Cheese after meals.** The European tradition of serving cheese after meals is healthier for the mouth than after-meal desserts. Cheese neutralizes oral acids and helps remove bacteria. It stimulates the flow of saliva, which also has acid-neutralizing properties.

The calcium and phosphorus in cheese and other dairy foods remineralizes tooth enamel, making it stronger and more impervious to acids.

Bonus: The ratio of phosphorus and calcium in cheese is optimal for the absorption of fluoride, which helps prevent decay.

If you don't eat dairy: Use MI Paste (a 40-gram tube is available online for about $29). It binds calcium and phosphate to tooth surfaces and makes teeth stronger. Apply twice daily after brushing with your regular toothpaste.

● **Tea.** Both green and black teas contain *polyphenols*, antioxidants that reduce inflammation and may decrease the risk for periodontal disease.

Researchers in Japan found that people who drank one cup of green tea daily were less likely to develop periodontal disease than those who didn't drink tea.

● **Vitamin C–rich foods.** The body uses vitamin C for the growth and repair of tissues. It is a necessary component of collagen, a protein that is one of the building blocks of cartilage, teeth and bones.

Why it matters: Patients with even mild periodontal disease can experience a weakening of tissues that support the teeth. In more advanced cases, periodontal disease can lead to tooth loss. A diet high in vitamin C can help repair and rebuild these tissues.

Vitamin C also is a potent antioxidant that can help counter the damaging effects of inflammation.

Foods rich in vitamin C include citrus fruits, peaches, papayas, strawberries, tomatoes, turnip greens, red and green peppers and broccoli.

If you are not getting enough vitamin C from food, consider taking a supplement. I recommend 500 milligrams (mg) daily.

Warning: Wait an hour after eating acidic foods to brush your teeth. If you brush after consuming acidic foods, such as tomato products, citrus fruits or vinegar—or after taking a chewable vitamin C tablet—the toothbrush can wear away small amounts of enamel as it rubs the acid against your teeth.

If you are drinking something acidic, such as fruit juice or soda, drink through a straw so the liquid bypasses tooth surfaces.

● **Garlic.** Garlic contains *diallyl sulfide*, an antimicrobial compound that can reduce the development of tartar and plaque. A laboratory study published in *The Journal of Food and Drug Analysis* found that garlic extracts almost completely suppressed the growth of *S. mutans*, an acid-producing organism that is the main cause of cavities.

Other foods that contain diallyl sulfide include onions, chives, leeks and shallots.

● **Sugarless gum.** Most people think that chewing gum is bad for the teeth. Not true. It's actually one of the most effective ways to prevent tooth decay and gum disease, particularly when you chew after meals.

Chewing gum greatly increases the flow of saliva, which washes away and neutralizes bacteria. Of course, it should always be sugarless.

● **Water.** Americans consume enormous quantities of sugar, particularly in soft drinks, sports drinks and juices. We've seen an increase in eroded tooth enamel in recent years because of high sugar intake. Even diet soft drinks cause problems because, like all carbonated beverages, they're acidic.

Cancer Concern

People with diabetes have about a 10% greater likelihood of all cancers combined and a much higher likelihood of certain other cancers, including cancers of the pancreas, bladder and kidney.

Possible reason: High blood levels of glucose and insulin, plus chronic inflammation.

Chaoyang Li, MD, an epidemiologist at the Centers for Disease Control and Prevention, Atlanta, and lead author of a study of nearly 400,000 people, published in *Diabetes Care.*

Better: Drink plain water or water with a little added fresh lemon juice or orange juice. When you do drink sweetened beverages, rinse your mouth with water when you're finished.

• **Avoid candy, cookies, cakes, crackers, muffins, potato chips, french fries, pretzels, bananas and dried fruits.** These provide a source of sugar that bacteria can use to produce acid.

■ ■ ■ ■

Surprising Cause of Memory Problems, Bladder Cancer and Other Dangerous Conditions

Ann Grandjean, EdD, associate professor of medical nutrition education at the University of Nebraska Medical Center in Omaha. She is coauthor of *Hydration: Fluids for Life,* published by the International Life Sciences Institute, *www.ilsi.org.*

We all know that water is essential for human life and dehydration is dangerous. But there are some surprising effects of even mild dehydration that you may not be aware of.

Little-known risks: In addition to impaired cognitive function and lethargy, dehydration is associated with increased risk for falls, gum disease and bladder cancer.

What you need to know about water's effect on your mental and physical well-being…

How Much Do You Need?

It's difficult to pinpoint exactly how much water we need.

Problem: Depending on activity levels, metabolism and environmental factors, such as heat and humidity, one person may require up to eight times as much water as someone else to stay hydrated.

Solution: Even though we often hear that most people should drink eight glasses of water a day, there isn't really any scientific evidence to support this approach. The first official recommendation for water consumption was issued in 2004 by the Institute of Medicine, the health arm of the government-sponsored National Academy of Sciences. This so-called *adequate intake* (AI) for males age 19 and older is 15 eight-ounce cups daily…for females of the same age group, 11 cups daily.

Sound like a lot of liquid? Remember this represents total water intake, including the water that comes from food—and for most people, this amounts to roughly 20% to 25% of the total. When focusing on water alone, the AI includes about 13 cups of beverages, including water, for males age 19 and older…and nine cups for females of the same age group.

Important: Contrary to what many people believe, there is no evidence to show that coffee, tea and other caffeinated beverages contribute to dehydration. So it's fine to count these beverages as part of your daily fluid intake.

Since it's so difficult to establish strict guidelines for water consumption, the most convenient indication may be your urine.

Simple self-test: If you urinate at least four times each day and the urine is colorless or pale yellow, you are probably well-hydrated.

Note: Some vitamin supplements, such as B vitamins, can cause urine to be yellow even if the person is hydrated.

Dangers of Dehydration

The first symptoms of dehydration usually are dry mouth and thirst. If dehydration progresses, headache, dizziness, sleepiness and muscle weakness may occur.

Dehydration that produces a 2% drop in body weight (due to water loss via sweat, vomiting, diarrhea, etc.) is associated with declines in short-term memory, attention and other mental functions. Similar levels of dehydration can lead to fatigue and reduce strength and endurance. *Chronic low-water intake can increase risk for illnesses such as…*

• **Urinary tract infection.** When female factory employees significantly increased their water intake and urination frequency by three times or more during their shifts for two years, the rate of urinary tract infections dropped from 9.8% to 1.6%.

• **Bladder cancer.** Not all research findings agree, but one large study that followed 47,000 men for 10 years found that those with the highest levels of fluid consumption (10.6 cups daily) had half the risk for bladder cancer as men who consumed the least fluids (5.5 cups).

When Your Risk Is High

Some people are at higher risk for acute and chronic dehydration than others. *Key risk factors…*

• **Illness.** Many chronic illnesses (diabetes and kidney disease among them) raise the risk for dehydration. Diarrhea and vomiting can present an acute dehydration danger—and water alone won't replace the minerals, such as sodium and potassium, that you lose. If either is severe or prolonged, or if you can't keep liquids down, consult your doctor.

• **Age.** The sensation of thirst is blunted as we age, so "drink when you're thirsty" becomes a less reliable guide. For many people, appetite also lessens with age—so you can end up getting less water from food. (See next article.)

Other indirect age-related factors also may come into play. For example, people troubled by incontinence often limit water intake.

• **Exercise.** During exercise, you lose more water through sweating. So make sure that you drink enough water when you exercise—generally one to two cups before… one to two cups during…and one to two cups after your workout. This is especially important in hot and humid weather or at high altitudes.

Treating Dehydration

When dehydration is mild to moderate, the treatment is simple—drink more liquids.

Severe dehydration is a medical emergency that requires immediate medical help. Some symptoms are the same as those for mild dehydration but greatly magnified—extreme thirst, profound sleepiness or lethargy and very dry mouth. Sweating and urination come to a virtual halt.

Older adults especially may experience irritability and lethargy, while severe dehydration also could lead to delirium (marked by disorientation and delusions) or unconsciousness.

If you experience any of these symptoms—or witness them in another person, especially an older adult—contact a doctor.

■ ■ ■ ■

More from Ann Grandjean, EdD…

Not Just Water

Drinking a glass of water is an ideal way to boost your daily fluid intake. But there is also water in frequently consumed beverages and foods. *Percentage of water in…*

• **Brewed tea or coffee,** diet soft drinks, sports drinks, lemonade and vegetable juice —90% to 100%

- **Fruit juice,** milk (skim, 1%, 2%, whole and chocolate) and regular soft drinks—85% to 90%
- **Soup** (chicken noodle, tomato)—80% to 90%
- **Fruits** (strawberries, melons, grapefruit, peaches, pears, oranges, apples, grapes)—80% to 85%
- **Vegetables** (lettuce, broccoli, onions, carrots, cucumbers)—80% to 85%
- **Cottage cheese and yogurt**—75% to 80%
- **Cooked rice and pasta**—65% to 80%
- **Pizza**—50% to 60%
- **Breads, bagels, biscuits**—30% to 45%
- **Chips, pretzels, dried fruit and popcorn**—1% to 10%

■ ■ ■ ■

Too Much Sugar in Your Diet Carries More Risk Than Weight Gain

Richard J. Johnson, MD, professor and chief of the division of renal diseases and hypertension at the University of Colorado, Denver. Dr. Johnson's medical research has appeared in *The New England Journal of Medicine,* the *American Journal of Clinical Nutrition,* the *International Journal of Obesity, Diabetes* and many other leading medical journals. He is the author of *The Sugar Fix: The High-Fructose Fallout That Is Making You Fat and Sick* (Gallery).

We all know that it's not good for our health to consume too much sugar. Excessive amounts of sugar in the diet are widely known to cause weight gain. But that's only part of the story.

Both table sugar and *high-fructose corn syrup* (HFCS) contain fructose, which recent research has shown can increase the risk for diabetes, fatty liver disease, high blood pressure and chronic kidney disease when consumed in excessive amounts. Currently,

most Americans consume way too much added sugar in their daily diets, putting them at risk for all these diseases.

What's the Trouble with Fructose?

Fructose is a simple sugar. It is found naturally in honey, fruits and some vegetables. But a typical fruit contains only about 8 grams (g) of fructose, compared with about 20 g in a sugary soda. Unlike soda, fruits and vegetables contain nutrients and antioxidants that are beneficial to health.

The two main sources of fructose in the American diet are table sugar (which is squeezed from beet and cane plants) and HFCS (which is processed using enzymes that turn corn starch into glucose and fructose). Table sugar and HFCS are almost identical in their chemical composition—and both, consumed in excess, can contribute to health problems.

But few Americans are aware of just how much added sugar they are getting in their diets. That's because many added sugars are often listed as ingredients that are not recognizable as sugar and are found in unexpected food sources (see next page for a list of these terms). For example, added sugar is found in not only obvious places like soft drinks and other sweet beverages, but also in great abundance in many salad dressings, condiments (such as ketchup), cereals, crackers and even bread.

My research and that of other scientists show that Americans' ever-increasing sugar consumption is hurting their health in unexpected—even deadly—ways.

- **High blood pressure (or hypertension).** About one in three American adults has hypertension, an underlying risk factor for heart attack, stroke and kidney disease. Historically, high blood pressure has been linked to excessive sodium intake. Now preliminary evidence shows that sugar may play a bigger role than was previously thought.

Important recent finding #1: In a study published in the journal *Circulation*, researchers found that among 810 overweight adults with stage 1 or borderline hypertension, those who drank one less drink sweetened with sugar or HFCS (such as soft drinks, fruit drinks and lemonade) per day for 18 months lowered their blood pressure. Although more research is needed, this study is a first step in confirming a sugar–blood pressure link.

Important finding #2: A *Journal of the American Society of Nephrology* study found that among 4,528 adults, those whose diets included 74 g or more of fructose daily had up to 77% higher risk for blood pressure problems than those who consumed less fructose daily.

• **Liver disease.** Traditionally, liver disease was widely linked to excessive alcohol intake. Then physicians began to identify a condition known as *nonalcoholic fatty liver disease* (NAFLD), in which fat builds up in the liver of a person who drinks little or no alcohol. Now research is showing that sugar may be involved in the development of NAFLD. For example, research at Duke University showed that those who ingested the most fructose had more rapid disease progression (fattening of the liver and formation of fibrous tissue) than those who ingested the least. NAFLD is common among people who have type 2 diabetes or are overweight and can progress to cirrhosis and liver cancer.

Emerging Research on Fructose

While there are many studies being conducted on different types of added sugars, there is important research that now focuses on various forms of fructose. For example, recent research suggests that fructose

Sugar Aliases

Take this list to the supermarket with you to help you identify the various terms for added sugars...

- Beet sugar
- Brown sugar
- Cane sugar
- Corn sweetener
- Corn syrup
- Demerara sugar
- Fruit juice concentrate
- Granulated sugar
- High-fructose corn syrup
- Honey
- Invert sugar
- Maple syrup
- Molasses
- Muscovado sugar
- Raw sugar
- Sucrose
- Syrup
- Table sugar
- Tagatose
- Turbinado sugar

is harmful because it increases levels of uric acid, a naturally occurring acid found in the urine. In crystalline form, uric acid can deposit in the joints and lead to gout.

Eating foods rich in a compound called *purines* (found in foods such as anchovies, beer, brewer's yeast supplements, clams, goose, gravy, herring, lobster, mackerel, meat extract, mincemeat, mussels, organ meats, oysters, sardines, scallops and shrimp) can also produce high levels of uric acid.

Smart Ways to Limit Sugar

It's important to remove added sugar from your diet—with a special focus on fructose due to its unique potential risks that are now being discovered in new research.

To minimize the health risks associated with added sugars, try these steps...

• **Beware of "hidden" sugar.** When buying processed foods, remember that added sugars can appear on food labels in various ways. (See box on page 293.)

• **Avoid any prepared or processed product that does not provide an ingredient list.**

• **Don't eat more than four fruits daily.** Even the naturally occurring fructose found in fruit counts toward your total daily intake of fructose. It's also important to limit your intake of fruit juice, which has been stripped of the nutritious fiber present in whole fruit and often contains added sugar.

• **Limit fructose intake to 25 g to 35 g per day.** Consuming more than that amount could trigger the physiological changes that may lead to disease.

To learn the sugar content of specific foods, go to the USDA Food Database at *www.nal.usda.gov/fnic/foodcomp/search*.

• **Take nutritional supplements.** Limiting fruit in your diet may lower your levels of important nutrients. To replace them, take a multivitamin plus an additional 250 milligrams (mg) of vitamin C daily.

• **Be cautious when eating in restaurants.** Limit restaurant meals and takeout food to those menu items for which you know the ingredients.

• **Be prepared for sugar withdrawal.** In rare cases, you could develop withdrawal symptoms from sugar and fructose, such as headache, fatigue and an intense craving for sweets.

To help ease these symptoms, be sure to drink plenty of water (five to eight cups daily).

Is It Just a Bladder Infection...or Are Your Kidneys in Danger?

Mildred Lam, MD, associate professor at Case Western Reserve University School of Medicine and an attending physician in the division of nephrology at MetroHealth System, both in Cleveland. She specializes in the care of patients with acute and chronic kidney disease.

My friend Jean was chagrined to have unwittingly risked her health. "It felt like a barely-there bladder infection, so I took some cranberry extract. The next day, I felt OK, so I forgot about it," Jean told me. "But on day three, I developed a fever and my back hurt like crazy, so I called my doctor. I wound up in the hospital getting intravenous [IV] antibiotics for a kidney infection that could have caused serious, or even fatal, complications! I am kicking myself for not checking with my doctor sooner, while the infection was still just in my bladder."

Jean's story is not unusual, I heard from kidney specialist Mildred Lam, MD, of Case Western Reserve University School of Medicine. She told me that, in most cases of *urinary tract infection* (UTI), bacteria get into the *urethra* (the tube that carries urine out of the body), travel into the bladder and multiply. Called a bladder infection or *cystitis*, this generally is easily treated with antibiotics.

But sometimes the bacteria travel farther and invade the kidney itself, causing a kidney infection. Possible consequences of this type of UTI can include temporary or permanent kidney failure...chronic kidney disease...and potentially life-threatening septicemia if bacteria enter the bloodstream.

Women are more vulnerable to UTIs than men because in women, the urethra and bacteria-laden anus are closer together...and the urethra is shorter, so bacteria don't have to travel as far to reach the bladder and kidneys. *Other risk factors…*

• **Being postmenopausal**—accompanying hormonal changes can diminish muscle tone in the urinary tract, making it easier for bacteria to invade.

• **Sexual activity, especially with a new partner**—perhaps because, over some time, a woman develops antibodies to her partner's bacteria.

• **Diabetes**—sugar in the urine promotes bacterial growth.

• **Kidney stones**—these provide a place for bacteria to grow and also impede the flow of urine (and therefore bacteria) out of the body.

• **Congenital defects** that let urine travel upward from the bladder to the kidney—normally urine only travels downward from kidney to bladder.

Because a kidney infection can quickly become serious, Dr. Lam urges women to be on the lookout for symptoms. *Call your doctor today if you notice…*

• **Any discomfort or burning pain when urinating.**

• **Frequent urge to urinate** (even if little comes out).

• **Cloudy or blood-tinged urine.**

• **Low-grade fever.**

• **Mild to moderate pain in the middle of the lower back.**

These symptoms suggest a bladder infection. Getting a urine test can confirm the diagnosis.

Remember: Prompt treatment—typically a three- to five-day course of oral antibiotics—helps keep a bladder infection from moving to the kidneys. If you need a pain reliever, your doctor may recommend *acetaminophen* (Tylenol). "High-dose aspi-

rin, ibuprofen and naproxen carry a small risk for kidney failure," Dr. Lam cautions.

• **Severe pain in the "flank" area of the back,** at the lower edge of the ribs on the left or right side.

• **Chills and/or fever above 102°.**

• **Nausea and vomiting.**

These symptoms suggest a kidney infection. "To minimize the risk for permanent kidney damage, high-dose IV antibiotics are needed to quickly achieve high antibiotic levels in both the blood and the urine," Dr. Lam says. You may be given IV fluids if dehydrated or very nauseated. Once fever subsides and you can take fluids and medication by mouth, you'll switch to oral antibiotics, taking these for 10 to 14 days to eradicate the bacteria.

Dr. Lam's bladder and kidney infection prevention strategies…

• **Don't hold your urine too long**—going when you need to go helps flush bacteria out of the bladder.

• **Always wipe from front to back after using the toilet.**

• **Drinking cranberry juice or taking cranberry supplements may help**—cranberries contain a compound that makes it difficult for bacteria to cling to the bladder walls.

• **Stay hydrated.**

• **Urinate before and after intercourse.**

If you are especially prone to UTIs (getting more than two in a six-month period), ask your doctor about taking a single dose of an antibiotic immediately after intercourse.

Diabetes May Link to Cognitive Decline

JoAnn E. Manson, MD, DrPH, professor of medicine and women's health at Harvard Medical School and chief of the division of preventive medicine at Brigham and Women's Hospital, both in Boston. She is one of the lead investigators for two highly influential studies on women's health—the Harvard Nurses' Health Study and the Women's Health Initiative. Dr. Manson is the author, with Shari Bassuk, ScD, of *Hot Flashes, Hormones & Your Health* (McGraw-Hill), and advisory board member for *HealthyWoman from Bottom Line.*

Memory loss is such a frightening and frustrating aspect of aging that, of course, we want to do what we can to keep our minds sharp. So it was a devastating disappointment to many people when a recent comprehensive analysis of studies concluded that there is simply not enough scientific evidence to support many of the strategies commonly recommended for preventing cognitive decline.

The big questions: How could the results of this analysis be so contradictory to those of numerous earlier studies? And what—if anything—can and should we do now to protect our minds?

Before we tackle those questions, let's first look at the recent analysis. An independent government panel reviewed the results from 165 scientific papers published in the last 25 years and concluded in *Annals of Internal Medicine* (AIM) that "the current literature does not provide adequate evidence to make recommendations for interventions" aimed at preventing cognitive decline. *Reasons for this conclusion…*

● **Genetic factors appear to affect susceptibility to cognitive decline**—and, of course, we can't change our genes.

● **Research on strategies to prevent cognitive decline is in a state of relative infancy.** There are numerous small studies with nonrigorous study designs—but few large-scale, long-term observational studies or randomized clinical trials. With many small studies of varying designs, it's not uncommon to get inconsistent findings and thus be unable to reach a definitive conclusion. In this regard, the panel's overall findings actually are not so surprising to me.

Still: A closer examination of the AIM report reveals some strategies that may indeed help.

Tentatively Linked to Lower Risk For Cognitive Decline...

● **Avoiding specific medical conditions, such as diabetes…depression or depressive symptoms…and metabolic syndrome**—a cluster of symptoms that increase risk for cardiovascular disease, including abdominal obesity, high triglycerides, high blood pressure, high blood sugar and low HDL (good) cholesterol.

● **Not smoking.** Individuals who never smoked or quit smoking appear to be 30% less likely to experience cognitive decline than current smokers.

● **Engaging in cognitively stimulating activities,** such as reading, crossword puzzles and the card game bridge.

● **Regular physical activity, such as walking, biking and gardening.**

● **A Mediterranean diet** that emphasizes fruits, vegetables, fish and whole grains and that limits unhealthy fats…a high intake of vegetables in particular…and a high intake of marine omega-3 fatty acids, which are found in fish and fish-oil supplements.

My recommendation: Although these strategies have not yet been proven to prevent cognitive decline, it seems likely to me that many, if not all, of them will ultimately be shown to do so. Why? A significant amount of cognitive decline is related to underlying vascular disease (diseased arteries supplying the brain or heart). There is conclusive evidence that a healthy lifestyle that includes most of the above strategies can prevent a large proportion of cases of stroke and heart disease, as well as vascular risk factors, such as diabetes and high blood pressure. This vascular protection would be expected to translate into reduced cognitive risk as well. Therefore, I'm hedging my bets and still recommending—and personally practicing—these strategies for prevention not only of vascular disease but also of cognitive decline.

What Appears *Not* to Help Prevent Cognitive Decline...

The AIM report noted that, although laboratory studies and some observational studies suggest cognitive benefit for the following interventions, they have not shown benefit in available randomized trials. *So, although the factors below may have other health benefits (as well as risks, in some cases), cognitive protection does not appear to be among the benefits of the following...*

• **Supplements of vitamin C...vitamin E ...beta-carotene...a combination of vitamins B-6, B-12 and folic acid...multivitamins...or the hormone DHEA.** Most of these supplements also have failed to protect against cardiovascular disease (or cancer) in large randomized trials.

• **Menopausal hormone therapy**—at least if started at age 65 or older. (We just don't know yet whether hormone therapy helps reduce dementia risk when started closer to menopause, because in most randomized trials, the women who used hormone therapy generally were older.)

• **Nonsteroidal anti-inflammatory drugs (aspirin, ibuprofen)...cholesterol-lowering statins...or blood pressure-lowering medications** (the quality of available data is particularly low for this last intervention).

• **Having an active social life and/or emotional support from friends and family.**

Get a Test

High blood pressure, memory problems and fatigue can be linked to *insulin resistance*. People who are insulin-resistant have an impaired ability to control their bodies' blood glucose levels. In addition to diabetes, the condition can lead to cardiovascular disease, decreased immunity, depression, increased inflammation, weight gain and breast and colon cancers.

Self-defense: Ask your doctor about getting tested for insulin resistance.

Allan Magaziner, DO, founder and director of Magaziner Center for Wellness, Cherry Hill, New Jersey, and author of *The All-Natural Cardio Cure* (Avery). *www.drmagaziner.com*

There's Just Too Little Data to Say...

The panel found too little evidence to hazard a guess whether the following factors increase, decrease or have no effect on cognitive function...

• **Changes in caloric intake...or dietary fat intake.**

• **Supplements of ginkgo biloba.**

• **Having sleep apnea.**

• **The presence of trace metals in the body...or toxic environmental exposures.**

Bottom line: My opinion is that there is no harm and much to be gained in terms of prevention of other health problems (including diabetes, heart disease, stroke, depression and physical disability) by adhering to a healthful diet...maintaining an active, involved lifestyle...and controlling blood pressure and cholesterol levels as needed. As more rigorous studies are conducted, hopefully we will find that our efforts have also kept cognitive decline at bay.

■ ■ ■ ■

Neuropathy: New Ways to Get Relief

John D. England, MD, the Grace Benson Professor and chairman of the department of neurology at Louisiana State University Health Sciences Center School of Medicine in New Orleans, and a fellow of the American Academy of Neurology (AAN). Dr. England has published more than 100 professional articles about neuropathy and other disorders and was the lead author of the recent AAN guidelines on peripheral neuropathy.

Until recently, there were no specific criteria for doctors to use when diagnosing the nerve disorder known as *peripheral neuropathy*. As a result, a patient might go for months or even years without getting the proper diagnosis for symptoms (such as numbness, tingling, burning or stabbing pain, a feeling of pins and needles or weakness) that typically occur in the hands and/or feet.

Development: Recent guidelines by the American Academy of Neurology can help patients get a prompt diagnosis and effective treatment that reduces their risk for permanent nerve damage.

The Diagnosis

Peripheral neuropathy can have various symptoms because there are many possible causes. If you suffer any of the symptoms mentioned above, see your primary care physician and describe them in as much detail as possible. Your doctor may refer you to a neurologist.

Your doctor will want to know…

● **Do you have weakness or feel clumsy at times?** Because nerves stimulate muscles, some neuropathies result in a loss of strength, causing patients to lose balance, trip and/or feel clumsy.

● **Where did you first notice the symptoms?** Peripheral neuropathy typically starts in the areas of the body farthest

ED Warning

Erectile dysfunction (ED) is linked to depression and heart disease. ED and cardiovascular disease share many risk factors, including hypertension and diabetes. ED also is one of the earliest manifestations of a forthcoming cardiovascular event. Men with ED, depression or both should talk to their doctors about being screened for possible heart problems.

Mario Maggi, MD, professor of sexual medicine, University of Florence, Italy, and coauthor of a study of 2,303 men, published in *The Journal of Sexual Medicine.*

from the spinal cord, usually the feet and/or hands.

● **Did the symptoms occur simultaneously on both sides of the body—for example, in both feet—or on only one side?** Peripheral neuropathy symptoms usually occur simultaneously on both sides of the body. If you experience symptoms on only one side, other possible causes, such as multiple sclerosis or a stroke, must be considered.

Be sure to tell your doctor about: All medications you have taken in the last year or are currently taking. *Among the drugs that can cause peripheral neuropathy…*

● **Chemotherapy drugs,** such as *vincristine* (Oncovin) or *cisplatin* (Platinol).

● **Antibiotics,** including *metronidazole* (Flagyl) or *nitrofurantoin* (Macrodantin).

● **Anticonvulsants,** such as *phenytoin* (Dilantin).

In addition, excessive doses of vitamin B-6 (*pyridoxine*) can bring on peripheral neuropathy.

Identifying the Cause

To find the cause of peripheral neuropathy, you should receive blood tests for…

● **High blood sugar (glucose).** This could indicate diabetes or glucose intolerance (impaired ability to convert glucose to energy). When prolonged, glucose elevation damages the small blood vessels, leading to slow nerve death.

To prevent further nerve damage: Control blood glucose through diet and/or the use of insulin and, if necessary, other diabetes medication.

• **Vitamin deficiency.** As many as one in three adults over age 50 does not efficiently absorb vitamin B-12, a nutrient required for proper nerve function. Vitamin B-12 deficiency also can result from heavy drinking or a poor diet. Because vitamin B-12 is found only in animal foods, such as meat, poultry and dairy products, some vegetarians are at increased risk for a deficiency unless they take a supplement.

To prevent further nerve damage: Ask your doctor about getting monthly vitamin B-12 injections and/or taking a daily B-12 oral supplements.

• **Infection and/or inflammation.** A *complete blood count* (CBC) and a test for the inflammation marker *C-reactive protein* (CRP) can help identify infections that can cause neuropathy, such as Lyme disease… HIV…hepatitis…and syphilis.

To prevent further nerve damage: Begin treatment immediately with an antibiotic or other medication.

What Other Tests Can Tell

The blood tests described above can usually identify the general cause of neuropathy, but other tests that may be needed include…

• **Nerve conduction study (NCS).** With this noninvasive test, electrodes are placed on the surface of the skin—on the hands and feet, for example—and mild electric shocks are delivered to help measure the speed of nerve signals. Some types of neuropathy, such as *Charcot-Marie-Tooth disease* (a hereditary disorder), strip the nerves of their protective coating (*myelin*), causing nerve impulses to travel more slowly.

• **Electromyography (EMG).** Often performed with NCS, this test helps evaluate the health of nerves that control muscles. A needle-thin electrode is inserted through the skin and into a muscle to track electrical activity that gives clues to the causes of muscle weakness.

• **Skin and nerve biopsies.** By taking a skin sample, doctors can examine the small nerve fibers that cause pain or numbness. A nerve biopsy can find less common causes of inflammation, including deposits of abnormal proteins, or unusual infections, such as leprosy.

The Best Treatment

If you identify neuropathy early, symptoms may disappear with proper treatment, such as improved blood sugar control or medication to treat infection or inflammation. By stopping the disease process, you often can avoid additional nerve damage.

Too often, however, nerve damage is permanent—and pain and numbness continue indefinitely.

In these cases, you should…

• **Get some exercise.** Physical activity helps maintain your physical abilities and prevent disabilities, such as muscle contractures (shortening of muscles). Exercise also triggers the release of natural painkilling compounds called *endorphins*.

For minor neuropathy, the best exercises include low-impact activities, such as walking and bicycling. Water exercises, which can build strength without risk for injury from falling, are especially good for people who have balance problems. Aim to exercise for 30 minutes three to four times weekly—as tolerated.

• **Avoid neuropathy-related injury.** If the body's pain signals are blunted, cuts and

Better Diabetes Control

New finding: Twenty-four percent of 716 people with diabetes who took an *alpha-lipoic acid* supplement daily for three weeks felt an improvement in pain, burning and numbness in their feet due to diabetic neuropathy (nerve damage caused by high blood sugar) compared with 16% of 542 diabetics taking a placebo.

Theory: Alpha-lipoic acid neutralizes the damage caused by small molecules that accumulate when blood sugar becomes elevated.

If you suffer from diabetic neuropathy: Ask your doctor about taking 1,200 milligrams (mg) to 1,800 mg daily of controlled-release alpha-lipoic acid, available at most health-food stores. Taking alpha-lipoic acid may alter insulin or drug requirements.

Ira Goldfine, MD, professor in residence, departments of medicine and physiology, University of California, San Francisco.

blisters are easily ignored and may become infected.

To prevent injury: Don't go barefoot... wash and examine your feet daily...and moisturize with a lotion or cream, when necessary, to avoid cracking skin.

• **Relieve the pain.** Pain can reduce your quality of life, limit your activities and may even "rewire" your brain so that your discomfort becomes more difficult to treat. *Best to try...*

• **Topical pain relievers.** When applied to the hands or feet, topical analgesics can relieve pain intensity in some people by reducing nerve sensation.

Example: Prescription *lidocaine* creams and patches.

Common side effects: Temporary tenderness at the application site.

• **Antidepressant medications.** Relatively new antidepressants called *selective serotonin* and *norepinephrine reuptake inhibitors* (SSNRIs) can increase levels of the brain chemicals serotonin and norepinephrine, both of which help regulate mood. The drugs inhibit pain impulses so that they don't "register" in awareness.

Examples: *Venlafaxine* (Effexor) and *duloxetine* (Cymbalta).

Common side effects: Nausea, insomnia and dry mouth.

• **Antiepileptic medications.** Developed to control seizures, these drugs can intercept the transmission of pain signals.

Examples: *Pregabalin* (Lyrica)...and *gabapentin* (Neurontin).

Common side effects: Sleepiness and dizziness.

• **Centrally acting analgesics.** These drugs bind to specific receptors in the brain to block pain and alter the patient's emotional response to the sensations. There is a risk for dependency with these drugs, so they are used only as a last resort.

Examples: *Oxycodone* (OxyContin)... and *hydrocodone* and *acetaminophen* (Vicodin, Lortab).

Common side effects: Sleepiness, dizziness and gastrointestinal upset.

When Wounds Won't Go Away...

Steven J. Kavros, DPM, a podiatrist, assistant professor of podiatric medicine and certified wound specialist at Mayo Clinic in Rochester, Minnesota. He has published several papers on diabetic and vascular wound care in peer-reviewed medical journals.

If you get a scrape or other superficial wound, it usually heals in a week or two. But some wounds do not go away so quickly—especially if you're an older adult, are confined to a bed or wheelchair, or have diabetes or some other condition that interferes with your blood flow.

Latest development: New, highly effective therapies and the proliferation of wound-care centers staffed by doctors and other health-care professionals (often located at large medical centers or university hospitals) are helping to prevent amputations, life-threatening infections and other serious complications.*

Why Wounds Become Chronic

If a wound doesn't heal within six weeks, it is considered chronic and requires special care. Poor blood flow, which cuts off the supply of oxygen and nutrients that are needed for healing, is a common cause of chronic wounds.

Basic care for all chronic wounds usually involves thorough cleansing (to remove foreign matter and bacteria-laden debris)... debridement (to remove dead and damaged tissue)...and dressing (often treated with a medicinal preparation, such as an antimicrobial solution, to prevent the growth of bacteria).

• **Diabetic foot ulcers.** Among Americans with diabetes, 15% will develop a foot ulcer, and many of them will ultimately require amputation of the foot—usually because the patient has developed a life-threatening condition, such as *gangrene* (decay and death of tissue due to insufficient blood supply).

Why are people with diabetes at such high risk for foot ulcers?

The disease not only impairs healthy blood flow, but also inhibits the body's ability to fight infection. In addition, *neuropathy* (a type of nerve damage that often occurs

*To find a wound-care specialist in your area, consult the American Board of Wound Management (202-457-8408, *www.aawm.org*).

in people with diabetes) can cause nerve pain and decrease sensation, so pressure and injury may go unnoticed.

Diabetic ulcers typically occur at points of prolonged or repeated pressure on the skin and underlying tissue—for example, on the big toe or front part of the foot.

Self-defense: People with diabetic foot ulcers should wear properly fitting shoes. They also may need a podiatrist to check for abnormalities in their gaits, perhaps with the aid of a computerized scan of pressure points on their feet. Special shoe inserts (*orthotics*) can help adjust the position of the foot to relieve pressure points.

Breakthrough Therapies

A chronic wound is a magnet for bacteria—the dead tissue and moisture provide a hospitable environment for germs to thrive.

Recent development: A treatment available at many wound-care centers uses low-frequency ultrasound to break up *biofilm* (a microscopically thin layer of film containing bacteria) on the wound. This stimulates the production of cells that fill in the wound with new tissue and help keep the area clean.

Caution: Notify your physician promptly if your wound shows signs of infection, such as pain, odor, redness, pus or streaks along the affected limb, or if you have a fever (above 99°F). Infections require antibiotic treatment.

Wounds that refuse to heal despite treatment may require one of the other latest therapies typically available at wound-care centers...

• **Cell therapy involves placing a bioengineered skin substitute over the wound.** This film-like material secretes substances that stimulate your own cells to grow tissue that will close the wound. Cell therapy is often used for resistant diabetic or venous ulcers.

- **Hyperbaric oxygen therapy,** which is mainly used for diabetic ulcers, involves sitting or lying for about 90 minutes in a room or chamber that contains 100% oxygen at two to three times the normal air pressure. Breathing this supercharged air promotes wound healing by raising oxygen levels in the blood.

- **Negative pressure wound therapy,** which is used for diabetic and arterial ulcers, involves placing a sponge or foam dressing over the wound and attaching a device that suctions off waste fluids and infectious material, thus stimulating the growth of new tissue.

Vitamin B-12 for Diabetic Neuropathy

Mariejane Braza, MD, internist, Valley Baptist Medical Center, Harlingen, Texas.

Jacob Teitelbaum, MD, author of *Pain-Free 1-2-3* McGraw-Hill) and *From Fatigued to Fantastic!* (Avery). *www. endfatigue.com*

A recent study says a vitamin can help reduce the pain associated with diabetic neuropathy.

Less Pain and Burning

Researchers in Iran studied 100 people with diabetic neuropathy, dividing them into two groups. One group received *nortriptyline* (Pamelor, Aventyl), an antidepressant medication that has been used to treat neuropathy. The other group received vitamin B-12, a nutrient known to nourish and protect nerves.

After several weeks of treatment, the B-12 group had…

- **8% greater reduction in pain.**

- **71% greater reduction in tingling and prickling.**

- **65% greater reduction in burning.**

Latest development: A few months after the Iranian doctors conducted their study, research in the US involving 76 people with diabetes showed that the widely prescribed diabetes drug *metformin* may cause vitamin B-12 deficiency—and that 77% of those with the deficiency also suffered from peripheral neuropathy!

Anyone already diagnosed with peripheral neuropathy who uses metformin should be tested for low blood levels of B-12, says Mariejane Braza, MD, internist at Valley Baptist Medical Center in Harlingen, Texas, and the study leader. If B-12 levels are low, she recommends supplementing with the vitamin, to reduce the risk of nerve damage.

Heal the Nerves

"If you take metformin, definitely take at least 500 micrograms (mcg) a day of vitamin B-12, in either a multivitamin or B-complex supplement," advises Jacob Teitelbaum, MD, author of *Pain-Free 1-2-3.*

"On a good day, the best that medications can do for neuropathy is mask the pain," he continues. "But vitamin B-12 gradually heals the nerves."

Best: If you already have neuropathy, Dr. Teitelbaum recommends finding a holistic physician and asking for 15 intramuscular injections of 3,000 micrograms (mcg) to 5,000 mcg of *methylcobalamin*, the best form of B-12 to treat peripheral neuropathy. "Receive those shots daily to weekly—at whatever speed is convenient to quickly optimize levels of B-12," says Dr. Teitelbaum.

If you cannot find a holistic physician near you, he suggests taking a daily *sublingual* (dissolving under the tongue) dose of 5,000 mcg for four weeks. (Daily, because you only absorb a small portion of the sublingual vitamin B-12, compared with intramuscular injections.)

At the same time that you take B-12, also take a high-dose B-complex supplement (B-50). "The body is happiest when it gets all the B-vitamins together," says Dr. Teitelbaum.

He points out that it can take three to twelve months for nerves to heal, but that the neuropathy should progressively improve during that time.

Also helpful: Other nutrients that Dr. Teitelbaum recommends to help ease peripheral neuropathy include...

● **Alpha-lipoic acid** (300 milligrams [mg], twice a day).

● **Acetyl-l-carnitine** (500 mg, three times a day).

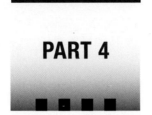

PART 4

Cancer Care, Recovery
& Nutrition

11

Alternative Cancer Care

Natural Cancer Treatments That Really Work

Keith I. Block, MD, medical director of Block Center for Integrative Care in Evanston, Illinois…director of Integrative Medical Education at University of Illinois College of Medicine, Chicago…and scientific director of the Institute for Integrative Cancer Research and Education, Evanston. He is editor of *Journal for Integrative Cancer Therapies* and author of *Life Over Cancer* (Bantam). *www.blockmd.com*

Many cancer patients augment conventional medical treatment with complementary medicine, such as nutritional or herbal supplements. The newest research and decades of successful clinical use show that some of these natural treatments work very effectively to fight cancer and reduce side effects.

Here are the best science-based complementary treatments for cancer. It's usually fine to take several of these supplements simultaneously, but be sure to talk to your doctor first. For help finding an integrative practitioner, go to *http://nccam.nih.gov/health/howtofind.htm.*

Antioxidants

Cancer specialists often advise patients not to take antioxidant supplements, such as vitamin A or vitamin E, during chemotherapy and radiation treatments.

Reason: One way chemotherapy and radiation destroy cancer cells is by causing oxidative stress. According to one theory, antioxidants may be counterproductive because they might have the ability to protect against this oxidative damage.

But new scientific research shows that the opposite is true—antioxidant supplements aren't powerful enough to counter chemotherapeutic medicines or radiation, but they can reduce the side effects of those treatments and also may battle tumors and extend life.

Recent study: Researchers from the University of Illinois at Chicago and the Institute for Integrative Cancer Research and Education analyzed 19 studies involving 1,554 cancer patients who took antioxidants during chemotherapy. They concluded that most cancer patients are better off using antioxidants in conjunction with chemotherapy and radiation than not using them.

Typical doses…

- **Vitamin A**—7,500 international units (IU) daily, which should only be taken under a doctor's supervision—patients should have their liver enzymes monitored on an ongoing basis.

- **Vitamin E**—400 IU daily, taken under a doctor's supervision (patients should have their platelet counts monitored). It's best to divide the dose, taking half in the morning and half in the evening. Ideally, take it on an empty stomach.

Astragalus

The herb astragalus has been used in traditional Chinese medicine for thousands of years. Scientific studies show that it strengthens the immune system, increasing the activity of cancer-fighting cells and inhibiting the activity of immune cells that increase inflammation and thereby worsen cancer. Research shows that the herb also can boost the power of certain types of chemotherapy.

Recent study: Researchers from the School of Public Health at the University of California, Berkeley, analyzed 34 studies involving 2,815 patients with non-small cell lung cancer who were treated with chemotherapy alone or who were treated with chemotherapy and astragalus. The patients taking astragalus had a 33% lower risk for death after 12 months and a 24% to 46% better tumor response than those not taking the herb.

Typical dose: 750 milligrams (mg) to 2,500 mg a day of astragalus extract.

Ginseng

Extracts from the root of this herb often are used as a natural stimulant—to boost mental and physical energy, improve athletic performance and relieve fatigue. Ginseng also may boost energy in cancer patients.

Recent study: Doctors from the North Central Cancer Treatment Group at the Mayo Clinic gave either a placebo or ginseng—at daily doses of 750 mg...1,000 mg... or 2,000 mg—to 282 cancer patients. Those taking 1,000 mg or 2,000 mg of ginseng had more energy and vitality and less fatigue. Those taking 750 mg or a placebo had no such improvement. The patients taking the higher doses of ginseng also reported greater physical, mental, emotional and spiritual well-being.

Typical dose: 500 mg to 1,000 mg twice daily of American ginseng (not Asian red ginseng). Medical supervision is needed for the higher dosage, particularly if you are taking blood-thinning medication.

Glutamine

Chemotherapy can damage the mucous lining of the digestive tract, which stretches from the inside of the mouth to the rectum. One common result is oral mucositis (OM), a condition in which the mucous lining of the mouth and throat becomes inflamed, painful, ulcerated and prone to infection. The amino acid glutamine fuels the daily maintenance of the mucous lining of the digestive tract—and supplemental glutamine can help limit or stop its destruction by chemotherapy.

Recent study: Researchers at the University of Connecticut Health Center gave either glutamine powder or a placebo to 326 cancer patients undergoing chemotherapy who were developing OM. Those taking glutamine experienced a significant reduction in the severity of the condition compared with those taking the placebo. In fact, many of those taking glutamine didn't develop OM at all during their second cycle of chemotherapy.

Typical dose: 5 grams (g) to 10 g, twice daily.

Omega-3 Fatty Acids

Chronic inflammation is known to fuel the growth of tumors. Omega-3 fatty acids, nutrients abundant in fish oil and flaxseed, are potent anti-inflammatories that slow tumor growth and shrink tumors in animal studies. Recent research shows that omega-3 fatty acids may do the same for men with prostate cancer.

Recent study: Researchers at Duke University Medical Center, the University of Michigan and the University of North Carolina studied 140 men with prostate cancer who were scheduled to undergo prostate surgery in 30 days. They divided the men into four presurgical groups—some took 30 g (about one ounce) of ground flaxseed daily...some ate a low-fat diet and took the flaxseed...some just ate a low-fat diet...and a control group used none of the regimens. After the surgery, researchers found that the tumors of the men who took flaxseed had grown more slowly—at a 30% to 40% slower rate than those of the other men. The men mixed the ground flaxseed in drinks or sprinkled it on yogurt and other foods. The study was reported at a meeting of the American Society of Clinical Oncology.

Typical dose: One ounce of ground flaxseed...or 3 g of fish oil.

Acupuncture

Acupuncture is a healing technique from traditional Chinese medicine. An acupuncturist inserts tiny needles into the skin along meridians (energy channels in the body) in order to restore and enhance chi, the fundamental force of health and well-being.

Recent study: Doctors at the Osher Center for Integrative Medicine at the University of California, San Francisco, studied 138 cancer patients undergoing surgery, dividing them into two groups. One group received acupuncture and massage after surgery, along with standard care, such as pain-relieving medications. The other group received standard care only. The acupuncture and massage group had 58% less post-surgical pain and less depression, reported the doctors in the *Journal of Pain and Symptom Management.* It's hard to tell specifically what role acupuncture played and what role massage played, but other studies that look at acupuncture and massage alone show that each has benefits, including reducing surgical pain.

Other studies show acupuncture may help prevent or relieve chemotherapy-induced nausea and fatigue...chemotherapy-induced decrease in white blood cell count...radiation-induced dry mouth...shortness of breath...and insomnia and anxiety.

Lifesaving Cancer Cocktails

Jeremy R. Geffen, MD, president of Geffen Visions International, Inc., and director of integrative oncology of P4 Healthcare and Caring4Cancer.com. Dr. Geffen is author of *The Journey Through Cancer: Healing and Transforming the Whole Person* (Three Rivers Press). *www.geffenvisions.com*

Roy S. Herbst, MD, PhD, professor of medicine and professor of cancer biology at the University of Texas, MD Anderson Cancer Center in Houston. Dr. Herbst has worked to develop a clinical/translational research program designed to test new therapies preclinically and then rapidly introduce them to the clinic to be studied in a scientific fashion using surrogate endpoints of tissue biopsy and imaging studies.

Cancer cocktails—or, more scientifically, combination molecular targeted therapies—are currently considered the most promising avenue for curing or prolonging the lives of many people with cancer. The potential is so encouraging that recent news stories have recounted how patients are working on their own to mix therapies they think might work—getting different prescriptions from different doctors or even going online for so-called expert assistance. The temptation to "do it yourself" is understandable because even the distant possibility of remission or cure gives hope to someone who may be running out of options and precious time —while for others, taking the matter into one's own hands seems like it might be the best route for a faster, more effective cure. Oncologists Jeremy R. Geffen, MD, a leading expert in integrative medicine and oncology (which combines state-of-the-art conventional cancer treatments with safe and effective complementary therapies) and founder of Geffen Visions International in Boulder, Colorado, and Roy S. Herbst, MD, a professor and researcher at the University of Texas MD Anderson Cancer Center in Houston, were asked whether this is ever a good idea, considering the plethora of reliable as well as unfounded information available on the Internet.

Promising Treatment or Risky Business?

Over the past two decades, the use of molecularly targeted drugs that kill tumor cells with minimal side effects has significantly improved the survival and quality of life for many cancer patients. While few of these drugs can cure cancer on their own, combinations of them, often used together with standard chemotherapy, can be highly effective. In fact, combination therapies have become conventional treatment in many cases, including for some kinds of colon cancer and non-Hodgkin's lymphoma.

However, physicians generally only prescribe combination therapies that have been proven safe and effective in carefully controlled clinical trials—and, frustratingly, the drug approval process for combination therapies is even slower than for single drugs. While doctors can prescribe drugs or combinations of drugs that haven't been formally approved for a specific condition, most avoid doing so, and for good reasons. "There are potentially serious consequences involved in giving patients unapproved drugs or unapproved drug combinations," says Dr. Geffen. "There are also significant ethical as well as medical-legal concerns. These concerns are part of the day-to-day challenge of practicing oncology in today's health care environment."

That's why some patients end up taking matters into their own hands, researching their options and finding different doctors to prescribe different drugs without disclosing what they are already taking. However, taking unapproved combinations of anticancer agents is a risky endeavor. The greatest risk, of course, is the possibility of adverse drug-to-drug interactions. "It's unpredictable at best, and can be harmful—or potentially even fatal—at worst," says Dr. Geffen.

Dietary Supplements and Cancer Drugs

Another version of the same story involves dietary supplements such as vitamins, minerals and herbs taken in combination with cancer therapies. According to the National Center for Complementary and Alternative Medicine (NCCAM), studies show that significant numbers of cancer patients are using complementary and alternative medicine (CAM) therapies as part of their cancer regimen. Others take supplements to reduce the side effects of their chemotherapies and boost their immune systems. Many of these herbs, such as ginger, flaxseed and ginseng, have been proven clinically effective in treating the symptoms of cancer and the side effects of drugs. Yet, though they are available without prescriptions, Dr. Geffen warns there are risks involved in combining natural substances with chemotherapy.

"The amount of reliable, scientifically rigorous information on the safety of these substances is relatively small," says Dr. Geffen. "Some herbs can indeed lower the toxicity of chemotherapy drugs—but they may also simultaneously lower the drugs' effectiveness. Ironically, some herbs can potentially increase the toxicity of chemotherapy, which could actually make people feel worse."

A variety of herbs and botanical supplements can interfere with the way cancer drugs work by altering how the drugs are metabolized in the liver or transported out of cancer cells. "These are two mechanisms that explain why combining natural substances with chemotherapy can be a risky proposition," says Dr. Geffen. "There are likely even more mechanisms that we don't fully understand yet, which is why more research is needed and why patients should be cautious about this."

Make Decisions Based on Knowledge, Not Fear

When it comes to do-it-yourself cancer cocktails, both Dr. Geffen and Dr. Herbst advise patients to "work with your oncologist and make informed, intelligent choices." In other words, let thoughtful, intelligent discussion between patient and doctor be the guide. *Here are some of their suggestions on how to make sure you are getting access to the best of what's available…*

• **Find an oncologist who is in sync with you,** including how aggressively you want to fight your disease. "Work with one who has extensive experience in treating your particular cancer," says Dr. Herbst. "By doing that, you could either learn about an early Phase I clinical trial to join or take the best combination of other drugs from studies that have proven effectiveness."

• **Ask your oncologist if he/she is willing to work with the latest combination therapies or a drug** (chemotherapy or non-chemotherapy) that is currently being explored "off-label" to treat the cancer, if this offers hope for your particular diagnosis. "Oncologists will combine drugs for you—that's what they're trained to do," says Dr. Herbst. "But these cocktails need to be rational combinations; they must be based on the findings of clinical data, even off-label." Mixing a personalized cancer cocktail should only be done with a physician.

• **If necessary, consider traveling to a major cancer center that is currently doing research with your particular kind of cancer.** "I encourage people to seek out major cancer centers to look at new cancer treatments, where they may be able to join an early clinical trial program and can potentially get on drugs that have more activity and less toxicity," says Dr. Herbst. You can find the latest information on early Phase I clinical trials or drugs being studied to treat your particular cancer from the National Cancer Institute at *www.cancer.gov/clinicaltrials/search.*

• **Don't fall prey to people who claim they can concoct a cancer cocktail for you.** "On the Internet there are people who advertise that they can help you design a cancer cocktail—but you want to go where the data is, and where the clinical trials are," says Dr. Herbst. "Until you know through exploring the research that something is better, it's safer to stick to what has already been proven safe and effective. There are many drugs that people thought would be better, but by Phase III we learn that they are actually worse."

The future remains promising for many cancer patients and for cancer cocktails, says Dr. Herbst. "Currently, in the general population, we're treating cancer based on what's already known about a particular cancer, and we may use some combinations that work together in a so-called cocktail," he says. "In the future, cancer cocktails will be custom-mixed for each individual patient based on the composition of his or her specific tumor."

But remember, these "mixes" aren't to be taken lightly based on something you read on a blog. It is understandable that when faced with a challenging circumstance like cancer, people may want to explore or even take desperate measures. In certain cases, risk-taking may even seem a logical choice. However, Dr. Geffen stresses that, "to maximize the chance for success, it is essential for patients and loved ones to make decisions based on knowledge and understanding, in partnership with their physician, rather than based on fear."

■ ■ ■ ■

Finding Optimal Cted Cancer Care

Lise Alschuler, ND, past president of the American Association of Naturopathic Physicians. She is a board-certified naturopathic oncologist at Naturopathic Specialists LLC in New Hampshire, and is coauthor of *Definitive Guide to Cancer: An Integrative Approach to Prevention, Treatment, and Healing* (Celestial Arts).

When a person is diagnosed with cancer, conventional doctors typically recommend surgery, chemotherapy and/or radiation.

Latest development: A growing body of research shows that complementary and alternative medicine (CAM) therapies benefit cancer patients in a number of ways, such as by reducing the adverse effects of conventional cancer treatments.*

*Integrative cancer centers can be found at major US medical institutions, such as Memorial Sloan-Kettering Cancer Center and MD Anderson Cancer Center.

An Attack on Cancer Cells

Normal cells divide in a predictable and orderly fashion—for example, in the growth of a fetus. When the DNA within cells is damaged—due to genetic abnormalities, for example, or lifestyle factors, such as smoking or getting too much sun exposure—the cells may become cancerous.

The cornerstone of integrative cancer care is to mobilize the body's natural ability to stimulate *apoptosis*—the selective destruction of cells, including cancer cells. Most patients still require surgery, chemotherapy and/or radiation. The integrative component—including dietary changes and the use of supplements simultaneously with conventional treatments—improves the patient's odds of living a longer and healthier life by altering the body processes closely linked with cancer.

Improved Immunity

The immune system is the first line of defense against cancer. For example, natural killer cells produce an estimated 100 biochemical poisons that attack foreign proteins, including those on the surface of cancer cells.

Key recommendations...**

• **Load up on antioxidants.** The average cell is subjected to 10,000 daily assaults from free radicals (unstable, negatively charged molecules that can harm DNA), and the resulting damage can overwhelm the ability of immune T cells (including natural killer cells) to destroy cancer cells.

Recommended: Antioxidant-rich fresh produce (at least five servings daily) and supplements, such as vitamin C (1,000 milligrams [mg] to 2,000 mg daily)...selenium (100 micrograms [mcg] to 200 mcg daily)... and zinc (30 mg to 45 mg daily).

• **Take mushroom extracts.** When scientists recently reviewed the results from

**Important: Consult an integrative health-care practitioner before taking any new supplements.

several randomized clinical trials in Japan, Korea and China, they found that the use of mushroom extracts (which contain a chemical compound that stimulates the immune system to destroy tumors) significantly improved survival rates for patients with malignancies of the stomach, colon, esophagus or breast.

A commonly recommended medicinal mushroom is *Coriolus versicolor* (or its chemical compound, PSK).

Typical dose: 3,000 mg daily.

Control Hormones

All cells have hormone receptors, molecular sites where hormones attach and cause biochemical reactions. One of the primary reactions is growth, which can be dangerous if a cell is cancerous.

Hormone-dependent cancers—such as some forms of breast cancer as well as many ovarian and prostate cancers—are most likely to be stimulated by certain hormones. But other cancers, such as malignancies of the lung or pancreas, are also influenced by hormones, particularly estrogen and cortisol, that compromise immunity or directly stimulate the growth of tumor cells. *Here, my advice…*

• **Consume phytoestrogens.** Estrogen-like compounds in plants (phytoestrogens) can reduce the potentially carcinogenic effects of estrogen in the body. Phytoestrogens occupy the estrogen receptor sites, thereby preventing the body's estrogens from binding to those sites. Foods such as soy and flaxseed are rich in phytoestrogens.

Recommended: One tablespoon daily of ground flaxseed and one to two servings weekly of soy foods.

• **Eat leafy greens.** They promote the health of hormone-producing glands, including the thyroid, and support the liver's detoxification of hormones.

Recommended: At least one cup of dark, leafy greens, such as kale and chard, daily.

• **Eat organic.** Many of the herbicides and pesticides used in commercial produce have strong hormonal and genotoxic (DNA-damaging) effects that can increase the risk of getting or having a recurrence of cancers of the breast, kidney, lung and prostate.

• **Exercise regularly.** It regulates the body's production of insulin as well as cortisol and other stress hormones, which, if elevated for too long, can have cancer-causing effects.

Recommended: Six 30-minute sessions weekly.

Remove Toxins

The body is constantly removing potentially carcinogenic toxins, such as benzene (commonly found in gasoline and tobacco).

One of the best herbs for detoxification is green tea. It supports the liver's elimination of toxins. Drink at least five cups of green tea daily.

Free Your Body And Brain from Toxic Metal Buildup

Mark Hyman, MD, founder of the UltraWellness Center in Lenox, Massachusetts, and chairman of the Institute for Functional Medicine. He is the author of several best-selling books, including *UltraMetabolism* (Atria) and *The UltraMind Solution* (Scribner). *www.ultrawellness.com*

Toxic metals are pervasive in our environment. Mercury is in the fish we eat, the vaccines we receive and the fillings in our teeth. Lead belches from coal-burning factories, and the residue of old leaded gasoline and paint remains in our soil and groundwater. Aluminum appears in medications that we swallow and personal-care products that we put on our skin.

These toxic metals can build up in the brain and body—and create big problems. *Examples…*

• **Mercury is linked to dementia,** depression, high blood pressure, autism and attention disorders. It disrupts hormones, mitochondria (the energy-producing parts of cells) and dopamine (a mood-affecting brain chemical). A large study of American women of childbearing age showed that 8% had toxic levels of mercury in the blood.

• **Lead exposure can lead to depression,** schizophrenia, reduced cognitive function, behavioral problems, heart attack, stroke and death.

Estimated: Nearly 40% of Americans have lead levels high enough to cause health problems.

• **Aluminum exposure** may be linked to increased risk for breast cancer and/or Alzheimer's disease.

New concern: Many people lack a gene called GSTM1 that appears to be key for proper functioning of the body's own natural detoxification mechanisms. This may explain at least in part why some people develop the chronic health problems linked to heavy metals while others who are similarly exposed do not.

To protect yourself, follow a dual strategy that maximizes your body's ability to rid itself of toxins and minimizes future toxic exposure.

To Boost Detox Power…

• **Maximize glutathione production.** The body's most important natural detoxifier is the amino acid–based antioxidant *glutathione*. It contains sulfur, which is like flypaper

—toxins stick to it, then are excreted via urine and stool.

To increase your glutathione levels, eat plenty of foods that contain sulfur.

Examples: Garlic, onions and radishes…cruciferous vegetables (bok choy, broccoli, cauliflower)…and egg yolks.

• **Take detox supplements.** Each day, take a multivitamin and follow this metal-chelating regimen—500 milligrams (mg) to 1,000 mg of vitamin C…10 mg to 30 mg of zinc…and 100 micrograms (mcg) to 200 mcg of selenium.

Also consider supplementing with any or all of the following glutathione building blocks—N-acetylcysteine (NAC) at 500 mg to 1,000 mg twice daily…milk thistle extract at 175 mg twice daily…and alpha-lipoic acid at 100 mg to 200 mg twice daily.

• **Sweat out toxins.** Take a dry-heat sauna or moist-heat steam bath, or soak in a hot bathtub five or so times per week, starting with 10-minute sessions and gradually increasing to 30 minutes. Drink 16 ounces of water before and after each session to help flush out toxins…shower with soap afterward to rinse toxins from your skin.

Cautions: If you take medication or have a chronic medical condition, get your doctor's okay first. If you are pregnant, do not use a sauna or steam bath or soak in a hot bathtub.

• **Fill your plate with colors.** Richly pigmented foods generally are high in phytonutrients, which help boost your body's own detoxification pathways. The more colorful your diet, the more different types of phytonutrients you get.

Simple: Each day, eat something red or purple (berries, pomegranate, red peppers)…yellow or orange (cantaloupe, sweet potatoes, yellow beans)…and dark green (collard greens, kale, spinach).

Best: Buy organic to limit exposure to chemical fertilizers and pesticides.

• **Get your metal levels measured,** especially if you have any symptoms of metal toxicity, such as unexplained fatigue, memory loss or depression. But don't rely on blood tests, which show what's happening in your bloodstream only at the moment.

More accurate: You swallow a chelating agent (which binds to heavy metals), then your urine is tested for toxins.

To find a doctor who performs this test, contact the Institute for Functional Medicine (800-228-0622, *www.functionalmedicine.org*). If your metal levels are high, the doctor can prescribe an oral chelating drug, such as *dimercaptosuccinic acid* (DMSA), to pull out metals.

To Reduce Metal Exposure...

• **Eat smaller fish.** Metal contamination is common in large fish (tuna, shark, swordfish, tilefish, sea bass) and river fish—so avoid eating these. Instead, to get omega-3 fatty acids that protect the heart and brain function, stick to fish small enough to fit whole in your frying pan—catfish, flounder, herring, mackerel, fresh or frozen sardines, shrimp and other shellfish.

Even small fish are not entirely free of toxic metals, however—so eat no more than two six-ounce servings per week. The limits apply to farm-raised fish, too, as these may be contaminated by their feed.

• **Drink only filtered water.** Economical faucet-mounted water filters, such as those from Brita or Pur, can reduce metal levels. Even more effective is a reverse osmosis filter installed under the sink. Avoid bottled water in plastic bottles—though probably free of metals, it may contain chemical contaminants from plastic, such as phthalates.

Guideline: Drink at least six to eight full glasses of filtered water daily to maximize the excretion of toxins.

• **Choose metal-free drugstore products.** Avoid underarm products and antacids that have any form of aluminum on the ingredients list...and contact lens fluid with thimerosol, a mercury-based preservative. Cosmetics can contain metals, too—for instance, some lipsticks have trace amounts of lead, so opt for chemical-free cosmetics (see *www.safecosmetics.org*). Limit use of *acetaminophen* (Tylenol), which depletes your stores of glutathione, to no more than twice weekly.

• **Consult a biological dentist.** Even though mercury-containing silver amalgam fillings are banned in some European countries, they still are used routinely in the US, and the American Dental Association continues to maintain that such fillings are not hazardous.

However: Some studies show that mercury migrates through the teeth into the bloodstream...and amalgam fillings are considered toxic waste when removed from the body.

Prudent: If you need a new filling, get one made of composite resin or another mercury-free material. If you have a chronic unexplained illness or if testing shows that your mercury levels are high, consider having your old amalgam fillings removed and replaced with a safer material. For this, consult a biological dentist—this type of professional is trained in the techniques required to remove amalgam safely.

Referrals: International Academy of Oral Medicine and Toxicology, 863-420-6373, *www.iaomt.org*.

Fungus Is Overlooked and Undetected—Could You Be Infected?

Mark A. Stengler, NMD, naturopathic medical doctor and leading authority on the practice of alternative and integrated medicine. Dr. Stengler is author of the *Health Revelations* newsletter, author of *The Natural Physician's Healing Therapies* (Bottom Line Books), founder and medical director of the Stengler Center for Integrative Medicine, Encinitas, California, and adjunct associate clinical professor at the National College of Natural Medicine in Portland, Oregon. *http://markstengler.com*

L ilia had uncontrolled asthma and wheezing. She had suffered from sinus infections and was repeatedly treated with antibiotics and anti-inflammatory steroids. Natural remedies cleared up her sinus infection but not her wheezing. Concerned, Mark Stengler, NMD, sent her to a lung specialist and asked for a fungal infection test. Antibiotics are known to destroy the body's healthful bacteria, which usually keep fungi in check. Sure enough, the test came back positive. Treatment with an antifungal protocol rapidly improved her respiratory problems. Fungal infections are the root cause of many illnesses—from sinusitis to kidney disease. And they are an area of medicine that is largely ignored by conventional physicians. *How to protect yourself…*

Fungus Is Everywhere

A fungus is a spore-producing, plantlike organism. Yeast, mold, mildew and mushrooms all are fungi. More than 100,000 species of fungus have been documented, and a few hundred can be detrimental to human health.

Fungi harm us by triggering allergic reactions…causing either localized or systemic infections…and exposing us to poisonous waste products called *mycotoxins*, which have been shown to depress immune function (and have been linked to certain types of cancers) and promote inflammation (associated with heart disease).

Fungi invade through our lungs, skin and digestive tract. Food, especially grains and peanuts, is rampant with fungi. Once inside our bodies, fungi can survive indefinitely. Fungal infections have been documented in every body part except teeth.

How Fungi Can Affect Health

Lifelong exposure to fungi leaves the body vulnerable to disease. There's growing evidence based on research in the US (at the Mayo Clinic) and around the world linking fungi to many ailments, including…

- **Eczema, psoriasis as well as other skin conditions**
- **Upper-respiratory tract symptoms**
- **Chronic sinusitis**
- **Kidney and bladder diseases**
- **Parkinson's disease**
- **Dementia and Alzheimer's disease**
- **Cancer of the liver**
- **Tumors of the kidneys, urinary tract and colon**
- **Endocarditis** (inflammation of the heart lining and valves)
- **Atherosclerosis**
- **Diabetes and hypoglycemia**
- **Hormone imbalance**
- **Weight gain**
- **Kidney stones**

How to Know If You Have A Fungal Infection

Blood tests that detect most fungal infections have not yet been developed, although sputum culture tests (for lungs) and stool tests (for the digestive system) can detect fungus. For those with the conditions listed above who get sick often or whose conditions do not improve with treatment, the best way to determine if your health is being affected by fungi is to go on an antifungal diet. This type of eating kills off the fungi inside your body by starving them of the nutrients that they need.

Going on an antifungal diet before you have a disease such as Alzheimer's can reduce your risk for the disease. If fungus is causing a disease (such as liver cancer) to thrive, getting rid of the fungus may slow the progression of the illness. If your chronic condition is caused by fungus, you may be able to relieve some of your symptoms.

The Antifungal Diet

One of the best sources of information on fungus is Doug Kaufmann, who has specialized in these infections for 30 years, after suffering from one himself. He teamed up with David Hollander, MD, to create Know the Cause, a Web site (*www.knowthecause. com*) and syndicated television show on the subject. They have created a multiphase antifungal diet that is high in protein and low in carbohydrates.

Fungi thrive on sugar and high-glycemic carbohydrates (which the body easily converts to sugar). The antifungal diet eliminates these foods and increases those that inhibit the growth of fungus. *For the first phase of the antifungal diet…*

Avoid

- **Grains, including rice, corn and wheat**
- **All sugars**
- **Pistachios and peanuts**
- **Potatoes and mushrooms**
- **Processed foods.**

Consume

- **Eggs**
- **Beef from cattle that has been grass-fed, which reduces the likelihood of fungus contamination**
- **Fish (all types) and chicken**
- **Nuts, other than pistachios and peanuts**
- **Vegetables, including carrots, broccoli, cabbage, onions**
- **Green apples (which have less naturally occurring sugar than other apples), berries, grapefruit, lemon, lime, avocados, flaxseeds**
- **Plain yogurt, real butter**
- **Oregano**
- **Coconut oil, olive oil, grapeseed oil, flaxseed oil.**

If your health improves after two to four weeks on this diet, there's a good chance that you have a fungal infection. Kaufmann then recommends a less restricted diet, gradually reintroducing some foods, including some grains.

Caution: Carbohydrates are an important energy source for young children and women who are pregnant or breast-feeding. They should not follow this diet unless monitored by a physician. People with advanced kidney disease (who should not consume a lot of protein) should avoid this diet.

Other Ways to Reduce Fungus

Antifungal remedies and medications can also help reduce fungus. If the antifungal diet does not improve your condition or if you want a more aggressive approach, try one or more natural remedies (in combination with the diet), sold separately as olive-leaf extract, grapefruit-seed extract, oregano (fresh, dried or oil), garlic, herbal pau d'arco tea, zinc, citrus bioflavonoids and d-limonene (oil extracted from citrus rind). Or look for a combination formula, such as CandiGONE by Renew Life (800-830-1800, *www.renewlife.com*). Take as directed on the label for one month.

If your symptoms do not improve, speak to a physician about a prescription antifungal medication, such as *nystatin* (Mycostatin) or *fluconazole* (Diflucan).

Is Your Air-Conditioning Poisoning Your Home?

Jeffrey C. May, MA, founder and principal scientist of May Indoor Air Investigations LLC, an air-quality assessment company in Tyngsborough, Massachusetts. He is author of several books on indoor environments, including *Jeff May's Healthy Home Tips* and *My House Is Killing Me!* (both from The Johns Hopkins University Press). *www.mayindoorair.com*

Mold and bacteria are probably spreading throughout your house right now.

If you have central air-conditioning or a forced-air heating, ventilation and air-conditioning (HVAC) system, inadequate air filtration could be allowing mold and bacteria inside your home. Fewer than 10% of residential forced-air systems have filters capable of preventing mold and bacteria growth.

Mold and bacteria contamination can trigger or exacerbate respiratory problems, including allergies and asthma. Certain molds even produce toxins that are linked to cancer.

Paying big money for high-end air-filtration devices does not necessarily solve this problem. Many expensive filtration products do little to improve air quality. *Here's what works and what doesn't work...*

Use a Better Filter

The cheapest, easiest way to improve your home's air quality is to improve the quality of the disposable filter you use in your forced-air system.

Most home owners use fiberglass panel filters that have a Minimum Efficiency Reporting Value (MERV) of just 3 or 4. To avoid mold or bacteria growth, instead use a "pleated" filter rated MERV 8 or higher.

Buying advice: MERV 8 filters are available at home-improvement stores, such as The Home Depot and Lowe's, and many hardware stores for between $5 and $10 apiece. Don't worry about the filter's brand—focus instead on its MERV rating, which usually is clearly marked on the package. Using the correct size is equally important—even the best filter will not improve air quality if air can get around it in your system's filter compartment or if the compartment does not close properly with the filter inside. Measure your system's filter compartment before buying.

Do not pay extra for expensive "electrostatic" filters for central air-conditioning. Manufacturers claim that these are washable and reusable, but in my experience, there is no way to clean them adequately.

Downside: Switching from a one-inch-deep MERV 3 to a one-inch-deep MERV 8 filter is likely to reduce your system's airflow by up to 10%, increasing your cooling and heating bills. (Deeper filters—two-inch, four-inch, six-inch—do not reduce the airflow as much but are too deep to fit most units.) Replacing filters every three months will minimize the energy consumption increase—dirty filters force heating and cooling systems to work even harder.

Keep the System Clean

If you have used filters rated lower than MERV 8 in the past, it is likely that mold and bacteria already are growing on your air conditioner's blower and coil unless you live in an arid region. Installing a filter with a higher MERV rating will not kill existing mold and bacteria, nor will it prevent their spores from spreading throughout your home—the air conditioner's blower and coil are located after the filter. The only reliable way to remove existing contamination is to hire a duct-cleaning service.

Contact the National Air Duct Cleaners Association (NADCA) to find a pro in your area (855-466-2322, *www.nadca.com*). The duct-cleaning sector is rife with scammers, but NADCA members usually are legitimate. Expect to spend around $1,000 to clean the ducts of an average-sized home of about 2,350 square feet. Any company that promises to clean ducts for significantly less is likely to either do a slipshod job or find excuses to pad your bill during the job. Ducts should be cleaned once every five years or so.

Before signing a contract, confirm that the duct cleaner will clean your air conditioner's blower and coil—some duct cleaners ignore these components and clean only the ducts.

Best and Worst Upgrades

If someone in your household has severe allergies or asthma, you might be tempted to invest in an air-filtration or purification system. *While some high-end products truly deliver cleaner air, others are a waste of money…*

● **MERV 10** or higher pleated filters do a wonderful job of trapping particulates and preventing mold and bacteria growth—but there's a catch. Filters with MERV ratings above 8 or so tend to be too deep to fit in the filter compartments of standard residential HVAC systems. Installing a larger filter holder is likely to cost $700 to $1,000.

MERV 10 replacement filters typically cost $40 to $60 each and last around six months.

Verdict: This is probably the most cost-effective high-end filtration option, even if you have to retrofit your system to accommodate the filter.

Whole-house air cleaners that accommodate high-MERV filters include: Aprilaire Models 2210/2310/2410/2250, which ship with a MERV 10 but have the option to upgrade to a MERV 13 (800-334-6011, *www.aprilaire.com*)…Honeywell F100 Whole-House Media Air Cleaner (877-271-8620, *http://yourhome.honeywell.com/home*).

● **High-Efficiency Particulate Air** (HEPA) whole-house filters have impressive MERV ratings of 16 and up. Unfortunately, residential whole-house HEPA filters are "bypass filters," which means that they subject only a small percentage of the air that passes through the HVAC system to extreme filtration on each circulation. Bypass systems do a fine job of removing particulates from the air, but they do little to prevent the growth of mold and bacteria within the HVAC system, which is the greater threat to residential air quality.

Verdict: Not worth the cost (around $2,000 to $3,000) except, perhaps, for those with severe allergies to particulates, such as pollen and pet dander.

● **Electronic filters attach an electrical charge to particles that pass through,** then collect the charged particles on an oppositely charged metal plate. In theory, that should be effective. In practice, these systems must be cleaned at least once a month to remain effective. Few home owners do this, so their electronic filters soon become useless.

Verdict: Don't bother. I've yet to see a residential electronic filter that's still functioning properly after a year.

● **Ultraviolet-light air purifiers** supposedly kill germs by irradiating the air that passes through the HVAC system. The technology works well in hospitals and other large industrial applications, but residential UV purifiers are so much less powerful that they are essentially worthless.

Verdict: A total waste of money.

● **A hot water–circulating heating system** reduces the odds of respiratory problems by perhaps 50%, compared with forced-air heating systems—even if central air-conditioning is still used a few months of the year. Unfortunately, making this change in an existing home could cost tens of thousands of dollars.

Verdict: Switching to a water-circulating heating system is worth considering if you are remodeling or building a home and a family member suffers from serious respiratory problems.

Portable Air Cleaners

These do an effective job of removing particulates, such as pollen, from the air, but they will not prevent mold and bacteria from growing inside your home's central-air system.

Buying advice: Choose a model with a "Clean Air Delivery Rate" (CADR) of at least 100. Avoid those with electronic filters regardless of their CADRs, however. Not only do electronic filters become useless if not cleaned frequently, they often produce ozone, a lung irritant, so they can create respiratory problems. Also, check portable air cleaners' decibel rating before buying—you don't want one much over 50 decibels. Noisy portable air filters are a common complaint.

Window Air Conditioners

Window air-conditioner units tend to use filters rated MERV 3 or lower.

Buying advice: A company called WEB Products makes a MERV 7 "Washable Electrostatic Filter" specifically for window air conditioners. It's the best filter on the market for window units—though I recommend disposing of these filters each cooling season rather than washing and reusing them (800-875-3212, *www.webproducts.com*, search for "WRAC," $6.99 each).

Helpful Test

To determine whether better air filters and a duct cleaning will help any respiratory problems you have, wear an N95 filter mask (available at home-improvement stores and drugstores for about $1 each) for a few days whenever you are inside your home. If the mask helps you breathe easier, improved air filtration is likely to help, too.

How Whole-Health Care Can Help You Feel Great...Live Longer

Henri Roca, MD, medical director, Integrative Medicine Program at Greenwich Hospital in Connecticut. He is a diplomate of both the American Academy of Family Practice and the American Board of Holistic Medicine and is on the clinical faculty of Yale University School of Medicines and LSU School of Medicine in Louisiana.

Think of your health as a pot on the stove that's about to come to a boil. Conventional medicine would try to slam a lid on the pot and hold it down tight. That may work at first, but unless the heat is also turned down, the pressure under the lid will build up and the pot will boil over anyway. What alternative therapies try to do is reduce the intensity of the flame under the pot. In both cases, we're trying to keep the pot from boiling over.

The difference is that with integrative medicine, we're trying to keep that flame turned way down and keep it from bringing the pot to a boil at all.

This combination of conventional medicine and alternative treatments works so well that today many hospitals (including the one where I work) offer integrative medicine centers. When we incorporate alternative treatments, we're looking at ways to help people with certain lifestyle issues that are out of balance and will eventually cause illness. We're looking at the whole person—mind, body and spirit.

Creating Balance

Our goal is to bring balance back—instead of allowing an imbalance to continue until it develops into serious symptoms. Through poor eating habits, lack of exercise and exposure to chemicals (pesticides and added hormones) in the air we breathe, water we drink and food we eat, we put a huge burden on the body. By using integrative medicine, we can reduce that burden and help the body detoxify.

How it works: By supporting the liver, the kidneys and the intestines. If any of these organs don't function correctly, we will develop serious disease sooner or later.

Do you suffer from such common disorders as acid reflux, stomach ulcers, obesity, diabetes, menstrual irregularities, skin rashes, allergies, asthma or digestive problems? Many of my patients do. All those diagnoses are related, because the human system is a web of interactions and no single diagnosis can stand alone. Instead of giving someone three or four or 10 diagnoses with three or four or 10 pills to treat them, we work to bring that entire system back into balance. *Treatments I use include…*

- **Herbal product.**
- **Biofeedback or other types of mind-body techniques, such as visualization.**
- **Meditation or deep breathing techniques.**
- **Traditional Chinese medicine, such as acupuncture.**
- **Homeopathy.**

There's no single best treatment that works for everyone. We look closely at the patient as an individual and choose treatments based on what is most likely to be effective for him/her. *But there are some important general guidelines that may apply to you…*

Chronic Diseases

When we have situations in life that impact our bodies significantly, such as chronic disease or stress, our nutrients are used up very quickly. We need to replenish them—if we don't, then chronic diseases worsen or we develop new disease.

Examples…

- **Depression often occurs after a person has been under significant stress that continues over a long period.** Under these circumstances, by replenishing basic nutrients necessary to create natural mood-regulating chemicals in the brain, we can potentially diminish depression symptoms. We don't automatically put any depressed person on an antidepressant medication. Sometimes we do so in conjunction with vitamin therapy, but the goal is to eventually lower the medication dosage or stop it altogether.

- **High blood pressure (hypertension) can be caused by a magnesium deficiency.** In that case, we might prescribe medication to lower blood pressure but also recommend a diet with more magnesium (or use magnesium supplements).

When to Choose Alternative Therapies

Conventional practitioners worry that by using alternative methods, some patients will end up delaying treatment until the condition has worsened…or even until it's "too late" in the case of life-threatening conditions. That's a valid concern, but rarely do I ever tell anyone that it's appropriate to use only conventional medicine or only an alternative approach.

Emergencies: When there's a truly dangerous medical condition—for example, blood pressure that's so high that the patient is in serious danger of having a heart attack or stroke…or a serious bacterial infection needing antibiotics…or cancer that might respond to chemotherapy, radiation and/or surgery—then conventional medicine, through the emergency room if necessary, is definitely the way to go.

But what if your blood pressure has just begun to increase? Then you could choose standard blood pressure medication to protect yourself from complications and worsening disease...and use an integrative approach to rebalance the system and turn off the fire. The ultimate goal is to reduce the medication dose or to stop the drugs completely.

In the case of a life-threatening illness, such as cancer, alternative therapies are not cures. Instead, integrative medicine focuses on supporting the person through the conventional treatment process and can be very effective in helping with the pain, fatigue and nausea associated with chemotherapy and radiation treatments. Similarly, integrative medicine can be very helpful for treating chronic diseases, such as multiple sclerosis, where fatigue is a big problem. Integrative medical doctors are board-certified by the American Board of Holistic Medicine. You can find a doctor near you by checking its Web site, *www.ho listicboard.org.*

Relax!

The most difficult thing for my patients to do is to prioritize their lives so that they have time for a different kind of therapy— relaxing. Yes, relaxing can be therapeutic. But it doesn't mean watching TV or reading a book. Sitting in a place of silence and meditating induces true relaxation.

Why this is so important: Focused relaxation reduces stress, and if there is one single thing I see that causes a tremendous amount of disease, it's stress, whether related to work, family, money or some combination.

Because of stress, people make poor diet choices, drink too much alcohol, take illegal drugs and don't get enough exercise. Stress is the underpinning of the current epidemic of obesity, among other health problems. By making the time for focused relaxation, you can reduce your stress level—and improved health will follow.

A Top Doc's Natural Cures

Brent A. Bauer, MD, director of the complementary and integrative medicine program and a physician in the department of internal medicine at Mayo Clinic, Rochester, Minnesota. He is professor of medicine in the College of Medicine, Mayo Clinic, and medical editor of Mayo Clinic *EmbodyHealth* newsletter. He is also medical editor of *Mayo Clinic Book of Alternative Medicine* (Time).

There are hundreds of supplements and health foods to choose from. Most haven't been thoroughly studied in large quantitative studies, but a few have been tested and found to work effectively— and, in many cases, with fewer side effects than drugs.

If you are interested in using any of these natural approaches, first talk with your doctor. He/she can help you make informed decisions based on your unique health needs.

Caution: If you are already taking a prescription medicine, don't stop taking it without your doctor's OK.

Here, some of the best natural remedies that the medical community has found effective...

• **Green tea,** which reduces heart disease and cancer risk.

Green tea is a highly concentrated source of antioxidants, particularly polyphenols, such as epigallocatechin gallate (EGCG). Most studies show that people who drink three or more cups of green tea daily are between 25% and 35% less likely to develop heart disease than those who don't drink tea.

Tea (both green and black) also seems to protect against a variety of cancers. Researchers at University of Minnesota School of Public Health tracked 35,369 postmenopausal women. Those who drank two or more cups of tea daily reduced their risk for digestive-tract cancers by about 68% and their risk for urinary-tract cancers by about 40%.

Asians, who typically drink much more green tea than Americans, often have significantly lower cancer rates. It's possible that substances in tea protect DNA from carcinogenic changes and/or promote the death of cancer cells. Also, people who drink a lot of tea aren't drinking as much soda and other unhealthy beverages.

Typical dosage: Three or more cups daily. Green tea also is available in extract form.

• **Probiotics,** which help prevent infections, including colds and flu.

The good bacteria that inhabit the large and small intestines do more than aid digestion—they play an important role in immunity. These beneficial organisms, known as probiotics, are thought to alter the signaling mechanisms in the intestinal wall and "switch off" inflammation throughout the body. This is important for preventing infections, including colds and flu.

In an 80-day Swedish study, volunteers given daily doses of the probiotic *Lactobacillus reuteri* were less than half as likely to require sick days (for either respiratory or gastrointestinal illnesses) as those who were taking placebos. A study of children in day-care settings showed a similar benefit.

There are many different types (and subtypes) of probiotics. The ones that have been most studied include the Lactobacillus and *Bifidobacterium* organisms.

Typical dosage: Most people find that food-based sources, such as the Activia and DanActive brands of yogurts and beverages, are a convenient way to try probiotics. You also can get probiotic supplements—follow directions on the label.

• **Ginger,** which fights nausea from motion sickness and chemotherapy.

A study funded by the National Cancer Institute found that patients undergoing chemotherapy experienced 40% less nausea when they took ginger. It also reduces motion sickness.

Typical dosage: The optimal dose isn't known. People sometimes chew a slice of fresh ginger. Ginger candies and ginger teas may work. Most ginger ales don't have enough ginger.

• **Saint John's wort,** an herb that eases depression.

Some studies indicate that this herb is as effective for mild-to-moderate depression as prescription antidepressants.

Recent finding: A large meta-analysis, which combined the results from previous studies, found that Saint John's wort also may be effective for severe depression.

Saint John's wort is less likely than prescription antidepressants to cause side effects, although some patients may experience stomach upset, dizziness, dry mouth, anxiety and/or sexual dysfunction.

Warning: Don't use Saint John's wort and a prescription antidepressant at the same time. It may interact with other drugs, such as *warfarin*, the heart drug *digoxin* (Digitalis) and birth control pills. Saint John's wort may also, in rare instances, cause a rash when the skin is exposed to the sun.

Typical dosage: Most studies used 900 milligrams (mg) to 1,800 mg daily.

Mayo Clinic's Top 10 Complementary Therapies

Amit Sood, MD, associate professor of medicine at Mayo Clinic College of Medicine and director of research at the Complementary and Integrative Medicine Program at Mayo Clinic, both in Rochester, Minnesota. He is a contributor to the *Mayo Clinic Book of Alternative Medicine* (Time).

Dozens of US hospitals and major medical centers now offer complementary treatments in addition to conventional medical care*—and some of these therapies are covered by health insurance.

Problem: With so many conflicting claims being made regarding complementary therapies, how do doctors at these institutions decide which to recommend to the patients they treat? *At the world-renowned Mayo Clinic, the following four criteria are used...*

• **Is it safe?** If a complementary treatment is completely safe, then it may be worth trying, even if its effectiveness has not been proven definitively by scientific studies.

• **Is it standardized?** Herbs and dietary supplements are subject to limited regulatory oversight by the FDA. Therefore, these products frequently are not standardized to contain a consistent level of ingredients, potency and purity. Some herbs and dietary supplements do provide benefits, but you should work closely with a knowledgeable doctor when using them.

• **Does it meet a need that cannot be met by conventional medicine?** When it comes to stress, for example, conventional medicine includes treatments, such as anti-anxiety drugs or antidepressants, that potentially

*To learn more about complementary therapies, go to *www.nccam.nih.gov*, the Web site of the National Center for Complementary and Alternative Medicine.

can help people. But such medications often have side effects and may not be suitable for long-term use. Complementary therapies, such as yoga, massage and meditation, can help relieve stress without the risk for serious side effects.

• **Does it positively affect not only patients, but also those with whom they interact?** The calming influence of several complementary treatments, such as meditation and music therapy, promotes a feeling of relaxation and well-being that helps bring harmony to one's interactions with family and friends. Positive, supportive relationships, in turn, are believed to help speed recovery from many types of illness.

Here is an alphabetical listing of Mayo Clinic's top 10 complementary treatments—and the research that supports their use...

Best Treatments

1. Acupuncture. In this treatment from traditional Chinese medicine, acupuncturists insert thin needles into strategic, energy-balancing points on the body. Acupuncture can prevent and treat nausea and vomiting and help relieve many types of pain, including that from osteoarthritis, low back pain, neck pain, headaches and postsurgical pain. Patients who receive acupuncture typically receive up to 12 treatments, usually given once or twice a week.

Standout scientific evidence: German researchers tracked more than 3,000 patients with hip or knee osteoarthritis and found that those receiving acupuncture experienced significantly more pain relief than those who did not receive acupuncture treatments.

2. Guided imagery. Patients imagine a beautiful, soothing environment, such as a warm beach. Guided imagery, also referred to as visualization, helps reduce anxiety in patients who become claustrophobic during magnetic resonance imaging (MRI) scans, who are having outpatient surgery without general anesthesia or who have been diagnosed with a life-threatening disease, such as cancer.

Standout scientific evidence: In a study conducted at the University of Akron in Ohio, a group of 53 women receiving radiation therapy for breast cancer either listened to guided imagery tapes once a day or did not. The women listening to the tapes felt more comfortable and less anxious, particularly during the first three weeks of treatment.

3. Hypnosis. The patient is led into a state of deep relaxation and focused attention by either a hypnotherapist or an instructional audio (self-hypnosis), and verbal suggestions are made to help relieve anxiety, pain, tension headaches and insomnia.

Standout scientific evidence: Doctors at the Mount Sinai School of Medicine in New York City analyzed 20 studies on hypnosis and surgical patients. In 89% of cases, surgical patients who were hypnotized had less pain, used less pain medication and recovered faster. (See page 328 for more information.)

4. Massage. A massage therapist manipulates the body's soft tissue—muscle, skin and tendons—using fingertips, hands and fists. Massage treats anxiety and low back pain and improves postsurgical healing.

Standout scientific evidence: Studies conducted at the University of Miami's Touch Research Institute show that massage can help relieve back pain and strengthen the immune system in women with breast cancer by increasing levels of natural disease-fighting cells.

5. Meditation. Attention is focused on breathing and/or on a word, phrase or sound (mantra), leading to a more relaxed body and calmer mind. Doctors at the Mayo Clinic use meditation to treat patients with anxiety and high blood pressure and to help people quit smoking without medication.

Standout scientific evidence: An analysis of 20 studies on meditation found that this treatment could help patients cope with epilepsy, premenstrual syndrome (PMS), menopausal symptoms, autoimmune disease and anxiety during cancer treatment.

6. Music therapy. Many complementary medical centers employ music therapists. However, you can use music therapy on your own by listening to soothing music or your favorite tunes.

Standout scientific evidence: At Abbott Northwestern Hospital in Minneapolis, a study of 86 patients recovering from heart surgery showed that those receiving music therapy experienced less anxiety and pain.

7. Spinal manipulation. Practiced by chiropractors, osteopaths (medical doctors whose training allows them to correct structural problems in the musculoskeletal system) and physical therapists, this hands-on technique adjusts the spine to properly align the vertebrae with muscles, joints and nerves. Spinal manipulation is an accepted medical practice for low back pain, but the evidence supporting its use for other medical problems is somewhat conflicting.

Standout scientific evidence: At the University of California, Los Angeles, School of Public Health, a study of 681 patients with low back pain showed that chiropractic care was as effective as medical care, including painkilling drugs, in relieving discomfort.

8. Spirituality. For some, this means religious observance, prayer or faith in a "higher being." For others, spirituality can be found through a deep appreciation of nature or art or participation in a secular community. Both praying for self and others have been shown to be therapeutic.

Standout scientific evidence: Researchers in Virginia who conducted an analysis of 16 studies on illness and "religious intervention"—praying or attending religious services—found that it can decrease the length of hospital stays and fever in patients with severe infections...increase immune function...help relieve rheumatoid arthritis symptoms...reduce anxiety...and improve outcomes in people with heart disease.

9. Tai chi. This gentle exercise, derived from Chinese martial arts, consists of a series of defined postures and movements performed slowly and gracefully. Medically, it is used to improve balance in older people who are prone to falls.

Standout scientific evidence: In a study of 278 elderly people at Vrije University in Amsterdam, The Netherlands, those who performed tai chi three times a week for six months had 50% fewer falls and fewer injury-causing falls.

10. Yoga. These stretching postures and breathing exercises, which originated in India, help calm body and mind. Yoga is particularly effective for stress relief, low back pain, carpal tunnel syndrome, osteoarthritis, anxiety and depression.

Standout scientific evidence: In a study conducted at All India Institute of Medical Sciences in New Delhi, 98 people with heart disease or diabetes who practiced the postures and breathing techniques of yoga had significant reductions in total cholesterol and blood sugar.

How Depression Can Make You Sick...and Vice Versa

Charles Raison, PhD, associate professor in the mind-body program, department of psychiatry and behavioral sciences at Emory University in Atlanta.

Esther M. Sternberg, MD, director of the integrative neural immune program at the National Institutes of Health in Rockville, Maryland. Dr. Sternberg is author of *The Balance Within: The Science of Connecting Health and Emotions* (W. H. Freeman).

It is an unfortunate double jeopardy—being sick can make you depressed...and being depressed can make you sick. New research shows that many chronic illnesses, including heart disease, diabetes and osteoporosis, have this two-way connection to depression.

Consequences can be grave. In a recent study, heart attack patients who were depressed had a two- to fourfold increased risk of dying within five years, compared with heart attack patients who were not depressed. In a global study from the World Health Organization involving 245,000 people, those with a chronic illness fared far worse if they also were depressed.

One in eight women experiences depression at some point, compared with only one in 16 men—a gender discrepancy due primarily to hormonal differences. That means it is especially important for women who are depressed to get regular checkups to screen for chronic illness...and for women who have a chronic disease to be alert for signs of depression. Self-help strategies and/or professional care can protect both your mental and physical well-being.

Explaining the Connection

Scientists are trying to discover how disease and depression interact. *What the evidence suggests...*

How disease can lead to depression: Common sense tells us that a woman with a chronic illness might feel sad—but physiologically speaking, the explanation may involve an overactive immune system.

● **Theory.** Inflammation is part of the body's normal healing process...but if the immune system fails to turn off the inflammatory mechanism at the appropriate time, inflammation becomes long-lasting and widespread. This can alter metabolism and damage blood vessels, bones and other body tissues, bringing on a variety of chronic illnesses and disrupting the balance of neurotransmitters (brain chemicals) that affect mood, triggering depression.

Recent studies show that the following conditions may be linked to depression—cancer...heart disease...diabetes...fibromyalgia (a syndrome of widespread pain)...psoriasis (patches of scaly, red skin)...rheumatoid arthritis (an autoimmune disease)...and stroke.

How depression can lead to disease: It is logical that a depressed woman may not take care of herself well enough to guard against illness, but this is only a partial explanation. Physiologically, depression is linked to high levels of stress hormones—which in turn may raise blood pressure and cholesterol levels...promote accumulation of harmful abdominal fat...impair digestion...and hamper immune function. Along with depression comes increased production of proteins called cytokines, which cause widespread inflammation. This can trigger changes in the brain that reduce its resistance to dementia.

Recent studies suggest that people who suffer from depression may be at increased risk for Alzheimer's disease...asthma... breast cancer...cardiovascular disease... diabetes...gastric ulcer...high blood pressure...osteoarthritis...osteoporosis...and thyroid disease.

Defense Against Depression

Getting relief from depression can help prevent chronic illness or make an existing illness easier to deal with. Yet even though up to 90% of depressed people can be treated effectively, only one in three seeks treatment. *To overcome depression...*

● **Develop realistic expectations.** You may pessimistically assume that your physical prognosis is worse than it really is...or you may be overly optimistic, then feel crushed if your progress is slow. Either attitude can negatively affect your motivation to participate actively in your own physical recovery.

What helps: Be proactive. Write down all of your questions about your condition, treatment and prognosis, and review them with your doctor. Use the Internet to find a national association that addresses your illness, or ask your doctor if he/she knows of one. Take medication as prescribed, and keep all of your doctor appointments.

● **Eat foods rich in omega-3 fatty acids.** Omega-3s reduce inflammation and aid neurotransmitter function. Research suggests that omega-3s may be better absorbed from food than from supplements.

What helps: Have at least four servings weekly of omega-3–rich foods.

Good choices: Two tablespoons of ground flaxseeds or flaxseed oil...one-quarter cup of walnuts...three ounces of herring, salmon or sturgeon...one cup of navy or kidney beans, cabbage, cauliflower, squash or leafy green vegetables.

● **Stay active.** Exercise releases endorphins, brain chemicals that lift mood and block pain.

What helps: Don't tell yourself, I feel too lousy to work out. Ask your doctor or physical therapist to recommend exercises that you can do—such as water aerobics, which is easy on joints and bones…or slow stationary cycling, which won't overtax the heart.

● **Strengthen social ties.** You may hesitate to tell loved ones how down your illness makes you feel for fear of burdening them—yet emotional support is vital to healing.

What helps: Remember that your illness affects your family and friends, too. Everyone will feel better if emotions and concerns are discussed honestly.

● **Know when to get professional help.** Many people incorrectly assume that depression is an unavoidable part of physical illness, so they don't seek treatment.

What helps: Learn the symptoms of depression—sleeping too much or too little, unintended weight gain or loss, low energy, persistent sadness, frequent crying, irritability, feelings of hopelessness, poor concentration, low libido or lack of interest in daily activities. If you have any thoughts of suicide or if you experience two or more of the symptoms above for more than two weeks, tell your doctor.

● **Consider psychotherapy.** A form called cognitive behavioral therapy helps depressed patients replace negative beliefs and behaviors with positive ones.

What helps: Talk to a therapist experienced in treating depression linked to chronic illness. Ask your primary care physician to refer you to a mental-health professional who meets your needs.

● **Try natural nonprescription supplements.** Sold at health-food stores, these may relieve mild-to-moderate depression. If you use pharmaceutical antidepressants or other medications, get your doctor's approval before taking natural supplements to avoid possible adverse interactions.

What helps: Ask your doctor about appropriate dosages and usage guidelines for the following…

● **5-adenosylmethionine** (SAMe)

● **5-hydroxytryptophan** (5-HTP)

● **Saint John's wort**

● **Vitamin D.**

● **Consider pharmaceutical antidepressants.** These pills work by slowing the removal of neurotransmitters from the brain synapses.

What helps: Antidepressants often are very effective, though it may take trial and error to find one that works for you and does not cause side effects (such as nausea, weight gain, drowsiness and low libido).

Useful: Ask your doctor about the *cytochrome P450* blood test, which helps identify genetic factors that influence your response to certain antidepressants.

Get Hypnotized, Get Healthier

Benjamin Kligler, MD, MPH, associate professor of family and social medicine at Albert Einstein College of Medicine, vice chair of the department of integrative medicine at Beth Israel Medical Center and research director of the Continuum Center for Health and Healing, an integrative medicine practice, all in New York City. *www.healthandhealingny.org.* Dr. Kligler, who is certified in Ericksonian hypnotherapy, is author of *Curriculum in Complementary Therapies* (Montefiore Medical Center).

Hear the word "hypnosis" and you may think of a stage show—a guy in a turban dangling a pocket watch and making you cluck like a chicken or behave in some other silly and uncharacteristic way.

This is not at all what modern hypnotherapy is like.

Reality: Ericksonian hypnosis (named after American psychiatrist Milton Erickson, who pioneered the techniques used today) is a collaboration between you and a trained health-care practitioner that can help you achieve specific health goals.

Hypnotherapy does not use commands, such as, "Now you will do what I say." Instead, the practitioner offers gentle, nonauthoritative suggestions when you are in a highly relaxed state. The idea behind hypnosis is that there is no separation between body and mind—so you can access the healing potential of the unconscious mind to move yourself in a healthful direction. Unlike classical hypnosis, which works on only a small subset of highly suggestible people, Ericksonian hypnosis can help almost anyone—though it is most effective for those who are motivated and accepting of treatment.

Help from Hypnosis

Research shows that hypnotherapy helps treat a variety of physical and psychological problems, including...

- **Anxiety**
- **Chronic pain**
- **Insomnia**
- **Irritable bowel syndrome** (recurring bouts of diarrhea and/or constipation)
- **Menopausal hot flashes**
- **Nausea**
- **Overeating**
- **Phobias, such as claustrophobia or fear of flying**
- **Sugar addiction**
- **Tobacco addiction.**

Examples: One study found that a single 15-minute hypnosis session significantly decreased pain and anxiety in women undergoing breast cancer surgery—and, for unknown reasons, also shortened the procedure time in the operating room. In another study, 68% of women with menopausal hot flashes showed reduced symptom severity and frequency, as well as decreased insomnia, after hypnosis.

How it works: Everybody has chatter in the conscious mind that can get in the way of healthful behaviors, such as controlling consumption of sweets or not panicking in an elevator. Hypnosis quiets the conscious mind so your unconscious can come in and say, "Wait a minute, we're trying to be healthier here"—making it easier to turn down that donut or stay calm in the elevator. Hypnosis relieves physical symptoms, such as pain or hot flashes, by reducing stress hormones that contribute to physical ailments.

Hypnosis by itself does not cure the problem—rather, it creates a heightened state of awareness that opens the way for your own willingness to bring about the desired changes. Hypnotherapy can focus on symptom reduction...strategies for coping with stress...resolution of personal problems...and/or personality development.

What to Expect
In Treatment

Typically, the first session with a hypnotherapist lasts one hour. During this visit, the practitioner asks questions about your particular problem—when symptoms began, other treatments you have tried, how the issue affects your life and stress level. Because hypnotherapy is highly individualized, this information helps determine the most appropriate treatment for you. Hypnosis may or may not be done during this first session.

A course of hypnotherapy generally ranges from three to eight sessions, with each weekly hypnosis session lasting about 30 to 40 minutes. Sometimes patients return months or years later for a "booster" session.

During a session, you sit on a comfortable chair or couch in a quiet and softly lit room. Usually your eyes are closed, but you can hear everything around you.

Speaking in a soothing voice, the practitioner leads you into an induction, a trancelike state of deep relaxation. One common technique is the body scan. The practitioner asks you to focus on your feet, relaxing the muscles there. Next you focus on feeling the relaxed sensation in your ankles, your calves, your knees. Over five to 10 minutes, the practitioner guides you to relax your entire body.

While you are in a state of deep relaxation, the practitioner makes therapeutic suggestions, prompting your unconscious mind to deal more effectively with your health issue. The practitioner does not say something like, "You will not be afraid of the airplane," but rather, "You may find yourself feeling much more relaxed on the airplane than you have in the past." Suggestions are tailored to the specific problem and person. The process generally is pleasant and completely safe. You do not reveal personal secrets or do anything that you don't want to do.

After the therapeutic suggestions, the practitioner typically brings you back to your normal state of consciousness by saying, "I'm going to be quiet now, and over the next few minutes, you can gradually bring yourself back to the room." You may or may not consciously remember what was said to you during hypnosis…you may come to the end of a session thinking that it lasted just a few minutes, when in reality it lasted half an hour.

Over the following few days or weeks, you may notice that your symptoms are improving—for instance, you sleep better, feel less nauseous or fearful, or find it easier to resist cravings for cigarettes.

Hypnotherapy Homework

The practitioner may assign you some simple self-hypnosis techniques to do on your own. For instance, if you are seeking to change a habit, such as compulsive overeating, self-hypnosis helps you handle cravings as they arise. These techniques typically include physical strategies, such as pressing two fingers together as a reminder of how to reach the relaxation state…or taking a series of deep breaths while focusing on a certain calming image or phrase.

For a physical problem, such as irritable bowel syndrome, the practitioner may tape-record an in-office hypnosis session and have you listen to it at home. As you reexperience the state of deep relaxation again and again, not only your mind but also your entire body benefits—making your gut less susceptible to digestive upsets.

Finding a practitioner: In addition to being a licensed doctor, psychologist or social worker, a qualified practitioner should have about one year of hypnotherapy training. To ensure that your practitioner has met educational standards and training requirements in clinical hypnosis, you may want to verify that he/she is certified through the American Society of Clinical Hypnosis (630-980-4740, *www.asch.net*).

Hypnotherapy costs about $125 to $300 per session. Although many insurance companies do not cover hypnosis per se, you may be able to collect under a mental-health benefit if your psychotherapist or integrative physician includes hypnosis among the treatments offered.

Coming to Terms with Cancer

Anne Coscarelli, PhD, director of the Simms/Mann–UCLA Center for Integrative Oncology at the Jonsson Comprehensive Cancer Center at the University of California, Los Angeles. Her articles on coping with cancer can be found at *www.cancerresources.mednet.ucla.edu* (click on "Information Resources" and then "Archives: Newsletters").

Emotional issues can profoundly affect quality of life before, during and after cancer treatment.

Helpful: Knowing what to expect at each stage…understanding your reactions…and taking steps to effectively handle the psychological upheaval.

Dealing with the Diagnosis

A woman diagnosed with cancer may struggle with intense anxiety…a sense of being betrayed by her body…guilt about lifestyle choices or missing warning signs…uncertainty as to her future…and fear about the effects on her family.

● **Beware of information overload.** Learning about your illness may help you feel in control, but being bombarded with data can be overwhelming and/or misleading. Your first source should be your doctor and his/her colleagues. Cancer encompasses more than 250 different diseases, so general information from friends may not apply to you.

Much of the information online is inaccurate. Stick to reliable Web sites, such as those of the American Cancer Society (*www.cancer.org*), National Cancer Institute (*www.cancer.gov*) and major cancer centers. If your anxiety increases when using the Web, take a break.

Do not feel obliged to respond positively to unsolicited advice. Select a standard courteous response, such as, "I appreciate your concern, but my doctor and I already have a plan"…or "I prefer not to hear stories about other cancer patients."

● **Avail yourself of support.** Many hospitals offer free or low-cost support groups and/or counseling from psychologists or social workers who specialize in oncology. Try them—you may learn useful coping strategies. A support group also offers the opportunity to share with others the strategies that work for you. Cancer threatens a person's sense of mastery. By helping others, you regain a feeling of control.

● **Be open with your family.** A cancer diagnosis disrupts the whole family. Your close relatives will feel anxious about the future. With youngsters, don't pretend everything is fine—they need to know that you will tell the truth—but keep it simple.

Example: "Grandma has a lump in her breast. The doctors say that surgery will help make her better. Her medicine makes her tired, so everyone needs to pitch in."

● **Establish a communications point person.** Responding to calls and questions from friends and extended family takes energy you need to conserve. Designate one person to pass on information via phone or e-mail or to set up a Web site to post news about your progress.

● **Reframe how you talk to yourself.** When you catch yourself worrying obsessively, identify and dispute irrational thoughts.

Examples: If you can't stop thinking, "I'm going to die," remind yourself, "There are more than 10 million cancer survivors in the US—I'm likely to be one of them." When you find yourself saying, "My family and friends have no idea what I'm going through," remind yourself, "They may not share my exact experience, but they have had other traumas that help them relate to mine."

Relief During Treatment

At this phase, cancer patients need practical ways to cope with fatigue and other side effects…plus psychological tools to handle stress.

• **Let people help.** Develop a list of tasks that need doing. When someone offers to help, suggest a task from the list.

Examples: Shopping for groceries…preparing meals…picking up prescriptions…helping with housework. Remind yourself, "My friends want to feel useful."

• **Don't rush through your sadness.** Losing part of your body to surgery can cause deep grief. So can side effects of treatment, such as losing your hair. Acknowledge and allow feelings of loss. Talk to people who can accept your emotions without launching into problem-solving mode. For this, a support group can be especially helpful.

• **Make time for intimacy.** It is not unusual for libido to disappear for a while as a side effect of treatment or from emotional depletion.

Remember: The most important part of intimacy is communication. Tell your partner, "Even though I'm not interested in sex now, I do want to be close to you." Explore ways of being intimate that feel comfortable to you both. If you and your partner have a hard time discussing these issues, consider couples therapy.

• **Take "vacations" from cancer.** Find simple, nonfatiguing ways to have fun.

Examples: Play board games with your family…drive to a nearby park and enjoy the natural surroundings…order pizza and invite a few friends over to watch a DVD… take a bath by candlelight.

Serenity in Survivorship

Cancer is understandably in the foreground of your awareness during diagnosis and treatment. The goal after treatment is to move it to the background.

• **Develop a fear-of-recurrence plan.** Every new ache may leave you wondering, "Is it cancer again?" Ask your doctor what symptoms of recurrence you should report immediately…and how long to wait before calling if you develop a new problem. Then, instead of ruminating, you can assure yourself, "I'm noting the date I first felt this pain in my leg. If it's still here after three days, I'll call the doctor."

Thoughts of cancer may move to the foreground again when you have a follow-up test or on the anniversary of your diagnosis. Compose statements you can use to calm yourself.

Examples: "The doctor said it is highly unlikely I will ever see this cancer again"… "My annual blood test is due, and that is why I am fearful. Every year it will get easier."

• **Appreciate the person you have become.** Many cancer survivors gain greater appreciation for life…stronger spirituality…deeper relationships with family and friends…more empathy…a fulfilling reordering of priorities…and a gratifying ability to live in the moment. No one would choose to have cancer in order to gain these benefits—but recognizing them helps you develop a sense of wholeness and peace.

12

Recovering from Cancer

America's Top Cancer Hospitals

Carey Gold, founder of The Health Advisory, a New York City–based medical consulting service that provides personalized medical advocacy to individuals faced with serious diagnoses, as well as undiagnosed symptoms, *www. thehealthadvisory.com.* Mr. Gold works with people globally, enabling them to access the specific type of medical care that most closely matches their health-care goals—including conventional, integrative and alternative medicine.

If you or a loved one has been diagnosed with a serious medical condition such as cancer, finding the right care can be a matter of life and death.

To identify the leading medical institutions in the country for cancer, we spoke with Carey Gold, a medical advocate who has provided expert guidance to individuals and families faced with serious medical diagnoses for the past 20 years.

Important: The "best" institution for one patient may be different for someone else. It's crucial to consider the individual patient's specific condition, medical history and personal needs.

Consider seeking care, or a second opinion, at one of these excellent institutions if your community lacks physicians who are specialized and experienced in your diagnosis, or if your diagnosis is in question.

Before traveling, obtain copies of all your pertinent medical records to take with you (or double-check to make sure that they have been forwarded). Also check with your insurance carrier about coverage and precertifications. If you are unable to travel, many of the institutions offer second opinions by mail and/or telephone.

Mr. Gold's recommendations for the top cancer hospitals…*

Dana-Farber/Brigham and Women's Cancer Center, Boston, 877-332-4294, *www.dfbw cc.org.* One of the outstanding teaching institutions of Harvard Medical School, Dana-Farber offers a roster of subspecialists covering common and rare types of cancer ranging from Hodgkin's disease and lung cancer to skull-base tumors.

Johns Hopkins Medicine, The Sidney Kimmel Comprehensive Cancer Center, Baltimore, 410-955-5000, *www.hopkinsmedicine.org/ kimmel_cancer_center.* While this is a large

*When seeking cancer care, whenever possible, it's wise to look for one of the 40 institutions (such as those listed here) that have been designated by the National Cancer Institute as a Comprehensive Cancer Center.

Postsurgery Help for Prostate Cancer Patients

One year after surgery to remove the prostate, 44% of patients studied at the University of Michigan reported worse-than-expected sexual function...and 46% reported worse-than-expected urinary continence.

Self-defense: Consider pelvic floor and penile rehab for the recovery of urinary and sexual function.

Daniela Wittmann, MSW, sexual health coordinator, prostate cancer survivorship program, University of Michigan, Ann Arbor, and leader of a study of 152 men with prostate cancer, published in *Journal of Urology.*

medical institution, the doctors work hard—though not always successfully—to humanize the patient experience. The pathology department is among the best in the US—some say the world—often being called on to offer highly valued second opinions on biopsies.

MD Anderson Cancer Center, The University of Texas, Houston, 877-632-6789, *www. mdanderson.org.* As the largest US cancer center (based on number of patient beds), MD Anderson has many of the assets—and a few of the liabilities—that result from sheer size. Subspecialists in most common and rare cancer types practice here.

Memorial Sloan-Kettering Cancer Center, New York City, 800-525-2225, *www.mskcc. org.* Memorial Sloan-Kettering has some of the country's leading physicians in medical and surgical oncology, hematology and research. Most patients speak favorably of inpatient experiences at Memorial Sloan-Kettering, but outpatients may experience delays and long waiting times.

Other excellent options: Mayo Clinic Cancer Center, Rochester, Minnesota...Duke Cancer Institute, Durham, North Carolina

...University of California, Los Angeles, Jonsson Comprehensive Cancer Center... University of Pittsburgh Cancer Institute.

■ ■ ■ ■

Complementary Therapies That Ease Cancer Treatment Side Effects

Roberta Lee, MD, vice chair of the department of integrative medicine at the Continuum Center for Health and Healing at Beth Israel Medical Center in New York City. She is also coeditor of *Integrative Medicine: Principles for Practice* (McGraw-Hill) and author of *The SuperStress Solution* (Random House). *www.superstresssolution.com*

A diagnosis of cancer presents a difficult battle not only with the disease, but also with the side effects of treatment. To destroy cancer, chemotherapy and radiation basically poison the body—which can bring on a host of miseries. Treatment may be essential, of course...but its side effects can be minimized with natural therapies that strengthen and support the body.

A study in *Breast Cancer Research and Treatment* found that 86% of newly diagnosed breast cancer patients incorporated complementary and alternative medicine (CAM) into their treatment. Roberta Lee, MD, is vice chair of the department of integrative medicine at the Continuum Center for Health and Healing at Beth Israel Medical Center. She recently talked about which CAM are most effective.

Dr. Lee recommended looking at life after cancer diagnosis as three separate phases—pretreatment, active treatment and posttreatment—because different CAM approaches work best during different phases.

Important: Before trying any complementary therapies, ask your oncologist which ones are safe and appropriate for you.

Before Treatment Begins

The focus is on ensuring that you will be as healthy and strong as possible, physically and emotionally, when treatment begins...

• **Work with a dietitian who specializes in oncology nutrition.** Visit *www.oncologynutrition.org* (a practice group of the American Dietetic Association) for a referral. Dr. Lee recommends lots of fruits and vegetables, whole grains and fish...low-fat organic chicken breast if desired...no red meat... and plenty of water.

• **Consider strengthening supplements.** Dr. Lee suggests folic acid and vitamin B-12, which help with proper cellular division and tissue recovery...vitamin D, which is good for immune regulation, bone health and mood...and probiotics, which help optimize immune function and reduce production of cancer-promoting chemicals. Ask your doctor about dosages.

• **Learn relaxation techniques.** An analysis published in *Psycho-Oncology* found that, when learned prior to rather than during cancer treatment, relaxation techniques were significantly more effective at reducing anxiety. Studies show that progressive muscle relaxation and guided imagery can improve cancer treatment–related nausea, pain, depression and anxiety. Practice a relaxation technique for 15 to 20 minutes daily, Dr. Lee suggests.

• **Exercise appropriately.** Gentle movements (simple stretches, leisurely walks) help you stay calm and centered. As for vigorous workouts, listen to your body—this is not the time to exhaust yourself.

• **If you work outside the home, plan ahead.** Calculating how long a leave you can afford and making arrangements now for your duties to be covered in your absence will give you less to worry about during treatment and ease your transition back to work afterward.

During Treatment

The primary consideration now is to avoid any CAM therapies that might lessen the effectiveness of your cancer treatment, Dr. Lee emphasizes, so your doctor may instruct you to discontinue certain herbs and supplements. *However, the following CAM approaches generally are safe during cancer treatment...*

• **Try acupuncture to minimize hair loss.** Chemotherapy drugs attack cells that are in the process of reproducing—but the drugs can't distinguish between rapidly dividing cancer cells and normal cells. In the body, hair follicle cells are among those that multiply fastest, which is why many patients experience hair loss. Acupuncture helps stimulate hair growth at a cellular level and reduces the stress that can exacerbate hair loss, Dr. Lee says.

Bonus: Acupuncture can ease chemo-related dry mouth.

• **Drink herbal teas for digestive woes.** Because digestive tract cells also multiply rapidly, chemo patients often develop gastrointestinal troubles. Dr. Lee suggests drinking chamomile tea, ginger tea and/or slippery elm tea as needed to reduce nausea and help smooth over any ulcerations in the intestinal tract. To ease cramping, try fennel tea.

• **For nerve damage, consider glutamine.** Ask your doctor about taking this amino acid to relieve tingling, burning or numbness from chemo-induced neuropathy.

• **Soothe skin with massage.** Skin exposed to radiation treatment often becomes sensitive, warm and red, as if sunburned. For relief, Dr. Lee suggests trying gentle massage with oils...acupressure...reiki (an energy healing technique in which the practitioner's hands are placed on or above certain spots on the patient's body)...or reflexology (massage of pressure points on the feet). To find a practitioner who works with cancer patients, check the Society for Oncology Massage (*www.s4om.org*).

• **Make each bite count.** You probably won't feel like eating much during treatment, so focus on foods that are easy to digest and nutritionally dense, such as protein shakes, soups and whole-grain breads. Avoid high-fat, spicy or acidic foods likely to aggravate nausea.

• **Do gentle yoga.** An analysis published in *Cancer Control* linked yoga to improvements in sleep quality, mood, physical function and overall quality of life.

• **Ease emotional distress.** Teas made with valerian, chamomile or hops flowers are calming, as are meditation and massage. Also consider hypnosis, which can help you process and release fear.

Referrals: American Society of Clinical Hypnosis (630-980-4740...*www.asch.net*, click on "Public" and "Member Referral Service").

After Treatment

Once chemo and radiation are over, attention shifts to restoring your health...

• **Have your doctor assess your nutrient levels.** Chemotherapy can deplete nutrients... blood tests can reveal whether a special diet and/or supplementation is appropriate to support your recovery. Ask your doctor and/or dietitian about magnesium...vitamin D...folic acid...and vitamin B-12, which, in addition to the aforementioned benefits, helps with mood and memory. Also discuss milk thistle, which helps your liver get rid of lingering toxins from chemotherapy.

• **To encourage hair growth, continue with acupuncture.** Folic acid and vitamin B-12 also can help with this, as can zinc and biotin, Dr. Lee says. Ask your physician about dosages.

• **As strength returns, gradually increase physical activity.** Dr. Lee suggests tai chi, Pilates and yoga, which are not too taxing.

Benefits for recovery: Exercise relieves stress, fortifies your body against further illness and improves overall well-being—all of which make it easier to get on with your life.

■ ■ ■ ■

Thrive as a Cancer Survivor

Mark A. Stengler, NMD, naturopathic medical doctor and leading authority on the practice of alternative and integrated medicine. Dr. Stengler is author of the *Health Revelations* newsletter, author of *The Natural Physician's Healing Therapies* (Bottom Line Books), founder and medical director of the Stengler Center for Integrative Medicine, Encinitas, California, and adjunct associate clinical professor at the National College of Natural Medicine in Portland, Oregon. *http://markstengler.com*

"Cancer survivor" is the title everyone diagnosed with this terrible disease hopes to own—and many do. According to the Centers for Disease Control and Prevention, the number of people who survive cancer has been steadily mounting since the mid-seventies, but the reality is that people who've survived cancer often have remnant health challenges, caused either by the disease or the treatment.

Once treatment is over, many people feel alone, no longer getting the close attention, advice and support they've received from their oncology team. In a survey done by the University of Pennsylvania Health System, 300 breast cancer survivors described their primary care doctors as "supportive and caring" but these same doctors were rated not very knowledgeable about how to guide the cancer survivors to rebuild their health following their chemotherapy, radiation and surgery.

Mark Stengler, NMD, shares his expertise on helping survivors thrive as they work through the damage left by the disease and/or treatment. *Specific challenges include...*

• **A build-up of cellular waste in remaining tissue,** due to the extreme toxicity of chemotherapy drugs. These powerful drugs kill healthy cells right along with the cancerous ones, leaving a residue that needs to be removed from the body.

• **Chemo depletes many important nutrient levels,** often causing digestive problems as the drugs destroy much of the good flora in the gastrointestinal tract in addition to the lining of the tract itself.

• **"Chemo brain" is a catch-all term for the common memory glitches,** lack of focus, mild cognitive impairment and fatigue that follow cancer treatment.

• **Peripheral neuropathy,** which causes tingling, burning and numbness in the feet and sometimes hands.

Diet and Supplements to Detox, Build Strength

Dr. Stengler advises taking control with both diet and natural supplements. These can help create a healthier cellular environment, clean out the damage done by treatment and rebuild digestive health. *Here are his dietary recommendations...*

• **Fermented foods.** Eat lots of miso, sauerkraut (the kind you buy at the health food store, not the deli), kefir and yogurt.

• **Water.** Drink 60 to 70 ounces daily to flush toxins from your system. (*Note:* Limit water with meals to eight ounces as more can dilute the effectiveness of stomach acid.)

• **Fruits and vegetables.** Enjoy these every day. If possible, buy organic, especially for soft fruits such as peaches, nectarines, strawberries and pears.

• **Avoid processed foods**—including sugar and white flour. This will eliminate refined sugars and unhealthy fats (trans fats,

partially hydrogenated or hydrogenated fats and interesterified fats), all of which can be harmful to health.

• **Eat plenty of healthy fats.** These are omega-3s (found in flaxseed, walnuts and fatty fish including salmon, herring and sardines), balanced by some omega-6s (in corn and soybeans).

• **Avoid tuna, king mackerel, shark, swordfish and others with potentially high levels of mercury.** You don't need to add yet more toxins to your system.

Many tissues in the body are challenged by chemotherapy. Dr. Stengler finds supplements helpful to strengthen health overall and detoxify the liver—which often endures the greatest insult. *He often prescribes the following...*

• **Antioxidants.** These can help rebuild health, potentially improve chemo outcomes and help to heal tissue damaged by radiation treatment. Among the supplements Dr. Stengler may prescribe—CoQ10...vitamin C...vitamin E mixed with tocopherol/tocotrienols and a carotenoid complex...vitamin D...lycopene and selenium.

• **Probiotics.** These can help balance the digestive system. Dr. Stengler typically prescribes one with a blend of *Lactobacillus acidophilus* and *Bifidobacterium bifidum.*

• **Greens-chlorella.** These deliver phytochemicals, which can be helpful to a system damaged by chemotherapy. Sun Chlorella is a brand he likes.

• **Wheatgrass.** It contains helpful vitamin K and chlorophyll antioxidants.

• **Milk thistle.** This herb helps support the liver and kidneys by protecting cells against damage caused by breakdown products of the cellular debris and chemo drugs.

• **NAC. N-acetylcysteine,** derived from a protein amino acid derivative L-cysteine, aids in the breakdown of drug and cellular wastes.

Other Strategies to Boost Health

Systemic inflammation is, not surprisingly, a problem that lingers long after cancer treatment. Dr. Stengler says that his patients who follow an improved diet and take many of the above supplements, along with getting regular exercise, often note reduced inflammation.

Dr. Stengler usually recommends an aerobic form of exercise for 30 minutes five times weekly and strength training for 15 minutes twice weekly. If you haven't already been exercising, go slowly in establishing a routine—fighting cancer and taking chemo or radiation exhaust many energy reserves in the body. Rest and recuperation are more important than pushing your workout to a higher level.

It can be challenging to keep your stress levels under control after dealing with cancer, but this too is important to strengthen your health. If you are having trouble with lack of focus, depression or anxiety, Dr. Stengler suggests that counseling may help you regain your physical and mental strength. Certain natural substances can also be helpful—Dr. Stengler may prescribe *phosphatidylserine* for cognitive dysfunction…*S-adenosylmethionine* (SAMe) for depression…and *5-hydroxytryptophan* (5-HTP) for anxiety and depression.

Kick-Start Immune System To Prevent Recurrence

Immunity levels may need a push after the challenges of treatment. There are several substances that may be supportive. These include Beta Glucan Formula, and mushroom extracts such as *Grifola frondosa* (Maitake), *Lentinula edodes* (Shiitake) and *Coriolus versicolor*. Fermented wheat germ extract in powder form (mixed in water or juice) may also be prescribed. Under your doctor's supervision, it is okay to use these supplements in combination, but your bank account may feel the pain. Ask your doctor what your priorities should be and choose a regimen accordingly.

If your immunity has been severely compromised, you may want to ask your physician about intravenous delivery of vitamin C and glutathione. If appropriate for you, this treatment may assist with tissue repair and will also help improve immune function.

Generally speaking, an excellent way to bridge the gap between your oncological treatment and your internist is to work with a naturopathic physician, who can prescribe and supervise a regimen such as the one Dr. Stengler presents here that may help fast-track you back to health.

How to Conquer Chemotherapy Side Effects

Sarah Hope Kagan, PhD, RN, professor of gerontological nursing at the University of Pennsylvania School of Nursing in Philadelphia, specializing in older adults with cancer. She received the 2006 Excellence in Care of the Older Adult with Cancer Award from the Oncology Nursing Society.

For someone recently diagnosed with cancer, facing the prospect of chemotherapy and the possibility of side effects can feel like a double whammy.

Good news: Advances in treatments designed to manage chemotherapy side effects have drastically reduced the discomfort associated with the use of this common cancer therapy.

The Downside of Chemo

Chemotherapy drugs (which come in oral, intravenous and topical forms, depending on the drug and its use) are prescribed alone or with radiation and/or surgery in an effort to cure or control many types of cancer, including malignancies of the breast, lung and colon.

Unfortunately, most of these drugs kill not only cancer cells but also some healthy cells found in many parts of the body, including the hair follicles, leading to such side effects as hair loss. The type of chemotherapy drug used largely determines which—if any—side effects will occur. Following chemotherapy, noncancerous cells that were affected by the drugs recover, allowing hair, for example, to grow back. *After 21 years of working with cancer patients, here's what Dr. Sarah Hope Kagan recommends to curb side effects…*

Appetite Loss

Chemotherapy can affect the taste buds and mucous membranes of the mouth, causing strong-tasting foods to taste offensive or less than palatable. This can result in a diminished appetite and other nutritional problems. *What to do…*

• **Talk to an oncology dietitian.*** People receiving chemotherapy often need more protein and calories in a relatively smaller amount of food (known as nutrient-dense food) because they feel too tired to eat or have experienced taste and/or smell changes. An oncology dietitian can suggest nutrient-dense foods, such as chicken and other lean meats, fish or eggs. Be sure these foods are fully cooked and eaten immediately or chilled to prevent the growth of bacteria.

Also helpful: If your dietitian, nurse or doctor recommends extra protein, try

*Ask your oncologist or oncology nurse to refer you to a dietitian who works with cancer patients.

adding nonfat, dry-milk powder to cereal, spaghetti sauce or other foods (as long as you're not lactose-intolerant). Also, eating five or six mini-meals each day can reduce the "work" of eating and make it easier to get the nutrition you need.

Fatigue

Fatigue is a common side effect of chemotherapy, especially for older adults who may have other chronic health conditions that also cause fatigue, such as arthritis or heart failure. *What to do…*

• **Set priorities.** It may seem obvious, but far too many cancer patients put pressure on themselves to maintain their normal schedules—even if they don't feel up to it. For example, if you're the family cook and typically prepare big breakfasts, ask yourself, "Do I value cooking more than showering in the morning?" If so, shower at night and just wash your face and brush your teeth in the morning, so you can cook. Or delegate the task of cooking to someone else.

• **Ask for help.** It's likely that many people know about your cancer and want to help but don't know how. If you're overwhelmed by multiple offers, appoint a friend or relative to coordinate help with meals, transportation, etc. If you don't have offers of help, contact people you may have met through volunteering, work and community activities.

Hair Loss

If hair loss occurs from chemotherapy, it is generally temporary. Still, it makes sense to plan ahead. *What to do…*

• **Get a haircut.** As surprising as this might sound, you can ease the psychological pain of losing your hair by getting a short haircut or your head shaved before long strands start falling out. (Men and women can follow this advice.) This allows you—rather than the chemotherapy—to be in charge.

• **Choose appropriate head coverings.** If you are comfortable with baldness, there's no reason to worry about head coverings. Just be sure to use sunblock on your head—as well as the rest of your body. Otherwise, go for a hat or a wig, depending on your own personal style. Head covers, including scarves and turbans, also are an option.

The American Cancer Society's Look Good…Feel Better program offers guidance on the use of head coverings. For more information, call 800-395-5665 or visit the Web site *www.cancer.org*. Or ask a hospital about boutiques that cater to cancer patients.

Nausea

Nausea is among the most dreaded potential side effects of chemotherapy. *What to do…*

• **Ask your doctor about anti-nausea medication.** A number of medications are available to prevent and treat nausea, including *ganisetron* (Kytril) and *ondansetron* (Zofran).

Also helpful: Lemon or ginger-flavored foods, such as lemon gelatin, ginger ale and candied ginger, may reduce nausea.

• **Get some exercise.** Mild aerobic exercise, such as walking, fights nausea by helping move food through the digestive tract. Ask your doctor or nurse about an exercise program that is suitable for you.

Skin Problems

Some chemo drugs affect skin cells, leading to cracking, itching or sensitive skin. *What to do…*

• **Use care when bathing.** Take a brief daily shower, using a non-irritating, soothing soap, such as Tone, Camay or Dove, only where you need it, such as your groin area and armpits. For dry skin, apply a fra-grance-free lotion or cream, such as Cetaphil or Eucerin.

For a line of skin-care products specifically formulated for people undergoing chemotherapy or radiation, contact Lindi Skin, 800-380-4704, *www.lindiskin.com*.

Weakened Immunity

Wash your hands often. Because chemotherapy can weaken immunity, scrupulous handwashing—in addition to avoiding large crowds and sick people—is an important defense against contracting a viral or bacterial infection. Wash up before preparing food and eating, after using the toilet and whenever you come in contact with something that may have been touched by someone else, such as an elevator button, a doorknob or a pen at the bank or drugstore. For convenience, carry your own pen and an alcohol-based hand sanitizer.

Natural Ways to Fight Side Effects of Cancer Treatment

Mark A. Stengler, NMD, naturopathic medical doctor and leading authority on the practice of alternative and integrated medicine. Dr. Stengler is author of the *Health Revelations* newsletter, author of *The Natural Physician's Healing Therapies* (Bottom Line Books), founder and medical director of the Stengler Center for Integrative Medicine, Encinitas, California, and adjunct associate clinical professor at the National College of Natural Medicine in Portland, Oregon. *http://markstengler.com*

The American Cancer Society estimates that 1.5 million Americans will be diagnosed with some form of cancer each year. The vast majority will choose to be treated with conventional therapies, such as chemotherapy, radiation, surgery or a combination. Mark Stengler, NMD, often advises patients who are undergoing these treatments and want to reduce their risk of side effects and optimize their outcome. An example is Yolanda, a 62-year-old woman who was diagnosed with a form of lymphoma (cancer of the lymphatic system). A program of nutrition and dietary supplements have given her more energy, promoted bowel regularity and boosted her immunity. Her oncologist was surprised with how well she tolerated her chemo treatments and remarked on her quick recovery.

Understanding Chemotherapy And Radiation

Chemotherapy involves the use of one or more drugs to destroy cancer cells. The treatments are most commonly given intravenously (IV) through a vein, orally or by injection into a muscle. These medications not only attack cancer cells but also harm healthy cells. This causes a variety of side effects, depending on the chemotherapeutic agents being used and the individual's response. Examples of short-term side effects include loss of appetite, memory impairment, constipation, diarrhea, hair loss, nausea, mouth sores, easy bruising, fluid retention and pain in muscles, bones, nerves and joints. It also can result in bone marrow suppression, which can lower white and red blood cell counts, causing fatigue and increasing a patient's susceptibility to infection. Long-term side effects can include infertility, chronic fatigue and continued bone marrow suppression. In addition, chemotherapy can result in secondary cancers—for example, a breast cancer patient might develop acute leukemia.

Radiation therapy also kills cancer cells and shrinks tumors. It is mainly used to attack localized cancers as opposed to cancer that has spread. Radiation treatments can be administered externally by a machine, internally through radioactive material placed in the body near cancer cells or via radioactive substances that are injected and circulate throughout the body. Side effects can be similar to those caused by chemotherapy, but symptoms such as redness, swelling and a burning sensation often are specific to the region being treated. Burned or reddened skin also can develop at the treated area.

Supplements That Help

The following supplements are recommended for people undergoing chemotherapy or radiation therapy. You can take all of them at once—with the exception of the mushrooms listed, which are typically taken one at a time, as directed. Always consult with your oncologist before taking any supplement. Supplements work best in conjunction with a healthful diet and lifestyle.

Detoxification Therapies

Toxic by-products are formed by cancer treatments. You can help eliminate these toxins from your body by supporting liver and kidney detoxification.

• **Milk thistle** is an excellent herb that supports liver detoxification and protects against liver and kidney cell damage. Studies show that it actually helps liver cells regenerate. Dr. Stengler recommends a 175-milligram (mg) to 250-milligram (mg) capsule of standardized extract (70% to 85% silymarin) taken three times daily. It can also be taken in liquid form. An excellent product is Thisilyn by Nature's Way, available in capsule form at most health-food stores, or you can contact the manufacturer to find a retailer (800-962-8873, *www. naturesway.com*).

• **Chlorella, spirulina, wheatgrass and other "super greens"** are nature's great detoxifiers. You can take chlorella by itself—it contains chlorophyll and a host of other detoxifying nutrients. A good choice, Sun-Chlorella A, is available at health-food stores or from Sun Chlorella USA (800-829-2828, *www.sunchlorellausa.com*). Follow label instructions. KyoGreen Energy by Kyolic is a good formula that contains a mixture of greens. It is available in tablet or powder form. To locate a store or mail-order company, contact Wakunaga (800-421-2998, *www.kyolic.com*).

Boosting Immunity

Because cancer treatments, especially chemotherapy, have a suppressive effect on the immune system—which makes you more vulnerable to infection—immunity boosting is critical. The following natural therapies can be used to support normal immune function without interfering with treatment.

• *Coriolus versicolor mushroom extract* is routinely used in Japan and China to support the immune function of people with cancer. It also is helpful in reducing the side effects of chemotherapy and radiation.

A study published in *The Lancet* examined the effects of coriolus on patients undergoing chemotherapy after surgical removal of stomach cancer. The 262 patients were randomly assigned chemotherapy alone or with coriolus extract. The survival rate of the group using the combination was 73% after five years, while the chemotherapy-only group had a survival rate of 60%. Researchers concluded that coriolus had "a restorative effect in patients who had been immunosuppressed by both recent surgery and subsequent chemotherapy." The recommended dose is 2,000 mg to 3,000 mg daily. The Mushroom Science brand of coriolus duplicates the formula that was used in the study and is available at health-food stores or by contacting Mushroom Science (888-283-6583, *www.mushroomscience.com*).

• **Maitake mushroom extract** is one of the most-studied mushroom extracts. Since the 1980s, Hiroaki Nanba, MD, a professor of microbiology at Kobe Pharmaceutical University, Kobe, Japan, has been researching maitake extract. It has been shown to enhance the activity of the body's natural killer cells against cancer cells. In addition, maitake extract has been shown to reduce the side effects of chemotherapy. A survey of 671 patients showed that the use of maitake during chemo reduced adverse effects such as hair loss, pain and nausea. Maitake Gold 404 is the form recommended by Dr. Nanba. Typical dosage is 1 mg per two pounds of body weight daily. It is available in capsule or liquid form at health-food stores. For a store locator, consult Natural Factors (800-322-8704, *www.naturalfactors.com*). Or you can buy Cellular Essentials NK-5 from Swanson Health Products (800-824-4491, *www.swansonvitamins.com*)—it contains Maitake Gold 404.

Note: Choose either coriolus or maitake based on the type of cancer being treated. Coriolus is a good general choice, especially for people with cancers of the throat, lungs and digestive tract. Maitake is better studied for cancers of the breast, prostate and liver.

• **Curcumin** is the yellow pigment found in turmeric, a prime ingredient in curry. It has been shown to have anticancer properties and to enhance the effectiveness of some chemotherapy drugs, such as *cisplatin* (Platinol). It has no known side effects. The recommended supplement dose is 400 mg twice daily. Many brands are available at health-food stores.

• **Whey protein,** derived from cow's milk, supplies all the essential amino acids the body needs for repair, including the amino acid glutamine, which prevents mouth sores and strengthens immunity. Take 20 grams (g) of whey protein powder twice daily, in water or a shake.

Digestive Help

Digestive function often is compromised by cancer treatments, particularly chemotherapy and radiation for cancers in the abdominal area. These treatments destroy "friendly" bacteria important for digestion, detoxification and immune function.

• **Probiotics** contain beneficial bacteria, such as *Lactobacillus acidophilus* and *Lactobacillus bifidus*. Take a daily dose of 10 billion or more active organisms. Good products include DDS Plus by UAS Laboratories (800-422-3371, *www.uaslabs.com*) and Bio-K Plus by Bio-K Plus International (for a store locator, go to *www.biokplus.com* or call 800-593-BIOK).

• **Ginger helps relieve indigestion,** nausea, bloating and diarrhea. Sip ginger tea throughout the day, or take two 300-mg capsules twice daily.

• **Homeopathic *Nux vomica*,** derived from the poison nut tree, combats nausea and constipation. Take two pellets of a 30C potency twice daily until symptoms subside, usually within two to three days.

Skin Soother

• **Aloe vera gel** can be applied topically to areas irritated or burned by radiation therapy. Choose a product that is 95% to 100% pure aloe vera. Aloe vera gel is available at health-food stores and pharmacies.

Antioxidants May Help

Antioxidants—such as vitamins A, C and E, selenium and coenzyme Q10—are controversial cancer treatments. Because conventional cancer treatments work in part by producing free radicals, and because antioxidants attack free radicals, the fear is that antioxidant supplements may neutralize the effects of chemotherapy or radiation. This is an area that needs to be better studied.

In Dr. Stengler's opinion, low doses of antioxidants are more helpful than harmful. In their excellent book *How to Prevent and Treat Cancer with Natural Medicine* (Riverhead), naturopathic doctors Michael Murray, Tim Birdsdall, Joseph Pizzorno and Paul Reilly state, "Antioxidant supplementation… offers about as much protection to the cancer cell as a bulletproof jacket would during a nuclear attack. However, normal cells are able to utilize the antioxidant to protect against the toxicity and damage caused by standard cancer treatments." Dr. Stengler recommends consulting your oncologist on this issue. Certainly, multivitamins and an antioxidant formula (containing CoQ10, mixed vitamin E, green tea extract and vitamin C) should be used after the completion of treatment for optimal recovery.

■ ■ ■ ■

Medical Marijuana— When It May Help

Donald I. Abrams, MD, professor of clinical medicine at the University of California, San Francisco, School of Medicine, chief of hematology and oncology at San Francisco General Hospital and president of the Society for Integrative Oncology. He has conducted clinical research on medical marijuana and other integrative approaches for treating cancer-related symptoms. He is the editor, with Andrew Weil, MD, of *Integrative Oncology* (Oxford University).

While the medicinal use of *cannabis* (more commonly known as marijuana) remains controversial in many parts of the US, researchers are discovering more about the plant's ability to help improve a variety of conditions.

There are now 16 states and Washington, DC, that have approved the use of medical marijuana for patients with chronic or debilitating diseases that cause pain, nausea, vomiting, loss of appetite and other serious symptoms.*

What you need to know…

Marijuana as Medicine

Medical marijuana is not the same as the prescription drug *dronabinol* (Marinol), which is derived from one of the plant's active compounds, *delta-9-tetrahydrocannabinol* (THC). Marinol was approved by the FDA in 1985 for cancer patients whose nausea and vomiting did not respond to conventional treatments. In 1992, the drug was approved for loss of appetite due to AIDS wasting syndrome.

Though Marinol is widely available, it contains just one of marijuana's estimated 70 compounds known as *cannabinoids*. For this reason, some researchers believe that it is important to investigate the medicinal use of marijuana because its many other cannabinoids may offer significant benefits beyond those conferred by THC alone.

However, marijuana has also been widely used as a recreational drug and remains illegal or "decriminalized" (regulated but not banned) in most parts of the world when used for this purpose.

Even now, when state laws permit the use of medical marijuana, federal law does not. Because of this, doctors can recommend marijuana only for medical conditions (such as cancer, chronic pain and glaucoma) for which medicinal use of the plant has been approved by state legislatures. In these cases, the physician generally writes a letter that allows patients to access medical marijuana from a dispensary.

*Marijuana is approved for medicinal use in Alaska, Arizona, California, Colorado, Delaware, Hawaii, Maine, Michigan, Montana, Nevada, New Jersey, New Mexico, Oregon, Rhode Island, Vermont, Washington and Washington, DC.

The legal and political issues surrounding medical marijuana have prevented it from being studied in the same ways that other medications are researched in the US. However, the Institute of Medicine (IOM), an independent organization that provides unbiased scientific opinions to government agencies, did issue an important analysis on medical marijuana.

Landmark report: The IOM concluded in 1999 that chemical compounds in marijuana, particularly cannabinoids, appear to have therapeutic value in treating…

• **Appetite loss, nausea and pain.** Cancer patients who undergo chemotherapy often experience nausea, pain, insomnia and/or depression. These symptoms can be treated separately with prescription drugs, but combining the drugs often results in drug-drug interactions. With marijuana, some patients get relief without this risk.

• **Nerve-related pain.** Research published in the *Journal of Pain* found that patients who smoked marijuana had less nerve-related pain from spinal cord injuries or other conditions.

• **Neurological conditions.** Some patients with multiple sclerosis who smoke marijuana report that they have less pain and fewer/less intense muscle spasms. Patients with seizure disorders may do better when they combine marijuana with antiseizure medications.

• **Glaucoma.** Marijuana has been found to help reduce eye pressure caused by glaucoma and is approved for this purpose in several of the states that permit its use.

Using Marijuana Safely

Marijuana is unlikely to cause serious side effects—but, like any drug, it's not appropriate for everyone. *Marijuana may…*

• **Lower blood pressure and increase heart rate.** For this reason, it may not be appropriate for people with a history of heart problems.

• **Cause unwanted sedation.** The use of marijuana might increase confusion in older adults with cognitive difficulties. Similarly, it shouldn't be used when driving or operating machinery.

Many people wonder about the potential health risks of smoking marijuana, but there's no evidence that the small amounts used for medicinal purposes are likely to increase the risk for lung cancer or serious respiratory diseases.

Best Ways to Use Marijuana...

Choose your delivery method wisely. Some patients choose to eat marijuana—in the form of brownies or other prepared foods—rather than inhale it. However, there are some potential problems when marijuana is eaten.

• **Taken by mouth,** marijuana takes two hours or longer to reach peak concentrations in the blood. Patients who don't feel the effects right away tend to eat a little more—and then discover that they've taken too much. Signs of taking too much include confusion, paranoia and dizziness.

Caution: When eaten, the patient's liver creates a metabolite that can accentuate the plant's psychoactive effect.

• **Inhaled marijuana,** on the other hand, reaches peak levels in the bloodstream within two to two-and-a-half minutes. Because the effects occur so quickly, patients can readily adjust the dose by inhaling more or less.

• **Consider using a "vaporizer."** Some patients use devices that heat, but don't actually burn, marijuana. Vapors go into a bag and can be extracted only through the mouthpiece. Studies show that fewer noxious gases are inhaled when marijuana is vaporized as opposed to smoked.

• **Be cautious with dosing.** Go slowly. Because the potency varies by plant, marijuana can't be standardized in the same ways that medications are standardized in a laboratory. In addition, a patient's sensitivity to marijuana will partly depend on his/her genetic makeup. Dr. Abrams recommends patient-titrated dosing—try a small amount...see how you feel...then increase/decrease the dose as needed.

Coping with Colon Cancer

Mark Bennett Pochapin, MD, director of The Jay Monahan Center for Gastrointestinal Health, chief of gastrointestinal endoscopy at NewYork-Presbyterian Hospital/Weill Cornell Medical College and associate professor of clinical medicine at Weill Cornell Medical College of Cornell University in New York City. He is the author of *What Your Doctor May Not Tell You About Colorectal Cancer: New Tests, New Treatments, New Hope* (Warner).

"It's colorectal cancer." More than 140,000 Americans will likely hear those words this year. Roughly half will be men, half women. The majority of them will be age 50 or older.

While 90% of colorectal cancer patients can be cured if the cancer is detected and treated in its early stages, the sad fact is that each year the disease claims an estimated 50,000 lives in the US. For those facing a diagnosis of colorectal cancer, the necessary tests, treatments and life changes can be daunting.

What you need to know...

Adjusting After Surgery

Removal of part of the colon or rectum is frequently part of the treatment for colorectal cancer (often it's the only treatment). About 20% of people may have changes in bowel function after surgery.

If the right side of the colon is removed, food that is digested in the small intestine will pour more rapidly into the colon, carrying bile salts that break down oils and fats. This may result in chronic diarrhea (frequent bowel movements that are soft or liquid).

Helpful: If you experience chronic diarrhea after surgery, consider asking your doctor about *cholestyramine* (Questran), a prescription resin-type medication that binds with bile salts to take them out of circulation…and motility-reducing agents, such as *loperamide hydrochloride* (Imodium A-D), an over-the-counter drug, or *diphenoxylate* with *atropine* (Lomotil), available by prescription.

If part of the lower colon or the rectum is removed, your body may not be able to store as much waste, which can result in more frequent bowel movements. If you develop this side effect, consult your doctor or a nutritionist, who may be able to suggest ways to retrain your gastrointestinal tract so that bowel movements are less frequent and more predictable.

Possible strategies to ask about…

• **Drink less fluid with meals.** This will slow down *peristalsis*, the muscular contractions that propel food through the digestive system. Avoiding hot liquids just before, during and just after eating also helps slow peristalsis.

• **Try fiber.** When bowel movements remain uncomfortably frequent, ask your doctor if this regimen may help: Use a fiber supplement, such as Metamucil, Citrucel or FiberCon, for five days. Take the amount of fiber recommended on the label with very little liquid after the same meal each day. Don't drink any fluid for one hour. The fiber will help to bulk the stool.

• **Consider probiotics.** Normally, the large intestine contains billions of bacteria. Many of these bacteria are harmless—and even helpful. They keep minerals and fluids in balance and help maintain good digestion. Surgery and the antibiotics that are prescribed afterward sometimes can destroy these helpful organisms.

In some cases, probiotics—beneficial bacteria like those that are found in yogurt—can firm up bowel movements, aid healing and improve digestive function after surgery.

Probiotics are sold as supplements at health-food stores. One product is *Lactobacillus GG* (sold as Culturelle). Others include *Bifidobacterium bifidum, Saccharomyces boulardii* (sold as Florastor) and other strains of Lactobacillus. Ask your doctor or a nutritionist whether probiotics might help you, and if so, what type you should take and in what amount.

A Healthy Future

When you get a disease like colorectal cancer, it may seem too late for "prevention." That's not true. The same lifestyle measures that reduce the risk of getting colon cancer also can help to improve your overall health afterward.

• **Eat healthfully.** Proper diet is crucial, so ask your doctor what type of diet is right for you. For many people, it should be low fat, high fiber, with lots of fruits, leafy greens and colorful, antioxidant-rich vegetables.

Because it can be difficult to know what to eat to meet your nutritional needs following surgery or during chemotherapy, consider adding a nutritionist to your medical team. Good nutrition not only makes you feel better, it also can strengthen the immune system and improve healing. (For more information about nutritional strategies, go to The Jay Monahan Center for Gastrointestinal Health Web site, *www.monahancenter.org/nutrition.*)

• **Exercise.** Physical activity has been linked to a reduced risk for colorectal cancer, increased bowel motility and improved stamina. Seek your doctor's advice on the type and amount of exercise best for you throughout your recovery process. Many people find it convenient to build short bursts of exercise into their normal routine—climb the stairs instead of riding the elevator, have a lunchtime walk, park at the far end of the lot, etc.

• **Consider supplements.** Several vitamins and minerals have been shown to reduce risk for colorectal cancer, including calcium, folic acid and vitamin D. While a calcium supplement is a good idea for women, it may not be recommended for men because early research has shown a possible increased risk for prostate cancer with high doses of calcium. Ask your physician about the dose that is right for you. Typical doses are 400 micrograms (mcg) daily of folic acid, 400 international units (IU) daily of vitamin D (although the recommended dose may soon be raised) and 1,000 milligrams (mg) daily of calcium (for women only).

• **Ask about aspirin.** People who use aspirin or other nonsteroidal anti-inflammatory drugs (NSAIDs), such as *ibuprofen* (Advil) and *naproxen* (Aleve), on a daily basis have been found to have fewer new colon polyps and malignancies. These drugs carry their own risks, such as gastrointestinal bleeding, so they may not be recommended to reduce colorectal polyp or cancer risk alone. However, if your doctor has already recommended aspirin for another purpose, such as heart attack and/or stroke prevention, or some other NSAID for arthritis treatment, the potential benefits also may include a reduced risk for colorectal cancer. Be sure to speak to your doctor before starting any regular regimen of aspirin or another NSAID.

• **Get support.** In-person support groups for people with colorectal cancer can help because they allow participants to share their concerns and swap practical information about diet, medication side effects and solutions to daily problems.

If you'd like the support of others but don't feel comfortable opening up in face-to-face encounters, or if transportation is a problem, consider a telephone or online support group. You may find it easier to talk about your feelings and difficulties via phone or computer.

To learn more about telephone, online or local support groups, contact the Colon Cancer Alliance, 877-422-2030, *www.ccalliance.org*...or CancerCare, 800-813-4673, *www.cancercare.org*.

Does Acupuncture Ease Chemo Side Effects?

Matthew D. Bauer, LAc, has practiced acupuncture for more than 20 years. He is a regular contributing columnist to *Acupuncture Today*, and formerly served on the executive committee of the California Acupuncture Association. His practice is in La Verne, California.

Nausea and vomiting are two of the most dreaded side effects of chemotherapy. Considering the cure can sometimes feel worse than the cancer it is meant to treat, some patients even elect to discontinue treatment. Although recent advances in anti-nausea and anti-vomiting medications have helped many cancer patients, the search for additional and more natural methods of relief for these hard-to-tolerate side effects continues. One method that was recently studied is acupuncture.

Study Pinpoints What Works

Can acupuncture reduce chemotherapy-induced nausea and vomiting? The Chinese healing method has been successfully used to treat a wide variety of ailments, including temporomandibular joint disorder (TMJ), drug addictions, alcoholism, allergies and back pain, by stimulating prescribed anatomical sites on the body.

In a review of 11 studies of acupuncture and its effects on chemotherapy-induced nausea and/or vomiting, the Cochrane Collaboration, an international organization that evaluates medical research, found a mixed bag of results, depending upon which acupuncture method was used and for which side effect.

A Review of the Findings

Electro-acupuncture (in which a small electrical current is passed through the needle) was effective in reducing vomiting during the first 24 hours after chemotherapy.

Traditional manual acupuncture using needles was not shown to be significantly effective for acute (within 24 hours of treatment) vomiting or nausea severity.

Based on similar principles, but using (highly trained) fingertip pressure on acupuncture points, "acupressure" was looked at as well. This method showed no benefit for vomiting, but did reduce acute nausea—although it was ineffective for delayed nausea (after 24 hours of treatment).

It is unclear why electro-acupuncture reduced acute vomiting while needles-only acupuncture did not, or why one method was successful with nausea while another was successful for vomiting. Of note is that all participants in all the trials reviewed were taking anti-vomiting drugs, so additional research is needed to determine whether acupuncture alone is effective, or whether it should be considered an effective adjunct to medications.

Expert Opinion

Acupuncturist Matthew D. Bauer, LAc, a former member of the Board of Directors for the California Acupuncture Association and a practicing acupuncturist with more than 20 years experience, spoke about these findings. In his view, it's hard to standardize this sort of study enough to make the findings meaningful. "So much depends on the practitioner's skill in placing needles at just the right angle in just the right place," he says. "In looking at this many trials, you're obviously dealing with many practitioners at varying levels of skill and experience, which, of course affects outcomes."

Acupuncture, he says, can be helpful in many ways for people undergoing treatment for cancer. It's worth a try since there's little risk and much potential benefit. It's important to work with a seasoned practitioner who has experience with oncology patients. And, of course, all cancer patients should check with their doctors before adding acupuncture or any other treatment to their cancer protocols.

■ ■ ■ ■

Music Therapy Speeds Recovery from Cancer Treatment

Amy Zabin, doctor of arts (DA), is the music therapist at Greenwich, Stamford and Norwalk hospitals in Connecticut. She is an adjunct clinical assistant professor in the graduate music therapy program at New York University in New York City.

As far back as World War II, music was used in Veterans Administration hospitals to treat soldiers suffering from shell shock. More recently, studies have shown that music therapy—which can include listening to and/or making music—

Acupuncture for Dry Mouth

Radiation for head or neck cancer can damage salivary glands, leading to severe dry mouth, loss of taste, difficulty swallowing, tooth decay and oral infections. Relief from medication lasts only a few hours and can cause sweating and slow heart rate.

Study: Patients who had completed radiation got twice-weekly acupuncture treatments for four weeks—and reported significant improvement in symptoms.

Referrals: American Association of Acupuncture and Oriental Medicine, 866-455-7999, *www.aaaomonline.org.*

M. Kay Garcia, DrPH, clinical nurse specialist and acupuncturist, Integrative Medicine Program, University of Texas MD Anderson Cancer Center, Houston, and leader of a study of 19 cancer patients.

reduces pain and other symptoms in cancer patients.

Example: A study published in *Cancer* looked at 69 patients who were undergoing high-dose chemotherapy and stem cell transplants. Those given music therapy reported having 37% fewer mood disturbances and 28% less anxiety than those who didn't get the treatments.

Benefits

What music therapy does…

• **Eases anxiety.** The brain and body synchronize their internal rhythms to external stimuli.

Example: A cancer patient who is suffering from anxiety might have a fast heartbeat and rapid breathing. Music with a slow, soothing tempo slows down both of these—and even slows brain waves, which reduces anxiety as well as pain sensations.

• **Blocks negative sensations.** According to the gateway theory of pain management, patients can't focus on opposing sensations simultaneously. Listening to or making music can reduce side effects from chemotherapy and other treatments.

Example: Researchers at University of Rochester Medical Center studied 42 patients undergoing bone marrow transplants. Those who received twice-weekly music therapy sessions reported significantly less pain and nausea than patients who were given only the standard care.

Patients who receive music therapy often require lower doses of painkillers.

• **Reduces nausea.** The drug cocktails used in modern chemotherapy are far less toxic than they used to be, but nausea still is among the main side effects. Much of this is due to anxiety about the disease and treatment. Patients who undergo music therapy have less stress, lower levels of the stress hormone cortisol and less nausea.

• **Helps healing.** The University of Rochester study found that patients given music therapy following bone marrow transplants started producing their own white blood cells in 13.5 days, on average, compared with 15.5 days in a control group. Music therapy also shortens the time that patients spend in intensive-care units by two to three days.

How to Use It

Music therapists design music sessions for individuals as well as groups. The sessions might include listening to music, making music or analyzing song lyrics. *To use music therapeutically…*

• **Set aside 15 to 30 minutes.** At home or in the hospital, close the door, turn off the phone and TV, and dim the lights. Get as comfortable as possible, and close your eyes.

349

● **Match the music to your mood.** A patient feeling agitated may respond more readily to music that matches that agitated mood at first...then the music therapist can gradually ease the patient into a more relaxed mental state. Soothing music with a slow tempo can slow the heart and make you feel more relaxed. If you would rather feel energized, uplifted or distracted, you might want to choose something lively.

● **Combine music with imagery.** Imagine yourself at a location that feels both safe and free, and try to use all your senses.

Example: Picture yourself on a mountain trail—what the ground feels like...the wind on your skin...the smell of the air, etc.

■ ■ ■ ■

Luxury Skin Products for Cancer Patients— Are They Safe?

Jennifer DeFazio, MD, dermatologist, Memorial Sloan-Kettering Cancer Center, New York City.

K. Simon Yeung, PharmD, LAc, research pharmacist and manager of the "About Herbs" Web site at the Integrative Medicine Service, Memorial Sloan-Kettering Cancer Center, New York City. *www.mskcc.org/aboutherbs*

If you or a dear friend has cancer, what's not to love about a gift package of skin care products specially formulated for cancer patients? Possible side effects, for one thing. Though these may seem like a sweet and thoughtful way to pamper someone, it's better to buy products that are basic—and bring along a basket of fresh fruit if you want to make it more special.

Cancer treatment can cause skin reactions, it's true, and they can last for weeks after treatment ends. Radiation often makes skin tender and sore and causes it to redden and peel, while treatment with various hormones and some of the more powerful chemo drugs may bring on dryness, skin rashes, blotching, itching and irritation.

To manage skin problems, dermatologists have long steered cancer patients toward mild and inexpensive drugstore skin-care products such as Cetaphil lotion. New luxurious lines of specialized creams and formulations specifically designed to soothe the skin and souls of cancer patients are appealingly scented with lavender and other herbs and botanicals and are beautifully packaged, but most also carry a top-of-the-line price tag. To get a professional's opinion on the matter, we spoke with dermatologist Jennifer DeFazio, MD, at Memorial Sloan-Kettering Cancer Center in New York City.

Dr. DeFazio first cautions that chemotherapy patients should discuss any skin changes after treatment with their doctor right away—the oncologist may want to adjust the drugs depending on the reaction. She also notes that good skin maintenance during cancer treatment is really no different than at other times in life—wash with a mild soap and moisturize daily for dry skin with application of a mild lotion while the skin is still damp after a bath or shower. Plain old time-tested petroleum jelly products, such as Vaseline and Aquaphor, are fine for skin irritated by treatment, she says. Your health-care professional may also advise using Biafine, a wound-healing cream, for more severe reactions.

As to specialized products, Dr. DeFazio expresses concern about those containing numerous botanicals. For example, the ingredient list accompanying one product line includes *astazanthin*, *bisabolol*, grape seed, red raspberry seed, white birch extract... and more. Dr. DeFazio says that some botanicals, such as aloe vera, green tea and oatmeal extracts are well-known for their soothing or anti-inflammatory properties, but we do not really know much about how well many others work. Furthermore, some common botanical and herbal extracts can actually cause side effects, and fragrances and preservatives in products can be irritating to sensitive skin. This is especially true for skin that has been subjected to radiation. Here are some side effects that K. Simon Yeung, PharmD, LAc, at Memorial Sloan-Kettering Cancer Center's Integrative Medicine Service, warns about…

• **Allergic reaction.** Some common essential oils, such as tea tree, lavender, bergamot and ylang-ylang, are known to cause contact dermatitis.

• **Transdermal absorption of phytoestrogens.** Many herbal skin products, like lavender or tea tree oil, have mild estrogenic effects. When applied in large quantities over prolonged periods of time, significant amounts can be absorbed through the skin. Patients with estrogen-receptor sensitive cancer should avoid these products.

It's important to check with an oncologist or dermatologist before using anything on your skin. While acknowledging that these lovely and aromatic skin products can give patients an important emotional lift, simpler ingredients may be a better choice in the long run.

■ ■ ■ ■

Six Essential Oils That Help Heal Cancer Patients

Cherie Perez, RN, quality assurance specialist in the department of GU Medical Oncology at MD Anderson Cancer Center in Houston.

Like so many New Age practices and beliefs, aromatherapy has ancient roots. The use of essential oils to affect mood and well-being can be found far back in Egyptian, Greek and Roman history. While scientific evidence about aromatherapy is scant, its long-standing role in spirituality and healing, along with anecdotal support of its benefits, gives essential oils an important role as a complementary alternative medicine therapy.

Boosting Immune Function

Cherie Perez, RN, quality assurance specialist in the department of GU (genitourinary) Medical Oncology at MD Anderson Cancer Center in Houston, is a strong proponent of aromatherapy, including as an adjunct for cancer treatment. She teaches monthly classes for patients on the topic. We asked Perez about how aromatherapy can be useful for people who are healthy, as well as those with chronic illnesses. Used properly, Perez says essential oils can indirectly help bolster immune function in cancer patients, strengthening their ability to fight back against the disease by helping to ease pain, depression, sleeplessness and stress. The oils can also help relieve anxiety and improve memory, both frequent problems for people in cancer treatment.

Essentials About Essential Oils

These essential oils have various scents such as floral, minty, citrus and masculine, and Perez advises using the ones you like best among the choices indicated for a specific treatment, since more than one oil may address the same problem. She explains that the limbic system, which is triggered by the sense of smell, is the emotional seat of the brain. It's the reason why people often respond strongly to certain scents positively or negatively. Lavender, for example, might bring back warm memories of a trip to Provence, or sour thoughts about a dour relative who wore it as a fragrance.

Dilution Required

All oils are highly concentrated distillations of plant parts, including the flowers, leaves, branches and roots. Because they are so potent (hundreds of times more concentrated than the culinary fresh or dried herb or herbal teas, and therefore easy to overdose on) they should be used only under the supervision of a knowledgeable practitioner, such as a naturopathic physician, registered nurse, massage therapist, clinical herbalist or aromatherapist. Some of the most popular oils include rosemary, eucalyptus, lavender and chamomile. Essential oils can be inhaled (safest with a simple diffuser), enjoyed in your bath or massaged onto your skin (but never directly in their undiluted form…because they can cause a rash or burning sensation).

Oils may come already diluted, and will say so on the ingredient label, but you can also dilute a pure oil yourself, with advice from your practitioner. Add three drops of an essential oil to a half tablespoon of scentless organic vegetable oil (such as sunflower or safflower) or to an unscented body lotion. People with sensitive skin should do a skin test before topical use. How much to dilute an oil depends on the type of oil and your skin's sensitivity. Thyme, for example, is quite irritating to some people, so it should be used more sparingly and with caution, whereas lavender is nonirritating to nearly everyone, says Perez. Citrus oils may cause sensitivity to sunlight, so avoid skin application if you are going to be in the sun. Because they're so pretty and fragrant yet highly toxic if ingested, they should be kept where children cannot reach them.

Menu of Options

Here's a list of popular oils that address some common problems, as well as those common among people in treatment for cancer…

- **Lavender.** Great as a general relaxant, it also treats migraines and relieves stress. It is excellent for insomnia resulting from cancer treatment.

- **Rosemary.** For muscle pain, low blood pressure (do not use if you have high blood pressure) and cold feet and hands. Rosemary stimulates appetite.

- **Spearmint.** Used to ease nausea and to help digestion. Can help ease gas and other treatment-related digestive problems.

- **Eucalyptus or peppermint.** For rubbing on sore muscles. Eucalyptus may also help joints, including arthritic ones. Eucalyptus may increase the absorption of certain cancer drugs that are applied topically, so use caution and try a patch test first, avoiding application to the same area as the cancer drug.

- **Pink grapefruit or juniper berry.** Used with massage to encourage lymphatic drainage of toxins and waste. Pink grapefruit is one of Perez's favorites for cancer patients, as she believes it helps energize them and raise their spirits. This and all citrus-type oils should be avoided during chemo and radiation and should not be used until you've spoken with your doctor.

- **Lemongrass, tea tree and orange.** Mix together into two cups of Epsom salts. Use five drops of each oil for a total of 15 drops to make soothing bath salts (use one-half cup per bath).

What to Look For

Aromatherapy has become so popular that essential oils are now widely available, including in health-food stores and supermarkets. However, Perez says that it is far better to purchase them from a shop with a staff knowledgeable in aromatherapy. Oils should come in dark blue or brown glass containers, which prevent light or heat damage. Avoid bottles with rubber droppers; the rubber breaks down and contaminates the oil. Finally, the label should feature both the common and the botanical name of the oil (for example, peppermint/*Mentha piperita*).

How to Try It

If you would like to learn more about how to incorporate aromatherapy in your life, Perez recommends *The Complete Book of Essential Oils & Aromatherapy*, by Valerie Ann Worwood (New World Library), which she says is both thorough and easily understood. Again, as in the case with skin sensitivities, people with asthma or allergies need to avoid things that might trigger an attack, for example, chamomile, which is in the ragweed family.

People who want to try inhalation aromatherapy should use only two or three drops of essential oils in a basin of water or diffuser, or on a napkin. And always consult with your doctor before using aromatherapy or any complementary therapy.

Break Through the Mental Fog of Cancer

Alan Hirsch, MD, founder and neurological director of the Smell & Taste Treatment and Research Foundation in Chicago. *www.scienceofsmell.com.* He is a neurologist and psychiatrist, and is author of *Life's a Smelling Success* (Authors of Unity) and *What's Your Food Sign?: How to Use Food Cues to Find True Love* (Stewart, Tabori & Chang).

Most adults find that they don't remember new information—telephone numbers, plot twists in a novel, etc.—as well as they used to. This can be especially true for cancer patients suffering from the mental fog known as "chemobrain"—a side effect of chemotherapy. Aromatherapy can be used to accelerate learning speed and promote better concentration and memory.

Proven effective: Floral scents. Sniffing a floral essential oil triggers the release of *norepinephrine* and *adrenocorticotropic hormone* (ACTH), hormones that increase attention. Floral scents have been shown to improve memory and learning speed by about 17%.

In one study, people were exposed to different scents prior to bowling. Those who smelled jasmine knocked down 28% more pins (it may have improved their concentration and hand/eye coordination).

Strategy: Sniff a floral scent when the material to be learned is initially presented, and repeat exposure to the same odor when the material must be recalled.

Also Good for Nausea

It's common for cancer patients who are undergoing chemotherapy to develop an intense aversion to the foods they ate immediately prior to treatments. There's little evidence that aromatherapy has a direct effect on nausea, but it can help prevent patients from developing a lifelong aversion to specific foods, which they may need for good health.

Proven effective: Smelling artificial cherry flavoring prior to chemotherapy. The best way to do this is to suck on a cherry candy. (This has the added benefit of stimulating saliva and helping to reduce hunger pangs.) Some patients will later associate the smell (and taste) of cherry with the treatments, but they can avoid cherry flavoring and continue to eat healthful foods, important for maintaining good nutrition.

What to Eat Before And After Chemo

Rebecca Katz, MS, senior chef-in-residence and nutrition educator at Commonweal Cancer Help Program in Bolinas, California. She is executive chef for The Center for Mind-Body Medicine's Food as Medicine and Cancer Guides Professional Training Programs. She is also author, with Mat Edelson, of *The Cancer-Fighting Kitchen: Nourishing, Big-Flavor Recipes for Cancer Treatment and Recovery* (Celestial Arts). *www.rebeccakatz.com*

Some people experience virtually no side effects from cancer chemotherapy, but this is rare. Most patients report at least some problems, including nausea, fatigue and diarrhea during the treatment.

Reason: The drugs that are used in chemotherapy are designed to kill fast-growing cancer cells. But they also damage fast-growing healthy cells, particularly in the mouth, digestive tract and hair follicles.

Good nutrition is critical if you're undergoing chemotherapy. It's estimated that up to 80% of cancer patients are malnourished. People who eat well before and during chemotherapy tend to have fewer side effects. They also are more likely to complete the full course of therapy than those who are poorly nourished and may feel too sick to continue. *What to do...*

• **Load up on nutrient-rich foods.** In the weeks before chemotherapy, patients should emphasize nutrient-dense foods, such as whole grains, vegetables and legumes. *The high nutrient load of a healthy diet helps strengthen healthy cells so that they're better able to withstand—and then recover from—the effects of chemotherapy. good choices...*

•Dark leafy greens, such as spinach, kale and Swiss chard. They're high in antioxidants, such as beta-carotene, lutein and other phytonutrients. These compounds help minimize the damaging effects of free radicals, tissue-damaging molecules that are produced in large amounts during chemotherapy. Kale is particularly good because it contains indole-3-carbinol, a compound that has anti-cancer properties.

•Olive oil, like green vegetables, is high in antioxidants. It's one of the best sources of oleic acid, an omega-9 fatty acid that strengthens cell membranes and improves the ability of the immune system to fight cancer cells. I like extra-virgin olive oil because it has been exposed to the least heat.

•Garlic. The National Cancer Institute reports that people who eat garlic regularly seem to have a lower risk for intestinal and other cancers, including breast cancer. The strong-tasting sulfur compounds in garlic, such as allicin, have strong antiviral and antibacterial effects—important for chemotherapy patients because they're susceptible to infection. Try fresh garlic in your cooking. Smash it and let it sit for 10 minutes to allow the antiviral properties to become more accessible—then chop and cook. (To smash garlic, set the side of a chef's knife on the clove, place the heel of your hand on the flat side of the knife and apply pressure.)

• **Increase protein.** It's the main structural component of muscle and other tissues. People who undergo chemotherapy need lots of protein to repair tissue damage that occurs during the treatments.

Recommended: About 80 grams of protein daily. That's nearly double the amount that healthy adults need. Cancer patients who increase their protein about a week before chemotherapy, and continue to get extra protein afterward, recover more quickly. They also will have more energy and less fatigue.

Try this: Two or more daily smoothies (made in a blender with juice or milk, a variety of fresh fruits and ice, if you like) that are supplemented with a scoop of whey powder. The protein in whey is easily absorbed by the intestine. And most people can enjoy a nutrient-rich smoothie even when they have nausea or digestive problems related to chemotherapy.

● **Drink to reduce discomfort.** Stay hydrated both before and after chemotherapy sessions to reduce nausea. Drink liquids until your urine runs clear—if it has more than a hint of yellow, you need to drink more.

Helpful: Soups and broths provide water, as well as protein, minerals and vitamins.

● **Avoid your favorite foods two days before treatments.** It's common for chemotherapy patients to develop food aversions when they get nauseated from treatments and then to associate the nausea with certain foods. It's sad when people develop aversions and can never again enjoy their favorite foods.

● **Eat lightly and frequently.** People tend to experience more nausea when the stomach is empty. During and after "chemo days," keep something in your stomach all the time—but not too much. Patients do better when they have a light snack, such as sautéed vegetables or a bowl of broth, than when they go hungry or eat a lot at one sitting.

● **Treat with ginger.** When your stomach is upset, steep three slices of fresh ginger in a cup of simmering water for 10 minutes, then drink the tea. Or grate fresh ginger with a very fine grater, such as a Microplane, and put the shavings under your tongue. Ginger alleviates nausea almost instantly.

● **Overcome "metal mouth."** The drugs used in chemotherapy can damage the nerves that control the taste buds. Some people complain about a metallic taste in their mouths after treatments. Others notice that foods taste "flat" or that their mouths are extremely sensitive to hot or cold.

These changes, known as transient taste changes, usually disappear a few weeks (or, in some cases, months) after treatments, but they can make it difficult for people to eat in the meantime.

Helpful: The FASS method. It stands for Fat, Acid, Salt and Sweet. Most people will find that it's easier to enjoy their meals, and therefore ingest enough nutrients, when they combine one or more of these elements in every meal.

For fat, add more olive oil than usual to meals…lemons are a good source of acid… sea salt has less of a chemical aftertaste than regular salt…and maple syrup gives sweetness with more nutrients (including immune-building manganese and zinc) than table sugar.

● **Try kudzu root.** Used in a powder form to thicken sauces, puddings and other foods, it soothes the intestine and can help prevent diarrhea. You also can dissolve one teaspoon of kudzu root in one teaspoon of cold liquid and drink that. Drink after meals, as needed. Kudzu root is available in most health-food stores.

● **Soothe mouth sores with soft,** easy-to-eat foods, such as granitas (similar to "Italian ices") or smoothies. The sores can be intensely painful, which makes it difficult to eat.

Recommended: Watermelon ice cubes. Purée watermelon, and put it in a tray to freeze. Then suck on the cubes. The cold acts like a topical anesthetic—you can numb the mouth before eating a regular meal. And the juice from the melon is just as hydrating as water but provides extra nutrients, including the antioxidant lycopene.

Use Your Mind to Ease Your Pain Without Pills

James N. Dillard, MD, DC, LAc, board-certified physician, doctor of chiropractic and certified medical acupuncturist who pioneered the integrative model in pain medicine. He is author of *The Chronic Pain Solution: Your Personal Path to Pain Relief* (Bantam). Dr. Dillard now maintains private practices in New York City and East Hampton, New York. www.drdillard.com

More people are disabled by chronic pain than by diabetes, heart disease and cancer put together. An estimated 27% of US women (and 29% of men) suffer from debilitating pain, yet the problem remains vastly undertreated. Pain medications do not always bring sufficient relief—plus they can lead to side effects and/or addiction.

The good news: Like everything in your body, pain is affected by the workings of your mind. No matter what the cause of your pain, you can harness the power of your brain to reduce your suffering. *Here's how…*

Your limbic system, the most primitive part of your brain, controls your involuntary nervous system and emotions. Pain activates the limbic system, triggering the fight-or-flight response. As stress hormones are released, your heart beats faster, blood pressure soars, muscles tense…and various emotions are sparked, including anxiety, panic, anger and sadness. Normally, these responses are temporary—but with chronic pain, the stress of these intense reactions creates a downward spiral.

Example: The pain of chronic arthritis provokes a continuous release of stress hormones, leading to headaches and insomnia that exacerbate discomfort. As your body weakens, it produces fewer mood-boosting endorphins. Soon you're too tired and despondent to socialize, and the resulting isolation only makes you feel worse.

Helpful: If you learn to cultivate a sense of distance from your pain, you can mute the limbic system's response, reducing physical pain signals and easing the accompanying emotional suffering.

At least twice a day, go somewhere quiet and safe where you won't be disturbed… sit or lie in whatever position is most comfortable…and practice one or more of the techniques below for five to 15 minutes.

Calming Breath

Pain can take your breath away, triggering a pattern of shallow breathing that increases muscle tension and deprives cells of oxygen. Deep breathing—especially when combined with a meditative focus—helps by relaxing muscles, stimulating endorphins and reducing emotional distress.

Remember: For both of the deep-breathing techniques below, inhale slowly through your nose and then exhale slowly through your mouth. Clear your mind, and focus only on your breath. If other thoughts intrude, let them float away and refocus on your breath.

• **Flare-control breath.** This is particularly effective for pain flare-ups. As you inhale, notice your lungs filling with the vitality of your breath. Imagine your breath flowing to the area of your pain, bringing healing energy to this spot. As you exhale, imagine the pain flowing out of your body along with your breath.

• **Purifying breath.** This is especially helpful for easing troubling emotions that accompany pain. Picture your body surrounded by pure, white light. Inhaling: Imagine this light being drawn into your lungs and then spreading until your whole body glows with healing light.

Exhaling: Picture a dark essence—representing fear, anger and sorrow—being expelled with your breath, leaving your body pain-free and your mind at ease.

Healing Imagery

The guided imagery method quiets the nervous system by convincing your mind that it does not feel pain. *Close your eyes and imagine either of these…*

• **A place of peace.** Picture yourself in an ideal setting of your choosing—a favorite vacation spot, a mountaintop, a lush garden, a tranquil lake. Immerse yourself in this scene by imagining what you see (majestic trees, an azure sky)…feel (a soft breeze, the warm sun)…smell (a campfire, fresh lilacs)…hear (singing birds, rustling leaves)…and taste (the salty sea, a perfect strawberry). The more details you can conjure up, the more effective the imagery is.

• **Soothing hues.** Take a few deep breaths, then focus on your pain. Note its location and intensity…describe its qualities (aching, throbbing, burning). Think of a color that represents pain (black, purple, hot pink), and imagine that your painful area is suffused with that color. Now choose a healing hue (such as white, silver or pale blue), and imagine that it has the power to dissolve your pain. Visualize the healing color pouring onto the painful area and spreading out wider and wider, until the painful color completely disappears. In your mind's eye, let that healing color continue to pour out for as long as you want—you have an unlimited supply.

Pain-Relieving Acupressure

Like acupuncture, acupressure is based on a principle of traditional Chinese medicine—that chi (energy) flows throughout the body along invisible channels called meridians, and that pain occurs when the chi becomes blocked or unbalanced. In terms of conventional Western medicine, the firm pressure applied during acupressure is thought to distract the nervous system, halting pain messages from traveling up the spinal cord to the brain.

The following techniques are particularly good for head, neck and shoulder pain, but they also ease the tension that pain elsewhere in the body can trigger in the neck area. Do each technique for several minutes per side.

• **Catwalk.** With your right hand, feel along the top of your left shoulder for any tender, tight or tense spot…then massage that area by "walking" your index, middle and ring fingers along it (like a cat kneading with its paws). Do this repeatedly and quickly—each finger press should last only about half a second. Repeat on the other side.

• **Thumb press.** Place your right hand behind your head, palm facing you and thumb pointing downward. With the pad of your thumb, press firmly into the base of your skull, working all the way across the right side and paying extra attention to any tight or tender spots. Repeat on the other side.

Soothing Aromatherapy

Certain scents can invigorate you when pain saps your energy…or calm you when pain leaves you tense or anxious. Aromatherapy also distracts your attention from pain and may relax muscles. Add a few drops of essential oil to a hot bath or sprinkle a few drops on a handkerchief that you hold near your nose (do not apply essential oil directly to skin).

• **Invigorating scents.** Try cedar…eucalyptus…or peppermint (this one also eases the nausea that can accompany pain).

• **Calming scents.** Try bergamot…geranium…lavender…rose…or sandalwood.

Breathe Like a Baby

Carol Krucoff, a registered yoga therapist at Duke Integrative Medicine and a yoga instructor at Duke University's Center for Living, both in Durham, North Carolina. She is also a certified personal trainer and the author of *Healing Yoga for Neck & Shoulder Pain* (New Harbinger). Ms. Krucoff's audiotaped lessons on breathing are available on her home-practice CD, Healing Moves Yoga (*www.healingmoves.com*).

As a yoga therapist, Carol Krucoff sees clients with different medical issues, from diabetes to chronic pain to cancer. No matter what they're dealing with, she always begins by teaching deep abdominal breathing—the way we all breathed when we were babies.

Deep abdominal breathing is one of the most effective ways to quickly reduce stress and unleash the body's natural vitality. By breathing this way, you calm down the sympathetic nervous system (involved in the body's "fight or flight" response)…reduce blood levels of stress hormones…increase the body's blood flow…reduce perception of pain…and induce the body's relaxation response, resulting in a slower heart rate, lower blood pressure, less muscle tension and a feeling of greater well-being.

These are powerful effects. If you're practicing breathing exercises but aren't getting these benefits, or tried them before but quit, you may simply be doing them improperly.

Soften Your Body

Abdominal breathing doesn't require a determined effort. You simply draw breath into the lower part of your lungs, the way babies do. Krucoff tells her clients to visualize their lungs as two big balloons that expand and contract in six directions when they inhale—front to back, top to bottom and side to side.

How to do it: Sit comfortably with one hand on your abdomen and the other on your chest. On an inhalation, breathe down to the deepest portion of your lungs, so that your belly rounds out into your hand as you fill with breath. On the exhalation, your belly gently contracts and your hand moves in. Continue for several slow, deep breaths, observing the out-and-in movement of your belly, while the hand at your chest stays relatively still. It may help to start by lying down and placing a book on your belly so that it rises and falls with each inhalation and exhalation.

Breathe Slowly

People often mistakenly think that abdominal breathing involves "gulping" air—taking big, swift inhalations. On the contrary, one of the most important aspects of abdominal breathing is that it slows and deepens the breath.

Why that's important: Slowing your breathing is the key to calming your nervous system and increasing oxygen flow throughout your body. One study of menopausal women, for example, found that lowering their breathing rates to seven to eight breath cycles (inhalations and exhalations) per minute, down from an average of 15 to 16, reduced hot flashes by about 50%.

To achieve this slow breathing rate, count slowly to five during each inhalation and again during each exhalation.

Make Exhalations Longer Than Inhalations

Once you're accustomed to the feeling of relaxed abdominal breathing, try gradually extending your exhalation until it's twice as long as your inhalation. Start by exhaling to a count of five, then work up to seven and finally to 10. Doing this triggers another deep-seated response—when you take longer to breathe out than in, it signals your brain that all is well, amplifying the relaxation effect.

Breathe Through Your Nose

If you have chronic congestion or other nasal obstruction, this may not be possible. But if you're able to breathe comfortably through your nose, this will help you control your breathing rate better while also ensuring the air you breathe is optimally warmed, moistened and filtered—all functions the nose is designed to perform.

Practice in a Relaxing Environment

Pick a calm, relaxing setting when first learning this technique. Choose a time when you don't have pressing concerns or deadlines. Select a place that's quiet, comfortable and free of distractions. Then spend at least several minutes exploring the techniques outlined above.

As you become more experienced with abdominal breathing, you can begin practicing it throughout the day—including when you awaken or go to sleep or during stressful situations, such as sitting in a traffic jam.

Employ a Mantra

Once you've become comfortable with your practice of inhalation and exhalation, try adding mantras that you can recite to yourself while breathing. This is often more interesting and can be even more effective —because you can choose a mantra with meaning to you or one that reinforces a desired emotional state.

Examples: The mantra offered by Zen master Thich Nhat Hanh, *Breathing in, I calm myself. Breathing out, I smile.* Or the Dorothy mantra, *There's no place like home.* You also can use a favorite phrase or make

up a phrase to fit the situation, such as *In energy, out fatigue* or *In peace, out anger.*

Begin by repeating your mantra silently, once while inhaling and once while exhaling. Then play with extending your exhalation to cover two repetitions of the mantra. Feel free to change mantras whenever you want.

Relax All Over with Guided Muscle Relaxation

Mark A. Stengler, NMD, naturopathic medical doctor and leading authority on the practice of alternative and integrated medicine. Dr. Stengler is author of the *Health Revelations* newsletter, author of *The Natural Physician's Healing Therapies* (Bottom Line Books), founder and medical director of the Stengler Center for Integrative Medicine, Encinitas, California, and adjunct associate clinical professor at the National College of Natural Medicine in Portland, Oregon. *http://markstengler.com*

Carol Krucoff, a registered yoga therapist at Duke Integrative Medicine and a yoga instructor at Duke University's Center for Living, both in Durham, North Carolina. She is also a certified personal trainer and the author of *Healing Yoga for Neck & Shoulder Pain* (New Harbinger). Ms. Krucoff's audiotaped lessons on breathing are available on her home-practice CD, Healing Moves Yoga (*www.healingmoves.com*).

When a patient is feeling stressed and has aches and pains and muscle tension all over, Mark Stengler, NMD, recommends a guided muscle relaxation technique. This easy-to-do stress- and anxiety-reducing sequence systematically relaxes the whole body. (It is especially helpful during the holiday season, which can be stressful and make muscle tension worse.) It also helps to ease the tense muscles and nerve pain of patients with diseases such as fibromyalgia and cancer. This technique doesn't take a lot of practice—in fact, you can do it right the very first time and feel results immediately. Many muscle-relaxation exercises involve contracting and relaxing muscles throughout the body. But the following technique, which was adapted by yoga therapist Carol Krucoff of Duke Integrative Medicine in Durham, North Carolina (*www.HealingMoves.com*), from her book *Healing Yoga for Neck and Shoulder Pain* (New Harbinger), is an awareness approach to stress relief that works well at relaxing every muscle group. People who do this sequence feel as though they are floating when they are finished. You'll feel that way, too!

The Setup

Do the entire sequence once daily, especially during stressful times or right before going to sleep (if you have trouble falling asleep).

Choose a quiet, relaxing place at home. For 10 to 15 minutes, lie on your back on the floor, in bed or in a reclining chair. When first learning the sequence, you may want to do it with a family member or friend, since it's more relaxing to have someone tell you which part of the body to relax. Or you can record the instructions and play them back.

Close your eyes and breathe in slowly and easily through your nose. Then breathe out again, relaxing and starting to release any stress or negative emotions as you exhale. Sink deeper into the floor or chair, feeling it support your head, back, buttocks and legs.

Let's begin…

Practice each step for three to five full breaths before moving to the next one.

- **Bring your attention to your face and its muscles.** Relax your face so that it becomes soft.
- **Relax your eyes so they rest back in their sockets.**
- **Bring your focus to your jaw.** Allow the hinge of your jaw to release, so your teeth part and your lips barely touch. Soften the inside of your mouth.

- **Let your head become heavy,** releasing its weight into the support of the floor or chair. Then allow your neck to relax.
- **Soften your throat…then bring your focus to your shoulders.** Freed of the weight of your head, your shoulders can rest back into the floor, bed or chair.
- **Bring your attention to your arms, hands and fingers.** Release any tension.
- **Focus on your internal organs, including your heart.** Let go of any emotional tension that you are holding on to, such as fear or anger.
- **Bring your attention to your hips, buttocks and groin, releasing any tension there.** Then do the same with your legs, feet and toes.
- **Next, focus on all the bones in your body.** Let them become heavy. Relax your muscles, so that they soften away from your bones.
- **Feel your whole body relax.** Stay like this for five minutes, focusing on your breath.

When you're ready to rise, gently wiggle your fingers and toes and stretch anywhere that feels comfortable. Roll onto your side and rest there for a minute, allowing your nervous system to readjust before standing.

What Guided Muscle Relaxation Can Do

While this type of sequence may look like you aren't doing much, the opposite is in fact true. You are focusing on completely relaxing and releasing all tension from the body. This type of relaxation has many health benefits—such as lowering blood pressure, relieving anxiety and enhancing sleep.

Massage OK for Cancer Patients?

In a three-year study of the effect of massage on more than 1,000 cancer patients—the largest study to date of massage used for cancer patients—patients rated their symptoms immediately before and after a single treatment of massage therapy.

Result: Anxiety declined by 52%...pain, 40%...fatigue, 41%...depression, 31%...and nausea, 21%. Massage was as effective as standard drug therapy for these symptoms.

Helpful: Insurance companies are more likely to pay for massage therapy if a doctor writes a referral to a certified therapist or if treatment is part of a hospital in-patient therapy. To locate a massage therapist in your area, contact the American Massage Therapy Association, 888-843-2682, or visit *www.amtamassage.org.*

Barrie R. Cassileth, PhD, chief, Integrative Medicine Service, Memorial Sloan-Kettering Cancer Center, New York City.

You Can Overcome the Emotional Challenges of Breast Cancer

Teresa L. Deshields, PhD, a licensed clinical psychologist, assistant professor of medicine at Washington University School of Medicine and manager of Psycho-Oncology Services for the Alvin J. Siteman Cancer Center at Barnes-Jewish Hospital, all in St. Louis.

Cancer patients often wonder, "When will things get back to normal?" Yet cancer is a life-changing experience—so even after treatment ends, the old "normal" life is gone forever.

This is difficult to accept, especially for women facing breast cancer. Unlike diseases that primarily affect the inner body, breast cancer leaves an external reminder—whether it's the loss of a breast to mastectomy, scars from lumpectomy or changes in breast shape and color from radiation. And because breasts are a symbol of femininity, many patients struggle to maintain a sense of themselves as sensual, strong, beautiful women. *Here's how to reestablish emotional equilibrium...*

Reawaken Sexual Identity

Breast cancer can wreak havoc with your image of your own sexuality. You may feel embarrassed about nudity, fearful of pain, disinterested in intimacy or worried about your partner's reaction to your scars.

Essential: Speak openly with your partner. Tell him what kind of caresses do and do not feel good to you now so that he can respond to your needs. If you feel self-conscious or unattractive when naked, wear a bra with a built-in prosthesis or a pretty camisole to bed, or try keeping the lights off until you and your partner feel more comfortable. To reignite interest in sex, read romantic books...watch sensual movies...develop fantasies that excite you...ask your doctor about libido-boosting medication.

Helpful: Visit the American Cancer Society (ACS) Web site at *www.cancer.org* and type "Sexuality for the Woman with Cancer" in the search box. Consult a sex therapist who specializes in treating couples facing cancer.

Referrals: American Association of Sexuality Educators, Counselors and Therapists, 202-449-1099, *www.aasect.org.*

Consider breast reconstruction, too. Health insurance policies that cover mastectomy also must cover reconstruction plus surgery on the other breast (a lift, reduction or enlargement) if necessary to achieve symmetry.

Referrals: American Society of Plastic Surgeons, 847-228-9900, *www.plasticsurgery. org*.

Rebuild Body Image

Even women who have always been healthy may wrestle with body image—berating themselves for having heavy thighs or crooked noses. Breast cancer exacerbates such insecurities.

To rebuild a positive body image, notice how you speak to yourself. Are you thinking, *I can never wear a bathing suit again* or *I should stick to baggy sweatshirts?* Try to imagine yourself speaking that way to a friend recovering from breast cancer. Unthinkable, isn't it? Speak to yourself with the same kindness that you would show to any loved one—I confront adversity with grace…I am beautiful inside and out.

Take practical steps to boost body image. "Look Good…Feel Better" is a free nationwide program that helps cancer patients deal with appearance-related changes by providing makeovers and lessons on cosmetics, skin care, hair care, wigs and head-scarf styling. Visit *www.lookgoodfeelbetter. org* or phone 800-395-5665.

For breast prosthetics, ask your doctor where to get professionally fitted.

Online option: For prosthetics and lingerie, check out The Pink Bra (888-838-0770, *www.thepinkbra.com*).

Regain Control

Feelings of helplessness that accompany cancer are heightened by loss of physical abilities. To recapture a sense of control, commit to exercise—it boosts energy, reduces stress, increases strength and stamina, and aids weight control. (Consult with your doctor before starting an exercise program.)

Don't be discouraged if you can't do as much as you used to.

To start: Walk for five to 10 minutes a day, gradually increasing your time and pace.

Motivating: Research suggests that physical activity equivalent to walking for three to five hours per week helps prevent breast cancer recurrence and increases survival.

Gilda's Club and The Wellness Community were two separate nonprofit organizations offering classes on exercise and nutrition for cancer patients, among other services. Now they are a united organization called the Cancer Support Community. Visit *www.cancersupportcommunity.org*, 888-793-9355.

Reclaim Connections

Breast cancer patients often feel alone… about 25% feel depressed at some point after treatment ends.

Helpful: Join a support group. You connect with other women who are on the same path…share your feelings and concerns… learn practical coping skills…and get satisfaction from helping others. To find local resources, visit the ACS Web site (*www.can cer.org*) and click on "Find Support & Treatment"…or call the Susan G. Komen for the Cure helpline at 877-465-6636.

For an Internet-based group, visit the Susan G. Komen Web site (*www.komen.org*) and click on "Message Boards." For support 24 hours a day, contact the Y-ME National Breast Cancer Organization hotline at 800-221-2141. Their Survivor Match Program will match you with a woman whose experience is similar to yours.

If you continue to feel depressed, see a mental-health professional who specializes in counseling cancer patients.

Referrals: American Psychosocial Oncology Society, 866-276-7443, *www.apossociety.org*.

Re-create Normalcy

Though your old "normal" life is no more, you can use this opportunity to create a new and even more satisfying definition of normal.

Look honestly at your former life. Are there negative aspects that you have clung to out of habit? Clear them away to make room for positive experiences—to let go of a job you loathe and pursue your dream career…to end destructive relationships and connect with new friends…to renounce bad habits and adopt a healthful lifestyle. As you move toward such rewarding goals, you cease to mourn what used to be—and embrace the new life ahead.

If Your Loved One Has Cancer, Offer Your Touch

William Collinge, PhD, director of Collinge and Associates, an independent research and consulting organization in Kittery, Maine. He is author of several books, including *Partners in Healing: Simple Ways to Offer Support, Comfort, and Care to a Loved One Facing Illness* (Shambhala), and executive producer of the Touch, Caring, and Cancer DVD program. *www.collinge.org, www.partnersinhealing.net*

Research sponsored by the National Cancer Institute has discovered a powerful treatment for people with cancer that can decrease stress, anxiety and depression…reduce fatigue…relieve pain…and ease nausea.

The Loving Touch of a Caregiver's Hands

The study looked at 97 cancer patients and their caregivers (spouse or family member), dividing them into two groups.

Half the caregivers watched a DVD called Touch, Caring and Cancer and read the accompanying manual—and then gave three massages a week for four weeks to the cancer patients. The other half read to the cancer patients three times a week from a book the patients said they would enjoy.

Those receiving the massages had less…

• **Stress/anxiety** (44% less, compared with 28% less for the reading group)

• **Pain** (34% less, compared with 18%)

• **Fatigue** (32% less, compared with 20%)

• **Depression** (31% less, compared with 22%)

• **Nausea** (29% less, compared with 12%).

The results were in the *Journal of the Society for Integrative Oncology*.

"It appears that caregivers receiving video instruction can achieve some of the same results as professional massage therapists," says William Collinge, PhD, the study leader, director of Collinge and Associates in Kittery, Maine, which provides consultation and research in integrative health care, and author of *Partners in Healing: Simple Ways to Offer Support, Comfort, and Care to a Loved One Facing Illness* (Shambhala).

"This has important implications for the quality of life of cancer patients, helping them feel better," says Dr. Collinge. "But it's also important for caregiver satisfaction. Cancer caregivers are at risk of distress themselves—they can feel helpless and frustrated at not being able to help. This gives them a way to help the patient feel better and increase their own effectiveness and satisfaction as a caregiver. It also appears to strengthen the relationship bond, which is important to both caregiver and patient."

The New Caregiver

"About one-third of adults have been in a caregiving role in the past year for a loved one with cancer or another chronic illness," says Dr. Collinge. "Caregiving is becoming a universal dynamic in relationships. And there are very simple complementary therapies—such as touch—that can make a big impact on both the person with the illness and the caregiver."

If you're a caregiver, here is what Dr. Collinge says you need to understand and do to help your loved one (and yourself) with the caring power of touch...

• **Know the benefits.** "A caring touch introduces so many dimensions of healing," says Dr. Collinge. "Skin to skin contact is so comforting by itself. It improves emotional intimacy between the person with cancer and the caregiver—it reassures the person with cancer of the presence and caring of the other person."

And then there are all the physiological benefits of touch—the relaxation from touch triggers the release of mood-boosting endorphins that can counter stress, anxiety and depression, and reduce pain, nausea and fatigue.

"Touch is unique. You won't find a single drug or other treatment that can yield all of its simultaneous benefits."

• **Be reassured about safety.** "The brief training of the Touch, Caring and Cancer video and manual can overcome some of the historical fears and misunderstandings about touch and cancer," says Dr. Collinge.

"It reassures the caregiver that touch and massage can't spread the cancer, or that cancer is somehow contagious.

"The manual also provides a precaution checklist to discuss with the cancer patient's doctors, so that the caregiver can simply and easily avoid any type of touch or area of touch that would cause pain or discomfort."

• **Understand that even simple touch works.** "For example, you can relax a person's whole body just by massaging their hand," says Dr. Collinge, "and you can do that while sitting in a waiting room or watching TV at home. Just lightly resting your hand on a loved one can provide comfort and relaxation."

• **Realize that you might offer more benefits than a massage professional.** "Some of the people in this study—such as older caregivers who were at home all day—would give short massages six or seven times a day," says Dr. Collinge. "When we asked them why, they'd say, 'We just enjoy it so much that we do five minutes here and five minutes there several times a day.' That means some people were giving 50 mini-massages a week—for enduring impact, that's so much greater than could be achieved by the patient seeing a massage therapist once a week."

• **Attitude matters more than technique.** "The bottom line is not how you touch, but receiving the permission and encouragement to touch," says Dr. Collinge. "The technique is really of minimal importance. What's important is the actual touching, and the compassionate presence of the caregiver."

• **Expand your concept of caregiving.** "We have the notion in our culture that caregiving is about changing the linens, monitoring medications, bringing good food, bathing, taking the patient to appointments and other similar tasks," says Dr. Collinge. "But we can expand the notion of home caregiving to include some simple complementary therapies such as touch that are deeply satisfying both to the person being cared for and the person doing the caring."

• **Watch the video and read the manual.** The DVD and manual used in the study—Touch, Caring and Cancer—is available at *www.partnersinhealing.net.*

Drug-Free Ways to Overcome Depression

Hyla Cass, MD, a board-certified psychiatrist and nationally recognized expert on integrative medicine based in Pacific Palisades, California. She is a frequent TV and radio commentator, author or coauthor of 10 books, including *Natural Highs: Feel Good All the Time* (Penguin) and a board member of the American College for Advancement in Medicine. *www.cassmd.com*

Everyone feels blue occasionally, but for the one in eight American women who are depressed, feelings of sadness and hopelessness persist for months or years.

Conventional treatment for depression includes medication, most often with a selective serotonin reuptake inhibitor (SSRI), such as *fluoxetine* (Prozac), or a *selective serotonin/norepinephrine reuptake inhibitor* (SSNRI), such as *venlafaxine* (Effexor). The mechanism is unclear, but these drugs may work by blocking reabsorption of the brain chemicals serotonin and/or norepinephrine, leaving more of these mood-lifting neurotransmitters in the brain.

Problem: Antidepressants' side effects can include lowered libido, weight gain, headache, fatigue, anxiety, zombie-like moods and even suicidal tendencies.

New finding: An analysis of numerous clinical studies concluded that SSRIs were not significantly more effective than a placebo against mild-to-moderate depression.

Other studies are more favorable for antidepressants, and medication is a vital part of treatment for some patients—but given the concerns about antidepressants, many experts believe that these drugs are overprescribed.

Better: A natural approach that treats depression with minimal side effects. *How it works…*

Getting Started

Research demonstrates the mood-elevating effects of regular exercise, proper diet, sufficient sleep and moderate sunshine—yet depression can erode motivation to pursue healthful habits.

What helps: Certain dietary supplements are natural mood enhancers, combating depression by correcting biochemical imbalances and increasing motivation to make healthful lifestyle changes.

Important: Before using supplements, check with a doctor knowledgeable about natural medicine, especially if you take medication, have a medical condition or are pregnant or breast-feeding. *Best…*

• **If you are not depressed,** take the nutrients listed below under "Mood Boosters for Everyone" to maintain healthful neurotransmitter levels.

• **If you are depressed but are not taking an antidepressant,** try natural remedies before considering drugs.

• **If you take an antidepressant but see no improvement in mood and/or suffer from side effects,** ask your doctor about weaning off the drug and starting natural therapies. Do not discontinue drugs on your own!

• **If an antidepressant is helping you and side effects are minimal,** continue your medication and ask your doctor about also taking supplements.

Supplements below are available in health-food stores and online.

Guideline: Begin at the low end of each recommended dosage range. If symptoms do not improve within a week, gradually increase the dosage.

Mood Boosters for Everyone

The following supplements are appropriate for most adults. Take all of them indefinitely to prevent or treat depression. They are safe to take while on antidepressants.

● **Omega-3 fatty acids.** These are essential for production of neurotransmitters that affect mood and thinking. Most effective are *eicosapentaenoic acid* (EPA) and *docosahexaenoic acid* (DHA), found in fish oil. Take 1,000 milligrams (mg) to 2,000 mg of combined EPA/DHA daily.

Caution: Fish oil may increase bleeding risk in people taking a blood thinner, such as *warfarin* (Coumadin).

● **B vitamins and magnesium.** The B vitamins help carry oxygen to the brain and produce neurotransmitters. They work best together and are absorbed best when taken with magnesium. Take a daily multivitamin or a vitamin-B complex that includes the following—25 mg each of vitamins B-1 and B-2...20 mg each of vitamins B-3 and B-6...50 mg each of B-5 and magnesium...and 100 micrograms (mcg) each of B-12 and folic acid.

Caution: Avoid supplements of B-3 if you have diabetes, gout or liver problems... avoid B-6 if you take L-dopa for Parkinson's disease.

● **Vitamins C, D and E.** These aid neurotransmitter production and/or protect brain cells. Take a daily multivitamin that includes 500 mg to 1,000 mg of vitamin C...2,000 international units (IU) of vitamin D...and 400 IU of vitamin E.

For Extra Help

If you still are depressed after taking the nutrients above for seven to 10 days, also take either of the following supplements. If symptoms do not improve within two weeks, switch to the other supplement. If you still see no improvement, take both.

Important: Though many patients are successfully treated with a combination of these supplements and antidepressants, this requires close medical supervision. Theoretically, the combination could lead to the rare but potentially fatal serotonin syndrome, caused by excess serotonin. Symptoms include headache, increased body temperature, fast heart rate, blood pressure changes, hallucinations and/or kidney damage.

Once you find an effective regimen, continue for several months. Then reduce your dose by one-quarter for one week. If symptoms return, resume the former dose. Otherwise, continue reducing until you find an effective maintenance dose or can stop completely.

● **Saint John's wort.** This herb raises serotonin and possibly the neurotransmitter dopamine, and may calm nerves. With breakfast, take 300 mg to 900 mg daily of a standardized extract of 0.3% hypericin (the active constituent).

Caution: Side effects may include digestive distress and a sun-sensitivity rash. Saint John's wort may interact with some drugs, including warfarin, the heart drug *digoxin* (Digitalis) and birth control pills.

● **5-HTP (5-hydroxytryptophan) or L-tryptophan.** These are forms of the amino acid tryptophan, which converts to serotonin. With fruit juice, take either 50 mg to 100 mg of 5-HTP or 500 mg to 1,000 mg of L-tryptophan once or twice daily.

Caution: Occasional side effects may include nausea and agitation.

To Rev Up...

If your symptoms include low energy and sleepiness, add either of the following to your regimen for as long as necessary. They may be taken with an antidepressant under close medical supervision.

• **Tyrosine.** This amino acid aids production of energizing adrenaline, dopamine and thyroid hormone. Take 500 mg to 1,000 mg before breakfast and in mid-afternoon.

Caution: Tyrosine may raise blood pressure—talk to your doctor. Do not use tyrosine if you have melanoma—it may worsen this cancer.

• **SAMe (s-adenosyl-methionine).** This compound boosts neurotransmitters and energy. Take on an empty stomach no less than 20 minutes before or after eating or taking any other supplement.

Dosage: Take 200 mg to 400 mg once or twice daily.

Caution: It may cause irritability and insomnia. Do not take SAMe if you have bipolar disorder—it could trigger a manic phase.

To wind down...

If depression symptoms include anxiety and/or insomnia, try...

• **Valerian.** This herb enhances activity of *gamma-aminobutyric acid* (GABA), a calming neurotransmitter. Take 150 mg to 300 mg one-half to one hour before bed. After one to two months, stop for a week. If insomnia returns, resume use. It is safe to take with an antidepressant.

Caution: Don't take valerian while using sedatives, such as muscle relaxants, antihistamines or alcohol.

Keep Cancer from Coming Back

Julie K. Silver, MD, cofounder of Oncology Rehab Partners, is on the medical staff at Massachusetts General, Brigham and Women's, and at Spaulding Rehabilitation Hospitals. She is also assistant professor of physical medicine at Harvard Medical School and author of *After Cancer Treatment: Heal Faster, Better, Stronger* (Johns Hopkins).

This year, an estimated 1.4 million Americans will be diagnosed with cancer. The primary cancer therapies—surgery, chemotherapy and/or radiation—are more effective than ever before, but these powerful weapons often leave cancer survivors weak and exhausted.

Until recently, doctors told cancer patients to go home following treatment and wait—sometimes for weeks or months—for their bodies to recover.

Now: Cancer specialists and physiatrists (doctors trained in rehabilitation medicine) have identified the best ways for cancer survivors to achieve a faster, fuller recovery—and perhaps even improve their odds against a recurrence.

As a physiatrist, Julie Silver, MD, worked with thousands of cancer survivors. But in 2003, when she was diagnosed with breast cancer, she experienced firsthand the debilitating effects of lifesaving cancer therapies. Medical research and personal experience convinced her that a positive outlook...supportive family and friends...a strong spiritual life...and effective pain relief all aid recovery.

Here she shares how to have an even greater impact on cancer recovery...

Eat the Right Foods

While attacking malignant tumors, chemotherapy and radiation treatments also kill normal cells. Your diet plays a crucial role in helping your body heal and replace lost and damaged tissue. *In addition to eating at least five daily servings of vegetables and fruits...whole grains at most meals...and legumes at least once daily, be sure your diet includes...* *

● **Protein.** During treatment and for several weeks afterward, increase your intake of protein. It helps prevent infection and repair damaged cells. How much protein do you need? Divide your weight in half and eat that many grams of protein daily.

Example: If you weigh 150 pounds, aim for 75 grams (g) daily.

Best protein sources: Fish, poultry, eggs and low-fat dairy products. Protein from plant sources, including most beans, nuts and seeds, also aids healing by providing cancer-fighting phytochemicals.

● **Organic foods.** The potential danger of pesticides is still being debated. But why take a chance? While your body is healing, protect it from potentially toxic pesticides by choosing organic fruits, vegetables and meats. (Look for "certified organic" on the label.)

While increasing your intake of the foods mentioned earlier, it's equally important to avoid...

● **Alcohol.** Relatively small amounts of alcohol have been linked to some types of malignancies, including colon, pancreatic and breast cancer. Limit your intake of alcohol to light drinking on social occasions, or abstain altogether.

Stay Active

Exercise improves mood, and there's increasing evidence that it also reduces the risk for breast, colon and possibly prostate cancer—and may help prevent a recurrence of these malignancies. *Your exercise program should include...*

● **Cardiovascular exercise.** Even while you're undergoing treatment, start using a pedometer to track how far you walk. These devices, which cost $15 or more at most sporting-goods stores, record the number of steps you take throughout the day.

Smart idea: Write down your daily step total (a mile equals about 2,000 steps) and aim to increase it by 10% a week until you reach 10,000 steps, or five miles a day.

When you feel strong enough, begin formal workout sessions. Use a treadmill and/or stationary exercise bike—or simply take brisk walks or swim. The American Cancer Society recommends working up to a 30-minute moderate-intensity workout (the equivalent of brisk walking), five days a week. Forty-five minute workouts may be even more beneficial.

Important: If you were active before your cancer diagnosis, aim for your earlier fitness level. If you were sedentary, simply try to exercise regularly for whatever period of time you are able to do so.

Helpful: Several shorter sessions each day—for example, three 10-minute sessions of brisk walking—may be less tiring than a single sustained workout.

● **Strength training.** Lifting weights or using resistance-type exercise machines, such as those made by Nautilus or Cybex, rebuilds muscle mass that is lost during inactivity and treatment, strengthens the bones and immune system, and improves balance.

Strength training should be performed two to three times per week to allow enough time for your muscles to recover between sessions.

During each workout...

● **Focus on all major muscle groups** and on strengthening your "core" (middle

*If your cancer therapy makes you tired or nauseated, it is best to start these practices after your treatment ends.

section of the body)—the core muscles support the rest of your body.

• **Find the maximum weight you can lift** 10 times—your "10 RM" (repetition maximum). Start by lifting 50% of this amount 10 times. Rest for one to two minutes or longer, then lift 60% of the same weight 10 times. After another one- to two-minute rest, lift 80% of the weight 10 times. Increase the weight as you grow stronger—a reasonable goal is 10% per week until you reach a plateau.

• **Flexibility exercises.** This type of exercise is less important than cardiovascular and strength training, but it will improve comfort and mobility, and make you more resilient and less prone to injury.

Tai chi and yoga are good forms of stretching exercise if you avoid movements that are painful.

Important: Before you start an exercise program, check with your doctor and consider working with a physical therapist or personal trainer. To avoid fatigue and injury, listen to your body. If you feel you're doing too much, cut back.

Although unstructured physical activity—for example, walking from your car to the mall, taking the stairs or gardening—is usually good for health, it provides less benefit than regular, structured exercise. Preserve your energy for exercise sessions by avoiding activities that tire you.

Get Enough Rest

Poor sleep compounds the fatigue that often follows radiation and chemotherapy. Research shows that sleep is vital to the cells and chemicals of the immune system, fortifying the body against infection and cancer growth.

Helpful: Plan for seven to eight hours of sleep a night, and follow the rules of "sleep hygiene"…

• **Avoid heavy meals and limit fluids** within two to three hours of going to bed. Stop drinking caffeine and alcohol (if you drink it) four to six hours before bedtime.

• **Go to bed and get up at the same time each day**—including the weekend. This "trains" your body to sleep.

• **Keep your bedroom dark and quiet, at a comfortable temperature.**

• **Don't watch television, play computer games or exercise** within one to two hours of going to bed. Allow an hour to unwind with music, reading, quiet conversation or a warm bath.

If worries about your health keep you awake, try meditation or relaxation exercises to lower anxiety. Talk out your concerns with friends and family. Counseling can teach you techniques to ease worrying.

If you find yourself sleeping more than 10 hours a night, tell your doctor—this could indicate depression or an underlying health problem. And if you have trouble falling asleep or staying asleep, ask your doctor about sleep aids (including natural remedies, such as low-dose melatonin).

Vanishing Cancers

Keith I. Block, MD, medical director of Block Center for Integrative Care in Evanston, Illinois…director of Integrative Medical Education at University of Illinois College of Medicine, Chicago…and scientific director of the Institute for Integrative Cancer Research and Education, Evanston. He is editor of *Journal for Integrative Cancer Therapies* and author of *Life Over Cancer* (Bantam). *www.blockmd.com*

A common belief about cancer is that it is an irreversible process. Normal cells become malignant and grow uncontrollably. The only way to stop the process is to remove or kill the cancer through surgery, chemotherapy and/or radiation. Cancer cannot just disappear.

That belief is proving to be untrue. In a recent study in *Archives of Internal Medicine*, researchers from Norway and the US analyzed the six-year incidence of invasive breast cancer in two very similar groups of Norwegian women.

About 119,000 of the women had mammograms every two years. Another 110,000 women in the study had not had mammograms and then had one mammogram.

To the surprise of the researchers, the six-year incidence of breast cancer in the two groups was quite different. The more frequently screened group had a 22% higher incidence of breast cancer.

So, what caused less cancer to be found in the second group? The intriguing theory is that cancer did indeed start in this group at an equal rate…and then spontaneously disappeared without ever being noticed (because the women were not being screened).

Other research has shown that spontaneous regression of cancer occurs in cases of advanced melanoma, advanced kidney cancer and neuroblastoma (a childhood cancer of nerve tissue). Regression also occurs in colonic adenomas (precancerous growths of the colon) and in precancerous lesions of the cervix.

Keith I. Block, MD, one of America's top integrative cancer therapy experts, explains that the number of documented cases of spontaneous cancer remission is quite low. He estimates that only one in 500 cancer tumors regress without surgery, chemotherapy or radiation.

However, he suggests that the unalterable, one-way trajectory of cancer is an outdated paradigm.

Cancer is not only mutagenic—propelled by damage to DNA—it also is mitogenic and the growth (mitogenesis) of cancer cells may be stopped by inhibiting molecular signaling and correcting disruption in the body's internal biochemical environment. This can be influenced by lifestyle factors that are alterable through personal choices.

Why Cancers Vanish

There are three main factors that can cause a cancer to regress…

- **Innate biology.** Some people are born with a naturally stronger constitution that is capable of stopping a cancer before it takes firm hold.

- **Transformation of the body's biochemical and molecular environment.** Many lifestyle factors influence the body's inner biochemical and molecular environment, including what you eat, how much you exercise and how much stress you're under.

The latest research shows that positive lifestyle factors can influence genes by turning on the tumor-suppressor genes and turning off the tumor-promoting genes.

- **Better communication.** This includes two types of communication—biochemical communication between cells and emotional communication with yourself and others.

What happens: In a normal biochemical environment, one cell sends a message to another, Don't grow, I'm using this space. One reason tumor cells can divide and grow is that they don't receive this message.

The breakdown in communication is fundamental in the biology of cancer in other ways. Studies show that meditation—one way to communicate with your inner spirit—reduces cancer-causing inflammation.

Close personal relationships also are relevant. A preclinical study from researchers at The University of Chicago suggested that social isolation and its impact on stress resulted in a greater than threefold increase in the onset of breast cancer.

Steps You Can Take

Various lifestyle factors can strengthen you against cancer…

● **Exercise and fitness.** Numerous studies link increased physical activity to lower incidence of cancers of the colon, lung, prostate, testicles, breast, ovaries and uterus.

Regular exercise can counter many cancer-causing biological factors, including cancer-fueling molecules called growth factors …oxidative stress (a kind of internal rust)…a weakened immune system…and poor response to inflammation. Aim for a minimum of 30 minutes of aerobic exercise daily, which can be divided into multiple sessions.

● **Whole-foods diet.** The right diet deprives a tumor of the compounds it most likes to feed on and supplies you with nutrients that help your body keep malignant cells in check.

Example: The Japanese have long had a diet rich in land and sea vegetables and fish—and low in meat, refined sugars and high-fat foods. Japan also has lower cancer rates than the US and better survival rates. For instance, men in Japan and the US are equally likely to have very early prostate cancer—the kind that never causes clinical problems—but American men have much higher rates of the clinical type that can lead to advanced prostate cancer.

Bottom line: If you eat too much dietary fat and refined carbohydrates, you run the risk of increasing body fat and weight while weakening your immune system and increasing oxidative stress, inflammation and

blood levels of substances that promote tumors.

● **Power foods.** There are "power foods" rich in phytochemicals that are uniquely anticancer. These include turmeric…grapes (they contain *resveratrol*)…green tea…milk thistle…ginger…and pomegranate.

But to get enough turmeric, resveratrol and all the rest, you would have to eat curry and guzzle grape juice until you exploded.

Best: Supplements and concentrates, such as "green drinks," often sold in health-food stores. Talk to your doctor about the best supplements for you.

● **Stress reduction.** Chronic anxiety and stress contribute to cancer's ability to thrive in your body.

What happens: Stress triggers biochemistry that is procancer—high levels of certain growth factors…an excess of oxidation-causing free radicals…high blood sugar…and raging inflammation.

Techniques such as relaxed abdominal breathing, progressive muscle relaxation and calming imagery can help you create emotional ease.

If You Have Cancer

The fact that a cancer can vanish without conventional treatments is important knowledge for a person diagnosed with cancer and for his/her doctor. However, a patient should never simply wait for a cancer to disappear. Getting started quickly on a plan of care can be essential for one's survival—losing time can be detrimental, even life-threatening.

Medical Miracles Really Do Happen

Larry Dossey, MD, executive editor of *Explore: The Journal of Science and Healing* and the former executive editor of the journal *Alternative Therapies in Health and Medicine.* He is the author of 10 books, including *Healing Words* and *Prayer Is Good Medicine* (both HarperOne) and *The Extraordinary Healing Power of Ordinary Things* (Harmony/Random House).

M ost of us have heard of people who recover from diseases that were considered incurable. The phenomenon, referred to in medical literature as spontaneous remission, occurs when serious, often deadly illnesses such as cancer quickly and inexplicably—some would even say miraculously—disappear.

No one knows exactly how often such cases occur. Approximately 3,500 medically documented cases of seeming miracles—based on reports from doctors in America and around the world dating to 1967—have appeared in 800 peer-reviewed medical journals and cover all major illnesses, including cancer, heart disease, diabetes and arthritis.*

Below, Larry Dossey, MD, answers questions on medically documented "miracles"—and what they might mean for improving everyday health and healing...

● **What is a "medically documented miracle"?** The word miracle is from the Latin *mirari*, meaning to look at in awe. For me, a medical miracle is an awe-inspiring healing event—a disease that goes away suddenly, unexpectedly and completely.

Attempts have been made to define and medically document miracle-type cures. For example, in 1954, the Catholic Church established the International

*These cases are found in *Spontaneous Remission* (The Institute of Noetic Sciences). An online version of the bibliography is available at *www. noetic.org.*

Medical Committee of Lourdes, a panel that includes dozens of experts from the European medical community. These doctors decide whether a cure reported by a person who has visited the healing shrine at Lourdes in southwestern France is an "authentic" miracle, using rigorous criteria, including a permanent remission of the disease. As of 2006, the committee had documented 67 cases.

● **Have any of your patients ever experienced this type of healing?** Early in my career, I had an elderly patient with cancer in both lungs that had spread throughout his body. We had no medical therapies for this type of cancer, but during visiting hours, people from his church stood near his bed, praying and singing gospel music. I expected him to die within days, and when he asked to go home, I respected his wishes and discharged him.

About a year later, this patient was back in the hospital—this time with a bad case of the flu. I went to the radiology department to look at his current chest X-ray, and it was completely normal. I thought that in the past year he must have had a dramatic response to additional therapy of some kind, but he hadn't undergone any therapy. To me, this was a true miracle cure.

● **Are religious and supernatural influences believed to play a role in most medical miracles?** Many medical miracles occur in a religious, spiritual or supernatural context—people pray to God, or to saints, or rely on what they believe to be the healing energies of the universe. Perhaps some unknown mind-body process is triggered by belief. But even this is pure speculation—because atheists and agnostics also experience what seem to be miracle cures.

Not knowing why something works is not necessarily a problem. Throughout the history of medicine, we often have known that a treatment works before we understand how it works. Aspirin and penicillin are two examples. We can add miracle-type cures to that list. Perhaps science will someday explain these occurrences. For now, they remain inexplicable.

● **How do people who experience these cures explain their recoveries?** In interviews conducted for a book called *Remarkable Recovery* (Riverhead), individuals whose illnesses were reversed pointed to a variety of factors they thought played an important role in their healing.

Paradoxically, the two most commonly cited factors seem like opposites—75% attributed the recovery to a "belief in a positive outcome," while 71% said it was based on "acceptance of the disease." This shows that there is no one "personality type" that experiences miracle-type healings.

Sixty-eight percent believed that prayer was responsible, followed by meditation and faith. Self-help regimens, including exercise, music and singing, were also cited.

● **Some doctors believe that telling patients about miracle-type cures instills "false hope."** What do you think? Yes, some doctors may believe that speaking about medically documented miracles promotes "false hope" in seriously ill patients. But I would say that not informing and educating patients about this possibility promotes "false pessimism"—a negative viewpoint that is not justified by the facts. Documented miracle cures are a fact of medical history. For someone who is ill, that knowledge can provide comfort and consolation.

■ ■ ■ ■

True Stories of Spontaneous

Joan Borysenko, Ph...
the mind-body clinical programs a... hospitals, now merged as Boston's Beth is... cal Center. Based in Boulder, Colorado, she runs... conducts lectures on mind-body healing. An updated e... her 1987 best seller *Minding the Body, Mending the Mind* is once again available (Da Capo). *www.joanborysenko.com*

On occasion, a health problem that was expected to be permanent or fatal instead disappears without medical intervention. The limited research that has been done suggests that the reason why one person recovers when most others do not might have as much to do with the mind as the body.

We interviewed Joan Borysenko, PhD, a former Harvard medical scientist who is a renowned expert in the field of mind/body healing. *She relays these true stories of spontaneous healing...*

Mind/Body Cure

In 1985, Alice Epstein, a sociology doctoral student at the University of Massachusetts, was diagnosed with kidney cancer. One of her kidneys was removed, but it was no use—the cancer had spread to her lungs, and treatment was impossible. Epstein was told she had only a few more months to live.

With no way to treat the physical problem, Epstein and her psychology-professor husband decided to treat her mind. Epstein used meditation to reduce her stress, and psychotherapy to deal with the angry, unhappy component of her personality. Within six weeks, tests showed that her cancer was going into remission. Her progress slowed when she took time off from the intensive psychotherapy but resumed once the psychotherapy resumed. The cancer eventually disappeared. Epstein earned her

D and is still alive today, more than 20 years later.

What may have happened: Eliminating stress and anger will not cure every disease, but it can trigger a host of biochemical changes in the body—including providing a boost to the immune system. It is possible that Epstein's aggressive mental treatments played a role in her return to physical health.

A Vision in Lourdes

Nearly 150 years ago, a teenage girl in Lourdes, France, reported seeing a vision of the Virgin Mary. Ever since, the waters in that area have been credited with healing powers. Most of these incidents involve cancer, multiple sclerosis and other diseases that occasionally go into remission, even without a visit to Lourdes.

The 1908 case of Marie Bire is more interesting. The 41-year-old French woman was blind as a result of optic atrophy—the degeneration of her optic nerve. According to medical science, it should not have been possible for optic nerves to recover from such a condition.

At Lourdes, the blind Bire attended Mass and received Holy Communion. Then, as the Blessed Sacrament in procession was passing the place where she sat, she suddenly regained her sight. Ten doctors examined Bire. They all found that her optic nerves were still withered but that she could see.

What may have happened: We do not have to believe in divine miracles to believe that Bire's faith might have played a role in her recovery. Studies have found that depending upon the medical condition, between 30% and 50% of people respond to placebos. If you tell these people that you have given them painkillers, their brain activity will show that they actually feel less pain.

Confidence Despite the Odds

In 1975, Ian Gawler, a 24-year-old Australian veterinarian and decathlete, learned that he had bone cancer in his right leg. The leg was amputated, but the cancer reappeared later that year and spread throughout his body. In 1976, Gawler was given two weeks to live. No one had ever been known to recover from such an advanced case of this form of cancer. As a doctor, Gawler knew that the reasonable response was to prepare for death. Instead, he remained certain that he would recover. He focused on meditation, positive thinking and a natural diet.

Gawler did recover. He now runs The Gawler Foundation (*www.gawler.org*), which provides support for others suffering from serious illnesses. The foundation stresses healthy food, meditation and belief in recovery.

What may have happened: We cannot simply imagine cancer away, but there is reason to think that believing in the desired health outcome might improve the odds that it will occur.

Surrounded by Love

Fifty years ago, the outlook was bleak for those suffering psychotic hallucinations. Today's pharmaceuticals and cognitive behavior therapy were not yet available. Recovery was very rare.

That was bad news for one previously healthy 10-year-old girl growing up in the 1950s. Her nightmares had entered her waking life—she saw snakes, scorpions and headhunters. The girl believed that these tormentors were going to kill her family and that the only way she could stop them was to repeat obsessive-compulsive behaviors, such as scraping the inside of her mouth with her fingernails, reading books only upside down and backward, rereading each sentence three times and erasing everything she wrote three times before continuing. The girl eventually was pulled from school and lived each day in a landscape of terror.

For months, she prayed intensely for a cure. One day during these prayers, she suddenly felt surrounded by love and wisdom, as though she were being held in the arms of God. Her fear instantly disappeared, and she stopped her obsessive-compulsive behavior cold turkey. Within days, all of her symptoms were gone, never to return.

I was that little girl. The experience sparked my lifelong interest in psychology and spirituality.

What may have happened: Most people with mental disorders cannot just pray their way to recovery. Still, it is worth noting that many people who experience spontaneous healing also experience a transformative spiritual episode similar to mine—a single moment when they feel aided by a loving, powerful outside force.

How to Use Your Mind to Heal

Here are some things we can do when we are seriously ill that will benefit our overall health…

• **Do not let your mind be pulled into worry or into the past or the future.** Spend time each day doing something that makes you feel good and keeps you in the present, whether it is gardening, meditating or walking in nature.

• **Forgive any wrongs that have been done to you.** Letting go of anger and regrets can reduce stress and boost your immune system.

• **Have gratitude.** Before going to bed, be truly grateful for something that happened that day. Wasn't it wonderful when someone smiled at you? Soak up these positive feelings.

• **Imagine the health outcome that you desire.** Picture the disease disappearing from your body. If you have trouble visualizing a positive health outcome, begin by picturing other things that make you happy.

Don't Let Grief Endanger Your Health

Phyllis Kosminsky, PhD, a clinical social worker specializing in grief, loss and trauma at the Darien, Connecticut–based Center for Hope/Family Centers. She also is in private practice in Pleasantville, New York, and Norwalk, Connecticut. She is the author of *Getting Back to Life When Grief Won't Heal* (McGraw-Hill).

When someone close to you dies, it's natural to grieve. The ache may never go away entirely, but you gradually accept that your loved one is gone, and you find a new way for life to feel normal.

But for up to 15% of bereaved people, intense grief can linger for years or even decades. This so-called complicated grief is powerful enough to disrupt the bereaved person's ability to work, get along with others and/or to find much pleasure in anything. Although elements of depression are present, complicated grief also is marked by chronic and persistent yearning and longing for the deceased…and an inability to accept the loss.

Especially in older adults, complicated grief can go undetected by doctors and family members—or even the sufferers themselves. Regardless of age, the condition can contribute to chronic depression, drug and alcohol abuse and certain infectious diseases (by weakening the immune system).

In people who have heart disease, the emotional stress created by complicated grief can worsen their condition.

Hurt but Healing

A person who is grieving is bound to experience feelings of sadness, emptiness, loss—and often anger. Physical symptoms are also common. You lack energy and feel fatigued. You may have trouble sleeping—or do nothing but sleep. You find it hard to concentrate and may even wonder about the meaning of life. Some people lose their appetites, while others eat uncontrollably. Headaches, digestive problems, and other aches and pains often occur.

These grief responses may actually serve a purpose. The psychological pain and physical symptoms force you to slow down, giving your mind and body the opportunity to heal.

Important: There's no fixed timetable for grieving. No one can say "you should be over it" in three months, six months or even a year. As long as the general trend is toward feeling better, it's normal to have ups and downs.

Grief Can Be Complicated

If painful feelings last for more than a few months—and don't seem to be getting better—something may have gone wrong with the grieving process.

Red flags: Thoughts of the lost person intrude throughout the day…or you're simply unable to speak about your loss…or normal life seems impossible, and you feel you can't survive without the person.

Complicated grief is more likely to occur if your relationship with the person you lost was characterized by…

• **Dependence.** We all depend on those we love. But such dependence is excessive when you can't let yourself acknowledge that the person you need so badly is dead and no longer there for you.

• **Ambivalence.** Virtually all relationships have some degree of ambivalence. For example, it's common to love a parent for his/her strength and reliability, but resent that person's tendency toward harsh judgment. Even in the most loving of marriages, anger comes up from time to time. Recognizing our negative feelings toward the deceased person can trigger guilt, so we instinctively push away those thoughts. However, the negative thoughts invariably find their way back into our consciousness, until we acknowledge them.

Regardless of the nature of the relationship, a sudden or otherwise traumatic death can complicate the task of grieving. You relive the moment—or keep trying to push it out of your mind. Problems also arise when death follows an extended illness, triggering both grief and guilt-inducing relief that the person is no longer suffering—and perhaps that you no longer have to take care of him.

Allowing Yourself to Grieve

Grieving involves experiencing your full range of emotions, including anger, resentment and relief as well as sadness. Some of these feelings may be hard to bear, especially if you have no one with whom to share them. Most people find it helpful to have the emotional support of others.

What to do…

• **Don't isolate yourself.** Spend time with compassionate, understanding friends and family members who are willing to listen, and tell them how you feel.

If you need to talk more than these people are willing to listen, consider joining a grief support group. Meeting regularly with people who share a similar loss gives you the opportunity to express your feelings. Local hospitals, hospices and mental-health facilities can help you find a support group.

Online support groups can be helpful if you live in a remote area, prefer not to deal with others face-to-face or lack transportation. To find an online support group, go to the Internet community Grief-Net, *www.griefnet.org*.

- **Be active.** For many people, doing is better than simply talking. Volunteer work can be especially healing—helping others diverts you from your own sadness and is a powerful way to help yourself.

Physical exercise also is a potent mood-lifter and a general aid to mental health. Anything that gets your body moving is a step in the right direction.

- **Take time to grieve.** Particularly if you have a busy schedule, spend five to 10 minutes a day in a quiet, private place where you feel safe and comfortable experiencing your grief. Focus on your feelings and on thoughts about the deceased. This way, if your grief intrudes during the day, you can remind yourself that you will have a chance to grieve at some point later.

When to Get Help

If your own efforts to deal with grief aren't enough, a professional can help you find where and why you're stuck.

Consider therapy or counseling if you're showing signs of depression—you can't work, can't sleep, can't eat, can't get interested in anything or can't deal with other people. Ask your physician to direct you to a therapist or counselor with experience in dealing with grief. Or you can find a list of "thanatologists"—grief specialists—from the Association for Death Education and Counseling, 847-509-0403, *www.adec.org*.

You also may want to consult your doctor about short-term use of medication to help you function in your day-to-day activities.

13

The Nutrients That Help Beat Cancer

The Secrets of Beating Recurrence

Keith Block, MD, medical director of the Block Center for Integrative Cancer Treatment in Skokie, Illinois, clinical assistant professor and director of integrative medicine, College of Medicine, University of Illinois at Chicago, editor-in-chief, *Integrative Cancer Therapies*, and author of *Life Over Cancer* (Bantam). *www.blockmd.com, www.lifeovercancer.com*

Xiao Ou Shu, MD, PhD, Vanderbilt University Medical Center in Nashville, Tennessee.

William E. Carson III, MD, professor of surgery and associate director for clinical research at Ohio State's Comprehensive Cancer Center.

Elizabeth Platz, ScD, MPH, associate professor at the Johns Hopkins Bloomberg School of Public Health and codirector of cancer prevention and control at the Johns Hopkins Sidney Kimmel Comprehensive Cancer Center.

Are you a cancer survivor? If so, you have a lot of company. Every year, hundreds of thousands of Americans diagnosed with cancer continue to live, says a new report from the Centers for Disease Control and Prevention (CDC). And that has added up to millions of people. Currently, one in 20 of us—approximately 11.7 million American adults—are cancer survivors. (Forty years ago, there were only three million cancer survivors in America.)

The CDC also found that 60% of survivors are 65 or older…22% were diagnosed with breast cancer…and 19% were diagnosed with prostate cancer.

Obviously, 100% of cancer survivors don't want their cancer to recur. But whether or not you have a recurrence isn't just a matter of chance. "There are steps you can take to reduce your risk of recurrence," says Keith Block, MD, medical director of the Block Center for Integrative Cancer Treatment in Skokie, Illinois, and author of *Life Over Cancer* (Bantam). It depends on what you do.

"If you return to the same diet and lifestyle as when you were diagnosed—the diet and lifestyle that may have contributed to your developing cancer in the first place—it's more likely your cancer will recur," he says. "You need to work as hard as possible to change the internal environment of the body so that it is less hospitable to cancer cells—and that effort includes a comprehensive revision of what you eat, how often you exercise, how well you manage stress levels and other lifestyle factors."

Preventing Recurrence

Several new studies highlight specific diet and lifestyle changes that may help stop cancer from recurring…

● **Soy and breast cancer.** In a seven-year study of more than 5,000 women with breast cancer, researchers at the Vanderbilt University Medical Center found that women with the highest intake of soy had a 32% lower rate of recurrence and a 29% lower rate of dying from the disease.

And the link between soy foods, recurrence and death rates followed a "linear dose-response pattern," say the researchers—the more soy the women ate, the lower their risk of recurrence and death from breast cancer, with benefits peaking at 11 grams (g) a day of soy protein. (Amounts over 11 g weren't more protective.) The study was published in the *Journal of the American Medical Association.*

"Soy foods are rich in isoflavones, a major group of phytoestrogens [an estrogen-like compound in plant foods] that has been hypothesized to reduce the risk of breast cancer," says Xiao Ou Shu, MD, PhD, the study leader. "However, the estrogen-like effect of isoflavones and the potential interaction between isoflavones and tamoxifen [an anti-estrogen cancer drug] have led to concern about soy food consumption among breast cancer patients.

"We found that soy food intake was associated with lower recurrence and mortality among breast cancer patients, is safe, and is potentially beneficial for women with breast cancer," she says.

What to do: To ensure an intake of 11 g of soy protein a day, eat a selection of foods from the following list, courtesy of the Soy Foods Association of North America…

● **Soy bar.** 14 g

● **Soy burger (one patty).** 13 to 14 g

● **Tofu (four ounces).** 13 g

● **Soy pasta (½ cup, cooked).** 13 g

● **Edamame (edible raw soybeans in the pod, ½ cup).** 11 g

● **Soy nuts (roasted, unsalted, ¼ cup).** 11 g

● **Soy breakfast patty (2 patties).** 11 g

● **Meatless soy ground (⅓ cup).** 10 g

● **Soy milk (1 cup).** 7 g

● **Soy cereal (1¼ cups).** 7 g

● **Soy chips (1 bag).** 7 g

● **Soy nut butter (2 tbsp).** 7 g

● **Soy yogurt (vanilla).** 6 g

● **Soy pudding (½ cup).** 6 g.

● **Stress reduction and breast cancer.** In an 11-year study of 227 women with breast cancer, researchers at Ohio State's Comprehensive Cancer Center found that women who were enrolled in a "psychological intervention program"—which taught patients how to cope with their disease—were 45% less likely to have a recurrence, and 56% less likely to die from the disease, compared with women not in the program. And even women who did have a recurrence were 59% less likely to die from the disease if they were in the program.

The program included many stress reduction techniques, such as progressive muscle relaxation…problem-solving for common difficulties of cancer such as fatigue…education on finding support from family and friends…as well as diet and exercise recommendations.

"Stress declined for those in the intervention group," says William E. Carson, III, MD, surgical oncologist and study researcher. "They learned how to cope and they put those lessons into practice. We're finding that reducing stress may be another powerful therapy to fight the disease."

What to do: There are many stress-reduction techniques that work, such as progressive muscle relaxation, mindfulness-based stress reduction or cognitive behavioral therapy, says Dr. Block. "Choose one that is practical and meaningful for you."

However: He points out that the women in the study were part of a comprehensive program that included a stress reduction technique, problem-solving, support from family and friends, nutrition and fitness recommendations, and encouragement to keep up with medical follow-ups. "In fighting recurrence, a comprehensive approach is preferable to a single strategy," says Dr. Block.

• **Green tea and breast cancer.** In an analysis of data from nearly 6,000 women with breast cancer, those who drank three or more cups of green tea daily had a 27% lower risk of recurrence, reported researchers from the Harvard School of Public Health in the journal *Breast Cancer Research and Treatment*.

What to do: Drinking even more green tea daily might produce better results, says Dr. Block.

Trap: "The potential benefits of green tea may not be realized if you don't make comprehensive dietary changes, emphasizing anticancer foods that include vegetables (particularly crucifers such as broccoli), fruits, whole grains, legumes and fish rich in omega-3 fatty acids such as salmon and sardines," says Dr. Block.

• **Weight control and prostate cancer.** In a 13-year study of more than 1,300 men with prostate cancer, those who gained five or more pounds in the five years before or one year after their surgery for the disease were two times more likely to have a recurrence, compared with men whose weight was stable, reported researchers from Johns Hopkins Bloomberg School of Public Health in the *Journal of Clinical Oncology*.

"By avoiding weight gain, men with prostate cancer may prevent recurrence and improve overall well-being," says Elizabeth Platz, ScD, MPH, a study researcher.

What to do: "The good news it that being physically active—exercising regularly—reduced the risk of recurrence associated with obesity," says Dr. Platz.

• **Quitting smoking and lung cancer.** People with early stage lung cancer who don't quit smoking at the time of diagnosis have a five-year survival rate of 29% to 33%—while those who do quit smoking have a survival rate of 63% to 70%, reported UK researchers in *BMJ* (*British Medical Journal* online).

These findings support the theory that continued smoking affects the behavior of a lung tumor, say the researchers, and provides a strong case for offering smoking cessation treatment to patients with early stage lung cancer.

What to do: "It's never too late to stop," says Dr. Block.

"It's also important to eat an antioxidant-rich diet low in saturated fat and high in fiber, plant-based sources of protein and omega-3 fatty acids. An individualized antioxidant supplement regimen may also improve lung function."

Dr. Oz's Simple Ways to Add Years to Your Life

Mehmet C. Oz, MD, medical director of the integrative medicine program and director of the Cardiovascular Institute at NewYork–Presbyterian Hospital/Columbia University Medical Center. Dr. Oz is coauthor, with Michael F. Roizen, MD, of several *You* books (Free Press) and is the host of his own TV show.

Today's life expectancy is 75 years for men and 80 years for women. That's better than it was in 1970—when life expectancy was 69 for men and 74 for women—but people still could be living much longer. Many of us can increase life expectancy and have a good chance of reaching 100. *Here Mehmet Oz, MD, tells how…*

Fight Free Radicals

Every cell has hundreds of mitochondria, which convert nutrients into energy. During this conversion process, mitochondria create waste—particularly free radicals, molecules that cause inflammation and cell damage. The mitochondria in someone over age 60 are 40% less efficient than the mitochondria in someone age 40.

Result: More inflammation…more damaged cells…and more age-related diseases.

Solution 1: Eat colorful produce. Fruits and vegetables with bright colors—red grapes, blueberries, tomatoes, etc.—are high in flavonoids and carotenoids, antioxidants that inhibit free radicals and reduce inflammation.

Solution 2: Try coenzyme Q10 (CoQ10). If you don't eat lots of produce—and most people don't—consider this supplement, which can improve the efficiency of mitochondria. It also is a potent antioxidant that helps neutralize free radicals. Dr. Oz usually recommends that people start taking CoQ10 after age 35.

Dose: 200 milligrams (mg) daily (100 mg in the morning and 100 mg in the afternoon). The gel-cap form is easier for the body to absorb than the tablets.

Eat Fish Instead of Meat

Americans eat a lot of red meat, one of the main sources of saturated fat. Saturated fat increases LDL "bad" cholesterol, one of the main risk factors for heart disease, and stimulates the body's production of inflammatory proteins, believed to be an underlying cause of most age-related diseases, including cancer.

Solution 1: Eat fish three times a week. The omega-3 fatty acids in fish reduce inflammation…increase joint lubrication…decrease risk for atherosclerosis (hardening of the arteries) and arterial clots…improve immunity…reduce menopausal discomfort…and improve memory and other cognitive functions.

Solution 2: Take DHA if you don't eat fish regularly. Fish oil supplements contain the omega-3s *docosahexaenoic acid* (DHA) and *eicosapentaenoic acid* (EPA)—but humans need only the DHA.

Daily dose: 400 mg of DHA for women, and 600 mg for men. Buy the algae form. It doesn't have the fishy taste—or the undesirable additives that prolong shelf life—found in many fish oil supplements.

Take Aspirin

It's estimated that about 50 million Americans should be taking aspirin daily, but only about 20 million are doing so.

Reasons: Some people don't know that they should be taking aspirin. Others experience stomach upset when using it. And some tend to think that a drug that's so cheap and readily available isn't likely to be effective.

Fact: In studies, taking 162 mg of aspirin daily reduces the risk for a heart attack by about 36% and the risk for colon, esophageal, throat and stomach cancers by about 45%. Serious side effects from aspirin are rare.

Solution: Take one-half of a regular aspirin or two 81-mg (baby) aspirins daily (162 mg total)—but check with your doctor first. Buy the cheapest tablets. These usually are unbuffered and dissolve more quickly in the stomach.

Also helpful: Drink half a glass of warm water before and after taking aspirin. It causes the aspirin to dissolve more rapidly, so it doesn't stick to the stomach wall—the main cause of discomfort.

Boost Nitric Oxide

Nitric oxide is a naturally occurring, short-lived gas that is produced mainly in the lining of blood vessels. It plays a critical role in vasodilation—the expansion of blood vessels that allows blood to circulate with less force. Nitric oxide is thought to lower blood pressure, reduce the buildup of plaque in atherosclerosis and foster better lung function. The traditional American diet, which promotes the accumulation of fat-laden deposits on artery walls, lowers nitric oxide in the blood.

Solution: Eat less saturated fat. Limit foods that are high in saturated fat, such as meats, butter and whole-milk dairy products. Studies show that the body's production of nitric oxide declines immediately after people eat a meal that is high in saturated fat—and nitric oxide levels stay depressed for about four hours after such a meal.

Reduce Stress

Researchers have found that chronic stress prematurely shortens telomeres, the tips of chromosomes that control the ability of cells to divide and repair damaged tissues. Impaired cell division is among the main causes of age-related diseases. Research has shown that people who achieve control over daily stress have lower levels of harmful stress hormones, lower blood pressure and better immunity.

Solution: Meditate for five minutes daily. Sit silently, and try to clear your mind of thoughts. To help do this, pick a word (it doesn't matter what it is), and repeat it to yourself over and over. Focusing on the one word helps prevent other thoughts from entering your mind. Another stress reducer is exercise, such as yoga or walking.

Limit Sugar

Sugar consumption in the US has increased almost every year since the early 1980s. The average American eats 20 teaspoons of added sugar a day—from sweets, soft drinks, table sugar, etc.

Because sugary foods often replace more healthful foods in the diet, they're a primary cause of heart disease, cancer and osteoporosis. Of course, a high-sugar diet contributes to obesity, a main cause of diabetes. Excessive sugar (glucose) in the blood can result in nerve damage, kidney failure, memory problems, eye disease and arthritis.

Solution: Avoid sugar. Also avoid other white carbohydrates, such as white rice, white potatoes and white flour. These "simple sugars" have few nutrients and cause blood sugar to spike.

Diabetes indicator: If you have to urinate more than 12 times a day, or more than three times in a three-hour period, ask your doctor to test your urine for sugar, an early indicator of diabetes.

Strengthen Bones

Falls—and the resulting broken bones and complications—are among the top five causes of death.

Solution: Regular exercise—particularly weight-bearing exercises, including lifting weights and using exercise bands—increases muscle strength and bone density. Taking a daily walk strengthens leg bones, but you also need exercises that target the upper body.

Self-test: Stand on one foot with your arms out to the sides. Close your eyes, and count the seconds until you fall off balance. If you can't stay balanced for 15 seconds at age 40 or seven seconds at age 60 or older, your balance and/or strength aren't optimal. Ask your doctor about balancing exercises, etc.

■ ■ ■ ■

Cancer Fighter: Modified Citrus Pectin

Mark A. Stengler, NMD, licensed naturopathic medical doctor in private practice, Stengler Center for Integrative Medicine, Encinitas, California…adjunct associate clinical professor at the National College of Natural Medicine, Portland, Oregon… author of many books, including *The Natural Physician's Healing Therapies* and coauthor of *Prescription for Natural Cures* (both from Bottom Line Books). *www.bottomlinepublications.com*

We usually think of the peels of oranges and grapefruit as good for compost heaps and garnish on foods and not much else. But research has found another use for a substance found in peels that is known as *pectin*—and it is at the root of a possible cancer therapy.

Where It Comes From

Pectin is a compound found in the peel and pith (the white strands attached to the peel) of citrus fruits. It also is found in the peel and core of other fruits, such as apples. Even if you were to eat an orange peel, you wouldn't get any pectin that your body could use because in its natural state, its molecules are too large for us to digest. But researchers have found that when they break down pectin molecules into smaller sizes, it can be absorbed into the bloodstream.

Modified citrus pectin (MCP), which is what the over-the-counter supplement is called, has been found to stop the spread of cancer. (The word "modified" in this case means that the substance has been

changed so that it can be absorbed by humans.) MCP is not meant to be used on its own as a cancer treatment, but it provides anticancer effects when used in conjunction with conventional cancer treatments such as chemotherapy. Its benefit is impressive because the spread (metastasis) of cancer from the original site to other parts of the body is the main cause of cancer-related death. MCP has been widely studied as a treatment for prostate and breast cancers and could help many other cancers.

How MCP Works

MCP prevents tumors from metastasizing by binding with a protein called *galectin-3*, a receptor molecule on the surface of cancer cells that usually carries out a number of cancer-promoting activities. One of galectin-3's most important functions involves helping cancer cells adhere to blood vessel walls and to other cancer cells, allowing the cells to colonize healthy body tissues. By binding with galectin-3, MCP blocks this adhesion process. MCP also blocks galectin-3's ability to stimulate the formation of blood vessels in new tumors, a process called angiogenesis that is essential to tumor growth…and it appears to encourage cancer-cell death (apoptosis) by interfering with signaling pathways related to cancer-cell proliferation and survival.

Galectin-3 also helps cancer cells survive chemotherapy treatment. MCP disrupts this, enabling chemotherapy to be more effective.

What the Studies Show

In a study published in *Integrative Cancer Therapies*, Columbia University researchers found that when prostate cancer cells were exposed to MCP in the laboratory, they died off.

Its effect on androgen-independent prostate cancer (a prostate cancer in which cells do not depend on the androgen hormone for growth) is especially exciting, because there are not many effective treatments for this form of cancer, which tends to be aggressive.

A study conducted at Miami Children's Hospital (and funded by a supplement company that makes MCP) and published in *BMC Complementary and Alternative Medicine* found that MCP had a powerful effect on the immune system's ability to fight cancer, inducing a dose-dependent increase in cytotoxic T-cells and natural killer (NK) cells—two immune system components that attack and kill tumor cells. Some forms of chemotherapy fight galectin-3 molecules, too, but they also kill healthy cells. MCP is the first natural substance shown to fight galectin-3—and the hope is that with MCP the body's normal NK cell activity will work overtime to kill cancer cells while leaving healthy cells alone.

MCP also has been found to improve quality of life. In a study published in *Clinical Medicine: Oncology*, German researchers found that MCP improved the quality of life (including pain level and weight) in patients with a variety of advanced cancers, such as breast, prostate, lung, cervical, liver and pancreatic cancers.

Who Should Take MCP

There's growing interest among holistic practitioners and some oncologists in MCP. One of MCP's most important features is that it is nontoxic. The only side effect is mild digestive upset. People can take MCP with other drugs—two hours apart is best, since MCP's fiber may hinder absorption of the other drugs. It also is safe for children.

MCP is a particularly good adjunct therapy for prostate and breast cancers, which have been the most studied. MCP's cancer-fighting ability also provides a protective benefit to cancer survivors and people with a family member (parent or sibling) who has had cancer.

Recommended brand: PectaSol-C, a proprietary formulation developed and manufactured by EcoNugenics. PectaSol-C MCP can be purchased online at *www.econugenics.com*. Follow directions on the label.

■ ■ ■ ■

More from Dr. Mark A. Stengler...

Glutathione...Your Body's Master Antioxidant

There's an antioxidant in your body, glutathione (pronounced glue-tuh-THIGH-own), that does more for you than any other. And as you already know, antioxidants do a lot. One of the primary roles of all antioxidants is to neutralize free radicals that damage cell DNA. Glutathione performs this main function and more—repairing DNA... preventing cell damage (which causes cancer and other diseases)...enhancing immune function...and breaking down toxins.

Your body makes glutathione in every cell, but many people still don't have enough glutathione in their bodies. One study published a decade ago in *The Lancet* found that healthy young people had the highest levels of glutathione...healthy elderly people had lower levels...and sick elderly people, even lower levels.

In addition to aging and illness, other factors that deplete our body's reserves of this important antioxidant include environmental toxins, medications and alcohol use.

What you may not know: Glutathione supplementation can help people who have chronic diseases feel better and help people who are healthy prevent disease.

Here's more on how glutathione helps you...

What Glutathione Does

● **Kills free radicals.** Free radicals (unbalanced oxygen molecules) attack cells, damage DNA and contribute to aging. They also are involved in every disease. While vitamins such as C and E help to neutralize free radicals, glutathione deactivates the most destructive free radicals. Other antioxidants are helpful, but they don't fight as many free radicals as glutathione.

● **Revitalizes other antioxidants.** When vitamins such as C and E neutralize free radicals, their "free-radical poison" gets used up. Glutathione works to restore the activity of these antioxidants so they can tackle more free radicals. Glutathione also helps to recycle coenzyme Q10, an enzyme found in the energy-producing mitochondria of all cells, back to full strength after it neutralizes free radicals. This is important work, since every cell in your body suffers about 10,000 free-radical hits daily.

● **Helps detoxification.** The vast majority of glutathione is found in the liver, where it plays a crucial role in the breakdown and removal of environmental toxins (such as food additives and pesticides) from the body. These toxins are known to cause cancer if they are left to roam freely through the body. Glutathione also helps dispose of hazardous by-products of normal metabolism, such as cellular waste products and excess hormones.

● **Protects the liver.** An example of glutathione's ability to protect the liver comes from two recent studies of children with acute lymphoblastic leukemia who were treated with chemotherapy. Like many drugs, whether prescription or over-the-counter, chemotherapy drugs increase the risk for liver damage and hepatitis. But studies published in *Advances in Hematology and Cancer* found that either of two glutathione boosters—*N-acetylcysteine* (NAC)

combined with vitamin E…or *silymarin*, the active ingredient in the herb milk thistle—protected against liver damage in these patients. Glutathione enables the liver to break down these drugs and to bounce back from its own toxic exposure.

Benefiting from Glutathione

Glutathione is available in several types of healthy foods, although not in therapeutic amounts. Because of this, I generally have patients improve their glutathione levels through supplementation rather than diet. Still, it's helpful to know that certain foods contribute to increased glutathione levels. These include proteins that contain the amino acids glutamate, cysteine and glycine (fish, turkey, eggs and whey protein, but not other dairy products that have been pasteurized because pasteurization breaks down the protein).

While I believe that everyone can benefit from supplementing with glutathione, the best way to determine how deficient you are is with a blood test. This can be helpful if you are ill and not getting better. Low glutathione levels may be preventing your recovery.

Depending on your health, there are different ways to boost your glutathione levels.

● **For patients with chronic diseases.** Most patients with chronic diseases (such as chronic fatigue, Parkinson's disease, mercury and lead toxicity, and immune system problems, including those due to cancer and chemotherapy) can be helped by glutathione supplementation. I often prescribe a pure form of glutathione delivered via an intravenous (IV) solution. Glutathione delivered directly into the bloodstream enables the body to get higher levels of this nutrient, compared with ingesting it. Patients who have had chronic fatigue for several years often improve their strength and vitality after just one or two treatments. These patients have about 10 treatments, either once a week or once every other week. Treatments have a cumulative effect—and the results can last from weeks to months, depending on the patient's condition.

• **For patients who are temporarily ill, have liver disease or take lots of medications.** Take any combination of the supplements below to boost your glutathione levels. This can include, for example, people who have colds, flu or asthma flare-ups.

• **For healthy patients.** Patients at any age who are healthy can benefit from taking any one of the supplements below daily. I usually tell my healthy patients to start out by taking NAC, since it is a great all-around antioxidant.

Supplements That Can Help

A variety of supplements work to boost glutathione levels. All of these supplements are safe to take—on their own and in combination. There are no side effects, except as noted.

• **Liquid glutathione.** After IV glutathione, the most effective form of this antioxidant comes in liquid form. (I don't recommend glutathione in capsules because it is not well-absorbed by the body.) Liposomal liquid glutathione uses technology that reduces the particle size of glutathione and enhances its absorption by the body.

Brand to try: Vitamin Research Products Lipoceutical Glutathione (800-877-2447, *www.vrp.com*).

Dose: One teaspoon daily. It costs $60 for four fluid ounces, which equals about 24 teaspoons.

For patients who want a less expensive way to boost glutathione, there are several supplements that help the body make glutathione on its own. These supplements are not as effective as the IV and liquid forms, but they do provide a huge health benefit by boosting glutathione levels…

• **N-acetylcysteine (NAC).** This antioxidant, which helps prevent flu and reduces the severity of respiratory infections, contains cysteine and sulfur, which increase levels of glutathione. Take 500 milligrams (mg) to 1,000 mg daily.

There is no better illustration of glutathione's—and NAC's—ability to protect the liver than in the case of *acetaminophen* (Tylenol) overdose. Unless treated quickly, the liver of a person who has overdosed loses its ability to detoxify, which can lead to liver failure and death. NAC, the standard medical treatment for acetaminophen overdose, restores normal liver function.

• **Alpha-lipoic acid (ALA) is another sulfur-rich antioxidant that boosts the liver's glutathione levels.** Take 100 mg to 300 mg daily. ALA can reduce blood glucose levels, so patients with diabetes should be monitored by a physician.

• **Silymarin,** the active ingredient in milk thistle, helps liver function and increases glutathione levels. Take 100 mg to 200 mg daily.

■ ■ ■ ■

All-Natural Cancer Helper

Andrew L. Rubman, ND, medical director, Southbury Clinic for Traditional Medicines, Southbury, Connecticut.

We are always on the lookout for new, interesting information on alternative or integrative treatments for health conditions, but something that sounds too good to be true can be a scam. That's why, when a report appeared in the highly respected newsletter *Alternatives* about a relatively new adjunct treatment for cancer called Avemar, we decided to check it out.

Background on Avemar

First, a bit of background. A defining characteristic of cancer is its uncontrolled metabolism and rampant cell division. Cancer cells really have only one function: proliferation. In the 1950s, a Nobel Prize-winning Hungarian scientist (named Albert Szent-Györgyi) made great strides in cancer research by examining how naturally occurring compounds could help control metabolism in cells, which controls cell profileration.

Another Hungarian doctor built on Szent-Györgyi's work in the 1990s by showing that fermented wheat germ extract could achieve this effect. Avemar is a fermented wheat germ product.

Avemar's Effectiveness

Avemar appears to have extraordinary abilities against cancer cells. The pedigree on this stuff is pretty impressive, says Andrew L. Rubman, ND. As of now there are more than 18 published studies in peer-reviewed journals, nearly all of them showing positive results. Research at the University of California, Los Angeles (UCLA) has demonstrated that Avemar reduces glucose flow into cancer cells, which inhibits their ability to reproduce.

Although no one is saying Avemar is a cure for cancer, it has been used as an adjunct to conventional therapies. It seems to be especially effective at reducing metastasis, or the spreading of the cancer to other sites throughout the body. It seems that Avemar boosts immune system function sufficiently to allow the natural process of the body routinely killing cells to succeed much more effectively, Dr. Rubman says. It's conceivable that its ability to boost the immune system is the reason it appears to be so effective at reducing the spread of cancer.

Who Should Use It

In Hungary, Avemar is an over-the-counter dietary supplement that is used by cancer patients in conjunction with other drugs. In one pilot study in Budapest, Dr. Rubman notes, a group of patients with advanced colorectal cancer were given Avemar and had no disease progression over nine months. And David Williams, MD, editor of *Alternatives*, has been quoted as saying, "There's absolutely no reason that Avemar shouldn't be used with every single cancer patient particularly in those with severely impaired immune systems and those who are undergoing conventional therapies."

Avemar is now being tested on patients with autoimmune conditions as well.

Availability

Avemar isn't cheap, but its benefits seem substantial. It's available in this country under the name of AvéULTRA, and contains Avemar. It's sold through The Harmony Company, P.O. Box 93, Northvale, New Jersey 07647, at 800-521-0543 or on the Web at *www.theharmonyco.com*. It comes in packets and is taken as a drink once per day or as prescribed by your oncology team. Of course, don't take Avemar without your doctor's consent.

With such great immune-boosting benefits, can noncancer patients benefit from Avemar, or even just plain wheat germ? Dr. Rubman says that eating wheat germ as a general immune booster can be good for many. As for taking Avemar prophylactically, if your health-care adviser believes that your immune system could stand improved function, Avemar may be a reasonable choice.

■ ■ ■ ■

Vitamin C—A Natural Form of Chemotherapy

Mark A. Stengler, NMD, naturopathic medical doctor and leading authority on the practice of alternative and integrated medicine. Dr. Stengler is author of the *Health Revelations* newsletter, author of *The Natural Physician's Healing Therapies* (Bottom Line Books), founder and medical director of the Stengler Center for Integrative Medicine, Encinitas, California, and adjunct associate clinical professor at the National College of Natural Medicine in Portland, Oregon. *http://markstengler.com*

Most people have never heard of intravenous (IV) vitamin C, and yet it is one of the best alternative therapies to fight cancer. Vitamin C is an antioxidant with an immune-boosting effect. But according to Mark A. Stengler, NMD, when administered at very high doses, it plays an altogether different role, acting like a type of natural chemotherapy and killing cancer cells. When used in conjunction with regular chemotherapy, IV vitamin C works right alongside it, helping to kill cancer cells while also boosting the immune system and helping the body to rid itself of unwanted waste products.

The use of vitamins in the treatment of cancer is controversial, extending back 40 years to when Nobel Laureate Linus Pauling, PhD, first proposed the use of high-dose vitamin C in the treatment of cancer. Many oncologists today remain skeptical about using any type of vitamin therapy in the treatment of cancer. Cancer specialists maintain that some types of chemotherapy and radiation kill cancer cells by generating large numbers of destructive free radicals. Because vitamin C is an antioxidant, they believe that it will neutralize these free radicals and reduce the effectiveness of chemotherapy and radiation.

Dr. Stengler thinks this view is simplistic. At low doses (under 25 grams [g], or 25,000 milligrams), vitamin C's antioxidant properties do help to neutralize disease-causing free radicals. But at doses higher than 25 g, vitamin C has a pro-oxidant effect that exploits a weakness in the biochemistry of cancer cells and increases production of hydrogen peroxide, an acid that has been shown to kill cancer cells without harming healthy cells.

It's impossible to achieve the required high concentrations of vitamin C through oral supplements alone. The body regulates the amount of vitamin C that can be absorbed through the gut, and very large amounts of the vitamin will cause diarrhea. Intravenous vitamin C bypasses this problem because it goes directly into the bloodstream. Dr. Stengler provides his patients with IV vitamin C in the office. They lie comfortably in a reclining chair during a one- to two-hour treatment session, at which time they receive doses of 30 g to 75 g of vitamin C.

Promising Research

The benefits of IV vitamin C for cancer patients has been demonstrated in studies, including those by researchers at the National Institutes of Health. Laboratory studies have shown that IV vitamin C kills cancer cells but not normal cells. Studies by physicians at University of Kansas Medical Center in Kansas City, for example, described two cases in which patients suffering from advanced ovarian cancer underwent surgery and then received chemotherapy and IV vitamin C. Three years after treatment, both women had no sign of disease, which is quite unusual, because the prognosis for ovarian cancer typically is quite poor. Other research has shown the benefit of this treatment for terminally ill patients. A Korean study found that a combination of IV and oral vitamin C improved quality of life, reducing nausea and increasing energy in terminally ill patients.

Most researchers agree that data from large clinical trials are needed. Several clinical trials are currently under way to assess the effect of IV vitamin C and other antioxidants on different types of cancers.

What You Can Do Now

Many oncologists will not advocate vitamin therapy in any form.

Good advice: While you're undergoing conventional therapy, look for a medical doctor or naturopathic physician experienced in IV therapies to work with your oncologist. You and your doctors can decide whether to administer IV vitamins during or immediately after receiving conventional therapies. Your doctor will determine the number of treatments you need. Some patients get one or two IV vitamin C infusions weekly for the first year after diagnosis and initial treatment for cancer, and then every other week for a few years to help prevent cancer cells from returning and to boost the immune system.

Large amounts of vitamin C are nontoxic and generally safe for everyone except those with kidney failure, who can't tolerate large amounts. In addition, a small percentage of people are deficient in the enzyme *glucose-6-phosphate dehydrogenase* (G6PD), which is needed to maintain normal red blood cells. Without this enzyme, large amounts of vitamin C can cause hemolytic anemia, a type of anemia that involves the abnormal breakdown of red blood cells. Before receiving IV vitamin C, ask your doctor to test you for this deficiency. If you have it, you should not have IV vitamin C.

Note that patients' response to cancer treatment of any kind varies, and no physician can ever know for certain how a tumor will respond to a specific treatment.

■ ■ ■ ■

More from Dr. Mark A. Stengler...

Mistletoe Extract for Cancer

It's not often that there is a proven natural treatment to recommend to the approximately 12 million people in the US who currently have cancer. One that has emerged recently is an extract made from European mistletoe (*Viscum album*), a plant that grows on apple, oak, maple and other trees. (You know it as a holiday decoration.)

Mistletoe extract has become one of the most well-studied compounds in complementary cancer therapy (with more than 120 published studies). It is widely used in Europe, particularly in Germany, Austria and Switzerland. In fact, in Germany, mistletoe extract is a licensed medicine that is partly reimbursable through the health-care system...and more than 50% of cancer patients are treated with the plant in some form. In Switzerland, it is fully reimbursable through health insurance.

Mistletoe extract has been used in medicine for centuries. It had multidimensional uses, including treating headache, menstrual symptoms, infertility and arthritis. Interest in mistletoe extract as a treatment for cancer was ignited in the 1920s.

Today several companies manufacture mistletoe extract under the brand names Iscador, Helixor, Isorel and others. One of the most studied formulations is Iscador.

Available from conventional medical and holistic doctors in the US and around the world, mistletoe extract is most often used in conjunction with standard cancer treatments such as chemotherapy and/or radiation. It has been found to increase the effectiveness of, and reduce the side effects from, conventional therapies and to improve patients' immunity and quality of life, including vitality, sleep and appetite.

I regularly prescribe mistletoe extract to my patients—to help those with cancer battle the disease and also as a postcancer treatment.

Find out what mistletoe extract can do...

How It Can Help

Medicinally, mistletoe extract's active compounds seem to be related to two main components—viscotoxins, proteins that exhibit cell-killing activity and stimulate the immune system...and lectins, molecules that bind to cells and induce biochemical changes in those cells. However, since the extract is made from the whole plant, including leaves, stems and berries, it contains hundreds of active compounds.

Studies have shown that mistletoe extract can help in a number of ways and with several different types of cancers. *What some studies have found...*

• **Patients with cancer of the colon, rectum, stomach, breast or lung** who took Iscador in addition to the conventional therapies reviewed in the study (chemotherapy and/or radiation) lived about 14 months, or 40%, longer than those who did not take mistletoe extract, according to a study published in *Alternative Therapies in Health and Medicine*.

• **Mistletoe extract extended survival time in patients with malignant melanoma** in a study published in a German journal. Patients had significantly lower rates of metastases compared with the control group.

• **Patients with colorectal cancer** who were treated with Iscador in addition to conventional treatment experienced fewer adverse side effects...better symptom relief...and improved disease-free survival rates compared with those treated with only conventional therapy, according to a study in the *Journal of Clinical Oncology*.

At last year's American Society for Clinical Oncology meeting in Washington, DC, researchers presented the results of a Phase I clinical trial that tested the safety of Helixor and the drug *gemcitabine* (Gemzar) in patients with advanced solid tumors of the breast, pancreas or colon.

Finding: 48% of patients taking both Helixor and Gemzar benefited from enhanced immune function and an increase in infection-fighting cells. Helixor also may allow for higher doses of chemotherapy.

Mistletoe extract improved the quality of life of 270 breast cancer patients undergoing chemotherapy, says a German study published in *Phytomedicine*. Physicians rated improvements in general well-being (87% of patients), mental health (71%) and disease coping (50%). Patients also reported improved appetite and sleep and less pain. Well-being is believed to result from mistletoe extract's anti-inflammatory effect, which can reduce pain and boost energy.

In addition, mistletoe extract has been found to inhibit growth of malignant cells and cause cancer-cell death (apoptosis)... and protect cell DNA.

How It Is Used

Mistletoe extract typically is given by injection. It also is available as a tincture and can be given intravenously—however, all the studies used the injection form. Cancer patients should use only the injection form because that's the form that has been studied. I teach my patients how to give themselves the injection in the abdomen or upper side of the thigh three times a week. We begin after a diagnosis and before surgery and/or chemotherapy/radiation. Even if mistletoe extract is not given immediately after diagnosis, it can be started at any time during the course of conventional cancer treatment.

Different species of mistletoe extract can treat different types of cancer. Doctors can use varying strengths depending on patients' responses to mistletoe extract. I like to have patients take mistletoe extract for five years after being diagnosed because it optimizes the immune system to continue fighting cancer.

As with most natural substances, the US Food and Drug Administration has not approved mistletoe extract as a cancer treatment. However, in this country, injectable mistletoe is available as a prescription. Any licensed primary care doctor can order and prescribe it. It costs about $200 a month and is not covered by insurance.

Patients with cancer should have this treatment only while being supervised by a doctor.

Side effects are uncommon but can include headache, dizziness, fatigue and itching. An allergic reaction is rare but possible. A normal reaction may include mild fever for one to two days after the first injection, swelling of local lymph nodes and redness or swelling at the injection site for 48 hours. Doctors look for this reaction—it means that the treatment is working and is prompting an immune response.

People who have an autoimmune disease such as rheumatoid arthritis or multiple sclerosis…high fever…active tuberculosis…or hyperthyroidism should be attentive to any symptoms that might occur because mistletoe extract can aggravate these conditions. Transplant patients and others who take immune-suppressing drugs should not use mistletoe extract.

Don't eat any part of the mistletoe plant—some species are toxic. For more information on mistletoe extract, speak to a holistic doctor who has experience using it.

Beware the Beef…and Poultry and Pork

Timothy C. Birdsall, ND, vice president of integrative medicine for Cancer Treatment Centers of America, a national network of cancer care facilities. Based in Zion, Illinois, he is the coauthor of *How to Prevent and Treat Cancer with Natural Medicine* (Riverhead). *www.cancercenter.com*

Are you a big meat eater? You may want to reconsider. A diet high in meat and poultry increases cancer risk. *Here's why…*

● **Sedentary farm animals tend to have more body fat than wild or free-range animals.** High-fat meat and poultry contain more arachidonic acid, a fatty acid that promotes cell-damaging inflammation.

● **Cattle often are given hormones to make them bigger.** When we eat their meat, we ingest residual hormones that may stimulate cancer growth.

● **Preserved, cured and smoked meats**—such as hot dogs, ham, bacon, smoked turkey and salami—contain preservatives called nitrites, which the body can convert into carcinogenic *nitrosamines.*

● **Grilling meat or poultry allows fat to drip onto coals,** forming carcinogenic *polycyclic aromatic hydrocarbons* (PAHs)—which smoke then deposits onto the food.

To decrease your risk…

● **Choose meats and poultry labeled "free-range,"** which generally contain less fat.

● **To avoid hormones, opt for poultry or pork** (the USDA prohibits hormone use in these animals)…or buy beef labeled "hormone-free."

● **Select nitrite-free brands** of deli meats, hot dogs and bacon.

● **When grilling, stick to vegetables,** which do not form PAHs. If you do grill meat, cut off charred bits.

- **Limit serving sizes of meat and poultry to three or four ounces**—about the size of a woman's palm.

■ ■ ■ ■

Mighty Mushrooms Combat Breast Cancer

Cynthia Bye, ND, a naturopathic physician specializing in complementary cancer care at Journey to Wellness, her private practice in Vancouver, Washington. She is a graduate of the National College of Naturopathic Medicine in Portland, Oregon, a past board member of the American Association of Naturopathic Physicians and a current member of the board of directors of the Ovarian Cancer Alliance of Oregon and Southwest Washington. *www.cynthiabye.com*

Breast cancer. Those two words strike fear into the heart of just about any woman—and with good reason. According to the American Cancer Society, nearly 290,000 new cases of breast cancer will be diagnosed in the US each year. Such statistics can leave us feeling that it is only a matter of time before breast cancer affects us or someone we love.

Cynthia Bye, ND, a naturopathic doctor based in Vancouver, Washington, often prescribes mushroom extracts for patients who want to be proactive in improving their immune function and reducing their cancer risk. And in fact, a growing body of research suggests that certain mushrooms are powerful weapons in the fight against breast cancer and other cancers. *For instance, various mushrooms…*

- **Contain chemicals** (including conjugated linoleic acid) that act as aromatase inhibitors. Aromatase is an enzyme in fat tissue that converts testosterone to estrogen. Since estrogen fuels many breast tumors, certain mushrooms combat breast cancer by suppressing aromatase activity.

- **Increase apoptosis,** the natural programmed death of old, worn-out cells. This acts as a check against the cells becoming cancerous (since cancer cells proliferate instead of undergoing apoptosis).

- **Stimulate the immune response through the action of beta glucans,** substances that support the production and/or function of various disease-fighting cells, including such disease-fighting white blood cells as T-cells and natural killer cells.

- **Simply eating more mushrooms may be good for you**—but for maximum therapeutic effects, consider mushroom extracts.

Reason: Beta glucans are in the mushrooms' cell walls, which you cannot digest. To get the beta glucans, Dr. Bye says, you need mushroom supplements prepared through a process called hot water extraction.

Dr. Bye recommends using mushroom extracts only under the guidance of a naturopathic doctor who is trained in their use,

Magnesium for Nerve Pain

Soaking in a bath with Epsom salts, which are granules of magnesium sulfate, is a well-known way to ease aches and pains. But I believe that magnesium's role in relieving severe pain has been barely tapped. In one study, British doctors used IV magnesium to treat people with postherpetic neuralgia, intense pain after a shingles (*herpes zoster*) outbreak. Pain was significantly reduced after just 30 minutes of receiving magnesium. Another study found that a onetime IV dose of 500 milligrams (mg) to 1,000 mg of magnesium sulfate eliminated nerve pain related to metastases in cancer patients. In my own practice, I find that a combination of IV and oral magnesium eases nerve pain.

Mark A. Stengler, NMD, naturopathic medical doctor and leading authority on the practice of alternative and integrated medicine. Dr. Stengler is author of the *Health Revelations* newsletter, author of *The Natural Physician's Healing Therapies* (Bottom Line Books), founder and medical director of the Stengler Center for Integrative Medicine, Encinitas, California, and adjunct associate clinical professor at the National College of Natural Medicine in Portland, Oregon. *http://markstengler.com*

to assure that you receive a formulation specifically tailored to your needs. Mushrooms come in many different varieties—*coriolus*, cremini, maitake, portobello, reishi, shiitake, white button, etc.—and each has its own distinct health benefits. The extracts best suited to helping a healthy person stay healthy are not the same as those that might be prescribed for a person with compromised immunity…or for a woman at high risk for cancer…or for a woman with a history of breast cancer who wants to reduce the risk for recurrence.

Referrals: American Association of Naturopathic Physicians (866-538-2267, *www. naturopathic.org*).

The New Cancer Prevention Plan

D. Barry Boyd, MD, director of the Integrative Medicine Program at Greenwich Hospital-Yale New Haven Health System, and the Boyd Center for Integrative Health, both in Greenwich, Connecticut. He is the author of *The Cancer Recovery Plan: Maximize Your Cancer Treatment with This Proven Nutrition, Exercise and Stress-Reduction Program* (Avery).

The best surgery, chemotherapy and radiation therapy are not always enough to prevent a cancer recurrence. In an estimated four out of every 10 cancer cases, the malignancy comes back despite state-of-the-art medicine.

To maximize the effectiveness of standard cancer treatment, you need an integrative program that includes a healthful diet, emotional support and regular exercise. This type of approach may give the millions of Americans who are cancer survivors the best possible chance of avoiding a recurrence—and help protect people who have never had cancer and want to do all they can to prevent it.

The Mystery of Metabolism

Conventional oncologists usually advise patients to avoid weight loss, a significant side effect of chemotherapy and radiation. But for most people with cancer, avoiding weight gain is just as important. Research shows that excess weight increases the risk for the development and recurrence of many cancers as well as associated mortality.

What's the link between weight and cancer? Insulin resistance is one theory that is being extensively studied. Insulin, a hormone produced by the pancreas, is vital for glucose (blood sugar) metabolism—it brings this simple sugar into the cells to be broken down for energy. Trouble develops when the cells become less sensitive to insulin, usually as a result of a person being overweight and/or underactive. The pancreas responds by producing more insulin, and higher levels of the hormone remain in the bloodstream.

Excessive insulin levels have been linked to persistent, low-grade inflammation, which releases chemicals that stimulate the growth of cells. Many experts believe that inflammation also stimulates the growth of cancer cells. Cancer and some cancer treatments, such as hormone therapy, may increase insulin resistance as a result of decreased metabolism, reduced activity levels and changes in nutritional intake.

People diagnosed with cancer, especially if they are overweight, should be tested for insulin resistance by checking levels of fasting blood sugar, insulin and lipids, and seek treatment with medication if necessary.

A Cancer-Fighting Diet

Weight control is one of the most important ways to help your body fight cancer and promote recovery. Unfortunately, many cancer patients seek fattening comfort food, or their doctors tell them to eat whatever they want.

The ideal cancer-fighting diet consists of 45% complex carbohydrates, 25% protein and no more than 30% fat. Strong evidence has shown that this kind of balanced diet is associated with lower rates of cancer and cancer recurrence.

The Mediterranean diet—including ample amounts of fruits and vegetables, whole-grain cereals and olive oil—is a wise choice. Small meals eaten four to six times a day also are recommended. That's because people who consume their food over the course of the day—rather than in one to three big meals—tend to take in fewer calories and stay healthier.

The same guidelines are important if your appetite is diminished by nausea caused by chemotherapy or the cancer itself. In these cases, a balanced diet is important because it helps prevent nutritional deficiencies that can result from appetite loss.

To create a cancer-fighting diet...

• **Choose the right carbs.** The amount of carbohydrates you consume isn't as critical as the kind. Sharply limit pastries, candies, beverages containing high-fructose corn syrup, such as soft drinks and some fruit-juice drinks, and refined grain products, such as white rice and bread made from white flour. The carbohydrates in these foods are broken down immediately and deposited into the bloodstream, triggering an insulin surge. With repeated exposure to insulin peaks, cells become less sensitive to the hormone.

Complex carbohydrates, such as fruits and vegetables, beans, brown rice, whole-grain cereals and whole-grain baked goods, are digested and absorbed gradually. Insulin is produced at a steady, moderate rate, fueling the body's cells with maximum efficiency. What's more, the fiber in complex carbs fills you up, so you can satisfy your hunger with fewer calories.

• **Eat a variety of vegetables and fruits.** Specific "superfoods," such as beans and blueberries, have received a great deal of attention for their healing properties, but it's crucial to get a broad selection of healthful foods.

Fruits and vegetables should be a mainstay of your diet—the American Cancer Society recommends at least five daily servings. Nine daily servings are even better. One-half cup is the standard serving size. In addition to fiber and complex carbohydrates, fruits and vegetables contain chemicals known as phytonutrients that protect against carcinogens and enhance the body's own healing powers.

Broccoli, cauliflower and cabbage have different phytonutrients than garlic and onion. Berries, citrus fruits and leafy, green vegetables each have their own nutrients. Eating a variety of fruits and vegetables ensures that you get them all.

• **Avoid dangerous fats.** Saturated fats, found mostly in meats and high-fat dairy products, promote insulin resistance, so limit your meat intake to two servings (three ounces per serving) of lean red meat per week and consume only low-fat or non-fat dairy products (one to three servings daily). Good protein sources include poultry, fish, nuts and legumes.

Trans fat, which is found in many baked goods and processed foods, can also cause inflammation.

Beware: Even in food products that claim "0" trans fat on the food labels, small amounts may be present and listed as "partially hydrogenated oil."

On the other hand, omega-3 fatty acids, found in cold-water fish, such as salmon, sardines and herring, have been shown to reduce inflammation and provide a range of other anticancer benefits. Other sources of omega-3s include walnuts and flaxseed.

Important: Food is the best way to get vitamins, minerals and other nutrients. High-dose supplements should be taken only under the supervision of a health-care professional who is knowledgeable about nutrition and cancer care.

Emotional Support

Serious illness, such as cancer, can trigger the release of stress hormones that increase your risk of developing excessive insulin levels. *Advice...*

• **Get emotional support.** In a Yale study that followed more than 300 women with breast cancer for 10 years, those who felt free to talk about their illness with others were significantly more likely to survive. Don't be reluctant to ask friends and family for help in performing difficult chores and for company during doctor visits.

• **Choose a doctor who gives you hope.** Hopelessness and helplessness are the worst stressors for people with cancer. Make sure your care is directed by a medical professional who focuses on the most positive possible outcome, even if the disease is severe.

Exercise Is Essential

Exercise reduces insulin resistance by building up lean, metabolically active tissue—which is better than fat tissue for cancer prevention.

In a study of 2,987 breast cancer patients, women who walked three to four hours a week had a 50% lower risk of dying from breast cancer than women who did little or no exercise. Researchers believe that physical activity also helps fight other types of malignancies.

For cancer prevention, strive for 30 minutes of brisk walking per day—or its equivalent in comparably strenuous activities, such as swimming or cycling.

■ ■ ■ ■

The Cancer Recovery Diet

Mitchell Gaynor, MD, assistant clinical professor of medicine at Weill Cornell Medical College of Cornell University in New York City. He is author of *Nurture Nature/Nurture Health* (Nurture Nature) and *Sounds of Healing: A Physician Reveals the Therapeutic Power of Sound, Voice and Music* (Broadway). *www.gaynoroncology.com*

When you are facing cancer, it is more important than ever to follow a nutritious diet that strengthens your immune system and helps your body detoxify. This often is challenging, however, because some cancer treatments interfere with the body's ability to take in or use nutrients. *Cancer patients undergoing chemotherapy and/or radiation often experience...*

• **Damage to salivary glands** resulting in a dry mouth, difficulty swallowing and unpleasant changes in taste.

• **Nausea and vomiting.**

• **Impaired absorption of nutrients and calories** due to changes in the normal intestinal bacteria.

These factors and the resulting loss of appetite deplete the body's stores of nutrients and can lead to excessive weight loss that impedes your recovery, strains your immune system and adds to fatigue.

The following nutrition plan is designed for cancer patients undergoing treatment—as well as for those who finished treatment within the past year—to help rebuild nutrient reserves. All supplements below are sold at health-food stores and/or online.

Important: Discuss your diet and supplement use with your oncologist—this helps the doctor determine the best treatment and follow-up regimen for you. *What to do...*

● **Eat plenty of protein.** Protein helps repair body tissues and prevent unwanted weight loss. It also helps minimize the memory and concentration problems ("chemo brain") common among patients on chemotherapy. The recommended dietary allowance (RDA) for women is 38 grams (g) of protein per day and for men it is 46 g—but for cancer patients, I recommend at least 70 g per day.

Example: With breakfast, include one egg (7 g) and eight ounces of unsweetened soy milk (8 g)...with lunch, a cup of lentil soup (10 g) and eight ounces of low-fat yogurt (12 g)...as a snack, two ounces of almonds (12 g)...with dinner, three ounces of chicken or fish (21 g) or one cup of soybeans (29 g).

Helpful: Consider a protein supplement—such as Biochem Sports Greens & Whey, which provides 20 g of protein per one-ounce serving.

Have eight ounces of low-fat yogurt or kefir daily. Check labels and choose unsweetened brands with live active cultures of *lactobacillus acidophilus* and *bifidobacterium*. Chemotherapy and radiation destroy beneficial bacteria in the gut. Restoring them with probiotics helps alleviate nausea, optimizes immune system function and reduces production of cancer-promoting chemicals.

Alternative: Try a probiotic supplement that contains at least one billion colony forming units (CFUs) per gram. Choose coated capsules to protect the probiotics from stomach acids. Take on an empty stomach upon awakening and also one hour before lunch and dinner.

Good brand: Natren Healthy Trinity (866-462-8736, *www.natren.com*).

● **Boost fiber.** This combats constipation, a common side effect of chemotherapy. Aim for six to 10 servings of whole grains daily.

Examples: One slice of whole-grain bread...one-half cup of cooked brown rice, rolled barley, millet or buckwheat...one-half cup of old-fashioned oatmeal.

Also eat seven to 10 servings of fruits and vegetables daily, which provide fiber and cancer-fighting phytonutrients (plant chemicals). If you have lost your taste for vegetables, have juice instead—it is easier to swallow. Carrots, celery, watercress and beets make delicious juices. Juicers are sold at kitchenware stores ($50 and up).

● **Focus on anti-inflammatory foods.** The same enzyme (called COX-2) that causes inflammation also may increase levels of compounds that allow cancer cells to grow. Lowering the body's inflammatory response may be protective.

Best: Eat cold-water fish (salmon, sardines, herring, mackerel, cod) at least three times per week—these are rich in anti-inflammatory omega-3 fatty acids. Avoid tuna, swordfish and shark, which may contain mercury and other metals.

Alternative: Take 2.5 g of a fish oil daily with food.

Also helpful: Use curry powder liberally to spice up vegetables, meats and poultry—it is a natural anti-inflammatory.

● **Eat foods rich in calcium, magnesium and vitamin D.** These bone-building nutrients are especially important for cancer patients who take steroid medication to control nausea, because steroids can weaken bones. Increase your intake of foods that provide calcium (low-fat dairy, fortified cereals, leafy green vegetables)...magnesium (nuts, beans, quinoa)…and vitamin D (fish, fortified dairy). Also supplement daily with 1,500 milligrams (mg) of calcium citrate…400 mg of magnesium…and 1,000 international units (IU) of vitamin D-3.

● **Minimize intake of sugar and white flour.** Eating these foods temporarily increases your levels of insulin-like growth factor (IGF), which has hormonelike effects. Although the long-term consequences are unclear, some research suggests a link between high IGF levels and cancer, especially of the breast and colon.

● **Drink plenty of fluids.** Dehydration contributes to decreased salivation…promotes inflammation…and stresses the kidneys and liver, making it harder for these organs to detoxify the body. Drink at least six eight-ounce glasses of water, broth or tea per day.

Beneficial: Green tea contains compounds that may inhibit *angiogenesis* (creation of blood vessels that feed cancer cells).

● **Opt for organic.** Conventionally grown produce often has pesticide and herbicide residues that stress the liver. Choose free-range chicken and beef from grass-fed cows to minimize exposure to antibiotics and hormones in the feed of nonorganic animals. Remove the skin from poultry and fish before cooking, even if organic—skin tends to store a high concentration of toxins.

Helpful: A dietitian who specializes in oncology nutrition can help monitor your nutrient intake and recommend alternatives if certain foods are difficult to eat.

Referrals: American Dietetic Association, 800-877-1600, *www.eatright.org*.

■ ■ ■ ■

The Anticancer Diet From a Doctor Who Fought Cancer

The late **David Servan-Schreiber, MD, PhD,** neuroscientist and clinical professor of psychiatry at University of Pittsburgh School of Medicine and author of *Anticancer: A New Way of Life* (Viking). He died after a 20-year battle with cancer. *www.anticancerbook.com*

At any given time, the average person might have thousands of cancer cells in his/her body. Individually, these abnormal cells are harmless, but any one of them could potentially proliferate and form a mass of cells (a tumor) that damages normal tissues and can spread to other parts of the body. About one-third of us eventually will get full-fledged cancer.

Often people who get cancer have created impairments in their natural defenses, allowing cancer cells to survive and proliferate. About 85% of all cancers are caused by environmental and lifestyle factors. We can't always control our environments, but we can control what we eat. Diet is one key factor that determines who gets cancer and who doesn't.

Example: Asian men have just as many precancerous microtumors in the prostate gland as American men, yet they are as much as 60 times less likely to develop prostate cancer. It's not a coincidence that their diets are far healthier, on average, than those consumed by men in the US. Asian men eat far more fruits and vegetables than Americans and relatively little red meat. They also tend to eat more fish and soy foods, and they drink more tea, especially green tea. These and other dietary factors allow their immune systems and other natural defenses to prevent cancer cells from proliferating.

My story: I was a physician in Pittsburgh when I was first diagnosed with a brain tumor in 1992. With the benefit of hindsight—and years of research into the origins and development of cancer—I have come to understand that my previous lifestyle, particularly my poor diet, fostered a procancer environment. For example, a typical lunch for me was chili con carne, a plain bagel and a can of Coke.

Causes of Cancer

It can take years for cancer cells to turn into tumors—assuming that they ever do. This lag time means that we have many opportunities to create an anticancer environment in our bodies.

There are three main factors that promote the development of cancer...

• **Weakened immunity.** The immune system normally patrols the body for bacteria and viruses, as well as for cancer cells. When it spots something foreign, it dispatches a variety of cells, including natural killer cells, to destroy the foreign substance. In people who eat an unhealthy diet—not enough produce, too much alcohol, very little fish and so on—the immune system works less efficiently. This means that cancer cells can potentially slip under the radar and eventually proliferate.

• **Inflammation.** Millions of Americans have subclinical chronic inflammation. It doesn't cause symptoms, but it can lead to heart disease and cancer. Chronic inflammation can be caused by infection, a diet low in antioxidant nutrients and even emotional stress. It's accompanied by the release of cytokines and other inflammatory chemicals. Inflammation also prevents the immune system from working efficiently.

• **Angiogenesis.** Cancer cells, like other cells in the body, need blood and nourishment to survive. They send out chemical signals that stimulate the growth of blood vessels that carry blood to and from the cancer.

This process is called angiogenesis—and it can be strongly influenced by what we eat.

Example: People who eat no more than 12 ounces of red meat weekly can reduce their overall risk for cancer by 30%. Red meat stimulates the release of inflammatory chemicals that inhibit apoptosis, the genetically programmed cell death that prevents uncontrolled growth.

Cancer Fighters

The best cancer-fighting foods...

• **Fatty fish.** The omega-3 fatty acids in fish reduce inflammation. Oncologists in Scotland have measured inflammatory markers in the blood of cancer patients since the 1990s. They have found that patients with the lowest levels of inflammation are twice as likely to live through the next several years as patients who have more inflammation.

Laboratory studies indicate that a high-fish diet can reduce the growth of lung, breast, colon, prostate and kidney cancers. And naturally, people who eat more fish tend to eat less red meat.

Important: The larger fatty fish, such as tuna, are more likely to be contaminated with mercury and other toxins. The best sources of omega-3s are smaller fatty fish, such as sardines, anchovies and small mackerel.

• **Low-glycemic carbohydrates.** The glycemic index measures the effects of the carbohydrates in foods on blood glucose levels. Foods with a high glycemic index, such as white bread and table sugar, cause a rapid rise in insulin as well as a rise in insulin-like growth factor (IGF). IGF stimulates cell growth, including the growth of cancer cells. Both insulin and IGF also promote inflammation.

Data from the Harvard Nurses' Health Study indicate that people who eat the most high-glycemic foods (these same people tend to be sedentary and overweight) are 260% more likely to get pancreatic cancer and 80% more likely to get colorectal cancer.

Recommended: Unprocessed carbohydrates that are low on the glycemic scale, such as whole-grain breakfast cereals and breads (with whole wheat, barley, oats, flaxseeds, etc.)...cooked whole grains, such as millet, quinoa and barley...and vegetables, such as broccoli and cauliflower.

Also important: Reduce or eliminate refined sugar as well as honey.

Better: Agave nectar, available at most health-food stores. Extracted from cactus sap, it's sweeter than sugar or honey, yet it has a glycemic index four to five times lower. You can use agave nectar just as you would sugar or honey—by adding it to cereals, tea and so on. Because of the liquid content of the syrup, you'll generally want to reduce the amount of other liquids in baked goods. Substitute three-quarter cup of agave nectar per one cup of any other sweetener.

- **Green tea.** Between three and five cups daily can significantly reduce your cancer risk. A chemical in green tea, *epigallocatechin gallate* (EGCG), inhibits angiogenesis. Green tea also contains polyphenols and other chemical compounds that reduce inflammation and activate liver enzymes that break down and eliminate potential carcinogens.

In men who already have prostate cancer, consuming five cups or more of green tea daily has been associated with reduced risk of progressing to advanced cancer by 50%. In women with certain types of breast cancer, three cups daily reduced relapses by 30%. Because black tea is fermented, it has a lower concentration of polyphenols and is less protective than green tea.

- **Soy foods.** The isoflavones in tofu, soy milk, edamame (green soybeans) and other soy foods help prevent breast cancer, particularly in women who started eating soy early in life. These compounds, known as phytoestrogens, have estrogen-like effects. They occupy the same cellular receptors as the body's estrogen yet are only about one-hundredth as active. This means that they may slow the development of estrogen-dependent tumors.

Recommended: Three servings of soy per week.

- **Turmeric.** No other food ingredient has more powerful anti-inflammatory effects. In laboratory studies, the active ingredient curcumin in the spice turmeric inhibits the growth of many different cancers. It helps prevent angiogenesis and promotes the death of cancer cells.

In India, people consume an average of one-quarter to one-half teaspoon of turmeric daily. They experience one-eighth as many lung cancers as Westerners of the same age...one-ninth as many colon cancers...and one-fifth as many breast cancers.

- **Asian mushrooms, such as shiitake, maitake and enokitake.** They're available in most supermarkets and gourmet stores and are one of the most potent immune system stimulants. Among people who eat a lot of these mushrooms, the rate of stomach cancer is 50% lower than it is among those who don't eat them. One to two half-cup servings weekly probably is enough to have measurable effects.

- **Berries.** Berries contain ellagic acid, which strongly inhibits angiogenesis. Aim for one-half cup per day.

- **Dark chocolate.** One ounce contains twice as many polyphenols as a glass of red wine and almost as much as a cup of green tea. Laboratory studies indicate that these compounds slow the growth of cancer cells.

Look for a chocolate with more than 70% cocoa. The lighter milk chocolates don't contain adequate amounts of polyphenols—and the dairy in milk chocolate blocks the absorption of polyphenols.

■ ■ ■ ■

Strawberries Join the Fight Against Cancer

Tong Chen, MD, PhD, assistant professor in medical oncology, The Ohio State University Comprehensive Cancer Center, Columbus.

Strawberries are high on a select list of super-healthy foods that virtually everyone likes. And listen up—now comes news that they are much more important to our health than previously thought. A new study done at The Ohio State University Comprehensive Cancer Center on freeze-dried strawberries and precancerous esophageal lesions found that the berries were extremely effective in slowing the development of those lesions.

Anything that helps the fight against esophageal cancer is very welcome news. Not only have the number of cases been growing, but it's also a very deadly cancer.

Berries Bring Reversals

The research (which was sponsored by the California Strawberry Commission) was done in China, where the incidence of esophageal cancer—the type known as squamous cell carcinoma—is extremely high. Americans more typically suffer from a different type of esophageal cancer, known as adenocarcinoma. Lead researcher Tong Chen, MD, PhD, assistant professor in medical oncology at Ohio State, says that strawberries may similarly affect the type of cancer common in the West because they impact some genes common to both types.

The study had 36 participants, average age 54, all of whom had precancerous lesions of the esophagus. Dr. Chen says that such precancerous lesions are graded mild or moderate (severe ones are clinically considered cancer) and that eventually about 25% of patients with mild lesions and 50% of those with moderate lesions progress to cancer. However, in her study, in which each participant ate about two ounces of freeze-dried strawberries a day, 29 of the 36 participants—about 80%—experienced at least some reversal of lesion progress, with some moderate lesions becoming mild and some mild ones reverting to normal. Dr. Chen says, "Our study is important because it shows that strawberries may be an alternative to—or may work together with—chemopreventive drugs to help stop esophageal cancer. But we will need to test this in randomized placebo-controlled trials in the future."

Big Power in a Little Berry

As a cancer fighter, strawberries have a powerful combination of molecular components, says Dr. Chen. They contain antioxidant polyphenols, of course, and also vitamins A, C and E, folic acid, calcium, selenium and zinc. As she points out, you can buy all of these in supplemental form, but in strawberries there seems to be a synergistic effect among the components that makes them more potent than the individual components are on their own. Freeze-drying the fruit takes it to an even more impressive level as a nutrient powerhouse—this process removes water from the fruit, leaving a much denser nutritional content within. In the case of strawberries, which are 90% water, when freeze-dried, the end product is 10 times more nutritious than the equivalent weight of fresh berries.

Freeze-dried strawberries are widely available now in supermarkets and health-food stores.

■ ■ ■ ■

Ginseng and Flaxseed a Boon for Cancer Patients

Robert F. Ozols, MD, PhD, former senior vice president for the medical science division at Fox Chase Cancer Center in Philadelphia, where he oversaw the center's patient care, clinical research and medical science laboratory research. He was a past chair of ASCO's Cancer Communications Committee.

Jeremy R. Geffen, MD, president of Geffen Visions International, Inc., and director of integrative oncology of P4 Healthcare and Caring4Cancer.com. Dr. Geffen is author of *The Journey Through Cancer: Healing and Transforming the Whole Person* (Three Rivers Press). *www.geffenvisions.com*

There's double good news in the area of cancer treatment. First is that two widely available dietary supplements, ginseng and flaxseed, have been shown in clinical studies to be potentially useful for some people with cancer. Second, these studies serve as further evidence that natural therapies as an adjunct to conventional ones are gaining increasing acceptance by the mainstream medical community. In the ginseng study, investigators found that the herb may help combat fatigue, one of the most common and debilitating side effects of cancer and its treatment. The flaxseed study found that flaxseed might slow the growth of prostate tumors. *Here are the important details...*

Evidence-Based Studies by Mainstream Physicians

The ginseng and flaxseed studies were highlighted at a meeting of the American Society of Clinical Oncology (ASCO), where the nation's cancer doctors convene to discuss the latest advances in cancer therapy.

We asked Robert F. Ozols, MD, PhD, oncologist and former senior VP for the medical science division at Fox Chase Cancer Center in Philadelphia, whether the presentation of complementary and alternative medicine (CAM) studies at a national medical conference indicates their greater acceptance as part of a standard of care for cancer. Noting that many oncologists have long been skeptical about whether CAM treatments have some potential benefit for cancer, he says, "As physicians, we live by the rule that we must have evidence-based results before we can recommend a treatment—anecdotal results don't really count. The positive results of these studies are very encouraging."

Until recently, few clinical trials have evaluated the effectiveness of CAM treatments for cancer. This may change, however, as more patients seek them out and discuss them with their doctors. We asked medical oncologist Jeremy R. Geffen, MD, if he notices a new trend in this area. Dr. Geffen, the founder of Geffen Visions International in Boulder, Colorado, is a pioneer in combining state-of-the-art conventional cancer treatments with safe and effective CAM therapies. "Up to 80% of all cancer patients use some form of CAM therapy during the course of their illness," he says. "As with most revolutions in medicine, mainstream physicians and medical centers understand and adopt new practices at different rates. It is unequivocally clear, however, that on a national level a fundamental paradigm shift has occurred. The ginseng and flaxseed studies are part of a trend in medicine in general, and oncology in particular, that is continuing to gain momentum. It's now clear that a variety of CAM therapies can indeed be safely and effectively integrated into mainstream care in a way that is meaningful for patients and health-care providers."

Ginseng May Help Combat Fatigue

While many cancer patients already take the herb ginseng to increase energy and combat fatigue, its effectiveness had never been rigorously tested. Conducted in part by the Mayo Clinic, the ginseng study involved 282 patients with different types of cancers and a history of fatigue, divided into four groups—one group took 750 milligrams (mg)/day of American ginseng…another group took 1,000 mg/day…and another group 2,000 mg/day. The final group took a placebo. Surveyed about their levels of fatigue throughout the eight-week study period, 25% of those who took 1,000 mg and 27% of those who took 2,000 mg reported that their fatigue levels were "moderately" to "very much" better, compared with only 10% of patients taking only 750 mg of ginseng and 10% of those who took the placebo.

Flaxseed May Slow Tumor Growth

For years flaxseed has been promoted as a dietary supplement with potential anticancer properties. Flaxseed has high quantities of lignan, a substance that binds to the metabolites of the hormones testosterone and estrogen and may block their cancer-promoting effects. In previous studies, lignan slowed the growth of prostate cancer cells grown in laboratories, and flaxseed reduced tumor size in mice with prostate cancer. Conducted by investigators at Duke University Medical Center and the University of Michigan, the flaxseed study involved 161 men with prostate cancer who were scheduled to have surgery to remove their prostate. The men were randomly divided into four groups—a control group who maintained their usual diets…men who consumed their usual diets but also took 30 grams of flaxseed per day…men who consumed a low-fat diet with less than 20% of their total calories coming from fat…and men who took flaxseed and also restricted their in-take of dietary fat. After roughly a month, the men's prostates were removed and the tumors were studied. Cancer cell growth had slowed in the two flaxseed groups compared with the placebo or dietary fat reduction groups.

Although the ginseng and flaxseed studies show promise for helping cancer patients, researchers stop short of recommending their usage as viable cancer treatments until more studies are conducted. "We need to explore flaxseed and ginseng in further controlled clinical studies," says Dr. Ozols. "As these therapies prove themselves in clinical trials, they will be added to our cancer-fighting armament."

Safe Use of Cam Treatments For Cancer

As with any therapy, natural or not, CAM treatments may have side effects or harmful interactions with other drugs or supplements. *If you are thinking about using CAM therapies for cancer…*

● **Be an informed consumer.** Don't use a CAM therapy simply because you've heard it may work. For your health and safety, learn as much as you can about the CAM treatment, including risks, benefits and side effects. Web sites where you can obtain information about the safety and effectiveness of CAM treatments, including scientific studies that may have been conducted, include the National Center for Complementary and Alternative Medicine (NCCAM) Web site, *nccam.nih.gov*…the Food and Drug Administration (FDA) Web site, *www.fda.gov*… and the American Cancer Society's Web site, *www.cancer.org*.

● **Make sure you receive the CAM treatment from a health-care practitioner who has knowledge and experience using it.** "Natural" isn't necessarily safe and all treatments should be prescribed by practitioners with experience and expertise in their use.

• **Tell your doctor about any and all CAM therapies you use.** Providing a complete picture of all therapies, including vitamins and supplements, will help ensure coordinated and safe care. "Many substances used in CAM can have potentially adverse interactions with conventional chemotherapy or radiation," warns Dr. Geffen.

• **Put together the best team to help you fight your cancer.** Any CAM practitioner to whom you go for treatment should work with your oncologist. Also, naturopathic physicians have extensive training and a wealth of knowledge about natural solutions to medical problems, but they are not formally trained to treat cancer. If you aren't already under the care of a naturopath, you might consider adding one to your team to work closely with your oncologist in order to be sure you are doing everything you can to feel your best and beat your cancer.

• **Discuss CAM therapies with your doctor before making decisions about treatment or care.** Be advised, however, that your doctor may not know anything about these treatments—and their particular risks or benefits. "Oncologists may not have clear answers to all of a patient's questions—sometimes the science just isn't there yet," says Dr. Geffen. "It's a real conundrum at times because we often don't have the information we need to make good recommendations—yet many people want to take a wide variety of substances despite the potential risks. That's why more research is so important, and why these studies reported at the ASCO conference are so meaningful."

Flaxseed Cautions

Jonathan Goodman, ND, naturopathic physician with private practices in Bristol and Bloomfield, Connecticut. An adjunct professor at the University of Bridgeport's College of Naturopathic Medicine, Dr. Goodman is author of *The Omega Solution* (Prima Lifestyles). www.drgoodmannd.com

Flax is one of the few plant foods that provide omega-3s, but you have to use a lot. That's because flaxseed contains short-chain fatty acids, mainly alpha-linolenic acid (ALA), that are converted to longer-chain omega-3s in the body.

The conversion process isn't efficient, so you would need to consume much more flaxseed to get the equivalent level of omega-3s found in fish oil. (For best absorption, flaxseed should be ground before consuming.)

Is flaxseed safe for everyone? Flaxseed contains lignans, substances that have complicated effects on estrogen metabolism and

Cancer-Fighting Food Combos

Many fruits and vegetables known for their cancer-fighting properties work even better when combined.

Broccoli and tomatoes: Broccoli contains sulforaphane, and tomatoes contain lycopene. Eaten together, they maximize each other's ability to fight cancer.

Soy and tea (black or green): A diet high in soy and tea can lower risk of prostate and breast cancers.

Selenium and sulforaphane: When combined, these can have a significant effect on the genes that control cancer development. Selenium can be found in poultry, tuna, eggs and sunflower seeds. Sulforaphane can be found in broccoli, cabbage and watercress.

Andrew L. Rubman, ND, director, Southbury Clinic for Traditional Medicines, Southbury, Connecticut.

may protect against estrogen-driven breast cancer. However, because the research is inconclusive, consult your doctor before using flax products if you have a personal or family history of breast cancer.

Because the high amounts of ALA in flaxseed oil may stimulate prostate cancer cells to grow, flaxseed oil should be avoided by men who have prostate cancer or risk factors for the disease, such as family history. However, flaxseed, which contains lower levels of ALA, appears to be safe for such men.

■ ■ ■ ■

Good and Easy...Eating The Mediterranean Way

Wendy Kohatsu, MD, assistant clinical professor of family medicine at the University of California, San Francisco, and director of the Integrative Medicine Fellowship at the Santa Rosa Family Medicine Residency Program in Santa Rosa, California. Dr. Kohatsu is also a graduate of the Oregon Culinary Institute.

There is abundant scientific evidence on the health benefits of the so-called Mediterranean diet, which promotes the traditional eating habits of long-lived people in such countries as Greece and Italy.

Landmark research: Among the most compelling evidence is one long-term European study of healthy men and women ages 70 to 90.

It found that following the Mediterranean diet as part of an overall healthful lifestyle, including regular exercise, was associated with a more than 50% lower rate of death from all causes over a decade. Numerous studies have associated this type of eating with reduced risk for heart disease, cancer, cognitive decline, and diabetes as well as obesity.

But many Americans are reluctant to try the Mediterranean diet for fear that it will be difficult or costly to follow because it emphasizes such foods as omega-3–rich fish, vegetables and nuts.

Surprising findings: Mediterranean eating does not increase food costs, according to a recent study—and this style of eating need not be complicated.

Below, Wendy Kohatsu, MD, an assistant clinical professor of family medicine at the University of California, San Francisco, and a chef who conducts cooking demonstrations for patients and doctors, explains the best ways to incorporate Mediterranean eating into your daily diet...

Easy Ways to Get Started

To effectively tap into the Mediterranean diet's powerful health benefits, it's important to know exactly which foods should be eaten—and in what quantities.

Start by getting four to five daily servings of whole grains (one serving equals one-half cup of cooked quinoa, brown rice or whole-wheat pasta, for example, or one slice of whole-wheat bread) and two to three daily servings of low- or nonfat dairy products (such as yogurt, cottage cheese or milk), which are an important source of bone-protecting calcium. *In addition, be sure to consume...*

• **Oily fish.** This high-quality protein contains abundant omega-3 fatty acids, which help fight the inflammation that plays a role in cardiovascular disease, Alzheimer's disease and asthma.

Best choices: Follow the acronym SMASH—salmon (wild)...mackerel (Spanish, not king, which tends to have higher levels of mercury)...anchovies...sardines... and herring.

How much: Three ounces (the size of a deck of cards), twice a week.

Chef's secret: Drain canned sardines (the large size), grill briefly, sprinkle with fresh lemon juice and chopped parsley.

Beware: Some fish—such as shark, swordfish, golden bass (tilefish), king mackerel and albacore tuna—can be high in mercury. Avoid these. If you eat tuna, choose the "light" version, which contains less mercury than albacore tuna does.

If you don't like fish: Take a fish oil supplement (1,000 milligrams [mg] daily). Choose a brand that guarantees that no lead or mercury is present.

My favorite brands: Carlson's and Nordic Naturals.

Vegetarians can get omega-3s from flaxseed, walnuts and other nonfish sources. However, nonfish food sources of omega-3s are largely in the form of alpha-linolenic acid (ALA), which is not as potent as the more biologically powerful fatty acids found in fish. Algae-derived *docosahexaenoic acid* (DHA) capsules contain one of the two main omega-3s found in fish. The recommended dose of DHA capsules is 1,000 mg daily.

What most people don't know: A small but important study shows that eating oily fish with beans, such as lentils and chickpeas (also known as garbanzo beans), improves absorption of the iron found in beans.

• **Olive oil.** Olive oil contains about 77% healthful monounsaturated fats. Olive oil is also high in sterols, plant extracts that help reduce LDL "bad" cholesterol and increase HDL "good" cholesterol.

Best choice: Look for extra-virgin (or "first-press") olive oil. ("Extra virgin" means that the oil is derived from the first pressing of the olives.)

How much: Use olive oil as your primary fat—in salad dressings, marinades and sautées. To minimize your total daily intake of fat, do not exceed 18 grams (g) to 20 g of saturated fat and 0 g of trans fat from all food sources.

Chef's secret: If you dislike the "grassy" taste of some extra-virgin olive oils, look for Spanish and Moroccan versions, which tend to be more mellow. One good choice is olive oil made from the arbequina olive, which has a buttery taste.

What most people don't know: Nutrients in extra-virgin olive oil may offer some pain-relieving qualities over the long term.

• **Nuts.** Like extra-virgin olive oil, nuts are high in healthful monounsaturated fats. In fact, a recent Spanish study found that a Mediterranean diet that included walnuts significantly lowered risk for heart disease.

What kinds: Besides walnuts, best choices include almonds and peanuts. Choose plain raw nuts—not salted or honey-roasted.

Broccoli Gets Cancer-Fighting Boost

When you eat broccoli with certain other vegetables, such as broccoli sprouts, arugula or radishes, you get twice the cancer-fighting power of broccoli consumed on its own, say University of Illinois researchers. These additional vegetables contain the enzyme *myrosinase*, which boosts the effectiveness of broccoli's cancer-preventive component, sulforaphane. To protect the nutrients and the enzyme, steam broccoli and vegetables for only two to four minutes.

Mark A. Stengler, NMD, naturopathic medical doctor and leading authority on the practice of alternative and integrated medicine. Dr. Stengler is author of the *Health Revelations* newsletter, author of *The Natural Physician's Healing Therapies* (Bottom Line Books), founder and medical director of the Stengler Center for Integrative Medicine, Encinitas, California, and adjunct associate clinical professor at the National College of Natural Medicine in Portland, Oregon. *http://markstengler.com*

Pomegranate Juice May Slow Prostate Cancer

In a study of 48 men who had undergone surgery or radiation therapy for prostate cancer, those who drank eight ounces of pomegranate juice daily for six years prolonged their "doubling time" from 15 months to 54 months. Doubling time is the amount of time it takes for levels of prostate-specific antigen (PSA) to double—a sign of prostate cancer progression.

Theory: The juice's antioxidants and/or anti-inflammatory substances may help slow cancer progression.

Allan J. Pantuck, MD, associate professor of urology, University of California, Los Angeles.

How much: One-quarter cup daily.

Beware: A quarter cup of nuts contains about 200 calories. Eat only a small handful daily—for example, about 23 almonds or 35 peanuts. If you're allergic to nuts, try pumpkin, sunflower or sesame seeds instead.

Chef's secret: Store nuts in your freezer to prevent them from going rancid.

• **Fruits and vegetables.** Many of the most healthful vegetables—including those of the brassica family, such as cabbage, kale, broccoli and cauliflower—originated in the Mediterranean area.

What kinds: Choose brightly colored fruit, such as citrus and berries, and vegetables, such as spinach, watercress, beets, carrots and broccoli.

How much: Five to nine servings daily. (A serving is one-half cup of cooked vegetables, one cup of leafy greens, one medium orange or one-half cup of berries.)

Contrary to popular belief, frozen vegetables, which are often far less costly than fresh produce, are just as nutritious—if not more so because they're frozen at their peak level of freshness and don't spoil in the freezer.

Chef's secret: Cooking tomatoes in olive oil concentrates the tomatoes' levels of lycopene, a powerful antioxidant that has been associated with a decreased risk for prostate, lung and stomach cancers.

Fruits and Veggies Can Boost Cancer-Killing Chemo

Xuan Liu, PhD, professor of biochemistry, University of California at Riverside, Riverside, California.

Recent research at the University of California Riverside showed that natural components in fruits and vegetables can improve cancer patients' response to chemotherapy.

Overcoming Tumor Resistance

In chemotherapy, the goal is to kill cancer cells. Theoretically, the treatments work by damaging DNA in cancer cells and causing them to die, but some forms of cancer are resistant and able to survive chemotherapy. At the University of California Riverside, Xuan Liu, PhD, and her colleagues were able to block this effect in lab studies using a concentrated form of *apigenin*, a naturally occurring flavonoid in fruits and vegetables, including apples, cilantro, basil, celery, cherries, grapes, parsley, tea and wine. For instance, pretreatment with apigenin raised the rate of death of cultured neuroblastoma (a rare cancer usually found in infants and children) cells to 53%, a success rate more than two-and-a-half times higher than with the chemotherapy drug etoposide alone. These results

Diet Changes and Stress Management Slow Prostate Cancer

Men who followed a plant-based diet and decreased their stress levels had a significant reduction in the rate of increase in levels of prostate-specific antigen (PSA), an indicator of prostate cancer. The men were asked to increase their intake of whole grains, cruciferous and leafy vegetables, beans, legumes and fruits, as well as decrease their intake of meat, poultry and dairy. Stress-management training included meditation, yoga and tai chi.

Gordon Saxe, MD, PhD, assistant professor of family and preventive medicine, University of California, San Diego, School of Medicine, and lead author of a study of prostate cancer, published in *Integrative Cancer Therapies.*

were published in the *Proceedings of the National Academy of Sciences.*

Eat Your Veggies

Apigenin has shown promise in slowing cancer cell growth of other types of cancer as well, including blastomas and certain types of breast cancer, as well as colon, skin, thyroid, leukemia and pancreatic cancer cells. Yet Dr. Liu cautions that we are still in the early stages of targeting particular types of cancers with specific strategies like these and says it's unclear what the practical applications of apigenin for chemotherapy will be. But she is optimistic that her research will add to our growing arsenal of more targeted treatment instruments against cancer, noting that it also serves as a reminder for everyone to include plenty of fresh fruits and vegetables in your daily diet.

PART 5

Digestive Distress
& Steps to Healthy Digestion

14

Keys to Healthy Digestion

Natural Ways to Improve Digestive Health

Jamison Starbuck, ND, a naturopathic physician in family practice and a guest lecturer at the University of Montana, both in Missoula. She is past president of the American Association of Naturopathic Physicians and a contributing editor to *The Alternative Advisor: The Complete Guide to Natural Therapies and Alternative Treatments* (Time Life).

Gastrointestinal (GI) health is fundamental to overall wellness. The GI tract, also known as the "gut," allows us to draw nourishment from our food and eliminate toxins. A variety of medications claim to promote intestinal health, but I prefer my own eight-step natural approach, which is both inexpensive and easy to follow. Add one new step each day. If you're like most people, your GI tract will be healthier within two weeks. *My advice…*

1. Avoid foods that cause indigestion. Indigestion is your body's way of telling you that a certain food is not readily digestible. Instead of trying to make a food digestible by taking drugs, choose foods that you can easily digest, such as fish, brown rice and steamed vegetables.

2. Shortly after awakening in the morning, drink an eight-ounce glass of room-temperature water. This "wakes up" the GI tract, preparing you for both digestion and elimination. Repeat this step five to 10 minutes before each meal. Avoid iced beverages, including water, with meals and 15 minutes before and afterward. Some research suggests that cold beverages decrease the secretion of digestive enzymes.

3. Squeeze fresh lemon or sprinkle vinegar on your food. For most people, one-half teaspoon of lemon or vinegar per meal fights indigestion by increasing stomach acidity and improving the digestion of fats.

4. Take a 15-minute walk after meals. Doing so will improve your digestion and elimination. If you can't do this after every meal, do so following the largest meal of the day.

5. Practice simple home hydrotherapy. This practice increases blood flow to your intestines, which helps them function properly.

What to do: Finish your daily shower or bath with a 30-second spray of cool or cold water to your entire abdomen. Towel dry with brisk strokes immediately after the cool water spray.

Caution: If you have a history of stroke, check with your doctor before trying hydrotherapy.

6. Drink chamomile or peppermint tea after dinner. These herbs soothe the lining of the stomach and intestines. Add one tea bag or two teaspoons of loose herb to eight ounces of water.

7. Use foot reflexology to relieve intestinal pain. Massaging reflexology points on the feet is thought to help increase blood flow to and improve the function of corresponding organs or body parts.

What to do: Whenever you have GI discomfort, firmly massage (for five to seven minutes) with your thumb and forefinger the outside portion of the middle one-third of the soles of the feet. According to reflexologists, this area corresponds to the colon. Your strokes should move toward the heel.

8. Never eat when you are stressed. Our bodies are not designed to simultaneously manage both stress and digestion. Studies show that just a few moments of relaxation, such as deep breathing or prayer, before a meal will improve the digestive process.

■ ■ ■ ■

Six Herbal Teas With Healing Powers

Jamison Starbuck, ND, a naturopathic physician in family practice and a guest lecturer at the University of Montana, both in Missoula. She is past president of the American Association of Naturopathic Physicians and a contributing editor to *The Alternative Advisor: The Complete Guide to Natural Therapies and Alternative Treatments* (Time Life).

With all the recent excitement about the health benefits of green tea, few people are taking advantage of the medicinal properties of many delicious herbal teas. Such teas are an excellent option for digestive ailments, including nausea, indigestion and stomach ulcer...and acute conditions, such as the common cold and the flu, anxiety and insomnia.

Even though herbs that are available in tea bags can be used for these purposes, you're much more likely to get medicinal benefits if the herbs are fresh, used in therapeutic amounts and steeped long enough. That's why I recommend infusions (for teas made from flowers, leaves and fresh stems) and decoctions (for teas made from roots, tubers or dried stems).

To make an infusion: Steep the herb in a covered pot of boiled water for 10 to 15 minutes.

To make a decoction: Simmer the herb in water for eight to 12 minutes. The typical "dose" is two teaspoons of herb per cup of water. For most medicinal purposes, one cup of tea should be taken on an empty stomach or 30 minutes after a meal, four times a day until the symptoms subside. All plants needed to make herbal teas are available at most natural-food stores (unless noted otherwise).

Homeopathy for Indigestion

A good remedy to keep in your medicine cabinet is nux vomica. It effectively treats indigestion as well as constipation, especially when these uncomfortable problems are caused by overindulgence. When you experience symptoms, dissolve three 30C pellets of nux vomica under your tongue. If you do not feel better within 45 minutes, repeat the dosage once or twice more. Do not exceed three doses in a day. Homeopathic remedies are sold at health-food stores and online.

Edward Shalts, MD, DHt (diplomate in homeotherapeutics), a private practitioner in New York City and author of two books, including *Easy Homeopathy* (McGraw-Hill). www.homeopathynewyork.com.

My favorite infusions…

● **Chamomile** has antispasmodic, anti-inflammatory and mild sedative properties that confer medicinal benefits if the tea is consumed or the scented steam is inhaled. For anxiety or insomnia, add a cup of chamomile tea directly to warm bathwater and sip another cup while enjoying a relaxing soak. Chamomile is also helpful in reducing indigestion and intestinal gas and in healing stomach ulcers.

● **Elder flower** contains healing compounds, including flavonoids, tannins and glycosides, that help "break" a fever and reduce mucus production, so it's ideal for the common cold or the flu.

● **Spearmint** has a milder flavor than its cousin peppermint but often is more effective in easing nausea and vomiting due to its healing compounds, such as bitters, tannins and volatile oils.

My favorite decoctions…

● **Gingerroot** contains plant compounds, such as volatile oils and alkaloids, that help ease motion sickness, improve digestion (if taken after a meal) and reduce mucus that accompanies a cold or the flu. Buy fresh gingerroot in your grocery store—peel, slice thinly and simmer (as described earlier).

● **Dandelion root** helps the gallbladder produce bile. I recommend dandelion root tea for people with high cholesterol, nonalcoholic fatty liver disease (in which fat accumulates in the liver of a person who drinks little or no alcohol) or gallbladder disease.

● **Licorice root** is an excellent antiviral agent that fights many viral ailments, including bronchitis and the common cold.

Caution: Avoid using licorice for more than 10 days if you have high blood pressure—the herb can affect blood pressure levels.

The Power of Enzymes For Better Digestion

Andrew L. Rubman, ND, director, Southbury Clinic for Traditional Medicines, Southbury, Connecticut, www.naturopath.org. Dr. Rubman is contributing editor to the free E-letter *Bottom Line's Daily Health News* (sign up at *www.bottomlinepublications.com*).

Healthy digestion is at the core of wellness—the nutrients in your food fuel your body and help build strong defenses against illness. But what is the key to healthy digestion? Believe it or not—despite all those TV ads you see about heartburn pills that "fight stomach acid"—it's stomach acid that you really need for healthy digestion.

What makes having acid in your stomach a good thing? Many of your body's digestive enzymes won't work properly unless they're in an acidic environment—and if your enzymes aren't working well, your digestion isn't working well either.

Enzyme Basics

Enzymes are natural chemicals manufactured by the body and present in many foods to make some kind of chemical reaction happen faster. Digestive enzymes work by breaking down the chemical bonds in your food and releasing the nutrients so you can absorb them. Without the enzymes, proper digestion doesn't happen. *Three major types…*

● **Proteolytic enzymes digest proteins.** The major proteolytic enzyme is pepsin, which breaks down the complex bonds in protein like a rock crusher.

● **Lipolytic enzymes digest fats.** Lipase is a major enzyme in this category.

● **Amylolytic enzymes digest carbohydrates.** Amylase, a major enzyme in this category, is primarily found in saliva, where it starts digesting as soon as you start chewing.

In your stomach, pepsin is the primary digestive enzyme—the others play a much bigger role later, when the food moves on to your small intestine. You make pepsin in your stomach lining, but it starts out in a preliminary form called pepsinogen.

The acid connection: Only when pepsinogen encounters sufficient stomach acid does it get converted to pepsin so it can do its job. Not enough acid in your stomach can prevent you from digesting protein, or anything else, well.

Not Enough Stomach Acid

Another naturally occurring and vital substance in the stomach is hydrochloric acid. By the time most people hit age 40, they no longer make as much hydrochloric acid as they used to. By then, most people aren't making enough to trigger proper pepsin production, and digestion and nutrient absorption begin to suffer. Low stomach acid can lead to trouble with gas and heartburn from incomplete breakdown of protein and other nutrients in the stomach.

The B connection: Animal protein is most people's major dietary source of B vitamins. When you don't digest it well, the B's aren't released to be absorbed—so you can start to run low on these vitamins. Serious consequences include anemia, poor healing, low resistance to illness and memory problems that can even resemble dementia.

Stomach acid production continues to drop gradually with stress and as you get older, to the point where many elderly people produce far less than they need for good nutrition.

What can you do to restore a good level of stomach acidity? My recommendations fall into two areas—better eating habits and acid-producing supplements.

Eating and Enzymes

How and what you eat has a lot to do with how well you digest it. *Some simple changes in the way you eat that can have a big positive effect…*

• **Chew more.** Digestion begins in your mouth. Chewing coats your food with saliva, which contains carbohydrate-digesting amylase. Chewing also breaks your food down into smaller pieces that can be digested more thoroughly.

What to do: Chew your food thoroughly. Consciously spend a little time on each mouthful.

Bonus: You'll enjoy your food more and feel more satisfied by it, and you'll probably eat less. If you need to lose weight, this is a painless way to do it—while improving your digestion at the same time.

• **Drink less.** Cut back on the liquids you drink while consuming a meal. When you chase your bites with sips, you dilute the acid in your stomach, and the enzymes themselves, which keeps them from working as well.

What to do: Limit the amount you drink during a meal. Skip sodas and drinks with caffeine. Sodas cause gassiness, and caffeine slows down your digestion of carbohydrates. Stick to plain water, well after you finish eating (wait at least a half hour).

• **Combine your foods carefully.** Different foods need to spend different amounts of time in your stomach to be fully digested. Simple carbohydrates, such as bread, pasta, rice, potatoes and sugary foods, are digested quickly. Complex carbohydrates—such as whole grains, beans and nuts—as well as proteins and fats, take longer. When you combine simple carbs with these complex foods, your stomach can empty too slowly, promoting fermentation (and growth of yeast) from improper carbohydrate digestion.

What to do: Eat small amounts of simple carbs along with more complex foods. Example: Have only a small portion of french fries along with a steak and salad. Skip prepared desserts completely. For a sweet treat, have fresh fruit—but fruit is sugary, so wait at least an hour after finishing your meal or eat it a half hour before.

Enzyme Supplements

Even with dietary changes, if you're older than age 40, you're probably not making enough stomach acid for good digestion, and are likely to experience such symptoms as increased irregularity and intestinal gas. *I often prescribe the following effective, safe supplements to help restore healthy stomach acid levels...*

• **Betaine HCL.** This generic supplement (available at health-food stores) works well to turn on the acid switch in your stomach. A 500-milligram dose just before each meal is often prescribed.

• **DuoZyme.** This combination supplement (available only through a health-care practitioner) contains betaine HCL, pepsin and other enzymes that help increase stomach acid, combined with additional enzymes that help later in the digestive process. Made by Karuna (800-826-7225, *www.karuna.com*).

• **Gastri-Gest.** Another combination supplement (also available only through a health-care practitioner), but made with plant-derived enzymes, Gastri-Gest helps increase stomach acid and also helps in the later phase of digestion. Made by Priority One Nutritional Supplements (800-443-2039, *www.priorityonevitamins.com*).

Digestive enzymes can be helpful to nearly anyone older than age 40, particularly those who experience acid stomach, mild nausea, gas, irregularity and other digestive upsets. Often betaine HCL is prescribed for a few weeks. If symptoms still persist,

DuoZyme or Gastri-Gest may follow. Both can help, but some people respond better to one or the other. Vegetarians and vegans will prefer Gastri-Gest, which doesn't contain animal products.

You'll probably need to take the supplements for a few weeks before you notice improvement. Digestive enzymes are generally very safe. But to avoid possible interactions, don't take them if you're taking an antibiotic or medication for an ulcer or other digestive problem, such as Crohn's disease. As with all medication, inform your doctor or other prescriber and follow his/her directions.

■ ■ ■ ■

Surprising, Little Known Digestive Problem Affects 30% of Population

Daniel Lustig, MD, pediatric gastroenterologist at the Mary Bridge Children's Hospital & Health Center in Tacoma, Washington.

Would you believe that there's yet another type of condition to consider if you are troubled by such common gastrointestinal (GI) symptoms as bloating, flatulence and the like? The problem is called fructose malabsorption, and it affects about one-third of the population. If you suffer frequent digestive distress and aren't sure why, this is a story that you really want to read closely.

How Bad Is It?

According to Daniel Lustig, MD, pediatric gastroenterologist at the Mary Bridge Children's Hospital & Health Center in Tacoma, Washington, the conditions is often misdiagnosed. The problem is fructose *malabsorption*, not fructose *intolerance*, which is what many people mistakenly call their affliction. These are separate issues, Dr. Lustig says.

The difference: Intolerance is a hereditary, lifelong condition present at birth that makes people unable to tolerate any fructose whatsoever. It is incurable and occasionally fatal, but fortunately it is also very rare. Conversely, the symptoms of fructose malabsorption generally range from mild to moderate, and Dr. Lustig says that the problem can develop at any time in life.

Fructose malabsorption often is misdiagnosed (when it is diagnosed at all) as lactose intolerance because the symptoms of both are strikingly similar—and, in fact, it is not unusual to have both conditions. It also affects 30% of people with irritable bowel syndrome (IBS).

Where's the Fructose?

Fructose is everywhere. It is a natural sugar found in virtually all fruits, and its equally problematic molecular cousin *fructan,* a starch, can be found in a few vegetables. Man-made products containing fructose are common, the best known example being the sweetener high-fructose corn syrup. Fructan is used in diet sweeteners in the form of inulin, maltitol and sorbitol.

Despite the ubiquity of fructose, the human body isn't designed to handle large amounts of it. It is the small intestine's job to absorb fructose, but excessive amounts can be overwhelming even for people who don't have problems with malabsorption. If fructose is not absorbed properly, it gets passed from the small intestine into the large one. Once there, colonic bacteria metabolize the fructose, producing abnormally high levels of hydrogen and methane as well as fructose fermentation—this, in turn, is what causes GI distress.

Anyone can suffer discomfort from eating lots of fructose in one sitting (say, 50 grams—what's in about two and one-half medium-sized apples), but in people with fructose malabsorption this threshold is about 25 grams, according to Dr. Lustig. Many people with this condition can't even handle that much without becoming uncomfortable.

There is good news: Unlike some conditions that require complete avoidance of the offending foods, people with fructose malabsorption do not have to avoid all fructose (see next article).

What to do? Read on to learn how to identify and solve your fructose malabsorption problem—including a list of foods you can and can't eat...

How to Handle Fructose Malabsorption

Daniel Lustig, MD, pediatric gastroenterologist at the Mary Bridge Children's Hospital & Health Center in Tacoma, Washington.

If you suspect that you suffer from fructose malabsorption, here is how you can get control of the problem.

Go Bananas!

It can be difficult to grasp why fructose in some fruits is more problematic than it is in others. Along with fructose, fruits generally contain *glucose,* another type of natural sugar (it's what is in sucrose, which is plain old table sugar). The presence of glucose in a food enhances absorption of its fructose, and so when you eat fruit with a high glucose-to-fructose ratio—ripe bananas, for example—you are unlikely to experience those unpleasant symptoms. On the other hand, if a person with fructose malabsorption eats more than a small quantity of fruits with more fructose than glucose—apples and pears are good examples—GI discomfort often follows. *What to do…*

● **Get a proper diagnosis.** A gastroenterologist will first eliminate serious digestive disease such Crohn's, ulcerative colitis or H. pylori, and after that give you a breath hydrogen test (it's simple, and just involves blowing into a special instrument). This may reveal abnormal levels of colonic hydrogen and carbon dioxide and tell whether the cause is fructose malabsorption or lactose intolerance or both. Dr. Lustig says the breath hydrogen test also reveals whether a small-bowel bacterial overgrowth is present, a condition that often coincides with fructose malabsorption and can be treated with a course of antibiotics.

● **Eat foods with more sucrose than fructose.**

● Stone fruit—apricots, nectarines, peaches, plums.

● Berries—blackberries…blueberries …boysenberries…cranberries…raspberries …strawberries.

● Citrus fruits—grapefruits…lemons …limes…mandarins…oranges (but not citrus juice, because it lacks the fiber)…tangerines …kumquats.

● Others—ripe bananas…kiwi…passion fruit…pineapple…surprisingly, rhubarb, which has a good balance of naturally occurring sugars.

● Table sugar—but in moderation because table sugar (the main source of sucrose) also contains fructose.

● **Limit or avoid foods that are higher in fructose than sucrose.** *This list includes…*

● High-fructose corn syrup because most (though not all) forms of it include more fructose than sucrose.

● Fruit juice concentrates.

● Agave nectar and syrup.

● Watermelon…honeydew…mango… guava and papaya…star fruit…apples… pears.

● All dried fruits.

● Honey.

● Fortified wines (sherry, port).

● **Limit foods containing fructan** (a carbohydrate polymer of fructose).

● These include asparagus…Jerusalem artichokes…leeks…onions…garlic…wheat. (Researchers are investigating how cooking might tame fructans, especially in garlic and onions.)

● Fine-tune your diet by finding which foods and how much fructose/fructan you can comfortably consume.

Ideally you should map this out with a dietitian trained in working with patients with fructose malabsorption, says Dr. Lustig, especially if your symptoms are frequent. However, if your symptoms are relatively mild, you may be able to manage your problems by keeping notes to see which fructose/fructan foods you can comfortably eat and which ones cause problems. For example, many people find that any amount of dried fruit brings on GI distress while a limited amount of fresh fruits daily is just fine. Don't overlook wheat-containing foods in your investigation—besides the fact that wheat contains fructans, it may be that fructose malabsorption is something you should check out if you have "gluten sensitivity."

Dr. Lustig says that there's research showing that carefully adhering to these food guidelines often brings improvement quickly, sometimes within a week, although it may take longer for complete relief. Yes, it is a bit of work—but if it frees you from all that gastric distress, it's worth doing.

What Makes Us Burp— Surprising Reasons Why Certain Foods Cause It

Andrew L. Rubman, ND, director, Southbury Clinic for Traditional Medicines, Southbury, Connecticut.

National Digestive Diseases Information Clearinghouse, http://digestive.niddk.nih.gov.

The curious thing about burping is that certain foods seem to have a tendency to produce more gas than others. Which are the worst culprits? What causes excess gas? And, how can you avoid it? Andrew L. Rubman, ND, director of the Southbury Clinic for Traditional Medicines in Connecticut, says that burping has many causes, from difficult-to-digest foods, to eating too fast, to our favorite culprit for anything and everything—plain, old-fashioned stress. *Dr. Rubman offers a number of common-sense suggestions on how to prevent burping, before it becomes a problem…*

A Normal (If Embarrassing) Body Function

Everyone has gas, so everyone occasionally burps, since it is one of only two ways to get gas out. It's a normal body function. While we all swallow small amounts of air when eating or drinking, when we eat or drink too quickly, we take in too much air…and we burp (or belch). Chewing gum, talking while eating, smoking and loose dentures can also be at the root of troublesome burping, since all can result in excess air entering the stomach.

It's All About Food Choices

However, when that lasagna with meat comes back to visit an hour after you eat it, it is often not because you swallowed air, but due to gas and fermentation from what you ate—particularly in combination, ex-plains Dr. Rubman. The most troublesome kind of food combination, says Dr. Rubman, is simple carbohydrates eaten with dense fats—think garlic bread and a well-marbled steak, or a bacon cheeseburger on a white bun…or lasagna with meat. Similarly, dessert (even fruit) eaten immediately following a fat-filled meal can cause fermentation, as the fat in the meal slows down digestion of the simple sugars in the dessert or refined carbohydrates, causing them to begin to react in your stomach. Not surprisingly, fried, fatty and processed foods present more of a challenge to the digestion than whole foods (e.g., fresh fish, steamed veggies and ripe fruits).

What You Can Do

An occasional burp is no big deal. Still, it's hardly the impression you want to make at a business dinner or on a date. The single most important thing you can do to avoid burping? Think about what you eat and drink, advises Dr. Rubman. If you eat fried clams followed by a hot fudge sundae, understand in advance that your body may make you pay a price for that choice, whether in burping, intestinal gas or a bellyache.

Other helpful strategies include…

• **Take it slow.** Try to eat at a leisurely pace, and chew food thoroughly. And, as mom always said, eat with your mouth closed.

• **Limit liquids with meals.** These dilute stomach acid, inhibiting digestion. The result is that the food ferments in your stomach, producing the CO_2 that comes back up as a burp.

• **Monitor food combinations.** Don't combine simple carbs with high saturated fatty foods…eat fruits at least one-half hour before meals…and skip dessert.

• **Forego the antacids.** Although they may help you feel better in the short run, insufficient stomach acid leads to insufficient

Common Causes of Flatulence

Diseases such as irritable bowel syndrome, Crohn's disease, ulcerative colitis and cancer can lead to excess gas and bloating. Certain medications, including calcium channel blockers, tricyclic antidepressants and narcotic-based painkillers, slow digestion and lead to excess gas. Diet changes, such as adding fiber to ease constipation, can create gas. Lactose intolerance leads to flatulence because lactose-laden foods are improperly digested. Loss of muscle tone around the anal sphincter and loss of elasticity of the valve itself can weaken control.

Self-defense: If you're lactose intolerant, limit intake of milk products, except for yogurt with active cultures, which consume much of the lactose during fermentation. Avoid carbonated beverages and foods that are heavy in carbohydrates, such as beans, brussels sprouts, broccoli and cauliflower. Also avoid foods that contain sugars such as fructose (including onions, artichokes, pears and wheat) and sorbitol (apples, peaches and prunes). Sorbitol also is used as an artificial sweetener, as is mannitol—both should be avoided. Eat slowly and chew food thoroughly. Consider taking Gas-X, sold over the counter.

Anil Minocha, MD, professor of medicine, Louisiana State University and staff gastroenterologist, Overton Brooks VA Medical Center, both in Shreveport, Louisiana.

digestion. You may be replacing a burp today with even more troublesome intestinal gas tomorrow.

● **No carbonated beverages.** They're made with CO_2, and therefore sure to generate a good belch.

● **Avoid chewing gum, hard candy, straws and smoking,** all of which permit more air to enter the stomach. If you smoke, here's yet one more good reason to quit.

● **If you wear dentures, check with your dentist to make certain they fit properly.** Poorly fitting dentures may cause you to take in air as you chew, which gets in the way of good digestion.

■ ■ ■ ■

The Right Way to Chew (It's Not as Simple as You Think)

Karyn Kahn, DDS, staff member of the Head and Neck Institute in the dentistry department and consultant for craniofacial pain and jaw dysfunction at Cleveland Clinic, and associate professor at Case Western Reserve University School of Dentistry, both in Cleveland.

Mastication, or chewing, begins the digestive process and prepares food for swallowing. Front teeth cut and tear the food...back teeth crush and grind it, increasing its surface area so that digestion of carbohydrates can begin. *Be careful about chewing...*

● **Too little.** Often the result of eating too fast, this can cause choking or pain upon swallowing. Additionally, heartburn or stomach pain can occur because saliva's digestive enzymes don't have time to work. And because gobbling food inhibits the release of hormones that tell you when you're full, you may overeat.

Solution: Start with smaller bites, and use your molars more—you should barely feel food going down when you swallow.

To slow down: Put your fork down between bites, and take a deep breath after each swallow.

● **Too long.** Once a bite is ready to be swallowed, teeth should separate and not touch. Chewing past the point when the normal swallowing reflex occurs can overload jaw muscles, resulting in muscle pain and/or dysfunction. This is one reason why gum chewing—in which teeth touch during chewing—can lead to disorders of the temporomandibular joint (TMJ), or jaw joint.

- **On just one side of your mouth.** If you have a full set of teeth and a normal diet, having a favorite side on which to chew—as many people do—is not a problem. But: If you wear full dentures, food must be distributed during the chewing process from one side of the mouth to the other to maintain the dentures' stability.

Important: If you avoid chewing on one side because it is painful, see your dentist.

Gas Be Gone!

Douglas A. Drossman, MD, professor in the division of gastroenterology and hepatology, and codirector of the Center for Functional Gastrointestinal and Motility Disorders at University of North Carolina, Chapel Hill, School of Medicine. He has published two books and more than 400 articles on gastrointestinal disorders.

The average person produces one to four pints of gas daily and expels it about 14 times a day. Sometimes gas gets trapped in the body, causing uncomfortable bloating. *What you should know…*

- **Flatulence occurs when bacteria ferment undigested carbohydrates in the colon.** The telltale noise is caused by vibration of the anal opening…odor depends on the foods eaten and types of bacteria present. Flatulence producers include asparagus, beans, bran, broccoli, brussels sprouts, cabbage, corn, onions, pasta, peas, potatoes, prunes and wheat. Dairy foods cause gas in people who lack the enzyme lactase needed to digest the milk sugar lactose. Called lactose intolerance, this gets more common with age.

Over-the-counter remedies: Charcoal tablets or *simethicone* (Gas-X) may help by breaking up big gas bubbles. Beano contains an enzyme that breaks down cellulose, a carbohydrate in legumes and cruciferous vegetables—take it just before eating. To help prevent gas, take a daily supplement that contains the probiotic *Bifidobacterium infantis,* such as the brand Align. For lactose intolerance, avoid dairy foods or try Lactaid supplements, which contain lactase.

- **Belching happens after you swallow air.**

Avoid: Fizzy drinks, gum, eating too fast, gulping, using a straw, smoking.

Another culprit: Anxiety makes people breathe rapidly and swallow more often.

Calming: Inhale for three seconds… hold three seconds…exhale for three seconds…hold three seconds…repeat.

See your doctor: If you are troubled by excess flatulence or belching, your doctor can check for underlying gastrointestinal problems.

Upset Stomach Cures— How to Prevent and Treat Transient Nausea

Sonja Pettersen, NMD, licensed in Arizona and Oregon to practice primary care medicine specializing in natural therapeutics. Her practice exemplifies a holistic approach to patient care through a variety of modalities, including clinical nutrition, botanical medicine and IV therapy, homeopathy, functional medicine, and mind-body techniques.

It is hardly uncommon to get a little queasy once in a while. Sonja Pettersen, NMD, explains why transient nausea happens and what we can do about it.

"Almost anything—from a headache to an antibiotic—can make you temporarily nauseated," she says. "But when there is no obvious cause, it frequently comes down to low stomach acid." According to Dr. Pettersen, when you have chronically low stomach acid you can get almost any symptom in the body, from a headache to poor skin... and of course, transient nausea. Low stomach acid can occur for a number of reasons, but the worst offenders are a high sugar (refined carbohydrate) diet…stress…and the use of acid-suppressing and/or neutralizing medications. When a meal enters your acid-impaired stomach you experience incomplete digestion of your food... ingested organisms that would otherwise be killed by stomach acid are able to survive… and fermentation of slowly digesting food results in an inflammatory response. Any and all of these processes are instigators of nausea.

Dr. Pettersen also points out that frequent nausea is highly related to sluggish or inadequate function of the gallbladder, which in turn is usually related to chronic stomach problems (impaired digestion, feeling overly full) and/or age and poor diet. In elderly people, constipation and dehydration are also common causes of nausea since they, too, are connected to the digestive process.

Nausea Self-Defense

What to do? Prepare the stomach for the meal to come. "This used to be the purpose of an aperitif or an appetizer. By having the diner relax, think about and smell food, the system has a chance to anticipate what's coming," Dr. Pettersen says. "But we don't prepare for eating anymore. We just pull up to a drive-in window. That could be part of the problem."

Dr. Pettersen often prescribes HCl (hydrochloric acid) in pill form, usually bound to a common material called *betaine*, derived from the common beet, to be taken with meals as a way to ensure thorough digestion. She also likes gingerroot in fresh, dried or capsule form, taken before the meal, as a way to get digestive juices flowing. "You can cut up fresh ginger and steep it in warm water and sip it," she says. "Lemon juice squeezed fresh into warm water also does the job very well." Sip the ginger or lemon beverage, or her favorite—apple cider vinegar (1 tablespoon with a little warm water)—about 15 minutes before a meal. "It's not fully understood how it works, but I suspect it helps prepare the digestive tract and gets digestive juices as well as blood flowing," she says.

Nausea First Aid

While these strategies are helpful for preventing nausea, we asked Andrew L. Rubman, ND, what to do when nausea strikes.

His response: "It depends on when it occurs."

If nausea occurs between meals, the fiber supplement *glucomannan* with a glass of sparkling water often works. If nausea occurs during a meal, digestive enzymes, particularly the betaine HCl described above, can help. If, however, nausea occurs an hour or more after a meal, it can be a sign of gall bladder disease or duodenitis. These conditions should always be addressed with a physician.

Of course, especially for frequent sufferers, it is important to have gastric pathology ruled out—and as always to have all interventions overseen by someone knowledgeable, such as your naturopathic physician. Read drug inserts of any medications you are taking because nausea is a common drug side effect.

Are You Using Probiotics Correctly?

Leo Galland, MD, founder and director of the Foundation for Integrated Medicine in New York City. He is the author of *The Fat Resistance Diet* (Broadway) and *The Heartburn and Indigestion Solution*, an e-book available online at *www.fat resistancediet.com/alternative-medicine/gerd.*

Known to help increase bowel regularity while decreasing gas and bloating, probiotics are making their way onto more and more top-10 health lists, so it's not so surprising to find them tucked into all manner of foods and beverages.

However, the formula for using probiotics to optimize your health is somewhat more nuanced than merely spooning up a daily serving of yogurt.

Probiotics Go Mainstream

Probiotics are definitely getting more respect. Doctors are beginning to suggest probiotic supplements along with antibiotic prescriptions. Probiotics have made their way into the hospital world, too—they're given to patients to help prevent deadly intestinal diseases that have resulted from antibiotic-resistant superbugs... researchers are studying their use for premature babies...and a few doctors even are urging consideration of a new hand-hygiene protocol that involves dipping caregivers' hands into probiotic solutions after scrubbing in order to recolonize the skin with good bacteria.

Maybe those doctors are also telling patients to buy probiotic-fortified foods at the supermarket—and there's nothing wrong with doing so. But Leo Galland, MD, director of the Foundation for Integrated Medicine in New York City, wants us to understand that we won't achieve any meaningful benefits by relying on these probiotic-fortified food sources alone.

Why We Need Supplements

Dr. Galland explains that acid naturally present in most probiotic-containing foods suppresses these helpful bacteria, at least partially—so it's impossible to know how many cultures survive and are of benefit. He believes that supplements are a better route since they reliably deliver a beneficial number of probiotic organisms.

However, he points out that specific types of probiotics can be used to address specific health concerns. This is another argument for supplements instead of probiotic-fortified foods and another reason why it's important to work with your doctor (or a naturopathic physician or a gastroenterologist experienced in working with prebiotics and probiotics) who can ascertain what's best for you, how much you should take and at what times of day.

Dr. Galland says that he tends to prescribe specific types of probiotics in certain situations. *For example…*

• **For people with no particular health concerns,** Dr. Galland might suggest 20 billion Colony Forming Units (CFUs) of combined *lactobacillus* and *bifidobacterium* "as a good general preventative for intestinal and respiratory tract infections."

• **For people taking antibiotics,** *Saccharomyces boulardii* (S. boulardii, brand name Florastor) usually is the best choice (though actually this particular probiotic is not a bacteria but a yeast). It's also helpful in boosting effectiveness of Flagyl (*metronidazole*) and is used to treat *Clostridium difficile colitis* and antibiotic-associated colitis, as well as other bacterial and nonbacterial intestinal infections.

Note: Dr. Galland says that S. boulardii should be taken only for the duration of antibiotic or Flagyl treatment, after which he switches his patients to a bacteria-based probiotic.

• **For patients having abdominal surgery,** Dr. Galland prescribes *Lactobacillus plantarum* for a few weeks before and after surgery, since research shows that it helps reduce postoperative infections. Other studies demonstrate that lactobacillus probiotics can help to reduce frequency of diarrhea and abdominal pain in cancer patients as well.

• **For gas and bloating,** Dr. Galland says that certain soil-based organisms (called "SBOs"—for instance, one kind is Bacillus laterosporus) can be helpful. These probiotics aren't normally found in the human digestive system and they won't take up permanent residence, so patients who find them beneficial may want to continue taking them daily even after their symptoms have subsided, he adds.

What's Best for You?

As with prebiotics, Dr. Galland says that it may take some trial and error to identify which probiotics are helpful in achieving the desired results without upsetting your system. He has found Lactobacillus plantarum beneficial for many of his patients, but it isn't always the right choice. Experienced doctors often use sophisticated stool test results to identify the types of bacteria already in a patient's system, since this information can help determine the best course of pre- and probiotic therapy, along with other natural supplements that will yield good results.

If you want to try adding probiotics to your personal health regimen, talk to a doctor with expertise in this area and expect to start slowly and watch closely to see what works best. (You'll know it's working if it helps diminish digestive difficulties, such as gas, indigestion and irregular bowel movements.) This may mean that you end up trying several different types of probiotics before you find what helps your system function best. Stick with it though, since these beneficial bacteria have the potential to transform your health for the better.

15

Food Allergies and Sensitivities

How to Protect Against Killer Food Allergies

Steve L. Taylor, PhD, professor of food science and codirector of the Food Allergy Research and Resource Program at the University of Nebraska, Lincoln. He is a leading expert on food allergies and serves on the editorial boards of the *Journal of Food Protection* and the *Journal of Natural Toxins.*

M any people with food allergies have mild symptoms, such as a rash, runny nose or itchy eyes, when they eat small amounts of a problem food. But they may still be at risk for a potentially deadly reaction.

In the US, food allergies cause up to 30,000 emergency room visits and 200 deaths annually due to anaphylaxis, an acute reaction that can cause respiratory distress and/or a heart arrhythmia (irregular heartbeat).

Recent development: The Food Allergen Labeling and Consumer Protection Act, which went into effect in January 2006, requires food manufacturers to list eight major allergens on food labels to help people with food allergies identify and avoid problem foods.

Is It Really an Allergy?

Not all reactions to food are due to allergies. Tens of millions of Americans suffer from food intolerance. A food intolerance, such as a sensitivity to the lactose in milk, can begin in childhood. The most common symptom of lactose intolerance is gastrointestinal discomfort, including diarrhea, cramping and flatulence.

Food allergies affect about 11 million to 12 million Americans. With a food allergy, the immune system mistakenly identifies as harmful the various proteins—or even a single kind of protein—within one or more foods. This triggers a cascade of events that causes immune cells to respond to the "threat" by releasing large amounts of histamine and other chemicals that produce the allergic symptoms.

The most common food allergen is shellfish. Up to 2% of Americans are allergic to shrimp and/or other shellfish, such as lobster, crab and crayfish. This type of allergy often is ignored—primarily because most people tend to eat shellfish far less often than other allergenic foods, such as eggs, peanuts and fish.

Testing for Allergies

A food allergy usually can be diagnosed with a thorough medical history taken by an allergist.

The doctor will want to know…

• **When do symptoms occur?** Food allergies typically cause symptoms within a few minutes to several hours after exposure. Symptoms include stomach cramping, hives, lip swelling, runny nose, congestion and asthma. With a food intolerance, symptoms may not occur until the next day.

• **How much did you eat?** With food allergies, any exposure can trigger symptoms. For some patients, 1 milligram—an amount that's almost impossible to see—will provoke an allergic response. A reaction can even be triggered by kissing—or sharing utensils with—someone who has eaten a substance to which you are allergic. A skin reaction can occur from touching the substance.

With a food intolerance, symptoms usually are linked to the amount consumed. Someone who's sensitive to milk, for example, can often drink a small amount without a reaction.

Two tests can identify most food allergies. *They are…*

• **Skin prick.** Extracts of suspected foods are introduced into the skin with a needle. The appearance of a rash within a few hours—or even a few minutes—indicates a food allergy.

Caution: The skin-prick test isn't advisable for patients with severe allergies. The tiny amounts of food used in the test could trigger a life-threatening reaction.

• **Radioallergosorbent test (RAST).** This blood test detects antibodies to specific food proteins. The test occasionally produces false positives—indicating an allergy where none is present. It's often combined with the skin-prick test for more accurate results.

Treatment

People with a history of serious food reactions must carry an EpiPen. Available by prescription, it's a self-injector that delivers a dose of epinephrine. Epinephrine stimulates the heart and respiration and helps counteract deadly anaphylaxis.

Important: Use the EpiPen immediately if you experience difficulty breathing or throat constriction. Even if you take the shot promptly, get to an emergency room as soon as possible for follow-up treatments.

Also helpful: Take an antihistamine, such as Benadryl, according to label instructions. It can lessen the severity of symptoms while you get to an emergency room.

New development: Omalizumab (Xolair), a medication currently used for asthma, appears to significantly blunt reactions in food-allergy patients who receive a monthly injection of the drug. In an early study, patients who reacted to trace amounts of peanuts were able to eat eight to 10 nuts without experiencing problems. Further studies must be completed to determine whether the FDA deems it an effective—and safe—therapy for food allergies.

Avoiding Problem Foods

Because there isn't a cure for food allergies—and even trace amounts of a protein can trigger reactions—strict avoidance is the best defense…

• **Always read food labels**—even if you've safely eaten that product in the past. Manufacturers frequently change or add ingredients.

• **Ask about "hidden" ingredients in medications.** Some prescription and over-the-counter (OTC) drugs, as well as vitamins and supplements, contain milk proteins or other common food allergens. This information should be on the label, but check with your doctor or pharmacist before taking any medication or supplement.

• **Talk to the chef or restaurant manager when eating out.** The waiter or waitress doesn't always have accurate information about food ingredients and preparation. Ask to speak to the chef or manager instead and tell him/her what you're allergic to. Explain that any contact with the offending food can be life-threatening.

• **If you're allergic to shellfish,** for example, tell the chef or manager you can't eat a hamburger that was cooked on the same grill used to cook shrimp.

Other hidden sources of food allergens: Cooking oils that are used to cook different foods…knives and cutting boards that aren't washed clean between uses.

• **Wear a medical alert bracelet/necklace.** Anaphylaxis can potentially cause a loss of consciousness within minutes. A medical alert bracelet/necklace lets medical personnel know that you require urgent treatment for your allergy.

■ ■ ■ ■

How to Enjoy Dairy When You're Lactose Intolerant

Jeannie Gazzaniga-Moloo, RD, PhD, a registered dietitian based in Sacramento, California. She is a spokesperson for the American Dietetic Association. *www.moloonutrition.com.*

As many as 50 million Americans suffer from lactose intolerance, the inability to fully digest the sugar found in milk and other dairy products. Sufferers typically experience cramping, diarrhea, nausea, gas and/or bloating 30 minutes to two hours after consuming dairy. Lactose intolerance

Calcium in Food

Milk is not the only source of calcium. Calcium-rich foods include leafy green vegetables (one cup of cooked collard greens contains 266 milligrams [mg] of calcium)… canned sardines with bones (324 mg per three ounces)…and blackstrap molasses (274 mg per two tablespoons).

Dennis A. Savaiano, PhD, dean of the College of Consumer and Family Sciences and professor in the department of foods and nutrition at Purdue University in Lafayette, Indiana.

can't be cured, but most sufferers can enjoy some dairy in their diet.

Who Gets It?

Lactose intolerance is caused by insufficient production of the lactase enzyme in the small intestine. This enzyme breaks down lactose into glucose and galactose, a pair of easier-to-digest sugars. The amount of lactase we produce can be determined by our genes, but because our small intestines produce lactase in the greatest quantities when we're young, the onset of lactose intolerance might not occur until adolescence or adulthood.

Smart Strategies

A recent study in *The American Journal of Clinical Nutrition* showed that calcium and vitamin D from dairy foods may improve bone density better than supplements. *Here's how to work dairy into your diet…*

• **Take lactase supplements immediately before consuming dairy.** These pills are available without a prescription at drugstores and supermarkets, and can be quite effective. Follow directions on the label.

• **Drink reduced-lactose milk.** Reduced-lactose milks are available in most supermarket dairy sections and typically contain 70% less lactose than conventional milk. If your intestines can't handle any lactose, 100% lactose-free milks are available. Lactose-free milk substitutes, such as soy milk and rice milk, are available as well, but these do not always deliver as much calcium and vitamins as dairy milk.

• **Consume dairy products in small amounts throughout the day,** rather than in one large serving. Lactose-intolerant digestive systems will have an easier time processing several two- to four-ounce glasses of milk drunk hours apart than one big glass in a sitting. Some lactose-intolerance sufferers even find that their ability to comfortably consume dairy increases when they make it a regular part of their diet.

• **Consume dairy products together with or following nondairy foods.** Eating dairy on an empty stomach is particularly likely to cause discomfort.

• **Select dairy products that are naturally low in lactose.** Milk and ice cream contain lots of lactose...but sour cream and cottage cheese have significantly less...and hard cheeses, such as cheddar and Swiss, contain still less. Goat's milk and goat cheeses contain nearly as much lactose as cow's milk and cheese.

• **Eat yogurt that contains active cultures.** If the words "active cultures" or "live cultures" appear on a yogurt container, live bacteria are among the ingredients. These helpful bacteria break down much of the lactose in the yogurt, making it easier to digest. Some buttermilk also contains these bacteria—check the label.

• **Look for hidden lactose.** Lactose sometimes is present in foods where it might not be expected, such as bread and other baked goods, margarine, salad dressing, instant cocoa mix, pancake mix, most lunch meats and even some "nondairy" creamers. Check the ingredients lists for dry milk solids...milk by-products...dry milk powder... curds...whey...and, of course, milk, cheese or butter. Look for products with the words "lactose-free" on the label.

■ ■ ■ ■

The Truth About Dairy Foods

Jamison Starbuck, ND, a naturopathic physician in family practice and a guest lecturer at the University of Montana, both in Missoula. She is past president of the American Association of Naturopathic Physicians and a contributing editor to *The Alternative Advisor: The Complete Guide to Natural Therapies and Alternative Treatments* (Time Life).

Most Americans grew up believing that dairy foods are synonymous with strong bones and good health. Many of my patients proudly tell me that they always have a glass of milk with dinner. These days, the dairy industry spends a fortune promoting milk as a healthful food. At the same time, many health experts suggest that dairy consumption (chiefly milk, yogurt, cheese, butter and ice cream) may lead to health problems. What's the truth?

Most people believe that dairy foods help prevent osteoporosis. Not so, according to the landmark Harvard Nurses' Health Study. In this study, scientists followed more than 77,000 women for 12 years to examine the possible link between calcium-rich foods, including milk, and osteoporosis. The researchers found no evidence that drinking milk prevents this bone-thinning disease. Some plant sources of calcium are more readily absorbed by the body and more likely to support healthy bone cells.

Example: Sesame butter is a good calcium source and is delicious on toast or rice crackers. Leafy, green vegetables are high in calcium, too. For example, one cup of cooked collard greens contains 266 milligrams (mg) of calcium.

There's also widespread confusion related to dairy's impact on heart disease. Whole-fat versions of dairy products are high in saturated fats, which increase the risk for cardiovascular disease. Studies also have linked dairy consumption to an increased risk for prostate cancer. Nonorganic dairy of any sort increases your exposure to toxins and hormones, possibly increasing cancer risk.

When it comes to dairy, people can be lactose intolerant (the inability to digest dairy sugar) or they can be allergic to the proteins in dairy. When lactose-intolerant people eat dairy, they suffer from indigestion, gas and irritable bowel symptoms.

People with a dairy allergy suffer from more than just bowel symptoms when they eat dairy. Allergic reactions cause inflammation throughout the body, most notably in the upper respiratory tract. Dairy allergy is a common cause of frequent sinusitis, ear infection and repeated colds.

Dairy foods do not promote disease as readily as soda, fried foods or candy, but it's clear that dairy can trigger some health problems. That's why I tell my patients to seek healthful alternatives to dairy. Vegetables, nuts, seeds, legumes and whole grains are excellent sources of essential minerals, such as calcium, magnesium and zinc. Avocado, olive oil, sesame oil and fish are more healthful sources of fat than cheese or whole milk.

My advice: If you don't have high cholesterol (LDL "bad" cholesterol above 129 milligrams per deciliter [mg/dL] in those who are not at risk for heart disease) and you are not allergic to dairy, enjoy small amounts as you would chocolate, wine or red meat. It's fine to sprinkle Parmesan cheese on a salad, have a slice of cheese on a sandwich or enjoy a cup of yogurt. Just watch your reactions to dairy and don't be taken in by the marketing hype. Some people may need a calcium supplement. Discuss this with your doctor.

■ ■ ■ ■

Surprising Facts About Cow's Milk

Dennis A. Savaiano, PhD, dean of the College of Consumer and Family Sciences and professor in the department of foods and nutrition at Purdue University in Lafayette, Indiana.

I f you grew up in the US, you were probably admonished to drink cow's milk for its bone-building calcium. But do you still follow that advice?

As adults, many people give up cow's milk because they don't like its taste...don't like the way cows are raised (on "factory farms")...or have difficulty digesting lactose (the primary sugar in cow's milk and other dairy products).

Good news: There are more good-tasting milk options now available than most people realize.

Milk from Animal Sources

Milk is a good source of calcium—one eight-ounce cup contains about 300 milligrams (mg) of the mineral (nearly one-third of the daily recommended intake for adults age 50 and under and about one-quarter of the daily recommended intake for adults over age 50). Milk also contains vitamin D (needed to absorb calcium) and protein, an important nutrient that helps us maintain strength and muscle tone as we age.

However, about 5% of infants are allergic to cow's milk. Symptoms include diarrhea, runny nose and hives. Most children outgrow the allergy by age two or three.

Because whole cow's milk contains saturated fat, which can contribute to obesity and heart disease, it's usually best to drink nonfat or 1% milk. *Milk options…*

- **Lactose-free cow's milk.** About one out of every four American adults has lactose intolerance. This condition, which is different from a milk allergy, causes stomach pain, diarrhea, bloating and/or gas after milk or other dairy products that contain lactose are consumed. But lactose can be removed from milk.

Examples: Lactaid and Land O Lakes Dairy Ease.

- **Cow's milk (with meals).** Studies show that many people who believe they are lactose intolerant can drink milk without suffering any symptoms as long as it's consumed with a meal, which helps slow the digestion of lactose.

If you've stopped drinking cow's milk due to lactose intolerance and would like to try reintroducing it: Drink one-quarter to one-half cup of milk with a meal twice daily. Within a few days, try drinking a full cup of milk with a meal. Most people who have identified themselves as being lactose intolerant can adapt to this level of milk consumption within two weeks—the length of time that it usually takes intestinal bacteria to activate the body's lactases (enzymes that break down lactose).

If you have gas or loose stools, reduce your milk intake to one-quarter cup daily until the symptoms subside. If this does not work, see a doctor. You may have another condition, such as irritable bowel syndrome, which causes cramping, abdominal pain, constipation and diarrhea.

- **Kefir.** Kefir is a slightly sour fermented milk drink produced by "friendly" probiotic bacteria and yeasts found in kefir grains. Kefir, which has a milkshake-like consistency, is an option for some people who are lactose intolerant.

Example: Lifeway Lowfat Kefir.

- **Goat's milk.** Like cow's milk, goat's milk contains lactose and is a good source of calcium, vitamin D and protein. Goat's milk has a refreshingly tart, almost sour taste.

Example: Meyenberg Goat Milk.

Kefir and goat's milk are available at health-food stores and some supermarkets.

Plant-Based Milks

Plant-based milks are lactose-free and offer health benefits of their own. Most of these milks contain only small amounts of calcium and vitamin D, so they are usually fortified with these nutrients. Some plant-based milks are flavored (vanilla and chocolate, for example), but these varieties can contain up to 20 grams (g) of sugar per cup. Check the label for the sugar content to avoid unnecessary calories. Choose a low-fat plant-based milk whenever possible. Plant-based milks, which can be used in baking and cooking, are available at health-food stores and most supermarkets. *Choices include…*

- **Soy milk.** This milk has a mild, bean-like flavor and contains heart-healthy soy protein. In addition, some studies, though inconclusive, suggest that the phytoestrogens (naturally occurring compounds with estrogen-like effects) in soy may help reduce the risk for breast and prostate cancer.

Example: Silk Soymilk Organic.

Caution: Anyone who has had breast or prostate cancer or who is at high risk (due to family history, for example) should consult a doctor before consuming soy—in some cases, phytoestrogens are believed to stimulate the growth of certain hormone-dependent malignancies.

- **Nut milks.** People who don't like the taste of soy milk often prefer almond or hazelnut milk.

Examples: Blue Diamond Almond Breeze and Pacific Foods Hazelnut Milk.

- **Oat milk.** The fiber in this milk, which has a mild, sweet taste, may help lower cholesterol levels.

  Example: Pacific Foods Oat Milk.

- **Hemp milk.** Derived from shelled hempseeds, this creamy, nutty milk contains a balance of fatty acids that are believed to fight heart disease and arthritis.

  Example: Living Harvest Hempmilk.

- **Rice milk.** For many people, rice milk, among all the plant-based milks, tastes the most like cow's milk. Rice milk has less protein than cow's milk and soy milk, but it can be consumed by some people who are allergic to cow's milk.

  Example: Rice Dream.

■ ■ ■ ■

Is Wheat Making You Sick?

Jamison Starbuck, ND, is a naturopathic physician in family practice and a guest lecturer at the University of Montana, both in Missoula. She is past president of the American Association of Naturopathic Physicians and a contributing editor to *The Alternative Advisor: The Complete Guide to Natural Therapies and Alternative Treatments* (Time Life).

These days, most people have heard of celiac disease. Affecting about one in every 100 Americans, it's a digestive disease in which the body reacts adversely to gluten (a protein found in wheat, barley and rye). But there's a similar condition, known as wheat intolerance, that few people know about and this food sensitivity can also cause significant problems.

Wheat-intolerant people have no symptoms when they eat barley or rye, but ingesting wheat often leads to such complaints as indigestion, bloating, canker sores, constipation, headache, sinusitis, respiratory problems, insomnia, joint pain and fatigue. Researchers don't yet know just how many

Food Allergy Head Count

More Americans are allergic to seafood than to any other food. Of the 11 million Americans who have food allergies, 6.5 million are allergic to seafood, most commonly shrimp, crab, lobster, salmon, tuna or halibut. Three million are allergic to peanuts and/or tree nuts. Severe allergic reactions to foods cause about 30,000 emergency room visits per year and 200 deaths.

Anne Munoz-Furlong, founder and CEO, Food Allergy and Anaphylaxis Network, Fairfax, Virginia. *www. foodallergy.org.*

people have wheat intolerance, but from what I see in my practice, the sufferers of wheat intolerance outnumber those with celiac disease.

Because people with either celiac disease or wheat intolerance experience similar symptoms after ingesting wheat, distinguishing the two conditions can be tricky. But a simple diagnostic clue helps—people with undiagnosed celiac disease are chronically unwell. Because celiac disease stresses the immune system, it drains a person's energy and can lead to other health problems, such as infertility and osteoporosis. People with wheat intolerance, on the other hand, are generally well but suffer episodic ailments, usually related to the amount of wheat consumed.

If you suspect that you may have celiac disease, see your doctor for an exam and blood tests. If you think wheat intolerance may be your problem, try a simple home test. Avoid wheat in any form for seven to 10 days, paying close attention to how you feel each day, then reintroduce it at each meal for two days (or less often if you get symptoms).

Read Labels!

Wheat is hidden in many unexpected products, such as candy bars, soy sauce, cream soups, pudding and luncheon meats. Since wheat is obviously a main component of bread, pasta, pizza and baked goods, wheat avoidance also can be a good way to shed a few pounds.

If you feel better when you avoid wheat than when you eat it, you very likely have wheat intolerance. You can determine the degree of your wheat intolerance through trial and error. Some people can tolerate one serving of wheat per day without experiencing symptoms, while others can eat wheat only once a week. Still others feel best if their diet is completely wheat free.

"What will I eat?" is a common response when I suggest a trial period—or a lifetime—of wheat avoidance. Fortunately, there are numerous wheat-free products, including wheat-free breads, pastas, pizzas and crackers, available at many supermarkets, health-food stores and online stores. For cooking, you can purchase flour made from rice, chickpeas, quinoa, millet or tapioca. Wheat-free recipes and cookbooks can be found at local libraries, bookstores and online.

Interestingly, many people with "hay fever"—a seasonal grass allergy—are wheat-intolerant. When they avoid wheat during the peak grass-growing seasons of spring and early summer, their hay fever symptoms are often reduced.

■ ■ ■ ■

Could You Have Celiac Disease and Not Even Know It?

Peter H.R. Green, MD, director of the Celiac Disease Center at Columbia University and professor of clinical medicine at Columbia University College of Physicians and Surgeons, both in New York City. Dr. Green is coauthor of *Celiac Disease: A Hidden Epidemic* (HarperCollins). *www.celiacdiseasecenter.org.*

Celiac disease is the most underdiagnosed autoimmune condition in the US. This gastrointestinal disorder affects one in every 100 Americans—yet only about 3% of those afflicted get properly diagnosed and treated. It takes 11 years, on average, from the time symptoms appear until the diagnosis is made. In the interim, as the disease progresses, patients grow increasingly at risk for complications that can harm their bones, blood and nervous system…or even lead to cancer.

Women are twice as likely as men to have celiac disease. Contrary to what many doctors believe, it can develop at any time, even among seniors.

New finding: Celiac disease is now four times as common as it was 50 years ago, tests of old blood samples show.

Confounding Symptoms

When a person who has celiac disease consumes gluten—a protein in wheat, rye, barley and triticale (a wheat-rye hybrid)—her immune system attacks the protein. This inflames and damages the intestinal lining and interferes with absorption of nutrients. *The person may develop…*

● **Classic, overt symptoms.** Typically, celiac disease causes severe chronic or recurrent diarrhea. Poor nutrient absorption leads to weight loss, smelly stools, gassiness and/or weakness. Many doctors, mistaking these symptoms for irritable bowel syndrome or inflammatory bowel disease, advise eating more high-fiber grains—which may make patients sicker.

- **Silent symptoms.** When there is no diarrhea, it's called silent celiac disease. In some silent cases, there are no symptoms at all. In others, atypical symptoms—abdominal pain, migraines, numbness or pain in hands and feet—lead to various wrong diagnoses. Silent celiac disease nonetheless continues to cause intestinal damage.

- **Skin symptoms.** Dermatitis herpetiformis (DH) is a chronic itchy, blistery rash. Only people with celiac disease get DH—but the vast majority of DH patients do not develop intestinal symptoms. Consequently, they often are misdiagnosed with eczema, psoriasis or "nerves."

Untreated, celiac disease creates an ever-increasing risk of developing very serious complications, such as osteoporosis, anemia, infertility, neurological problems (poor balance, seizures, dementia) and/or various cancers (melanoma, lymphoma). A missed diagnosis also represents a missed opportunity to watch for other autoimmune disorders that often go hand-in-hand with celiac disease, including thyroid disease, rheumatoid arthritis and alopecia areata (patchy hair loss).

Getting Diagnosed at Last

Celiac disease is genetic—you cannot get it by eating too much gluten. The genes can "express" themselves at any point in life, and the disease is never outgrown.

Vital: Get tested if you have any of the following…

- **Possible celiac symptoms.**

- **A family history of the disease.** Almost 10% of family members of celiac patients also have it, even if they have no symptoms.

- **Type 1 diabetes.** Genetic factors link this autoimmune disorder to an increased risk for celiac disease.

- **Down syndrome.** Again, there appears to be a genetic link.

Celiac disease usually can be diagnosed with blood tests for certain antibodies. A biopsy of tissue from the small intestine then is needed to confirm the diagnosis. If a patient has skin symptoms, a skin biopsy that confirms the DH rash also confirms the celiac diagnosis.

Sometimes nutritionists or naturopaths will recommend that patients adopt the gluten-free diet used to control celiac disease—but without first confirming the diagnosis with a blood test or biopsy.

Problem: Starting a gluten-free diet before you complete the diagnostic tests may yield a false-negative result, i.e., a normal reading even though you have the disease. If you do not actually have celiac disease, you subject yourself to needless limitations…you incur the extra cost of buying gluten-free foods…and your diet may lack adequate fiber.

The Diet Solution

Currently there are no drugs or supplements available to treat celiac disease. However, following a strict gluten-free diet can work wonders at alleviating celiac symptoms.

Important: If tests confirm celiac disease, the diet is essential even if you have no symptoms—otherwise, intestinal damage continues.

The diet can be tricky because gluten is in all foods that contain wheat, rye, barley and triticale. What's more, gluten grains have many aliases.

Example: Bulgur, couscous, dinkle, durum, einkorn, emmer, fu, graham, kamut, matzah, mir, seitan, semolina and spelt all are wheat products. Avoid oats, too—these

Gluten-Free Grains

What grains are safe to eat if you are sensitive to gluten?

You can eat brown rice, corn, wild rice and buckwheat (also called kasha), all of which are easy to find. Less common grains that also are fine—but you may have to hunt a bit for them—are amaranth, millet and quinoa.

Caution: If you have a gluten sensitivity, it is not enough to avoid wheat. You also must stay away from products containing rye, barley and spelt. Gluten can cause digestive problems in people who are sensitive to it.

Thomas Brunoski, MD, a specialist in food and environmental allergies and nutritional medicine in private practice in Westport, Connecticut.

often get tainted from being processed in proximity to gluten grains—unless labeled "gluten-free."

Unexpected: Gluten may be found in processed luncheon meat, imitation seafood, canned soup, frozen entrées, soy sauce, beer, medications, supplements and lipsticks.

Adhering to a gluten-free diet is easier than it used to be because all products with wheat now must be labeled as such. Though products containing gluten-grain–derived ingredients are not all necessarily labeled that way, requirements for allowing a food to be labeled gluten-free have become stricter. Now, gluten-free breads, cereals, pastas and other foods are sold in supermarkets and health-food stores. Do be sure to get enough fiber from gluten-free grains and other sources.

After adopting a gluten-free diet, some patients see radical improvement within weeks...for others, it takes months or longer. If improvement is slow, your gastroenterologist should investigate possible underlying conditions (such as infection or hormonal problems) that can exacerbate celiac symptoms.

Information: Contact the American Celiac Disease Alliance (703-622-3331, *www. americanceliac.org*)...Celiac Disease Foundation (818-990-2354, *www.celiac.org*)...Celiac Sprue Association/USA (877-272-4272, *www.csaceliacs.org*).

■ ■ ■ ■

Age and Celiac Disease— Going Against the Grain?

Joseph A. Murray, MD, gastroenterologist, professor of medicine, department of gastroenterology, Mayo Clinic, Rochester, Minnesota.

It's a good thing that age brings wisdom, because it also brings lots of other less desirable changes. One of the more surprising ones we've heard about lately is an increased susceptibility to celiac disease (or gluten intolerance). According to Joseph Murray, MD, a Mayo Clinic gastroenterologist, it was once unusual for a new case of celiac disease to be diagnosed in an older man or woman, but that's no longer the case. "Now it's as common as in younger people, and we're making diagnoses in 70- and even 80-year-olds," he says. This means that seniors should be alert to the possibility that while new digestive difficulties that seem to develop as they get older could be the result of age, they also could be celiac disease.

Celiac disease is a tough diagnosis to pin down, Dr. Murray acknowledges, so it is possible that at least some of those older folks have gone undiagnosed for years. But he emphasizes that incidence of the disease is unquestionably rising dramatically, most particularly among older people who are now known to be twice as likely as the general population to develop celiac disease.

Why Is This Happening?

Genetics definitely play a role in susceptibility to celiac disease, but Dr. Murray and others believe that environmental factors are contributing to the problem. Looking for antibodies that accompany celiac disease, he and his team analyzed three sets of blood samples—blood (taken for other reasons) from Air Force recruits that was drawn 50 years earlier and stored in a lab freezer…blood taken recently from young men whose ages matched those of the airmen at the time that their blood had been drawn…and new blood samples taken from elderly men who are contemporaries of the now elderly Air Force recruits. Using modern testing methods, the researchers found evidence of undiagnosed celiac disease in some of those old frozen blood samples.

Their comparisons of the groups showed that the elderly men today have four times the incidence of celiac disease compared with the young recruits of 50 years ago and that the disease is 4.5 times more common among today's young men than the young men of the 1950s. Also, in investigating the health records of the 1950s recruits, Dr. Murray learned that the ones who'd had undiagnosed celiac disease were four times more likely than the other recruits to have died since then.

"These results tell us that whatever happened to increase celiac disease happened after 1950," says Dr. Murray—hence the theory that some change in the environment is responsible.

Two possibilities: Dr. Murray says one reason might be that our "clean" lifestyles have so dramatically reduced the number of germs in our environment that our immune systems have been left with too little

to do, so they've turned against us…or that changes in how much wheat we eat as well as how wheat is grown and processed may be partially or fully to blame.

Should You Get Tested?

It's generally thought that the majority of people with celiac disease remain undiagnosed (estimates vary, but some believe that 90% of cases aren't identified), so it makes sense to be highly suspicious if you have certain types of digestive symptoms. These include abdominal bloating and pain, diarrhea, vomiting, gas, constipation and unexplained weight loss. Some folks should be especially on guard, says Dr. Murray, citing those who have a sibling, child, grandchild or indeed any other blood relative with known celiac disease. If any of those symptoms or categories describes you, you may want to ask your doctor to order a blood test for celiac disease. Don't first experiment with a gluten-free diet, since doing so can result in a false-negative result when you do get the test. And, speaking of false-negative results, these occur quite often with celiac disease, so if your test is negative but your symptoms persist, you may want to seek further evaluation.

People with celiac disease need to follow a gluten-free diet. You can obtain a list of foods to eat and foods to avoid by going to *www.mayoclinic.com/health/gluten-free-diet/MY01140* or *http://Digestive.niddk.nih.gov/ddiseases/pubs/celiac*, which is the National Institute of Diabetes, Digestive, and Kidney Disorders (NIDDK) Web site. "The good news is, this diet works," says Dr. Murray. "Most older people with celiac disease do well after diagnosis—in fact, 80% to 90% of patients feel completely better."

Stay Healthy with Celiac Disease

Jamison Starbuck, ND, a naturopathic physician in family practice and a lecturer at the University of Montana, both in Missoula. She is past president of the American Association of Naturopathic Physicians and a contributing editor to *The Alternative Advisor: The Complete Guide to Natural Therapies and Alternative Treatments* (Time Life).

Experts believe that at least one out of every 100 American adults has celiac disease, a condition that can make sufferers ill after eating even a single slice of bread. The culprit is gluten—a type of protein found in wheat, barley, rye and, in some cases, oats that creates an autoimmune, inflammatory reaction in the small intestine. The usual symptoms are bloating and diarrhea, but some people also experience abdominal pain and/or constipation. In some cases, celiac disease causes only a blistery, itchy skin condition (dermatitis herpetiformis) or fatigue.

If you think you might have celiac disease, discuss it with your doctor. A diagnosis requires specific blood tests and, in some cases, an intestinal biopsy. If you do have celiac disease, your medical doctor will tell you to completely avoid gluten. This may sound like hard work, since gluten is in all sorts of things you might not suspect, such as many kinds of soy sauce, creamed soups and salad dressings. But it is definitely doable and gets easier as you learn where gluten-free products (even bread and pasta) are available—for example, in many health-food stores and a growing number of restaurants.

Payoff: Once you start avoiding gluten, your celiac symptoms will disappear over a period of weeks and months. *Other steps to consider…**

*To minimize inflammation, follow the dietary advice indefinitely—and also continue to take the vitamin supplements to guard against a nutritional deficiency.

• **Take supplements.** Inflammation in the small intestine interferes with the absorption of key nutrients. I advise my celiac patients to take a daily regimen that includes 5 milligrams (mg) of folic acid…800 international units (IU) each of vitamins E and D…25,000 IU of vitamin A…and 2 mg of vitamin K.

Note: Vitamin K supplements should be avoided by patients taking *warfarin* (Coumadin) or another blood thinner. I also recommend taking a botanical formula that contains one or more of these herbs (in powdered form)—deglycyrrhizinated licorice root, slippery elm and marshmallow root. Follow label instructions and take until inflammatory bowel symptoms abate.

• **Eat healthful fats daily and fish twice a week.** Olive oil, avocado, soy milk and small portions of unsalted nuts (eight to 12) are good sources of healthful fat. (However, celiac patients should avoid peanuts, which can be hard for them to digest.) Fatty fish, such as salmon or halibut, is an easily digested protein source.

Warning: In people with celiac disease, high-fat dairy products, as well as fried foods, tend to worsen diarrhea.

• **Use plant-based enzymes.** Enzyme supplementation helps break down food and reduces post-meal bloating. Plant-based enzymes (available at natural-food stores) are usually derived from pineapple or papaya, and they are safe for just about everyone unless you have ulcers or you are allergic to pineapple or papaya.

Typical dose: One or two capsules per meal.

• **Get support.** Avoiding gluten isn't easy, but you'll feel much better if you do. For more advice, consult the Celiac Sprue Association/USA, 877-272-4272, *www.csaceliacs.org.*

16

Preventing and Relieving Heartburn

Beware of Heartburn Drugs

Leo Galland, MD, founder and director of the Foundation for Integrated Medicine in New York City. He is the author of *The Fat Resistance Diet* (Broadway) and *The Heartburn and Indigestion Solution*, an e-book available online at *www.fat resistancediet.com/alternative-medicine/gerd.*

Popular heartburn medications known as proton-pump inhibitors (PPIs) are the third-highest-selling class of drugs in the US with an estimated one of every 20 Americans taking them. However, recent research shows that PPIs can be harmful—and frequently are overprescribed.

FDA warns of danger: Based on a review of several studies, the FDA has issued a warning about a possible increased risk for fractures of the hip, wrist and spine in people who take high doses of prescription PPIs or use them for more than a year.

Other important findings: A recent study of hospital patients treated for infection caused by the bacterium *Clostridium difficile* (which leads to severe diarrhea) found that those who took a PPI were 42% more likely to have a recurrence of the infection than those not taking the drug. A number of studies have also linked PPIs to possible

increased pneumonia risk—the drugs make it more likely that pneumonia-causing microbes will survive in the stomach and migrate into the lungs.

The irony is that PPIs, such as *esomeprazole* (Nexium), *omeprazole* (Prilosec) and *lansoprazole* (Prevacid), don't actually address the underlying cause of heartburn. Instead, these drugs work by shutting down production of stomach acid—but this acid is essential for absorbing nutrients as well as controlling harmful stomach bacteria. Reduced stomach acid can increase susceptibility to foodborne illness, such as salmonella, and can increase risk for small intestine overgrowth (which causes faulty digestion and absorption).

However, a number of natural remedies do attack the root cause of heartburn very effectively—without harming your health.

The Problem with PPIs

Heartburn occurs when the contents of the stomach back up into the esophagus (acid reflux), causing a sensation of burning and discomfort. Contrary to popular belief, heartburn is not caused by excess stomach acid. In fact, most people with heartburn have normal levels of stomach acid.

Instead, acid reflux occurs because the valve that is supposed to keep the stomach's contents in the stomach—called the lower esophageal sphincter (LES)—relaxes at the wrong time.

Taking medications that neutralize stomach acid (as antacids do) or reduce production of stomach acid (as PPIs and similar drugs known as H2 antagonists do) makes the reflux from your stomach less acidic, but it does nothing to make the faulty valve work better.

What's more, since acid reflux contains digestive enzymes—which can be just as irritating to the esophagus as stomach acid—your reflux may still cause you problems, such as heartburn, belching or sore throat, even after taking these acid-fighting medications.

Addressing the Root Cause

If you use a PPI drug and want to stop, taper off gradually.

Here's how: Talk to your doctor about switching to a 20- milligram (mg) dose of omeprazole, the mildest PPI, for several weeks. From there, switch to an H2 antagonist, such as *cimetidine* (Tagamet) or *ranitidine* (Zantac), for a week or two. These drugs are less potent acid inhibitors.

At that point, ask your doctor about stopping acid-suppressing medication altogether. *While tapering off the drug, begin working on correcting the underlying problem of your leaky LES valve…*

• **Eat more frequent, smaller meals.** Aim for five small meals daily. A distended stomach is the biggest stimulus for the LES to open.

• **Chew your food well.** The act of chewing signals the LES to stay closed. Chew each mouthful of food 10 to 20 times.

• **Don't eat within three hours of bedtime.** This allows your stomach to empty into the small intestine before you go to sleep.

• **Switch to a reduced-fat diet (no fried, fatty or greasy foods)—**and minimize your intake of chocolate, coffee and alcohol. All of these foods can impair the function of the LES. These dietary changes help reduce symptoms in 70% to 80% of my heartburn patients. Try it for one week to see if it helps you. If the reduced-fat diet doesn't improve your symptoms, try cutting back on carbohydrates instead. In about 10% of people with heartburn, the reflux is triggered by high-carbohydrate foods, such as bread, pasta and potatoes.

Follow these dietary changes until you have been totally off acid-suppressing drugs for at least six weeks. Then experiment to see if changing the diet provokes symptoms such as heartburn.

The Natural Approach

If the lifestyle changes described above don't adequately ease your heartburn symptoms, a number of natural products can be very effective at improving LES function. After checking with your doctor, you can try the following supplements (available at most health-food stores or online) one at a time. If a supplement doesn't improve symptoms after one week, discontinue it. If it does help but you need more relief, continue taking it while adding the next supplement on the list.

Continue taking these supplements for at least six weeks. Then try stopping the supplements to see if you still need them. They are safe to use indefinitely if necessary.

• **Calcium citrate powder.** This is the most important supplement you can take for acid reflux. Calcium in your body's cells stimulates the LES to close, but studies have shown that when the esophagus becomes inflamed from chronic reflux, the LES no longer responds to these cellular signals. This leads to even more inflammation, creating a vicious cycle.

To be effective in these cases, the calcium needs to have direct contact with the esophagus. That's why I recommend a solution of calcium powder in water rather than pills.

Typical dose: 250 mg mixed in two to four ounces of water after dinner and after other meals as needed (up to four doses per day).

Good brands: NOW Foods (888-669-3663, *www.nowfoods.com*)…ProThera, Inc. (888-488-2488, *www.protherainc.com*).

Caution: People with kidney stones or chronic constipation should consult their doctors before taking calcium citrate powder.

• **Digestive enzymes.** While these products help acid reflux in many people, it's not completely clear why. One possible reason is that they help the stomach empty faster.

Typical dose: One to two capsules or one-half teaspoon powder mixed with two to four ounces of water after each meal.

Good brands: AbsorbAid (866-328-1171, *www.iherb.com*)…NOW Foods Optimal Digestive System 90.

• **Betaine hydrochloride.** This digestive aid is typically used by people who do not produce adequate levels of stomach acid. In people with heartburn, betaine hydrochloride helps the stomach empty, thus reducing the possibility of reflux.

Typical dose: One to two capsules (typically 360 mg each) after meals.

Good brands: Country Life (800-645-5768, *www.country-life.com*)…NOW Foods.

• **Deglycyrrhizinated licorice.** This supplement appears to have a direct soothing effect on the esophagus, reducing inflam-

Painful GERD

Acid reflux can cause chest pain, according to Julia Liu, MD.

New finding: In a study of 31 emergency room patients (median age 46) who complained of chest pain, 57% had acid levels in the esophagus high enough to indicate gastroesophageal reflux disease (GERD). Heartburn is the most common symptom of GERD, but the disorder also can cause chest pain, hoarseness and chronic cough with or without heartburn.

If you have any of these symptoms: Ask your doctor if GERD is a possible cause.

Caution: If you suffer severe chest pain that does not go away within five minutes, seek immediate medical care to rule out a heart-related cause.

Julia Liu, MD, assistant professor, division of gastroenterology, University of Alberta Hospital, Edmonton, Canada.

mation—which, in turn, helps improve LES function.

Typical dose: 150 mg to 300 mg, just before or after meals.

Good brands: Integrative Therapeutics, Inc. (800-931-1709, *www.integrativeinc.com*)…NOW Foods.

• **Aloe liquid.** Derived from the aloe vera plant, this supplement reduces heartburn by soothing the esophagus.

Typical dose: Four ounces, just before or after meals.

Good brands: George's Aloe (254-580-9990, *www.warrenlabsaloe.com*)…Lily of the Desert (800-229-5459, *www.lilyofthe desert.com*).

• **Sustained-release melatonin.** Most people think of the hormone melatonin as a sleep aid, but it also affects a number of gastrointestinal functions, including tightening the LES.

Typical dose: 3 mg to 6 mg, taken shortly before bedtime.

Good brands: NutriCology (800-545-9960, *www.nutricology.com*)...Jarrow Formulas (310-204-6936, *www.jarrow.com*).

Caution: People with certain autoimmune diseases (including rheumatoid arthritis) should avoid melatonin.

■ ■ ■ ■

Heartburn Relief

Ara DerMarderosian, PhD, professor of pharmacognosy (the study of natural products used in medicine) and Roth chair of natural products at the University of the Sciences in Philadelphia. He also is the scientific director of the university's Complementary and Alternative Medicines Institute.

Barry L. Zaret, MD, professor emeritus and senior research scientist in medicine and professor of radiology at Yale University School of Medicine in New Haven, Connecticut. He is coauthor of *Heart Care for Life* (Yale University Press).

Many people who suffer from heartburn take over-the-counter antacids or expensive prescription medication, such as *esomeprazole* (Nexium) and *lansoprazole* (Prevacid). These treatments can help but often cause side effects, such as diarrhea and dry mouth.

Heartburn, a sharp, burning pain under the rib cage, occurs when stomach contents "back up" (reflux) into the esophagus.

Chamomile, ginger and deglycyrrhizinated licorice have long been used (in tea, extract and tincture) to relieve heartburn as well as indigestion and intestinal irritation. Their effectiveness is supported by anecdotal evidence.

For relief proven in clinical studies, try pectin, a substance found in the outer skin and rind of fruits and vegetables. Apples and bananas are among the best sources of

PPI Warning

Acid blockers, such as Nexium, Prevacid and Prilosec, can lead to fractures in people with osteoporosis. Proton-pump inhibitors (PPIs) are potent acid-blocking drugs prescribed for people with heartburn and chronic indigestion. Doctors often tell patients that they must take these drugs for life—but long-term use can interfere with the body's absorption of calcium and minerals, increasing the risk for broken bones and hip fractures.

Self-defense: Ask your doctor about alternatives, such as digestive enzyme combinations prescribed by naturopathic physicians. If you must take PPIs, ask about limiting their use to as short a time as possible.

Andrew L. Rubman, ND, adjunct professor of clinical medicine, Florida College of Integrative Medicine, Orlando, and director, Southbury Clinic for Traditional Medicines, Southbury, Connecticut.

pectin. If you suffer from heartburn, try eating an apple (do not choose green or other tart varieties) or a banana to see if it relieves your symptoms.

Pectin supplements, which are available at most health-food stores, are another option. Take at the onset of heartburn until it subsides. For dosage, follow label instructions. Pectin supplements are generally safe but may interfere with the absorption of some medications, so check with your doctor before trying this supplement.

Caution: Chronic heartburn (more than twice a week) may indicate gastroesophageal reflux disease (GERD), a condition that should be treated by a gastroenterologist.

Don't Let Heartburn Turn Deadly

Anil Minocha, MD, professor of medicine at Louisiana State University and staff gastroenterologist at Overton Brooks VA Medical Center, both in Shreveport, Louisiana. He is the author of *How to Stop Heartburn* (Wiley).

Nearly everyone suffers from heartburn from time to time, but frequent episodes (two or more times weekly) can signal a condition that must be taken seriously. Chronic heartburn, also known as gastroesophageal reflux disease (GERD), can lead to internal bleeding and scarring—even a deadly form of cancer. More than 20 million Americans have GERD.

Alarming new finding: The number of people hospitalized for conditions related to GERD doubled between 1998 and 2005, according to the US government's Agency for Healthcare Research and Quality.

What Goes Wrong

When you eat or drink, food and liquid move from your mouth to the esophagus, where a valve, called the lower esophageal sphincter, relaxes to allow the food and liquid to pass into your stomach. The lower esophageal sphincter then squeezes shut to keep stomach contents from backing up (a process known as reflux) into the esophagus.

Some degree of reflux occurs normally—including after meals. But when reflux becomes excessive, causes complications or affects quality of life, it is called GERD.

Symptoms that may be misdiagnosed: GERD—with or without heartburn—also can be characterized by chronic hoarseness or cough, sore throat or asthma, conditions that occur when gastric contents come in contact with the upper respiratory tract.

A Life-Threatening Danger

Chronic reflux can lead to injury and bleeding in the esophagus, which sometimes affects swallowing. With time (sometimes just a few years), cells lining the esophagus can become precancerous as a result of chronic inflammation. This condition, known as Barrett's esophagus, can lead to esophageal cancer, which is often fatal and is the most rapidly increasing cancer in the US.

Important: Because GERD can lead to serious, even life-threatening complications, see a doctor if you have heartburn two or more times weekly—or if you have symptoms, such as difficulty swallowing, unexplained chronic cough or hoarseness, that don't respond to standard treatment, such as medication and lifestyle changes.

Getting the Right Diagnosis

A primary care doctor or gastroenterologist usually diagnoses GERD on the basis of the symptoms described earlier. In some cases, the doctor will perform endoscopy, in which a thin, flexible, fiber-optic tube is passed through the throat to examine the esophagus and upper part of the stomach.

Ask your doctor about: An esophageal acidity test. With this procedure, a tiny device is placed in the esophagus to monitor levels of acidity for 24 hours (very high levels usually indicate GERD). This test typically is used when a patient has not responded to treatment or has atypical symptoms (such as chronic cough or hoarseness).

Best Medication Choices

Over-the-counter (OTC) antacids, such as TUMS, Rolaids and Maalox, neutralize stomach acid and may help relieve heartburn, but they do not heal the injury to the esophagus caused by reflux.

People who have frequent heartburn usually get better results from acid-reducing

Sleep on the Left

Sleeping on your right side worsens heartburn. People who sleep on their right side suffer reflux for longer periods than people who sleep on their left side. Left-side sleeping may keep the junction between the stomach and esophagus above the level of gastric acid, reducing heartburn symptoms.

Self-defense: If you have heartburn, sleep on an incline so that gravity helps keep stomach contents in place. And if you tend to sleep on your side, make it your left side.

Donald O. Castell, MD, professor, division of gastroenterology at Medical University of South Carolina, Charleston, and leader of two studies of acid reflux, published in *The Journal of Clinical Gastroenterology* and *The American Journal of Gastroenterology.*

prescription medication, such as H2 blockers, including *ranitidine* (Zantac) and *famotidine* (Pepcid), or proton pump inhibitors (PPIs), including *omeprazole* (Prilosec) and *esomeprazole* (Nexium). Some of these medications are available OTC.

Ask your doctor about: Potential side effects of long-term use of PPIs, which include reduced absorption of vitamin B-12, calcium and magnesium, higher risk for bone fractures and increased risk for respiratory infections.

Small Changes That Help

If followed conscientiously, lifestyle changes can eliminate the need for medication in up to 20% of GERD sufferers. *My advice…*

• **Check your medications.** Calcium channel blockers and beta-blockers taken for high blood pressure or heart disease, as well as some antidepressants and anti-anxiety medication, can reduce lower esophageal sphincter (LES) pressure and may worsen GERD. If you have heartburn symptoms, ask the doctor who prescribed your medication about alternatives.

• **Modify your eating habits.** Small, frequent meals leave the stomach quickly, thus providing less opportunity for reflux.

Avoid foods that may worsen GERD: Onions, chocolate and fatty foods reduce LES pressure, allowing reflux to occur.

• **Sleep right.** If you're troubled by reflux when you sleep, place a foam wedge under the mattress or wooden blocks under the bedposts to elevate the head of your bed by four to six inches.

Important: Extra pillows under your head will not do the job. They will raise your head, but won't change the angle between your stomach contents and your LES.

Alternative Approaches

Stress causes the LES to relax more often, increasing reflux episodes. Practicing a regular stress-reduction technique, such as deep-breathing exercises, has been shown to reduce the amount of acid in the esophagus. *Also helpful…*

• **Acupuncture.** This ancient Chinese practice is most likely to help people diagnosed with "slow stomach"—that is, their GERD is worsened by food taking longer to leave the stomach. Acupuncture can improve the movement and emptying of stomach contents.

• **Probiotics,** such as Lactobacillus acidophilus, are "friendly" bacteria that reduce the harmful effects of acid in the esophagus.

My advice: Eat yogurt or kefir containing "live, active" cultures twice daily.

The Surgical Option

Surgery usually is an option if drug treatment and alternative approaches have failed.

In the standard procedure, called *fundoplication*, part of the upper stomach is wrapped around the LES to strengthen it. This operation can be performed with tiny incisions (laparoscopically), rather than by opening the chest.

In one study of 100 individuals, 90% expressed overall satisfaction with the surgery. Although 80% continued to take anti-reflux medications, most took lower doses than before the surgery. Some new procedures, which involve injections or sutures to tighten the LES, are promising but unproven.

Postmenopausal Heartburn

Leo Galland, MD, director, Foundation for Integrated Medicine, New York City. He is author of *The Fat Resistance Diet* (Broadway). *www.fatresistancediet.com.* Dr. Galland is a recipient of the Linus Pauling award.

Does hormone replacement therapy (HRT) cause heartburn? That was the implication of reports associating the heartburn suffered by many postmenopausal women with use of either over-the-counter (OTC) estrogen (phytoestrogens/botanicals) or HRT. The data was from the Nurses' Health Study, which has been gathering information from more than 121,000 registered nurses since the 1970s.

Published in the *Archives of Internal Medicine*, the study reported that women who were using OTC products that are estrogen-based or who were on hormone replacement therapy were one-and-a-half times more likely to report having symptoms of heartburn or other gastroesophageal reflux disease (GERD) symptoms. Leo Galland, MD, director of the Foundation for Integrated Medicine, and author of the downloadable e-book *The Heartburn and Indigestion Solution*, believes the heartburn connection is more complex.

Hormones and GERD

The study associates the use of estrogen products with GERD (defined in the study as heartburn that occurs one or more times a week). However as we know, a correlation isn't the same as causation. Dr. Galland says that many factors may account for the increased risk of heartburn associated with hormone therapy used during or after menopause. Hormones like estrogen and progesterone affect how well muscles are able to contract, and therefore may contribute to heartburn by relaxing the LES valve that separates the stomach from the esophagus. This relaxation of the smooth muscle tissue in the lower esophagus lets stomach acid back up—that's what causes the burning sensation, Dr. Galland explains.

Plavix and PPI

Heartburn pills may impair the effectiveness of a popular drug, warns Paul A. Gurbel, MD. Millions of Americans take the anti-platelet agent *clopidogrel* (Plavix) to prevent blood clots and reduce heart attack and stroke risk. Plavix can cause stomach bleeding—so some patients also take heartburn drugs (PPIs), such as *omeprazole* (Prilosec) or *lansoprazole* (Prevacid). According to a recent study, people who take Plavix and PPIs are about 50% more likely to have a heart attack than people who take only Plavix.

Self-defense: Talk to your doctor.

Paul A. Gurbel, MD, director of Sinai Center for Thrombosis Research and associate professor of medicine, Johns Hopkins University, both in Baltimore.

PPIs Are All Alike

Heartburn drugs are equally effective, says Mark Ebell, MD. Researchers recently analyzed 19 studies involving more than 9,000 patients who took proton pump inhibitors (PPIs) for gastroesophageal reflux disease (GERD) for about four weeks.

Result: Equivalent doses (10 milligrams [mg] to 40 mg daily) of several PPIs, including *esomeprazole* (Nexium) and *omeprazole* (Prilosec), worked equally well.

If you take a PPI for GERD: Ask your doctor to prescribe the least expensive drug that is effective for you.

Mark Ebell, MD, associate professor, College of Human Medicine, Michigan State University, Ann Arbor.

It's thought that the presence of extra progesterone is probably responsible for heartburn that occurs during pregnancy and it's also a component in many treatments for menopausal symptoms.

It's important to take these and all GERD symptoms seriously, as left untreated, it can lead to precancerous tissue changes. "Prevention is important," says Dr. Galland. Taking calcium supplements is among the most effective ways to prevent GERD, he notes. He recommends following meals immediately with either a chewable product (like Viactiv or a drugstore brand) or powdered calcium citrate that you dissolve in water and drink (several brands are available online). "These increase the tightness of the LES valve and also improve the ability of the esophagus to expel stomach acid back into the stomach," he explains.

For more information on soothing symptoms of GERD and, even better, how to avoid them altogether, see Dr. Galland's Web site, *http://fatresistancediet.com/alternative-medicine/gerd/.*

In the meantime, if you experience heartburn, consider the possibility that hormones, drugs or dietary supplements you're taking may contribute to the symptoms and understand that these symptoms are likely not due to excess stomach acid, but to weakness of the LES valve. See a doctor for proper hormonal assessment and symptomatic management.

Peppermint and Reflux Don't Mix

Elaine Magee, RD, MPH, registered dietitian and the author of *Tell Me What to Eat If I Have Acid Reflux* (New Page).

Anything you suck on or chew (such as hard candies or gum) increases saliva production, which is thought to help reduce acid reflux. However, some foods and beverages can aggravate reflux symptoms. Peppermint, in particular, can weaken the lower esophageal sphincter (a muscle that prevents food and acid from backing up into the esophagus). Therefore, it should be consumed sparingly by people with gastroesophageal reflux disease (GERD), a condition in which certain stomach contents (including acid) rise from the stomach into the esophagus, causing heartburn and other symptoms. To determine whether the peppermint candies are aggravating your symptoms, try eating just one and see how you feel. Then eat a few more and note how you feel. It may be possible that you can tolerate one candy at a time—but not half a pack.

The Best Healing Herbs

David Hoffmann, a clinical medical herbalist based in Sonoma County, California, a fellow of Britain's National Institute of Medical Herbalists and one of the founding members of the American Herbalists Guild. He is the author of 17 books, including *Herbal Prescriptions After 50* (Healing Arts).

Anyone who has taken prescription drugs is well aware that these medications can not only be costly, but they also can cause a variety of uncomfortable or even dangerous side effects, such as excessive bleeding, headache, nausea and dizziness.

Recently reported problem: A study of 150,000 older adults (who are among the heaviest users of prescription medications) found that 29% were taking at least one inappropriate drug—including medications that were ineffective or even dangerous.

Often-overlooked alternative to drugs: Herbal medicine. Herbs should not be substituted for all prescription medications, but the careful use of medicinal plants can improve overall health and reduce or eliminate the need for some medications—as well as the risks for drug-related side effects.

Common conditions—and the best herbal treatments…

Chronic Bronchitis

More than 5% of Americans suffer from chronic bronchitis (a mucus-producing cough that occurs on most days of the month at least three months of the year).

Best herbal treatment: Horehound (leaves and flowering tops). It relaxes the bronchi (airways that connect the windpipe to the lungs) and makes it easier to expel mucus.

How to use: Add 1 milliliter (ml) to 2 ml of horehound tincture (concentrated liquid) to one ounce of hot or cold water. Drink this amount three times daily during bronchitis flare-ups.

Important: Most herbs are available in various forms, such as dry leaf, capsules and powders, but tinctures are convenient, among the quickest to be absorbed and have a long shelf life.

Heartburn

When acid from the stomach backs up into the esophagus, the result is often heartburn (a burning pain behind the breastbone).

Best herbal treatment: Marshmallow root. It coats and soothes the esophageal lining.

How to use: Make an infusion by adding one heaping teaspoon of powdered marshmallow root to a cup of cold water and letting it sit at room temperature for 12 hours. Drink the entire mixture when heartburn occurs. If you get heartburn more than three times a week, drink one infusion in the morning and another at bedtime until the heartburn eases. If you make more than one cup in advance, you can refrigerate the unused portion for 24 hours.

Low-Acid Coffees

"Stomach-friendly" coffees are less likely to cause heartburn and acid reflux. Puroast Low Acid Coffee (877-569-2243, *www.puroast. com*) is a Venezuelan blend that was ranked first among testers for its nutty aroma, robust flavor and smooth, almost chocolaty taste. Folgers Simply Smooth, available in grocery stores, uses a special roasting process to reduce acidity. For more on coffee and heartburn, see page 446.

Newsweek, 251 W. 57 St., New York City 10019.

Quit Soda to Beat Reflux

Prone to heartburn? Stop drinking soda, says Stuart F. Quan, MD. Consumption of carbonated beverages is a risk factor for nighttime heartburn—which can cause more damage to the esophagus than daytime heartburn. Acid that comes up into the esophagus is not cleared as easily by the body during sleep. Even people who usually don't have heartburn should stop drinking soda at least three hours before bedtime to reduce the chance of nighttime acid reflux.

Stuart F. Quan, MD, professor of medicine, University of Arizona, Tucson, and coauthor of a recent study of 3,806 people with nighttime heartburn, published in *Chest.*

Important: Do not use hot water. It will provide only about one-fourth of the soothing mucilage (lubricating substance) of a cold-water infusion.

Insomnia

Stress, poor sleep habits and health problems that cause pain are common causes of insomnia (an inability to fall asleep or remain asleep).

Best herbal treatment: Passionflower (leaves or whole plant). Its depressant effect on the central nervous system helps promote restful sleep.

How to use: Add 1 ml to 4 ml of passionflower tincture to one ounce of cold water, or make an infusion by pouring one cup of boiling water over one teaspoon of dried passionflower and letting it sit for 15 minutes. Drink the entire tincture mixture or infusion at bedtime when you suffer from insomnia.

Caution: People who take drugs with sedative effects, such as certain antihistamines, antianxiety medications and insomnia supplements or drugs, should not use passionflower, which can increase these sedative effects.

Irritable Bowel Syndrome

Alternating bouts of constipation and diarrhea are characteristic of irritable bowel syndrome (IBS).

Best herbal treatment: Yarrow (leaves and other parts that grow above ground) for the diarrhea phase...mugwort (leaves) for constipation. These herbs also are effective for episodes of diarrhea and constipation that are not related to IBS.

Yarrow contains tannins, substances that reduce the amount of water released by the intestinal lining. Mugwort is a bitter herb that promotes the intestinal contractions needed for bowel movements.

How to use: Add 1 ml to 2 ml of yarrow or mugwort tincture to one ounce of hot or cold water. Drink this amount three times daily when you have diarrhea or constipation.

Osteoarthritis

Age-related changes in the joints are the primary cause of osteoarthritis. Most patients can get temporary relief with pain relievers, such as *ibuprofen* (Advil), but these drugs often cause side effects, such as gastrointestinal bleeding.

Best herbal treatment: Black mustard (for external use) and meadowsweet (for internal use). A poultice of black mustard causes mild, temporary inflammation that stimulates circulation—good for muscle and/or joint pain.

How to use: Make a black-mustard poultice by grinding the seeds in a coffee grinder and mixing one-half cup of the mustard powder with one cup of flour. Add enough hot water to make a paste. Spread the mixture on a piece of heavy brown paper, cotton or muslin that has been soaked in hot water, then cover it with a second piece of dry material. Lay the moist side of the poultice across the painful area, leaving it on for 15 to 30 minutes once daily.

Caution: Consult a doctor before using the poultice on a young child, or on anyone who is age 70 or older or seriously ill.

Meadowsweet is a pain reliever that contains aspirin-like chemicals called salicylates.

How to use: Add 1 ml to 2 ml of meadowsweet tincture to one ounce of hot or cold water. Drink this amount three times daily until symptoms subside.

Periodontal Disease

Bacterial buildup in the spaces between the teeth and gums leads to periodontal (gum) disease—the most common cause of tooth loss in older adults. Gum infection has been linked to an increased risk for heart attack and stroke. Regular dental care and cleanings (at least annually) are essential.

Best herbal treatment: Goldenseal and/or myrrh. Goldenseal acts as a topical antibiotic. Myrrh strengthens mucous membranes. Start treatment when you first notice gum tenderness and/or bleeding— the first signs of periodontal disease.

How to use: Mix equal amounts of goldenseal and myrrh tinctures. Use a very fine paintbrush to apply the mixture to the gum line. Leave it on as long as you can—the taste is unpleasant—then rinse your mouth with water and spit it out. Repeat two or three times daily.

Better Coffee Choice

When human stomach cells were exposed to decaffeinated and regular coffees roasted in a lab setting, less gastric acid was produced from the decaffeinated, dark-roasted coffees.

Theory: The compound N-methylpyridinium, generated during roasting, prevents the stomach from producing acid—particularly if caffeine, which stimulates gastric acid secretion, has been removed.

If coffee gives you heartburn: Try a decaffeinated, dark-roasted variety.

Veronika Somoza, PhD, professor of bioactive food compounds, University of Vienna, Austria.

The Fastest-Growing Cancer Threat

Herman Kattlove, MD, a medical oncologist and medical editor with the American Cancer Society. He is based in Los Angeles.

Cancer rates are generally declining in the US, but the incidence of adenocarcinoma, the most common type of esophageal cancer, has increased more rapidly since the 1970s than any other cancer.

Until recently, cancer of the esophagus—the foot-long muscular tube that carries food from the mouth to the stomach—has been considered deadly, though relatively rare. Now both of these beliefs are being challenged.

At one time, people diagnosed with esophageal cancer who underwent surgery had a low chance of surviving for five years. That survival rate is now as high as 50%, most likely due to earlier screening and diagnosis.

Fortunately, healthy lifestyle changes can reduce your risk of developing esophageal cancer.

Who Is At Risk?

As with many cancers, the risk for esophageal cancer increases with age—nearly 80% of new cases are diagnosed in people ages 55 to 85.

There are two main types of esophageal cancer—squamous cell carcinoma, which develops in the cells that line the entire esophagus, and adenocarcinoma, which occurs in the part of the esophagus closest to the stomach.

More than half of all squamous cell carcinomas are linked to smoking. Risk of adenocarcinoma is doubled in people who smoke a pack of cigarettes or more per day. Carcinogens in tobacco are believed to enter the bloodstream and contribute to the development of esophageal cancer. Excessive alcohol consumption—more than two drinks daily—also increases the risk for the squamous cell type of cancer, although it is not known why.

Tobacco and alcohol are a potentially deadly combination. A person who drinks excessively and smokes one to two packs of cigarettes a day has a 44 times higher risk of getting esophageal cancer than someone who does neither.

A diet low in fruits and vegetables accounts for approximately 15% of esophageal cancer risk. To help avoid the disease, eat at least five daily servings. Some scientific evidence suggests that berries, particularly black raspberries, which are rich in cancer-fighting antioxidants, protect against esophageal cancer.

Body weight also is a factor. Obese men are twice as likely to die from adenocarcinoma of the esophagus as men of normal weight.

The Heartburn Connection

Frequent heartburn, known as gastroesophageal reflux disease (GERD), is caused by stomach acid backing up into the esophagus. Up to 14% of Americans experience heartburn at least weekly, while 44% suffer from it monthly. GERD is linked to nearly one-third of esophageal cancer cases.

An additional factor for esophageal adenocarcinoma is a condition called Barrett's esophagus, in which cells of the esophagus begin to resemble those that line the stomach. People with Barrett's esophagus are about 50 times more likely to develop esophageal cancer than those without the condition.

People who suffer from chronic heartburn (three or more times per week for more than three months) should be screened for Barrett's esophagus. If they are found to have the condition, screenings every year may be recommended to detect esophageal cancer.

Screening involves the use of endoscopy, an invasive procedure that requires sedation. During the test, the doctor passes a thin, flexible tube (endoscope) through the mouth to view the entire length of the esophagus.

Prompt and effective treatment of GERD might reduce the risk for esophageal cancer, although this has never been proven. A number of effective prescription and over-the-counter GERD remedies, which block the production of stomach acid, are available. These include H2 blockers, such as *ranitidine* (Zantac) and *famotidine* (Pepcid), and proton pump inhibitors, such as *omeprazole* (Prilosec).

Symptoms and Diagnosis

Difficulty swallowing is the most common symptom of esophageal cancer. If you notice that swallowing has become even slightly harder—you must swallow more firmly or food doesn't go down properly—see your doctor immediately. It could save your life.

Weight loss commonly occurs because of difficulty swallowing and loss of appetite. Frequent bouts of hiccups, another sign of esophageal cancer, may result when cancer irritates the nerves leading to the diaghragm. More advanced cancer may compress the nerves that control the vocal cords, which can lead to hoarseness.

If your doctor suspects cancer, endoscopy will be performed and a biopsy taken. Additional tests may be necessary—endoscopic ultrasound, a procedure that involves the use of high-frequency sound waves, to pinpoint the tumor thickness... and a computed tomography (CT) scan and a positron emission tomography (PET) scan to determine whether the tumor has spread to nearby lymph nodes.

Treatment

Surgery is the main treatment for esophageal cancer. Most often, the surgeon will perform esophagectomy, in which the cancerous part of the esophagus and nearby lymph nodes are removed, or esophagogastrectomy, in which the lower part of the esophagus and upper part of the stomach are removed. With both procedures, the remaining part of the esophagus is reconnected to the stomach, often with a segment of the large intestine.

These procedures are extremely complex and demand a high degree of surgical expertise, as well as a skilled team of nurses and other personnel to provide after-care. Choose a major cancer center that performs more than 10 esophageal cancer surgeries a year.

Chemotherapy and radiation before surgery have been shown to improve the outcome, possibly because they destroy microscopic tumor tissue before it can spread.

In one study of 802 patients, 42% of those who had two rounds of chemotherapy before surgery were still alive two years later, compared with 34% of those who had surgery alone.

New finding: A long-term clinical trial showed that esophageal cancer patients who received so-called "triple therapy"—treatment with two cancer drugs (5-fluorouracil and cisplatin) and daily radiation for five weeks before surgery—had a 39% chance of surviving for five years, compared with 16% of patients who received only surgery.

17

Natural Help for Constipation

Constipation: What Your Doctor May Not Tell You

Norton J. Greenberger, MD, a clinical professor of medicine at Harvard Medical School and a senior physician at Brigham and Women's Hospital, both in Boston. He is a former president of the American Gastroenterological Association and coauthor, with Roanne Weisman, of *Four Weeks to Healthy Digestion* (McGraw-Hill).

Constipation is one of those ailments that most people think they know how to treat—the majority believe that simply eating more fiber is the answer. But this often doesn't work.

What few people realize: Chronic constipation can have some very surprising causes...and dietary changes alone help only about one-third of those with the condition. What's more, if overused, some of the same laxatives that relieve constipation initially can exacerbate it in the long run, so most people need additional help to really get rid of their constipation.

What's Normal?

Most people have one to three bowel movements daily, while others have as few as three a week. This variability is normal.

What's more important are changes in bowel habits, particularly if you're having fewer bowel movements than usual and also are experiencing other symptoms that could indicate a more serious problem—such as blood in stool (colon cancer)...unexplained weight loss (diabetes or colon cancer)...or weight gain (low thyroid function).

The first step: Even though not all people with constipation will improve by eating a fiber-rich diet, it's still wise to start by eating more fruits, vegetables, legumes and whole grains that are high in fiber. In general, people who consume 20 grams (g) to 35 g of dietary fiber daily—and who exercise regularly—are less likely to suffer from constipation than those who mainly eat a meat-and-potatoes diet.

Examples of fiber sources: One cup of oatmeal or a bran muffin provides 4 g to 5 g of fiber.

Helpful: Be sure to eat the vegetables and fruits that are most likely to draw water into the stool to facilitate soft, bulky bowel movements.

Best vegetables to ease constipation: Those in the Brassica family, such as broccoli, asparagus, brussels sprouts, cauliflower and cabbage.

Best fruits to ease constipation: Peaches, pears, cherries and apples (or apple juice).

If your constipation doesn't improve within a few weeks, then…

1. Check your medications. Many prescription and over-the-counter medications slow intestinal movements and cause constipation. Narcotic painkillers, such as *oxycodone* (OxyContin) and the combination of *acetaminophen* and *oxycodone* (Percocet), are among the worst offenders. Tricyclic antidepressants, such as *amitriptyline*, also can cause it. So can medications that treat high blood pressure (calcium channel blockers) and Parkinson's disease.

Helpful: Constipation also can be triggered by the antihistamines used in allergy medications, such as *cetirizine* (Zyrtec) and *diphenhydramine* (Benadryl), if used daily. Lowering the dose of an antihistamine drug or taking it less often may reduce constipation.

2. Get your magnesium and potassium levels tested. Most people get sufficient amounts of both minerals in their diets. But if you take a daily diuretic or laxative or have an intolerance to gluten (a protein found in wheat, barley and rye), you may be deficient. Low magnesium or potassium decreases the strength of intestinal contractions—this may contribute to diarrhea or constipation.

Important: If constipation doesn't improve within a month of boosting your fiber intake, see your doctor. The problem could be due to a deficiency of either or both minerals. If a blood test shows that you have low magnesium and/or potassium, supplements can restore normal levels within a week or two (ask your doctor for the appropriate dosage).

3. Be cautious with calcium. High-dose calcium often causes constipation, particularly in people who take antihistamines or other drugs that slow intestinal transit time (how long it takes food to pass through the bowel).

My advice: Get most of your calcium from calcium-rich foods. If your constipation is related to high-dose calcium supplements, talk to your doctor about limiting the supplement dose to 500 milligrams (mg) to 1,000 mg daily—and be sure to eat plenty of high-fiber foods and drink lots of fluids.

4. Drink at least two quarts of fluids daily— more if you exercise or engage in activities that cause you to perspire heavily. Drinking this much fluid increases lubrication and makes stools larger, which helps them pass more easily (and frequently). Water is best—it has no calories and usually is the most readily available fluid.

5. Avoid laxatives. Some of the most popular products actually can increase constipation. So-called stimulant laxatives, such as Dulcolax and castor oil, cause the intestinal muscles to stretch and weaken with continued use. People who use these products frequently may become dependent—they can't have a bowel movement without them.

Important: It's fine to use these products occasionally—when, for example, you haven't had a bowel movement for several days and are feeling uncomfortable. But if you use them more than once or twice a week, it's too much. Talk to your doctor about healthier methods such as those described in this article.

6. Relax and reregulate. If you get enough fiber and drink enough fluids but still are constipated, see your doctor. You may have a type of constipation known as dyssynergic defecation (different parts of the anorectal area—pertaining to the anus and rectum— contract and relax at the wrong time).

This type of constipation can be diagnosed by giving patients oral radiopaque markers that allow the doctor to view intestinal movements on an abdominal X-ray.

Normally, people initiate a bowel movement by instinctively contracting the upper part of the rectum while relaxing the lower part. People with dyssynergic defecation constipation often do the opposite. Stools aren't propelled through the colon, or they get "hung up" due to inappropriate muscle movements.

People with this type of constipation usually are referred to a gastroenterologist, who often uses biofeedback, along with exercises such as Kegels (a type of pelvic-muscle exercise), to help them learn to relax and contract different parts of the anorectal area. They're also taught not to strain during bowel movements—this decreases the force of intestinal contractions and impairs one's ability to have a bowel movement.

■ ■ ■ ■

Prebiotics for Constipation

Leo Galland, MD, founder and director of the Foundation for Integrated Medicine in New York City. He is the author of *The Fat Resistance Diet* (Broadway) and *The Heartburn and Indigestion Solution,* an e-book available online at *www.fat resistancediet.com/alternative-medicine/gerd.*

If you don't know much (or anything) about prebiotics—with an "e"—you are far from alone. Many people don't know the difference between prebiotics and their better known cousins, probiotics...so we decided to explain more about how both can be used to optimize digestive health and boost immunity. We placed a call to a medical doctor who also is highly active and respected in the world of natural medicine, Leo M. Galland, MD.

Prebiotics—What Probiotics Eat

Your high school Latin provides an easy and obvious way to differentiate prebiotics from probiotics—focus on the "pre." *Pre*biotics are the predecessor. Their primary purpose is to provide nourishment to probiotics, thus helping to sustain a healthy level of these good bacteria in the gut.

Research has shown prebiotics to be beneficial for people with Crohn's disease and ulcerative colitis. Prebiotics can serve as a natural remedy to ease constipation, and they can be helpful for a number of other digestive complaints, including constipation-associated irritable bowel syndrome (IBS) and some cases of inflammatory bowel disease. Prebiotics also help absorption of calcium and magnesium in people who have low mineral levels in their diets, and there's some evidence that they might help prevent colon cancer as well.

Unlike probiotics, prebiotics are not bacteria—they're a form of soluble fiber that can be found in a few complex carbohydrates. What makes them unique is their ability to pass unabsorbed through the small intestine, which makes them available to feed tissue and probiotics in the large intestine. One of the most common prebiotics is a kind of complex fructose polymer found in some plant foods called *inulin* (which, in spite of the similarity in names, has nothing to do with insulin). There are other kinds, too, including non-inulin prebiotics and a type called *fructo-oligosaccharides* (or FOS).

Are Dietary Sources Sufficient?

Some foods are rich sources of prebiotics. For instance, inulin can be found in generous amounts in Jerusalem artichokes (a potato-like tuber)...chicory...icama...and dandelion. And many common foods contain lesser amounts of inulin and/or FOS, such as onions, garlic, leeks, bananas, tomatoes, spinach and whole wheat.

Since prebiotics aren't abundant in these foods, it can be useful to take prebiotic supplements if you have certain types of problems.

Constipation Concern

Constipation may signal Parkinson's disease. In a study of 392 adults, those with Parkinson's disease were about twice as likely to report a history of constipation as those without the disease.

Theory: Parkinson's may begin to affect the autonomic nervous system—which controls digestion, bowel movements and other body functions—years or even decades before motor symptoms of the illness (such as tremors and rigid muscles) appear.

Self-defense: If you have a history of constipation and are suffering Parkinson's-like symptoms, see your doctor.

Walter A. Rocca, MD, MPH, professor of epidemiology and neurology, College of Medicine, Mayo Clinic, Rochester, Minnesota.

Dr. Galland prescribes prebiotic supplements for many of his patients, noting that a typical dose can range from 4 grams to 8 grams. They come in various forms, including powders and capsules. *He often prescribes...*

• **Extracts of Jerusalem artichokes** or extracts of chicory, best for chronic constipation.

• **FOS extracted from fruits and grains,** which can be helpful for constipation and colitis.

• **Non-inulin prebiotics,** which include oat beta-glucan—a soluble fiber that is separated from oats to make supplements. These have the additional benefit of lowering cholesterol. Oat beta-glucan is less likely to cause gas or bloating than inulin and can be excellent for boosting immune function, Dr. Galland says.

Start Slowly and Talk to Your Doctor

Since this is all fairly complex, it is important to consult with a physician who has expertise in treating patients with prebiotic supplements. If you and your doctor agree that prebiotics may be helpful to you, plan to start slowly and increase the dosage gradually, or your body may overrespond to added prebiotics, Dr. Galland cautions. "Let your GI tract get used to the prebiotics and shift the bacteria slowly," he says. Stop taking them if you notice an upset stomach, gas, diarrhea, bloating and other uncomfortable digestive symptoms that don't dissipate within a few days.

A group that is especially likely to experience such difficulties, Dr. Galland says, is people with inflammatory bowel disease—as well as some folks with other types of digestive problems. Why? While the prebiotics are not themselves irritating, they may increase production of irritants by stimulating the growth of beneficial intestinal bacteria, Dr. Galland explains.

Note: Unpleasant as it may be, this actually may be a sign that the prebiotics are beginning to do their job.

Some people should avoid prebiotics altogether, including people who have fructose malabsorption, a limited ability to absorb fructose (including that found in inulin-based prebiotic supplements and inulin-containing foods such as Jerusalem artichokes). If you have this problem, you may experience gastrointestinal problems (gassiness, bloating, diarrhea) that get worse and worse if you take prebiotics. Don't know whether this might apply to you? Here's a clue. People with fructose malabsorption are very likely to get gassy and/or bloated or have diarrhea if they consume the sweeteners sorbitol or xylitol, because these are fermented by the same bacteria that ferment inulin.

Suffering from Constipation? How to Keep Things Moving

Brian Lacy, MD, PhD, director of the gastrointestinal motility lab, Dartmouth-Hitchcock Medical Center, Lebanon, New Hampshire, and associate professor of medicine, Dartmouth Medical School, Hanover, New Hampshire.

The word "constipation" comes from the Latin meaning "to press or crowd together." And that's just what happens in this common digestive disorder—stool becomes hard and compressed...and/or difficult to expel from the body. There are traditional remedies—some of which can work in the right circumstances—and there's also a new drug that has been created to help with chronic constipation.

We all get constipation sometimes. *Here's what you need to know to remedy constipation and keep it from becoming chronic…*

What's Normal?

While most people think of constipation as the inability to have a daily bowel movement, the definition is broader than that. Studies show that the "normal" frequency of bowel movements varies. Some people may have more than one bowel movement per day, while others may routinely have a bowel movement every couple of days. I generally consider someone constipated if he/she typically goes three or four days between bowel movements. On the other hand, you may have a daily bowel movement that involves lengthy straining—which also qualifies as constipation.

While constipation can cause discomfort and may affect your quality of life, it doesn't pose a health threat in and of itself. Until recently, it had been thought that infrequent bowel movements could increase the risk for colorectal cancer. But a recent large-scale study in Japan found that only very infrequent bowel movements (every 10 to 14 days) could increase the risk. Some of the main health risks associated with constipation arise from the physical stress of passing hard stools—which may cause hemorrhoids and, in some cases, a fissure or tearing of the rectum.

Causes of Constipation

Most people experience constipation as a temporary condition brought on by a change in diet...medication (constipation can be caused by narcotic pain relievers, high-dose iron supplements and some blood-pressure drugs)...or travel (when you are thrown off your routine, not following your normal diet or not able to make regular bathroom visits). For this group, self-treatment with an over-the-counter laxative will usually restore regular bowel function.

For others, constipation is chronic—it does not go away. *The two main causes of chronic constipation are…*

- **Irritable bowel syndrome (IBS).** This occurs when the nerves and muscles of the colon fail to function properly. It accounts for 30% to 40% of all chronic constipation and is usually associated with bloating and pain in the lower abdomen.

- **Pelvic floor dysfunction.** This condition accounts for another 30% to 40% of chronic constipation. More common in women than men, it occurs when the muscles and nerves in the pelvic floor (the muscles under the pelvis) aren't coordinating properly. Constipation due to pelvic floor dysfunction won't respond to laxatives but can usually be cured through physical therapy.

Chronic constipation also can result from other disorders including neurological disorders (such as Parkinson's, multiple sclerosis and stroke)...metabolic and endocrine conditions (such as diabetes and an underactive thyroid)...and systemic disorders

Chronic Constipation

Are you chronically constipated? What's the cause—and what should you do?

A low-fiber diet or medications that slow gastrointestinal movement, including calcium channel blockers, diuretics and Parkinson's drugs, are among possible causes.

Advice: Schedule daily bathroom times, such as 30 minutes after breakfast or dinner, when gut activity increases and prompts the bowel-movement urge. Consume about 30 grams of fiber daily from fiber-rich foods, such as fruits, vegetables and whole grains, including brown rice and wheat germ. To avoid bloating and gas, slowly increase your fiber intake to this level.

If you have trouble getting enough fiber in your diet, try taking one to three tablespoons daily of the natural high-fiber laxative flaxseed, crushed or mixed with juice. Drink eight ounces of water with flaxseed or any fiber supplement to help it add bulk to stool. Lastly, don't ever ignore the urge to have a bowel movement—you could eventually lose this sensation. Rarely, constipation can signal cancer. See a doctor if it's coupled with unintentional weight loss and/or blood in the stool and symptoms last longer than three weeks.

Brian Lacy, MD, PhD, director, Gastrointestinal Motility Laboratory, Dartmouth Medical School, Hanover, New Hampshire.

(such as lupus or scleroderma). A problem in the colon, such as diverticulosis or cancer, can also cause constipation, although this is not common.

Whatever the cause, constipation becomes much more prevalent over age 65, and women are more likely than men to become constipated.

Treatments That Work

For occasional constipation or constipation due to IBS, the first line of treatment involves establishing a regular bathroom schedule, dietary changes and over-the-counter medications. What to do...

• **Establish a regular bathroom schedule.** A wave of motility goes through everyone's GI tract around 5 am, which is why many people feel the urge to have a bowel movement in the morning. A similar wave occurs after eating. I encourage my patients to listen to their bodies and to arrange for scheduled bathroom times that coincide with their urges to have bowel movements. Give yourself three to four weeks to adjust to this schedule.

• **Add fiber to your diet.** Dietary fiber speeds movement of food through the GI tract and binds with water, causing stools to become bulkier and pass out of the colon more easily. Optimal fiber intake is 25 to 30 grams a day, but the average American consumes less than half this amount.

Solution: Eat more high-fiber foods, such as legumes (split peas, lentils, black beans, lima beans, baked beans, etc.), fresh fruits and vegetables (artichokes, raspberries, pears, broccoli), whole-wheat pasta and cereals and other foods containing whole bran or oats. You can also boost fiber intake with supplements, such as psyllium husk powder (Metamucil, Serutan) or *methylcellulose* (Citrucel). It may take three or four days to notice positive effects.

• **Try an over-the-counter laxative.** If regular bathroom visits and additional fiber don't solve the problem, add an over-the-counter laxative. There are different types—for example, osmotic, which draw water into the area, or lubricant, which help stools move more easily. Milk of magnesia is a safe, effective and inexpensive choice. To avoid elevated magnesium levels, however, it shouldn't be taken for longer than two weeks—and should be avoided by anyone with kidney disease. Miralax, another laxative, also is safe and effective for seven days, but some people don't like mixing the powder. Stimulant laxatives, such as *bisaco-dyl* (Dulcolax), have been shown to improve constipation with short-term use, though they may cause cramping. After two weeks, however, the body develops a tolerance to them. If your constipation is not improved within two weeks, consult your doctor.

Not recommended: Stool softeners. These popular laxatives are a waste of money. They are supposed to work by drawing water into the stool, making it softer and easier to pass. But they bulk up stool by only 3%—not enough to make any difference in your bowel movements.

Also not helpful: Exercise. While regular physical activity is beneficial in many ways, studies have shown conclusively that it has no effect on chronic constipation.

When to Seek Medical Help

Most people are helped by the steps above. But if you see no improvement after several weeks, ask your primary care doctor for a prescription-strength laxative. An osmotic agent called lactulose (Chronulac, Constilac)—which is made of sugar molecules that make the gut more acidic and causes more water to be drawn in—makes bowel movements easier. Although side effects can include gas and bloating, people can take lactulose indefinitely. There is also a new medication for chronic constipation called *lubiprostone* (Amitiza) that has been found to be safe and effective. It is the first medication for constipation that works by stimulating intestinal fluid secretions that help the bowels move. Most patients prefer lubiprostone because it comes in a pill, not a sugary drink (like lactulose) and because there is no bloating.

If these prescriptions drugs still don't help, there may be an underlying condition that is causing the problem and you may need to see your primary care provider or a gastroenterologist for testing. This may include a complete blood count (CBC) test to make sure that you are not anemic and a thyroid-stimulating hormone (TSH) test to make sure that you do not have an underactive thyroid gland. This visit should also include a physical exam to check for pelvic floor dysfunction or any neuromuscular disorder. Since constipation can sometimes be a sign of colon cancer, a colonoscopy may be recommended.

Lastly, some patients with severe constipation swallow a capsule with markers to determine how quickly the markers pass through the gastrointestinal tract.

If pelvic floor dysfunction is detected, the patient will be referred to a physical therapist for a series of specific exercises for the pelvic floor and surrounding muscles.

If the constipation still doesn't improve and is seriously affecting quality of life, the last resort is a surgical procedure, called a colectomy, in which the colon is removed and the small intestine connected directly to the rectum. While this relieves constipation, it also results in frequent bowel movements—up to four per day.

When to Worry About Constipation and Diarrhea

Andrew L. Rubman, ND, medical director, Southbury Clinic for Traditional Medicines, Southbury, Connecticut. *www.naturopath.org.*

Bowel movements are hardly the stuff of polite dinner table conversation, so it's not surprising that many people don't know exactly what healthy, normal bowel habits are. The reality is that "normal" varies from person to person.

And whatever normal is, it needs to stay that way in order for you to avoid other health challenges down the road. What changes might be worrisome?

Normal or Not?

Bowel movements vary in their degree of regularity, color, texture, odor and difficulty. It can be normal to have three a day or as few as three a week. The normal, healthy stool color is dark butterscotch, says Andrew L. Rubman, ND, but that can be affected by what you eat—especially if you had spinach or beets, for instance. The shape should be something like a sausage—soft but solid...relatively easy to pass...and emerging in one nearly continuous movement, as the different segments of the colon consecutively empty.

Constipation and Diarrhea: When to Worry

Constipation and diarrhea are the most common complaints, affecting most people from time to time, and not particularly worrisome on an occasional basis. You qualify as constipated if you have fewer than three bowel movements a week, with stools that are hard, dry and difficult to pass. There's often related abdominal discomfort and bloating as well. Dehydration, inadequate dietary fiber and a lack of exercise are the usual causes, according to Dr. Rubman.

As many people already know, you can help move matters along by eating more fiber-rich foods (e.g., whole grains, vegetables and fruits) and fewer processed foods. Various fiber supplements may also be helpful. Discuss with your doctor what type you should take. Exercising about 30 minutes most days of the week will also help ease constipation.

Diarrhea refers to loose, watery stools more than three times in a day. It's usually temporary—perhaps caused by food, antibiotics or the stomach flu—and typically

clears on its own without treatment. In the meantime, good foods to eat include bananas, rice, applesauce and toast (called the BRAT diet) and Dr. Rubman also recommends egg drop soup, since diarrhea depletes not only water but salt and albumin (protein) as well. Consult your doctor if diarrhea persists longer than three days...if you become dehydrated...or you see blood, frothiness or large amounts of mucus.

What Changes Do You Need to Report?

Occasional digestive disturbances are part of life, but if you notice significant changes in regularity, color, texture or experience difficulty in passing stool for longer than a few weeks, it's time to take notice. Dr. Rubman suggests keeping a journal to help you identify what is different, including dietary factors, and advises seeing your doctor. Such changes may signal any of a number of digestive challenges—e.g., hemorrhoids, irritable bowel syndrome, ulcerative colitis or colorectal cancer (especially if you're 50 or older). In particular, always call your doctor if you see blood in the stool. Any abnormal color that lasts more than a few days and can't be traced to something you ate is a reason to call your doctor—most especially if it is accompanied by other symptoms, such as abdominal pain or unexplained weight loss. The earlier you diagnose and address any gastrointestinal disorder, the more successful the treatment.

Keep Your Digestive Tract On Track

To keep digestion on the right track, Dr. Rubman advises that you watch your diet and get regular exercise....avoid prolonged use of antacids or anti-inflammatory drugs such as ibuprofen, naproxen or aspirin...refrain from alcohol or tobacco use...chew food thoroughly...and limit water with meals. If you notice changes or are concerned about any symptoms, a naturopathic physician, specially trained and attuned to digestive issues, will be able to examine the state of your digestive function by ordering diagnostic tests, recommending diet and lifestyle changes and prescribing medicines, such as nutrients in which you are deficient. If necessary, he/she will refer you to a gastroenterologist for further treatment.

■ ■ ■ ■

Deli Cure for Constipation

Joanne Slavin, PhD, RD, a professor of food science and nutrition at the University of Minnesota, St. Paul, and a specialist in the gastrointestinal effects of whole grains.

Constipation is the butt of many jokes (sorry), but you won't hear any laughter from the 15% of Americans who suffer from it day in and day out, a percentage that soars to as high as 40% of people (women two to three times as often as men) in their mid-60s. A study from Finland, published in the *Journal of Nutrition*, reveals a seemingly simple and appealing solution for mild constipation—whole-grain rye bread!

The researchers found that rye bread was more effective in relieving constipation than laxatives...buttermilk (naturally rich in probiotics—*lactobacillus rhamnosus GG* specifically—and thought to have a laxative effect)...or "white wheat bread" (which has a bit of whole grain in it). Study authors report that the particular sort of fiber in rye is abundant in *arabinoxylan* (a type of *polysaccharide*), which adds water to stools and also produces short-chain fatty acids (SCFAs). Both of these help move waste more efficiently through the colon. So—could it be this simple to improve your constipation?

Other Great Grains

The 51 constipated adults in the study consumed about 8.5 ounces of rye bread daily (this was seven to 14 slices, depending on how thickly it was sliced) for three weeks. This improved their "transit time" (from ingestion to defecation) by 21% to 43% and enabled them to move their bowels an average of 1.4 more times per week.

According to Joanne Slavin, PhD, RD, a professor of food science and nutrition at the University of Minnesota and a specialist in the gastrointestinal effects of whole grains, rye is by no means unique in containing arabinoxylan in generous amounts—whole-grain wheat has a lot, too (though somewhat less) and oats are a plentiful source.

It's important to note that what you need is *whole-grain* rye bread, and that is not so easy to find here in America—at least not the flavor- and fiber-filled sort that lucky Europeans eat all the time. Our supermarket rye breads (the ones that come in plastic bags) are of limited value in that even most of the "whole-grain" rye breads contain nongrain fibers that do little to help constipation. However, Dr. Slavin says that some whole grain is better than none.

Dr. Slavin offers the following advice on how to identify the breads that are most apt to improve your colon health and reduce constipation...

It's best to buy your whole-grain breads from a bakery, where you can ask which ones are made with the most whole grain.

If you must buy packaged bread, choose carefully. Look for breads where the first word on the "whole-grain" label (whether rye, wheat or any other) is "whole," which establishes that at least some of its fiber is indeed from whole grains. A good rule of thumb is, the denser the bread, the more whole grain it contains. The best choices are 100% whole grain, of course.

Choose breads that have a lot of crunch. Crunchy breads have bigger grain particles, and these contribute directly to regularity by adding bulk to the stool and helping to push it through the colon.

What a great reason to do what many people would prefer to do anyway—bypass the "bread" aisle in the supermarket and buy baked goods fresh from a local bakery! They're not only more delicious, but clearly more healthful, too.

■ ■ ■ ■

The Power of Pickles

Andrew L. Rubman, ND, medical director, Southbury Clinic for Traditional Medicines, Southbury, Connecticut. *www.naturopath.org.*

Foods that are pickled (fermented) dish up serious health benefits. Specifically, they are really good for soothing digestive discomfort of all kinds. Counterintuitive as it may be, eating fermented foods—not only pickled cucumbers, but also peppers, tomatoes and sauerkraut—is a simple and tasty way to resolve heartburn, bellyaches and other intestinal distress.

Pickling is an ancient preservation technique with healthful results. British seamen ate sauerkraut to ward off scurvy… Bulgarians were believed to live longer because they drank fermented milk…and Koreans today eat more than 40 pounds per year of kimchi (a blend of cabbage, garlic, chilis and other ingredients) both for taste and to ease digestion.

Pickling Promotes Digestion

The fermentation of foods takes place through the breakdown of carbohydrates by live microorganisms such as bacteria (for instance, *Lactobacillus acidophilus* or *Lactobacillus bulgaricus*), yeasts and molds.

Kimchi, pickles, sauerkraut and the like act as probiotics, encouraging the growth of positive intestinal microbes. These fermented foods promote efficient digestion, support immune function and boost good nutrition overall. They support availability of B vitamins in certain foods and essential amino acids. They also serve to counteract the ill effects of antibiotics.

According to Dr. Rubman, fermented foods are far better than the over-the-counter antacids or the proton pump inhibitors (PPIs) people routinely swallow to relieve heartburn and stomach upset, which end up causing more harm than good. While they may provide temporary relief, use of antacids or PPIs can backfire because you need acid to efficiently digest foods…and insufficient stomach acid can upset the proper environmental balance of intestinal flora. In contrast, fermented foods encourage the growth of good gut flora while also helping to neutralize the small amounts of stomach acid left in the system between meals, which is a common problem for people with gastritis and GERD.

Pick a Peck…

Eating fermented foods a few times a week can make a real difference in how well your digestive system functions. It's easy enough to do—you can spice up stews with a dollop of chutney or a ¼ cup of kimchi, enjoy a bowl of miso soup, slice pickled cucumbers or peppers onto sandwiches or spoon yogurt over fresh fruit. *To find fermented foods, visit your local health or gourmet store or shop online…*

● **Order fermented foods** from farms such as Wills Valley Farm Products (*www. willsvalley.com*) in Lancaster County, Pennsylvania, which offers fermented vegetables including kimchi, red cabbage, red beets and ginger carrots. Other American picklers include Adamah Farm in Falls Village,

Mind Over Constipation

Biofeedback—which helps the mind to control involuntary body functions, such as blood pressure—can work if constipation is caused by rectal spasm or spasm of the pelvic muscles. In these cases of dyssynergic defecation—when muscles responsible for bowel movements don't work well due to a failure to relax pelvic floor muscles—biofeedback can retrain muscles to push more effectively. There is as yet no home-based biofeedback program—one is under development.

To find a doctor who works with biofeedback: Contact the Biofeedback Certification Institute of America (303-420-2902, *www.bcia.org*).

Leo Galland, MD, founder and director of the Foundation for Integrated Medicine in New York City. He is the author of *The Fat Resistance Diet* (Broadway) and *The Heartburn and Indigestion Solution*, an e-book available online at *www.fatresistancediet.com/alternative-medicine/gerd.*

and on Web sites such as *www.kushistore.com*. To explore the extensive world of Indian chutneys, visit *www.kalustyans.com*.

● **Choose carefully.** Read labels and buy fermented products that are low in sugar and contain live or active cultures. Dr. Rubman warns that most brands of yogurt, in particular, are loaded with sugar and artificial flavoring, but he notes that Stonyfield Farm and Nancy's are two organic brands that contain live bacterial cultures and no artificial ingredients.

In cases of active intestinal disturbances such as irritable bowel syndrome or gastritis, Dr. Rubman sometimes prescribes fermented foods and/or probiotics (supplements that you can take if you don't enjoy the taste of fermented foods), but he does not recommend that you try this on your own. See a qualified and experienced naturopathic physician who can assess your condition and prescribe an appropriate dosage. But if you're in good health, pile pickles on your plate...pucker up...and enjoy.

■ ■ ■ ■

Natural Cures for Constipation

Jamison Starbuck, ND, a naturopathic physician in family practice and a lecturer at the University of Montana, both in Missoula. She is past president of the American Association of Naturopathic Physicians and a contributing editor to *The Alternative Advisor: The Complete Guide to Natural Therapies and Alternative Treatments* (Time Life).

So-called herbal "bowel cleansers" are touted as a healthy and effective treatment for chronic constipation. In my clinical experience, this claim simply is not true. Bowel-cleansing formulas typically contain strong laxative herbs, such as aloe resin (sometimes listed as "aloe leaf"), buckthorn, cascara, rhubarb and senna.

Connecticut (*www.isabellafreedman.org/adamah/products*) and Sonoma Brinery in Healdsburg, California (*www.sonomabrinery.com*). In New York City, classic Lower East Side vendors Russ & Daughters (*www.russanddaughters.com*) and Pickle Guys (*www.pickleguys.com*) are great sources. You can find many more online.

● **Visit food festivals that celebrate pickling,** such as New York City's International Pickle Day (*www.nyfoodmuseum.org*).

● **Go international.** Explore fermented foods from around the world, such as the pickled Asian plums known as umeboshi. In Japan, these have been consumed for thousands of years for their purported ability to counter nausea, stimulate the digestive system and promote the elimination of toxins. Find them in Asian and gourmet markets

These herbs increase peristalsis, the wave-like movement of the bowel that facilitates elimination of stool, but they also irritate the gut wall. Like any good laxative, these herbs will promote a bowel movement, but repeated or large doses create cramping, diarrhea and blood in the stool.

I define constipation as having less than one bowel movement per day. Common causes of constipation include irregular bowel habits (ignoring the urge to go or not allowing enough time)...inadequate fiber and/or water...lack of exercise...and poor digestive function (due to low secretion of digestive enzymes). Medications such as antihypertensives, tricyclic antidepressants, antacids and opiate pain relievers (such as codeine) can cause constipation. Unless your constipation is temporary (caused, for example, by the use of opiate medication following surgery), avoid strong laxatives—even if they are natural or herbal products. The bowel becomes reliant on laxatives, which can worsen your constipation and create inflammation and irritation in your intestinal tract.

Rather than seeking a temporary solution, people who are constipated should slowly retrain their bowels to work correctly. This process usually takes about four weeks. *Here's how...*

1. Eat fiber. Fiber helps retain water in the colon, which promotes softer and larger stool. While a healthy, toned bowel will respond to a moderate amount of fiber, a bowel that has become slack and weak (due to the effects of insufficient fiber) will need much more fiber. Start with five half-cup servings of vegetables and four half-cup servings of fruit per day. Have at least one cup daily of a whole grain, such as brown rice, oatmeal, quinoa or millet.

2. Exercise. Physical activity improves peristalsis. Get at least 20 minutes each day. My favorite exercises are yoga and aerobic activity, such as brisk walking, cycling or swimming.

3. Drink lemon water. To expand stool size and encourage elimination, drink 64 ounces of water daily. Twice a day, before meals, drink 16 ounces of water that contains the juice from half a fresh lemon (bottled lemon juice also can be used, but it is not as healthful). Lemon water encourages the secretion of bile, a digestive fluid that acts as a laxative.

4. Use small doses of herbs. A tea made with equal parts dandelion, yellow dock, burdock and licorice root has a mild laxative effect. What to do: Mix one-half ounce of each dried herb. Use two teaspoons of the mix per eight ounces of water, simmer for eight minutes, strain and drink. Start with one cup four times daily during the first week of bowel retraining. Reduce by one cup per week until you are able to eliminate regularly without the tea.

■ ■ ■ ■

18

Preventing and Treating Diarrhea

What You May Not Know About Diarrhea

Douglas L. Seidner, MD, director of nutrition in the department of gastroenterology and hepatology at the Cleveland Clinic.

Diarrhea—bowel movements that are looser and more frequent than usual—is the second most common medical complaint (after respiratory infections) in the US.

Most people associate a bout of diarrhea with a viral infection or food poisoning.

Now: Researchers are identifying new —and sometimes surprising—triggers, including the use of some medications.

Development: The Journal of the American Medical Association recently published a study that links the use of acid-lowering heartburn drugs, such as *omeprazole* (Prilosec), *lansoprazole* (Prevacid) and *ranitidine* (Zantac), to increased infection with the bacterium *Clostridium difficile*—a cause of severe and persistent diarrhea.

In an unexpected finding, the same researchers identified an association between diarrhea and regular use of *nonsteroidal anti-inflammatory drugs* (NSAIDs). More study is needed to confirm this NSAID-diarrhea link.

How Diarrhea Develops

What's left of food after most of it has been digested reaches the large intestine as a sort of slurry. There, the body absorbs water from this material, creating a solid mass to be excreted. Normal stool is 60% to 90% water. Diarrhea occurs when stool is more than 90% water.

When stool does not remain in the large intestine long enough, it is excreted in a watery form. This "rapid transit" diarrhea can be caused by stress, overactive thyroid (hyperthyroidism) and certain drugs, such as antacids and laxatives that contain magnesium, and chemotherapy for cancer.

Other types of diarrhea...

● **Osmotic diarrhea occurs when too much food remains undigested or unabsorbed.** Water is drawn into the colon to dilute unabsorbed chemicals, which makes the stool looser.

Large amounts of certain fruits and beans as well as sugar substitutes (sorbitol and xylitol) that are used in some brands of fruit juice, chewing gum and candy are

461

common causes of osmotic diarrhea. When the diarrhea sufferer stops eating the offending food, the condition stops.

Lactase deficiency—a lack of the enzyme needed to break down milk sugar (lactose)—is another cause of osmotic diarrhea. Most people know if they have this deficiency and avoid milk products.

Osmotic diarrhea also may develop in people taking antibiotics. That's because the drug eliminates beneficial bacteria that live in the intestinal tract, allowing harmful bacteria to proliferate. These microorganisms normally help the body process and absorb the small amount of food that hasn't been digested yet. Diarrhea usually develops within a few days of treatment. If it's bothersome enough, your doctor may prescribe a different antibiotic.

More rarely, diarrhea develops toward the end of antibiotic treatment—or even up to a month later. This may be caused by C. difficile or another bacterium that can flourish and cause inflammation of the large intestine when beneficial bacteria are eliminated.

Helpful: This infection is usually treated with the antibiotics *vancomycin* (Vancocin) or *metronidazole* (Flagyl).

• **Secretory diarrhea occurs when an excessive amount of water, salt and digestive fluids are secreted into the stool.** Viral infections, bacterial toxins that cause some types of food poisoning and rare tumors of the small intestine and pancreas can trigger the secretions that lead to secretory diarrhea.

With food poisoning, excess secretions are stimulated by chemicals produced by bacteria that have contaminated something you ate. This diarrhea usually lasts for 12 to 24 hours and stops without treatment. If it persists, your doctor may order tests, such as stool cultures, to determine whether a virulent bacterium, such as *Salmonella*, *Shigella* or *Campylobacter*, is involved and will require medication.

• **Travelers' diarrhea has a similar cause.** The culprit is generally a mild strain of a toxin-producing bacterium, such as *Escherichia coli*, that is present in food and/or water. Natives of the region you're visiting have been exposed to the microorganism for years and usually are immune to it. You're not. Traveler's diarrhea typically goes away within one to two days.

• **Exudative diarrhea occurs when the large intestine's lining becomes inflamed.** This triggers the release of blood, mucus, proteins and other fluids. Infection with the bacterium Shigella can cause this type of diarrhea. Crohn's disease (chronic inflammation of the small bowel or colon) and ulcerative colitis (chronic inflammation and ulceration of the colon) can also cause exudative diarrhea.

An antibiotic is sometimes used to treat a bacterial infection. Medication, such as the corticosteroid *prednisone*, and sometimes surgery are used to treat the inflammatory conditions.

Best Relief Strategies

In some cases, diarrhea can be a sign of a serious infection and should be treated by a doctor. Even though most types of diarrhea run their course within a few days, the following steps can hasten the process and ease your discomfort…

• **Eat right.** If food poisoning is the problem, you should abstain from all food until symptoms resolve, usually one to two days.

For other acute diarrhea, follow the "BRAT" diet: bananas, rice, applesauce and toast. Bananas and applesauce contain pectin, a water-soluble substance that helps firm up the stool…the carbohydrates in white rice and white toast are easy to digest. If you eat other foods, stick to small portions and avoid dairy products.

Yogurt is an exception. If it's made from live and active cultures, such as Lactobacillus

Bananas Fight Depression, Heartburn and More

Most people know that bananas are an excellent source of potassium (one ripe banana supplies more than 10% of an adult's daily requirement of the mineral). That's important because people with a low dietary intake of potassium are 28% more likely to suffer a stroke than those who consume higher levels, according to a study conducted at Tulane University.

Lesser-known medicinal uses of bananas...

• **Depression.** Bananas are a good source of tryptophan (a precursor to serotonin, a brain chemical that helps regulate mood).

• **Diarrhea.** Unripe bananas and plantains (high-starch, green bananas that are typically cooked) are a rich source of tannins, astringent plant compounds that help stop water accumulation in the intestines, thus diminishing diarrhea.

• **Heartburn and ulcers.** Bananas neutralize acidity and soothe and coat esophageal tissue with pectin (a substance used as a thickener and stabilizer in jellies).

Important: In rare cases, bananas may cause an allergic reaction. Bananas with blackened skin can increase blood sugar levels. Because bananas have high levels of potassium, people with kidney problems should check with their doctors before eating this fruit.

Ara DerMarderosian, PhD, professor of pharmacognosy (the study of natural products used in medicine) at the University of the Sciences in Philadelphia.

bulgaricus and Streptococcus thermophilus, yogurt may replace beneficial bacteria in the colon, helping to relieve antibiotic-related diarrhea.

When the diarrhea subsides, return to your normal diet cautiously. For the first few days, avoid fatty foods (they're harder to digest).

Important: Drink 64 ounces of fluids daily to replace what you're losing. Choose weak tea, water and/or small amounts of clear juice or soda, such as apple juice or ginger ale.

If diarrhea is severe: Drink "replacement fluids," such as CeraLyte, Pedialyte or Enfalyte. These contain salt and simple sugars that help the body retain water. Diarrhea-related dehydration isn't a danger for most adults, but it is a danger for children and many adults over age 65. Young children do not have as large of a reserve of water in the body as healthy adults. Older adults may have heart or kidney disease, which can be exacerbated by dehydration.

• **Medication.** Several over-the-counter preparations can help relieve diarrhea...

• Loperamide (Imodium) is a semi-synthetic narcotic that slows food as it passes through the bowel, allowing more time for water to be absorbed. Try loperamide if diarrhea is mild and hasn't been resolved in one to two days. It should not be taken if you have a fever or the stools are bloody.

• Bismuth subsalicylate (Pepto-Bismol, Kaopectate) absorbs toxins—it's quite effective for traveler's diarrhea. It should not be taken with aspirin. Do not take it if you have a fever or bloody stools. Children should not take this product.

C. Difficile Bacteria—The Latest Dangerous, Antibiotic-Resistant Microbe

Cliff McDonald, MD, chief, Prevention and Response Branch, Division of Healthcare Quality Promotion, Centers for Disease Control and Prevention. Dr. McDonald is a former officer in the Epidemic Intelligence Service.

Clostridium difficile (C. difficile), a toxin-producing bacterium long associated with elderly folks in hospitals and nursing homes, has now morphed into a virulent epidemic strain, threatening people of all ages. C. difficile can range from an annoyance, causing mild symptoms such as watery diarrhea, fever, nausea and cramps, to more severe troubles including inflammation of the colon, sepsis (blood poisoning), kidney failure and, in the worst cases, death.

As its name suggests, *C. difficile* can be difficult to treat. It is a real challenge to control in hospitals, since it produces spores that are difficult to eradicate and are easily passed from one person to another. And its antibiotic resistance has led to the selection of more virulent strains of C. difficile, leading to hospital outbreaks all around the United States.

Is It an Epidemic?

According to Cliff McDonald, MD, chief of the Prevention and Response Branch in the Division of Healthcare Quality Promotion at the Centers for Disease Control and Prevention (CDC), C. difficile has been known about as a cause of human disease for 30 years. "It was previously uncommon, but it has now reached epidemic proportions," he says. He estimates the number of C. difficile cases may reach 500,000 annually (including up to 30,000 deaths), reflecting approximately a five-fold increase since 2000.

The cause of the C. difficile epidemic is a newly identified strain called NAP1, which, when tested in the laboratory, produces 16 times more toxin A and 23 times more toxin B than other common strains. NAP1 is more resistant than other strains to the fluoroquinolones, a group of antibiotics that are commonly used to treat pneumonia in hospitals. "The overuse of antibiotics and the general resistance to fluoroquinolones has given NAP1 C. difficile a one-up on other strains," says Dr. McDonald. "Because it had a selective advantage over susceptible strains, it quickly spread and became epidemic in health-care facilities."

Are You a Carrier?

About 3% to 5% of healthy people actually carry C. difficile in their large intestines, Dr. McDonald explains, but typically without symptoms—it is held in check by the "good" bacteria that we also harbor, at least optimally. Ironically, this is often disturbed by the use of antibiotics, leaving some people vulnerable and allowing C. difficile to flourish.

Typically cases of C. difficile originate in hospitals, spread unwittingly by health-care workers as they handle infected patients and then touch other patients and medical equipment or other surfaces. C. difficile spores are unaffected by most hospital disinfectants...nor are they inactivated by alcohol-based hand sanitizers commonly in use. Special measures are required in hospitals to keep C. difficile infection from spreading.

Making matters worse is that C. difficile has a high recurrence rate. One out of five (20%) patients who get sick with it experience a recurrence and the chances increase following subsequent recurrences. Some cases are so severe that the only

Prevent Stool Leaks

Diarrhea can lead to stool leaks. Fiber helps —so eat more whole grains and take a fiber supplement, such as Citracel. Avoid artificial sweeteners, which often make stool looser. Constipation also could be the culprit, because when it is difficult to have a complete bowel movement, leftover stool may leak out later. Again, add fiber—it softens stool and makes it easier to expel.

Another possible reason for leaking is weak sphincter muscles. Biofeedback can help you learn to strengthen these. To find a practitioner, contact the Biofeedback Certification Institute of America (866-908-8713, *www.bcia.org*). In some cases, surgery is needed.

Hemorrhoids can keep the anal sphincter from closing, allowing leaks. If you have large hemorrhoids, see a colorectal specialist.

Referrals: The American Society of Colon and Rectal Surgeons, 847-290-9184, *www.fascrs.org.*

Madhulika G. Varma, MD, associate professor and chief of colorectal surgery, University of California, San Francisco.

option has been removal of the affected part of the colon. "People can actually have a mild infection the first time and then die of a recurrence," Dr. McDonald explains.

Tips for Consumers

We can do our part, suggests Dr. McDonald, by keeping our antibiotic usage to a minimum. "As a society we need to rethink the way we approach antibiotics. People need to understand that antibiotics are not vitamins and they are not sugar pills—they can carry some very significant risks, and C. difficile is one of them. Don't push for a prescription when you don't really need one. *In addition…*

● **Wash hands after using the bathroom and before eating or touching your face—**C. difficile must be ingested in order to cause disease. Dr. McDonald notes that it's important to remember that alcohol-based sanitizers don't work against C. difficile, so it may be better to wash with soap and water at these times.

● **Keep your household clean.** If you are exposed to C. difficile, or indeed to any individual with diarrhea, scrupulously clean all exposed surfaces in the room and/or that you or that person may have touched. Use a solution that is 1/10 household chlorine bleach, 9/10 cold water…made fresh daily… and scrub thoroughly to effectively kill C. difficile spores.

● **Realize that not all cases of diarrhea are C. difficile.** However, if you have severe diarrhea that occurs several times a day for two or more days, see your doctor immediately. A stool test can confirm the presence of the disease.

Remember, the drugs many people take in order to feel better—including antibiotics and proton pump inhibitors (PPIs) —alter the natural composition in the body in many different ways, making it vulnerable to disease. Though drugs can play an important role in medicine, in the end, less medicine is often the best medicine.

19

Natural Ways to Treat Ulcers

Natural Therapies for Ulcers

James N. Dillard, MD, DC, in private practice, New York City and East Hampton, New York. He is a former assistant clinical professor at Columbia University College of Physicians and Surgeons and clinical director of Columbia's Rosenthal Center for Complementary and Alternative Medicine, both in New York City. *www.drdillard.com.*

I f you've got an ulcer, chances are you're taking an over-the-counter (OTC) antacid and/or prescription medication to neutralize gastric acid or inhibit its production. These medications include proton pump inhibitors (PPIs), such as *esomeprazole* (Nexium) and *lansoprazole* (Prevacid), and H2-blocking drugs, such as *cimetidine* (Tagamet) and *ranitidine* (Zantac).

What most people don't realize: There are several natural, complementary remedies that help reduce ulcer symptoms and promote healing while conventional treatment is under way. Some of these treatments also can help prevent ulcers in some patients.

What Causes Ulcers

It's been more than 20 years since doctors learned that an infectious disease—rather than emotional stress—was the primary cause of most ulcers.

A screw-shaped bacterium, Helicobacter pylori, or H. pylori, burrows through the protective mucous lining in the small intestine and/or stomach, allowing harsh digestive fluids to accumulate and ulcerate the lining. About 50% of Americans over age 60 are infected with H. pylori. The bacterium doesn't always cause ulcers—but about 60% of patients with ulcers harbor H. pylori.

Most of the remainder of ulcers are caused by regular use of stomach-damaging nonsteroidal anti-inflammatory drugs (NSAIDs), such as aspirin, ibuprofen (Advil) and naproxen (Aleve)…alcohol…and/or smoking. Excessive alcohol wears down the lining of the stomach and intestines. Nicotine causes the stomach to produce more acid.

Best complementary treatments…*

Nondrug Therapies

● **Probiotics.** The intestine contains up to four pounds of "friendly" bacteria, which aid digestion. There's some evidence that

*Check with your doctor before taking supplements. They can interact with prescription medications.

maintaining adequate levels of beneficial bacteria helps create an inhospitable environment for H. pylori and makes it harder for this ulcer-causing bacterium to thrive.

Self-defense: Take a probiotic supplement that contains *Lactobacillus acidophilus* and *Bifidobacterium bifidus*. These organisms create a healthful mix of bacteria and can inhibit the growth of harmful organisms. Probiotics are helpful if you've taken antibiotics, which can kill off some beneficial bacteria.

The optimal dose for probiotics hasn't been determined. Preliminary research cites a daily dose of up to 10 billion organisms—the amount usually included in one to two capsules. Probiotics are available at health-food stores.

• **Cabbage juice.** This folk remedy has some evidence to support it. Cabbage is high in vitamin C, which seems to inhibit growth of H. pylori. It also contains glutamine, an amino acid that may strengthen the protective lining in the stomach.

A small Stanford University School of Medicine study found that ulcer patients who drank about a quart of cabbage juice daily healed significantly faster than those who didn't drink it.

Self-defense: If you have an active ulcer, consider drinking a quart of cabbage juice (about the amount in half a head of cabbage) once daily for up to two weeks.

• **Deglycyrrhizinated licorice (DGL).** Herbalists often recommend fresh licorice root to heal ulcers. Licorice contains mucin, a substance that protects the stomach lining, and antioxidants that may inhibit H. pylori growth.

However, natural licorice can increase the effects of aldosterone, a hormone that promotes water retention and can increase blood pressure in some people. DGL supplements (available at health-food stores) are a better option because the substances that increase blood pressure have been removed.

Self-defense: Take one DGL tablet before meals and another before bed. DGL may be effective for people with ulcers whose H. pylori has been successfully treated with antibiotics but who still have some stomach irritation.

• **Vitamin A.** Vitamin A helps repair damaged mucous membranes. A report in the British medical journal *The Lancet* suggests that ulcers heal more quickly in patients given supplemental vitamin A.

Caution: High-dose vitamin A therapy can be toxic, so get your vitamin A from dietary sources along with a daily multivitamin—not from a separate vitamin A supplement.

Self-defense: Get 10,000 international units (IU) of vitamin A daily if you're undergoing ulcer treatment. (A multivitamin typically contains 3,500 IU to 5,000 IU of vitamin A.)

Good food sources: Beef liver (one-and-one-half ounces contains 13,593 IU)...carrots (one raw carrot contains 8,666 IU)...and spinach (one cup of raw spinach contains 2,813 IU).

• **Zinc.** Like vitamin A, zinc is involved in tissue healing. In Europe, a drug compound made with zinc plus an anti-inflammatory is often used for treating ulcers. Early studies indicate that zinc alone can speed ulcer healing and possibly even help prevent some ulcers.

Self-defense: Don't exceed the recommended daily intake (15 milligrams [mg]) of zinc. Take a daily multivitamin that includes zinc...and get adequate intake from dietary sources (five medium fried oysters, 13 mg...¾ cup fortified breakfast cereal, 15 mg...three ounces lean beef tenderloin, 5 mg).

Another Way to Fight Ulcers

NSAIDs alleviate pain by inhibiting the production of pain-causing chemicals called *prostaglandins*. However, the body produces several kinds of prostaglandins, including some that protect the stomach lining. That's why NSAIDs, which block the production of pain-causing and stomach-protecting prostaglandins, make people who regularly use the drugs more susceptible to ulcers.

Self-defense: If you require regular pain relief, start with *acetaminophen* (Tylenol). It relieves pain without depleting stomach-protecting prostaglandins.

Caution: Taking more than the recommended dosage or drinking alcohol with acetaminophen can cause liver damage.

Also helpful: Ask your doctor about taking Arthrotec, a prescription drug combination that includes the NSAID *diclofenac* along with *misoprostol*, which protects the stomach and intestinal lining. One study found that patients taking Arthrotec experienced up to 80% fewer ulcers than those taking an NSAID alone.

Natural Cures for Heartburn and Ulcers

Jamison Starbuck, ND, a naturopathic physician in family practice and a lecturer at the University of Montana, both in Missoula. She is past president of the American Association of Naturopathic Physicians and a contributing editor to *The Alternative Advisor: The Complete Guide to Natural Therapies and Alternative Treatments* (Time Life).

"Doctor, I have heartburn, but I don't want to take a prescription drug. What can I do?" Many people have asked me for such advice—especially since the media have publicized risks associated with popular heartburn and ulcer medica-

New Treatment for Ulcer-Causing Bacteria

The traditional treatment—a triple therapy of two antibiotics with a proton pump inhibitor (PPI) drug, such as *omeprazole* (Prilosec)—eradicates 80% of bacteria.

New finding: Sequential therapy—in which a different PPI/antibiotic combination is followed by the traditional treatment—eradicates more than 90% of bacteria.

Better: Ask your physician about using *bismuth subsalicylate* (Pepto-Bismol) instead of a PPI. Pepto-Bismol soothes the stomach and prolongs the effects of the other medications.

Andrew L. Rubman, ND, director of Southbury Clinic for Traditional Medicines, Southbury, Connecticut.

tions called proton pump inhibitors (PPIs). These drugs, including *omeprazole* (Prilosec), lansoprazole (Prevacid) and *esomeprazole* (Nexium), offer short-term relief by reducing stomach acid, but they do not cure the underlying problem. Even worse, long-term use (more than a year) of PPIs increases risks for hip fracture (because of decreased mineral absorption)…and the bacterial intestinal infection *Clostridium difficile* (because stomach acid is needed to fight bacteria). For my patients, I use a different approach that focuses on improving digestion and healing the lining of the stomach and the esophagus. *My advice…*

If you suffer from heartburn and/or have an ulcer, avoid any foods that may irritate your condition, such as fried foods, citrus, tomato-based foods and spicy meals. Don't overeat. Large meals increase the demand for stomach acid. Chew thoroughly and eat nothing within two hours of going to bed. Avoid smoking and pain relievers, such as aspirin or ibuprofen (Advil), that can cause gastrointestinal irritation.

Herbal tea also can be surprisingly effective for heartburn and ulcers. Chamomile and licorice root are two herbs with a long medicinal history for treating the digestive tract lining.* Drink three cups of either tea daily, on an empty stomach. Use two teaspoons of dried plant or one teabag per eight ounces of water.

For heartburn (without ulcer), I suggest that you add stomach acid—which is necessary for good digestion—rather than reduce it with an acid blocker. At the end of your meal, sip on a four-ounce glass of water to which you have added one teaspoon of either apple cider vinegar or fresh lemon juice.

Caution: Do not drink vinegar or lemon water if you have an ulcer or gastritis (inflammation of the lining of the stomach). Discontinue this practice if it causes pain or worsens symptoms.

If you have an ulcer (with or without heartburn), I recommend adding other botanical medicines. The antiseptic herbs echinacea, cranesbill root and Oregon grape root (50 milligrams [mg] each) help reduce bacteria associated with ulcers. The herbs cabbage leaf, marshmallow root and slippery elm bark (200 mg each) help restore the gut's protective lining. Take these herbs three times daily on an empty stomach until the ulcer symptoms have eased, usually for two to eight weeks.

If you take a PPI but want to stop using it, gradually wean yourself off the drug while you add this protocol. Consult your doctor about your plan and schedule a follow-up visit in a month. You can review your condition and discuss what I hope will be good news about your progress.

*If you have high blood pressure, avoid licorice tea.

■ ■ ■ ■

Natural Ulcer Treatments

Andrew Rubman, ND, founder and director, Southbury Clinic for Traditional Medicines, Southbury, Connecticut. *www.naturopath.org*

Gastric ulcers are a perfect illustration of the way medical thinking can change dramatically over a relatively brief period of time. It wasn't long ago that most people—including doctors—believed stomach ulcers were the result of intemperate living, primarily caused by spicy foods and stress. Scientists then discovered that in many cases, the real culprit was *Helicobacter pylori* bacteria, so that became the new target of treatment. Then they learned that killing off H. pylori can increase risk of cancer, so now the latest thinking represents another shift—instead of aiming for eradication of H. pylori altogether, the goal is control of the bacteria so that it remains in a healthy balance. This, it's believed, can fortify the digestive system…and ultimately support optimal overall health.

What Causes Ulcers?

One important role of the linings of the stomach and intestine is to protect against stomach acid and bacteria, but when intestinal balance is disturbed—for example, when H. pylori bacteria run rampant and begin replicating uncontrollably—the digestive tract becomes irritated and inflamed (gastritis), a condition that over time weakens and damages the protective mucus coating. If a sore or erosion then develops in the lining of the stomach or duodenum (the first part of the small intestine), you have an ulcer. In addition to H. pylori, other possible causes of ulcers include a high intake of aspirin, ibuprofen or other NSAIDs (nonsteroidal anti-inflammatory drugs), alcohol use or smoking. Some people believe stress contributes to ulcers, but scientists continue to debate the issue.

Ancient Remedy for Ulcers

Dracaena, a treelike plant used in traditional Chinese medicine for stomach ailments, contains two compounds that slow the growth of Helicobacter pylori, the bacterium that causes most ulcers. More research is needed before Dracaena can be recommended for use in the US as a treatment for ulcers.

The Journal of Natural Products.

Whatever their cause, ulcers are painful and can disrupt your life. To prevent that from happening, treatment for serious ulcers generally consists of seven to 10 days of prescription proton pump inhibitors (PPIs) to suppress stomach acid and give the tissue a chance to heal, plus a longer course of antibiotics to suppress H. pylori bacteria. Taking PPIs for much longer than 10 days—a common mistake—can backfire and alter the natural acid-producing abilities of the stomach. As for antibiotics, bacteria are becoming increasingly resistant to these drugs, which makes it all the more important to identify other means of treatment.

Give Your Stomach a Rest

Andrew L. Rubman, ND, stresses that the single most important rule in treatment and recovery is to give your stomach and digestive tract a rest. Just as you need additional rest to recover from illness or injury, Dr. Rubman advises taking measures to allow your digestive system to heal. He says that natural care is also beneficial, even as an adjunct to the pharmaceutical drugs necessary to treat severe ulcers. Specific advice includes eating smaller meals, three or four times a day, consisting of light proteins with easier to digest fats, like boiled eggs and steamed chicken...fresh low-fiber vegetables and their juices...and soft rice. Chew food slowly and thoroughly...limit fluid with meals...don't eat within two hours of bedtime...don't smoke or take NSAIDs... and avoid stomach irritants such as heavy animal protein (including beef, lamb and others), fatty and fried foods, stimulating spices like black pepper, spicy dishes, refined sugars, colas, caffeine and alcohol.

In his practice, Dr. Rubman also prescribes some combination of the following to ulcer patients...

• **L-glutamine.** In a study at Beth Israel Deaconess Medical Center in Boston, mice that were infected with H. pylori and given supplemental L-glutamine experienced a significant improvement in gastric inflammation and early immune response, which helps to minimize further inflammation and damage. Dr. Rubman prescribes this simple amino acid to support mucosa and protect against gastric damage. Take it in the form of gelatin capsules, apart from meals in a little applesauce.

• **Botanical medicines.** To soothe the stomach and speed healing of delicate mucus membranes, Dr. Rubman prescribes Glyconda, a ready-made mixture of Turkey rhubarb root, cinnamon and goldenseal. Dr. Rubman tells his patients to dissolve 10 to 20 drops in two ounces of warm tea or water and drink before meals. Ask your doctor about the right dosing for you.

Preventive Strategies

Digestive enzymes can help you better absorb nutrients by working alongside the natural enzymes produced by your body to break down chemical bonds in foods. This process helps reestablish a more balanced environment in the gastrointestinal tract so your gastritis and the scar left by the ulcer will heal completely. Though it may seem counterintuitive to take additional

What Is Gastric Erosion?

Gastric erosions are small cracks in the gastric mucosa (stomach lining) that are most commonly caused by bacteria called Helicobacter pylori or by nonsteroidal anti-inflammatory medications (NSAIDs), such as *ibuprofen* (Advil, Motrin) and *naproxen* (Aleve)—even at normal doses—and may be associated with a gastric ulcer. Symptoms may include stomach pain or nausea, but the majority of patients have none. However, even if a patient does not have symptoms, gastric erosions may be detected when he/she undergoes an upper endoscopy (examination of the esophagus, stomach and part of the small intestine using a video camera on a flexible tube) for other conditions, such as esophageal reflux (backup of stomach contents). In rare cases, gastric erosion may have other causes, including inflammatory bowel disease and gastric cancer. Gastric erosions generally are harmless, unless they cause bleeding. Treatment usually includes a proton pump inhibitor (PPI), such as *esomeprazole* (Nexium) or *dexlansoprazole* (Kapidex), oral medications that reduce stomach acid and allow the stomach lining to heal.

David P. Jones, DO, chief of gastroenterology, Brooke Army Medical Center, San Antonio, Texas.

acids when your stomach lining is irritated, supplemental digestive enzymes properly prescribed can in fact be helpful to the digestive process for middle-aged and older individuals whose natural stomach acid levels are waning. Dr. Rubman often prescribes DuoZyme by Karuna (*www.karunahealth.com*) due to its combination of assorted enzymes. Take the dose prescribed by your doctor at the beginning of meals (check whether you should adjust for meal size and composition). Don't self-prescribe—taking the wrong amount can cause inappropriate acid release when the stomach is empty, of particular concern for those with a history of acute gastritis or ulcers.

• **Ulcers are dangerous.** Dr. Rubman emphasizes the importance of not undertaking treatment—natural or otherwise—on your own. It's far better and more effective, he says, to work with a physician who is expert in digestive issues and can help you learn to encourage your body's own natural healing processes to successfully cope with ulcers and other stomach and digestive challenges.

■ ■ ■ ■

20

Relief for Irritable Bowel Syndrome

Use Your Mind to Soothe Your Stomach

Mary-Joan Gerson, PhD, clinical professor of psychology at New York University, and *Charles D. Gerson, MD,* clinical professor of medicine at Mount Sinai School of Medicine, both in New York City. They are codirectors of the Mind-Body Digestive Center in New York City, which offers a comprehensive treatment program for digestive disorders.

When *tegaserod* (Zelnorm) was pulled from the market, it was bad news for many sufferers of irritable bowel syndrome (IBS). Tegaserod was the first—and only—drug approved by the FDA for IBS with constipation. A heightened risk for heart attack and stroke made tegaserod too risky for most sufferers to use.*

Fortunately, IBS sufferers can still help themselves and perhaps even eliminate the need for medication.

Here's how...

A Mind-Body Problem

IBS is one of the most common digestive problems—one of every five Americans

*Patients who meet strict FDA-approved criteria can now be considered for restricted access to tegaserod.

has it, according to the American Gastroenterological Association. The condition often forces sufferers to curtail their activities and become isolated because they cannot anticipate whether they will experience a bout of diarrhea or severe cramping.

No one knows exactly what causes IBS, but the interaction between the bowels and nervous system seems to be a key factor. The digestive system includes a rich supply of nerves that regulate secretions, muscle contractions and other physical processes. In people with IBS, this control system goes awry, causing diarrhea or constipation (usually one or the other predominates), bloating and cramps.

Our research has shown that a mind-body treatment program is significantly more successful than medical treatment alone.

Know Your Illness

The pattern of IBS differs widely from person to person. That's why it is important to observe what triggers your symptoms.

What to do...

• **Watch your diet.** Not all IBS sufferers are affected by the same foods. For example, high-fiber fruits and vegetables can cause intestinal distress for some people, but these foods may help other IBS sufferers control constipation.

● **Keep a journal.** Use a notebook to record when your symptoms flare up—and when they improve. At the same time, keep a record of triggers, such as diet and distressing events or emotions. Also, record how your symptoms affect you—do they limit your activities? What feelings do they arouse?

Personalized Stress Control

Stress and anxiety affect digestive function in perfectly healthy people—for example, it's common to experience "butterflies in the stomach" before a speech. IBS sufferers are especially sensitive to such triggers. Your journal will allow you to track stressful situations that precipitate digestive distress so that you can think of ways to lessen their impact.

Example: For many people, rushing to be on time triggers an episode of cramps or diarrhea. To avoid this, try time management strategies, such as waking up a half hour to one hour earlier, so you have more time in the morning.

Other approaches…

● **Tend to your personal relationships.** In our research, we have found that IBS patients with supportive families fare much better than patients whose family relationships are high in conflict. Try to identify areas of conflict in your intimate relationships and reduce the stress that can result. Be specific about the kinds of support you need from those who are close to you, such as help with dietary restrictions.

Helpful: Don't let concerns or disagreements fester. Talk out feelings about your illness and others' reactions to it.

● **Relax.** When anxiety and feelings of stress occur, it's crucial to practice a relaxation technique.

Helpful: Try meditation or yoga. Or distract yourself by listening to soothing music and/or reading.

● **Break the cycle.** Many people who track their experiences find that stress triggers the first stirrings of abdominal discomfort, which then leads to anxiety that worsens IBS symptoms. Practicing a relaxation technique at such times is useful.

Helpful: Try to recognize when symptoms start but don't escalate—you will increase your sense of mastery and control.

See a Professional

Tell your doctor if you suffer recurrent abdominal discomfort or a change in bowel habits. There is no specific diagnostic tool for IBS, but your doctor may perform various tests, such as stool tests and imaging tests, to rule out other causes, such as inflammatory bowel disease and cancer.

If you have IBS and need more than self-help, you should consider psychotherapy to explore how IBS symptoms affect your life. Cognitive behavioral therapy (CBT)—which helps IBS sufferers identify thought patterns that may worsen their symptoms—and psychodynamically oriented psychotherapy—which explores conflicts, particularly in relation to how past experiences influence present coping behavior—are both effective. In addition, hypnotherapy may help.

If You Need More Help

Medication also may be necessary to help control symptoms. The prescription drug *alosetron* (Lotronex) is available (with monitoring by your physician) if IBS causes severe diarrhea that has not responded to other treatments, such as antidiarrheal drugs. *Other options...*

• **Antidepressants,** such as *amitriptyline* (Elavil), taken in low doses can calm the nerves that control intestinal function and reduce diarrhea and pain.

• **Antispasmodic drugs,** such as *dicyclomine* (Bentyl), reduce intestinal contractions but often have limited effectiveness.

• **Diarrhea drugs,** such as *loperamide* (Imodium), are available over the counter (OTC).

• **Fiber supplements,** such as Metamucil or Citrucel, help fight constipation.

• **Probiotics containing healthful bacteria,** such as acidophilus, may help ease gas and bloating. Probiotics are available at health-food stores and most drugstores.

■ ■ ■ ■

IBS Breakthroughs

Brian E. Lacy, MD, PhD, associate professor of medicine at Dartmouth Medical School and director of the gastrointestinal motility laboratory at Dartmouth–Hitchcock Medical Center in Lebanon, New Hampshire. He is author of *Making Sense of IBS* (Johns Hopkins).

If you're among the estimated one in six American adults who suffers from chronic abdominal pain or discomfort due to irritable bowel syndrome (IBS), you know that effective, long-lasting treatment remains elusive.

Good news: The American College of Gastroenterology recently published a review of the most effective treatments, including dietary approaches, nondrug therapies and medications, that should finally give relief to people with IBS.

What Is IBS?

Irritable bowel syndrome (IBS) is a gastrointestinal disorder that causes diarrhea and/or constipation, bloating and abdominal cramps. IBS, also known as spastic colon or a nervous stomach, occurs when muscle contractions that move food through the intestine are too fast, too slow or erratic. Psychological distress is believed to worsen IBS symptoms.

Mary-Joan Gerson, PhD, clinical professor of psychology at New York University, and *Charles D. Gerson, MD,* clinical professor of medicine at Mount Sinai School of Medicine, both in New York City. They are co-directors of the Mind-Body Digestive Center in New York City, which offers a comprehensive treatment program for digestive disorders.

Do You Have IBS?

With IBS, the nerves that control the gastrointestinal tract are hypersensitive—that is, sensations that other people wouldn't notice, including those produced by the ordinary process of digestion, are amplified and often painful.

Research has shown that many times IBS begins after a severe bout of digestive upset caused by a bacterial or viral infection, such as "stomach flu" or "traveler's diarrhea"—perhaps because such infections temporarily or permanently affect nerves in the gastrointestinal tract.

What most people don't know: Researchers have found that people with a history of abuse (physical, emotional or sexual) are at heightened risk for IBS—probably due to stress on the intestinal nervous system.

Diagnosis of IBS can be tricky because symptoms, including abdominal pain, bloating and troublesome bowel patterns (frequent or persistent bouts of diarrhea, constipation or both, generally occurring at least three days a month), often wax and wane in severity. So-called "flares" (episodes of severe symptoms) may occur weeks, months—or even years—apart.

IBS symptoms that may be missed: Mucus in the stool or straining during, or a feeling of incomplete evacuation after, a bowel movement.

If you think you may have IBS: See your primary care doctor. IBS almost always can be identified with a standard history and physical exam.

When Food Is the Trigger

Lactose intolerance (the inability to digest dairy sugar) can lead to misdiagnosis because its classic symptoms—bloating and diarrhea—mimic those caused by IBS.

My advice: If your digestive problems seem to worsen when you consume dairy products, follow an elimination diet.

What to do: Go without all dairy products for seven to 10 days—and slowly reintroduce each type of dairy product, such as yogurt or cheese, to see how much you can tolerate before symptoms return.

IBS food triggers that often are overlooked—try the elimination diet (as described above) with each…

• **Soft drinks and other high-fructose drinks and foods.** Fructose—a sugar commonly added to carbonated soft drinks and sports drinks and naturally occurring in fruit juices and high-sugar fruits (such as dried fruits)—can cause bloating, gas and diarrhea in people with IBS.

• **Caffeine.** It stimulates the digestive tract and may cause cramps and more frequent bowel movements in people with IBS.

The Fiber Factor

For many people with IBS—especially those with recurrent constipation—adequate fiber intake (25 milligrams [mg] to 30 mg per day) helps relieve symptoms. If you are not consuming this much fiber, increase your intake of fruits and whole grains or take a fiber supplement containing psyllium (such as Metamucil or Konsyl).

Fiber-rich foods I recommend most often: Raspberries, artichokes, green peas, almonds, oatmeal, oat bran and whole-grain bread.

Important: IBS patients who have recurrent diarrhea should limit fiber intake to about 10 grams daily and avoid leafy greens and cruciferous vegetables (such as cauliflower) because high-fiber foods can worsen symptoms in these patients.

Best Alternative Approaches

If dietary changes (described above) do not relieve IBS symptoms, there is credible scientific evidence to support the use of two natural remedies for IBS…

• **Peppermint oil.** In enteric-coated capsule form, peppermint oil appears to relax smooth muscle in the gastrointestinal tract and therefore reduce IBS abdominal pain caused by muscle spasms. For dosage, follow label instructions.

• **Probiotics.** Probiotics augment the "friendly" bacteria in the large intestine. Probiotic dietary supplements containing the *Bifidobacterium* species are worth trying when bloating and diarrhea are prominent. Look for probiotic supplements providing at least 100 million colony-forming units per dose. Be patient—it may take up to three months to produce substantial benefits.

Best IBS Medications

If your IBS persists, there are medication options for…

• **Diarrhea.** Try an antidiarrheal medication, such as the over-the-counter (OTC) product loperamide (Imodium) or the prescription drug diphenoxylate and atropine

Better IBS Remedy

In a 12-week study, 275 men and women with irritable bowel syndrome (chronic abdominal pain with diarrhea and/or constipation) took 10 grams (g) daily of psyllium (a vegetable fiber), bran or a placebo. Using a standard scale, the severity of symptoms dropped by 90 points, on average, in the psyllium group, compared with 58 points, on average, for the bran and placebo groups.

Theory: Psyllium is a soluble fiber, which slows the rate at which the stomach empties—an effect that reduces IBS symptoms.

If you have IBS: Ask your doctor about taking 10 g (about two tablespoons) daily of psyllium, which can be mixed with water, taken in capsule form or added to foods, such as yogurt.

C.J. Bijkerk, MD, PhD, researcher, University Medical Center, Utrecht, the Netherlands.

(Lomotil). For diarrhea and abdominal pain, consider adding a low dose of a tricyclic antidepressant, such as *imipramine* (Tofranil) or *amitriptyline* (Elavil). These antidepressants may affect how the brain interprets pain.

• **Pain and bloating.** A tricyclic antidepressant often reduces discomfort and other symptoms, including diarrhea, pain and bloating, to a tolerable level. If the drug causes side effects, such as dry mouth or dizziness, a selective *serotonin reuptake inhibitor* (SSRI), such as *citalopram* (Celexa) or *fluoxetine* (Prozac), can be used, but there is less proof that SSRIs are effective for IBS symptoms.

• **Constipation.** If you're consuming adequate levels of fiber (described earlier) but still have constipation, you may want to try an OTC laxative, such as *polyethylene glycol* (Miralax) or Milk of Magnesia for seven to 14 days. (See your doctor if symptoms persist after that trial period.) For more extended use, the prescription medication *lubiprostone* (Amitiza) has been shown to be effective for IBS with constipation.

■ ■ ■ ■

Relief from IBS Naturally

Alexander C. Ford, MD, gastroenterology division, Hamilton Health Sciences Centre, McMaster University, Hamilton, Ontario, Canada.

Andrew L. Rubman, ND, medical director, Southbury Clinic for Traditional Medicines, Southbury, Connecticut. www.southburyclinic.com.

Sometimes old-fashioned remedies work best, and for the millions of people with one very hard-to-treat condition—irritable bowel syndrome (IBS)—an old remedy beats everything modern science has dreamed up. If you or someone you know has IBS, please read on.

As many as one in five Americans suffer from IBS, a miserable disorder that can bring an endless progression of constipation, diarrhea, gas, bloating and stomach cramps. Where expensive new IBS drugs have been disappointing, it turns out that a classic stomachache remedy, peppermint oil, can often get the job done more effectively.

In With the Old, Out With the New

At McMaster University in Ontario, Alexander C. Ford, MD, and his colleagues analyzed the results of many previously published studies on adults with IBS, including 12 comparing fiber with placebo, 22 comparing antispasmodics with placebo, and four comparing peppermint oil with placebo. Peppermint oil was surprisingly

New Treatment for Irritable Bowel Syndrome (IBS)

Lubiprostone (Amitiza) is the only FDA-approved prescription drug therapy for constipation-predominant IBS (which also can cause cramping, abdominal pain, bloating and diarrhea). Lubiprostone increases secretions of intestinal fluid, which increases intestinal motility and reduces symptoms of chronic constipation.

Julie Beitz, MD, director, Office of Drug Evaluation III, FDA Center for Drug Evaluation and Research, Silver Spring, Maryland.

effective, bringing relief to 74% of patients. This compares very favorably with antispasmodics, which helped only 61%, and fiber, which was beneficial to just 48%.

Peppermint oil may be most helpful in soothing the abdominal pain and cramping that are common IBS symptoms and, over time, it may also help ease diarrhea or constipation. Scientists believe it works by blocking the movement of calcium into muscle cells in the gastrointestinal tract, thereby reducing muscle contractions, discomfort and bloating.

How to Make Your IBS Better

Look for "enteric-coated" peppermint oil capsules at your health-food store, since taking peppermint oil straight can produce reflux symptoms, suggests *Daily Health News* contributing medical editor Andrew L. Rubman, ND. Dr. Rubman often prescribes doses of 200 milligrams (mg) to 300 mg to be taken once, twice or three times daily—but not more often, as larger doses can be toxic. He says most patients find it helpful to take a dose just before eating a meal.

Several factors should be considered when identifying the right treatment for an IBS patient, including whether symptoms are dominated by diarrhea or constipation or whether both occur about equally. If your doctor seems quick to recommend newer pharmaceuticals, consider seeing a specialist in natural medicine to discuss the older remedies and over-the-counter medicines.

As Dr. Ford points out, even though peppermint oil helped the most people in his analysis, the other two treatments—fiber and antispasmodics (which lessen spasms in the gastrointestinal tract)—were effective for many, and they are safe, inexpensive and readily available over the counter at most pharmacies. Also, Dr. Rubman says that there are many other useful botanical extracts that are antispasmodic as well, including valerian, skullcap, viburnum, juniper berry, hyoscamus niger, gentian and gelsemium. "Their effects may vary from minor to profound, so it's best to use these only under physician care," he adds.

■ ■ ■ ■

Foods That Explode in Your Bowel

Elizabeth Lipski, PhD, CCN, has been working in the field of holistic and complementary medicine for more than 25 years. She is author of *Digestive Wellness* (McGraw-Hill)...*Digestive Wellness for Children* (Basic Health) and *Leaky Gut Syndrome* (McGraw-Hill). *www.lizlipski.com.*

Your abdomen bloats and cramps. You pass so much gas that you think you might be contributing to global warming. You have diarrhea or constipation or an alternating assault of both.

Your problem: Irritable bowel syndrome (IBS), the most common gastrointestinal complaint, accounting for 10% of doctor's visits and about 50% of referrals to gastroenterologists. But the fact that doctors see a lot of IBS doesn't mean that they understand the condition or treat it effectively.

IBS is a well-recognized but unexplained set of symptoms—medical science knows what is happening but not exactly why. A diagnosis isn't made by detecting telltale biochemical or structural changes unique to IBS—it's made after other digestive disorders, such as colorectal cancer and inflammatory bowel disease, have been ruled out.

At that point, the typical doctor offers a predictable prescription—eat more fiber, drink more water, get more exercise, reduce stress.

While that regimen may work for some, it fails many because it overlooks a common but often ignored trigger of IBS—food hypersensitivity.

Trigger Foods

To understand food hypersensitivity, you first need to understand what it is not—a food allergy. Food allergies are relatively rare, affecting 1% to 2% of the adult population. The ingested food attracts the immune system's immunoglobulin E (IgE) antibodies, which identify the food as "foreign" and attack it, sparking the release of histamine and cytokines, inflammatory chemicals that cause tissue to swell, eyes to tear, skin to itch and other allergic symptoms. Eggs, milk, nuts, shellfish, soy and wheat are common allergy-causing foods.

Food hypersensitivity involves other antibodies, such as IgA, IgG and IgM. Their attack isn't immediate—it can occur hours or days after eating an offending food and cause bloating, cramping, constipation and/or diarrhea.

What to do: For one week, eat an "elimination diet" consisting solely of foods that almost never cause hypersensitivity—fruits (except citrus), vegetables (except tomatoes, eggplant, white potatoes and peppers), white rice, fish and chicken. You can use olive and safflower oils. If after seven days you are symptom-free, food hypersensitivity is triggering your IBS. *Follow these steps...*

Step 1: Reintroduce one category of food every two to three days. Start with one of the foods that together account for 80% of food hypersensitivity—beef, citrus, dairy products, eggs, pork and wheat. For two days, stay on the elimination diet and eat as much of the reintroduced food as you like.

If IBS symptoms return, you have detected a hypersensitivity. Stop eating the offending food, and wait until symptoms disappear to reintroduce another food.

If you don't get symptoms, try the next food after the two days of eating the previous one. Repeat this process, reintroducing foods one by one.

Step 2: For the next six months, avoid all foods that caused IBS during the elimination testing. This will help your bowel heal.

Acupuncture for IBS

People who received six acupuncture treatments over a three-week period experienced less abdominal pain, bloating, diarrhea, constipation and other IBS symptoms than those who received no treatment. Needles were inserted at various points, including near the stomach, liver, spleen and large intestine. Researchers believe acupuncture may help by balancing hormones and triggering a relaxation response. To find a board-certified acupuncturist, go to *www.nccaom.org*—the Web site for the National Certification Commission for Acupuncture and Oriental Medicine.

Anthony Lembo, MD, associate professor of medicine, Harvard Medical School, Boston, and leader of a study of 230 adult IBS patients, published in *The American Journal of Gastroenterology.*

Step 3: After the six months, you can try a "rotation diet"—reintroduce the offending foods (as long as they don't cause symptoms), but eat any offending food no more than once every four days. Now that your digestive tract is healed, you may be able to handle small amounts of the offending foods.

Also helpful: Digestive enzyme supplements can help reduce gas and bloating. Effective products include Tyler Enterogenics…Transformation Enzymes DigestZyme and TPP Digest…Enzymedica Digest and Digest Gold…and Enzymatic Therapy Mega-Zyme. These products are available at most health-food stores and many drugstores.

Infections

Food hypersensitivity triggers 50% to 75% of all cases of IBS. Another 25% or so is caused by infections.

Research: Israeli doctors studied 564 travelers. While traveling, people are more likely to be exposed to new microbes that can cause diarrhea. Those who developed traveler's diarrhea were five times more likely to later develop IBS. In reviewing eight studies, American scientists found a seven times higher risk of IBS among those who had infections in the gastrointestinal tract.

What to do: See your doctor—he/she can perform tests to detect abnormal bacteria, fungi and parasites, and prescribe the appropriate treatment.

Natural Remedies

Supplements to help relieve IBS symptoms…

• **For diarrhea.** Probiotic supplements provide friendly intestinal bacteria that can help restore normal bowel function. Saccharomyces boulardii is an unusual probiotic—it's yeast, not bacteria—but doctors have used it for decades to control diarrhea effectively.

Look for a product called Florastor or other probiotic brands containing the yeast. Take 250 milligrams (mg), three times a day. If that works, try twice a day and then once a day, finding the lowest dosage that works for you.

• **For constipation.** You've probably tried fiber supplements—and found that they didn't work. Instead, take a magnesium supplement, which naturally loosens bowels.

Use magnesium glycinate, starting with 300 mg a day. If that dosage doesn't work, increase the dose by 100 mg per day, until you develop diarrhea. Then cut back by 100 mg—to produce regular bowel movements.

Probiotic supplements can help as well (see above).

The Problem With Medications

Doctors have tried a range of drugs for IBS—bulking agents for constipation, antidepressants to affect brain chemicals that play a role in digestion, spasmolytics to decrease cramping. A review by Dutch doctors of 40 studies on medications for IBS concluded, "The evidence of efficacy of drug therapies for IBS is weak."

The drugs also can be dangerous. In March 2007, the FDA pulled the IBS drug Zelnorm (*tegaserod maleate*) from the market when studies showed that it increased the risk for heart attack and stroke 10-fold.

21

Treating Colitis and Crohn's Disease

The Common Fat That Triggers Ulcerative Colitis

Floyd Chilton, PhD, professor, physiology and pharmacology, Wake Forest University, Winston-Salem, North Carolina, and author of *Inflammation Nation* (Fireside).

Jennifer Adler, CN, nutritionist, natural foods chef and adjunct faculty member at Bastyr University in Seattle, Washington.

You definitely don't want ulcerative colitis—an inflammatory bowel disease (IBD) that strikes the lining of the colon and rectum. (Crohn's, another IBD, can inflame any part of the intestinal lining.)

You don't want diarrhea that forces you to urgently seek out a bathroom… bloody stools…abdominal pain and cramping…and an increased risk of bowel cancer.

But for reasons scientists haven't figured out, more and more people are joining the estimated 500,000 Americans with the disease—a recent study shows a 49% jump in new cases over the past decade.

Fortunately, another new study shows that changing your dietary mixture of fatty acids—the building blocks of fat—might keep ulcerative colitis out of your life.

Linoleic Aid Burns the Gut

Researchers in the UK analyzed four years of health data from more than 200,000 Europeans, aged 30 to 74. They found that those with the highest intake of linoleic acid were 2.6 times more likely to develop ulcerative colitis, compared with those with the lowest intake. Linoleic acid is a polyunsaturated omega-6 fatty acid found in beef and pork, in vegetable oils such as corn and safflower and in many margarines.

Red flag: Many fried foods served in restaurants are cooked in oils loaded with linoleic acid.

The researchers also found that those with the highest intake of *docosahexaenoic acid* (DHA) were 77% less likely to develop the disease. DHA is an omega-3 polyunsaturated fatty acid found in fatty fish that live in cold water, such as salmon, mackerel and sardines.

The average age of those in the study diagnosed with ulcerative colitis was 60—and the researchers estimate that 30% of those and other new cases of ulcerative colitis might be caused by high dietary intakes of linoleic acid.

Why is linoleic acid a risk factor for ulcerative colitis?

Theory: In the body, linoleic acid turns into *arachidonic acid*…which is incorporated into the lining of bowel cells…where it breaks down into three inflammatory compounds…all of which are found in high levels in people with ulcerative colitis.

DHA, on the other hand, helps produce compounds that calm inflammation.

Bottom line: A diet lower in linoleic acid might not only help prevent the disease—it might help control the disease in people who already have it, say the researchers.

Protect Against Inflammation

"The omega-6 to omega-3 ratio of the typical diet is about 15-to-1," says Floyd Chilton, PhD, a professor at Wake Forest University in Winston-Salem, North Carolina, and author of *Inflammation Nation* (Fireside). "If we change that ratio to be closer to 5-to-1—and, ideally, to 2-to-1—we can make changes that are very protective against inflammation."

"There are many ways you can increase your intake of omega-3 fatty acids and decrease your intake of omega-6s," says Jennifer Adler, CN, nutritionist, natural foods chef, and adjunct faculty member at Bastyr University in Seattle, Washington.

Their recommendations…

● **Limit vegetable oils.** Cut back on vegetable oils and margarine, says Dr. Chilton.

Smart idea: If a recipe calls for vegetable oil, use olive oil instead. Use "light" or 100% pure olive oil for high-heat cooking.

● **Eat fish with over 500 mg of omega-3 per serving.** These include mackerel, canned albacore tuna, canned sardines, canned wild Alaskan salmon and canned skinless pink salmon.

● **Eat grass-fed beef.** In our modern society, cows are typically fed on a diet of corn and soy, which increases the meat's content of linoleic acid.

Better: Purchase grass-fed beef, which is low in linoleic acid and high in omega-3s. "One study put the omega-6 to omega-3 ratio in conventional beef at 4-to-1, compared with 2-to-1 in grass-fed beef," says Dr. Chilton.

"Look for a label that says, '100% Grass-Fed,' which means the animal has been fed on grass their entire life," says Adler. "Otherwise, the animal may have been fed on corn for the last 90 days of its life—increasing linoleic acid and decreasing omega-3s."

● **Take cod liver oil.** "I frequently recommend that a client take a cod liver oil supplement to increase the intake of omega-3s," she says. "One reason I like cod liver oil more than omega-3 fish oil supplements is that it is also loaded with vitamins A and D."

Product: Carlson's (*www.carlsonlabs.com*, 888-234-5656) or Nordic Naturals (*www.nordicnaturals.com*, 800-662-2544). "These brands have third-party testing to guarantee that they are free of contaminants," says Adler. "And they both have a range of flavored products, so the cod liver oil doesn't have an objectionable taste."

Recommended amount: Two tablespoons a day.

● **Make bone broth.** "Simmering bones for 12 hours produces a broth that is rich in collagen, elastin and gelatin, protein compounds that help heal a damaged intestinal tract," says Adler. "For someone with ulcerative colitis, I recommend one to three cups of the broth a day."

Use bone broth instead of water in soup, or in making rice and other grains, says Adler. Or you can drink it like a tea, salting to taste.

To make the broth: Fill a large soup pot with water, leftover bones from a roasted or baked chicken, four carrots, ½ bunch of celery and one or two whole onions. Bring to a gentle boil, then lower heat. Simmer slowly for 12 hours. Strain and refrigerate or freeze for future use.

■ ■ ■ ■

The Amazing Healing Power of Probiotics

Tracy Olgeaty Gensler, RD, dietitian in Chevy Chase, Maryland, and author of *Probiotic and Prebiotic Recipes for Health* (Fair Winds).

Elizabeth Lipski, PhD, CNN, clinical nutritionist in Ashville, North Carolina, and author of *Digestive Wellness* (McGraw-Hill). *www.lizlipski.com*

The cells in your body are outnumbered—by the bacteria in your intestines! "A total of one hundred trillion bacteria live in our digestive system—10 times more than the number of cells in our body," says Elizabeth Lipski, PhD, CNN, a clinical nutritionist in Ashville, North Carolina, and author of *Digestive Wellness* (McGraw-Hill).

Some of these bacteria can produce harmful toxins and carcinogens. But many of them are helpful—the so-called probiotics. And they're helpful in lots of different ways, says Dr. Lipski. *They…*

- **Protect the intestinal lining,** preventing colonization by bad bacteria and yeast;
- **Stop the growth of bacteria that produce nitrates,** a cause of cancer;
- **Decrease the side effects of antibiotics,** such as diarrhea;
- **Stop the absorption of toxins from the gut;**
- **Manufacture B-complex vitamins;**
- **Help regulate peristalsis,** the contraction of the intestinal walls that pushes waste matter through the digestive tract;
- **Strengthen immunity;**
- **Help normalize cholesterol and triglycerides,** blood fats that can cause heart disease;
- **Break down and rebuild hormones.**

"The overall composition of these helpful and harmful bacteria—our intestinal flora—usually remains fairly constant in healthy people," says Dr. Lipski. "However, the intestinal flora can become unbalanced—with the harmful bacteria no longer held in check—by aging, poor diet, disease, medications such as antibiotics or stress." In fact, she says, "digestive problems due to imbalanced flora have become widespread."

But, she adds, taking a probiotic supplement or eating foods rich in probiotics can help restore your helpful bacteria and counter those health problems.

Latest Research

- **Improving digestive well-being.** Researchers in France studied 197 women with "minor digestive symptoms," dividing them into two groups. One group ate yogurt rich in the probiotic bifidobacteria; the other didn't.

After four weeks, 69% more women in the probiotic group reported an improvement in "GI well-being" and had fewer digestive symptoms.

Products: Yogurts and other food products rich in *bifidobacteria* include General Mills YoPlus yogurt, TCBY frozen yogurt and Attune Wellness bars, says Tracy Olgeaty Gensler, RD, a dietitian in Chevy Chase, Maryland, and author of *Probiotic and Prebiotic Recipes for Health* (Fair Winds).

- **Relieving irritable bowel syndrome.** Researchers in the US studied 44 people with irritable bowel syndrome—a constellation of digestive symptoms such as abdominal pain, cramping, bloating and diarrhea and/or constipation that affects 10% to 20% of Americans. Half received a daily probiotic supplement of bacillus coagulans and half didn't. After two months, those taking the supplement had much less abdominal pain and bloating.

Supplement: Sustenex, with Ganeden-BC, which is widely available. The dosage used in the study was one capsule a day.

You can find out more about the product at *www.sustenex.com*.

● **Easing ulcerative colitis.** This digestive disease—a severe inflammation of the lining of the colon and rectum—afflicts 500,000 Americans with symptoms such as diarrhea, bloody stools, abdominal pain and cramping, which come and go in flare-ups.

Researchers in India studied 77 people with "mild to moderate" ulcerative colitis, dividing them into two groups. One received a probiotic supplement twice daily for 12 weeks; one didn't.

After three months, 43% of the patients taking the probiotic were in remission. Only 11% of those taking the placebo saw improvement.

Supplement: VSL#3, a supplement with eight different strains of friendly bacteria. It is available at *www.vsl3.com*, or by calling 866-438-8753. Use it with your doctor's approval and supervision.

● **Better health after gastric bypass.** Researchers at Stanford University in California studied 44 patients who had gastric bypass weight-loss surgery. After the surgery, half the patients took a daily supplement of the probiotic lactobacillus, and half didn't.

After six months, the probiotic group had lost more weight, had less "bacterial overgrowth" in the stomach (a possible side effect of the surgery), and had higher vitamin B-12 levels (B-12 deficiency is another possible side effect).

Dosage: Lactobacillus supplements are widely available. In this study, the dosage was 2.4 billion organisms daily. (Supplement manufacturers use a number of different ways to indicate the number of bacteria in a probiotic, such as 600 million organisms or 1 billion microbes, or simply a number after the name of the bacteria.)

● **Controlling gum disease.** Researchers in Japan studied 66 people, giving half of them a daily supplement of lactobacillus salivarius, a probiotic found in the mouth.

After two months, those taking the supplement had much lower levels of five types of oral bacteria that cause gum disease.

Probiotic supplements could beneficially affect gum disease, say the researchers, in the *Journal of Clinical Periodontology*.

Dosage: Supplements of lactobacillus salivarius are widely available. In this study, the daily dosage was 2 billion organisms.

● **Boosting immunity after a flu shot.** Researchers in France studied more than 300 people over 70 years of age. For four weeks before receiving a flu (influenza) shot, they drank either a dairy drink rich in the probiotic lactobacillus casei or a nonprobiotic dairy drink.

In the five months after receiving the shot, those using the probiotic drink manufactured many more "influenza-specific antibodies"—the drink had powered up the immune system's ability to respond to the vaccine.

Product: DanActive yogurt, from Dannon.

● **Lowering cholesterol.** Researchers in Iran studied 14 people with high cholesterol, asking them to eat 10 ounces a day of either "ordinary" yogurt or probiotic yogurt with lactobacillus acidophilus and bifidobacteria.

After six weeks, those eating the probiotic yogurt had a "significant decrease" in total cholesterol, compared with those eating the ordinary yogurt.

Product: Yogurts containing these two bacteria include Stonyfield Farm low-fat and nonfat frozen yogurts, and TCBY frozen yogurt, says Gensler.

■ ■ ■ ■

Is There a Place for Medical Nicotine?

Luis Ulloa, PhD, The Feinstein Institute for Medical Research, North Shore Long Island Jewish Health System, Manhasset, New York.

According to researcher Luis Ulloa, PhD, of The Feinstein Institute for Medical Research in Manhasset, New York, nicotine has a long and rich healing history. Nicotine? That devil of a drug that addicts smokers to deadly cigarettes? In 1560, Jean Nicot, after whom the present name of the tobacco plant *Nicotiana tabacum* was named, introduced tobacco to the queen of France for her migraines. Nicot promoted tobacco's therapeutic properties for various other ailments as well.

Now modern researchers, including Dr. Ulloa, have some evidence that supports some of the theories dating back to the 1500s. They have discovered that nicotine possesses anti-inflammatory properties that ease the symptoms of conditions involving inflammation, such as Alzheimer's disease and ulcerative colitis. It is possible that one day you may see medicinal compounds derived from nicotine beyond its current prescriptive use for tobacco addiction.

Nicotine and Inflammation

Until recently, no one understood how nicotine affected inflammation in the body. The problem with nicotine was that we didn't know its mechanism of action, and it cannot be used extensively in humans due to the risk of secondary effects, explains Dr.

Ulloa. Nicotine is known to be an addictive chemical in tobacco, and tobacco products contribute to cardiovascular disease and cancer risk.

To unravel the mystery of nicotine's anti-inflammatory benefits and risky side effects, Dr. Ulloa and his colleagues studied its impact on mice infected with severe sepsis. This dangerous inflammatory condition occurs as a complication (secondary infection) after an underlying illness has progressed.

While the initial problem in sepsis is infection, this is dwarfed by the extremely aggressive inflammatory response that follows. To defend itself, the body mobilizes infection-fighting white blood cells known as macrophages, which respond by furiously pumping out pro-inflammatory immune system proteins called *cytokines*. Instead of protecting the body, however, this backfires in lethal fashion, resulting in life-threatening tissue damage, organ failure and cardiovascular complications.

This is where nicotine comes in. The working hypothesis is that nicotine blocks a pathway involved in inflammation and the production of cytokines by macrophages. In his research, Dr. Ulloa found that the effect of nicotine appears to be mediated by a specific nicotinic receptor. He points out that this is a major breakthrough because researchers can now design specific agonists for that receptor in order to overcome the clinical limitations of nicotine by hopefully minimizing risky side effects, such as toxicity, cardiovascular and tumor-causing risk and addiction.

Looking Toward the Future

In the future, researchers hope to develop healing compounds that harness nicotine's healing qualities while limiting its toxicity. While this study focused on sepsis, some physicians suggest that it may be possible to use nicotine patches for inflammatory disorders such as ulcerative colitis. Stay tuned...but don't start smoking.

■ ■ ■ ■

7 Steps to Controlling Crohn's Disease

Andrew L. Rubman, ND, director, Southbury Clinic for Traditional Medicines, Southbury, Connecticut.
American Society for Microbiology, *www.asm.org/.*

For people with digestive issues, life tends to revolve around what you can and can't eat and how far away from the nearest bathroom you dare to venture. That's certainly the case with Crohn's disease, which along with ulcerative colitis is one of the two most common forms of inflammatory bowel disease. Symptoms include wrenching stomach pain soon after eating (typically in the lower right side) and relentless diarrhea. It's relatively rare, but a new research finding suggests that people with Crohn's are seven times more apt to carry bacteria that cause a related gastrointestinal disease in cattle. The bacteria —*Mycobacterium avium* subspecies paratuberculosis or MAP—has been found in milk in American supermarkets, and some studies have found it in meat and cheese, raising the possibility that it may be passed up the food chain to people.

It's Gut Wrenching

Whether or not bacteria such as MAP cause disease in the intestinal tract is largely a matter of threshold, explains Andrew L. Rubman, ND. A person with a healthy, intact digestive tract will likely be able to resist infectious bacteria. But the large intestine is the body's center of immunity, and when the digestive tissue becomes damaged and

Better Crohn's Disease Therapy

In a two-year study of 129 patients with Crohn's disease (chronic inflammation of the digestive tract), half the patients received conventional treatment—including steroid drugs to reduce inflammation followed by the immune-suppressing drugs *azathioprine* (Imuran) and, if needed, *infliximab* (Remicade), given via infusion. The others received the same regimen without steroids. After 26 weeks, 60% of the steroid-free group was symptom-free versus 36% of the conventional therapy group.

Geert D'Haens, MD, PhD, director, Imelda Gastrointestinal Clinical Research Center, Imelda General Hospital, Bonheiden, Belgium.

inflamed, it becomes more susceptible to invasive microorganisms, be it MAP or the increasingly infectious species of E. coli, *Salmonella*, and other causes of food poisoning. If the balance of healthy versus harmful bacteria is disrupted and/or tissue is damaged, people become less able to resist disease and it becomes more difficult to treat.

Little is known about the causes of Crohn's disease, although family history, an overactive immune system and inflammation response, and environmental triggers are all believed to play a role. It differs from ulcerative colitis (which causes similar symptoms) because inflammation is deeper in the intestinal wall and also potentially affects the entire gastrointestinal tract from mouth to anus. Ulcerative colitis primarily affects the colon. There's no known cure for Crohn's and remedies offered by conventional medicine are riddled with problems. In September 2008, the FDA ordered stronger warnings for common Crohn's drugs— *infliximab* (Remicade), *adalimumab* (Humira) and *certolizumab pegol* (Cimzia)—after an

Breakthrough Crohn's Disease Treatment

The medication *Certolizumab pegol* may be especially useful for patients who have stopped responding to *infliximab* or *adalimumab*, standard treatments for this incurable disease. Crohn's, an inflammatory disease of the digestive tract, affects an estimated 500,000 people in the US. Symptoms include abdominal pain, fever, nausea, vomiting, weight loss and diarrhea. Certolizumab pegol works by blocking tumor necrosis factor, which is a main cause of inflammation in Crohn's patients. The drug is administered through subcutaneous (under the skin) injections that patients can administer themselves. Ask your doctor for details.

William Sandborn, MD, gastroenterologist, Mayo Clinic, Rochester, Minnesota, and leader of a study of 662 adults with Crohn's disease, published in *The New England Journal of Medicine.*

association with the risk of developing fungal and yeast infections such as Candidiasis was found. Because conventional treatments have significant side effects—even when they work, and they don't always—more than half of people with Crohn's disease turn to natural therapies.

Natural Solutions

Since Crohn's disease affects different people in different ways, Dr. Rubman individualizes treatment for each patient, working in collaboration with his/her gastroenterologist—a strategy he suggests for all Crohn's patients since a combination of natural and mainstream treatments seems to be most effective.

Dr. Rubman's natural solutions include....

- **Probiotics.** Health requires maintaining a balance between good and bad bacteria in the digestive tract. Poor diet, stress or a digestive disorder such as Crohn's can result in a takeover of the system by "bad" bacteria, resulting in symptoms such as diarrhea and gas. To restore a proper floral balance, Dr. Rubman frequently prescribes a seven- to 10-day course of a probiotic supplement composed of *Lactobacillus acidophilus* and *Bifidobacterium bifidus*. However, he notes that it is important to have a stool test before treatment, in order to ensure the proper probiotic formula is administered.

- **Fish oil.** A small British study found that fish oil taken with antioxidants may help reduce the inflammation associated with Crohn's disease. Eat fatty fish such as salmon, mackerel or sardines two or three times a week. In addition, Dr. Rubman often prescribes one or more grams of an EPA-DHA fish oil capsule or liquid daily.

- **Vitamin B-12.** When the bowel has been damaged by Crohn's disease, it may no longer effectively absorb B-12. If you are tired and rundown, ask your doctor to test you. Dr. Rubman prefers to prescribe sublingual B-12 rather than B-12 shots. "It's as effective, less expensive and certainly more comfortable," he notes.

- **Acupuncture.** Acupuncture has traditionally been used to treat inflammatory bowel disease in China and is meeting with increasing mainstream acceptance in the US. A small German study suggests that acupuncture may help improve quality of life and general well-being in people with Crohn's disease by modulating symptoms and may even result in a small decrease in inflammatory markers in the blood. Find an acupuncturist in your area at the Web site of the American Association of Acupuncture & Oriental Medicine at *www.aaaomonline.org.*

Crohn's Disease Relief

In a 12-week study, 17 people with Crohn's disease (a chronic disorder of the digestive tract) took 4.5 milligrams daily of *naltrexone* (ReVia), a drug normally used to treat alcohol and drug addiction.

Result: Crohn's symptoms improved in 89% of the patients studied. Researchers don't yet know how the drug alleviates Crohn's disease symptoms, but say it is a safe alternative to current standard therapy, including steroid drugs, which can suppress the immune system.

Jill P. Smith, MD, professor of medicine, Pennsylvania State University College of Medicine, Hershey, Pennsylvania.

● **Focus on whole foods, fresh fruits and vegetables.** A diet that contains lots of processed and fast foods—like white bread, sugary desserts, etc.—stresses the bowel and may trigger inflammation and worsen symptoms of Crohn's disease. Disease-causing microorganisms thrive on foods like these. Many people with Crohn's report that they feel better when they eliminate or significantly cut back on processed foods and place a greater emphasis on whole foods, fresh fruits and vegetables and moderate amounts of protein. Avoid milk and dairy products as well as trans fats, as they can also irritate the intestinal track.

● **Decompress.** Many people with Crohn's find that their symptoms worsen during stressful periods. If you find this to be the case, take steps to effectively manage stress. Do whatever works best for you —whether that is yoga or meditation or dancing or tennis.

● **Stay away from colonics.** Many people are tempted to turn to this "quick fix," but Dr. Rubman warns that colonics can backfire and worsen symptoms. The large intestine requires a healthy balance of microorganisms to function properly, and colonics indiscriminately wipe out the good with the bad under the thinly supported premise of detoxification.

To feel more in control of your disease and your life, learn more about Crohn's and connect with others who are going through the same things you are. Join message boards, chats, blogs and support groups (online or offline) at Web sites such as *www.ccfa.org,* or those listed at *http://www. crohns-disease-and-stress.com/support.html* and *http://ibdcrohns.about.com/od/online-support/a/supportgroups.htm.*

Acknowledging that a diagnosis of Crohn's disease is never good news, Dr. Rubman urges those who have the problem to be optimistic—it can often be controlled without drastic drugs or a draconian diet, and quality of life need not suffer.

Index

Continuous positive airway pressure. *See* CPAP (continuous positive airway pressure)

Contraceptives, resistant hypertension and, 23

Copper
  avoiding, for brain health, 114
  supplements, 211

CoQ10 (Coenzyme Q10)
  for brain health, 154
  depleted by fibrate drugs, 244
  for fatigue in diabetes, 271
  free radicals and longevity, 381
  for heart health, 80
  for high blood pressure, 46, 55–56

Coriolus versicolor mushroom extract, 342

Coronary angiograms, 94

Coronary calcium CT scan, 71

Cow's milk, 428–29

CPAP (continuous positive airway pressure), 132

C-reactive protein levels
  diabetes and, 269–70
  hs-CRP, heart attack risk and, 79
  peripheral neuropathy and, 299
  SSBs and, 208

Crohn's disease, 451–52, 485–87

Cruciferous vegetables, brain health and, 150

CT heart scan, 71, 93–94

Curcumin
  Alzheimer's disease, prevention of, 120
  in cancer care, 399
  as immune booster, 342

Curry, and prevention of Alzheimer's disease, 120

CVD (cardiovascular disease). *See* Heart disease

Cytochrome P450 blood test, 328

D

Dairy products
  alternatives to, 427–28
  cow's milk, 428–29
  in the DASH diet, 4
  diabetes and, 195–96, 270, 272
  lactose intolerance and, 426–27
  low-fat, kidney disease and, 284
  See also specific dairy products

Dandelion root, 413

DASH diet, for blood pressure problems, 3–5, 22

Decoctions, how to make, 412

Decongestants, resistant hypertension and, 23

Deglycyrrhizinated licorice (DGL), 438, 467

Dehydration. *See* Water, drinking

Dementia
  atrial fibrillation (AF) and, 126
  communications problems, 134–35
  depression and, 327
  as drug side-effect, 140
  elevated insulin and, 150
  Frontotemporal dementia, 137
  Lewy body dementia, 137
  mercury toxicity and, 314

personality and, 128
risk of, and coffee, 124
sepsis and, 127
tai chi for, 132
vascular dementia, 136–37
vitamin D and, 216
See also Alzheimer's disease

Dentistry
  dentures, burping and, 419
  fillings, recommendations for, 315
  silver amalgam fillings, 315

Dependence relationships, grief and, 376

Depression
  bananas for, 463
  breast cancer and, 362
  chronic illness and, 326–28
  circadian rhythms and, 222
  drug-free help for, 365–67
  heart disease and, 98
  lead exposure, 314
  natural approach to, 321
  pain relief and, 256
  See also Antidepressants

Desserts, low-carb suggestions, 259–60

Detoxification
  from cancer treatments, 337, 341–42
  glutathione for, 385
  green tea for, 313
  of heavy metals, 313–15

DHA (docosahexaenoic acid), 405, 480

"diabesity," 193–94

Diabetes
  Alzheimer's risk and, 119
  animal protein and, 199–200
  astaxanthin for, 267
  belly fat and, 226
  berberine for, 250–51
  beverages to avoid, 208–9
  black tea for, 239
  brain health and, 142
  cancer risk and, 289
  celiac disease and, 432
  circadian rhythms and, 221
  coffee to reduce risk of, 232–33
  cognitive decline and, 296–97
  and cold products, OTC, 25
  complications from, preventing, 272–74
  "diabesity," 193–94
  diabetic neuropathy, 172, 302–3
  diabetic retinopathy, 271
  diets for, 200–201
  drugs, and fracture risk, 246
  drugs, possibility of eliminating, 236–38
  drugs, safer, 246
  education and help for, one-on-one, 262–63
  exercise regimes for, 240
  eye damage and, 272–73
  flexitarian diet, 206
  foot ulcers, 301
  full-fat dairy products and, 195–96
  and hbA1C levels, 66
  heart disease and, 273

inflammation, best and worst foods, 206–8
kidney disease and, 273, 274–75
managing, 235–36
metformin (drug), 192, 241
nuts to reduce risk of, 231
periodontal disease and, 273
peripheral neuropathy and, 272
prediabetes, 189–91
prevention, lifestyle *vs.* drugs, 191–93
pycnogenol for, 50
qigong for, 260
resveratrol for protection against, 230
sleep problems and, 265–66
sugar consumption and, 382
sun exposure and, 195–96
sweets and, 196–97
tests for, 191
urination, profuse, 257
vinegar and, 239
viruses, using, 267–68
vision problems and, 276–77
vitamin D and, 216
whole wheat and, 197–98
wound healing, 300–302
See also Peripheral neuropathy

"Dialysis" to reduce LDL cholesterol, 76–77

Diarrhea
  bananas for, 463
  C. difficile and, 465
  with IBS, medications for, 475–76
  with IBS, probiotics for, 479
  stool leaks and, 465
  when to worry about, 456

Diet pills, resistant hypertension and, 23

Diet soda, diabetes and, 237
  See also Soda

Dietary Approaches to Stop Hypertension (DASH). *See* DASH diet

Diets
  antifungal diet, 317
  BRAT diet, for diarrhea, 456
  cancer care, 367–68, 371, 393–94, 395–97
  for celiac disease, 432–33
  flexitarian diet, 206
  Paleolithic diet, 282
  Perfect 10 diet plan, 204–5
  See also Mediterranean diet

Digestive health
  burping, causes of, 418–19
  during cancer therapy, 343
  chewing correctly, 419–20
  enzymes for, 413–15, 438, 470–71
  flatulence, causes of, 419, 420
  fructose malabsorption and, 415–17
  homeopathy for indigestion, 412
  natural ways to improve, 411–12
  prebiotics for, 451–52
  probiotics and, 422–23, 482–83
  See also Food allergies and sensitivities; Heartburn; Nausea

Digital blood pressure monitors, 45

Dinner, low-carb suggestions, 259